Lecture Notes in Computer Scie

T0230053

Commenced Publication in 1973
Founding and Former Series Editors:
Gerhard Goos, Juris Hartmanis, and Jan van Leeuwen

Maarten van Steen   Michi Henning (Eds.)

Middleware 2006

ACM/IFIP/USENIX 7th International Middleware Conference
Melbourne, Austrlia, November 27-December 1, 2006
Proceedings

 Springer

Volume Editors

Maarten van Steen
Vrije Universiteit Amsterdam
Faculty of Sciences
Department of Computer Sciences
De Boelelaan 1081a, 1081 HV Amsterdam, Netherlands
E-mail: steen@cs.vu.nl

Michi Henning
Triodia Technologies Pty Ltd
150 Sapphire St, Holland Park 4121, Brisbane, Australia
E-mail: michi@triodia.com

Library of Congress Control Number: Applied for

CR Subject Classification (1998): C.2.4, D.4, C.2, D.1.3, D.3.2, D.2, H.2, H.4

LNCS Sublibrary: SL 2 – Programming and Software Engineering

ISSN   0302-9743
ISBN-10   3-540-49023-X Springer Berlin Heidelberg New York
ISBN-13   978-3-540-49023-4 Springer Berlin Heidelberg New York

Springer is a part of Springer Science+Business Media

springer.com

© Springer-Verlag Berlin Heidelberg 2006
Printed in Germany

Typesetting: Camera-ready by author, data conversion by Scientific Publishing Services, Chennai, India
Printed on acid-free paper   SPIN: 11925071   06/3142   5 4 3 2 1 0

Preface

Middleware is one of those topics in computer science for which it appears difficult to reach consensus on its exact meaning. Broadly speaking, one could say that middleware contains solutions to the distribution of processes, data, and control that are more or less independent from applications, and that allow underlying platforms and hardware to be hidden from applications. In other words, it covers a lot.

However, there does seem to be consensus on the fact that middleware is about distributed systems, and that the solutions incorporated into middleware are applicable to a wide range of applications. Following the trend of past Middleware conferences, this seventh edition has continued to take a broad perspective on what middleware is all about, and there was general agreement among the Program Committee members that we should be open-minded as to what should be considered on topic or not. This open-mindedness is reflected in an interesting collection of papers that cover many fields of middleware, and even touch upon areas that have traditionally belonged more to the systems arena, such as virtualization.

However, not everything changes. As usual, the number of strong submissions was remarkably high, and there were many discussions among committee members as to which papers to accept. (Almost every paper was reviewed by four committee members.) Eventually, we selected 21 out of the 122 submissions, with space limitations forcing us to reject even papers that reflected good and original research.

We would like to thank all authors who submitted papers for Middleware 2006. Also, we both feel that we had a strong committee with members who not only did an excellent job reviewing submissions, but also submitted their reviews on time and acted promptly during the discussion phase, which allowed us to send out notifications to the authors as originally planned. We also gratefully acknowledge the work done by external reviewers, who often provided detailed and high-quality reports.

September 2006   Maarten van Steen and Michi Henning

Organization

Middleware 2005 was organized under the auspices of IFIP TC6WG6.1 (International Federation for Information Processing, Technical Committee 6 [Communication Systems],Working Group 6.1 [Architecture and Protocols for Computer Networks]).

Executive Committee

General Chairs:	Joe Sventek (University of Glasgow, UK)
	Shanika Karunasekera (University of Melbourne, Australia)
Program Chairs:	Michi Henning (ZeroC, USA)
	Maarten van Steen (Vrije Universiteit Amsterdam, Netherlands)
Local Arrangements Chairs:	Aaron Harwood and Lars Kulik (University of Melbourne, Australia)
	Lars Kulik and Lars Kulik (University of Melbourne, Australia)
Workshop Chair:	Antony Rowstron (Microsoft Research Cambridge, UK)
Doctoral Symposium Chair:	Karen Henricksen (National ICT Australia, Australia)
Industry Track Chair:	Rajkumar Buyya (University of Melbourne, Australia)
Publicity Chair:	Egemen Tanin (University of Melbourne, Australia)

Steering Committee

Gordon Blair
Elie Najm
Clem Cole
Joe Sventek
Jan de Meer
Doug Schmidt
Markus Endler
Steve Vinoski
Arno Jacobsen
Jean-Bernard Stefani
Gustavo Alonso

Program Committee

Christiana Amza (University of Toronto, Canada)
Ozalp Babaoglu (University of Bologna, Italy)
Mark Baker (Independent Consultant)
Alberto Bartoli (University of Trieste, Italy)
Yolande Berbers (Leuven University, Belgium)
Gordon Blair (Lancaster University, UK)
Chi-Hung Chi (Tsinghua University, China)
Michele Colajanni (University of Modena, Italy)
Geoff Coulson (Lancaster University, UK)
Fred Douglis (IBM Watson, USA)
Pascal Felber (University of Neuchâtel, Switzerland)
Indranil Gupta (University of Illinois, Urbana-Champaign, USA)
Franz Hauck (Ulm University, Germany)
Bettina Kemme (McGill University, Canada)
Anne-Marie Kermarrec (INRIA Rennes, France)
Fabio Kon (IME/USP, Brazil)
Ihor Kuz (NICTA, Australia)
Doug Lea (Oswego State University, USA)
Mark Little (Arjuna Technologies, UK)
Ted McFadden (Latent Ventures, USA)
Philip McKinley (Michigan State University, USA)
Jishnu Mukerji (HP Labs, USA)
Bernard Normier (ZeroC, USA)
Tamer Ozsu (University of Waterloo, Canada)
Gian Pietro Picco (Politecnico di Milano, Italy)
Frank Pilhofer (Mercury Computer Systems, USA)
Misha Rabinovich (Case Western Reserve University, USA)
Alexander Reinefeld (ZIB, Germany)
Luis Rodrigues (University of Lisbon, Portugal)
Emin Gun Sirer (Cornell University, USA)
Peter Steenkiste (CMU, USA)
Stefan Tai (IBM Watson, USA)
Amin Vahdat (UCSD, USA)
Aad van Moorsel (Newcastle University, UK)
Steve Vinoski (IONA, USA)
Craig Wills (Worchester Polytechnic Institute, USA)

Referees

Jeannie Albrecht	Trevor Armstrong	Ben Beckmann
Gustavo Alonso	Dhouha Ayed	Marin Bertier
Mauro Andreolini	Gilbert Babin	Lindsay Bradford
Artur Andrzejak	Hitesh Ballani	Ryan Braud

Ciaran Bryce
Ramon Caceres
Raphael Y. Camargo
Claudia Canali
Antonio Carzaniga
Yatin Chawathe
Jin Chen
Lei Chen
Fabio Moreira Costa
Paolo Costa
Raphael Y. de Camargo
Dave Dice
Joerg Domaschka
Markus Endler
Onyeka Ezenwoye
Luis Garces
Vittorio Ghini
Lukasz Golab
Alfredo Goldman
Charles Gray
Gernot Heiser
Kirsten Hildrum
Mikael Hoegqvist
Yyun Huang
Danny Hughes
Felix Hupfeld

Eric Kasten
Oliver Kennedy
Chip Killian
David Knoester
Manolis Koubarakis
Riccardo Lancellotti
Tobias Langhammer
Guoli Li
Yi Lin
Giorgia Lodi
Francesca Mazzoni
Madalin Mihailescu
Hugo Miranda
Alberto Montresor
Luca Mottola
Erich Nahum
David Oppenheimer
Sujay Parekh
Cesare Pautasso
Kathrin Peter
Milan Pirca
Marius Pirvu
Christian Plattner
Barry Porter
Davy Preuveneers
Hans P. Reiser

Patrick Reynolds
Thomas Rblitz
Thomas Roeblitz
Bin Rong
Leonid Ryzhyk
S. Masoud Sadjadi
Farshad Samimi
Florian Schintke
Holger Schmidt
Thorsten Schuett
Sabina Serbu
Nir Shavit
Santosh Shrivastava
Gokul Soundararajan
Kevin Walsh
Qiang Wang
Zhihua Wen
Stuart Wheater
Alex Wun
Zhen Xiao
Yun Yuan
Jingdi Zeng
Zhinan Zhou

Sponsoring Institutions

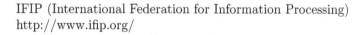

IFIP (International Federation for Information Processing)
http://www.ifip.org/

Advanced Computing Systems Association
http://www.usenix.org/

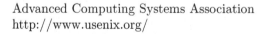
Association for Computing Machinery
http://www.acm.org

The Melbourne Convention and Visitors Bureau
http://www.mcvb.com.au/

The University of Melbourne, Australia
http://www.unimelb.edu.au/

P2P Networks and Applications Research Group,
Univ. Melbourne
http://mundula.cs.mu.oz.au:8080/p2p

Grid Computing and Distributed Systems Laboratory,
Univ. Melbourne
http://www.gridbus.org

BBN Technologies
http://www.bbn.com/

National ICT Australia
http://www.nicta.com.au/

ZeroC
http://www.zeroc.com/

ARC Res. Netw. on Intell. Sensors, Sensor Netw. & Info.
Proc.
http://www.ee.unimelb.edu.au/ISSNIP/

Table of Contents

Databases

Mobile and Ubiquitous Computing

Security

Datamining Techniques

Performance II

Management II

Caching Dynamic Web Content: Designing and Analysing an Aspect-Oriented Solution

Sara Bouchenak[1], Alan Cox[2], Steven Dropsho[3],
Sumit Mittal[4,*], and Willy Zwaenepoel[3]

[1] INRIA, 655, av. de l'Europe, Montbonnot, 38334 St. Ismier Cedex, France
Sara.Bouchenak@inria.fr
[2] Rice University, Department of Computer Science, Houston, TX USA
alc@cs.rice.edu
[3] EPFL, Department of Computer Science, CH-1015 Lausanne, Switzerland
{Steven.Dropsho, Willy.Zwaenepoel}@epfl.ch
[4] IBM India Research Lab, Block-1, IIT, Hauz Khas, New Delhi, India
sumittal@in.ibm.com

Abstract. Caching dynamic web content is an effective approach to reduce Internet latency and server load. An ideal caching solution is one that can be added transparently by the developers and provides complete consistency of the cached documents, while minimizing false cache invalidations. In this paper, we design and implement AutoWebCache, a middleware system for adding caching of dynamic content transparently to J2EE server-side applications having a backend database. For this purpose, we first present the principles involved in caching dynamic web content, including our logic to ensure consistency of the cached entries. Thereafter, we demonstrate the use of aspect-oriented (AOP) techniques to implement our system, showing how AOP provides modularity and transparency to the entire process. Further, we evaluate the effectiveness of AutoWebCache in reducing response times of applications, thereby improving throughput. We also analyze the transparency of our system for a general application suite, considering issues such as dynamic web pages aggregating data from multiple sources, presence of insufficiently structured interfaces for exchanging information and the use of application semantics while caching. We use two standard J2EE web benchmark applications, RUBiS and TPC-W, to conduct our experiments and discuss the results obtained.

Keywords: Caching, aspect-oriented programming, J2EE applications, dynamic content.

1 Introduction

Dynamically generated web content represents a large portion of web requests. The rate at which dynamic documents are delivered is often orders of magnitudes slower than static documents [9,11]. Therefore, caching dynamic web content is

---

* Work done while being at Rice University, Houston and EPFL University, Lausanne.

M. van Steen and M. Henning (Eds.): Middleware 2006, LNCS 4290, pp. 1–21, 2006.
© IFIP International Federation for Information Processing 2006

an appealing approach to reduce Internet latency and server load. Web sites for dynamic content are usually based on a multi-tier J2EE architecture using several middleware systems [27]: an HTTP server as a web front-end and provider of static content, an application server to execute the business logic and generate the dynamic web content, and a database to store the persistent data required by the application. Dynamic content generation places a significant burden on the servers, often leading to performance bottlenecks. Caching dynamic web content can directly address these bottlenecks.

Implementing caching as a middleware solution is particularly attractive. Of course, an ideal solution is one that can be added transparently by the developers, possibly even as an after-thought. Some examples of transparently adding caching to an application are given in [17,6,4], but these ignore consistency of the cached entries. Other solutions provide consistency, but ignore transparency, requiring manual insertion [10]. There are some projects that provide both consistency and transparency, such as those caching SQL query result sets [8] at the back-end. The interesting property of data from result sets of SQL queries is that it is from a single interface and hence, of one type (homogeneous). An open question is whether similar techniques can be successful for more complex content such as web pages that aggregate data from multiple sources (*i.e.*, heterogeneous).

In this paper, we present the design and implementation of *AutoWebCache*, a middleware solution for caching dynamically generated content in J2EE applications. A goal is to move the caching as far forward in the multi-tier architecture to not only reduce the database activity in the back-end but also the business logic activity, which is becoming ever more complex and costly at the middle tier. Unlike caching data such as JDBC SQL results at a single well-specified interface, caching fully formed web pages requires interfacing to both the front-end (e.g., Tomcat servlet engine) *and* the back-end (e.g., JDBC interface). Caching at this level requires information from both interfaces to maintain consistency of the cached documents. To keep the caching transparent, we cast caching as an aspect of the application and use an aspect oriented programming (AOP) framework to capture the information flowing through various interfaces. We give details of the AutoWebCache cache system based on AOP principles and the AspectJ [2] weaving rules that add the caching logic transparently to the application.

We evaluate the performance of our middleware solution with the help of two J2EE benchmarks - RUBiS and TPC-W. RUBiS implements the core functionality of an auction-site: selling, browsing and bidding [1], while TPC-W simulates an online-bookstore [30]. We demonstrate the gains in response times using AutoWebCache for each. We also analyze the transparency of AutoWebCache for a general application suite. We argue that for the general case, issues can arise when caching dynamic content at the front-end due to 1) dynamic web pages aggregating data from multiple sources, 2) some sources not having sufficiently structured interfaces for exchanging information and 3) the need to consider semantics of the application while caching. Although our benchmark applications are servlets-based and use SQL queries to incorporate dynamism, we believe that the results and arguments presented in this paper hold true for a general architecture as well.

The contributions of this paper can be summarized as follows:

1. Design, implementation and evaluation of AutoWebCache, a middleware solution that caches dynamic web pages at the front-end while maintaining consistency with the back-end database(s).
2. Demonstrating that dynamic web caching can be considered a crosscutting aspect and, therefore, AOP methods should be considered as a flexible and easy-to-use tool to develop the middleware support.

The remainder of this paper is organized as follows. Section 2 gives some background on dynamic web applications and aspect-oriented programming. Section 3 outlines the principles involved in designing a dynamic web cache and gives an overview of our AutoWebCache system. Section 4 describes the implementation of AutoWebCache using aspect-oriented techniques, and analyzes its transparency with respect to an application. Sections 5 and 6 present our evaluation environment and the results of our evaluation, respectively. Section 7 provides a discussion of our experiences. Section 8 discusses some related work and finally, Section 9 draws our conclusions.

2 Background

2.1 J2EE Web Applications

Java 2 Platform, Enterprise Edition (J2EE) defines a model for developing distributed applications, *e.g.*, web applications, in a multi-tiered architecture [27]. Such applications usually start with requests from web clients that flow through an HTTP server front-end and provider of static content, then to an application server to execute the business logic and generate web pages on-the-fly, and finally to a database that stores resources and data (see Figure 1).

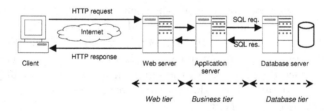

Fig. 1. Architecture of Dynamic Web Applications

Upon an HTTP client request, either the request targets a static web document that the web server can return directly; or the request refers to a dynamic document, in which case the web server forwards that request to the application server. The application server runs one or more software components (e.g., Servlets, EJB) that query a database through a JDBC driver (Java DataBase Connection driver) [28] and retrieve data to generate a web document on-the-fly.

2.2 Aspect-Oriented Programming

Aspect-Oriented Programming (AOP) is a methodology with concepts and constructs to modularize crosscutting concerns (i.e., *aspects*) [15]. With AOP, the different aspects involved in a system are separately implemented in different modules. The developer can also specify the manner in which these modules need to be woven to form the final system. Aspects are woven together via the *join point* model, a fundamental concept in AOP specifying identifiable execution points in a system. Such join points include method calls and executions, constructor calls, read and write access to fields, exception handler invocations, etc. *Pointcuts* allow a programmer to capture certain join points while an *advice* provides a way to express crosscutting actions to be performed at a certain pointcut. At a pointcut, an advice specifies the weaving rules involving that point, such as performing some actions *before* or *after* the execution of the pointcut. Figure 2 shows the basic principle of adding caching transparently to a web application, using aspect weaving.

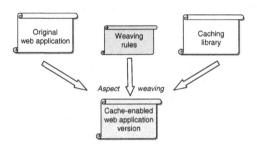

Fig. 2. Aspectizing Caching

3 Dynamic Web Caching

Caching dynamic web content prevents the client from remotely re-accessing the database server to re-execute SQL queries, and from regenerating dynamic web pages on the application server. In this section, we first present the principles involved in designing a dynamic web cache, including our logic to ensure consistency of the cached documents. We then give an overview of our implemented system. Concrete details about the implementation based on aspectizing web caching are provided in the next section.

3.1 Designing a Web Cache

Designing a cache for web documents is rendered complicated by the dynamic nature of web applications, requiring mechanisms to maintain consistency between the data and its cached copy. Specifically, dependency needs to be established between requests that read the data in the back-end (read-only requests) and those that make updates to the back-end (write-requests). We divide the design of such a caching system into the following mechanisms:

- **Cache checks.** Upon a client read-only request, the cache is first checked to look up the requested document. In case of a hit, the cached document (e.g. a web page) is simply returned to the client, bypassing the request execution.
- **Cache inserts.** Upon a miss in the cache during a client read-only request, the request is executed by the application server (and SQL queries are possibly executed on the database server) to dynamically generate a web document that is returned to the client; and a copy of that document is stored in the cache.
- **Collecting consistency information.** For a read request, we attach the information mapping the underlying database set used in the generation of response to this request (dependency information). Similarly, for a write request, we associate information regarding the database set updated by this request (invalidation information).
- **Cache invalidations.** Upon a client write request, the cache entries that are affected by the write must be invalidated. This would require making use of the consistency information.

Index: URI (readHandlerName + readHandlerArgs)	Cached web page	Index: SQL String	<value vector, URI> pair
URI_1	WebPage1	ReadQueryTemplate$_1$	<instance values$_{1a}$, URI_1> <instance values$_{1b}$, URI_{41}> <instance values$_{1c}$, URI_{57}>
URI_2	WebPage2	ReadQueryTemplate$_2$	<instance values$_{2a}$, URI_7>
		ReadQueryTemplate$_3$	<instance values$_{3a}$, URI_{12}>
...	...	...	...

Fig. 3. Cache Structure

Figure 3 shows the basic structure of our cache. The first table stores the entries of web pages, indexed by URI of the client requests including the request arguments (input info). The second table maintains details about the read-only queries (template + vector of dynamic values = dependency info) used in the formation of the cached pages. When a write query occurs, a query analysis engine determines the set of read queries affected by the update. This information is then used to remove the invalidated entries from the cache.

3.2 Maintaining Cache Consistency

Determining if a client write request invalidates the cached page resulting from a previous client read-only request is equivalent to determining if the set of SQL queries associated with the former request invalidates one of the SQL queries underlying the latter request. For this purpose, our implemented solution includes a query analysis engine that has the task of determining the dependencies between SQL queries. Query analysis has two primary components:

- **Determining possible dependencies between queries.** SQL queries are given as templates (the vector of dynamic values for a particular instance to be known at run-time). If a read query template shares common tables and columns with an update query template, then a dependency is established.
- **Actual intersection testing to reveal true dependencies.** A true intersection between a read query and an update query (with a dependency established) exists if the update modifies one or more columns in the row(s) being read, and/or results in changing the set of rows satisfying the selection clause of the read query [20].

It is interesting to note that while the first component of this analysis is based on the static portion of the query string (i.e. query template), the second component comes into play at run-time, once we know the actual values used in the selection criteria. For efficiency, our system caches the results of the first component and re-uses them while encountering the same queries again. In practice, there are usually a small fixed number of different query templates, thus, the query analysis cache stabilizes very quickly (Figure 4).

Benchmark	Read queries	Write queries	Number Clients	Time to stabilize
RUBiS	22 types	10 types	1000	< 4 min
TPC-W	10 types	14 types	400	< 1 min

Fig. 4. Query Analysis Cache Statistics for RUBiS and TPC-W

Our analysis engine explores a balance between invalidation precision and its associated evaluation cost, the cost of precision being determined by the detail of query analysis required to extract the relationship needed. The engine supports three cache invalidation policies that increase precision by providing progressively more refined analysis:

1. A simple method is to check if the columns used in the read query are also updated in the write query. This column-only check may result in many *false positive* indications that an intersection exists when, in fact, there is none. E.g., reading then updating column a from table T creates an intersection, but reading column a and updating column c does not.
   (a) "SELECT a FROM T WHERE b=X" vs "UPDATE T SET a=new_val..." *may* intersect if the column updated is a (as here) or b.
   (b) "SELECT a FROM T WHERE b=X" vs "UPDATE T SET c=new_val..." does not intersect (assuming c != a,b).

2. To make the test for intersection more precise, selection criteria in the read query's WHERE-clause are matched to values from the write query to see if the same rows are being updated. E.g., if a read's selection clause requires that T.b=X, but for the write query T.b=Y and $X \neq Y$, then the queries do not intersect.
   (a) "SELECT a FROM T WHERE b=X" vs "UPDATE T SET a=new_val WHERE b=Y", does not intersect if $X \neq Y$.

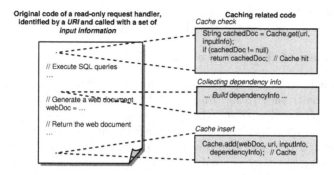

Fig. 5. Caching Read Requests

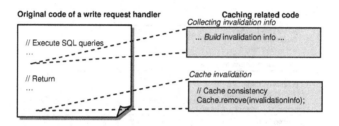

Fig. 6. Handling Write Requests

3. Invalidates can be made even more precise by executing *extra queries* to retrieve missing data needed to test for intersection. Continuing with the prior example, if the value of the field T.b is not specified in the write query itself, then an extra query can be made to the database to read the value of T.b in the row(s) being updated. This option generates additional queries (by the cache) to the back-end but reduces unnecessary webpage invalidations. E.g.,

   (a) "SELECT a FROM T WHERE b=X" vs "UPDATE T SET a=new_val WHERE d=W", but there is no reference to the value of b in the update query.
   (b) Therefore, the cache generates a query for column b of the row being updated: "SELECT b FROM T WHERE d=W".
   (c) The read and update queries intersect if the value returned equals X (from the read query).

We refer the reader to [20] for detailed descriptions of the engine's handling of various query types for each of the above three cases. The last (and most aggressive) technique which we call the *AC-extraQuery* strategy is used in this study.

Figure 5 and Figure 6 show how collecting dependency and invalidation information, and how cache check, insert and invalidation operations take place within web application request handlers. From the figures, it is clear that to provide consistency, information is gathered both at the front-end (request arguments in the servlet engine) as well as the back-end (queries being shuttled to the database).

This is in contrast to caching of SQL query result sets, which requires capturing calls to the database at the JDBC interface only [8].

3.3 Overview of the AutoWebCache System

Our design is called *AutoWebCache*, a system for caching web pages and managing their consistency [3,20]. In AutoWebCache, the cache is located on (in front of) the application server (though it could easily be used in a proxy cache formation), and it consists of a set of web pages from read-only requests indexed by the request URI + set of arguments. A page is invalidated if a client update request modifies the data set used to generate the cached page. AutoWebCache uses the most precise cache invalidation strategy discussed prior, namely the *AC-extraQuery* strategy. Web pages resulting from client write requests are not cached.

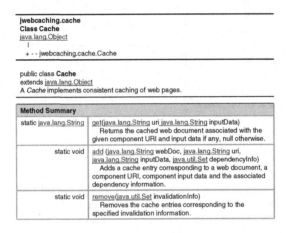

Fig. 7. Cache API

The main package of the AutoWebCache system is the *jwebcaching.cache* package. It provides several classes, among which the *Cache* class provides the necessary features for cache management, including interaction with the query analysis engine to maintain consistency of the cached web pages. Figure 7 illustrates a part of the API of this class.

4   Aspectizing Web Caching

Aspect-oriented programming (AOP) hands us an efficient tool to perform caching by treating it as a concern that cuts across the application. In this section, we describe our implementation of AutoWebCache, an AOP based caching middleware system. We will also analyze the transparency of the caching aspect with respect to a general application suite.

4.1   Implementing an AOP Based Caching

AspectJ [2] is an aspect-oriented environment that provides the AOP constructs and set of tools for aspects written in the Java programming language. The AspectJ language exposes a set of join points that are well-defined places in the execution of a Java program flow.

```
(a)   aspect ServletExecution {
(b)       // Pointcut definition
(c)       pointcut doGetExecution() :
(d)           execution(
(e)               void HttpServlet+.doGet(
(f)                   HttpServletRequest, HttpServletResponse)) ;
(g)       // Advice definition
(h)       before() : doGetExecution() { ... crosscutting actions  ...}
(i)   }
```

Fig. 8. Pointcut and Advice Examples

Figure 8 gives an example of a pointcut and advice declaration in the AspectJ language. This example defines a pointcut called *doGetExecution* that designates the execution of the *doGet* method in the *HttpServlet* class or its subclasses[1] that takes a first argument of type *HttpServletRequest* and a second argument of type *HttpServletResponse* (lines (c)-(f) in Figure 8). This example also defines an advice that executes prior to the specified pointcut (the *doGet* method, line (h) in Figure 8). Please notice that the pointcuts and advices that define the weaving rules to be applied are specified as entities separate from the individual aspect modules. Weaving the final system from individual aspects is performed by the *ajc* tool, the AspectJ compiler.

In order to apply aspect-oriented techniques for caching dynamic web pages in J2EE applications, the following properties are needed:

– The entry and exit points of request handlers in web applications must be well-known points. This is necessary to automatically inject cache check, insert and invalidation operations to those handlers.
– The call to SQL queries that underlie the request handlers in web applications must be well-known points. This is necessary to collect dependency and invalidation information.

4.2   AutoWebCache-An AOP Based Web Cache

We implemented AutoWebCache as an AOP-based solution that helps in transparently injecting caching mechanisms to web applications. This involved the following steps:

– **Weaving rules specification** - defines how to integrate the caching aspect into the web application core aspect. The weaving rules specify the points in the application where mechanisms for cache check, insert, invalidation operations etc. need to be injected (see Figure 5 and Figure 6).

---

[1] The + sign following the *HttpServlet* class name in Figure 8 designates its subclasses.

– **Aspect weaving** - the process of composing the final cache-enabled system
from individual web application and AutoWebCache aspects by following
the weaving rules, using the AOP compiler (see Figure 2).

```
// Pointcut for Servlets' main method
pointcut servletMainMethodExecution(...) :
    execution(
        void HttpServlet+.doGet(
            HttpServletRequest, HttpServletResponse))
    || execution(
        void HttpServlet+.doPost(
            HttpServletRequest, HttpServletResponse));
```

Fig. 9. Capturing Servlets' main method

Figure 9 shows how to capture the execution of a Servlet's main method in
AspectJ; this is necessary to inject cache checks, inserts and invalidations. Since
Java Servlets are defined with a standard API, their main methods are known
as being either *doGet* or *doPost* that respectively implement HTTP GET and
POST; and the AspectJ's *execution* keyword used in the pointcut captures the
execution of those methods [2].

Cache checks and inserts. Figure 10 describes the rules for tackling read-only
Servlets. The *around* advice surrounds the normal execution of the main method
of a Servlet with cache checks and inserts (the *proceed* keyword calls the normal
execution of the method). In case of a cache hit, the normal execution of this
Servlet is bypassed. For a cache miss, an entry is added in the cache along with
the dependency information associated with this request (c.f., Figure 5).

```
// Advice for read-only requests
around(...) : servletMainMethodExecution (...) {
    // Pre-processing: Cache check
    String cachedDoc;
    cachedDoc = ... call Cache.get of JWebCaching
    if (cachedDoc != null)  {
        ... return cachedDoc
    }

    // Normal execution of the request
    proceed(...);

    // Post-processing: Cache insert
    ... call Cache.add of JWebCaching
}
```

Fig. 10. Weaving rules for cache checks and inserts

Cache invalidations. Figure 11 describes an advice that is aimed at tackling
write Servlets; it defines the *after* advice that executes following a Servlet's

---

[2] In case a Servlet's *doGet* and *doPost* methods are interleaved, it is necessary not
to capture the execution of both methods, but only the top-level one. This can be
achieved in AspectJ using a *cflowbelow* pointcut (see [17], Chapter 3). For simplicity
purposes, we do not use it here.

```
// Advice for write requests
after(...) : servletMainMethodExecution (...) {
    // Cache invalidation
    ... call Cache.remove of JWebCaching
}
```

Fig. 11. Weaving rules for cache invalidations

main method. Specifically, it uses the invalidation information attached with this request (c.f., Figure 6) to invalidate the affected cache entries.

Collecting consistency information. Figure 12 declares a pointcut that captures calls to read-only and write SQL queries (through standard JDBC API calls, e.g., *executeQuery, executeUpdate*). The *after* advice executes following an SQL query and collects the consistency information - dependency (read query templates + value vectors for a read-only request handler) or invalidation (write query templates + value vectors for a write request), derived from that query.

If a read query is aborted during the formation of response for a client request, the corresponding web page is not stored in the cache. Further, if a write query does not complete successfully, it is not considered for determining the cache entries affected. For simplicity, implementation details concerning these points have been omitted from our presentation.

```
// Pointcut for SQL query calls
pointcut sqlQueryCall() :
    call(ResultSet PreparedStatement.executeQuery())
    || call(int PreparedStatement.executeUpdate());
// Advice for SQL query calls
after() : sqlQueryCall () { ... collect consistency info  ...}
```

Fig. 12. Collecting Consistency Information

4.3   Analysing Transparency of AutoWebCache

Caching of dynamic web content can not be considered as an aspect completely orthogonal to the application, in general. In this subsection, we outline some issues that affect the transparency of AutoWebCache with respect to a general application suite.

Capturing Information Flow through various Interfaces. To maintain complete consistency of the cache with the back-end databases, the caching scheme must capture all flow of information in the application, from front-to-back. Such information can flow through various interfaces:

- *Entry and Exit points.* AutoWebCache requires well-defined interfaces for identifying the entry and exit points of a request. In our benchmarks, the Java Servlet APIs provide a standard way to capture entry and exit of a http client request. Further, each cached document is uniquely identified by the URI and Servlet parameters specified in the request.

- *Modification to underlying Data Sets.* When time-lagged weak consistency is employed, once cached, entries are valid until some timeout occurs. To provide a strong consistency of cached documents, however, changes must be tracked on the data used to generate the documents. In our case, we capture modifications to the data sets by capturing the associated SQL requests.

- *Cookies.* Some web applications store part of their request parameters in cookies, instead of specifying them explicitly in the http requests (e.g., the user name and password). In this case, the client includes its cookie [21] in all requests to the server. A cookie is a small amount of state with no defined structure. Thus, if each web application defines its own ad-hoc cookie structure, transparency is difficult to achieve in AutoWebCache.

- *Multiple Sources of Dynamism.* A dynamic web page can be formed by aggregating data from multiple sources. Currently, AutoWebCache handles dynamism resulting out of SQL queries to a database. However, as long as the interfaces for accessing such sources of dynamism are well-defined, AutoWebCache can be extended easily to provide a high degree of transparency.

The Hidden State Problem. Implied in the design of AutoWebCache is that the http request contains all the information necessary for the servlet to create the web page, thus, identical requests (which will map to the same cache entry) result in the same page being generated. Any other state that affects the web page content is considered *hidden state*. For example, some applications employ randomly generated information for advertisement banners [25]. Another instance is the use of static variables inside the application. In such setups, each subsequent identical http request results in generation of different web pages. Such requests should be marked as uncacheable by the developer.

Use of Application Semantics. For aspect-orientedness to be used, the key semantic concepts must be conveyed via the syntax of the code and, therefore, must be rather straightforward. In some cases, however, understanding the nature of application provides avenues for improving performance of the caching system. For instance, in one of our benchmarks, the TPC-W application, the expensive *Best Seller* web interaction uses a 30 second window allowing dirty reads. In essence, the effects of a change committed to the database by any web interaction which completed less than 30 seconds before the *Best Seller* is permitted to be not reflected in the response page for *Best Seller*. This conforms to clauses 3.1.4.1 and 6.3.3.1 of the TPC-W v1.8 specification [30]. Such concepts form a part of the complex application semantics, and as we demonstrate in the results section, can be quite effective in performance improvement.

5   Evaluation Environment

Test-bed J2EE Web Applications. We tested with the J2EE applications on-line bookstore TPC-W and auction site RUBiS. TPC-W implements an on-line bookstore [30] and defines 14 different interactions among which are accessing a user home page, listing new products and best sellers, registering a new user, updating the shopping cart, ordering. We used an implementation of TPC-W proposed by the University of Wisconsin [18]. RUBiS implements the core functionality of an auction site modeled over eBay [1]. It defines 26 interactions including registering new users, browsing items by category or region, bidding, buying or selling items, and leaving comments. Both TPC-W and RUBiS provide a benchmarking tool that emulates web client behavior and provides statistics (e.g., client response time). For evaluation, we use the shopping mix for TPCW (80% read requests), and the bidding mix for RUBiS (85% read requests). We vary the client load but the size of the database is fixed.

Client Emulator. Both benchmarks use a client-browser emulator to generate requests. A client session is a sequence of interactions for the same client. For each client session, the client emulator opens a persistent HTTP connection to the Web server and closes it at the end of the session. The average think time between requests (7 sec) and session time (15 min) conform to clauses 5.3.1.1 and 6.2.1.2 of the TPC-W v1.8 specification [30]. All our experiments warm the cache for 15 minutes before collecting statistics over the next 30 minutes.

Software & Hardware. We use the Apache v.1.3.22 web server and the Jakarta Tomcat v3.2.4 servlet engine, with the MySQL v2.04 type 4 JDBC driver, running on Sun JDK 1.4.2. The database is MySQL v.3.23.43-max with MyISAM tables. All machines have an Intel Xeon 2.4GHz CPU, 1GB ECC SDRAM, the 2.4.20 Linux kernel, and a 120GB 7200 rpm disk drive. All machines are connected through a switched 1Gbps Ethernet LAN.

Using this setup, we next analyse the AutoWebCache system, and shed light on some of these important questions:

- What is the effect of AutoWebCache on the performance of an application?
- How does the semantics of an application relate to cache efficiency?
- What is the relative benefit of caching on different read-only requests?
- How much do AOP techniques help in implementing the caching system?

6   Results

In our first experiment, we study the effectiveness of AutoWebCache in reducing the response time of applications. Figure 13 shows the response time for RUBiS, comparing the results of the cache-enabled version (AutoWebCache) with the original application (No cache). Here, RUBiS is running the bidding mix which has updates. Thus, we need to generate cache invalidations to ensure cache consistency. For this mix, the cache hit rate is 54% [3]. We see that AutoWebCache provides a clear performance benefit, improving response time by upto 64%.

---

[3] All numbers reported here are for the most optimal *AC-extraQuery* cache invalidation strategy of AutoWebCache. See [20] for results comparing different strategies.

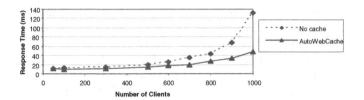

Fig. 13. Response Time for RUBiS - Bidding Mix

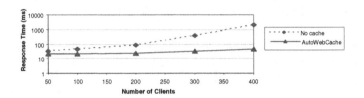

Fig. 14. Response Time for TPC-W - Shopping Mix

Figure 14 shows the results for TPC-W, using the primary reporting mix of shopping which has updates. Please note the log scale of the y-axis. From the graph, we again see that AutoWebCache version of the application has significantly faster response times than the No cache version. In this case, the response time is reduced by up to 98%, and the cache hit rate is 43%. The overhead of processing cache lookups can be measured by forcing a cache miss on every lookup. The performance difference to NoCache is negligible (not distinguishable at the millisecond scale) so it is not shown in the graph.

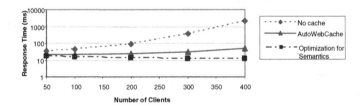

Fig. 15. Cache Improvement in TPC-W based on Application Semantics

In our second experiment, we present how knowledge of the application semantics can help in improving the efficiency of AutoWebCache. In TPC-W application, the expensive `BestSeller` request uses a 30 second window allowing dirty reads, permitting those changes committed to the database less than 30 seconds before this request to be not reflected in the response (c.f., Section 4.3). Making use of this semantics, the best seller pages were marked cacheable for a full 30 second window. The performance improvement with this optimization is shown in Figure 15.

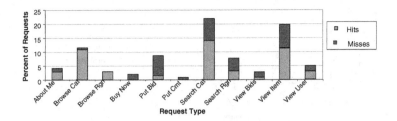

Fig. 16. Relative Benefits for different Requests in RUBiS

In our next experiment, we analyze the relative benefit of caching on different individual read-only requests. Figure 16 shows that for RUBis (with 1000 clients), as expected, requests benefit by varying degree using the AutoWebCache system. Requests BrowseCategories and BrowseRegions have an almost 100% hit rate, while requests BuyNow and PutComment have the least cache hit ratios. While most of the misses in the last two categories were cold misses,[4] for ViewItem and ViewBids, most of the misses were due to invalidation of the cached entries.

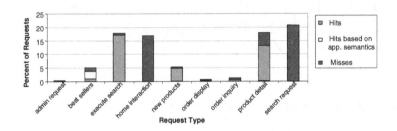

Fig. 17. Relative Benefits for different Requests in TPCW

Figure 17 shows the relative benefits experienced by different requests for TPCW, running with 400 clients. However, there are two differences in this graph from the one we obtained for RUBiS. Firstly, in the case of TPCW, two requests (unlike any in RUBiS), SearchRequest and HomeInteraction were explicity marked uncacheable because they use a random number generator to produce advertisement banners. Secondly, most of the hits for BestSeller request were obtained using a 30 second window for invalidation (described earlier). Such application semantics were not used for any request in RUBiS.

Figures 18 and 19 report the improvement in response times of individual requests with AutoWebCache, for RUBiS and TPCW with 1000 and 400 clients, respectively. For each request, the graphs show the average extra time required to generate the response for that request in case of a cache miss. Hence, for a miss, the response time for a request is the sum of the two components. In the case of RUBiS, AboutMe has high penalty for a miss. However, this is compensated by

---

[4] Hits for these requests require the same customer *and* item as a previous request.

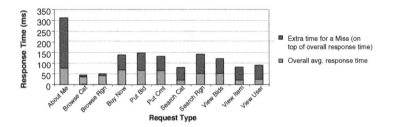

Fig. 18. Breakdown of different Requests in RUBiS w.r.t. Response Time

a high rate for this request. Same arguments can be applied for `BestSeller`, `ExecuteSearch` and `NewProducts` requests in TPCW. Also, since the requests `SearchRequest` and `HomeInteraction` have low response times, marking them uncacheable does not impact the performance of AutoWebCache a great deal.

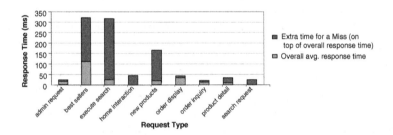

Fig. 19. Breakdown of different Requests in TPCW w.r.t. Response Time

Application	Web application		Caching library		AOP-based caching	
	# Java classes	Java code size	# Java classes	Java code size	# AspectJ files (weaving rules)	Size of AspectJ code
TPC-W	46	12K lines	13	4.6K lines	1	150 lines
RUBiS	25	5.8K lines				

Fig. 20. Web App & Cache Library Code Size vs. Aspect-J Code Size

Figure 20 compares the code size of the individual aspects, the TPC-W and RUBiS testbed applications and the JWebCaching library. Most of the code for the AutoWebCache system, including the query analysis engine, lies in the JWebCaching library. This library implements the cache interfaces and can be reused for various applications. Size of code written in AspectJ for weaving caching into the application is much smaller. Thus, it is easy to maintain and customize for different applications.

7 Discussion

A goal in web cache research has been to develop designs that are completely transparent to the application yet supports strong consistency. Complete transparency means that no effort is required from the application programmer to achieve caching - such a cache would be easy to add. Support for strong consistency means the cache can ensure it is always synchronized with the state of the persistent backing store - such a cache would have a wide audience. Caching of static content achieves both goals. Strong consistency is trivial by the fact that the content does not change. Transparency is easily achieved as the final content can be captured at a well-known point - while being sent as the response to a client's request.

The complexity of maintaining consistency in our case is due to caching *derived data*. We call data such as web pages derived because they are obtained using some set of data in the persistent store of the application (e.g., rows in the database tables). In contrast, non-derived data objects map directly to *unique* items in the persistent store. Thus, checking for inclusion in the cache is a simple matter of checking for the existence of a unique global identifier (e.g., a simple id). When caching derived data, however, the mapping relationship is obscured. Complexities arise as more than one document can depend on the same field in the database. Also, dynamic web pages can aggregate data from multiple databases. Therefore, detecting if a change to a database affects a web page involves testing for inclusion of the changes in each page's input set.

Aspect-oriented programming is an efficient tool to capture the information flow in an application and can be used to inject the caching calls at appropriate points. Working with AOP gives several benefits:

Modularity. Separation of concerns is inherent to AOP-based systems. The implementation of each individual aspect (e.g., the J2EE web application and the logic for caching dynamic content) may evolve separately without inducing a change in the implementation of the others.

Generality. The AutoWebCache prototype uses AOP to add caching of dynamic web pages to a Servlet-based web application that interfaces a database with JDBC. This methodology is general enough to encompass other sources of dynamic data. Specifically, individual aspects can be developed separately for each source and then woven together.

Transparency. Any modification/extension to the application interfaces is captured by making appropriate changes in the pointcut specifications, and not the way individual aspects have been developed or woven. This provides a clean way to make caching look oblivious to the developer.

Our AOP-based framework combines simplicity with flexibility to achieve a good level of transparency. Let us compare our technique with a compiler-based approach as in [8]. The compiler does a similar query analysis at compile time and embeds the results for simple look-up at run-time. The proposed AutoWebCache system also achieves almost zero run-time analysis overhead via result caching [3], but is much easier to develop than compiler techniques, making use of AOP tools. Another subtle advantage of our approach is that it is robust even if the SQL queries are dynamically formed, as it captures the run-time value of the string at the point of SQL call. For a compiler, query strings must be statically available. This assumption might not hold for real-life, complex applications.

We believe that achieving the simultaneous goals of complete transparency and strong consistency in web caching is not possible for the general case. The key problem is in automatically verifying that no essential data in an application needed for caching flows through unexpected interfaces and, thus, elude the consistency logic. Cookies, randomly generated data and application semantics are some examples of this phenomena from our benchmarks. If an application presents a fairly orthogonal caching aspect, AutoWebCache would require only minimal developer intervention. If not, a special weaving rule would be constructed for each non-orthogonal concept. In the worst case, AOP would extend only modularity as a benefit, same as that offered by object-oriented techniques.

8   Related Work

Caching of dynamic content with weak consistency can achieve transparency because, as for static content, no information is needed to synchronize the cached documents with the backing store. Typically, pages can be set to timeout so that the cache content is periodically refreshed. CachePortal [4] has a unique form of weak, time-lagged consistency. It relies on timestamps and HTTP logs to conservatively determine which pages to invalidate. Inconsistencies can exist for a time between the cache and the backing store.

While caching the contents of the persistent store (non-derived data) directly, a high degree of transparency with strong consistency can be achieved. Examples include caching direct copies of raw DBMS tables [29] or caching copies of persistent Java objects [13]. A framework where business rule SQL query result sets are cached is presented in [8,12]. As with our work, strong consistency is maintained through complex analysis of the SQL queries. A high degree of transparency is achieved through the compiler-based solution to insert the cache API calls tuned to the Websphere environment. In contrast, our work uses much simpler AOP tools.

Examples of caching derived data with strong consistency suffer from a low level of transparency that requires considerable developer input about request structure or dependencies. DynamicWeb [10] provides a strongly consistent web page cache, but not transparently as developers must define the dependencies between events, e.g., read and write queries. Similarly, form-based proxy caching [19] of web pages requires developers to pre-define configurations of web page formats. Weave [33] requires the programmer to use a specialized language to describe dynamic web pages and event handlers to specify invalidations. Various commercial solutions such as SpiderCache [26], Xcache [32], and Oracle9iAS [22] provide an event API to the developers to add consistency management.

The current prototype of AutoWebCache is implemented as a generic solution for a J2EE web application that uses Servlets embedding SQL queries based on JDBC [27] since this pattern is widely used in many J2EE applications [5]. It can be easily extended to include other sources of dynamism, as well as other ways of forming dynamic content, such as PHP [31]. Furthermore, the proposed caching solution is completely transparent when all database updates go through the server-side application. However, if some updates are directly performed on the database, transparency is difficult to achieve. A possible solution is to extend the caching system with an API similar to the ones provided by the DynamicWeb and Weave systems to allow an external entity to invalidate cache entries [10,33]. This external entity could, for instance, work through database triggers.

AOP techniques were experimented for profiling [7], persistence [23], distribution [14], web cache pre-fetching [24], caching static content [17], caching (non-derived) Java objects [13], and also for transactions [16] where the authors conclude that, as for consistent caching of dynamic web content, transactions can not be aspectized in general.

9 Conclusions

In this paper, we presented AutoWebCache, a middleware system for adding caching of dynamic content transparently to J2EE server-side applications having a backend database. Caching fully-formed webpages reduces the work at both the increasingly costly business logic tier as well as the back-end database tier. We first outlined the principles involved in caching dynamic web content, including the logic to ensure consistency of the cached documents. Thereafter, we demonstrated the use of aspect-oriented techniques to implement our system. We showed how aspect-oriented techniques improve modularity and transparency of the entire solution.

Using two standard J2EE web benchmarks, RUBiS and TPC-W, we evaluated AutoWebCache along various dimensions. First, we studied the effectiveness of AutoWebCache in reducing the response time of applications. Second, we analyzed the transparency of our system for a general application suite. We argued that for the general case, issues may arise when caching at the front-end as dynamic web pages can aggregate data from multiple sources and also some sources might not have sufficiently structured interfaces for exchanging the information necessary for tracking coherency. Furthermore, we showed that knowledge about application semantics can improve the efficiency of caching.

Our work presents itself several avenues for extension. A database query-results cache is complementary to webpage caching. Complex SQL queries that cannot be efficiently parsed for coherency dependency information (e.g., range queries) can be declared uncacheable at the front-end webpage cache but have its result sets cached at the back-end, thus, reducing the database costs if not the business logic costs for those requests. We also want to extend the AutoWebCache system to incorporate sources of dynamism other than SQL queries, and study their transparency w.r.t. AOP. Finally, we want to analyze the effect of varying cache size on the hit rates of requests and investigate different cache replacement strategies in this context.

References

1. C. Amza, E. Cecchet, A. Chanda, A. Cox, S. Elnikety, R. Gil, J. Marguerite, K. Rajamani and W. Zwaenepoel: Specification and Implementation of Dynamic Web Site Benchmarks. IEEE 5th Annual Workshop on Workload Characterization (WWC-5), Austin, TX, USA, Nov. 2002. http://rubis.objectweb.org
2. AspectJ 1.1, 2004. http://www.eclipse.org/aspectj/
3. S. Bouchenak, A. Cox, S. Dropsho, S. Mittal and W. Zwaenepoel: Caching Dynamic Web Content in J2EE Applications. EPFL Tech. Report IC/2004/82, Oct. 2004.
4. K. S. Candan, W.S. Li, Q. Luo, W.P. Hsiung and D. Agrawal: Enabling Dynamic Content Caching for Database-driven Web Sites. ACM SIGMOD'2001, Santa Barbara, CA, USA, 2001.
5. R. Cattell and J. Inscore: J2EE Technology in Practice: Building Business Applications with the Java 2 Platform, Enterprise Edition. Pearson Education, 2001.
6. A. Colyer: Implementing Caching with AOP. TheServerSide.COM, June 2004. http://www.theserverside.com/blogs/showblog.tss?id=AspectJCaching
7. J. Davies, N. Huismans, R. Slaney, S. Whiting, M. Webster and R. Berry: Aspect Oriented Profiler. 2nd Intl. Conference on AOSD, Boston, USA, Mar. 2003.
8. L. Denagro, A. Iyengar, I. Lipkind and I. Rouvellou: A Middleware System Which Intelligently Caches Query Results. Middleware Conference, NY, USA, Apr. 2000.
9. A. Feldmann, R. Cceres, F. Douglis, G. Glass and M. Rabinovich: Performance of Web Proxy Caching in Heterogeneous Bandwidth Environments. IEEE Conference on Computer Communications (INFOCOM), New York, Mar. 1999.
10. A. Iyengar and J. Challenger: Improving Web Server Performance by Caching Dynamic Data. In proceedings of USITS'97, Monterey, CA, USA, Dec. 1997.
11. A. Iyengar, E. MarcNair and T. Nguyen: An Analysis of Web Server Performance. IEEE Global Telecommunications Conference (GLOBECOM), Phoenix, 1997.
12. A. Iyengar and J. Challenger: Data Update Propagation: A Method for Determining How Changes to Underlying Data Affect Cached Objects on the Web. IBM Technical Report RC 21093(94368), IBM Research Division, Feb. 1998.
13. JBoss Inc. JBossCache. http://www.jboss.org/products/jbosscache
14. M. A. Kersten and G. C. Murphy: Atlas: A Case Study in Building a Web-based Learning Environment using Aspect-oriented Programming. ACM Conference on OOPSLA, Denver, Colorado, USA; Nov. 1999.
15. G. Kickzales, J. Lamping, A. Mendhekar, C. Maeda, C. V. Lopes, J. M. Loingtier and J. Irwin: Aspect-Oriented Programming. ECOOP'97, Jyvskyl, Finland.
16. J. Kienzle and R. Guerraoui: AOP: Does it Make Sense? The Case of Concurrency and Failures. In proceedings of ECOOP'2002, Mlaga, Spain, June 2002.
17. R. Laddad: AspectJ in Action - Practical Aspect-Oriented Programming. Manning Publications, 2003.
18. M. H. Lipasti: Java TPC-W Implementation Distribution. http://www.ece.wisc.edu/ pharm/tpcw.shtml
19. Q. Luo, J. F. Naughton: Form-Based Proxy Caching for Database-Backend Web Sites. 27th Very Large Data Bases Conference (VLDB'2001), Roma, Italy, 2001.
20. S. Mittal: A Consistent and Transparent Solution for Caching Dynamic Web Content. Masters thesis, Rice University, 2004. http://www.cs.rice.edu/ mittal/presentations/thesis_mittal.pdf
21. Netscape. Persistent Client State - HTTP Cookies. http://wp.netscape.com/ newsref/std/cookie_spec.html

22. Oracle. Oracle9iAS Caching Solutions. Oracle Technical White Paper, Dec. 2001. http://otn.oracle.com/products/ias/web_cache/pdf/9ias_caching_twp.pdf
23. A. Rashid and R. Chitchyan: Persistence as an Aspect. 2nd International Conference on Aspect-Oriented Software Development (AOSD), Boston, 2003.
24. M. Sgura-Devillechaise, J. M. Menaud, G. Muller and J. Lawall: Web Cache Prefetching as an Aspect : Towards a Dynamic-Weaving Based Solution. 2nd International Conference on AOSD, Boston, USA, Mar. 2003.
25. S. Sol and G. Berznieks: Instant Web Scripts with Cgi Perl. M & T Books, 1996.
26. Spider Software. SpiderCache Enterprise 2.0:Dynamic Content Delivered Faster. Spider Software Technical White Paper, Sep. 2001. http://www.spidercache.com/
27. Sun Microsystems. Enterprise Applications with J2EE Platform, 2nd Edition. http://java.sun.com/blueprints/guidelines/designing_enterprise_applications_2e/
28. Sun Microsystems. Java DataBase Connection (JDBC). http://java.sun.com/jdbc/
29. TimesTen. TimesTen Real-Time Event Processing System. TimesTen White Paper, 2003. http://www.timesten.com
30. Transation Processing Performance Council. TPC-W: a transactional web e-Commerce benchmark. http://www.tpc.org/tpcw/
31. PHP: Hypertext Preprocessor. Visual PHP Web Development and Web Reporting. http://www.yessoftware.com/content_simple.php?content_id=php_org.
32. XCache Technologies. XCache Overview. 2004. http://www.xcache.com
33. K. Yagoub, D. Florescu, V. Issarny and P. Valduriez: Caching Strategies for Data-Intensive Web Sites. 26th Very Large Databases Conference (VLDB), Egypt, 2000.

Non-intrusive Performance Management for Computer Services

Magnus Karlsson[1] and Christos Karamanolis[2]

[1] Enea, Stockholm, Sweden
magnus.karlsson@enea.com
[2] VMware Inc., Palo Alto, U.S.A.
christos@vmware.com

Abstract. Networked computer services are increasingly hosted on shared consolidated physical resources (servers, storage, network) in data centers. Thus, some form of resource control is required to ensure contractual performance targets for service customers under dynamic workload and system conditions. This paper proposes a solution for resource control that maximizes the yield of the performance contracts given the available physical resources, while it does not require any modifications to the clients' and the computing services' software or hardware. Our approach achieves this by manipulating the flow of requests into the service by using one or more proxies between the clients and the service.

This paper evaluates Proteus, a prototype implementation of the proposed approach, on two different services: a 3-tier e-commerce system and a networked file service. We show that existing proxies for the two respective protocols (HTTP and NFS RPC) can easily be modified to use Proteus to schedule their requests. Once the modified proxies have been deployed, our approach is transparent to clients and services. Moreover, we show that, in contrast to prior art, our solution (1) is stable when workloads and systems change, (2) automatically tunes itself to different services, (3) can enforce flexible quality of service specifications, and (4) correctly detects and reacts to contention of internal service resources.

1 Introduction

Increasingly, computing services are hosted using clustered architectures, rather than single servers, where a number of distributed physical resources (servers, storage, network) together offer a service. Moreover, service providers and enterprises use shared pools of resources to host multiple customers of a service and/or more than one service. Multiplexing services onto a shared infrastructure allows for on-demand assignment of resources and, thus, improves resource efficiency and cuts management costs.

This paper is concerned with how to manage the performance of a shared computing infrastructure. Negotiated *Service Level Agreements* (SLAs) define contractual performance objectives, such as throughput and response time bounds, and corresponding monetary returns for those performance objectives. The yield derives from the revenue for serving the service workloads, less any penalties for failing to meet contract terms. This paper focuses on the problem of *performance management*, i.e., how to share resources between customers/workloads given the choices already made for admission control and provisioning. These policies usually overbook resources to improve

M. van Steen and M. Henning (Eds.): Middleware 2006, LNCS 4290, pp. 22–41, 2006.

resource utilization and efficiency, assuming a statistical multiplexing of the service demands of different customers. When the total demand exceeds the capacity of the provisioned resources, then a performance management mechanism is needed to share the available capacity, in a way that first isolates workloads from each other and second maximizes the yield obtained from the service given the SLAs in place.

A lot of existing research and commercial systems that provide performance management depend on modifications in the operating system [1,2], middleware [3], or application code [4]. Clearly, such intrusive approaches are not generally applicable. Thus, a number of non-intrusive approaches have been proposed to intercept and control the workloads as they enter the service infrastructure [5,6,7,8,9]. All these approaches suffer from drawbacks that affect their general applicability.

First, all non-intrusive approaches depend on some form of feedback about the performance delivered to each performance class. The feedback loops of existing solutions are implemented in some ad hoc way, usually employing heuristic algorithms. As a result, there is no guarantee that the system is stable and that it converges to the desirable performance goals when workloads and systems outside the experimental evaluation are used. Second, prior art requires tuning according to the specific service, infrastructure configuration and workload characteristics, something that is ever changing. Third, they may unfairly penalize the performance of workloads given that they do not know who contends for what resources in the infrastructure. For example, if we have ten workloads and one of them has poor performance because it contends for resources with only one other class, then the only way to improve its performance is to reduce the throughput of the contending class. Reducing the others, as usually happens with prior approaches [5,6,7,8,9], will only decrease the total system throughput.

Finally, none of them allows for enforcing *flexible performance goals* that take into account the state of the workloads and resource usage. Prior approaches [5,7,8] assume simple static SLAs in the form of a single latency goal that will be guaranteed up to a throughput limit. If demand exceeds the throughput limit or the service cannot provide the latency goal due to workload or system variations, then either no performance guarantees are made [9], the client application is required to throttle back requests [8], or requests are dropped from mainly the performance class with the strictest latency goal [5]. Clearly, such approaches are not acceptable by all applications and services. E.g., dropping requests destined for a disk array is not an option and penalizing the class with the strictest latency goal is unacceptable if that one workload is more important than the others. A more flexible way of specifying performance goals is required.

To address these needs, we propose a new non-intrusive approach for performance management of computing services. Our approach uses standard proxies to intercept service requests before entering the system. These proxies have been modified to use our Proteus library to schedule their requests. Once the modified proxies have been deployed, our approach is transparent to clients and services. Internally, Proteus uses a *control-theoretic adaptive controller* to schedule the requests so that the performance of the service is automatically adjusted according to the specified SLAs. The controller automatically adapts to system and workload characteristics. Thus, it requires no tuning between different services or as the system and workloads change. We prove that the proposed closed-loop design is stable for throughput goals. Last, the controller automatically detects workloads that contend for internal service resources without any prior knowledge about those resources. Thus, control actions do not penalize workloads that do not use bottleneck resources. We report on an prototype of our approach and on experimental results with two diverse computing services: a 3-tier e-commerce system and an NFS service. In both cases, we show that Proteus can achieve all the previously mentioned goals and that the proxies can easily be modified to use Proteus.

2 Overview

This section introduces the basic system model in Section 2.1 and a flexible and generic way of describing performance goals and performance differentiation policies in Section 2.2. In Section 2.3, we show that the performance of a real service varies quickly and often. Thus a static solution or a human in the loop is not an option. Instead, we need an automatic controller that we develop in Section 3.

2.1 System Model

We assume that the system consists of a stream of requests dispatched from a set of clients. The requests are processed by a service and returned to the clients in some arbitrary order. Each request can be associated with a *performance class*. A class can be made up of e.g., a specific set of clients or any client using a set of services. A service usually uses a multitude of compute, storage and networking resources. The actual number, layout and performance characteristics of these resources are assumed to be unknown.

In order to be able to isolate and differentiate performance classes, one or more proxies are interposed on the network path between the service and its clients as in Figure 1. The proxies are modified to use our software library to schedule their requests through the API discussed in Section 4. The library consists of two parts: a controller and a scheduler. The scheduler intercepts requests and re-orders or delays them to achieve the partition of throughput capacity corresponding to a configurable *share* setting. For example, with two classes, setting the share to 2:1 means that one class will get 2/3 of the throughput, while the other one gets 1/3. The second scheduler parameter is the *concurrency level* that decides the maximum number of requests inside the system at any given point in time from all the classes. The premise is that the performance (latency and/or throughput) of a class varies with the amount of resources available to execute it. Thus, the scheduler enforces approximate proportional sharing of the service's capacity to serve requests aiming at meeting the performance goals of the different classes. The controller (described in Section 3) will then set these parameters so that the performance goals are met.

The scheduler in our system implements Controllable Start-Time Weighted Fair Queuing ($C\text{-}SFQ(D)$) [10], a scheduling algorithm common in computer systems, for four reasons. First, it is computationally efficient; second, being work conserving it results in high resource utilization; third, it is responsive to parameter changes; and fourth, it works in systems with high degree of concurrency.

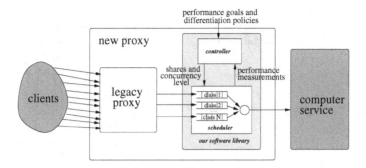

Fig. 1. Our software layer is integrated into a proxy and consists of two parts: a scheduler and a controller. The scheduler controls how a resource is shared by a number of performance classes, while the controller sets the scheduling parameters based on performance feedback.

2.2 Specifying Performance Goals

In contrast to prior approaches, we provide a way to generically specify any performance goal and performance differentiation policy. A *performance differentiation policy* is used to modify the performance goals when there is not enough capacity in the system to satisfy all the classes' performance goals. The reason for this is that we do not believe that a single policy or goal formulation is good for all possible services, workloads and systems. For a web service with gold, silver and bronze class customers, it might be enough to have a simple priority differentiation policy to prioritize gold over silver over bronze when the system is overloaded. On the other hand, for a shared remote file system in a company, we might want to provide low latency for business critical workloads, but at the same time ensure some slice of the throughput to guarantee forward progress of the backup application. Other situations require completely different performance goals and differentiation policies.

Utility functions [11] provide a way to flexibly specify performance goals and differentiation policies. These are monotonically increasing (for throughput and bandwidth) or decreasing (for latency) functions of one or more performance measurement. The measurements can either be averages or percentiles and there is one utility function per class. The goal of the system is to maximize the total utility obtained, given the utility functions of the classes. In the example of Figure 2, a user of performance class 1 does not want the request latencies to be above 300 ms. In that case the provider should pay 40 monetary units as a penalty. The user is willing to pay for performance above 300 ms, but at the most 100 monetary units for 100 ms. Simpler goals such as "provide at the most 100 ms latency and nothing else" of prior work [5,8,9] can be achieved by a utility function that gives x monetary units for 100 ms or less and $-x$ for anything above 100 ms. It is also possible to describe the utility as a function of more than one goal, e.g., utility as a function of both latency and throughput is useful. With these, throughput and latency can be traded off against each other according to user specifications, or we can specify strict goals for both of them.

The performance differentiation policy is captured by the difference between the utility functions of the classes. If one class consistently pays more than another, as is

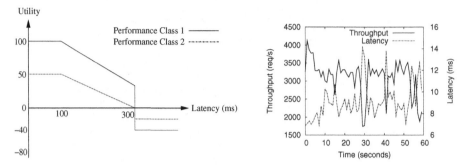

Fig. 2. A utility function example to the left. The right graph shows that a fixed share of the service capacity result in widely varying throughput and latency in our experimental service.

the case in Figure 2 where class 1 always pays more than class 2, we have a priority policy preferring the high-paying class. If the utility functions alternately pay more than each other for each performance level, we have a fair sharing policy, as maximum utility is achieved by alternately giving each class a little bit more of performance. A plethora of other differentiation policies are possible. This way, the users of our system are not locked into a specific differentiation policy or performance goal specification as in prior art [5,8,9].

Throughout the paper we will mostly talk about high level performance goals such as "provide 100 ms request latency" or "give me between 100 and 400 req/s" combined with high level performance differentiation policies such as "priority", "fair share" and "best effort". The reason for this is that these are easier both to understand and to validate than arbitrary chosen utility functions. Note, that these performance goals and differentiation policies are all specified with utility functions and, as we will see in Section 3, utility functions are the only performance specification that is used internally by our library to achieve our goal of flexibility.

2.3   Need to Vary Shares and Concurrency

A key problem is that, in the general case, certain share and concurrency level assignments do not result in steady and predictable performance, because of the dynamic nature of workloads and systems. The right graph in Figure 2 depicts the example of a typical workload of a remote file service. Even in this static example where the system does not change (there is a fixed number of clients running the same workload on a fixed set of resources), a fixed share and concurrency level (80% and 16 in this example) for one class results in widely oscillating throughput and latency. If for example, we would like to provide exactly 2,000 req/s to a class, that would mean 100% of the share around 30 s. and around 50% of the share at the beginning of the execution. Clearly, the shares need to change dynamically. A solution that does not dynamically vary the shares [5,8,9] can fundamentally not provide a flexible performance differentiation policy, as the sharing of the system is fixed.

The concurrency level also needs to vary dynamically. When the concurrency level is high, the system is used efficiently as it provides the highest total throughput. But the more requests inside the service, the higher the request latencies will be, given a fixed amount of resources. There is thus a trade-off between these goals. The concurrency level that achieves the best trade-off varies with for example, what other requests are inside the system, what resources are used and resource lay-out. As this changes, the concurrency level also needs to vary dynamically.

3   Adaptive Resource Control

In this section, we will design a controller for automatically and dynamically setting the shares and the level of concurrency of the scheduler. We will use *adaptive control theory* [12] described in Section 3.1, as it provides a well understood methodology for designing closed-loop systems that are stable, efficient and meet their goals. On a high level, an adaptive controller has two sets of inputs, a set of performance measurements from the system and a set of desired performance references. The goal of the controller is to get the performance measurements to equal the desired references by adjusting one or more system parameters. In order to achieve this, one of the most important tasks for it is to internally estimate a model of how the system parameters affect the measurements.

Figure 3 shows an overview of the control architecture we propose to provide adaptive resource control. It consists of one controller for setting the shares and one for setting the level of concurrency. The share controller in Section 3.2 sets the shares of the performance classes so that their performance goals are met. The concurrency controller in Section 3.3 adjusts the level of concurrency as to achieve the best trade-off between high capacity and meeting the strictest latency goal. An optimizer, described in Section 3.4, computes the performance targets for the classes, using the utility functions of the classes and the performance model produced in the share controller. These performance targets are then fed as references to both controllers, that they can adjust the shares and concurrency so that the classes achieve their performance targets. The targets are continuously modified so that they are always possible to achieve. The extension to distributed proxies is described in Section 3.5.

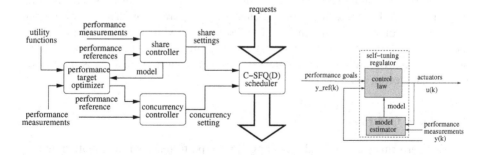

Fig. 3. Overview of our solution to the left and a self-tuning regulator to the right

3.1   Adaptive Optimal Control Theory

In order to explain the controllers, we need to introduce some notation. Assume that there are N measurements of interest made in a system, and let $y(k)$ be a column vector of the N measurements sampled at time k. These measurements are statistical metrics (e.g., average or percentile) computed over the sample period $(k-1, k]$. The elapsed wall clock time between $k-1$ and k is called the *sample interval* and is assumed to be constant over time. Let column vector $y_{ref}(k)$ denote the desired values for the N measurements at time k, and let $u(k)$ capture M actuator settings at time k. An *actuator* is a system parameter that can be dynamically set. For example, it can be the resource share of each performance class. Informally, the problem is to have the N measurements converge to the specified desired values by dynamically setting the M actuators in the system. This can be formalized as the following optimization problem:

$$minimize\ J(u(k)) = \|W(y(k+1) - y_{ref}(k+1))\|^2 + \|Q(u(k) - u(k-1))\|^2 \quad (1)$$

$W \in \mathbb{R}^{N \times N}$ and $Q \in \mathbb{R}^{N \times M}$ are positive-semidefinite weighting matrices. W captures the importance of meeting the reference values for different measurements, and Q reflects the penalties for large actuation changes. This objective function J is expressed as a function of $u(k)$, as the latter is the only input that can affect the state of the system. Note that $J(u(k)) \geq 0$ in all cases. It becomes zero when all the measurement references are met and there is no change to the actuators between consecutive intervals, i.e. the desired state.

The advantage of the problem formulation in (1) is that there are well-understood controllers that can be applied to solve it. More specifically, *optimal control* [13] is a field of control theory, in which control goals are formulated as optimization problems. Controllers designed following this approach are constructed so that they aim for the optimal solution to (1), while guaranteeing that the system is stable and converges fast.

There are a number of requirements that such a controller should meet. It has to be computationally efficient—as it needs to perform on-line control of the system. The controller should require little or no knowledge of the target system and should need little or no manual tuning before being applied. It should also quickly adapt to changes to the system and its workloads and the closed-loop should always be stable.

We propose using a certain type of adaptive controllers called *Self-Tuning Regulators* (*STR*) [12], that can enforce on-line optimization of optimal control problems while they satisfy the above practical requirements. The structure of an *STR* is shown in the right diagram of Figure 3. It consists of an *estimator* module that on-line estimates a model that describes how actuator setting affect the measurements. That model is then used by a *control law* that decides how to set the actuators so that (1) is minimized while guaranteeing stability.

3.2   Shares Controller

Meeting performance goals and providing flexible performance differentiation by manipulating the share of resources each class gets, can be formulated as an optimization problem using (1). In this case, the vector $y(k)$ refers to the performance measurements of each of the N performance classes, sampled at time k. These measurements can refer to either request latencies, throughput, or both. Vector $y_{ref}(k)$ represents the desired performance. When these targets cannot be met, $y_{ref}(k)$ will be adjusted by the optimizer in Section 3.4 according to the performance differentiation policy. $u(k)$ captures the individual share settings of each of the N performance classes. Minimizing $J(u(k))$ in this case means that the system converges to the performance targets for the N classes, while minimizing the necessary changes in share settings.

For model estimation in the *STR* we use a linear model of the following form:

$$y(k) = \sum_{i=1}^{n} A_i y(k - i) + \sum_{i=0}^{n-1} B_i u(k - i - d_0) \qquad (2)$$

Here A_i and B_i are the model parameters. Note that $A_i \in \mathbb{R}^{N \times N}$, $B_j \in \mathbb{R}^{N \times M}$, $0 < i \le n, 0 \le j < n$, where n is the *model order* that captures how much history the model takes into account. Parameter d_0 is the delay between an actuation and the time the first effects of that actuation are observed. The diagonals of A_i and B_i state what performance a class receives from a given share setting, while the anti-diagonals describe the effect changing the shares of the other classes have on a given class. Thus, the first advantage of the model is that it models how the classes are contending for resources. To correctly capture and react to this was one of our goals of the architecture. A second advantage is that it is simple and generic, a prerequisite for wide system applicability. A third advantage of this model is that it captures the dynamics of the system. This is important as higher share many times results in worse performance for a short period before the performance gets better. The underlying reason for this is e.g., warming up of caches. If the model in the controller did not take this into account, it might increase the share even further as a response to the worse performance observed shortly after the change, leading to oscillations and in the worst case to instability. The final advantage with this model is that it does not assume that all requests in all classes consume the same amount of resources. One class can have a higher entry in B_i than the others reflecting requests that take longer to serve. Prior work [5,9] does not take any of these four effects into account.

We know that the relation between actuation and performance is not always linear. For example, latency is inversely related to the share. However, even in the case of nonlinear metrics, a linear model is a good enough local approximation for the controller, as it usually only makes small changes to actuator settings. But the estimation can be improved by inputting the inverse of the latency, which we do for the rest of the paper. The advantage of using linear models is that they can be estimated in computationally efficient ways, that result in tractable control laws and there are stability proofs for them.

The unknown model parameters A_i and B_i are estimated using *Recursive Least-Squares* (RLS) estimation [12]. This is a standard, computationally fast estimation technique that fits (2) to a number of measurements, so that the sum of squared errors between the measurements and the model is minimized. RLS is able to estimate even the performance correlation between the classes (the anti-diagonals of A_i and B_i).

The control law is a function that, based on the estimated system model (2), decides what the actuator settings should be so that objective function (1) is minimized. One of the reasons we specifically chose (1) and (2) is that $u(k)$ can be computed using a computationally efficient closed-form expression. The full derivation can be found in Karlsson *et al.* [14].

From a systems perspective, the important point is that the control law provides a computationally efficient way to calculate $u(k)$ which can be performed on-line. This *STR* requires little system-specific tuning as it uses a dynamically estimated model of the system, the control law automatically adapts to system and workload dynamics.

It has been shown [12] that this *STR* is stable iff the following is true of the system: (i) the initial delay (d_0) is known and bounded; (ii) the system is minimum phase[1]; (iii) the signs of the triangular elements of B_0 are known; (iv) the upper bound on the order (n) of the system is known; and (v) the measurements are linearly related to the actuators. If true, our control-loop is stable and the performance converges to the performance goals in steady state. Independently of the system we run on, we know that the diagonal of B_0 is positive for throughput and negative for latency, and that throughput is linearly related to the share, while latency is nonlinearly related. The other parameters are system dependent and hold for our experimental systems. This means that the controller is provably stable for throughput goals and for latency goals when the changes to the system and workloads are small (as linearity is a good approximation). It is a topic of future work to analyze the stability of the loop for latency goals under arbitrary workload and system changes.

3.3 Concurrency Controller

For the concurrency level controller we are going to use the same control law and estimator as for the share controller, though with different measurements and actuators in $y(k)$ and $u(k)$, respectively. $u(k)$ will now contain the concurrency level as that is what we desire to set. The trade-off in setting this is between high total throughput of the system and being able to meet the tightest latency goal. Generally, the higher the concurrency, the higher the total throughput (until we get into overload). The end-to-end latency consists of the sum of two parts: the waiting time inside the scheduler ($w(k)$) and the service time[2] ($\sigma(k)$) inside the service itself. As the service times also monotonically increase with an increase in concurrency level, we can achieve the best total throughput while still being able to satisfy the tightest latency goal by having the system operate around a service time that will provide that end-to-end latency goal. Thus, $y_{ref}(k)$ of the concurrency controller should contain the service time it should aim for, that is the tightest latency goal minus the wait time $w(k)$ for that class. The corresponding measured service time is put in $y(k)$. This computation of $y_{ref}(k)$ is performed by the performance target optimizer and fed to this controller. The control law is then used to compute the concurrency level in $u(k)$. Note, that we do not need to care about the other classes' latency goals here, as they will be met by adjusting the shares with the share controller.

The stability conditions are the same as for the share controller. Note that these two stability proofs are only valid when the two controllers are applied to the scheduler

---

[1] This basically means that new actuator settings have precedence over old actuator settings.
[2] Queuing time plus processing time inside the service.

1   $s_{ip} = 0 \ \forall i \in classes, \ \forall p \in proxies$
2   $U_i^{curr} = -\infty \ \forall i \in classes$
3   while $\sum_{i=1}^{N} s_{ip} < 1 \ \forall p \in proxies$
4   for all performance classes i and proxies p
5   find smallest integer $d_{ip} > 0$ for which $U_i(\hat{X}_p(s_{ip} + d_{ip}/T_{tot,p}(k))) > U_i^{curr}$
6   if no such d_{ip} or $d_{ip} + \sum_{i=1}^{N} s_{ip} > 1$
7               $d_{ip} = 1$
8   end for
9   find j and p that maximize $U_j(\hat{X}_p(s_{jp} + d_{jp}/T_{tot,p}(k)))/d_{jp} - U_j^{curr}$
10      $s_{jp} = s_{jp} + d_{jp}/T_{tot,p}(k)$
11      $U_j^{curr} = U_j(\hat{X}_p(s_{jp}))$
12 end while
13 $y_{ref,p}(k) = \hat{X}_p(s_p) \ \forall p \in proxies$

Fig. 4. Pseudo-code of the performance target optimizer used to compute $y_{ref,p}(k)$

individually. It is a topic of future work to analyze the stability of the two loops together. Currently, we make sure that the concurrency controller's effect on the share controller's measurements are small by increasing Q in (1) for the concurrency controller, making it less aggressive than the share controller.

3.4   Performance Target Optimizer

As noted in the beginning of Section 3, the utility functions we use to describe performance goals and differentiation policies need to be translated into a setting of the references ($y_{ref}(k)$) for the controllers at each time interval. The problem is to find the share settings or resource partitioning that maximize the utility of the system given the current service capacity. Fortunately, we can derive a function relating shares to utility, as utility (U) is a given function of performance and RLS estimates a model correlating performance with shares inside the share controller. For notational convenience, we will here denote that model from (2) as $\hat{X}_p(s)$ where s is a vector of shares for the N classes and p indicates what proxy this is from. We have so far only presented the solution for one proxy, so this p can be ignored for now. But in the next section, we will present a distributed solution that will use multiple proxies.

Throughput is linearly dependent on the shares, so this optimization problem can be easily solved using linear algebra. But for latency, the model $\hat{X}_p(s)$ has a nonlinear dependency on the shares (in contrast to the latency inverse that was entered). Thus we cannot solve this optimization problem using standard linear algebra. Instead, we use a greedy optimization heuristic depicted in Figure 4 that works as follows. Each performance class is initially given 0 in share (s) in line 1 and the current utility (U_i^{curr}) provided by class i is initialized to minus infinity in line 2. We then find the smallest increase in share that will provide an increase in utility for each class in line 5. (The granularity of share increases is set to the share that one request consumed on average during the last interval, i.e. $1/T_{tot,p}(k)$.) The reason we do this is to deal with utility functions that have sections that are flat (as in Figure 2 for latencies above 300 ms). If there is no such share increase or this increase would be larger than giving that class the rest of the system capacity, the share increase is set to its minimal value in line 7. In line 9, we then find the class that provides the largest increase in utility per share by giving it a share corresponding to the share increase computed in line 5. This class is then given this amount of extra share in line 10, and the process is repeated until the sum of all shares given equals 1. Finally in line 13, we enter the computed shares into the estimated model to compute the latency values to put into $y_{ref}(k)$ for the share controller. The concurrency controller is fed the strictest latency goal found in $y_{ref}(k)$ minus the queue wait time for that class. Note, that changing the reference values does not affect the stability of the controllers, only the time it takes for them to reach the desired goals.

3.5 Distributed Proxies

A solution with multiple distributed proxies can be employed in front of the service when there are multiple entry points or when the request rate is so high that one proxy cannot handle it. In this case, the controllers and the scheduler are run on each proxy using local information. However, the optimizer is only executed on one node using measurements gathered from all the distributed proxies, thus it becomes a global optimizer for all the proxies. The same algorithm as in Figure 4 is used, but now there are multiple proxies so the algorithm will iterate over all proxies. That way, we now loop through line 3 to 12 until we have used up all shares on all proxies. Once the algorithm terminates, the individual references for each proxy are distributed to the local controllers on each proxy. The amount of floating point numbers transmitted over the network per sample period is $(4N + 2N^2)(P - 1)$, where N is the number of performance classes and P is the number of proxies. The quadratic term stems from transferring the model and the linear term from the measurements and results. The physical location of this global optimizer is statically defined at start up.

4 Implementation and API of Proteus

Our implementation of the controllers, optimizer and scheduler is called Proteus. We have implemented it as a library weighting in at slightly over 10,000 lines of C++. Proteus exports the API tabulated in Table 1. It consists of two parts. The first part is used to initialize the library and register and unregister performance classes and their goals. The second part of the interface is related to the handling of application requests. Whenever a request arrives at the proxy, the request is queued in the proxy and is registered with prRequest(), which returns a unique handle for the request. Similarly, when a reply to a request goes through the proxy, the reply is also registered with prReply() using the handle of the corresponding request. Proteus specifies the next request to be submitted to the backend service in either of two ways, depending on whether the proxy is implemented as an event-driven or a multi-threaded program. Event-driven proxies register a call-back function using prInit(). Whenever one of the Proteus functions are called, Proteus may invoke the call-back with the handle of the next request to be sent out. Threaded proxies, instead, may use a thread to call prDequeueRequest() to obtain the handle of the next request to be sent to the service or return an error if there is no request for delivery.

Table 1. The API of Proteus

Function name	Description
void **prInit**(cb1, cb2)	Initializes Proteus and registers application callbacks for sending the next request (for event-driven proxies) and dropping requests.
ClassID **prClassInit**(PerfGoal)	Registers a class and its performance goals. Returns a unique ID for this class.
void **prPerfGoal**(ClassID, PerfGoal)	Changes the performance goal of the class identified by ClassID.
void **prExecCtrl**()	To be called repeatedly by the proxy. Once every sample interval, a call to this function will execute the controllers.
QoSReqID **prRequest**(AppReqID, ClassID)	Register an incoming client request to belong to class ClassID. AppReqID is the proxy's request ID. Returns a unique identifier for this request.
void **prReply**(QoSReqID, AppReqID)	Registers a reply with Proteus. The reply is uniquely identified by the <QoSReqID,AppReqID> tuple.
<QoSReqID,AppReqID> **prDequeueRequest**()	Synchronous call to dequeue the next request for submission to the system. QoSReqID is -1 if there is no request to send. Used by threaded proxies.
void **prRemoveRequest** (QoSReqID, AppReqID)	Explicitly remove a pending request from Proteus.

The running time of Proteus is around 150 μs on our machines, a low overhead to incur at every sample interval. The sample interval is 1 s which we found to work well empirically. The overhead of Proteus incurred when registering requests and replies is negligible.

5 Evaluation

In this section, we present our prototype implementation Proteus and experimental results showing that it can achieve the goals stated in the introduction.

5.1 Experimental Methodology

Our evaluation demonstrates the effectiveness of Proteus using two different network services: a 3-tier e-commerce system and an NFS service. The 3-tier system consists of a web server, two application servers and one database server. They are hosted on separate server blades, each with two 1 GHz Pentium III processors, 2 GB of RAM, one 46 GB 15 krpm SCSI Ultra160 disk, and two 100 Mbps Ethernet cards. The web server is Apache version 2.0.48 with a BEA WebLogic plug-in. The application server is BEA WebLogic 7.0 SP4 over Java SDK version 1.3.1 from Sun. The database client and server are Oracle 9iR2. All three tiers run on Windows 2000 Server SP4. The site hosted on the 3-tier system is the Java PetStore[3].

---

[3] http://java.sun.com/developer/releases/petstore/

The workload applied to this system mimics real-world client behavior on shopping sites. These clients log in, browse and search for products, put products in their carts, and sometimes checkout the cart which gives rise to credit card verifications, adjustment of inventory, etc. The response latencies vary between 10 ms and 700 ms for the various operations. The workload also captures the corresponding time scales and probabilities these occur with and is generated using httperf on a separate machine. Proteus has been integrated into tinyproxy v1.6.3 that intercepts the traffic between the client machine and the 3-tier system. Only 15 lines of code had to be added to tinyproxy to use Proteus. For the experiments in the rest of this section, we generate 80 concurrent client sessions and we consider 2 performance classes of 40 clients each, unless noted.

We generate three workload patterns in order to stress the system. Smooth keeps the number of clients and their shopping behavior steady with a minimum of changes. In Ramp, more clients are gradually added as in TPC-W. After 80 is reached, they gradually start to check out more things which gives rise to even higher load on the system, especially on the database tier. The third pattern, Step, makes the same changes as ramp but all at once. This change is repeated in a square wave pattern with a change occurring every 30 s. Note that it is not possible to perform this change instantaneously, as clients must add products to their carts before they can check them out. Thus, the step takes 3-4 s in practice.

Second, we use an NFS file service consisting of five blades with the same hardware specification as the ones above. All blades run Linux 2.4.20. Two blades are used as clients, two as servers and one as an NFS proxy. Both clients and servers use NFS v.3 with asynchronous writes. In order to stress the system, the clients make random reads and writes to individual files on the NFS servers. The full data set is large enough that it does not fit in the in-memory cache of the file server. The traffic between clients and servers is intercepted by a user-space NFS v.3 proxy. Only 20 lines of code were added to integrate Proteus into this proxy. There are 16 concurrent client threads generating requests on each client node. Each node belong forms a different performance class.

5.2 Comparison Against Prior Art

First we will compare Proteus to prior art. We will only compare against non-intrusive techniques as another non-intrusive technique [5] already showed it was comparable to the best intrusive ones. Of the non-intrusive techniques, we did not consider techniques that cannot provide performance isolation [7,9], nor do we think it is fair to compare a technique [6,8] not designed for 3-tier systems or NFS servers. This leaves us with Quorum [5] designed for Internet services. We implemented Quorum according to the algorithmic pseudo code reported in their paper. Their scheduler and dropping module was used instead of C-$SFQ(D)$ and their controller replaced ours.

In order to make the comparison fair, we will only consider the case which Quorum was designed for; a 3-tier system when there is a combined latency and throughput goal per class and achievable goals. Quorum adjusts the concurrency dynamically based on the latency goal, while the shares (called weights in Quorum) are static and set off-line according to the ratio between the throughput goals. Class one (C1) has a latency goal of 200 ms and a throughput goal of 60 req/s. Class two (C2) has a latency goal of 5,000 ms (effectively best effort so that we can ignore it for the comparison) and a

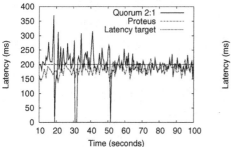 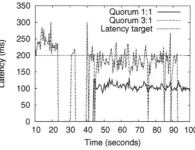

Fig. 5. A comparison against Quorum on the 3-tier system. C1 has a 200 ms latency goal and C2 has a best-effort goal and is not shown in the graphs. Quorum shows unstable behavior when the workload is changing between 10 s and 60 s. As can be seen in the right graph, the stability of Quorum is also dependent on the throughput goals used to statically set the shares.

throughput goal of 30 req/s. The static share ratio is then set to $60 : 30 = 2/1$ in the Quorum scheduler. The workload used is `ramp` as we want to evaluate how Quorum deals with change.

The left graph in Figure 5 shows the provided latency over time for Quorum and for Proteus. A latency of zero means that there were no requests at all during that interval. From this figure we can see that Quorum oscillates widely and misses the latency target during the period the `ramp` workload changes between 10 s and 50 s. Quorum exhibits instabilities around 20, 30 and 50 s when the dropping module of Quorum drops all requests from C1. Proteus with the same latency and throughput goals, on the other hand, has no problem with the changing workload and varies smoothly slightly under the latency target most of the time. After 60 s, when the workload and system is not changing, Quorum and Proteus are comparable.

If we then change the throughput goals to 60:60 (a 1:1 share ratio) or 60:20 (a 3:1 share ratio) we expect Quorum to provide similar latency measurements as for the 60:30 case, as the throughput goals are still easily going to be met (the total capacity is around 150 req/s) and therefore have no impact on the system. But this is not the case as seen in the right graph of Figure 5. Quorum oscillates widely when the share ratio is 3:1 and shows complete starvation for 1:1 during the ramp up, then undershoots the goal by a wide margin once the workload stabilizes. One of the reasons for this is that shares have an impact on not only the throughput but also the request latencies as seen in Figure 2. Proteus, on the other hand, automatically adjusts the shares to produce the desired performance goals. Proteus behaves the same in all these three cases as the references produced by the optimizer are the same in all three cases, because the throughput goals are always met. Clearly, the shares need to be set dynamically in response to both latency and throughput goals and measurements, and not set statically according to the throughput goals only. Moreover, if we would like to support flexible performance differentiation policies and react to internal resource contentions as in Proteus, being able to vary the shares is imperative.

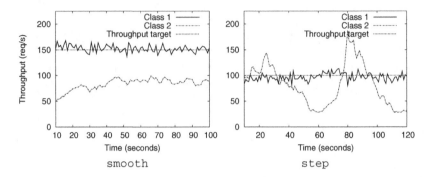

Fig. 6. Proteus on the 3-tier system with throughput goals. C2 has a best-effort goal.

5.3   3-Tier e-Commerce System

For the rest of the evaluation we will evaluate how well Proteus can achieve the objectives stated previously. That is, to be able to provide flexible performance goals and differentiation policies, show that it works between systems without any system-specific modifications or tuning, it is stable, and show that Proteus can successfully detect and deal with workload and system changes as well as contention for unknown internal service resources.

In this section, we will focus on the 3-tier system. We will start to show that Proteus works for throughput goals with a strict prioritization between the classes. C1 has higher priority than C2. The throughput target of C1 and C2 is given in the graphs and C2 gets any spare capacity. In this case, the goal of C1 can be met for the workloads shown in Figure 6. The throughput does vary a little around the performance target, because the total throughput of the 3-tier system is not constant as was shown in Figure 2.

Figure 7 shows that we can also enforce latency goals. In these experiments, C1 and C2 have the same latency goal, but C1 has higher priority. If it is not possible to meet both class goals, then the latency goal of C1 is met at the expense of C2. To introduce even more variation from the previous experiment, if both goals can be met, then any remaining resources are shared fairly resulting in better latency for both classes. We can see from the graphs that this indeed is the case for all three workloads: for smooth, C1 gets a latency around its requested target value, while C2 gets only what is possible; with step we can also see that when the capacity is high enough to satisfy both classes, they equally share the excess capacity (with the exception of the initial start up period).

The previous experiments have only considered absolute performance goals with prioritization. However, any other performance goal or performance differentiation policy is possible as long as it can be described by utility functions. Figure 8 shows results for proportional performance goals: in the left graph, throughput is shared 2/3 to C1 and 1/3 to C2; and in the right graph, C1 has to have half of C2's latency. The ramp workload is used for both experiments. We see that Proteus effectively also enforces proportional performance goals. Note that C2's latency varies more than C1's. The reason is that the higher the latency, the more sensitive it is to even slight throughput changes. When few requests are let into the system from a class, admitting one more or less will have a

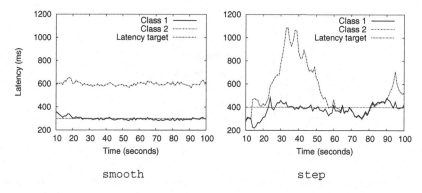

smooth   step

Fig. 7. Proteus on the 3-tier system with latency goals. C1 has higher priority than C2.

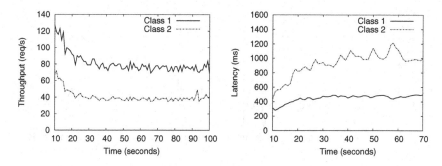

Fig. 8. Demonstrating the enforcement of proportional performance goals in the 3-tier system with ramp. On the left, C1 gets 2/3 of the throughput; and on the right, C1 has half the latency of C2.

large impact on the average latency measured for that class. One the other hand, when there are many requests from one class, one more or less makes little difference in the measured latency.

To show that Proteus can handle more than two performance classes, we ran an experiment with 4 classes. The results are shown in Figure 9. Each class has a throughput goal of 70 req/s. Priorities are set as C1 > C2 > C3 > C4. We use the ramp workload to show how Proteus reacts to changes. As specified, a class receives some throughput only if there is spare capacity after the goals of higher priority classes have been met. C4 is the first one to get throttled back to 0 req/s, followed by C3. Then C2 is scaled back to around 45 req/s, while C1 receives its requested 70 req/s throughout the run.

5.4 A Shared NFS Service

To demonstrate that Proteus can be effectively used in different systems, we applied the same library used for the 3-tier system to enforce performance differentiation in a shared NFS service. The two services have workloads with different types of requests, response latencies that are orders of magnitude different, and internal structures that are

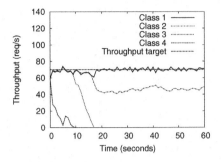

Fig. 9. Showing that Proteus can handle more than 2 performance classes. Here is an example with 4 classes with strict priority amongst them.

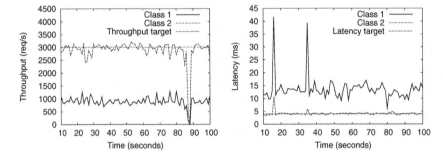

Fig. 10. Using Proteus to meet performance goals in an NFS server. Throughput goals are shown on the left and latency goals to the right.

representative of different types of resource contentions. For example, the application server in the 3-tier system is mostly CPU-bound, while the NFS servers are disk-bound.

Figure 10 demonstrates performance differentiation in the NFS service. Class 1 is the high priority one, while class 2 is best effort. Note, that the performance of the NFS system varies more than the performance of the 3-tier system. The dip in throughput right before 90 s is due to the kswapd daemon in Linux being invoked to write pages to disk. During those 1-2 s the throughput of the NFS server is close to zero.

To show that Proteus can successfully detect and deal with changing internal bottleneck resources due to workload variations and/or resource failures, we conducted an experiment where the two classes are accessing different NFS servers during the first 30 s. After that, class 2 switches to accessing the same server as class 1. In this experiment we mounted the NFS partitions in synchronous mode to be able to load the servers more, hence the lower performance numbers. The results of this experiment are shown in Figure 11 for throughput goals. Before time 30 s, both classes are getting their desired 150 req/s as they are accessing disjoint servers. But at time 30 s, they start to share the same server, which cannot meet the goals of both workloads. This is detected by the model estimator in the share controller, and the model starts to show that the performance of the two classes is now correlated. This is taken into account by the

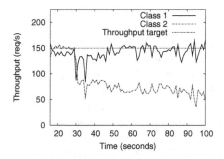

Fig. 11. Proteus can adapt to dynamic resource contention inside the system. At time 30 s, Class 2 switches from its own NFS server to accessing the same server as Class 1.

optimizer that adjusts the performance target of the low priority C2 downwards so that the target of the high priority C1 can be met. This takes Proteus only a few seconds.

6 Related Work

During the last few years, there has been a surge of research on automatic performance management of systems. For on-line management problems, most existing solutions consider some form of feedback approach. Many of them use classical non-adaptive controllers [4,15,16,17,18], which for most practical purposes are not adequate in computer systems due to their ever changing characteristics [7,8,19]. Some approaches have addressed this problem by proposing some form of adaptive controller designed in an ad-hoc manner [6,7,9,20,21,22]. Given that the analysis of the controller is based on empirical data, it is unknown whether the resulting controller is stable and performs well beyond the generally narrow experimental evaluation performed. Moreover, they are designed for a specific service and many require modifications to the target service.

To the best of our knowledge, there are six published papers that use adaptive controllers designed using a formal control-theoretic approach to achieve performance goals in computer systems. All of them are intrusive, target a specific system, cannot detect contention between performance classes, and have a static performance differentiation policy, if any at all. Proteus addresses all of these problems. Lu *et al.* [23] constructed an *STR* to satisfy absolute latency goals in web servers by partitioning the cache space. Wu *et al.* [24] used a dual *STR* to control the hit ratio of a web cache by allocating cache space to different users. Karlsson *et al.* [8] used an *STR* to achieve latency differentiation in a clustered file-system. Zhu *et al.* [25] use a adaptive pole placement controller to set the CPU resources given to a performance class in a web server, while Wei *et al.* [19] use an adaptive fuzzy controller to guarantee latency goals in web servers. Finally, Lu *et al.* [26] used another type of adaptive controller called model-based predictive controller to satisfy end-to-end latency bounds in distributed real-time systems. The controller we use here is of the same general type (*STR*) as the first three approaches, though they only design single input and single output controllers and do not use optimal control.

7   Conclusions

In this paper, we proposed a solution for performance management that maximizes the yield of the performance contracts given the available physical resources, while it does not require any modifications to the software or hardware of the computing services or the clients. Our approach achieves this by manipulating the flow of requests into the service by using one or more proxies between the clients and the service. In contrast to prior art, our solution is stable, runs on different services and can enforce flexible performance goals.

We implemented a prototype of our design called Proteus, that was evaluated on two systems, a 3-tier e-commerce system and an NFS file service. We show that existing proxies for the two respective protocols (HTTP and NFS RPC) can easily be modified to use Proteus to schedule their requests. Once the modified proxies have been deployed, our approach is transparent to clients and services. Proteus ensures that both services effectively conform to the SLAs of multiple competing workloads and enforces flexible performance specifications. It adapts within a few seconds to system and workload dynamics, is more stable than prior art, and automatically detects contention on internal service resources to improve overall resource utilization. We also show that it can be used on both systems without any tuning between them.

References

1. Shenoy, P., Vin, H.: Cello: A Disk Scheduling Framework for Next Generation Operating Systems. In: International Conference on Measurement and Modelling of Computer Systems (SIGMETRICS), Madison, WI (1998) 44–55
2. Voigt, T., Tewari, R., Freimuth, D., Mehra, A.: Kernel Mechanisms for Service Differentiation in Overloaded Web Servers. In: USENIX Annual Technical Conference, Boston, MA (2001) 189–202
3. Shen, K., Tang, H., Yang, T., Chu, L.: Integrated resource management for cluster-based internet services. In: USENIX Symposium on Operating Systems Design and Implementation (OSDI), Boston, MA (2002) 225–238
4. Abdelzaher, T., Shin, K.G., Bhatti, N.: Performance guarantees for web server end-systems: A control-theoretical approach. IEEE Transactions on Parallel and Distributed Systems 13(1) (2002) 80–96
5. Blanquer, J., Batchelli, A., Schauser, K., Wolski, R.: Quorum: Flexible Quality of Service for Internet Services. In: USENIX Symposium on Networked System Design and Implementation (NSDI), Boston, MA (2005) 159–174
6. Chambliss, D., Alvarez, G., Pandey, P., Jadav, D., Xu, J., Menon, R., Lee, T.: Performance virtulization for large-scale storage systems. In: Symposium on Reliable Distributed Systems (SRDS), Florence, Italy (2003) 109–118
7. Kamra, A., Misra, V., Nahum, E.: Yaksha: A Self-Tuning Controller for Managing the Performance of 3-Tiered Web sites. In: International Workshop on Quality of Service (IWQoS), Montreal, Canada (2004) 47–56
8. Karlsson, M., Karamanolis, C., Zhu, X.: Triage: Performance isolation and differentiation for storage systems. In: International Workshop on Quality of Service (IWQoS), Montreal, Canada (2004) 67–74

9. Lumb, C., Merchant, A., Alvarez, G.: Façade: Virtual storage devices with performance guarantees. In: International Conference on File and Storage Technologies (FAST), San Francisco, CA (2003) 131–144

10. Karlsson, M., Karamanolis, C., Chase, J.: Controllable fair queuing for meeting performance goals. In: IFIP International Symposium on Computer Performance Modeling, Measurement and Evaluation (PERFORMANCE), Juan-les-Pins, France (2005) 278–294

11. Chase, J., Anderson, D., Thakar, P., Vahdat, A., Doyle, R.: Managing Energy and Server Resources in Hosting Centres. In: ACM Symposium on Operating Systems Principles (SOSP), Banff, Canada (2001) 103–116

12. Åström, K.J., Wittenmark, B.: Adaptive Control. 2 edn. Electrical Engineering: Control Engineering. Addison-Wesley Publishing Company (1995) ISBN 0-201-55866-1.

13. Bryson, A., Ho, Y.C.: Applied Optimal Control – Optimization, Estimation, and Control. Taylor & Francis (1975) ISBN 0-89116-228-3.

14. Karlsson, M., Zhu, X., Karamanolis, C.: An Adaptive Optimal Controller for Non-Intrusive Performance Differentiation in Computing Services. In: IEEE Conference on Control and Automation (ICCA), Budapest, Hungary (2005)

15. Diao, Y., Hellerstein, J., Parekh, S.: MIMO control of an Apache web server: Modeling and controller design. In: American Control Conference (ACC), Anchorage, AK (2002) 4922–4927

16. Li, B., Nahrstedt, K.: A control theoretical model for quality of service adaptations. In: International Workshop on Quality of Service (IWQoS), Napa, CA (1998) 145–153

17. Lu, C., Abdelzaher, T., Stankovic, J., Son, S.: A feedback control approach for guaranteeing relative delays in web servers. In: IEEE Real Time Technology and Applications Symposium (RTAS), Taipei, Taiwan (2001) 51–62

18. Robertsson, A., Wittenmark, B., Kihl, M., Andersson, M.: Design and Evaluation of Load Control in Web Server Systems. In: American Control Conference (ACC), Boston, MA (2004) 1980–1985

19. Wei, J., Xu, C.Z.: A Self-tuning Fuzzy Control Approach for End-to-End QoS Guarantees in Web Servers. In: International Workshop on Quality of Service (IWQoS), Passau, Germany (2005) 123–135

20. Diao, Y., Lui, X., Froehlich, S., Hellerstein, J., Parekh, S., Sha, L.: On-line response time optimization of an apache web server. In: International Workshop on Quality of Service (IWQoS), Monterey, CA (2003) 461–478

21. Sundaram, V., Shenoy, P.: A practical learning-based approach for dynamic storage bandwidth allocation. In: International Workshop on Quality of Service (IWQoS), Monterey, CA (2003) 479–497

22. Welsh, M., Culler, D.: Adaptive overload control for busy internet servers. In: USENIX Symposium on Internet Technologies and Systems (USITS), Seattle, WA (2003) 43–56

23. Lu, Y., Abdelzaher, T., Lu, C., Tao, G.: An adaptive control framework for QoS guarantees and its application to differentiated caching services. In: International Workshop on Quality of Service (IWQoS), Miami Beach, FL (2002) 23–32

24. Wu, K., Lilja, D., Bai, H.: The Applicability of Adaptive Control Theory to QoS Design: Limitations and Solutions. In: International Workshop on Performance Modeling, Evaluation, and Optimization of Parallel and Distributed Systems (PMEO-PDS), Denver, CO (2005)

25. Liu, X., Zhu, X., Singhal, S., Arlitt, M.: Adaptive entitlement control of resource containers on shared servers. In: IFIP/IEEE International Symposium on Integrated Network Management (IM), Nice, France (2005) 163–176

26. Lu, C., Wang, X., Koutsoukos, X.: End-to-end utilization control in distributed real-time systems. In: International Conference on Distributed Computing Systems (ICDCS), Hachioji, Japan (2004) 456–466

True and Transparent Distributed Composition of Aspect-Components

Bert Lagaisse and Wouter Joosen

Dept. of Computer Science, K.U.Leuven, Belgium
{Bert.Lagaisse, Wouter.Joosen}@cs.kuleuven.be

Abstract. Next-generation middleware must support complex compositions that involve dependencies between multiple components residing in different contexts and locations in the network.

In this paper we present DyMAC, an aspect-oriented middleware platform that offers an aspect-component model to support such complex distributed compositions by means of advanced remote pointcuts, transparent remote advice and distributed instantiation scopes for aspects. The remote pointcuts can evaluate on calls and executions of remote method invocations and can also evaluate on the distributed context. The remote advice can be executed transparently in a remote environment while still respecting the full semantics of existing types of advice, including around advice. The component model unifies aspects and components into one entity with one interaction standard.

To our knowledge, DyMAC middleware is the first AO middleware platform that distributes the concepts of aspect-oriented composition completely and transparently.

1   Introduction

The environments in which distributed software applications must execute have become very dynamic and heterogeneous. As a result, software must be dynamically composed and even be adapted at runtime. This is for instance the case in ubiquitous computing environments. Typical enterprise applications expose similar needs.

Distributed applications are typically built on middleware, the software that sits between lower level system software (such as the OS) and the distributed programming platform. A dominant trend in (typical) enterprise middleware is the fact that specialized servers combine many middleware functions with specific component frameworks (e.g. J2EE, .NET etc.). The value of such a middleware component framework is twofold [1,2]: first, a specific component model enables the construction of applications from independently developed third party components - at least in principle - and second, built-in services facilitate covering non-functional requirements of a distributed application. The presence of built-in (container managed) services is often the basis for acceptance of a specific middleware platform. However, this critical success factor is at the same time the basis for the limitations of such a middleware platform. Built-in services support modularized, declarative composition of concerns of a cross-cutting nature:

M. van Steen and M. Henning (Eds.): Middleware 2006, LNCS 4290, pp. 42–61, 2006.

these are concerns that cannot easily be addressed without creating code that is scattered over the application and middleware artifacts. However, these built-in services are hard to modify or customize. Solutions for these shortcomings have been proposed in [3,13]. But, the services also cannot be used in complex compositions. This observation characterizes the limited flexibility that is supported by state-of-the-art middleware: more complex compositions must be enabled. The types of compositions that should be supported are very broad. Many of these compositions involve dependencies between multiple components residing in different contexts and locations in the network. This is extremely hard if one has to rely purely on state-of-the-art software development technologies - i.e. object-oriented and component based software engineering.

To address this problem, aspect-oriented software development (AOSD[7]) often has been put forward as a possible solution. AOSD addresses this shortcoming by focusing on the systematic identification, modularization, representation and composition of (often crosscutting) concerns or requirements throughout the entire software development process. The core concept in AOSD is an aspect [4,5]: a coherent entity that addresses one specific concern and that has the properties of a module that can be changed independently of other modules. An aspect defines behaviour that can be executed (so called advice) and defines composition logic to describe complex and dynamic dependencies between this behaviour and the rest of the software system. This composition logic is expressed using a joinpoint model. A common definition of a joinpoint refers to well-defined places in the structure or execution flow of a program [5,7]. In any case, joinpoints represent dynamic, runtime conditions that arise during program execution. The occurrence of such a condition is an event that can trigger the execution of aspect behaviour (advice). A set of joinpoints can typically be specified with pointcut designators that address and describe the kind and context of the joinpoints [7]. By the *kind* of a joinpoint we mean for instance a method call or a field access, etc. By the *context* we refer to additional information that can be made available to constrain the condition, such as the method signature, type and identity of the caller or callee of a method, further credentials and properties of the caller etc. The statically decidable conditions of a pointcut can be evaluated at compiletime or loadtime. The dynamic conditions are evaluated at runtime.

In state-of-the-art AOP, context information is essentially limited to local information, managed in a single VM. In a realistic distributed application however, joinpoints must refer to context information that is inherently distributed. Relative to state-of-the-art AOP, *distributed* joinpoints are advanced in that they transparently distribute the basic concept of a joinpoint: they refer to sophisticated conditions in distributed systems that are required to express composition in a distributed application. In general, the context information that is needed must refer to (potentially multiple) components that are not local, and possibly to distributed infrastructure. In particular, to express these runtime conditions and express compositions, we need support for aspects with three key features.

1. We need remote pointcuts, that can evaluate on calls and executions of remote method invocations and also can evaluate on distributed context.
2. Remote advice is required, which can be transparently executed in a remote environment (different from the pointcut evaluation), while still respecting the full semantics of existing types of advice, including *around* advice[1].
3. To be part of a mature middleware concept, aspects need component semantics, including clearly defined interfaces, supporting third party composition and interaction with other aspects.

Many initiatives in the domain of aspect-oriented middleware (AO middleware) have started to support creation, deployment and execution of distributed aspects for a distributed environment [9,15,18,17]. However, so far none of these research results have defined and illustrated a *complete* solution to the above mentioned challenges. In this paper, we present DyMAC, a middleware architecture that offers true and transparent distributed composition of aspect-components. Its component and composition model offers a solution for the three key challenges.

The rest of this paper is structured as follows. In section 2 we refine the problem statement and motivate why true and transparent distributed composition of aspect-components will be an important feature of next-generation middleware. Section 3 describes the model, architecture and implementation of our solution, DyMAC middleware. Section 4 evaluates our prototype. We discuss related work in section 5 and we conclude in section 6.

2   Problem Refinement

We use an example of a banking application that manages checking accounts and offers support to perform transactions on the checking accounts. The core business component is *BasicBanking*, which is a component offering operations to create new checking accounts, and execute transactions: withdrawals, deposits and transfers. This component is located at the application server. The employees at the branch offices use the *EmployeeClient* component at their workstations to handle the requests of the customers to create a new checking account or perform a transaction. The clients send the requested operations to the BasicBanking service at the application server. We have depicted the deployment architecture of the application in Figure 1. It also describes the set of additional middleware services that are part of the application:

1. A client-side, local component asking the employees for credentials, before the EmployeeClient component starts up.
2. An authentication service to authenticate the credentials of the employees and add an authentication token to their execution context. This authentication service is located at the central authentication server and is called after the client has provided his credentials.

---

[1] Around advice replaces the advised method invocation.

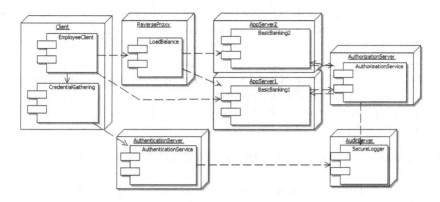

Fig. 1. The deployment architecture of the banking application

3. An authorization service at a central authorization server that verifies the application-level rights associated with the authenticated user. Before the execution of a remote method invocation at the BasicBanking service, this authorization server is called.
4. A load-balancing and fail-over service that delegates the calls of the clients to one of the application servers, based on the load or availability of the servers. This middleware service is located at a dedicated server (called reverse proxy-server).
5. A secure logging component at the central audit server that keeps track of all authentication and authorization attempts and the results.

The composition policies of these middleware services should solve the problem of crosscutting calls to the services in the core business components, and should allow a clean separation of concerns. Therefore the component and composition model needs to support the three key features from section 1. We motivate and refine the three key features with illustrations from the example.

Advanced remote pointcuts

1. Remote pointcuts that are able to refer to joinpoints before and after calling and executing remote method invocations in a distributed system. This notion extends the *kind* of the joinpoint for distributed systems. E.g. for the load balancing service: whenever a client machine calls the BasicBanking service, before that call load balancing advice should be called.
2. Remote pointcuts that can evaluate over the contextual properties about the components involved: the calling and receiving component name, the interface of the receiving component or the dependency name [2] of the sending component. E.g. for the authorization service: it has to be called each time a method is executed at the BasicBanking service. But this service is duplicated for load balancing as different components and has different names. By

---

[2] A dependency defines a required interface to be fulfilled by another component.

using the interface of the component as contextual property of the receiving component, all duplicated BasicBanking components can be captured in one pointcut.

3. Remote pointcuts that allow to evaluate over the contextual properties about the distributed location of sending an receiving component. E.g. for the load balancing service: the composition policy above uses the contextual property *hostgroup*[3] of the calling component. This scales better when other client-side components are using the BasicBanking service.

Transparent remote advice with full semantics

4. Transparent remote execution of advices, based on the deployment specification of an advising component. E.g. for the authorization service. The deployment location of that service should be transparent when defining the composition.

5. Remote before, after and around advice with full remote semantics. This allows to capture remote behaviour that is associated with calling and executing remote invocations.

   - E.g. for the validation at the authentication server of the given credentials, remote after advice is needed after the client has provided the credentials.
   - E.g. for the evaluation of the load balancing policy, remote around advice is needed: based on the load or availability of the application server it can *replace* the original call with a call to a backup server or it can just let the original call continue.

Unified aspect-component model

6. Unification of the entities. Components are aspects and aspects are components. E.g. the logger entity to log executing messages. This should be a reusable component, offering support for aspect-oriented composition in its interface. And it should be reusable and deployable in third party compositions and deployment infrastructures.

7. Unification of interaction: advices and methods are considered normal remote method invocations and are both subject to aspect-oriented composition. E.g. the remote authentication advice for validating the credentials is remotely advised by the logging component at the audit server.

State-of-the-art aspect-oriented middleware fails to define the complete range of compositions as sketched above. For instance, the contextual information provided for pointcut expressions is too limited and remote around advice with full semantics is not supported. We further discuss the shortcomings and the consequences in the related work section.

---

[3] A name for a group of hosts in the application, e.g. workstations.

3   DyMAC Middleware

In this section we discuss the DyMAC middleware platform. First, we briefly describe the basic concepts of the component model. Second, we explain the support for aspect-oriented composition in a distributed environment. Third, we explain how the middleware supports the concepts of the component and composition model. We explain the basic architecture of the middleware and describe the important subsystems that support distributed joinpoints, remote pointcuts and the coordination of remote advices. We also motivate the architectural decisions in the middleware that manage performance overhead. Fourth, we present a brief description of the .NET implementation of DyMAC.

The component model has been inspired by two evolutions: the first one is the evolution to distributed object-based component technology, such as EJB [8]. The second one is the evolution in AOSD towards the concept of an aspect with component semantics[10,11,15,14], and even towards a unified concept of aspect and component [19]. A pure object-based approach to the latter is currently supported for single-process applications [23]. Aspects are reduced to normal Java classes and advices are reduced to normal object methods, having a special signature. The resulting programming model offers one entity with one interaction standard. The aspect-oriented composition itself is defined in a separate specification file. These specifications define a pointcut, and which class and advice to bind. This way the advising entities become more reusable in third party compositions, an essential property for component based software development. DyMAC leverages the unified, object-based approach to aspects to the level of distributed object-based component models.

3.1   DyMAC's Basic Component Model

DyMAC components are object-based entities that separate interfaces and implementation. DyMAC components declare their required interfaces by means of dependencies. Components are composed in an application and are deployed on a distributed infrastructure. We explain these different concepts.

Components have two interfaces: a create-interface that specifies how to instantiate a component, and an instance-interface that specifies which methods are offered by a component instance. We illustrate this for the BasicBanking component in listing 1.1.[4]

The implementation of the component implements the members of the two interfaces as follows. First, it implements a constructor for each create-method specified in the create-interface. Second, it explicitly implements the instance interface. Client components implement the predefined interface IExecutable, which defines a main method, as an entry point for execution. Each component implementation also inherits from *ComponentInstance*, which binds a component to the DyMAC framework. Listing 1.2 illustrates the implementation of the BasicBanking component and the EmployeeClient component. It also illustrates

---

[4] The examples are implemented on the DyMAC.NET prototype and use plain C#.

Listing 1.1. BasicBanking interfaces

```
interface IBasicBankingCreate {
  IBasicBanking Create();}
interface IBasicBanking {
  void CreateAccount(string id);
  void WithDraw(string account, double amount);
  void Deposit(string account, double amount);
  void Transfer(string from, string to, double amount, string msg);}
```

Listing 1.2. Component implementations

```
class BasicBankingImpl : IBasicBanking, ComponentInstance {
  public BasicBanking(){}
  public void WithDraw(string account, double amount){...}
  ...}
class EmployeeClientImpl : IExecutable, ComponentInstance{
  public void Main(string[] args){
    ...
    //create an instance
    IBasicBanking ibb = Factory.Create("mybanking") as IBasicBanking;
    ...
    ibb.WithDraw(accountid, amount); //call an instance method
}}
```

how to create instances and how to do remote method invocations using the instance interface.

The component descriptor defines the component name, the provided interfaces, the implementation file and the dependencies of the component. A dependency is defined by a dependency name and the interfaces that are expected of the component that will be bound to the dependency. This is similar to the approach that is used in the EJB component model.

The application descriptor first defines a name for the distributed application, then it defines the set of components that is used, by referring to their descriptor. Then the compositions of the components are defined. These compositions can be normal compositions between dependencies and components, as well as aspect-oriented compositions.

Deployment descriptor. A distributed DyMAC application consists of a set of components that are deployed across a distributed infrastructure. This distributed infrastructure has a hierarchical structure: a hostgroup contains multiple hosts, (E.g. the client workstations), a host can contain multiple framework instances, which are processes. A framework instance can host multiple applications, each in an application domain. Multiple application domains are typically used on web servers and application servers to host multiple applications in one process. An application domain is a contextual unit of isolation for an application. The isolation guarantees that an application can be independently stopped. Furthermore an application cannot directly access code or resources in another application. A fault in an application cannot affect other applications. Processes with multiple application domains are only used for server processes; for the client tier of distributed applications, each application starts a different process at the client, containing one application domain with the client tier components. For one distributed application, the deployment infrastructure consists of a set of application domains that are located on multiple processes and hosts. The deployment descriptor of an application defines those deployment locations of the components. For a remotely accessible component, this location is unique in the infrastructure and is defined by the name of a host, framework instance and application domain. A component can also be deployed as a local component, then it is deployed in every application domain of the distributed application. When components are deployed locally, then an instantiation call always creates a local instance of the component.

3.2 Support for Aspect-Oriented Composition

In DyMAC, aspect-oriented compositions are defined in the application descriptor. They consist of two main parts.

1. The component providing the aspect behaviour and its instantiation scope.
2. A set of bindings in which each binding defines a pointcut, refers to an advice-method of the advising component, and specifies an advice type (before, after or around).

We first explain the pointcut expressions, then we explain advice and the instantiation scopes of an advising component. For each concept, we emphasize how it supports AO composition in a distributed environment. Finally we illustrate AO compositions in DyMAC by means of the example from section 2.

Pointcut expressions. Pointcuts are logical expressions that evaluate over the kind and context properties of the joinpoints. The kind of the joinpoint can be restricted to calling and executing remote method invocations. The pointcut expressions to support that are a *call and execution* pointcut. Pointcuts can further evaluate over two sets of contextual properties. First, the *component-related properties* of the joinpoint model: the message signature, the dependency name of the sending component, the interface of the receiving component, and the names of the sending and receiving component and the name of the distributed application they belong to. Second, the *infrastructure-related properties* of the joinpoint model: the host names of sending and receiving component, their hostgroups, their framework and the application domain they belong to. If pointcuts do not specify a value for a certain property, it has the default value *all*. This breakdown of the contextual properties implies that pointcuts can be *remote in an implicit and explicit way*. Pointcuts evaluating on the component-related contextual properties only, are implicit remote pointcuts. They allow to refer to distributed components, without being aware (containing no information) of their distributed location. Notice that in this way the concept of a pointcut is transparently remote. Pointcuts that evaluate on the infrastructure-related contextual properties are explicitly aware of remote locations of components in the infrastructure. But, even with explicit remote pointcuts, AO compositions in applications can be made reusable in third party deployment scenarios by means of hostgroups. These are deployment-independent groups of hosts, defined by the application. The deployment descriptor defines which hosts belong to the groups.

Advice. First we describe briefly the different types of advice that are supported in DyMAC. Second we describe the definition of advice methods in the interfaces of components. Third, we explain the implementation of advice and the joinpoint API. Last, we discuss the execution semantics of advice.

Types of advice. In DyMAC, three types of advice are supported: before, after and around. Before and after advices are respectively called after and before the call or execution of a remote method invocation. Around advice replaces the actual invocation it advises, but a *proceed* operation can be called in the advice to continue with the original remote method invocation. In case multiple advices have to be called on a certain joinpoint, the proceed call continues with the next advice in the advice chain. In case the advice is terminal in the chain, the call or execution of the original method invocation continues. After the execution of the advices later in the chain, the control flow returns to the rest of the around advice where the proceed was called.

Specifying Advice Methods. Methods, defined in the interface of a component, that are used as advice in an aspect-oriented composition, need to have a special signature. The advice can also be annotated with the kind of the joinpoint that the advice *supports, requires* or *prohibits* to be composed with. The possible advice kinds are BeforeCall, AfterCall, AroundCall, BeforeExection, AfterExecution and AroundExecution. Multiple *prohibits* and *supports* annotations can be defined. Only one requires annotation can be defined. These annotations are part of the interface (and thus the contract of the component [1]) because they express explicit requirements of the component when composed with other components. These need to be fulfilled to guarantee correct behaviour of the component. We specify the log method of the secure logger as an example. It only supports to be composed after an execution or call, because it needs the return message to check for exceptions.

```
[Supports(Kind.AfterExecution)]
[Supports(Kind.AfterCall)]
void Log(RuntimeJoinPoint rjp);
```

Advice implementation and the joinpoint API. The implementation of a component implements the behaviour of the advice methods specified in the interface. In this implementation the joinpoint API can be used to reflect on the current joinpoint. In DyMAC the current joinpoint is accessed using the RuntimeJoinPoint parameter of the advice. It contains information about the kind and context of the joinpoint. The joinpoint API contains contextual properties about the remote method invocation that is being advised and the calling and executing component instance of that invocation. Component properties like component name, interface and dependency names are read only. Infrastructure properties are read only too. Arguments of the method invocation can be altered. In case the joinpoint's kind is after a call or execution, the return message can also be inspected and altered. The joinpoint API also contains the proxies to the sending and receiving component instance. Remote method invocations can be called on those remote instances out of the advices. This can be required to pull state of the component instances, that is needed in the advice, for example to evaluate an authorization policy using application-level domain knowledge. Another advantage of those proxies is that additional application-level behaviour can be called out of the advice.

Execution semantics of advice. Advice is considered a normal remote method invocation when it is called from the joinpoint context and executed at the receiving component. It is advisable like any other method invocation. The sending component of an advice is the component instance in whose context the advised joinpoint is situated. In case of a call, the sending component instance of the advice is the sending component of the invocation that currently is being advised. In case of an execution, the sending component instance of the advice is the receiving component of the invocation that currently is being advised.

Defining Distributed Instantiation Scopes. Instances of advising components are created implicitly. Aspect scopes [5,7] define the creation moment and usage scope of the instance. Typical instantiation scopes in single-process AOP systems are: per joinpoint, per class, per instance, per thread, per VM. The per instance instantiation scope, for example, means that there is one instance of the advising aspect for each object instance that is advised. For every new object a new aspect instance is created. That instance is reused for all advised method invocations on the advised object. DyMAC supports distributed instantiation scopes for components that are used to remotely advise in a distributed system, and thus includes scopes beyond process boundaries.

- Singleton : one instance in the distributed system.
- Per hostgroup : one instance per group of hosts.
- Per host : one instance per host.
- Per application domain : one instance per application domain.
- Per application : one instance per distributed application
- Per component type : one instance per component type in the distributed system
- Per component instance : one instance per component instance in the distributed system
- Per logical thread : one instance per logical thread (or distributed thread), which is used for remote control flows.

Example. We define the AO compositions of the load balancer and the secure logger in detail. They illustrate true remote around advice and after advice, but also the supported kinds of pointcuts and their evaluation on contextual properties. The load balancing composition in listing 1.3 expresses first that the LoadBalancing component is used as a singleton for this composition. The pointcut refers to all calls from the *workstations* hostgroup to the components with the *IBasicBanking* interface. They are advised by the *LoadBalancer* using the method *Balance* as around advice. Based on load and availability of the application servers, the load balancer decides to proceed with the message or it calls one of the backup servers itself, thus replacing the original call of the client. We assume that the BasicBanking service is stateless, and therefore, all remote invocations to the instances can be redirected to another instance on another server. The location of the LoadBalancer is transparent in this composition. It is defined in a separate deployment descriptor.

The composition of the SecureLogger in listing 1.4 specifies that advice *log* is called after each execution on the authentication server. This log method uses the joinpoint API to check the return message. If it contains an exception, an authentication failure is logged with the contextual properties of the caller in the joinpoint. The binding with the authorization server is similar.

The concrete syntax of the application descriptor is XML based in the .NET implementation of DyMAC, but for readability and conciseness we use the Java configuration file syntax. The structure or abstract syntax of the composition is the same in both notations.

Listing 1.3. LoadBalancer

```
ao−composition{
  AdvisingComponent: LoadBalancer;
  Scope: Singleton;
  Binding{
   Pointcut{
    Kind: call;
    MethodMessage: * * (..);
    Caller{
     Hostgroup: workstations;}
    Callee{
     Interface: IBasicBanking;}}
   Advice{
    Kind: around;
    MethodMessage: Balance;
   }}
}
```

Listing 1.4. SecureLogger

```
ao−composition{
  AdvisingComponent: SecureLogger;
  Scope: Singleton;
  Binding{
   Pointcut{
    Kind: execution;
    MethodMessage: * *(..);
    Callee{
     Host: AuthenticationServer;}}
   Advice{
    Kind: after;
    MethodMessage: Log;
   }}
  Binding{
   //authorization logging
  }}
```

3.3 The Middleware Architecture

In this description of the middleware architecture we first describe briefly the top-level global architecture and its distributed deployment on the network. Then we focus on the essential subsystems that support the key features of the component and composition model: the aspectbinder and interception core that process the remote pointcuts at loadtime and at runtime, the distributed joinpoint architecture that supports advanced remote pointcuts with acceptable performance overhead, and the advice coordination infrastructure supporting multi-threaded, remote around-advices. In addition we discuss instance management, especially the component factory and instance registry for distributed instantiation scopes of advising components.

The top-level architecture. Each DyMAC framework can host multiple application domains for different distributed DyMAC applications. The framework middleware offers a remote interface *framework facade* to deploy, startup, stop

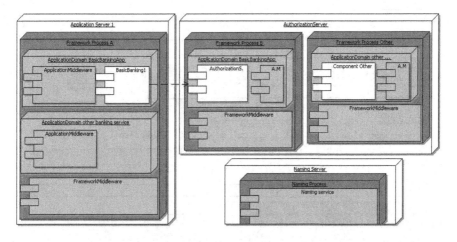

Fig. 2. DyMAC deployment view

and undeploy applications on the framework. The *deployer* distributes the application binaries and descriptors to the framework middleware to store them on the *application repository.* Then the distributed application can start up. The framework middleware first instantiates an application domain and loads the application middleware into it. The *application middleware* loads and manages the different components that are deployed in its application domain. A deployment scenario for the framework middleware, application domains, application middleware and some application components is depicted in Figure 2 . We now focus on the different subsystems of the middleware. An overview of these subsystems is depicted in Figure 3. The following subsystems are involved in the loading process. First the application descriptor is handled by the *ApplicationParser* and an *ApplicationSpec* model is built. After parsing successfully, the application domain loads the binaries and the *ApplicationVerifier* checks the Application-Spec model to verify if it conforms to the component model, and whether all binaries referenced are loaded. If the ApplicationSpec is sound, the application builder builds an application metamodel (*ApplicationType*). This model contains a component type for each component spec in the application spec model. Each component type contains a list of dependencies with a list of method definitions. The component type also contains a list of provided method definitions. In this step of the loading process all method definitions have an empty advice chain. The *AspectBinder* then handles the bindings defined in the AO compositions.

The AspectBinder. We first explain the common approach for call-pointcuts as well as execution-pointcuts in the bindings. Then we refine the explanation for each kind of pointcut. *For each binding,* the properties of the pointcut that are known at loadtime are evaluated. If the loadtime known properties of a method definition match, an *advice thunk* is inserted into the advice chain of the method. Advice thunks define a set of properties to evaluate at runtime (the *pointcut residue*[6]) and an advice method to be called when the runtime properties

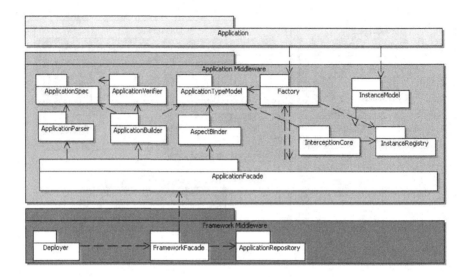

Fig. 3. DyMAC subsystem view

evaluate to true. *In case of an execution pointcut,* the method signature and
the properties of the callee in the pointcut are evaluated at loadtime. The properties of the caller can only be evaluated at runtime when a method message
arrives at the component. *In case of a call pointcut,* the method signature and the
properties of the caller in the pointcut are evaluated at loadtime. The properties
of the callee are evaluated at runtime when the message is sent to the component instance that is bound to the dependency. This binding can be different
at runtime because of possible runtime changes to the component satisfying the
dependency, such as its location.

Once the application is running, the *interception core* processes the remote
invocations between components. This interception core has two important services. The first one is the distributed joinpoint infrastructure, that manages the
runtime representations of distributed joinpoints. The second service is the remote advice coordinator. This service selects and evaluates the advice thunks
for a joinpoint, iterates the resulting advices and handles the execution of them.

The distributed joinpoint infrastructure. Joinpoints in DyMAC contain runtime
information about calling or executing method invocations between component
instances in the distributed infrastructure. Four different kinds of joinpoints are
distinguished at runtime : before a call, before an execution, after an execution
and after a call. The distributed joinpoint infrastructure creates a runtime representation of these joinpoints, that *localizes all information* that is needed to
select and evaluate the advice thunk.

Before a remote invocation is called a before-call joinpoint is constructed using
the following information: (1) the contextual properties of the sending component, which are locally stored in the component type model, and (2) the contextual properties of the receiving component, stored in the proxy to the receiving

component instance. The properties of the sending component are added to the *call context* of the method message. The call context containing the caller properties is serialized as a piggy back on the remote invocation. *Before a remote invocation is executed* at the destination component, a before-execution joinpoint is created. The call context of the message is deserialized and the caller's contextual properties are added to the execution-joinpoint. The callee's contextual properties are stored local in the typemodel of the receiving application middleware platform and are added to the joinpoint *After the execution* the kind of the before-execution joinpoint is changed to after-execution, and the return message is added to the joinpoint. *After the call,* the call-joinpoint's kind is changed to after-call and the received return message is added to the joinpoint.

Architectural decisions about the management of the contextual properties are incorporated to avoid chattiness. Chattiness could have occurred when the information that is remote to the location of a joinpoint is pulled from the remote host *by need.* This could have occurred during call-joinpoint evaluation, when information about the callee is needed and during execution-joinpoint evaluation when information is needed about the caller. It could have occurred when contextual information about caller and callee is accessed using the joinpoint API at the execution location of the remote advice.

Therefore, when a component is instantiated, its contextual properties are stored in its proxy. Every remote client of the component receives the contextual properties along with the proxy. This does involve an initial transport overhead when the proxy is created, but the properties of the callee are always local for the call-joinpoint. To achieve locality of the caller-properties for an execution-joinpoint, the properties of the caller are added as a piggy back on the remote message to the callee. This omits a call-back of the callee to the caller to query contextual information during runtime evaluation. When the remote advice methods access the contextual properties of the joinpoint parameter, that information is local. The joinpoint object is a composite value object, and therefor a complete local copy is available in the execution context of remote advice methods.

The remote advice coordination infrastructure. The interception core of DyMAC coordinates remote advice with the advice handler. The advice handler of DyMAC is instantiated when advice needs to be executed for a certain joinpoint. The list of advices matching the joinpoint is handed over to the new advice handler instance. In case the advice chain contains a remote around advice, the advice coordinator is a remotely accessible instance. This remote access is necessary to give back the control flow in case a *proceed* is called in the remote around advice. In case the advice bindings do not contain remote around advices, the advice handler instance is a local object. This avoids expensive instantiation of a remotely accessible advice handler. In case the advice is local around advice, the proceed call to the advice handler is also local, and no remote advice handler is needed. In case the advice is remote before advice or remote after advice, the control flow returns to the local advice handler automatically after the execution of advice. We show the message flow for the execution of the withdraw operation in figure 4. Only the around advice of the load balancer and the AdviceHandler at the client are illustrated.

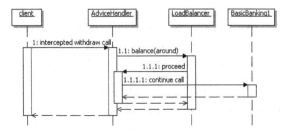

Fig. 4. Remote AdviceHandler for Remote Around Advice

Component Factory. Instantiation of components is supported by the DyMAC factory. This service provides a create-operation with as first argument a dependency name and then a variable number of arguments. When the create-operation is called, the factory looks up the dependency name, binds a component to it and creates an instance of the component, using the appropriate constructor in the implementation. This instance can be remote, depending on the deployment location of the component. The remote interface of the application middleware containing the component is called to create the remote instance.

Distributed instance registry. The instance of an advising component is implicitly created when it is needed in an AO composition. It is registered in the aspect registry at the deployment location of the component. If a new instantiation request arrives at the instance registry, the registry checks if there is already an instance bound to the requested instantiation context. This can be deducted from the caller properties that are a piggyback on the instantiation call. If such an instance exists, a proxy to the existing instance is returned to the requesting advice binding.

The application middleware of an application domain has a local cache of the aspect registry. It contains the proxies to the remote instances that are related to the application domain. This avoids expensive remote lookups before advice is executed, and also reduces chattiness. Concretely, the application middleware has a hash-based cache structure that is divided into substructures for the different instantiation scopes : group, host, framework, application domain, distributed application, component type and component instance.

For the logical thread instantiation scope, DyMAC supports another optimization for the distribution of the instance proxy along the distributed call flow. The proxy is piggy backed with a method message whenever the call flow is transferred to the next application middleware instance. This again avoids a lot of chattiness. Chattiness could have occurred due to lookups for the remote component instance handling the advice. In fact, these lookups would be performed at every application domain.

3.4   Prototype Implementation

The DyMAC middleware platform has been prototyped on .NET 2.0. It is implemented as a framework and does not involve any language extension. Component interfaces and implementation can be defined in any CTS/CLS compliant language. Remote method invocations are normal method calls and do not involve any meta object protocol as in some other AO middleware approaches [15]. This implies that components and their interactions are statically verified by a production .NET compiler.

The InterceptionCore in the middleware is built on the Context Bound Object technology to intercept remote messages. This interception happens in the .NET CLR. The CLR then activates the DyMAC message sink of the InterceptionCore, which creates a runtime joinpoint and starts the DyMAC AdviceCombiner. This way of dynamic interception does not require byte code weaving on components and does not require the CLR to run in debug mode.

The remote method invocations between component instances are implemented on .NET remoting. Piggy backs added by the DyMAC middleware are stored in the *call context* of a remote message. This is a hashtable associated with the call flow and .NET remoting serializes this information along with the remote method invocation.

4   Evaluation

We evaluate the runtime overhead introduced by the middleware platform to support the features of the component model. This runtime overhead is evaluated in terms of three kinds of resource usage: increased data access, increased network usage and increased usage of computation resources. We compare the runtime overhead of a DyMAC based application with an application based on state-of-the-art distributed component technology. For this comparison we use the .NET implementation of DyMAC. The distributed aspect-component model of DyMAC.NET is built on top of .NET remoting. So the first version of the application has been built on DyMAC, the second version of the application uses only the .NET remoting infrastructure.

Performance analysis. The runtime overhead of the DyMAC is evaluated in terms of increased data access, increased number of remote messages, increased size of remote messages, and increased usage of computation resources. DyMAC does not introduce additional data access at runtime. The application descriptors and configuration files are loaded at startup time of the application. So in case data access is involved in an application operation, that latency is the main performance bottle neck, because it is orders of magnitude larger than the networking and computing overhead. If we ignore data access, then the network overhead is the next important performance overhead. We evaluate network overhead in the next paragraph in detail. The overhead of calculating advice activation caused by the middleware layer is neglectable in comparison with the latencies of the network access. However, when using the framework for pure single-process, single-user AOP applications, without network communication or data access, the framework's overhead is significant. Offering features like client-specific middleware extensions and dynamic adaptability does involve a large computation overhead, due to the use of runtime interception, reflection and access of data-structures containing component metadata. That overhead is acceptable for large-scale distributed enterprise applications, and even unavoidable for the features required in that domain. [5]

Network overhead. The network overhead of DyMAC has to be evaluated on two properties : the number of additional messages involved, and the increased message size. If a remote before or after advice is used in stead of an ordinary method message, the number of messages stays the same. If an around advice is used with a proceed call, the proceed call seems to involve an additional remote call: i.e. the call-back to the advice coordinator. But, implementing the behaviour of around advice in the pure .NET remoting environment also involves two normal method messages: one to query if the remote message should be executed, and then another message to execute the behaviour that normally would come after the proceed call. The second element to compare is the overhead caused by increased message sizes. A method message in DyMAC carries additional information about the caller in its call context. This causes overhead in the transmission time. The parameter of advising method messages in DyMAC is a value copy of the joinpoint object, which contains kind and distributed context information. This also introduces a transmission overhead. To measure the network overhead, we compare the execution time of four kind of messages:

1. A pure .NET remoting method message with empty body, no parameters and no return value. We call this a minimal method message.
2. A DyMAC method message with the caller properties piggybacked.
3. A DyMAC advising method message, with caller properties piggybacked, but without the joinpoint object (the parameter is null).
4. A DyMAC advising method message with the joinpoint object.

First, the messages are sent between two processes on the localhost and second, between two different hosts on a 100MBit network. The first test simulates an optimal network. The second one compares messages in a real-life network. Timing started after 10 calls, to avoid delays by the .NET JIT compiler, because that would scale down the overhead. The timing results for each 1000 executions are:

```
Localhost:              100 Mbit:
1:  1.1093750  sec      1:  1.3785850  sec
2:  1.1875000  sec      2:  1.4935000  sec
3:  1.1875000  sec      3:  1.5175150  sec
4:  1.4075000  sec      4:  1.7695000  sec
```

The caller properties add a 6 to 7 % overhead maximally, on a minimal method message. The runtime joinpoint object adds another 18-20 % compared to the minimal method message. These overheads are calculated for minimal method messages and thus are an upper limit. As the method message gets more or

---

[5] For AOP systems focusing on single-user, single-process applications, different requirements exist. It is one of the key features to minimize overhead of activation of advice added by aspects. The application domain of one of the first AOP papers was the implementation of computation intensive algorithms for image processing[4]. In that domain, the performance overhead of activating added advice is crucial. Appropriate AOP tools, focusing on optimal advice weaving should be used then.

larger parameters, the relative overhead gets substantially smaller. In distributed enterprise applications, the facade pattern [8] is applied for remote components. In this pattern, remote messages have more parameters, and also have larger value objects as parameters or as return value. The average overhead will be smaller in that type of applications.

Based on our initial measurements, we claim that the runtime overhead of DyMAC is acceptable in a distributed application. We have illustrated that the penalty of fully distributed aspect-oriented middleware can be limited to network (message size) overhead as no additional messages are required to support remote pointcuts and remote advices. Recall that the figures presented above present an upper limit. Moreover we are working on optimizations that leverage pro-active distribution of useful context information, again without additional messages.

5   Related Work

This section focuses on existing AO middleware technologies that support to a certain extent distributed aspects with a notion of remote pointcut and remote advice: JAC[9], CAM/DAOP[15,16] and AWED[18].

JAC (Java Aspect Components [9]) is a Java-based framework that offers an aspect model to advice objects locally. Using this aspect model, a lot of internal middleware services of the framework itself are developed as aspects on the framework. The framework also supports distribution of components and distributed deployment. Both services are even implemented as aspects on the framework. JAC simulates the semantics of remote advice by executing local advice on a local copy of the aspect (aspects are replicated on each host). The states of the aspect instances are synchronized at each state change. The example from section 2 cannot be modeled using JAC. For instance, the security of the authentication service would be broken by duplicating private keys. Moreover, the workaround in JAC causes a lot of extra communication (chattiness). Finally, JAC has a limited join point model when it comes to evaluating distributed context information.

CAM/DAOP[15,16] is a framework for distributed applications that offers aspect-components and regular distributed components supporting broadcasting, events, synchronous and asynchronous messages. The aspect-components can offer remote before and after advice on sending and receiving messages. The CAM component model supports defining provided and required interfaces for components and aspect-components. DAOP does not offer remote around advice. The example from section 2 needs remote around advice for security services and for load balancing. The security services could be simulated with critical aspects, in which the before advice has to evaluate to true in order to let the message continue. But for the load balancing service this is not a solution. DAOP also has very limited pointcut expressions that do not allow to evaluate on contextual properties apart from the sending and receiving component role. Support for context properties concerning the distributed location or other component-related properties like interfaces are not supported.

AWED[18] is a language for distributed AOP and offers explicit remote point-cuts and explicit remote advice. The pointcut language offers the keyword host() to evaluate on the host of the joinpoint. Remote advice is explicitly remote us-ing the on() keyword to specify the host on which the advice should execute. AWED's approach to distributed aspects and remote around advice does not offer the abstraction of around advice in a fully distributed way. The proceed statement in the remote around advice has local semantics. The original inter-cepted message is executed at the host where the around advice is executed. This approach only works if the destination component is a static class or singleton deployed in every VM. In the example of section 2, the effect of the proceed call is that the messages to the application server are executed on the reverse-proxy server. AWED deploys each aspect and each class on every host to realize this. AWED also doesn't support transparent execution of remote advice: the host on which the advice should be executed is explicitly stated in the pointcut using the on() construct. Defining the deployment location of the advising component in the pointcut destroys the separation of composition and deployment. This also mixes up the separation of the specification of pointcut and advice. A pointcut should express the events in the system that need to be advised. The host of the advice itself is not part of that, but part of the advice's deployment specification.

Other approaches have been proposed to integrate AOP into middleware, but without integrating the component model, only the class model of the program-ming language: JBOSS AOP[12,21], AspectWerkz[23], Spring AOP[22]. This de-sign choice is clearly reflected in the kind and context of joinpoints that can be specified in pointcut expressions. The above mentioned approaches do not offer true support for distributed aspect composition anyway: they do not support a distributed joinpoint model, remote pointcuts or remote advice. AspectJ2EE[20] however, has the same approach offering a local AOP framework on Java classes, but with the difference that it offers one special kind of pointcut: remotecall, to advise remote calls from clients to EJBs. The use of contextual properties about location or components is not supported.

6   Conclusion

Complex compositions cannot be expressed effectively in state-of-the-art mid-dleware and AOSD is a promising technology that can assist in improving the situation. In this paper we presented DyMAC middleware. The AO middleware platform offers true and transparent distributed composition by means of ad-vanced remote pointcuts that can evaluate on distributed context, transparently remote advice with full semantics and a unified distributed component model. To our knowledge, this is the first middleware architecture that transparently and completely extends the power of aspect composition (join point model and advice execution) in a distributed context. We have prototyped DyMAC in a .NET environment and initial benchmarks show promising performance results.

References

1. C. Szyperski. Component software: beyond object-oriented programming. Second Edition. ACM Press/Addison-Wesley.
2. G. Heineman & W. Councill. Component-based Software Engineering. Addison-Wesley.
3. G. Blair, G. Coulson, et al. The design and implementation of OpenORB version 2. IEEE Distributed Systems Online Journal, 2(6), 2001
4. G. Kiczales. Aspect-Oriented Programming. In Proc. ECOOP'97.
5. G. Kiczales, E. Hilsdale, J. Hugunin, M. Kersten, J. Palm & W. Griswold. An Overview of AspectJ. In Proc. ECOOP'01.
6. E. Hilsdale & J. Hugunin. Advice Weaving in AspectJ. In proc. AOSD'04.
7. R. Filman, T. Elrad, S. Clarke & M. Aksit. Aspect-Oriented Software Development. Addison-Wesley, 2004.
8. Sun Microsystems. Inc. Enterprise Java-Beans (EJB) Specification v2.0, 2001.
9. R. Pawlak, L. Seinturier, L. Duchien & G. Florin. JAC: A Flexible Solution for Aspect-oriented Programming in Java. In Proc. Reflection'01.
10. D. Suvée, W. Vanderperren & V. Jonckers. JAsCo: An aspect-oriented approach tailored for component-based software development. In Proc. AOSD'03.
11. M. Mezini & K. Ostermann. Conquering Aspects with Caesar. In Proc. AOSD'03.
12. M. Fleury & F. Reverbel. The JBoss extensible server. In Proc. Middleware 2003.
13. E. Truyen, B. Vanhaute, B.N. Jorgensen, W. Joosen & P. Verbaeten. Dynamic and Selective Combination of Extensions in Component-Based Applications. In Proc. ICSE'01.
14. B. Lagaisse & W. Joosen. Component-Based Open Middleware Supporting Aspect-Oriented Software Composition. In Proc. CBSE'05.
15. M. Pinto, L. Fuentes & J.M. Troya. A Dynamic Component and Aspect-Oriented Platform. The Computer Journal,2005.
16. M. Pinto, L. Fuentes, M.E. Fayad & J.M. Troya. Separation of coordination in a dynamic aspect oriented framework. In Proc. AOSD'02.
17. M. Nishizawa, S. Chiba & M. Tatsubori. Remote pointcut: a language construct for distributed AOP. In Proc. AOSD'04.
18. L.D.B. Navarro, M. Südholt, W. Vanderperren, B. De Fraine & D. Suvée. Explicitly distributed AOP using AWED. In Proc. AOSD'06.
19. D. Suvée, W. Vanderperren, D. Wagelaar & V. Jonckers. There are no Aspects. In Proc. Software Composition 2004.
20. T. Cohen & J.Y. Gil. AspectJ2EE = AOP + J2EE: Towards an Aspect Based, Programmable and Extensible Middleware Framework. In Proc. ECOOP'04.
21. JBoss AOP homepage, http://labs.jboss.com/jbossaop
22. Spring Framework website. http://www.springframework.org/
23. AspectWerkz homepage, http://aspectwerkz.codehaus.org/

Policy-Driven Middleware for Self-adaptation of Web Services Compositions

Abdelkarim Erradi[1], Piyush Maheshwari[1,2], and Vladimir Tosic[1,3]

[1] Shool of Computer Science and Engineering, The University of New South Wales,
Sydney, Australia
[2] IBM India Research Lab, New Delhi, India
[3] Department of Computer Science, The University of Western Ontario, Canada
aerradi@cse.unsw.edu.au, pimahesh@in.ibm.com,
vladat@computer.org

Abstract. We present our policy-based middleware, called Manageable and Adaptive Service Compositions (MASC), for dynamic self-adaptation of Web services compositions to various changes. MASC integrates and extends our earlier middleware called the Web Services Message Bus (wsBus). In particular, we discuss MASC support for customization of Web services compositions to address business exceptions and wsBus support for correction (fault management) of Web services compositions to improve reliability. We have evaluated the former support on a stock trading case study and the latter support on a supply chain management case study. Our solutions are complementary to the existing approaches and provide: coordination of fault management between SOAP messaging and business process orchestration, greater diversity of monitoring and control constructs, specification of both technical and business aspects used for adaptation decisions, higher level of abstraction easier for use by non-technical people, and externalization of monitoring and adaptation actions from definitions of business processes.

Keywords: Web services middleware, Web services composition, policy-based management and adaptation, Microsoft .NET.

1 Introduction and Motivation

Web services compositions (orchestrations and choreographies) are rapidly becoming a dominant approach for implementing business processes and building open distributed systems. The widely accepted Web services technologies (the Web Services Description Language – WSDL, SOAP, and the Universal Description, Discovery, and Integration – UDDI) are not enough for implementing Web services compositions [4]. Several languages for describing Web services compositions have appeared and the Web Services Business Process Execution Language (WSBPEL or BPEL) is the most widely accepted among them. A number of additional technologies (often named 'WS-*') have been developed to address requirements such as security, reliable messaging and transactional service coordination. However, a number of important issues are not completely solved. Many of them are related to building more powerful

M. van Steen and M. Henning (Eds.): Middleware 2006, LNCS 4290, pp. 62–80, 2006.

middleware to support creation, execution, and management of Web services compositions. Such an important research question, discussed in this paper, is how to build more powerful middleware to enable autonomous self-adaptation of Web services compositions to various runtime changes.

In preparation for this research, we had studied different types of adaptations of Web services composition and decided to classify them based on 3 dimensions, each orthogonal to the other 2. The first dimension is whether the complete class of compositions (e.g., an abstract process in BPEL) is changed or whether only a particular composition instance is changed. In this paper, we focus on the latter, because the need for such adaptations is much more frequent. The second dimension is the relative time when a Web services composition instance is changed. Adaptation is *static* when a composition instance is changed before it is started, while it is *dynamic* when a running composition instance is changed without being stopped and restarted from the beginning. In this paper, we focus on dynamic adaptation, because it is much more challenging. The third dimension describes the reason why the adaptation is done, which impacts how the adaptation is done. On this dimension, adaptation can be: a) *customization* – to add/remove/replace activities specific to the composition instance (but not to the complete class of compositions); b) *correction* – to handle faults reported during execution of this composition instance; c) *optimization* – to improve extra-functional (usually performance or billing) issues noticed during correct execution of this instance; or d) *prevention* – to prevent future faults or extra-functional issues before they occur. This classification is similar to the classification of software evolution into adaptive, corrective, perfective, and preventive [17]. In this paper we focus on customization and correction. While we have some results related to optimization, they will be discussed only in relationship to using corrective adaptation (i.e., fault management) to improve reliability of Web services compositions. A long-term goal of our research is to study and enable all identified adaptation types.

Special cases ('business exceptions') can occur relatively frequently in business processes. Such a special case has almost all activities as in a regularly occurring base business process, but some activities are removed or replaced and/or new activities are added. An example is when a company has set up a complex business process for domestic business partners (e.g., within one country), but an unexpected request comes to set up a version of this business process for some international partners with additional activities to handle payment in multiple currencies. This special case can be addressed with customization of the base business process for domestic partners. Such a customization can be performed in different ways. One way is to add into the description of the base business process (e.g., in BPEL) appropriate new exceptions, event handling constructs (e.g., timeouts), compensation activities, and/or message correlation. While this is a simple and straightforward approach, it has several drawbacks, which reduce its applicability to advanced scenarios. The most important drawbacks are that (1) it enables only static and not dynamic customization (i.e., change of running process instance), and that (2) it cannot be applied in cases when the base business process is defined by a standardization body and its description cannot be changed easily. The latter drawback can be addressed if the base process description is copied and then manually changed into a description of a new business process. However, this approach also does not address dynamic customization. In addition, it significantly reduces maintainability because if a change in the base process occurs, descriptions of all customized processes have to be updated manually. When dynamic customization is needed, it is usually advantageous to externalize descriptions of specifics of individual cases from the description of the base process. This simplifies development, composition, and management activities (and corresponding software) and fosters reuse. Such separation of concerns is used frequently in software engineering, e.g., in aspect-oriented programming, and distributed systems and network management, particularly policy-based management [12].

Additionally, various faults can occur relatively often and unexpectedly in distributed systems. For example, remote computers can be down or unavailable (e.g., due to denial of service attacks), network links can be congested or broken, or remote applications can produce unexpected results due to semantic misunderstandings. In Web services compositions, the diversity of possible faults is particularly high because implementations of Web services have to be treated as 'black boxes', participants in business-to-business (B2B) interactions usually relinquish no or very little control to other participants, and SOAP communication mostly uses unmanaged Internet infrastructure. On the other hand, Web services compositions often implement business-critical processes whose correct and uninterrupted operation is paramount. Therefore, to achieve dependable business processes, Web services compositions have to be made reliable. Reliability can be defined as the continuity of correct service delivery. This implies zero or, at worst, relatively few failures and rapid recovery time. Reliability of Web services compositions is a complex and challenging task that has to be addressed at several layers: service provider layer (e.g., service hosting containers), transport layer, SOAP messaging layer, and business process layer. Some reliability aspects (e.g., invocation retries) can be solved at different layers with different trade-offs, but some reliability aspects are best solved only at one particular layer (e.g., influences of dependencies between activities on the reliability of the whole process can be determined only at the business process layer). In our approach, events can trigger cross-layer adaptation that could span both the process layer and the messaging layer. Among the advantages of the adaptation at the messaging layer is the potential reusability across process instances and process types. In particular, executing faults handling policies at the messaging layer shields faults from the process orchestration.

During the last several years, a number of academic papers (e.g., [13]), industrial standardization efforts (e.g., WS-ReliableMessaging, WS-Reliability, WS-Transaction), and industrial products have made contributions to improving reliability at different layers. However, they have limitations, particularly in the diversity of events (e.g., QoS degradations that cause faults) that they can monitor and handle, customizability and diversity of actions (apart from rollback and compensation) that they can perform in different contexts, specification of technical (e.g., performance, security) and business benefits/costs of particular actions, and cross-layer integration of reliability solutions at different layers (e.g., retries considered only at the SOAP messaging layer could cause business process timeout). One of the recent research trends to address reliability issues is augmenting Web services middleware with autonomous behavior capabilities such as self-healing and self-configuring [15]. Our work belongs to this emerging direction.

Policies can be used for representation of all types of adaptation and monitoring activities. The term 'policy' is used in different ways in the literature. A general definition is that a policy is a declarative, high-level description of goals to be achieved and actions to be taken in different situations. There are different types of policies, but in this paper we focus on Event-Condition-Action (ECA) rules [9]. Such a rule specifies a triggering event (e.g., arrival of a message, start of a process instance, runtime fault, or performance problem), additional conditions to be satisfied (e.g., referring to process state or history), and actions to be taken (e.g., change of a process instance) when the event occurs and the conditions are satisfied. The main advantage of policies over alternatives (e.g., aspect-oriented programming) is that policies are higher-level abstractions, so humans (e.g., business analysts) can specify them more easily.

In this paper, we present our work on policy-based middleware, called Manageable and Adaptive Service Compositions (MASC) (http://masc.web.cse.unsw.edu.au), for dynamic self-adaptation of Web services compositions to various changes. While some of our previous publications, particularly [6], also discuss some aspects of our work in this area, this paper complements them by providing both an overall picture of our research and additional technical details about our recent solutions. MASC is an evolution of our previous research of middleware for Web services. It integrates and extends our previous middleware-related projects, the Web Services Message Bus (wsBus) [5] and AdaptiveBPEL [7]. In addition, we have performed a technology switch – while our previous projects were built with Java-based technologies, the new implementation of MASC is based on the novel Microsoft .NET Framework 3.0 technologies and C#. An important aspect of our work on the MASC middleware is that we aim to provide policy-based adaptation (particularly optimization and prevention) based on maximizing business metrics (e.g., profit). This complements current works on dynamic adaptation of Web services compositions, which mostly focus on maximizing technical QoS metrics (e.g., throughput), but rarely ([11]) study business metrics in detail.

This section provided an introduction to our research and summarized our motivation. The second section presents MASC middleware solutions for customization of Web services compositions. We elaborate our .NET-based architecture and implementation and explain their evaluation on a stock trading case study. The third section presents our middleware solutions for corrective adaptation of Web services compositions to improve their reliability. We discuss our Java-based architecture and implementation of wsBus and its evaluation on a supply chain management case study. wsBus is now a part of the MASC project, so their relationships are discussed in the third section. The fourth section compares our research with related work, while the last section summarizes conclusions and outlines our future work.

2   Middleware for Policy-Based Customization

To be able to perform policy-based management, it is necessary to define an appropriate machine processeable and precise format for policy specification. We have been developing a novel XML (Extensible Markup Language) format, called WS-Policy4MASC. Its goal is to enable specification of policies for monitoring of functional and QoS aspects (such as performance and reliability) and different types of adaptation for Web services and their compositions, in a way that can be used for automatic configuration of our MASC middleware presented in this section. Our language is an extension of the Web Services Policy Framework (WS-Policy) [16], an industrial specification standardized by the World Wide Web Consortium (W3C). In WS-Policy, policies are collections of policy alternatives, which are collections of policy assertions. WS-Policy Attachment defines a generic mechanism to associate a policy with subjects (e.g., WSDL elements) to which the policy applies. WS-Policy is a general and extensible framework for specification of policies for Web services and it has very good properties in this respect. However, it does not contain detailed rules for specification of policies in particular areas, such as security, QoS monitoring, and adaptation. Specification of such detailed rules is left for WS-Policy extensions. Unfortunately, only extensions for security, reliable messaging, and a few other management areas that are not the focus of our project have been suggested. Therefore, we had to develop a new WS-Policy extension for use in our middleware. WS-Policy4MASC is also compatible with other Web services standards such as WSDL and BPEL, as well as Microsoft .NET 3.0 technologies. Since our MASC middleware has ambitious goals in several areas, WS-Policy4MASC offers a number of constructs for powerful and precise policy specification. Details and examples of the WS-Policy4MASC expressive power and syntax will be given in a future publication. We only provide here a short overview of the current support for customization policies.

An adaptation (including customization) policy in the current version of WS-Policy4MASC can define events which cause its evaluation, optional conditions on its relevance (e.g., a policy may be relevant only in particular contexts), a state in which the adapted system (e.g., a Web services composition) should be before the adaptation, additional conditions on the adapted system (e.g., historical values of QoS metrics), a set of actions to be taken if all previous conditions are met, a state in which the system will be after the adaptation, and change of business value (e.g., monetary payments) associated with this adaptation. The basic adaptation actions include removal, addition, and replacement. In removal and replacement, an activity or an activity block in a base business process is deleted. All business processes, including base processes and variation processes, are defined in appropriate other documents (e.g., BPEL files), so they are only referenced in WS-Policy4MASC policies. Thus, an activity block is specified using beginning and ending points. In addition and replacement, a new variation process or a single activity is inserted into a particular point in a base process. If the inserted single activity is a Web services call, the policy can specify a particular Web service or a set of criteria for dynamically selecting the best Web service from a directory. Data exchange (i.e., required parameters binding and value passing) between a base process and a variation process/activity is also described.

2.1 Architecture of MASC Support for Customization and Its Implementation

To enable different types of adaptation of Web services compositions, we have been developing the MASC middleware. It extends the new Microsoft .NET Framework 3.0 (currently in pre-release - http://www.netfx3.com/), particularly its components the Windows Communication Foundation (WCF) and the Windows Workflow Foundation (WF). For the MASC solutions presented in this section, the extensions of WF are more important. WF provides an extensible framework for building processes

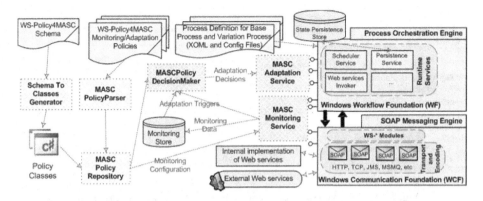

Fig. 1. Architecture of MASC support for customization of Web services compositions

(workflows) and embedding them into .NET applications to orchestrate activities of objects and services. In this respect, a WF process can represent a Web services composition (orchestration). WF processes are defined in Microsoft's Extensible Applications Markup Language (XAML, but file extension for WF is '.xoml') and not BPEL. Translation between XAML and BPEL is promised for a future version. The glue code for connecting activities, such as activity input validation, can be encapsulated into a 'code beside' .NET class. To execute a process, WF has a lightweight WF runtime engine that can be hosted in any .NET application. The WF runtime engine manages the instantiation and execution of the workflow activities. Additionally, it takes care of different middleware concerns through an extensible set of WF runtime services (e.g., Tracking, Persistence and Transaction support are built-in). Therefore, we designed and implemented another WF runtime service, named MASCAdaptationService, for policy-based adaptation of Web services compositions implemented as WF processes. It currently enables static and dynamic customization, while its future version will provide support for static and dynamic corrective, optimizing, and preventive adaptation based on maximizing business metrics. The support for dynamic adaptation means that MASCAdaptationService can use policies to change a running process instance without any changes to process definition or implementation of activities (e.g., composed Web services). The WF runtime engine can be configured to include MASCAdaptationService and support its operation. MASC is a complex middleware with many modules (some of which are not yet implemented). For readability purposes, we will describe in this section only MASC support for customization. The overall architecture of MASC will be given in another publication.

The conceptual architecture of the MASC support for policy-based customization is shown in Figure 1. We have implemented its prototype in C#. Monitoring and adaptation policy assertions are stored in a policy repository, which is a collection of instances of policy classes. The policy classes are generated automatically from the WS-Policy4MASC schema, using an XML-schema-to-C#-classes generator (in our case, the XSD tool from .NET). When the MASCAdaptationService starts, our MASCPolicy-Parser imports WS-Policy4MASC files, creates instances of corresponding policy classes, and stores these instances in the policy repository. Static customization

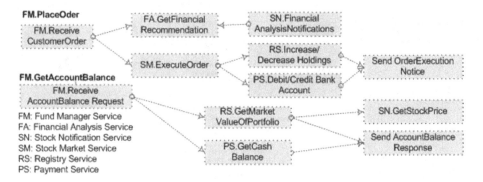

Fig. 2. Example Web services interactions in the Stock Trading case study

is started when the WF runtime raises an event that a process instance is created. Dynamic customization is started when the MASCMonitoringService module raises an event that for a particular process instance it detected (e.g., by introspecting exchanged SOAP messages and/or measuring QoS metrics such as response time) adaptation pre-conditions specified in monitoring policies. Such events can also be raised by the MonitoringStore database in situations when adaptation pre-conditions refer to several different SOAP messages. For both static and dynamic adaptation, the raised events are handled by MASCPolicyDecisionMaker, which determines adaptation policy assertions to be applied to the process instance and sends an event to MASCAdaptationService. Policy priorities are used to determine the order of execution if several policy assertions apply per event. In case of dynamic adaptation, MASCAdaptationService suspends the running process instance to be adapted. Then, it asks the WF runtime engine for a description of the process to be adapted and gets back a transient copy of the process' object representation. For this copy, MASCAdaptationService performs the changes specified in the policies, using primitives built into the WF runtime. If data exchange is required between the base process and the variation processes/activities, our service also takes care of required parameters binding and value passing between base processes and their variation processes. When MASCAdaptationService passes the modified copy of the process' object representation back to the WF runtime, the latter applies the changes using built-in algorithms. After this, the execution of the adapted process instance is resumed.

2.2 MASC Evaluation on the Stock Trading Case Study

The MASC support for customization has been evaluated and demonstrated in various adaptation scenarios using a simplified Stock Trading case study implemented with C#, .NET 3.0, and MASC. Parts of this case study are shown in Figure 2. The base Trading Process is initiated when a human investor places an investment or redemption order with their FundManagerService. The latter, after verifying the order, invokes the FinancialAnalysisService to get a recommendation to enable an informed investment/redemption decision. The FinancialAnalysisService gets periodic notifications from the StockNotificationService about the current stock values and real-time market surveillance, announcements, quotes, and other information. Based on this information, historical records, and predictive models built into the service (for our prototype, we used very simple models), the FinancialAnalysisService informs the FundManagerService about how well certain stocks are performing. The FundManagerService makes a decision which stock to buy/sell for the monetary amount requested by the investor. (In our prototype, this decision is very simple, e.g., buy one best stock or sell as many poorly performing stocks as needed to get the redeemed money.) Then, the FundManagerService sends the buying/selling request to the StockMarketService. The latter performs a simple trade matching between the buy orders and the sell orders. When a trade match is formed, the StockMarketService invokes in parallel the StockRegistryService to transfer the stock share ownership and the PaymentService to transfer funds. Note that, with the exception of the FundManagerService, there can be multiple different services of the same type in the composition. For example, there can be more than one FinancialAnalysisService, e.g., provided by different vendors and/or performing different types of financial analyses.

To evaluate MASC's static and dynamic adaptation capabilities, we have conducted several experiments to customize the base business process for national stock trading, described above, to support international stock trading. WS-Policy4MASC was used for policy description. Among the conducted experiments was dynamic addition of a CurrencyConversion Web service (CC_1, CC_2...CC_n) to convert stock prices of foreign stocks to a local currency. Also, depending on the country of foreign stock, a PESTAnalysis Web service (PS_1, PS_2...PS_n) was added to assess the non-financial aspects (political, economic, social and technology) that influence the trade. Additionally, monitoring policies were used to define constraints over the trade transaction amount and/or the customer's profile (e.g., personal investor vs. corporate investor) to dynamically add a CreditRating Web service (CR_1, CR_2...CR_n) before processing the trade. In terms of removing activities, we have experimented with dynamic removal of the invocation of MarketComplianceService when the trade amount is less than a particular threshold. The conducted experiments were successful and demonstrated feasibility and usefulness of the MASC approach in adding dynamic customization capabilities to existing Web services compositions, guided by declarative policies specified in WS-Policy4MASC. MASC has provided a solution for policy-based static and dynamic customization without any changes to either the process definition or the constituent services implementations. All that is needed is a WS-Policy4MASC document describing monitoring and adaptation policies to be enforced. When a WS-Policy4MASC document changes, these changes are automatically enforced the next time adaptation is needed with no need to restart any software component. The above scenarios will be further extended to evaluate MASC and WS-Policy4MASC support for corrective, optimizing, and preventive optimization, once they are completed.

3   Middleware for Policy-Based Corrective Adaptation

Our work addresses reliability at the business process layer and the SOAP messaging layer by specifying and enforcing monitoring policies to help in fault detection and corrective adaptation policies to guide fault correction. It is complementary to the existing approaches and provides: (1) coordination of fault handling across these two layers, (2) greater diversity of monitoring and control constructs, (3) specification of both technical and business aspects that can be used for adaptation decisions, (4) higher level of abstraction easier for use by non-technical people, and (5) externalization of monitoring and adaptation actions from definitions of business processes.

Our main past project in the area of reliability of Web services compositions was the wsBus middleware built using Java-based technologies and an early version of our WS-Policy extensions in this area (the name 'WS-Policy4MASC' was not used at that time). As mentioned in the introductory section, our focus has recently shifted towards the more general MASC middleware built upon .NET technologies. WS-Policy4MASC grammar was also updated. We have been working on integrating wsBus solutions with other parts of MASC, including .NET and C# reimplementation and support for the new WS-Policy4MASC grammar. However, since our results are still more complete for the Java-based implementation of wsBus, we will describe it in this paper and leave discussion of recent improvement for another publication.

Policies that can be enforced by the Java-based version of wsBus are specified in a WS-Policy extension described and illustrated in [6]. The main types of actions in these policies are: invocation retries, Web services substitution, concurrent invocation of multiple equivalent services, skipping of activities, and relatively simple dynamic changes of process instances (e.g., add/remove/skip an activity, change sequence of activities, delay/suspend/resume/terminate process). Only the latter is at the business process layer, while the others are at the SOAP messaging layer. In this way, they complement the policies described in the previous section, which are all at the business process layer.

3.1 Architecture of wsBus and Its Implementation

This section presents the architecture of wsBus with emphasis on the modules that facilitate the enactment of adaptation policies. As shown in Figure 3, adaptation policies supported by wsBus work via injecting runtime inspectors and custom Message Processing Modules into a messaging pipeline at different message processing stages such as before sending a request and after receiving a response. These custom modules can be applied at different scopes such as the whole service, a particular endpoint or a particular service operation. For example, the Invocation Retry Handler places the messages that fail to be delivered in a retry queue and the queue reader tries redelivery using the pattern specified by the used recovery policy. Messages for which processing repeatedly fails are placed in a 'dead letter' queue after exhausting the maximum number of allowed retries and no further delivery will be attempted.

wsBus key architectural abstraction is the concept of a Virtual End Point (VEP). A VEP allows virtualization by grouping a set of functionally equivalent services and exposes an abstract WSDL for accessing the configured services (e.g., Web search service exposing Google, Yahoo and MSN search as one virtual service). The grouped services might have different QoS properties. The VEP acts as a recovery block and various runtime policies can be associating with it.

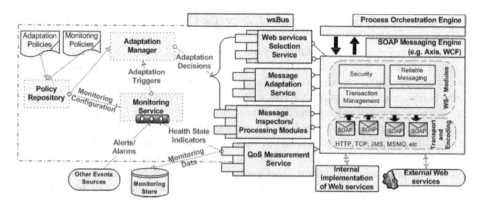

Fig. 3. wsBus Architecture

wsBus can be deployed either as a gateway to a Process Orchestration Engine or it can act as a transparent HTTP Proxy. In the first case the Process Orchestration Engine should be configured to explicitly direct service calls to the virtual endpoints configured in wsBus and the later routes request messages to the real services. The VEP takes care of the dynamic Find, Select, Bind and Invoke on behalf of the BPEL engine, using the configured selection and binding policies. The VEP does 'on the fly' selection of service provider or intermediary based on a selection criteria specified in the policy attached to the VEP, such as message content and context (e.g., requester profile), or the service provider's capabilities or QoS of prior interactions. The VEP then manages the automatic enforcement of adaptation policies (e.g., retry and substitute policies) by inspecting messages going into and out of the composed services and interposing additional Message Processing Modules along the message pipeline. To decide the relevant Message Processing Modules applicable to a given message, the VEP uses simple rules expressed as a regular expression or XPath query against the header or the payload of the message. Additionally, the VEP provides middleware services to service compositions such as QoS measurement and monitoring, conversation management and fault management. Our fault management approach is based on two models: (1) the capturing model uses assertion-based monitoring to detect faults and to notify the relevant middleware component, and (2) the handling model uses adaptation policies represents to resolve faults. For example, a policy might stipulate that for particular type of faults, the VEP should retry to the original service and if the fault persists then it should select an equivalent backup service.

The enactment of adaptation policies is managed by the following key components:

1) *QoS Measurement Service* is responsible for management data collection and analysis either through direct computation of QoS metrics (e.g., collecting statistical metrics about the performance) or via periodic probing for management information from other management intermediaries (e.g., third QoS measurement entity). The key QoS metrics measured by this component are: (a) Reliability (calculated as a ratio of successful invocations over the number of total invocations in given period of time); (b) Response Time (the time interval between when a service is requested and when it is delivered; (c) Availability: the percentage of time that a service is available during

some time interval. Because the lack of space, the QoS measurement algorithms are not presented is this paper.

2) *Monitoring service* continuously monitors interactions with the participating services to verify that the configured monitoring policies are being satisfied and to detect any condition changes such as faults. The monitoring policies specify the desired behavior of the system in terms of (a) pre-conditions and post-conditions that express constraints over exchanged messages (b) thresholds over QoS guarantees (e.g. service response time) as stipulated in pre-established Service Level Agreements (SLAs). The monitoring policies can be attached to Monitoring Points at various levels of granularity such as a Service Endpoint or a Service Operation. For example, the monitoring policies could specify that exchanged messages between participant services must be validated to ensure conformance to the service contract expected by the service composition. The Monitoring Service also supports events-based monitoring to detect fault events and recognize their type. Various techniques are used to achieve this. First, the Monitoring Service listens to fault messages returned by invoked services as specified in their WSDL interface. Faults can also be identified based on management events coming from internal or external management systems, such as hardware or network failure faults. Also, the Web services Invoker component can use timers to raise timeout faults when the service does not respond within the set timeout interval.

The monitoring policy uses XPath to reference variables defined in the header or the body of the WSDL contract of constituent services (e.g., the CustomerID of PurchaseOrder message). During the evaluation of the monitoring assertions, the Monitoring Service might reference data from external sources to obtain data not available in the exchange messages. The source of such external data as specified as Web service calls in the monitoring assertions, such as calling a QoS measurement service or querying the log of prior interactions to get some historical data.

When an undesirable condition is detected, then the Monitoring service uses ECA rules to assign a meaningful fault type to the violation event, such as Service Unavailable Fault, SLA Violation Fault, Service Failure Fault and Timeout Fault. The fault is then passed to the Adaptation Manager along with all the data required for recovery (i.e., ProcessInstanceID of the process instance to be adapted, and a Context Collection that contains relevant data that could be needed during the adaptation.)

3) *Adaptation Manager* decides and coordinates the execution of appropriate adaptation action(s) to restore the system to an acceptable state using adaptation policies configured at the VEP. Currently our adaptation policies use a rule-based approach to specify the necessary adaptations per fault type. Such a rule-based approach is more flexible as it can handle wider variety of faults whether coming from the infrastructure or from the partner services. Also the process specification is kept simple and uncluttered through the separation of the process logic and fault handling policies. The adaptation action could be simple or composite. It could be specified to be enacted either at the SOAP messaging layer (such as retry a service call) or at the process orchestration layer (such as skip a process activity or add/remove activity) or sometimes at both layers. For example, before retrying invocation of a faulty service, the adaptation policy might stipulate that MASCAdaptationService should first suspend the calling process instance (until the execution of the adaptation actions is completed) or increase its timeout interval to avoid the calling process timing out. To

be able to decide the process instance to be adapted, MASCAdaptationService transparently adds the ProcessInstanceID of the calling process to outgoing SOAP messages (using the RelatesTo Message Addressing Header). When multiple adaptation policies are specified per fault type, policy priorities are used to determine the order of execution of the adaptation actions. For example, a policy could stipulate that the VEP should first attempt *n* retries before failover to a known backup service. The policy decision manager passes an object representation of the adaptation actions to the relevant policy enforcement point(s) to execute the adaptation policy.

4) *Web services Selection service* manages the dynamic mapping of abstract Web services defined in the composition to concrete Web services. This allows shielding the orchestration engine from changes to available services. Hence, adding, modifying and selecting among available services could be done without the need to complicate the process with the routing logic for deciding which concrete services to use. The selection of services among the equivalent services registered with a VEP is done using various selection policies. A VEP can be configured to choose between registered services in round-robin fashion, or to select the best performing service (based on the QoS metrics gathered from prior interactions or from other management entities), or to 'broadcast' the request message to multiple targets service providers concurrently and consider the first one that respond, all pending invocations are then aborted and their responses are ignored. The concurrent invocation of equivalent services is accomplished by making a copy of the message and modifying its route, then invoking multiple target services using concurrent invocation threads. This strategy is more suitable for data lookup services and freely available services such as Web search.

5) *Message Inspectors/Processing Modules* implements common handlers for enforcing typical adaptation policies. These handlers can be configured as a pipeline to manipulate and pre/post-process both request and response messages as instructed by adaptation policies. Among the handlers provided by this component is a Message Logger to log the messages as they pass through the messaging layer. This is useful for debugging problems, meter usage for subsequent billing to users, or trace business-level events, such as transaction over a certain amount. It can also be used for data inspection, or for service management.

6) *Message Adaptation Service* is a Message Processing Module that handles data transformation and enrichment to resolve incompatibilities between services registered with a particular VEP (i.e., structural, value and encoding mismatches). Various transformation patterns are supported, such as transform a message payload from the one schema to another; attach additional data from external sources, such as Web services calls or from database queries; split/merge messages; buffer multiple messages and aggregate them into a single one before sending them to the destination service. These transformation modules can be composed into a pipeline to transform and relay messages.

3.2 wsBus Evaluation on the WS-I Supply Chain Management Case Study

We conducted a series of benchmarking tests to assess effectiveness (i.e., impact on reliability) and efficiency (i.e., impact on performance) of wsBus in enhancing

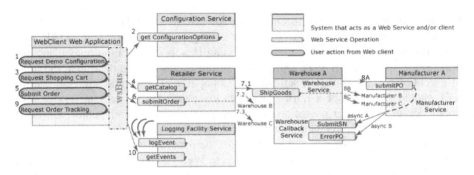

Fig. 4. WS-I Supply Chain Management (SCM) application process (adapted from [17])

reliability of Web services interactions. Our secondary aim for these tests was to discover areas of the platform that need further improvement. We used an extended Java-based implementation of WS-I (Web Services Interoperability) Supply Chain Management (SCM) application [17]. The SCM scenarios, as shown in Figure 4, are designed as Web services based interactions that simulate business activity of an online supplier of electronic goods. First a Web client calls the Retailer service's *getCatalog* operation. When the user submits the order, the Web client calls the Retailer service's *submitOrder* operation. To fulfill orders, the Retailer Web service manages stock levels in three warehouses (WA, WB, and WC). If Warehouse A cannot fulfill an order, the Retailer checks Warehouse B; if Warehouse B cannot, the Retailer checks Warehouse C. When an item in a Warehouse stock falls below a certain threshold, the Warehouse must restock the item from the Manufacturer's inventory (MA, MB, and MC). Each use case includes a logging call to a Logging Service to monitor activities of the services. A customer can track orders by using the *getEvents* operation of the Logging Facility Web service. During the SCM process enactment, participating Web services can log events by calling the *logEvent* operation of the Logging Facility Web service. Optionally, there is a Configuration Web service that lists all implementations registered in the UDDI registry for each of the Web Services in the sample application.

Our experimental setup consisted of 2 run-time configurations: 1) wsBus was not used and all invocations were direct (point-to-point) between the Web services, and 2) wsBus was placed at the client side and acted as an intermediary (broker, mediator). Both configurations used identical application logic implemented in Java. We simulated multiple concurrent Web service clients, each of which invoked deployed services multiple times. We used Apache's JMeter 2.1.1, a load generator toolset, to generate the workload and to measure the observed performance. We deployed the SCM backend Web services (Retailers, Warehouses, and Manufacturers) at a P4 2.8GHz, 1GB RAM server running Windows 2003, Tomcat 5.5 and Axis 2. JMeter stress tool (acting as the client) and wsBus were deployed at a Windows XP laptop with P4 2.8GHz and 500MB RAM. The machines were connected by a 100MB LAN.

To estimate the impact on reliability and robustness of the wsBus solution in response to QoS changes and service failures, we wrote test code that occasionally (at random times) injected exception events in the tested system. For service failures, we randomly picked some of available services and made them unavailable for a random amount of time. For service QoS degradations, test code occasionally picked some service instances and changed their QoS values (e.g., introduced delays). We have defined monitoring policies and corrective adaptation policies for the experiments using wsBus. Monitoring policies configured messaging pipeline inspectors to intercept faults (e.g., fault message returned from the service provider, timeout fault message returned from the Web services invoker, QoS degradation event raised by the QoS constraints evaluator). When a fault was detected, the wsBus VEP used corrective adaptation policies to decide the adaptation actions. For timeout faults, these policies configured the VEP for the Retailers to first retry the invocation of the faulty services three times with a delay between retry cycles of two seconds. After exhausting the maximum number of allowed retries, the policies configured the VEP to route the request message to a different Retailer based on the response time gathered from prior interactions. (In other experiments, we have defined policies that configured concurrent invocation of the four Retailer services and considered the results coming from the first responding service.) For the Logging service we have configured a skip policy since the functionality provided by the Logging service is not business critical.

Table 1. Reliability and availability of direct interactions vs. channeling through wsBus

		Reliability	Availability
Direct Web services invocations without wsBus mediation	Only Retailer A used by the client	105 failures per 1000 requests	0.952
	Only Retailer B used by the client	81 failures per 1000 requests	0.992
	Only Retailer C used by the client	17 failures per 1000 requests	0.998
	Only Retailer D used by the client	91 failures per 1000 requests	0.983
Web services invocations with wsBus mediation	All 4 Retailer services exposed as 1 wsBus VEP	6 failures per 1000 requests	0.998

In a representative experiment, we compared reliability and availability of the *get-Catalog* operation in cases when a client directly calls one of the Retailer Web services (which have occasional random faults) and cases when the client calls Retailer Web services (with the same occasional random faults) through 1 VEP of the client-side wsBus. Reliability was measured as a number of failures seen by the client per 1000 requests. Availability was calculated as mean time between failures divided with the sum of mean time between failures and mean time to recover. The test results in Table 1 show that reliability and availability in cases when wsBus was used improved compared to cases when only direct interaction with individual Retailers was used. This is a simple experiment that enabled us to perform quantitative comparisons. Qualitative comparisons are more straightforward – when there are complex failures, wsBus adds useful corrective adaptation. How much useful and appropriate the adaptation is in particular circumstances, depends solely on the policies and their priorities – if a human defines an inappropriate policy, wsBus will try to enforce it.

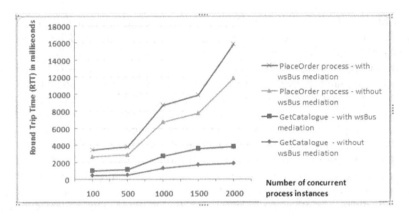

Fig. 5. Round trip time (RTT) for direct interactions vs. channeling through wsBus

To estimate the impact of introducing wsBus on performance of Web services compositions, we used the implemented SCM Web services composition to measure and examine 2 key performance metrics: round trip time and throughput. *Round Trip Time (RTT)* is defined as the period from the time a service consumer sends a request to the time when it successfully receives full reply from its service provider. It includes execution time of the service implementation, time consumed by the supporting provider-side software (e.g., application server, Web server, database server), queue waiting time (if any) inside wsBus, and network delays. *Throughput* is defined as the average number of successful requests processed in a sampling period.

Figure 5 shows round trip time for *getCatalogue* and *submitOrder* requests with varying request sizes. Each data point represents the average latency value over three independent runs of up to 2000 requests each and performed measures at different load levels. The delay between requests is set to zero to increase the load on the server. These data show that channeling of SOAP through wsBus is slower (usually about 10%, which is not drastic) than direct SOAP-over-HTTP, due to the overheads introduces by the added QoS features in wsBus. Our analysis of the main reasons of delays introduced by wsBus points to the high number of threads created to serve the requests. When a message arrives at the Listener component, a thread is created to serve the request, and this does not scale well with high number of requests. This will be avoided in our new .NET reimplementation of wsBus. Another important source of wsBus delays is the need to import, parse, and process policies. In our .NET reimplementation of wsBus we will minimize this overhead by working with object representation of policies, which is updated only when policies change.

4 Related Work

While Web services based business processes are gaining wider adoption, tools and middleware frameworks in this space do not yet provide adequate support for modeling and enacting dynamic process adaptations. Several ongoing academic and industrial efforts recognize the need to extend Web services composition middleware with mechanisms to provide dynamic adaptation. However, our work has unique characteristics. We adopt a policy-based approach that builds on the established policy-based management principles [12], while decoupling between sensors that monitor and detect adaptation triggers and effectors that react to and handle such triggers. Our middleware performs different types of adaptation and contains solutions at different Web services middleware layers. Also, our technological base is different (extensions of WS-Policy and Microsoft. NET 3.0 have not been previously studied in detail), which leads to different architectural solutions. Furthermore, the ultimate goal of our research in this area is business-driven adaptation of Web services compositions, while related works aim at improvement of technical metrics. We briefly discuss next how our work differs from and complements the main recently published works.

Probably the closest related work is the service monitoring approach presented in [1]. The authors proposed the Web Service Constraint Language (WS-CoL) for specifying client-side monitoring policies, particularly those related to security. At deployment time, WS-CoL constraints attached to a process are translated into BPEL invoke activities that call the Monitoring Manager, the component in charge of runtime evaluation of monitoring policies to detect anomalous conditions. This approach is similar to ours in that monitoring policies are specified externally rather than being embedded into the process specification. The proposed approach achieves the desired reusability and separation of concerns. However, it only provides support for monitoring and focuses mainly on security. On the other hand, our approach is more focused on adaptation (rather than just monitoring) to customize the process to cater for special cases or to handle faults and address anomalous situations.

Another related work is [3], which suggested an aspect-oriented extension to BPEL to enable dynamic weaving of aspects into Web services compositions. In their work, a process runs inside a process container that provides middleware services to BPEL processes. However, we believe that some of the QoS aspects that they tried to address, e.g. security and state persistence, can be addressed more naturally via interception at lower-layer messaging middleware rather than augmenting a BPEL engine with the ability to call low-level middleware services. We argue that a process should focus solely on the control flow and message routing between composed services. On the other hand, enforcement of adaptation policies in our approach can be either delegated to the underlying SOAP messaging middleware that mediates the Web services interactions or enacted by the process orchestration engine via dynamic adaptation of Web services composition instances. This operation at the SOAP messaging layer can shield the process orchestration layer from the need to provide fault management.

In [8], the authors presented RobustBPEL as an approach to improve reliability of BPEL processes via automatic generation of exceptions handling BPEL constructs, as well as generation of a Web services proxy for each participating service to discover and bind to equivalent Web services that can substitute a faulty service. However, the proposed approach does not consider potential dependencies between Web service operations. Our approach is more general and controls adaptation using policies that can be checked for consistency.

Significant progress (e.g., see [14]) has been achieved in the field of dynamic composition of Web services by leveraging artificial intelligence planning and semantic Web services to obtain new Web service compositions when the measured QoS violates a Service Level Agreement (SLA). However, such approaches incur considerable overhead and their practical applicability to business problems is still to be proven. We argue that our approach is more practical and lightweight.

Our MASC middleware can also be seen as a complement to Web services management (WSM) systems, such as the Web Service Offerings Infrastructure (WSOI) [16]. These systems provided mechanisms for measuring, evaluating, and managing Web services to ensure that QoS objectives are met. The central concept in such systems is often an XML-based contract that formally specifies QoS assurances (e.g., about response time, throughput, availability, and reliability). However, most of the proposed approaches focus on monitoring and/or QoS-based selection of individual Web services. Our work aims to go beyond the past approaches towards self-adaptive and more agile business processes implemented as Web services compositions.

The work in [2] proposed a general extension of the service oriented architecture to support autonomic behavior of Web services, but the proposed architecture does not address the requirements of adaptive business process execution.

5 Conclusions and Future Work

Dynamic adaptation of Web services compositions is an important step towards agile business processes that need to continually adapt to keep fulfilling the functional and QoS requirements of their dynamic business environment. In this paper, we presented MASC – a policy-based middleware for monitoring and adaptation of Web services compositions. The underlying design principle of our approach is the separation of concerns between the process definition and the monitoring and control, considerably simplifying Web services composition development and management. The benefits of the work presented in this paper are of twofold:

(1) A novel language, WS-Policy4MASC, is used to declaratively specify monitoring policies for detection of adaptation needs (e.g., special cases and faults) and adaptation policies that guide process reconfiguration (e.g., fault correction). The externalization and explicit definition of such policies helps in keeping the Web services composition simple and uncluttered. Further, these policies can evolve independently, while allowing potential reuse.

(2) The new MASC middleware architecture has been designed and implemented to autonomously make and coordinate enforcement of runtime adaptation decisions across both the business process orchestration layer and the SOAP messaging layer. Currently, MASC supports both static and dynamic customization of Web services composition instances, as well as corrective adaptation at the messaging layer.

The paper reports the progress on MASC middleware design and implementation and highlights how our previous work on the wsBus and adaptation strategies fits into the overall MASC architecture. To demonstrate feasibility and evaluate effectiveness of our adaptation techniques at the SOAP messaging layer, wsBus was deployed in a supply chain management Web services composition. The preliminary measurements confirmed improved availability and reliability at an acceptable increase in latency. Also, feasibility of our process-level static and dynamic customization was assessed using scenarios from the stock trading domain.

Our ongoing work is on providing support for other types of adaptation, i.e., corrective adaptation at the business process orchestration layer to handle process-level faults, optimizing adaptation to improve extra-functional properties, and preventive adaptation to avoid future faults and/or QoS degradations before they occur. We are also extending our middleware to enable making and enacting adaptation decisions (e.g., optimal configuration of running Web services compositions) based on not only event-condition-action rules, but also more abstract utility/goal policies describing how to determine business benefits/costs and maximize business value by performing adaptations. These ambitious extensions aim to position MASC as a middleware for autonomic business-driven management of Web services compositions.

Acknowledgments. This work is a part of the research project "Building Policy-Driven Middleware for QoS-Aware and Adaptive Web Services Composition" sponsored by the Australian Research Council (ARC) and Microsoft Australia. We also thank A/Prof. Boualem Benattallah for insightful discussions and his comments.

References

1. Baresi, L., Guinea, S., Plebani, P.: WS-Policy for Service Monitoring. Proc. of the 6th International Workshop on Technologies for E-Services (TES 2005, Trondheim, Norway), Lecture Notes in Computer Science (LNCS), Vol. 3811. Springer (2005) 72-83
2. Birman, K., Van Renesse, R., Vogels, W.: Adding High Availability and Autonomic behavior to Web Services. Proc. of the 26th International Conference on Software Engineering (ICSE 2004, Edinburgh, Scotland, UK). IEEE-CS (2004) 17-26
3. Charfi, A., Mezini, M.: An Aspect-Based Process Container for BPEL. Proc. of the First Workshop on Aspect-Oriented Middleware Development (AOMD 2005, Grenoble, France). ACM (2005) #4
4. Curbera, F., Leymann, F., Storey, T., Ferguson, D., Weerawarana, S.: Web Services Platform Architecture: SOAP, WSDL, WS-Policy, WS-Addressing, WS-BPEL, WS-ReliableMessaging and More. Prentice Hall (2005)
5. Erradi, A., Maheshwari, P.: A Broker-Based Approach for Improving Web Services Reliability. Proc. of the IEEE International Conference on Web Services 2005 (ICWS'05, Orlando, Florida, USA). IEEE -CS (2005) 355 - 362
6. Erradi, A., Maheshwari, P., Tosic, V.: Recovery Policies for Enhancing Web Services Reliability. Proc. of the IEEE International Conference on Web Services 2006 (ICWS'06, Chicago, Illinois, USA). IEEE-CS (2006)
7. Erradi, A., Maheshwari, P.: AdaptiveBPEL: Policy-Driven Middleware for Flexible Web Services Composition. In Proc. of the EDOC 2005 Middleware for Web Services Workshop (MWS'05, Enschede, The Netherlands). IEEE-CS (2005) 5-12
8. Ezenwoye, O. Sadjadi, S.M.: Enabling Robustness in Existing BPEL Processes. Proc. of the 8th International Conference on Enterprise Information Systems (ICEIS-06, Paphos, Cyprus). INSTICC (2006)
9. Geppert, A., Tombros, D., Dittrich, K.: Defining the Semantics of Reactive Components in Event-Driven Workflow Execution with Event Histories. Information Systems, Vol. 23, No. 3/4. Elsevier (1998) 235-252.
10. Mens, T., Buckley, J., Zenger, M., Rashid, A.: Towards a Taxonomy of Software Evolution. Proc. of the Workshop on Unanticipated Software Evolution (Warsaw, Poland). (2005)

11. Salle, M., Bartolini, C.: Management by Contract. Proc. of the IFIP/IEEE International Symposium on Network Operations and Management (NOMS'04, Seoul, South Korea). IEEE (2004) 787-800
12. Sloman, M.: Policy-Driven Management for Distributed Systems. Journal of Network and Systems Management, Vol. 2, No. 4. Kluwer (1994) 333-360
13. Tai, S., Mikalsen, T., Wohlstadter, E., Desai, N., Rouvellou, I.: Transaction Policies for Service-Oriented Computing. Data & Knowledge Engineering, Vol. 51, No. 1. Elsevier (2004) 59-79
14. Verma, K., Doshi, P., Gomadam, K., Miller, J., Sheth, A.: Optimal Adaptation in Web Processes with Coordination Constraints. Proc. of the IEEE International Conference on Web Services 2006 (ICWS'06, Chicago, Illinois, USA). IEEE-CS (2006)
15. Verma, K., Sheth, A.P.: Autonomic Web Processes. Proc. of the Third International Conference Service-Oriented Computing (ICSOC'05, Amsterdam, The Netherlands), Lecture Notes in Computer Science (LNCS), Vol. 3826. Springer (2005) 1-11
16. Tosic, V., Lutfiyya, H., Tang Y.: Extending Web Service Offerings Infrastructure (WSOI) for Management of Mobile/Embedded XML Web Services. Proc. of the 8th IEEE International Conference on E-Commerce Technology and The 3rd IEEE International Conference on Enterprise Computing, E-Commerce, and E-Services (CEC/EEE'06, San Francisco, California, USA). IEEE-CS (2006) 87-95
17. The Web Services Interoperability Organization (WS-I): Supply Chain Management Sample Application Architecture. Web resource (version Dec. 9, 2003; accessed Sept. 1, 2006). On-line at: http://www.ws-i.org/SampleApplications/SupplyChainManagement/2003-12/SCMArchitecture1.01.pdf (2003)

Living with Nondeterminism in Replicated Middleware Applications

Joseph Slember and Priya Narasimhan

Carnegie Mellon University, Pittsburgh PA 15213, USA
jslember@ece.cmu.edu, priya@cs.cmu.edu

Abstract. Application-level nondeterminism can lead to inconsistent state that defeats the purpose of replication as a fault-tolerance strategy. We present Midas, a new approach for living with nondeterminism in distributed, replicated, middleware applications. Midas exploits (i) the static program analysis of the application's source code prior to replica deployment and (ii) the online compensation of replica divergence even as replicas execute. We identify the sources of nondeterminism within the application, discriminate between actual and superficial nondeterminism, and track the propagation of actual nondeterminism. We evaluate our techniques for the active replication of servers using micro-benchmarks that contain various sources (multi-threading, system calls and propagation) of nondeterminism.

1 Motivation

Replication is a common technique used to build fault-tolerant, distributed systems. The idea behind replication is the creation and distribution of multiple, identical copies (replicas) of a component across a system so that the failure of a replica can be masked by the availability of the other replicas. Determinism is a fundamental property required in order for replication to work. A component is said to be deterministic if it contains no characteristics that could cause replicas to become inconsistent with each other. In other words, identical replicas, when started from the same initial state and supplied the same ordered sequence of input messages, should reach the same final state and produce the same output.

A simplistic, but effective, strategy is to disallow the use of any nondeterministic functionality within applications that are to be replicated – effectively, this forbids the use of multithreading, shared memory, local I/O, system calls, random numbers, timers, etc. This is, in fact, the approach adopted by industrial standards, such as Fault-Tolerant CORBA [14].

Clearly, this approach is unrealistic for real-world applications that wish to use all of these nondeterministic functions. Current approaches to handling nondeterminism, covered in Section 8, allow nondeterminism to exist within the application, but handle it transparently. Transparency has its accompanying benefits, but does not exploit application-level information that might facilitate the handling of nondeterminism. In addition, architecture/application programmers often need to able to exercise control and "want to worry about replica

M. van Steen and M. Henning (Eds.): Middleware 2006, LNCS 4290, pp. 81–100, 2006.
© IFIP International Federation for Information Processing 2006

configuration, intervene in failure detection or enabling explicit synchronization between replicas" [21]. With this motivation, we have developed a program-analysis approach to handling all forms of nondeterminism (including system calls and multithreading) – this allows us to *exploit application-level insight in handling nondeterminism*. Active replication is the predominant replication style that falls prey to nondeterminism. Therefore, our techniques are focused on how to handle nondeterminism in architectures using active replication. However, our techniques are easily applicable to other replication styles as well.

Contributions of this paper: Our previous research [18] showed that program analysis could assist in handling one specific form of nondeterminism, namely, system calls, such as `gettimeofday`. In our enhanced approach, Midas, described in this paper, we handle all forms of nondeterminism, including multithreading and contaminated nondeterminism. More specifically, the contributions of this paper include the following:

- Taxonomy and technique that distinguishes between nondeterminism that is superficial (looks like a nondeterministic call, but its effects do not lead to replica divergence) vs. actual (effects do lead to replica divergence) – this allows us to be discriminating in that we only need to worry about *addressing the actual, and not the superficial, nondeterminism*;
- Tracking the *propagation (or "contamination") of nondeterminism* through the application code – this allows us to capture the effects of nondeterministic execution and variables on otherwise deterministic code;
- Design and empirical evaluation of various application-centric *performance-sensitive techniques that compensate for the nondeterminism* that we detect and track – these techniques range from re-executing the contaminated non-determinism to transferring the entire application state.

2 Taxonomy of Nondeterminism

Program analysis allows us to identify the true causes in the divergence of replicated state. Application state can be classified into one of three mutually exclusive categories: pure nondeterminism, contaminated nondeterminism, and pure determinism.

1. Pure nondeterminism: This covers any function that is the originating source of nondeterminism and that affects the server's state. Examples include system calls such as `gettimeofday` or `random`, all inputs, and all `read` calls that change the server's state nondeterministically. An example is

```
for (int j = 0; j < 100; j++ ) foo[ j ] = random();
```

Shared state among threads also falls within this category. However, we treat shared state in a special way – each access of shared state by a thread is considered to be a separate source of nondeterminism. For example, consider a single shared variable between two threads; if each thread accesses this variable four times, then, there exist eight separate instances of pure nondeterminism. It is immaterial that these eight instances happen to involve the same variable. This view of shared state among threads frees us from having to worry about thread interleaving or the actual point in time when the threads execute.

2. Contaminated nondeterminism: This covers state that has any dependency, direct or indirect, on an instance of pure nondeterminism. Contaminated state captures the effect of pure nondeterminism when it propagates to the rest of the application. In other words, the pure nondeterministic state marks the beginning of nondeterministic execution. Anything that the pure nondeterministic state then touches is contaminated. If there was no pure nondeterminism, then, there would be no contamination. An example is the contaminated variable bar that depends on the purely nondeterministic variable foo:

```
for (int j = 0; j < 100; j++ ) {
    foo[ j ] = random();
    bar[ j + 100 ] = foo[ j ]; }
```

3. Pure determinism: This covers state that has no dependency whatsoever on the identified pure nondeterminism. This category of state will always be consistent across all server replicas. Assuming that the values in bar are initialized to zero, an example is:

```
for (int j = 0; j < 100; j++ ) bar[ j ] = bar[ j ] + 10;
```

4. Superficial nondeterminism: This falls under the category of pure determinism, but might be misclassified if a transparent approach to handling nondeterminism were used. In this category, a nondeterministic call is executed, but the end-result does not affect the application's persistent state and does not contaminate the rest of the application, either. An example is:

```
int a = random(); b = 5; return b;
```

Here, variable a is nondeterministic, but its value does not affect the server's state. More realistic examples of superficial nondeterminism are not shown here due to lack of space. A significant source of superficial nondeterminism arises in multithreaded applications where threads do not share any variables and do not modify any persistent application state, or where the shared state is split up across the threads such that each thread has its own distinct piece of state.

The value of this taxonomy, lies in its utility in compensating for nondeterminism. Only pure and contaminated nondeterminism need to be addressed for replica consistency – the other categories (pure determinism and superficial nondeterminism) can be disregarded. Thus, the compensation overhead will depend on the relative amounts of each category within an application.

3 Objectives

Our aim is to permit programmers to continue to create distributed applications that are nondeterministic (e.g., containing performance features such as multithreading) and yet allow these applications to be made fault-tolerant. Midas is independent of the target application and middleware and could be readily applied to any distributed, nondeterministic application.

In this paper, we exploit client-server middleware as the vehicle for exploring the issues underlying nondeterminism. In particular, we target CORBA C++ applications for the application of Midas. MEAD [12], the fault-tolerant middleware that we use, enables CORBA applications to be made fault-tolerant in multiple ways, including active, or state-machine, replication [17]. With the active replication of a server, every server replica receives and processes each request; every server replica also sends a response to the client, leading to duplicate responses that need to be filtered. The MEAD infrastructure performs this filtering and delivers only one response to the client, thereby masking the server's replication from the client. Clearly, for active replication to work, the server replicas must receive the same set of messages in the same order, which MEAD assures because it conveys messages over the underlying totally-ordered group communication system, Spread [3]. Active replication traditionally requires the supported application to be deterministic; however, we relax this requirement to allow MEAD to support the active replication even of applications containing nondeterministic features.

Midas' approach involves a synergistic combination of two aspects: *compile-time* knowledge with *run-time* compensation. By exploiting program analysis to isolate the possible places where nondeterminism can affect the system state or behavior, we then perform code transformations (that do not violate application semantics or expected functional behavior) to ensure consistent results across all of the replicas. We offer the programmer various options to deal with nondeterminism. A side-benefit of our analysis lies in its software engineering aspect. Because our program analysis tracks all live variables and their dependencies on detected nondeterminism, we can assess to what extent nondeterminism pervades the application. This information can be beneficial to the application programmer in understanding the trade-offs and deciding between various choices in compensating for nondeterminism.

Assumptions. Midas relies on having complete access to the application's source code, along with the ability to modify it prior to deployment. Specifically, we assume that we are allowed to modify the source code for the client, the server, and the IDL interfaces of all objects. Both the client and server source code must be available for analysis, although only the server is replicated. We also assume that all of the application state can be determined statically – thus, program analysis techniques that can handle dynamic state (e.g., dynamically allocated variables whose size is unknown at compile time) are outside the scope of this paper. Pointer-aliasing analysis is currently outside the scope of the techniques highlighted in this paper; our most recent work does incorporate advanced compiler techniques to handle dynamic memory and pointers.

For the purpose of this paper, and to describe how we handle *application-level nondeterminism*, we assume the deterministic, reproducible behavior of the operating system and the underlying middleware. While we make this simplifying assumption in order to demonstrate our approach to handling nondeterminism, we emphasize that Midas is general enough that we could apply it equally to the middleware/OS source-code and address their inherent nondeterminism as well, as describe in [19]. We also require homogeneous platforms, i.e., all of the

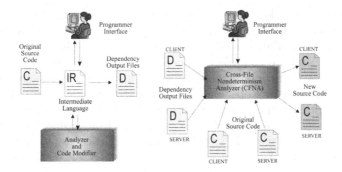

Fig. 1. Midas' program analysis framework for analyzing nondeterminism

replicas of the application must be hosted over identical hardware and operating systems; future versions of our approach will be extended to cover heterogeneous platforms. We assume an independent-failures model across distinct nodes and replicas, and aim to tolerate crash and communication faults.

4   Program Analysis Framework

To perform program analysis, we needed to convert the C++ CORBA application source-code into an intermediate format that is more suitable for program analysis. We first transformed our target C++ applications into C code using EDG [1], and then used the SUIF2 [2] compiler to transform the resulting C code into the intermediate representation. Conversion from C++ to C allows for easier analysis because it eliminates some complexities (e.g., object-oriented issues) that C++ introduces. It also allows us to leverage current compiler tools that expedite the transformation of C code into a workable, efficient intermediate form (referred to as an annotated parse-tree henceforth).

As shown in Figure 1, Midas' analyzer makes multiple passes through each intermediate file, and highlights the sources of nondeterminism in the code. For instance, a pass that discovers a nondeterministic call will annotate the return value of that call and then track that variable as potential (contaminated) nondeterminism. For each source file, the analyzer creates a dependency file that captures the nondeterministic behavior of the source code in that file. We then modify the original application source-code to insert specific code-snippets for the tracking and subsequent compensation of nondeterminism.

Enhancements to Analysis Framework. In our current program-analysis framework, we use SUIF to generate the initial abstract syntax tree (AST). All of the subsequent application analysis-passes are custom extensions to SUIF because of our specific needs in analyzing nondeterminism. For instance, our enhanced Midas framework supports thread analysis, as long as we can statically determine the entry, exit, and launch of all threads. In addition, we perform a complete dependency analysis to identify not only pure nondeterminism, but also the contaminated state that depends on it.

Some information is lost in the conversion from C++ to C, and we traverse the C++ code to mark up the SUIF-generated AST tree to fill in this information. The declaration of variables needs to be updated as scope is defined differently in C and C++, and this can affect the dependency chain between variables. For instance, in C++, the conditional block within an if, while, do-while, or for is considered to be a new scope, unlike in C. Another example of lost information relates to exception-handling code in try-catch blocks; try-catch blocks that form the top-level statements of functions, constructors, or destructors must be updated because they can affect the propagation of exceptions. Midas' current automated generation and insertion of code to handle our categorized nondeterminism includes:

- Tracking to assign unique identifiers to nondeterminism that is embedded within specific elements of a non-scalar data structure (e.g., nondeterminism that affects only one element of an entire array);
- Data structures to hold the variable-size state of the application;
- State-transfer operations (get_state and set_state) to copy state back and forth from the application into the appropriate data structures for transfer over the network;
- Execution that re-generates the contaminated state from the pure nondeterministic state, only if the latter has been transferred.

Data-Flow Passes. We perform multiple passes over the annotated parse tree. The first set of passes identifies all of the persistent state within the server code. Ultimately, this represents the only state that might be affected by nondeterminism and the state that we need to worry about for consistent server replication. The second set of passes identifies the pure nondeterminism within the application; these passes find and mark nondeterministic system calls, inputs, I/O, etc. Shared state between threads is initially considered as potentially nondeterministic, and another pass is made to discover all accesses to this shared state; these accesses are then marked as pure nondeterminism. Subsequently, these accesses are treated as sources of nondeterminism in their own right, and effectively constitute state. def-use chains (that determine where a specific variable is defined, and where it is used or assigned to another variable) are then calculated for all marked pure nondeterministic variables – this represents the first phase of dependency-tracking.

Control-Flow Passes. The next phase involves evaluating all of the possible execution paths that the server code might take. We determine the order of variable assignments along a particular control path, and for every discovered control path, we link together the def-use chains that we determined in the previous data-flow phase. This allows us to calculate dependencies of every variable for every possible execution path. Carrying this argument forward, we can now mark as contaminated nondeterminism all of the state that depends on the pure nondeterministic state identified in the data-flow phase. This is recursive – as we mark more contaminated state, we need make further passes to determine if there are further dependencies on this newly discovered contaminated state. We

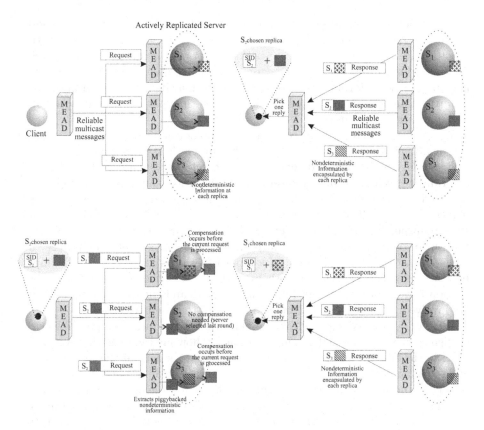

Fig. 2. Underlying approach for Midas' various compensation techniques. The techniques differ in the nature/amount of the information passed back and forth between the client and the server, and in the actual compensation work done on the server-side.

perform an exhaustive search of the server source-code to ensure that all such contaminated state is found. All persistent state that remains unmarked at the end of the control-flow phase can be considered as pure determinism.

5   Midas' Compensation Approaches

During our compile-time phases, we insert the compensation and state-transfer code snippets that will actually execute at runtime within the application. In this section, we describe how and when these code-snippets accomplish the compensation. For the remainder of the text, we assume that the server is actively replicated.

In our approach, the client is an integral participant in the compensation of the server's nondeterminism. Consider any two consecutive requests from the client to the replicated server, as shown in Figure 2. Each server replica piggybacks the relevant information(this information is specific to the technique described below) about its nondeterminism to the client in its response to the first request. Then, this information, piggybacked onto the second request, is echoed by the client to all of the server replicas so that they can perform individual, local compensation actions *before* they begin to process the second request. All of the piggybacked nondeterministic information, as well as its associated transfer and compensation code, is generated by our compile-time phase, without burdening the application programmer.

We emphasize here that the server replicas do not need to be in lock-step synchronization in order to do this – each replica proceeds asynchronously to service its incoming, totally-ordered requests and to return responses. Thus, through the runtime execution of our inserted compensation snippets, each replica is rendered logically identical with its peers before it starts to process any new request from the client; between requests, the server replicas (if each's internal state is inspected individually) might, in fact, be divergent in state. However, this out-of-band divergence does no harm because it does not compromise the fault-tolerance of the application. If a replica fails or is recovered, it will simply be rendered consistent with the others at the *start* of the next new request. In Section 7, we address how this divergence becomes an issue when multiple clients are involved, with each controlling some part of the compensation.

All of our performance-sensitive compensation techniques undergo two rounds of client-server interaction for compensation, as shown in Figure 2. However, they differ in the amount and nature of compensation work done at the server replica and the amount/kind of relevant information transferred back and forth between the client and the server replicas. While all of our techniques are common in exploiting program analysis, the range of choices allow an application programmer to make an application-centric, performance-sensitive choice in compensating for nondeterminism. The techniques described below can be broadly classified as:

- Transfer of state, or the `transfer-*` techniques:
  `transfer-ckpt`, `transfer-diff-ckpt`, `transfer-contam` and
  `transfer-contam-track`;
- Re-execution of code, or the the `reexec-*` techniques:
  `reexec-contam` and `reexec-contam-track`.

In Figure 3, we depict the decision process that an application/system developer would undergo in order to decide among the various techniques.

5.1   Full-Checkpoint Transfer (`transfer-ckpt`)

After processing each request, every replica marshals its entire state (checkpoint) and passes this state, along with its response, to the client. The client accepts the first response[1], stores the identifier of the corresponding (selected) replica

---

[1] The client always sees only one response from the entire set of replicas because MEAD delivers the first-received response from the replicated server and suppresses the other responses. The replica whose response makes it first to the client is called the *selected replica* in the processing of the client's *next* request. The selected replica can vary from one request to the next, and is not dictated by the client or the server.

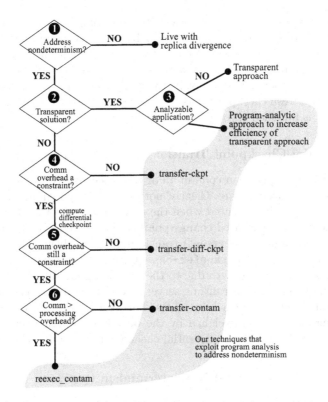

Fig. 3. Decision tree for determining appropriate technique for handling nondeterminism in an application. (1) Yes: Nondeterminism must be dealt with; No: Either no nondeterminism or can live with potential replica divergence. (2) Yes: Application code cannot be modified or designer prefers a transparent approach; No: Application code can be modified. (3) Yes: Pure deterministic code can be highlighted by program analysis, enabling a more efficient transparent technique that addresses only actual, and not superficial, nondeterminism; No: Program analysis cannot be performed on application source code, requiring a transparent approach that unnecessarily handles even superficial nondeterminism. (4) Yes: Communication overhead is an issue and a more efficient technique must be found. Only the state that has changed needs to be handled; No: Communication overhead is not a constraint and `transfer-ckpt` technique can be used. (5) Yes: Communication overhead is still a constraint and further analysis is required; No: Communication overhead is within reason and `transfer-diff-ckpt` can be used. (6) Yes: Communication overhead is a greater constraint than processing overhead, and `reexec-contam` can be used; No: Processing overhead is a greater constraint than communication overhead and `transfer-contam` can be used.

and that replica's state. On its next request to the server, the client piggybacks this saved information (including the checkpoint of the selected replica).

Each receiving replica examines this information to see if it was the selected replica, at the client-side, for the previous request. The selected replica does not need to compensate and can proceed with processing the current request; a replica that was not selected by the client in the previous round must apply the piggybacked checkpoint before proceeding to service the current request. Thus, these checkpoints are passed back and forth between the client and the server to ensure replica consistency. Effectively, the compensation is as if a new replica was started and a fresh checkpoint was transferred to it, except that, in our case, the checkpoint is funneled through the client in its next request.

5.2 Differential-Checkpoint Transfer (`transfer-diff-ckpt`)

We instrument the application code in all of the places where the processing of a request might modify its state. Clearly, not all of these potential state-change points might actually be executed when the server processes a request. At runtime, only the actually executed change-points are captured and the associated state (called a differential checkpoint) transferred to the client. The remainder of the technique is similar to `transfer-ckpt`. Compared to `transfer-ckpt`, we have increased static code growth due to the additional instrumentation. There should be a slight increase in runtime server-side latency due to the additional scaffolding code required to track variables. This technique performs best when the scaffolding latency is outweighed by the benefit in communication latency obtained with transferring the differential checkpoint vs. the full checkpoint.

5.3 Transfer Contaminated-Nondeterminism (`transfer-contam`)

The `transfer-ckpt` and `transfer-diff-ckpt` techniques do not discriminate between actual and superficial nondeterminism. In the `transfer-contam` technique, each server replica piggybacks only its actual nondeterministic state (both pure and contaminated) back to the client.

Based on the output of our data-flow and control-flow analyses, we create a server-side `struct` that holds the pure and contaminated nondeterminism within each replica. Because this `struct` needs to be marshaled over the standard middleware protocol, we need to augment the IDL interface specifications of the server so that this nondeterministic `struct` contains (and serves as) the return value of the server's methods and is also an input parameter to the server's methods – this allows us to piggyback the nondeterministic `struct` onto messages passed back and forth between the client and the server. The remainder of the algorithm is similar to the `transfer-ckpt` technique, except that the client-side and the server-side extract, copy, and piggyback the nondeterministic `struct` instead of a checkpoint.

5.4 Reexecute Contaminated-Nondeterminism (`reexec-contam`)

We insert prepared portions of code that can be executed to re-generate the contaminated nondeterminism, if provided the pure nondeterminism (i.e., the origin of the contamination) as an input. In `reexec-contam`, every receiving server replica extracts the piggybacked nondeterministic `struct`, as in `transfer-contam`. As with all of the other techniques, the selected replica for one request has no compensation work to do for the next request. On the other hand, each of the remaining (non-selected) replicas for a request performs compensation, before processing the next request, by first setting the pure nondeterministic part of its state to the received nondeterministic `struct`, and then re-executing the inserted code-snippets to regenerate the corresponding contaminated nondeterminism. At the end of this compensation, each replica is consistent and is ready to process the current request.

Compared to `transfer-contam`, the `reexec-contam` technique should incur lower communication overheads due to the reduced amount of nondeterministic state being piggybacked back and forth; however, the tradeoff is that runtime latency is increased by the reexecution of the compensation snippets at the server side. Also, `reexec-contam` requires more compile-time analysis and source-code modification to the server-side than `transfer-contam`. This is because additional control-flow passes are needed to isolate the code that encapsulates the contaminated nondeterministic state. The client-side code is the same as in `transfer-contam`.

Obviously, reexecution is justified when the compensation overhead is outweighed by the communication overhead of the `transfer-*` techniques.

5.5 Incorporating Tracking (`transfer-contam-track`, `reexec-contam-track`)

The complexity of the data structures that constitute application state, along with the way these structure are accessed or referenced, affects how we track changes in that application's state. The nondeterministic `struct`s that we create for compensation purposes must be flexible and able to hold a dynamic amount of information, ranging from no state all the way to a full checkpoint. We use the CORBA `sequence` type for this purpose because it can hold, and marshal over the wire, a dynamic amount of information.

If state variables are all scalar types (e.g., `int a`), then, there is no need for tracking. However, if data structures are more complex or non-scalar (e.g., `int a[10000]`), then, additional information might be needed to track which of the member items of the non-scalar structure have changed.

To cover the worst possible case, we identify each piece of state with an additional identifier. This identifier can be used to directly reference its associated piece of state. For example, if `int a[500]` is a part of the state, then another shadow array of the same size is created to hold the indexes of array `a[]`. If only one value in the array `a[]` changes at runtime, the shadow array tracks the change and allows us to know which index in `a[]` changed. The additional compile-time work to support tracking is minimal because it involves creating sequences of `long`s to hold all the identification information to reference non-scalar types.

5.6 Additional Clarification

The above techniques encapsulate all of the nondeterminism that is present in a distributed application. However, nondeterminism might be introduced if different replicas of the same server talk to different external servers. In other words, we assume that a replicates server receives the same messages in the same order using totally ordered multicast. Therefore, consistency is maintained and nondeterminism is handled properly in the above techniques.

Midas' techniques will handle *all* nondeterminism that is present in an application. This, however, can present a problem if the nondeterminism is built into the application for a specific reason and, therefore, should not be compensated for. In order to allow for nondeterminism to exist in the application without being compensated for, it is possible for a programmer to mark parts of code or variables that Midas would consider deterministic and, therefore, would not handle by its compensation techniques. Additionally, we could allow the programmer to specify when and/or what replicas responses would be used for the compensation. This would allow for greater control for the application programmer and for more flexibility in the architecture. However, this is outside the scope of this paper, even though the implementation would be relatively straight-forward.

The main idea behind using program analysis to handle nondeterminism is to target only the nondeterminism that actually causes replica divergence. Thus, it should not result in higher overheads than other transparent approaches, such as full-state transfer. While it is possible that an application will be strife with nondeterminism and, therefore, will involve significant overhead on Midas' part, this overhead should not exceed that of a basic transparent approach.

6 Experimental Evaluation

Because our techniques are non-transparent, the overheads that we incur should be directly proportional to the amount of actual nondeterminism that exists within the application, e.g., if only 5% of the application is actually nondeterministic, our compensation overheads should be incurred only for that portion of the application. We also note that the runtime overheads and behavior of MEAD will undoubtedly influence our runtime overheads. Where possible, we distinguish between MEAD's performance and our compensation performance.

We conducted our experiments using the Emulab distributed environment [22], with a homogeneous test-bed of nodes that each run the RedHat 9 Linux, 2.4.18 kernel operating system on a 850MHz processor, 256KB cache, and 512MB RAM over a 100 Mbps LAN. We use MEAD version 1.5 that uses Spread version 3.17.3 as its group communication protocol. In our experiments, we do not load the nodes with any other running programs other than MEAD, Spread, our micro-benchmarks, and the native OS utilities that typically run on each node. Each replica runs on a separate node.

We evaluate a number of metrics (communication overhead, compensation overhead, server-side processing time, and round-trip time) under fault-free conditions.

Table 1. Description of the various micro-benchmarks

Compensation technique	no_sha micro-benchmark	sha micro-benchmark
vanilla (baseline)	Replicas are nondeterministic and inconsistent; no compensation performed	Same as no_sha, except that a 20-byte digest is computed and stored at each replica at the end of each request
transfer-ckpt	Entire checkpoint piggybacked on each server's reply to the client, compensation according to Section 5.1	Same as no_sha, with digest considered part of the checkpoint and piggybacked on each server's reply
transfer-contam	Pure and contaminated nondeterminism piggybacked on each server's reply to the client, compensation according to Section 5.3	Same as no_sha, with digest considered part of the contaminated nondeterminism
transfer-contam -track	Same as transfer-contam above, but with tracking enabled	Same as transfer-contam above, but with tracking enabled
reexec-contam	Pure nondeterminism piggybacked on each server's reply to the client, contaminated nondeterminism re-generated through re-execution, compensation according to Section 5.4	Same as no_sha, with digest needing to be re-computed as a part of the re-execution
reexec-contam -track	Same as reexec-contam above, but with tracking enabled	Same as reexec-contam above, but with tracking enabled

6.1   Micro-benchmarks

We have developed two micro-benchmarks to compare our various compensation techniques. The two micro-benchmarks are identical in many ways. They both constitute a two-tier application, i.e., with a single client and a single replicated server. Both micro-benchmarks use multi-threading with homogeneous threads (to simplify experimentation), identical code at each of the server replicas (except for the fact that each replica stores a unique, hard-coded server_id SID), and identical initial state to start out with. The difference is that the sha micro-benchmark involves the computation of a 20-byte digest, and therefore, requires significantly more processing time at the server-side, as compared with the no_sha micro-benchmark. The two micro-benchmarks are compared in Table 1. The sha version is used to give an example of an application that has increased reexecution time.

Each micro-benchmark contains an array of 10,000 longs that represents its state. Pure nondeterminism involves generating a random number and assigning it to one of the elements in the array. Contaminated state is subsequently created by performing arithmetic on the random number and assigning the result to

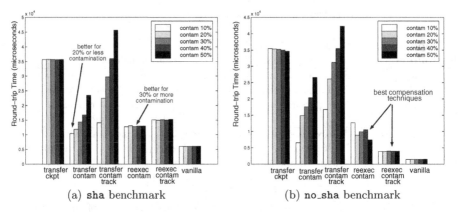

(a) sha benchmark   (b) no_sha benchmark

Fig. 4. Compensation approaches with varying amount of contaminated state for 10% pure deterministic state for the two micro-benchmarks. The cross-over between the transfer-contam and the reexec-contam is visible for both the tracking and the no-tracking cases.

another element in the array. The server state is changed in 15 different ways: varying the pure nondeterminism to 10%, 30% and 50%. For each value of pure nondeterminism, we vary the amount of contaminated nondeterminism to 10%, 20%, 30%, 40% and 50%. For each of the 15 state combinations, we evaluate each of our five techniques: transfer-ckpt, transfer-contam, transfer-contam-track, reexec-contam and reexec-contam-track. Note that we can compare all of the techniques for a given $x\%$ of nondeterminism. However, we cannot fairly compare a single technique for $x\%$ vs. $y\%$ of nondeterminism because these represent two entirely different applications (while the % of nondeterminism varies, the application is, in fact, functionally different). The vanilla case simply serves as a baseline for performance comparison. We also vary other parameters, such as the number of replicas (1–4), amount of multithreading (2–6 threads), and amount of state (100, 1000 and 10,000 longs).

6.2   Empirical Observations

Varying amount of contamination. Graph 4(b) shows the effect on the round-trip time of increasing the amount of contaminated nondeterminism within the no_sha micro-benchmark. The amount of pure nondeterminism for these results is fixed at 10%, and 3 replicas are used. Because pure nondeterministic state is handled identically across all of our various techniques, the graph demonstrates how each technique handles an increase in contaminated state.

The transfer-ckpt technique shows a fairly constant round-trip time regardless of the amount of contaminated state. The processing time increases slightly across all techniques because additional work is done due to the increased amount of contaminated state. However, the processing time is relatively small compared to the communication overhead of passing the entire state of back and forth.

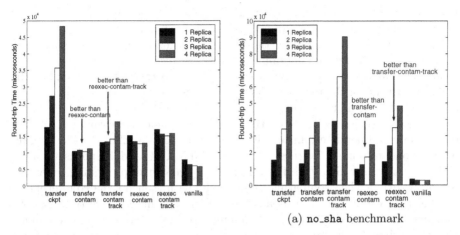

(a) no_sha benchmark

Fig. 5. (a) transfer-contam-* techniques are better than reexec-contam-* techniques for increasing number of replicas for the sha micro-benchmark for 10% pure deterministic state and 10% contaminated state. (b) reexec-contam-* techniques are better than transfer-contam-* techniques for increasing number of replicas for the no_sha micro-benchmark for 50% pure deterministic state and 30% contaminated state.

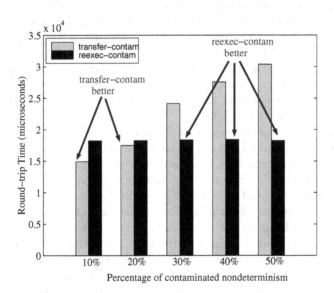

Fig. 6. Cross-over between the transfer-contam and the reexec-contam techniques for the sha micro-benchmark for 30% pure deterministic state

The transfer-contam-* techniques show a linear increase in round-trip time with increased amount of contaminated state. This is because the communication overhead is proportional to contaminated state. Note that transfer-contam-track has the higher overheads of the two because more information is being passed by the replicas. Also, `transfer-contam-track` becomes worse than `transfer-ckpt` when more than 50% of the state is nondeterministic.

There is very little change in the round-trip time of the `reexec-contam-*` techniques with increased contaminated state because the communication overhead dominates over re-execution time. Again, `reexec-contam-track` has the higher overheads of the two. We observe that the `reexec-contam-*` techniques are better than their `transfer-contam-*` counterparts.

Figure 4(a) shows the effect on the round-trip time of increasing the amount of contaminated nondeterminism within the `sha` micro-benchmark. The amount of pure nondeterminism for these results is fixed at 10%, and 3 replicas are used. Note that the sha1 algorithm has a significant amount of processing time; this is readily visible when comparing these results with their `no_sha` counterparts.

The same trends are seen as in Figure 4(b). The most interesting observation here is due to the fact that communication overhead does not dominate processing time. For instance, with 10% and 20% contamination, `transfer-ckpt` appears to have lower overheads. Once contamination reaches 30% or more, `reexec-contam` once again displays lower overheads. This is because the increased processing time outweighs the communication overhead for lower amounts of contaminated state.

Varying degree of replication. In Figures 6.2 and 5(a), the amount of pure and contaminated nondeterminism is constant, but the number of replicas is varied. Figure 6.2 shows the `sha` micro-benchmark for 10% pure nondeterminism and 10% contaminated nondeterminism. Figure 5(a) shows the `no_sha` micro-benchmark for 50% pure nondeterminism and 30% contaminated nondeterminism. Note that, for every additional replica, the communication load increases because all of the replicas send their nondeterministic state, along with their responses, to the client.

In Figure 6.2, all of the techniques. except for `transfer-ckpt`, demonstrate a minimal increase in round-trip time with increased number of replicas. This is because, apart from `transfer-ckpt`, which sends the entire state over, the other techniques only deal with 10% pure and 10% contaminated nondeterminism. Because the communication overhead is relatively lower due to the small amount of nondeterministic state, `reexec-contam` performs worse than `transfer-contam` technique, except in the 4-replica case where the communication overhead overcomes the re-execution time. Thus, the number of replicas, along with the amount of transferred state, can dictate which technique is appropriate for a given application.

Figure 5(a) demonstrates lower processing time with higher communication overhead. As in the previous case, the tracking counterpart of a technique adds more overhead than its corresponding no-tracking version. Here, `reexec-contam` is always better regardless of the number of replicas. In fact, with an increased number of replicas, the relative performance of the `reexec-contam` technique becomes markedly better.

Trade-offs. Figure 6 shows the round-trip time for the `sha` micro-benchmark with the amount of pure nondeterminism fixed at 30% for 3 replicas, and with the amount of contaminated state varying from 10-50%. We focus only on the performance of the `reexec-contam` and the `transfer-contam` techniques. The `reexec-contam` technique shows relatively no change as contaminated state increases because of the overwhelming communication overhead and the low processing time. The `transfer-contam` technique demonstrates a linear increase in overhead with respect to the amount of contaminated state. This graph clearly shows the cross-over between the two techniques, demonstrating that no technique works for all cases to provide the best performance. Many factors, including the number of replicas, the amount of contaminated state, the communication overhead, the processing overhead, etc., need to be weighed in deciding which technique is appropriate. Figures 6.2 and 5(a) also support our insights about the trade-offs between re-execution vs. the transfer of contaminated state, based on the relative amount of communication overhead and processing time.

Code growth. Code growth is inevitable in our technique. The `transfer-ckpt` technique will typically have the least code growth because it is perform simple checkpointing. The `transfer-contam` technique is next in code growth; `transfer-contam-track` will have even larger code growth. The `reexec-contam` will likely have the largest code growth of the all of techniques, because of the inserted compensation snippets. However, we note that `reexec-contam` will have smaller code growth if the amount of contaminated state as large and the re-execution snippets are small. Thus, while code growth matters and should be considered, using it as a metric for comparison might be subjective since it depends on the application's functionality.

7   Future Work

We note that our current implementations of the `transfer-*` and `reexec-*` techniques leave much room for optimization, but efficiency considerations form a part of our ongoing investigation. Multi-tier applications and nested end-to-end requests introduce increased complexity in handling nondeterminism, especially with actively replicated tiers. The propagation of nondeterministic state is no longer contained at the client or at any one tier. We need to handle any nondeterministic state or execution that propagates to other tiers. This is especially evident when a failure occurs during an end-to-end request, resulting in some of the replicas at every tier becoming inconsistent. Multiple clients can also complicate the techniques described in this paper because each client is an active participant in the back-and-forth compensation of nondeterminism, and we would then require coordination across clients or some alternative way of ensuring consistency across multiple clients. Both multi-tier and multi-client fault-tolerant architectures are part of our ongoing research on the scalable compensation of nondeterminism, but remain outside the scope of this paper.

8   Related Work

Gaifman [10] targets nondeterminism that arises in concurrent programs due to environmental interaction. This technique involves backup replicas lagging behind the primary to ensure consistency. The technique is transparent to the user, but the application is actually modified by transformations that handle multithreading. The Multithreaded Deterministic Scheduling Algorithm [11] aims to handle multithreading transparently by providing for internal and external queues that together enforce consistency. The external queue contains a sequence of ordered messages received via multicast, while each internal queue focuses on thread dispatching, with an internal queue for each process that spawns threads. Basile [5] addresses multithreading using a preemptive deterministic scheduler for active replication. The approach uses mutexes between threads and the execution is split into several rounds. Because the mutexes are known at each round, a deterministic schedule can be created. This approach does not require any communication between replicas.

Delta-4 XPA's semi-active replication [4] addresses nondeterminism through a hybrid replication style that employs primary-backup replication for all nondeterministic operations and active replication for all other operations. In SCEPTRE 2 [6], nondeterminism arises from preemptive scheduling. Semi-active replication is used, with deterministic behavior enforced through the transmission of messages from a coordination entity to backup replicas for every nondeterministic decision of the primary's. Similarly, Wolf's piecewise deterministic approach [23] handle nondeterminism by having a primary replica that actually executes all nondeterministic events, with the results being propagated to the backups at an observable, deterministic event.

The fault-tolerant real-time MARS system requires deterministic behavior [16] in highly responsive automotive applications that are nondeterministic due to time-triggered event activation and preemptive scheduling. Determinism is enforced using a combination of timed messages and a communication protocol for agreement on external events.

X-Ability [9] is based predominantly on the execution history resulting from previous invocation. The approach is not necessarily transparent to the programmer because the proposed correctness criterion must be followed for consistency. The advantage is that it is independent of the replication style. Slye et al. [20] track and record the nondeterminism due to asynchronous events and multithreading. The nondeterministic executions are recorded so that they can be replayed to restore replica consistency in the event of rollback.

The Transparent Fault Tolerance (TFT) system [7] enforces deterministic computation on replicas at the level of the operating system interface. The object code of the application binaries is edited to insert code that redirects all nondeterministic system calls to a software layer that returns identical results at all replicas. Hypervisor-based fault tolerance [8] involves a virtual machine that ensures that all nondeterministic data is consistent across replicas. A simulator executes all environmental instructions, and then requires system-wide lock-step synchronization on this execution.

TCP tapping [15] captures and forwards nondeterministic execution information from a primary to other replicas. The backup replicas gain information from the primary after it has done the work. The approach is transparent, but involves setting up routing tables to snoop on the client-to-server TCP stream, with the aim of extracting the primary's nondeterministic output. Zagorodnov et al. [24] target nondeterminism that is inherent to service protocols used by network servers. The solution involves the interception of I/O streams of replicas, and the appropriate handling of input and output streams.

9   Conclusions

We present Midas, a new approach, for living with nondeterminism in distributed, replicated applications by exploiting static program analysis on the application's source code, along with the runtime compensation of nondeterminism. We identify the sources of nondeterminism within the application, discriminate between actual and superficial nondeterminism, and track the propagation/contamination of nondeterminism within the application.

We describe two different techniques, one that involves the reexecution of contaminated nondeterministic code and another that involves the transfer of checkpoints or nondeterministic state. We can support even the active replication of nondeterministic applications in this manner. Our empirical evaluation involves various performance-sensitive techniques for distributed middleware micro-benchmarks that contain various sources (multi-threading, system calls and contamination) of nondeterminism.

Acknowledgements

We gratefully acknowledge the feedback that we received on early drafts of this paper from John Wilkes, Dan Siewiorek and Greg Ganger. This work has been partially supported by the NSF CAREER grant CCR-0238381.

References

1. http://www.edg.com/.
2. G. Aigner, A. Diwan, D. L. Heine, M. S. Lam, D. L. Moore, B. R. Murphy, and C. Sapuntzakis. *The Basic SUIF Programming Guide.*
3. Y. Amir, C. Danilov, and J. Stanton. A low latency, loss tolerant architecture and protocol for wide area group communication. In *The International Conference on Dependable Systems and Networks*, pages 327–336, New York, NY, June 2000.
4. P. Barrett, P. Bond, A. Hilborne, L. Rodrigues, D. Seaton, N. Speirs, and P. Verissimo. The Delta-4 extra performance architecture (XPA). In *Fault-Tolerant Computing Symposium*, pages 481–488, Newcastle, UK, June 1990.
5. C. Basile, Z. Kalbarczyk, and R. Iyer. A preemptive deterministic scheduling algorithm for multithreaded replicas. In *The International Conference on Dependable Systems and Networks*, pages 149–158, San Francisco, CA, June 2003.
6. S. Bestaoui. One solution for the nondeterminism problem in the SCEPTRE 2 fault tolerance technique. In *Euromicro Workshop on Real-Time Systems*, pages 352–358, Odense, Denmark, June 1995.

7. T. C. Bressoud. TFT: A software system for application-transparent fault tolerance. In *Fault-Tolerant Computing Symposium*, pages 128–137, Munich, Germany, June 1998.

8. T. C. Bressoud and F. B. Schneider. Hypervisor-based fault-tolerance. *ACM Transactions on Computer Systems*, 14(1), pages 90–107, Feb. 1996.

9. S. Frolund and R. Guerraoui. X-ability: A theory of replication. In *Principles of Distributed Computing*, pages 229–237, Portland, OR, 2000.

10. H. Gaifman, M. J. Maher, and E. Shapiro. Replay, recovery, replication, and snapshots of nondeterministic concurrent programs. In *Principles of Distributed Computing*, pages 241–255, Montreal, Canada, Aug. 1991.

11. R. Jimenez-Peris, M. Patino-Martinez, and S. Arevalo. Deterministic scheduling for transactional multithreaded replicas. In *Symposium on Reliable Distributed Systems*, pages 164–173, Nurnberg, Germany, October 2000.

12. P. Narasimhan, T. A. Dumitraş, S. M. Pertet, C. F. Reverte, J. G. Slember, and D. Srivastava. MEAD: Support for real-time fault-tolerant CORBA. *Concurrency and Computation: Practice and Experience*, 17(12):1527–1545, 2005.

13. P. Narasimhan, L. E. Moser, and P. M. Melliar-Smith. Enforcing determinism for the consistent replication of multithreaded CORBA applications. In *Symposium on Reliable Distributed Systems*, pages 263–273, Lausanne, Switzerland, Oct. 1999.

14. Object Management Group. Fault Tolerant CORBA. OMG Technical Committee Document formal/2001-09-29, September 2001.

15. M. Orgiyan and C. Fetzer. Tapping TCP streams. In *IEEE International Symposium on Network Computing and Applications*, pages 278–289, Cambridge, MA, Oct. 2001.

16. S. Poledna. *Replica Determinism in Fault-Tolerant Real-Time Systems*. PhD thesis, Technical University of Vienna, Vienna, Austria, Apr. 1994.

17. F. B. Schneider. Implementing fault-tolerant services using the state machine approach: A tutorial. *ACM Computing Surveys*, 22(4):299–319, 1990.

18. J. G. Slember and P. Narasimhan. Exploiting program analysis to identify and sanitize nondeterminism in fault-tolerant, replicated systems. In *Symposium on Reliable Distributed Systems*, pages 251–263, Florianopolis, Brazil, Oct. 2004.

19. J. G. Slember and P. Narasimhan. Nondeterminism in ORBs: The perception and the reality. In *Workshop on High Availability of Distributed Systems*, Krakow, Poland, September, 2006.

20. J. H. Slye and E. N. Elnozahy. Supporting nondeterministic execution in fault-tolerant systems. In *Fault-Tolerant Computing Symposium*, pages 250–259, Sendai, Japan, June 1996.

21. W. Vogels, R. van Renesse, and K. Birman. Six misconceptions about reliable distributed computing. In *ACM Special Interest Group on Operating Systems, European Workshop*, Sintra, Portugal, Sept. 1998.

22. B. White, J. Lepreau, L. Stoller, R. Ricci, S. Guruprasad, M. Newbold, M. Hibler, C. Barb, and A. Joglekar. An integrated experimental environment for distributed systems and networks. In *Symposium on Operating Systems Design and Implementation*, pages 255–270, Boston, MA, December 2002.

23. T. Wolf. *Replication of Non-Deterministic Objects*. PhD thesis, Ecole Polytechnique Federale de Lausanne, Switzerland, Nov. 1988.

24. D. Zagorodnov and K. Marzullo. Managing self-inflicted nondeterminism. In *Hot-Dep, International Conference on Dependable Systems and Networks*, pages 323–328, Yokohama, Japan, June 2005.

Trading Off Resources Between Overlapping Overlays

Brian F. Cooper

College of Computing, Georgia Institute of Technology
cooperb@cc.gatech.edu

Abstract. Many different overlays with different properties have been proposed. Rather than using one overlay for all applications, it is likely that multiple overlapping overlays will be deployed on the same computing resources for different purposes. We present an architecture, called ODIN-S, for mediating the resources used by overlapping overlays. We can specify priorities for different overlays, and then allow ODIN-S to allocate computation and bandwidth across the network to respect priorities. The key features of ODIN-S include a common middleware runtime supporting multiple overlay logics, and "filters" for throttling, ordering and dropping messages in order to manage resources. We present experimental results that demonstrate ODIN-S's ability to manage resources between different types of overlapping overlays.

1 Introduction

Middleware-level overlays have proven to be a useful abstraction for building scalable distributed systems. Many different kinds of overlays have been designed and built; a small sample includes [12,14,22,28,27,29,33,36]. Each of these overlays has strengths and weaknesses, and each aims for different design goals, which means that different kinds of overlays are useful for different applications. As a result it is unlikely that all applications will be built on one, general purpose overlay. Instead, there are likely to be many overlays using the same infrastructure resources, each deployed for a different purpose. For example, an enterprise might deploy a Narada overlay for message brokering, a super-peer overlay for information discovery, a Chord overlay for LDAP directory services, and so on. A simple example of two such overlapping overlays is shown in Figure 1. Several recently developed overlay toolkits have the ability to deploy overlapping overlays, including P2 [23] and GridKit [18].

It is important to mediate resource usage between all these overlapping overlays. A particularly resource intensive overlay should not starve other overlays that are not as greedy. Moreover, in many cases we want to assign priorities to overlays, and to give more resources to higher priority overlays (but again, without starving lower priority overlays.) For example, an enterprise may give the highest priority to the messaging overlay that is supporting its day-to-day operations, and less priority to an information discovery overlay that merely supplements its internal document search apparatus.

How can we mediate resource usage between overlapping overlays? We must allocate both bandwidth resources and processing resources in a fair but prioritized way between overlays. Existing overlay toolkits lack the ability to trade off resources between multiple overlays, or do not enforce fine grained priorities over all of these resources. In

M. van Steen and M. Henning (Eds.): Middleware 2006, LNCS 4290, pp. 101–120, 2006.

Fig. 1. Overlapping overlays. Solid lines represent a super-peer overlay; thick lines for connections between super-peers, and thin lines for connections to leaf-peers. Dashed lines represent a flat mesh network, such as a Narada broker network or unstructured peer-to-peer overlay.

this paper, we present a middleware system we have built, called *Overlay Dynamic Information Networks - Shared* (ODIN-S), that manages this resource mediation. The key architectural aspects of ODIN-S are (1) a common middleware runtime that supports the logic for multiple overlay clients on a single host, and (2) filters that manage the sending and processing of messages by these clients to enforce fairness and resource quotas.

Filters are the primary mechanism in ODIN-S for trading off resources between overlays. Filters can be used to throttle, schedule and drop messages to enforce quotas and overlay priorities. As such, filters must be used both to filter incoming messages and outgoing messages sent by a peer. We describe how to construct filters to manage the processing load, upload bandwidth and download bandwidth for a peer.

The primary contribution of this work is an architecture that integrates and adapts multiple techniques from other domains for the purpose of mediating resource usage among overlapping overlays. For example, we apply a weighted fair queuing discipline [17,16], typically used in network routers, to the problem of scheduling messages that are delivered and sent by the middleware. We develop an adaptive algorithm, inspired by a similar algorithm used in database replication [26], to allocate download bandwidth among multiple upstream peers. We use the concept of ingress and egress filters, typically used at network boundaries (for example, to detect and defeat denial of service attacks) to manage message flows between individual peers. In this paper, we describe how to combine and extend all of these techniques into a comprehensive middleware system for managing the resource usage of multiple overlays.

The remainder of this paper is organized as follows. In Section 2, we place ODIN-S in context with related work. Section 3 describes the overall architecture of ODIN-S, focusing on the support for overlapping overlays. In Section 4 we demonstrate how to use filters for a variety of resource management goals. Section 5 presents experimental results, and we conclude in Section 6.

2 Related Work

General scheduling of resources for data flows is a well known problem. Queuing disciplines for scheduling packets have been studied in depth in the networking domain [16,17,6]. Scheduling of flowing data has been studied both in operating systems research [9] and database research [3]. We view the traffic on an overlay as a data flow, and then adopt and extend techniques from different domains to manage the resources used by this traffic. Queuing of traffic from a single overlay is used in data stream systems such as Borealis [13] and overlay toolkits such as P2 [23]. We generalize this approach to queue messages from multiple overlays to enforce priorities across general overlay types. Some recent work has been done on scheduling for overlays, such as operator scheduling for distributed data stream processing [32,27,13], or load-based rearrangement of query streams in peer-to-peer overlays [25]. Our work generalizes these approaches for arbitrary, and overlapping, overlays.

In addition to throttling and scheduling, ODIN-S's filters can be used for load shedding, dropping messages when buffer resources are saturated. This approach is used to drop packets at overloaded routers [19], and tuples in overloaded data stream processors [15]. Our current implementation provides only simple tail drop of messages, but other policies could be easily added just by implementing a new filter. Moreover, it may be desirable to implement application-level endpoint congestion control (such as the congestion control schemes used in TCP) in addition to the in-network filters; we have not yet explored this approach.

Our upstream/downstream filter sets distribute a fair queuing algorithm among multiple upstream filters. A similar approach is taken in Core Stateless Fair Queuing (CSFQ) [34], where packets entering a core network are labeled by multiple upstream edge nodes to achieve approximate fair queuing behavior inside the core. Unlike the "core-stateless" approach where the core has no fair queues, ODIN-S can place filters at all overlay peers, ensuring per-link fair queuing and finer-grained control over resource usage. Other approaches to network QoS include Integrated Services (IntServ), in which flows must reserve resources that will be needed [10], and Differentiated Services (DiffServ), in which classes of flows (say, from the same ISP) are provided service based on a service level agreement [8]. Our techniques borrow the notion of using control messages to configure resource management from these approaches. Furthermore, we integrate aspects of each approach: our per-peer filters are similar to the per-router states maintained in IntServ, while our approach to managing the traffic of an entire overlay (as opposed to the flow of a single request) is similar to the classes of flows in DiffServ.

Packet and message filters are used in a variety of systems for different purposes. Examples include security filters at network boundaries, message filters in Web middleware such as mod_perl, content filters in publish/subscribe middleware [5], and so on. We apply the concept of filters to provide pluggable middleware components for managing resources in overlapping overlays.

Orthogonal to our approach to overlapping overlays is to have distinct overlays interoperate, as in PPPP [4]. In this approach, the overlays are using different hardware resources, and thus resource mediation is not as important.

3 Architectural Support for Overlapping Overlays

In this section, we describe the architecture of ODIN-S, focusing particularly on the features that support overlapping overlays. ODIN-S is a middleware toolkit designed to support various types of overlays, including unstructured peer-to-peer overlays [25,36], structured overlays [33,28,31], message and event dissemination overlays [14], data

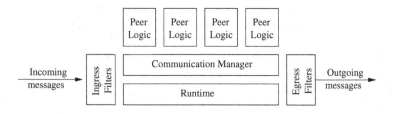

Fig. 2. ODIN-S peer architecture

stream transport and processing overlays [27], and so on. In each of these overlay types, many distributed "peers" or "nodes" are connected by middleware-level, logically persistent communication "links." For clarity in the rest of our discussion, we will refer to "peers" to mean either "peers" or "nodes."

The architecture of an ODIN-S peer is shown in Figure 2. We now describe each of the components of the architecture. As a running example, we will use both a super-peer network and a completely unstructured overlay (e.g. as in the original Gnutella protocol). There are many other types of overlays, but these relatively simple overlays are used to clarify the discussion. In a super-peer network, "leaf-peers" send a summary of their content to "super-peers." Super-peers, which typically are high capacity nodes, handle all of the searching, both looking for matches in the summaries of their leaf peers and forwarding messages to other super-peers. Leaf-peers are thus unloaded. An unstructured network has only one type of peer, and each peer connects to some number of neighbors. Each peer processes searches over its local content, and forwards the search to some or all of its neighbors. The peer can "flood" the search (as in the original Gnutella) by sending it to all of its neighbors, or may choose a more efficient routing strategy [1,24,35,21,11].

3.1 Peer Logic

A *peer logic* handles the routing and topology management for a single overlay. A peer that is participating in multiple overlays will have multiple peer logics, one per overlay. In order to join a new overlay, the peer creates and starts a new peer logic. Similarly, to leave an overlay, the peer stops and destroys a peer logic.

A peer logic in ODIN-S is comprised of two sub-components: the *routing logic* and the *topology manager*. The routing logic receives messages from other peers, processes them, and decides which neighbors (if any) to forward the messages. For example, a routing logic for a super-peer will receive search messages from leaf-peers and other super-peers, look for matching content in its indexes, return result messages if any content is found, and forward the search messages to other super-peers. In contrast, a topology manager manages the set of neighbors that the peer has in the overlay, by making and breaking connections to other neighbors based on the overlay's neighbor policy. For example, a topology manager for a super-peer will always try to have at least N super-peer neighbors, making connections to new neighbors if existing neighbors leave the overlay. Similarly, the super-peer topology manager will accept connections from leaf-peers, possibly enforcing some upper limit on the number of connected leaf-peers. By separating the peer logic into routing and topology components, we can easily mix and match different routing and topology algorithms in different overlays. These reusable components makes it easier to extend ODIN-S to support different overlays.

Peer logics in ODIN-S also provide some key functionality available in other overlay toolkits [23,30]. For example, peer logics can set and respond to timers, and pass events to and from the application (such as a GUI or other application logic.)

3.2   Communication Manager

The communication manager handles the setting up/tearing down of connections, and the sending/receiving of messages, for all peer logics residing at a peer. The communication manager API allows peer logics to create connections to other peers and send messages, abstracting away the details of the underlying transport layer. Thus, the same unmodified peer logic could be used over a variety of underlying transports, including raw TCP sockets, SOAP calls, JXTA connections, and so on. Our system currently uses TCP sockets.

The communication layer also provides multiplexing and demultiplexing of messages from different peer logics over the same underlying transport. Each overlay is identified by an integer *overlay ID* that is a constant value across the entire overlay. This overlay ID is included in the header of each message sent, so that the receiving communication manager can dispatch it to the appropriate peer logic.

In this way, the overlay ID "names" the overlay. For example, we could have different but overlapping super-peer networks if each super-peer network was identified by a different overlay ID. Creating a new overlay involves choosing a new overlay ID, starting a peer logic for that overlay ID at some peer, and publicizing the overlay ID so that other peers can join (for example, by advertising it on a registry). The only requirement is that logically different overlays have different IDs (no *overlay ID collisions*). If the overlays exists within a single organization, the organization's IT department can hand out overlay IDs. On the Internet, the problem of avoiding ID collisions is somewhat more complex. There might be an ICANN-style service for handing out overlay IDs, or IDs may be cryptographic hashes of some meaningful description string. If we choose a large enough ID space (e.g., 256 bits), then we can even choose overlay IDs randomly and have minimal chance of collisions.

3.3   Runtime

The runtime provides the base functionality for each peer. The runtime creates and destroys peer logics, schedules timers, dispatches events between the application layer and the peer logics, provides a logging facility, and provides other services. Creating a peer means starting the runtime. The runtime will then construct a communication manager. The runtime will also accept "create peer logic" events, and create the appropriate peer logic according to a set of properties embedded in the event. The runtime is thus like a simplified application server that creates and destroys individual components as needed.

3.4   Filters

The resource mediation capability in ODIN-S is provided by *filters*. In particular, filters manage messages according to resource quotas and policies. Filters provide:

- *Throttling* of message rates to enforce quotas,
- *Ordering* of message sending and delivery to enforce priorities, and
- *Dropping* of messages to shed load when necessary.

For example, a filter might enqueue (and hence delay) messages to perform throttling, prioritize the queue to reorder messages, and drop new messages if the queue of existing messages reaches a pre-defined limit.

Two types of filters can be created. An *ingress filter* filters incoming messages before they are delivered to the appropriate peer logic. An *egress filter* filters outgoing messages that are generated by a peer logic, before they are actually handed over to the transport layer for sending. Both ingress and egress filters are installed in the communication manager and shared across peer logics, so that one filter can manage resources shared across overlays. For example, an ingress filter can enforce a quota per minute on the overall number of messages processed by the peer for any overlay; any incoming messages over the quota in a given minute would be enqueued, regardless of which peer logic they were destined for. At the same time, filters can be used to enforce policies for a particular overlay, passing through (without filtering) any message on other overlays.

Filters are pluggable components, so that multiple ingress and egress filters can be installed at a peer. For example, one egress filter might enforce an overall quota on the upload bandwidth used, while another egress filter might be used to throttle the message rate of a particular overlay. Filters process messages in the order they were installed, and only if all filters approve a message will the message be delivered/sent (respectively, for ingress/egress filters). If a filter delays a message, when it is eventually approved by that filter it will be passed to the next filter in the list before delivery/sending. Filters can also be created dynamically, as needed. For example, when a peer in one overlay joins a second overlay, it might dynamically create a filter to manage the two overlays.

Filters do not have to be passive components, responding only to incoming or outgoing messages. Filters can also set timers, and be notified when the timer expires. In addition, filters send messages to communicate with filters on other peers. In this case, the filter receiving the message should install itself as an ingress filter so it can receive the message and avoid its dispatch to any peer logic. (Because the same filter object instance can be installed as an ingress and egress filter, this mechanism allows even egress filters to communicate with each other.)

The generality of our filtering architecture means that filters can also be used to perform other functionality for overlays, such as gathering statistics about traffic, filtering out ill-formatted messages, or logging messages for recovery purposes. Such functionality is outside of the scope of this paper, and we focus on using filters for resource mediation here. We examine specific examples of using filters to mediate resources among overlapping overlays in the next section.

4   Mediating Resources Using Filters

We now illustrate how filters in ODIN-S can be used to mediate different types of resources shared among overlays. We focus on techniques for mediating *processing load*, *upload bandwidth* and *download bandwidth*. A typical peer will want to manage its overall load, and thus will likely install filters simultaneously for all three goals. The techniques presented here are representative examples; filters are a general architectural feature that can be used to implement a wide range of load and resource management techniques. Experiments in Section 5 demonstrate that the filters described here are effective at trading off resources between overlapping overlays.

4.1   Processing Load – Priority-Based Ingress Filter

A machine hosting multiple overlays can experience CPU overload as it processes all of the messages arriving on all of the overlays. Therefore, it is important to be able to limit the amount of CPU used by the ODIN-S middleware. This limit can be enforced by operating system mechanisms, such as UNIX "nice." Another approach is to create an ingress filter that enforces a limit on the messages processed per unit time. One advantage of the ingress filter-based approach is that the limit can be expressed in high-level terms (e.g., "process no more than 10 search messages per second"). A disadvantage of enforcing an absolute quota using a filter is that if the machine is otherwise idle, the spare CPU cycles will not be used by ODIN-S. Most likely, combining OS priority and filter-based quotas will be useful.

In either case, ODIN-S will be given a limited amount of processing capacity in which to handle messages. This capacity must be allocated to different peer logics in accordance with the priority of their overlay. For example, if a machine is participating in a high priority super-peer overlay and a low priority unstructured overlay, then proportionally more processing capacity should be given to the messages from the super-peer overlay (without starving the unstructured overlay.) We assume that each overlay is assigned a global priority, for example by the enterprise using the overlays. If different peers have different notions of priority for different overlays, then they can use ODIN-S filters to enforce those priorities locally. However, in this case, there will be no global enforcement of priority, which is appropriate given that there is no global agreement on overlay priority.

A filter that implements queuing can enforce both an absolute quota on messages processed (e.g., throttling) as well as enforcing priority (e.g., message ordering.) Arriving messages are automatically enqueued. Messages are dequeued and delivered to the appropriate peer logic in an order determined by priority. If the filter is enforcing a quota, then messages are only delivered periodically. For example, if the quota is 10 messages per second, then a new message will be taken off the queue and delivered every 100 milliseconds. If the filter is only enforcing priority (and not a quota), then a new message is taken off the queue as soon as the previous message has been processed. The filter can also enforce a maximum queue size, and drop messages according to some drop policy when the queue is full.

Priority-Based Ordering of Messages. An important consideration is the order in which we dequeue messages. A simple approach is to always dequeue the message from the highest priority overlay. However, as is well known from experience with network routing and operating systems scheduling, such an approach can lead to starvation for lower priority processes. Another possible approach is to divide the quota among overlays according to priority, for example giving 1/3 to the low priority overlay and 2/3 to the high priority overlay. However, this approach is not *work-conserving*: when the super-peer network is not using all of its quota, the unused portion is wasted, when it should be given the unstructured overlay. Instead, we need a fair and work-conserving algorithm for dequeuing messages.

These properties are provided by a class of *weighted fair queuing* (WFQ) algorithms, traditionally used to schedule packets in network routing. WFQ allocates an overloaded network channel to a flow in proportion to the flow's relative priority. Thus, if the sum of flow priorities is P, and a particular flow has priority p_i, that flow should receive p_i/P of the channel bandwidth. WFQ is work conserving because it schedules packets eagerly: if there are no queued packets for some other flow j, then WFQ schedules more of flow i's packets, beyond i's guaranteed bandwidth proportion of p_i/P. We adapt the WFQ approach to CPU scheduling in ODIN-S: if an overlay i has priority p_i, and the sum of priorities over all the overlays the peer participates in is P, then the overlay i should receive p_i/P of the CPU (or of the CPU quota, if one is enforced.) Practically, this means that if we dequeue P total messages in a time period, p_i of those should be from overlay i. If some overlay is not using its full allocation, the unused portion is fairly divided among the remaining overlays, again respecting priority.

WFQ was proposed originally in [16]. We actually use a follow-on proposal called *start-time fair queuing* (SFQ) [17] in ODIN-S. SFQ has two key advantages over the original WFQ algorithm: 1. SFQ has less computational complexity than WFQ, and 2. SFQ is more fair when the sender's rate is not constant. SFQ also has advantages over other queuing disciplines; these advantages are outlined by Goyal, Vin and Cheng [17]. Other queuing disciplines can be enforced by implementing an appropriate filter.

Briefly, SFQ operates as follows. (For more details, see [17]). Each message m that is enqueued is given a start tag S_m and a finish tag F_m, and messages are dequeued and serviced in order of increasing S_m (with ties broken randomly). The start tag S_m is set equal to either the start tag of the message that was being sent when m arrived, or the finish tag of the previous message enqueued for m's overlay, whichever is greater. The finish tag F_m is set equal to $S_m + c_m/p_m$, where c_m is the cost of sending the message, and p_m is the priority of m's overlay. The c_m value can be the length of the message in bytes, the estimated processing time, or some constant (if all messages are roughly equally expensive to process.) In this way, successive messages on the same overlay are given progressively higher finish (and hence start) tags, while messages on different overlays are given finish (and hence start) tags that are interleaved proportionally to their c_m/p_m ratio, resulting in proportionally more service for higher priority messages.

4.2   Upload Bandwidth – Priority-Based Egress Filter

Another resource used by the peer is upload bandwidth (link capacity used for sending messages). With asymmetric connections (such as residential DSL), the upload

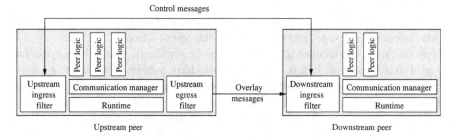

Fig. 3. Upstream/downstream filter set

bandwidth may be different than the download bandwidth. Thus, we often have to manage the upload bandwidth separately from download bandwidth. Even with symmetric connections (e.g. a machine connected to a LAN via Ethernet), it is important to manage the number of messages sent in order to mediate the usage of the link bandwidth.

Upload bandwidth is managed by an egress filter. When any peer logic attempts to send a message, the message is automatically enqueued. The filter takes messages off the queue for actual sending according to the overlay priority. The filter can also enforce a quota on the upload bandwidth used by sending (dequeuing) no more than N bytes in any time unit. In fact, the same priority based filter described in Section 4.1 can be used, except that the filter is installed as an egress filter instead of an ingress filter. Therefore, we can use SFQ (or any desired queuing discipline) here as well.

4.3 Download Bandwidth – Upstream/Downstream Filter Set

Download bandwidth is more difficult to manage than upload bandwidth, which can be managed by installing a single egress filter. In contrast, a peer cannot manage its download bandwidth by installing a single ingress filter; by the time the ingress filter touches the arriving message, the download bandwidth has already been used. Instead, a peer needs to cooperate with its neighbors in order to manage its download bandwidth. Consider a peer i that wishes to cap the amount of download bandwidth used for overlay messages. Peer i can contact each of its neighbors, regardless of which overlays they participate in, and ask them to throttle their message sending rate so that the total bandwidth used is no more than the cap.

Figure 3 shows an *upstream/downstream filter set* that implements the cooperative management of download bandwidth. The upstream filter is installed at each of peer i's neighbors, while the downstream filter is installed at peer i itself. The downstream filter determines how much bandwidth can be used by each upstream neighbor, and sends control messages to the upstream filters to ask them not to use more bandwidth. Both the upstream and downstream filters are ingress filters so that they can receive control messages. However, the upstream ingress filter creates egress filters on the upstream peer to enforce the downstream peer's bandwidth limitation requests. For example, if peer i asks peer j to send no more than 10 Kbps, then peer j will install an egress filter with a quota of 10 Kbps. This egress filter will apply only to peer i, so messages sent by peer j to peers other than i will be passed through the filter without delay. In fact, peer j may create multiple egress filters, one per downstream neighbor that requests a cap. However, peer j would only have a single instance of an upstream ingress filter to respond to control messages and manage all of the egress filters.

Note that since connections in an overlay can be symmetric, j may be downstream of i as well as upstream. In this case, j will also have a downstream filter and i will have an upstream filter, and i will install egress filters at j's request (just as j installs them at i's request.) Then, the total complement of filters at both i and j would include: a upstream ingress filter, a downstream ingress filter, and quota-enforcing egress filters.

If two peers are neighbors in multiple overlays, then the upstream egress filter must enforce overlay priority as well as a download quota when determining which messages to send to the downstream peer. To do this, the egress filter created by the upstream filter can be the same filter as described in Section 4.2: the priority-based egress filter, perhaps based on SFQ.

Allocating Bandwidth Quotas to Upstream Neighbors. Consider a peer i that wants to enforce a total quota of D bytes per second on its download bandwidth. Peer i must ask its upstream peers to throttle their message sending so that the total bandwidth is no more than D for all messages sent by i's neighbors. The simplest way to do this is for i to divide the quota equally among all of its neighbors: if i has n neighbors, then each neighbor is given a quota of D/n. However, this simple approach may waste quota, since the same quota is given to each neighbor regardless of the number of overlays the neighbor wants to send traffic on. Neighbors that want to send traffic on one or only a few overlays will have a larger quota than is necessary. Similarly, it makes no allowance for the fact that some neighbors may only be members of low priority overlays, and thus should not get an equal allocation of the quota as neighbors who are members of higher priority overlays.

We now describe how to allocate the quota D to upstream neighbors according to the priority of overlays those neighbors are participating in. Our algorithm divides the total quota proportionally based on the priority of overlays, and then further divides these fractional quotas evenly among the neighbors that wish to send traffic on a particular overlay. The algorithm operates as follows. Peer y tracks which upstream neighbors want to send traffic on each overlay, either by tracking received messages or by having upstream peers send control messages listing the overlays on which they want to send messages. Periodically, peer y adjusts the quota assigned to each upstream neighbor as follows. First, it divides the total quota into per-overlay fractional quotas, proportional to the relative priority of each overlay: each overlay i is given quota $d_i = D \times \frac{p_i}{P}$. These fractional quotas are then evenly divided among the neighbors that wish to send traffic: if there are c_i neighbors sending traffic on overlay i, each neighbor receives a slice of the fractional quota equal to $\frac{D}{c_i} \times \frac{p_i}{P}$. The total quota given to an upstream peer is the sum of the slices for that peer. That is, define $t_{i,j}$ as 1 if neighbor x_j wants to send traffic on overlay i, and 0 otherwise, and m as the number of overlays. The quota assigned to an upstream neighbor x_j is $\sum_{i=1}^{m} t_{i,j} \times \frac{D}{c_i} \times \frac{p_i}{P}$. Each upstream neighbor manages its quota using an egress (SFQ) filter.

As an example, consider a peer Y, with a download quota of 9 messages/second, and its three upstream neighbors A, B and C. A and B both want to send traffic on overlay 1. C wants to send traffic on both overlay 1 and overlay 2. Assume that overlay 2 has twice the priority of overlay 1. Then, the total quota on messages delivered to Y from any peer should be divided into one-third for overlay 1 and two-thirds for overlay 2. The quota for overlay 1 (3 messages/second) will be divided evenly among A, B and C (each receiving 1 message/second). The entire quota for overlay 2 (6 messages/second) will be given to C. The total quota given to C will be 7 messages/second.

It is also possible to extend this algorithm to give more quota to upstream neighbors that wish to send more traffic on a given overlay. Then, instead of dividing the fractional quotas into equally sized slices, we would divide the fractional quota based on the observed traffic rate from each neighbor. However, experiments in Section 5 demonstrate that in practice, this approach does not work as well as the equal division in the algorithm detailed above.

5   Experimental Results

We have conducted experiments to determine how effective the ODIN-S architecture is at fairly managing resources between overlapping overlays. Our experiments utilize ODIN-S components both in a discrete event simulation, and as actual peers. Our simulator allowed us to quickly examine many overlay combinations and parameter settings, while the prototype allowed us to examine the real system in action. It is important to note that the peer logic and filter implementations were the same in the simulator and prototype; in other words, in the simulations each peer was processing and sending actual messages. This philosophy of simultaneously implementing a simulator and peer client software using the same components was proposed in [30,20]. For the experiments in this paper, we used the peer implementation to calibrate and validate our simulations. Here, we report simulation results.

The primary metric we have considered is *throughput*, measured in terms of messages processed by the overlay per second. Although we are examining different overlays providing different functionality, this throughput metric allows us to examine a common performance measure across all overlays.

5.1   Experimental Setup

We experimented with three types of overlays: an *unstructured peer-to-peer overlay*, with searches routed via optimized random walks [1,24], a *super-peer overlay*, with searches flooded between super-peers [36], and a *multicast tree overlay*, with a single source multicasting updates to multiple clients. The multicast overlay is modeled on the end-system multicast trees provided by the Narada system [14], although we have only implemented the multicast tree construction and not yet the topology-aware optimizations that Narada provides.

In most of our experiments, there were 1,000 total peers participating in multiple overlays. Each peer remained alive during the entire experiment. This scale and lack of peer "churn" represents enterprise-scale overlays. A typical Internet peer-to-peer overlay would likely have more peers and more churn. Given the priority-based nature of our techniques, and the need to use a common runtime, we expect enterprises or other similar organizations to be the most immediate target of our techniques. However, we also examined the scalability of our techniques to larger networks: due to space restrictions, we do not report the results, which were consistent with the results for 1,000 peers. We also examine the effectiveness of our techniques in the presence of peer churn (in Section 5.5).

For the unstructured and super-peer overlays, we downloaded HTML data from real web sites, and each peer provided full-text keyword search over the data from one website (using standard IR techniques: scored using a normalized cosine distance of TF/IDF weighted queries and documents, and a document match had score > 0.1). If a peer participated in multiple overlays, each peer logic searched documents from a different site. We used real keyword searches from the search.com search engine. In the super-peer network, only high capacity peers (capacity greater than the average) chose to become super-peers, with a probability 0.1. In the multicast overlay, a single source generated small (< 100 bytes) updates, and propagated the updates along the multicast tree. Each multicast peer had up to five children in the tree.

Each peer was given a quota, measured in messages/second, that it could receive, process, and transmit. Alternatively, the quota could have been measured in message size, time to process, etc. We chose number of messages both because it generalizes across bandwidth and CPU time (which would otherwise be measured in different units), and different types of overlays (which would have different processing costs, message sizes, and so on). To determine appropriate quotas for peers, we measured the maximum throughput achievable with our current prototype. We started an unstructured overlay using real ODIN-S peers, each on separate, otherwise unloaded machines connected by gigabit Ethernet. Each machine had dual 3.0 GHz Pentium4 Xeon CPUs and 4 GB RAM. The maximum throughput measured was 135.5 messages per second. We expect this type of machine to be in the mid to high range for overlay peers; some machines (e.g. servers) will be more powerful while many will be less powerful (both in terms of CPU and bandwidth.) Therefore, in our experiments, our simulation models machines as having capacity randomly chosen in the range 20-200 messages per second. Of course, machines that are conducting other work besides hosting an overlay node may decide to set a quota less than their maximum capacity. In such a situation, the absolute values of the quotas would be less but the range (e.g., an order of magnitude) would likely be similar.

5.2 Overlapping Unstructured Overlays

Our first set of experiments measured the throughput provided by ODIN-S for overlapping unstructured overlays. We started with unstructured overlays because they are the most traffic-intensive of the three overlay types we implemented, and thus they give a sense of how the system performs under heavy load. Other overlay types are considered in the next section. The experiments here examine two overlapping overlays; in other results (not shown here) we have increased the number of overlapping unstructured overlays and observed similar results.

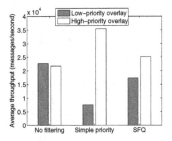

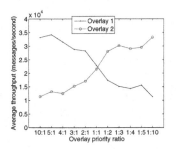

Fig. 4. Throughput without filtering, with simple priority filtering, and with SFQ filters

Fig. 5. Throughput with varying priority ratio

Ingress Filters for Managing Processing Load. We created two overlapping unstructured overlays: a *low priority* overlay, and a *high priority* overlay, with priority equal to twice that of the low priority overlay. Each peer participated in both overlays. We ran the system for 100 simulated seconds, generating a total of 25,000 search requests per overlay during this time. In simulations of peers with unlimited capacity, this setup results in an average of 99,000 messages per overlay per second (across the whole overlay). However, the limited capacity of peers sharply reduces the actual throughput.

Figure 4 shows the average throughput for no ingress filtering, ingress filtering using a simple priority scheme (always prefer higher priority messages), and ingress filtering using SFQ. As the figure shows, in each case the total throughput over both overlays is about 44,000 messages per second. However, without filters, that throughput is allocated unfairly: the low and high priority overlays receive the same service. The throughput is also unfairly balanced with simple priority filters, as the low priority overlay is starved (7,500 messages/second) compared to the high priority overlay (35,000 messages/second). In contrast, the SFQ ingress filters result in service that more properly reflects the overlay priorities: the high priority overlay receives 60 percent of the total throughput. This result is not exactly the 2:1 ratio of high/low priority, and reflects overlay-wide queuing effects that disproportionately affect the high priority overlay. In particular, since more high priority messages are approved by filters at some nodes, there are disproportionately long queues of high priority messages at other nodes, and these queuing delays reduce throughput of the high priority overlay somewhat. Despite this issue, the ingress filter using SFQ queuing most effectively preserves the overlay priority. We also ran experiments with larger and smaller rates of search requests, and observed similar effects.

Varying Priorities. In the next experiment, we used the same overlays and traffic as in the previous experiments, but varied the priority ratio between the two overlays from 1:10 to 10:1 (each different ratio represents a different experimental run). As Figure 5 shows, the changing relative priority results in changing relative throughput. In the middle of the figure (for ratios near 1:1), the ratio of throughput nearly exactly reflects the ratio of priorities. For larger ratios (on the left and right of the figure), the throughput of the high priority overlay flattens, while the lower priority overlay receives less through-

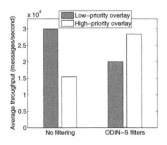

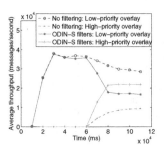

Fig. 6. Throughput when the low priority overlay has double the traffic of the high priority overlay

Fig. 7. Throughput when the high priority overlay starts 50 seconds after the low priority overlay

put. In all cases, the high priority overlay properly receives more service. The flattening results from an increasing number of "bottleneck" peers as more high priority messages are sent. Bottleneck peers are low capacity peers that have long queues and effectively throttle the throughput of the entire overlay. Thus, even as more priority is allocated to the overlay, the network simply cannot provide it more service. (This effect is the reason the SFQ filter provides only a 60/40 throughput allocation in the previous section.)

Varying Traffic Rates. So far, both the high and low priority overlays have had the same, constant rate of traffic to send. We also experimented with cases where the traffic rates varied between overlays and over time.

First, we ran an experiment where the low priority overlay had twice the query rate of the high priority overlay. Figure 6 shows the results. Without filtering, the low priority overlay receives significantly more service than the high priority overlay. ODIN-S filters properly preserve priority; even though the low priority overlay has more traffic to send, it still receives less service than the high priority overlay.

Next, we ran an experiment where both overlays had the same query rate, except that the low priority overlay experienced a load spike, doubling its traffic for 20 seconds (starting at 50 seconds.) The results (not shown) indicate that the high priority overlay is not affected, and continues to receive higher service than the low priority overlay.

Third, we ran an experiment where both overlays had the same query rate, but the high priority overlay was created halfway through the simulation. This models a scenario where an overlay exists, and then another overlay is started using the same machines. As Figure 7 shows, initially the low priority overlay is receiving high service, because it is the only overlay. In the no-filtering case, the low priority overlay continues to receive the most throughput even after the high priority overlay begins to transmit traffic. In contrast, with ODIN-S filters, when the high priority overlay starts, it quickly achieves higher throughput than the low priority overlay.

These results all show that ODIN-S filters can effectively trade off resources between overlays, even when the traffic rates change.

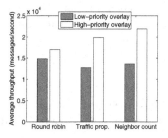

Fig. 8. Approaches to allocating quota to upstream peers

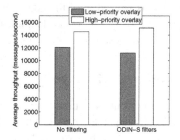

Fig. 9. Two overlapping multicast overlays

5.3   Upstream/Downstream Filter Sets for Managing Link Bandwidth

Next, we examined the effect of our adaptive algorithm for allocating quota to upstream egress filters. We used the same overlapping unstructured overlays and message load as in the previous section. We compared three methods of allocating upstream quota:

- *simple round-robin*: the quota was divided evenly among upstream neighbors.
- *adaptive, neighbor count*: our algorithm from Section 4.3 was used to adjust upstream quota based on which overlays at neighbors participate in.
- *adaptive, traffic-proportional*: we extended our adaptive algorithm to adjust upstream quota based on the traffic rates at upstream neighbors.

The traffic-proportional algorithm gives more quota to neighbors that wish to send more traffic. In this case, the upstream neighbor measures its traffic rate and sends updates to the downstream neighbor. The total quota is divided proportionally based on overlay priority into fractional quotas, and then further divided proportionally to the amount of traffic that the upstream neighbors of each overlay want to send. In all cases, the dynamically created upstream egress filters were SFQ filters.

Figure 8 shows the results. As the figure shows, in the simple round-robin method, the throughput experienced by both overlays is roughly equal. In contrast, both adaptive algorithms allocate total throughput according to priority, such that the high priority overlay receives more throughput than the low priority overlay (again, split 60/40). Another key difference between the three techniques is that the adaptive algorithms provide greater total bandwidth over both overlays than the simple round robin. In fact, the adaptive, neighbor count algorithm results in the highest total throughput, with 9 percent more total throughput than the traffic-proportional algorithm, and 11 percent more total throughput than the round-robin approach. Round-robin wastes quota by allocating the same amount to neighbors that host only one overlay as to those that host multiple overlays. The traffic-proportional approach would seem to effectively allocate quota based on traffic rates (and in fact was our first approach.) However, our experiments show that this approach also wastes quota when traffic is bursty. A burst causes a large quota window to open on one neighbor, consequently reducing the quota on other neighbors. When the burst is over, another burst typically arrives at another neighbor, who now has a small quota. The result is that the large quota on the formerly bursty neighbor is wasted until the adaptive algorithm reallocates quota. The neighbor count approach provides more stable quotas, but does so in recognition of the actual overlays of neighbors, resulting in both fairness and larger total throughput.

5.4   Other Overlay Types

In addition to unstructured overlays, we also examined super-peer and multicast overlays. First, we present results where the overlapping overlays are of the same type, and then we present results where the overlays are different.

Overlapping Overlays of the Same Type. We examined a network with two overlapping super-peer overlays. In this case, super-peers handle almost all of the overlay messages, since search messages are never sent to leaf peers. Therefore, there is only contention for resources when the same peer hosts super-peers for both overlays. We again generated 25,000 searches per overlay. The results (not shown) demonstrate that at the nodes where there is resource contention, the higher priority overlay receives higher throughput, consistent with the relative priorities between the two overlays.

Next, we ran an experiment with two overlapping multicast trees. Each multicast source generated 25,000 events. The high priority tree had twice the priority of the low priority tree. Figure 9 shows the resulting throughput. As the figure shows, the effect of filtering is less prominent. Although filtering results in the high priority overlay receiving more throughput, the allocation is not as fair: the high priority overlay only receives 57 percent of the throughput. In an application-level multicast tree, the total throughput is heavily dependent on the capacity of the root peer and peers near the root, since they are the bottlenecks for dissemination to the rest of the tree. If a peer is a bottleneck node in both multicast overlays, then ODIN-S filters can mediate the resources at the bottleneck; otherwise, the filters have only a minor effect. The result is that ODIN-S filters allocates total throughput more effectively than in the no filtering case, but not as well as for other types of overlays.

Because performance of the multicast overlay depends so heavily on the topology and nature of the bottleneck nodes, to ensure an apples-to-apples comparison we had to hardwire our system to construct the same overlay topology in both the filtering and no filtering scenario. We do the same for multicast tree experiments in the next section.

Overlapping Overlays of Different Types. We examined four combinations of heterogeneous overlapping overlays: (1) unstructured + super-peer, (2) flooding-based unstructured + random-walk based unstructured, (3) super-peer + multicast, and (4) unstructured + multicast. These experiments are just a subset of all of the possible combinations of overlays. However, they allow us to examine how well ODIN-S trades off resources between overlapping overlays of different types.

First, we ran an experiment where an unstructured overlay overlapped with a super-peer overlay. We assigned the super-peer overlay twice the priority of the unstructured overlay. In this case, the super-peer overlay's resource requirements are concentrated at super-peers (approximately 5 percent of the total nodes), which have high traffic volumes. As shown in Figure 10, without priority filtering, the super-peers become a bottleneck for both overlays, effectively starving the unstructured overlay. In contrast,

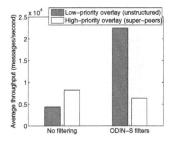
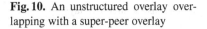

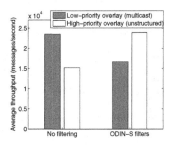

Fig. 10. An unstructured overlay over-lapping with a super-peer overlay

Fig. 11. An unstructured overlay over-lapping with a multicast overlay

with ODIN-S filtering, the unstructured overlay is given its fair share of priority at the super-peers, reducing the bottleneck effect and resulting in more than a factor of five increased throughput. This demonstrates how ODIN-S can prevent the topology features and hotspots of one overlay from impeding the throughput of the other overlay. Note that the super-peer overlay, which is high priority, sends relatively few messages, since it is more efficient than the unstructured overlay. However, at peers hosting a super-peer, the super-peer overlay is receiving twice the service of the unstructured overlay, without starving the unstructured overlay.

Next, we examined two different types of unstructured overlays: a flooding-based unstructured overlay (as in the original Gnutella) and a random-walk based overlay. Flooding, which is not scalable for Internet overlays, might be used in enterprise-scale overlays because it offers low result latency. For this reason, some domain-specific tools use a flooding-based overlay [2]. Our results (not shown) indicate that despite the difference in routing method, ODIN-S filters result in both overlays receiving throughput in proportion to their priority. Without filtering, both overlays receive approximately the same throughput, despite their priority difference.

We also examined a super-peer overlay overlapping with a multicast overlay. The results (not shown) are similar to the case of the two overlapping multicast trees (Section 5.4): filtering improves the fairness of the allocation of throughput, but the effect is not as dramatic as in the other overlay types. Again, the unique topology features of the multicast tree (bottleneck nodes are near the root) means that unless a bottleneck node and super-peer are hosted on the same peer, ODIN-S filters have limited effect.

Finally, we examined an unstructured high priority overlay overlapping with a low priority multicast tree. The results are shown in Figure 11. As the figure shows, ODIN-S has a large effect on the throughput, effectively allocating more throughput to the high priority overlay, while no filtering allows the low priority multicast tree to grab most of the service. In this case, the bottleneck nodes of the multicast tree are always overlapping with a traffic-bearing node in the unstructured network (since all peers in unstructured network forward traffic.) Then, ODIN-S can effectively allocate the throughput at the bottleneck nodes between the two overlays, resulting in an overall fair allocation of throughput.

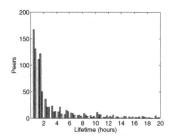

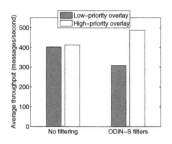

Fig. 12. Distribution of peer lifetimes in the dynamic scenario. 51 peers with lifetimes >20 hours are not shown. The maximum lifetime is 120 hours.

Fig. 13. High churn scenario: two overlapping unstructured overlays

5.5 Dynamic Scenario

We examined a scenario in which overlay peers joined and left frequently, as frequently occurs in many Internet peer-to-peer overlays. Although we primarily envision our system being used for more stable networks where priority can be effectively assigned to overlays (such as in enterprise networks), we wanted to see how a large amount of churn affected the throughput. We used a real trace of peer joins and leaves from the Overnet system [7], and extracted the first 1,000 peers from the trace (representing roughly the first 14 hours of the trace.) This trace is highly dynamic: the average peer is alive for only 5 hours, while the shortest lived peers are alive for 20 minutes. Figure 12 shows a histogram for the distribution of peer lifetimes. Each peer participated in two overlapping unstructured overlays. Since Internet peers are not usually dedicated but instead used for multiple tasks besides the overlay, peers allocated 10 percent of their capacity to the overlay; hence the capacity range was 2-20 messages/second.

Figure 13 shows the results. As the figure shows, even in the presence of high churn the system performs as before: without filtering, both overlays receive the same service, but with ODIN-S filters, the higher priority overlay receives an appropriately higher level of service.

5.6 Summary of Results

We can draw the following conclusions from our results:

– ODIN-S is effective at enforcing fair allocation of resources between overlapping overlays, respecting priority but avoiding starvation.
– Using the SFQ filter as an ingress filter is effective across different priority ratios, traffic patterns, and overlay types. It is least effective for overlapping multicast overlays, where the topology characteristics often outweigh what the filtering can achieve. Even in this case, however, filtering is more fair than no filtering.
– The adaptive, neighbor-count algorithm for allocating quota to an upstream neighbor is more fair, and results in better overall throughput, than a simple round robin scheme (allocate equal quota to all neighbors), or a scheme where quota is allocated proportionally to the traffic each neighbor wants to send.

- Heterogeneous overlapping overlays can have complex interactions as hotspots in one overlay impact the throughput of another. ODIN-S filters can effectively mitigate the impact one overlay has on another.
- Our architecture is effective both for overlays with little or no churn, as well as for overlays with a high amount of churn.

6   Conclusion

We have presented ODIN-S, a middleware system for trading off resources between overlapping overlays. Our architecture can be used to mediate the resource demands of different overlays deployed to provide different functionality on the same hardware. The system demonstrates how to integrate and extend techniques from multiple domains into a comprehensive middleware toolkit for deploying and managing multiple overlays. ODIN-S provides a common runtime that supports multiple peer logics, one per overlay. Our system also provides a flexible and extensible filtering mechanism. Filters can be used for a variety of tasks, and we focus on their use for allocating resources to different overlays based on priority. We describe ingress, egress and upstream/downstream filters to manage CPU usage, upload and download bandwidth (respectively). Experiments demonstrate the effectiveness of ODIN-S at enforcing fair, priority-based sharing of resources among overlapping overlays.

References

1. L. Adamic, R. Lukose, A. Puniyani, and B. Huberman. Search in power-law networks. *Phys. Rev. E*, 64:46135–46143, 2001.
2. D. Agarwal and K. Berket. Supporting dynamic ad hoc collaboration capabilities. In *Proc. Conf. for Computing in High-Energy and Nuclear Physics (CHEP)*, 2003.
3. D. Aksoy, M. F. Franklin, and S. B. Zdonik. Data staging for on-demand broadcast. In *Proc. Conference on Very Large Databases (VLDB)*, 2001.
4. H. Balakrishnan, S. Shenker, and M. Walfish. Peering peer-to-peer providers. In *Proc. Int'l Workshop on Peer-to-Peer Systems (IPTPS)*, 2005.
5. G. Banavar, T. Chandra, B. Mukherjee, J. Nagarajarao, R. E. Strom, and D. C. Sturman. An efficient multicast protocol for content-based publish-subscribe systems. In *Proc. IEEE International Conference on Distributed Computing Systems*, 1999.
6. Jon C.R. Bennett and Hui Zhang. Hierarchical packet fair queueing algorithms. In *Proc. SIGCOMM*, 1996.
7. R. Bhagwan, S. Savage, and G. Voelker. Understanding availability. In *Proc. of the 2nd Int'l Workshop on Peer to Peer Systems (IPTPS)*, 2003.
8. S. Blake, D. Black, M. Carlson, E. Davies, Z. Wang, and W. Weiss. Rfc 2475 - an architecture for differentiated services. http://www.ietf.org/rfc/rfc2475.txt, 1998.
9. William J. Bolosky, Robert P. Fitzgerald, and John R. Douceur. Distributed schedule management in the tiger video fileserver. In *Proc. SOSP*, 1997.
10. R. Braden, D. Clark, and S. Shenker. Rfc 1633 - integrated services in the internet architecture: an overview. http://www.ietf.org/rfc/rfc1633.txt, 1994.
11. A. Carzaniga and A. L. Wolf. Forwarding in a content-based network. In *Proc. SIGCOMM*, 2003.

12. Y. Chawathe, S. Ratnasamy, L. Breslau, N. Lanham, and S. Shenker. Making Gnutella-like P2P systems scalable. In *Proc. SIGCOMM*, 2003.
13. M. Cherniack, H. Balakrishnan, M. Balazinska, D. Carney, U. Cetintemel, Y. Xing, and S. Zdonik. Scalable distributed stream processing. In *Proc. of the First Biennial Conference on Innovative Data Systems Research (CIDR)*, 2003.
14. Y. Chu, S. G. Rao, and H. Zhang. A case for end system multicast. In *Proc. SIGMETRICS*, 2000.
15. A. Das, J. Gehrke, and M. Riedewald. Approximate join processing over data streams. In *Proc. SIGMOD*, 2003.
16. A. Demers, S. Keshav, and S. Shenker. Analysis and simulation of a fair queueing algorithm. In *Proc. SIGCOMM*, 1989.
17. P. Goyal, H. M. Vin, and H. Cheng. Start-time fair queuing: A scheduling algorithm for integrated services packet switching networks. In *Proc. SIGCOMM*, 1996.
18. P. Grace, G. Coulson, G. S. Blair, and B. Porter. Deep middleware for the divergent grid. In *Proc. Middleware*, 2005.
19. G. Iannaccone, M. May, and C. Diot. Aggregate traffic performance with active queue management and drop from tail. *Computer Communication Review*, 31(3):4–13, 2001.
20. M. B. Jones and J. Dunagan. Engineering realities of building a working peer-to-peer system. Microsoft Research Technical Report MSR-TR-2004-54, available at ftp://ftp.research.microsoft.com/pub/tr/TR-2004-54.pdf, 2004.
21. V. Kalogeraki, D. Gunopulos, and D. Zeinalipour-Yazti. A local search mechanism for peer-to-peer networks. In *Proc. CIKM*, 2002.
22. A. Keromytis, V. Misra, and D. Rubenstein. SOS: Secure overlay services. In *Proc. SIGCOMM*, Aug. 2002.
23. B. T. Loo, T. Condie, J. Hellerstein, P. Maniatis, T. Roscoe, and I. Stoica. Implementing declarative overlays. In *Proc. SOSP*, 2005.
24. Q. Lv, P. Cao, E. Cohen, K. Li, and S. Shenker. Search and replication in unstructured peer-to-peer networks. In *Proc. of ACM Int'l Conf. on Supercomputing (ICS'02)*, June 2002.
25. Q. Lv, S. Ratnasamy, and S. Shenker. Can heterogeneity make gnutella scalable? In *Proc. of the 1st Int'l Workshop on Peer to Peer Systems (IPTPS)*, March 2002.
26. C. Olston, B. T. Loo, and J. Widom. Adaptive precision setting for cached approximate values. In *Proc. SIGMOD*, 2001.
27. P. Pietzuch, J. Ledlie, J. Shneidman, M. Welsh, M. Seltzer, and M. Roussopoulos. Network-aware operator placement for stream-processing systems. In *Proc. Int'l Conf. on Data Engineering (ICDE)*, 2006.
28. S. Ratnasamy, P. Francis, M. Handley, R. Karp, and S. Shenker. A scalable content-addressable network. In *Proc. SIGCOMM*, Aug. 2001.
29. P. Reynolds and A. Vahdat. Efficient peer-to-peer keyword searching. In *Proc. ACM/IFIP/USENIX International Middleware Conference*, 2003.
30. A. Rodriguez, C. Killian, S. Bhat, D. Kostic, and A. Vahdat. MACEDON: Methodology for automatically creating, evaluating, and designing overlay networks. In *Proc. NSDI*, 2004.
31. A. Rowstron and P. Druschel. Pastry: Scalable, decentralized object location and routing for large-scale peer-to-peer systems. In *Proc. Middleware*, 2001.
32. U. Srivastava, K. Munagala, and J. Widom. Operator placement for in-network stream query processing. In *Proc. ACM Symp. on Principles of Database Systems (PODS)*, 2005.
33. I. Stoica, R. Morris, D. Karger, M. F. Kaashoek, and H. Balakrishnan. Chord: A scalable peer-to-peer lookup service for internet applications. In *Proc. SIGCOMM*, Aug. 2001.
34. I. Stoica, S. Shenker, and H. Zhang. Core-stateless fair queueing: A scalable architecture to approximate fair bandwidth allocations in high speed networks. In *Proc. SIGCOMM*, 1998.
35. B. Yang and H. Garcia-Molina. Efficient search in peer-to-peer networks. In *ICDCS*, 2002.
36. B. Yang and H. Garcia-Molina. Designing a super-peer network. In *Proc. ICDE*, 2003.

Efficient Probabilistic Subsumption Checking for Content-Based Publish/Subscribe Systems

Aris M. Ouksel[1,*], Oana Jurca[2], Ivana Podnar[2], and Karl Aberer[2,**]

[1] The University of Illinois at Chicago
Depts. Of Information and Decision Sciences and Computer Science
`aris@uic.edu`
[2] School of Computer and Communication Sciences
Ecole Polytechnique Fédérale de Lausanne (EPFL)
CH-1015 Lausanne, Switzerland
{`oana.jurca, ivana.podnar, karl.aberer`}`@epfl.ch`

Abstract. Efficient subsumption checking, deciding whether a subscription or publication is covered by a set of previously defined subscriptions, is of paramount importance for publish/subscribe systems. It provides the core system functionality—matching of publications to subscriber needs expressed as subscriptions—and additionally, reduces the overall system load and generated traffic since the covered subscriptions are not propagated in distributed environments. As the subsumption problem was shown previously to be co-NP complete and existing solutions typically apply pairwise comparisons to detect the subsumption relationship, we propose a 'Monte Carlo type' probabilistic algorithm for the general subsumption problem. It determines whether a publication/subscription is covered by a disjunction of subscriptions in $O(k\,m\,d)$, where k is the number of subscriptions, m is the number of distinct attributes in subscriptions, and d is the number of tests performed to answer a subsumption question. The probability of error is problem-specific and typically very small, and sets an upper bound on d. Our experimental results show significant gains in term of subscription set reduction which has favorable impact on the overall system performance as it reduces the total computational costs and networking traffic. Furthermore, the expected theoretical bounds underestimate algorithm performance because it performs much better in practice due to introduced optimizations, and is adequate for fast forwarding of subscriptions in case of high subscription rate.

1 Introduction

Content-based publish/subscribe systems are receiving growing interest with a large number of relevant applications such as stock tickers, RSS news feeds, network monitoring, traffic monitoring, and electronic commerce requiring selective information

---

* Research supported in part by the National Science Foundation grant IIS-0326284.
** Research supported in part by the National Competence Center in Research on Mobile Information and Communication Systems (NCCR-MICS), a center supported by the Swiss National Science Foundation under grant number 5005-67322 and carried out (partly) in the framework of the EPFL Center for Global Computing.

M. van Steen and M. Henning (Eds.): Middleware 2006, LNCS 4290, pp. 121–140, 2006.

dissemination. Traditional content-based publish/subscribe systems usually employ high-performance servers to handle high rates of publications and serve millions of subscribers in static environments. They have been optimized for fast matching of publications to subscriptions [1,2,3,4] and typically maintain a special subscription index that does not frequently change as the rate of subscription changes is negligible compared to the publication rate.

Distributed content-based publish/subscribe systems traditionally assume static environments and use a network of brokers to divide the publication and subscription load. Brokers implement routing protocols to provide a consistent service with the goal of reducing networking costs generated by publications and subscriptions [5,6]: Subscriptions are typically routed through the network toward publishers to enable filtering of publications close to their sources. Subscription traffic, on the other hand, is reduced by not propagating covered subscriptions, as they are redundant, or by subscription merging [7,8].

Although the importance of subscription set reduction for content-based publish/subscribe systems has been stressed, e.g. in [8], existing deterministic algorithms [9,6,7] focus either on efficient matching of publications to subscriptions only or rely on basic heuristics for subscription set reduction such as pairwise subscription comparison or subscription merging. In this paper we take a more fundamental approach to subscription set reduction for (distributed) content-based publish/subscribe systems. In particular we show that when using general subsumption checking, where the covering of subscriptions by multiple other subscriptions is exploited, important performance improvements can be achieved. However, efficient general subsumption checking is non-trivial. Publications and subscriptions are typically modeled as logical expressions–conjunctions of predicates–where each predicate defines a simple constraint on an attribute. Geometrically, subscriptions can be viewed as convex polyhedra. Therefore, the general subsumption checking problem corresponds to the problem of checking whether a disjunction of subscriptions covers a subscription/publication, which can geometrically be interpreted as checking whether a convex polyhedron is contained within a finite union of convex polyhedra. This problem was proven to be co-NP complete in [10].

Since the general subsumption problem is practically unfeasible, for solving it, we introduce a probabilistic 'Monte Carlo type' algorithm. This is the first probabilistic approach to test the subscription coverage by a union of subscriptions. The algorithm solves the subsumption problem in $O(k \cdot m \cdot d)$, where k is the number of subscriptions, m is the number of distinct attributes in subscriptions and d is the number of tests performed to answer the subscription coverage question. The value of parameter d is dependent on an acceptable predefined probability of error which is problem specific and can be computed in polynomial time a-priori. Using this algorithm a subscription set can be efficiently reduced to a minimized subscription set matching the same set of publications. Experiments show that in practice our algorithmic approach performs much better than the theoretical bound $O(k \cdot m \cdot d)$. The same algorithm can also be used to efficiently match publications from imprecise data sources, by representing publications also as convex polyhedra, as it is advocated in recent publish/subscribe models with approximate matching [11].

The importance of subscription set reduction is highly significant in distributed content-based publish/subscribe system for the following reasons:

- The publish/subscribe systems architecture is increasingly used in environments with highly variable subscriptions, such as MANETs and sensor networks, where the assumption of both network [12] and subscription stability no longer holds. The rate of subscription changes may drastically increase as a consequence of both changing interests and context changes, and also may substantially exceed the publication rate if rare events are monitored; therefore, novel indexing techniques have been investigated that trade-off precision to performance [13], however they do not solve the essential problem of subscription set reduction.
- As publish/subscribe systems mainly target usage scenarios where a subscription space is moderately populated and subscriptions typically overlap due to similar but not equal interest, there is a higher probability of a subscription being covered by a set of subscriptions rather than a single one. Covered subscriptions are redundant. Therefore, they are not propagated further which reduces the total number of subscriptions in the system saving memory and reducing traffic. This in turn reduces computational costs for matching publications to subscriptions and new subscriptions to existing subscriptions as the set of subscriptions is reduced.
- As publish/subscribe systems are growing in scale to very large networks of brokers, the benefit of any reduction in the number of subscriptions forwarded locally by a broker, is amplified exponentially in the network diameter while broadcasting subscriptions in the broker network. Thus even modest local reductions lead to substantial global reductions in network traffic during subscription propagation.

Due to the probabilistic nature of the algorithm a concern about lost publications (false negatives) may be raised. However, many recent applications are tolerant to lost publications, because e.g. the data sources are already unreliable themselves, as in sensor networks. Furthermore, the error probability can be controlled and adapted to application needs, trading off computational cost for precision. Therefore, we expect that for a wide range of important applications the probabilistic nature of the approach is fully acceptable.

To summarize, the algorithm has the potential to significantly decrease costs in terms of computation, memory, and bandwidth consumption in content-based and distributed publish/subscribe systems by fully exploiting the potential subscription set reduction and achieving computational efficiency through a probabilistic approach. In our experimental evaluations we verify both the performance gain with respect to subscription set reduction by comparing to the standard technique of pairwise reduction and the performance characteristics of the algorithm as compared to the pessimistic theoretical bounds.

The remainder of the paper is structured in the following way. We review the basic principles of content-based publish/subscribe communication model in Section 2. To motivate the presentation, Section 3 sketches a usage scenario and formally defines the subsumption problem. Section 4 presents our novel probabilistic algorithm with specific optimizations, and we investigate it's properties in a distributed setting in Section 5. Section 6 presents an evaluation of the algorithm using extensive experimentation, and in Section 7 we compare it to the related work in the field. We complete the paper with our conclusions in Section 8.

2   Distributed Publish/Subscribe Communication

The publish/subscribe interaction model enables asynchronous communication between information *publishers* and *subscribers*. Subscribers express interest in receiving publications that comply to specific criteria by defining *subscriptions* that change the set of active subscriptions maintained by the publish/subscribe system. When a publisher defines a new *publication*, it is compared against all active subscriptions, and the system notifies subscribers with a matching subscription about the published content. Thus, the publish/subscribe service performs content filtering and enables push-style group communication, where group members are determined dynamically per each publication.

In a distributed system a set of publishers $P_i, 1 \leq i \leq n$ and a set of subscribers $S_j, 1 \leq j \leq m$ interact over a set of nodes, *brokers*, $B_k, 1 \leq k \leq N$. Brokers are responsible for matching publications to subscriptions and for disseminating publications to neighboring brokers with subscribers interested in the published content. A publication matches a subscription if all publication attributes satisfy constraints defined by the subscription. The simplest approach to route publications in a broker network is publication flooding, where end brokers perform publication filtering prior to final delivery to local subscribers. This approach is an obvious solution for scenarios with a densely covered subscription space where most brokers have interested subscribers for all publications; however, it wastes a lot of bandwidth in cases with few or no subscribers interested in a large fraction of publications.

To decrease the publication traffic, subscriptions are disseminated through the network close to publishers to enable publication filtering 'at the source'. Upon receiving a new subscription, a broker will forward it to its neighbors that are potential publishers of content matching the defined subscription. A commonly used technique for subscription dissemination is flooding: A subscription is sent to all neighbors except to the one from which it was received. Note that brokers maintain a routing table with a set of active subscriptions per each neighboring broker, and consider this neighbor to be a subscriber without knowing the 'real' end subscribers. Upon receiving a publication, a broker B_i forwards it to its neighboring broker B_j only if it matches any of B_j's subscriptions. In other words, publications follow the reverse direction of subscriptions. The technique originates from IP muticast and is commonly known as *reverse path forwarding* [5,6].

To reduce the subscription traffic, subscription covering and merging is applied. Informally, a subscription s_1 covers subscription s_2 if all publications matching s_2 will also match s_1, but the opposite does not hold. Since a covered subscription does not influence the propagation of publications, there is no need to forward it to neighboring brokers. Therefore, when a broker B_i receives s_2 which is covered by s_1, it will not forward s_2 to B_j if B_i has previously forwarded s_1 to B_j. Nevertheless, s_2 has to be stored in the *passive set of subscriptions* (s_1 would be an element of the *active set*), because it must be activated in case s_1 expires, i.e. a subscriber unsubscribes from s_2. The process of merging proposes a single merged subscription for similar subscriptions, but will not be discussed in detail as it is beyond the scope of this paper.

3   Problem Statement

Scenario. To motivate the need for an efficient subsumption checking mechanism, we introduce a usage scenario potentially generating a large number of subscriptions. *Resource discovery in Grids* assigns computation requests (jobs) to available services. Current systems use server-based solutions and recently P2P-based solutions have been investigated [14] to deal with the scalability problem caused by a large number of jobs and services. Let us discuss the problem of resource discovery in terms of publish/subscribe. Services offering computational resources may announce their capabilities and availability through subscriptions to enable efficient matching and scheduling of jobs searching for available services. Jobs define their requirements from the services using publications. An example subscription with two publications are presented in Table 1.

Table 1. Subscription and publication examples

	$CPU cycles$	$disk$	$memory$	$service$	$time$
s_1	[3000, 3500]	[40, 50kB]	1GB	a.service.org	[2006-03-31T16:00:00, 2006-03-31T20:00:00]
p_1	3500	45kB	1GB	*.service.org	2006-03-31T16:00:00
p_2	1035	45kB	0.5GB	*.*.org	2006-03-31T12:23:05

The basic characteristic of the presented usage scenario is the potentially large number of services and jobs that generate huge amounts of both subscriptions and publications. Dynamic changes of subscriptions are significant because as the context changes, i.e. services get allocated to new jobs, subscriptions will consequently change. Therefore, this scenario exemplifies a setting where context changes induce higher subscription rate, as it can also be observed in mobile environments. Next, the subscription space may have high dimensionality: Even in our simple example without detailed job and resource descriptions, 5 different attributes have been defined. Thus, we propose a method for reducing the total number of active subscriptions in the system by means of group coverage. Due to large numbers and inherently distributed characteristics of Grid services, the publish/subscribe service for resource discovery would be distributed. As in this paper we are focusing on the subsumption process performed within a single node, we are not assuming neither an underlying network topology nor stability of the broker network. It can be applied with various routing protocols, and our goal is to point out potential impact of the proposed algorithm on the performance of a distributed system regardless of its topology and applied routing strategy.

Let us consider the following example of subscription coverage in a 2-dimensional subscription space. Table 2 defines two existing subscriptions, s_1 and s_2, and new subscription s. We want to determine whether s_1 and s_2 jointly cover s. As it is visible from the graphical representation of subscriptions in Figure 1, the subsumption relationship indeed exists. Even though neither s_1 nor s_2 cover s, their union entirely covers s. Note that constraints in this example define ranges to simplify the presentation, and can straightforwardly be extended to finite sets [15].

Table 3 lists the notation used in the paper.

Table 2. Subsumption example: $s \sqsubseteq (s_1 \vee s_2)$

Subscription s
$[x_1 \geq 830 \wedge x_1 \leq 870 \wedge$
$x_2 \geq 1003 \wedge x_2 \leq 1006]$
Subscription s_1
$[x_1 \geq 820 \wedge x_1 \leq 850 \wedge$
$x_2 \geq 1001 \wedge x_2 \leq 1007]$
Subscription s_2
$[x_1 \geq 840 \wedge x_1 \leq 880 \wedge$
$x_2 \geq 1002 \wedge x_2 \leq 1009]$

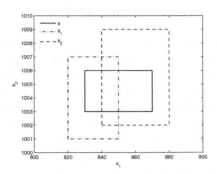

Fig. 1. Graphical representation of subscriptions in Table 2

Table 3. Notations

Symbol	Meaning
s	New subscription
p	Publication
S	Disjunction of existing subscriptions $s_i, 1 \leq i \leq k$
k	$|S|$
s_i	Existing subscription $s_i \in S$
s_i^j	j^{th} predicate in s_i
x_j	Attribute j
m	number of distinct attributes in S
T	Conflict table
T_i^j	Value in row i, column j of T
t_i	Number of defined elements in row i of T
f_{c_i}	Number of conflict-free elements in row i of T
δ	Error probability
ρ_w	Probability of guessing a point witness

Definition 1. *Subscription s_i is a conjunction of predicates $s_i = s_i^1 \wedge s_i^2 \wedge \ldots \wedge s_i^{r_i}$ where each s_i^j is a simple predicate, and $r_i \geq 1$, where r_i is the number of simple predicates forming subscription s_i. Let us define m, as the number of distinct attributes in the set of k subscriptions $s_i, 1 \leq i \leq k$.*

Without restricting the applicability of the algorithm and to simplify the analysis, we consider that each simple predicate defines a constraint on an attribute $x_j, 1 \leq j \leq m$, where each x_j has a lower ($x_j \geq low_j$) and upper limit ($x_j \leq high_j$). Each attribute is therefore defined as a range. Furthermore, we assume that all subscriptions define constraints for the same number of attributes $m_1 = m_2 = \ldots = m_k = m$, and since there is a lower and upper bound on each x_j, $r = 2 \cdot m$. In fact, this is not a restriction as the bounds $(-\infty, +\infty)$ mean the attribute is not significant for a particular subscription, and remains undefined.

The *general subsumption* problem tests whether a subscription s is covered by a disjunction of subscriptions, $s \sqsubseteq (s_1 \vee s_2 \vee \ldots \vee s_k)$, where k is the total number of existing subscriptions.

Definition 2. A *conflict table* T is a $k \times (2 \cdot m)$ table relating a subscription s to all simple predicates defined by $S = \{s_1 \vee s_2 \vee \ldots \vee s_k\}$. An element in table T, T_i^j is $\neg s_i^j$ if $s \wedge \neg s_i^j$ is satisfiable or is otherwise *undefined*.

A conflict table points out conflicting and not covered intervals between a tested subscription and a set of subscriptions. To construct the conflict table, we process each subscription $s_i \in S$ to verify the satisfiability of the negation of each simple predicate s_i^j against subscription s. If the condition is true, T_i^j is assigned the value $\neg s_i^j$, otherwise it is assigned the *undefined* value. Thus, the decision whether a specific T_i^j is defined is done in $O(1)$ and the construction of the table requires $O(m \cdot k)$.

For the example in Table 2, $s \wedge \neg s_1^1$ is *not satisfiable*, because the intersection between s and $\neg s_1^1 = \{x_1 < 820\}$ is empty, while $s \wedge \neg s_1^2$ is *satisfiable* because the intersection between s and $\neg s_1^2 = \{x_1 > 850\}$ is non-empty. Both $s \wedge \neg s_1^3$ and $s \wedge \neg s_1^4$ are *not satisfiable* and thus the corresponding table cells are $undefined$. The same procedure is performed to compare s to s_2.

Table 4. Conflict table for the example in Figure 1

s_i	$x_1 < low_i^1$	$x_1 > high_i^1$	$x_2 < low_i^2$	$x_2 > high_i^2$
s_1	$undefined$	$x_1 > 850$	$undefined$	$undefined$
s_2	$x_1 < 840$	$undefined$	$undefined$	$undefined$

The conflict table relating subscription s from Table 2 to the set of subscriptions s_1 and s_2 is given in Table 4. The first row represents a template for the content of the actual conflict table relating s to s_1 and s_2. The first line corresponding to s_1 has only one defined element, $\neg s_1^2 = \{x_1 > 850\}$ because, as it is visible in the graphical representation, s_1 does not cover s for $x_1 > 850$. Analogously, the only defined element in the second line corresponding to s_2 is $\neg s_2^1 = \{x_1 < 840\}$.

Definition 3. A *polyhedron witness* to non-cover is a set of elements from a conflict table T, $\left\{ T_1^{j_1}, \ldots, T_k^{j_k} \right\}$, such that $s \wedge \neg s_1^{j_1} \wedge \ldots \wedge \neg s_k^{j_k}$ is satisfiable, defining a convex polyhedron. In other words, a polyhedron witness is a convex polyhedron contained in s, but not in S.

Let us consider the example graphically represented in Figure 2, defining two subscriptions s_1 and s_2 that do not cover subscription s. The *polyhedron witness* to non-cover is a rectangle in this case, and is defined by the intersection of s and the element $\neg s_2^2 = \{x_1 > 870\}$. This rectangle is contained in s, but not in s_1 nor s_2.

Definition 4. A *point witness* to non-cover is a point that satisfies s, but does not satisfy S. A point witness is inside a polyhedron witness, but not inside S.

Table 5. Non cover example: subscriptions

Subscription s
$[x_1 \leq 890 \wedge x_1 \geq 830 \wedge$
$x_2 \leq 1006 \wedge x_2 \geq 1003]$
Subscription s_1
$[x_1 \leq 850 \wedge x_1 \geq 820 \wedge$
$x_2 \leq 1009 \wedge x_2 \geq 1002]$
Subscription s_2
$[x_1 \leq 870 \wedge x_1 \geq 840 \wedge$
$x_2 \leq 1007 \wedge x_2 \geq 1001]$

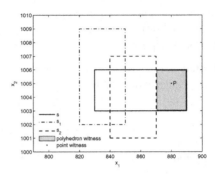

Fig. 2. Non-cover example: graphical presentation of a polyhedron witness and point witness

In the previous example, any point inside the polyhedron witness rectangle defined by $s \wedge \neg s_2^2$ is a point witness. The following 2 corollaries are based on the properties of the conflict table, polyhedron witness and point witness.

Corollary 1. If all T_i^j for $1 \leq j \leq r$ are undefined, then s is covered by s_i.

Proof. If all $T_i^1, \ldots, T_i^r$ are undefined, then $(s \wedge \neg s_i^1, \ldots, s \wedge \neg s_i^r)$ are all not satisfiable, and thus $(s \sqsubseteq s_i^1) \wedge \ldots \wedge (s \sqsubseteq s_i^r)$, or alternatively, $s \sqsubseteq (s_i^1 \wedge \ldots \wedge s_i^r)$. In effect s is covered by s_i. Thus, as a side-effect, the use of the conflict table provides a sufficient condition, tested in $O(m \cdot k)$, to check whether s is covered by any of the subscriptions individually.   □

Corollary 2. If all T_i^j for $1 \leq j \leq r$ are defined, then s covers s_i.

Proof sketch. If all $T_i^1, \ldots, T_i^r$ are defined, then $(s \wedge \neg s_i^1, \ldots, s \wedge \neg s_i^r)$ are all satisfiable, and thus s includes s_i on all attributes.   □

Corollary 3. Let $t_{i_1}, t_{i_2} \ldots t_{i_k}$ be the list resulting from sorting $t_1, t_2 \ldots t_k$ in ascending order, where t_i represents the number of defined entries in row i of the conflict table T. If all $t_{i_j} \geq j$ for $1 \leq i_j \leq k$, then s is not covered by S.

Proof sketch. If $t_{i_j} \geq j$ for $1 \leq i_j \leq k$, then a polyhedron witness exists. It can be constructed in the following way: Choose any element $s_{i_1}^{j_{i_1}}$ to be part of a polyhedron witness, and then eliminate any conflicting entries from other rows. Since each row will have a maximum of one conflicting element with $s_{i_1}^{j_{i_1}}$, then at most one element in each row will be eliminated. If this step is repeated k times a polyhedron witness will be derived. Thus, s is not covered by S.   □

4   Probabilistic Cover Algorithm

In this section we describe the probabilistic cover algorithm to solve the defined subsumption problem. This algorithm has direct implications on the effectiveness of routing both publications and subscriptions in a distributed environment, and the efficiency to discover matching publications. The probabilistic core of the algorithm is the 'Monte Carlo type' Random Simple Predicates Cover part. It runs in a fixed number of iterations, but may produce an incorrect result with a certain pre-determined probability of error. The probability of error is problem specific, and we show that an upper bound on this error is derived in polynomial time prior to the execution of the algorithm. Thus, the performance of the algorithm can be decided in advance based on particular application requirements. The Random Simple Predicates Cover can be executed independently or in conjunction with the minimized cover set algorithm which reduces the original set of subscriptions S to a non-reducible set against which a new subscription s has to be checked. We also introduce a number of optimizations used for making fast decisions under specific conditions that can be detected from the conflict table.

4.1 Random Simple Predicates Cover

The Random Simple Predicates Cover (RSPC) algorithm exploits the property of *point witnesses*. If the algorithm guesses a point in s that is a *point witness* to non-cover for the set of subscriptions S, then the subsumption problem is solved with a definite NO, i.e. $s \not\sqsubseteq S$. On the other hand, in case a subsumption relationship exists, the algorithm would try in vain to find such a witness. To prevent this situation, we define a threshold d for the number of guesses, and the algorithm may output a probabilistic YES, i.e. $s \sqsubseteq S$ with a predefined probability of error.

Algorithm 1. Random-Simple-Predicates-Cover

1: /* Decide whether a subscription s is covered by the existing subscriptions set S */
2: **for** $i = 1$ to d **do**
3:     **GUESS** a point P inside s
4:     **if** P **does not satisfy** subscriptions set S **then**
5:         **RETURN** false
6:     **end if**
7: **end for**
8: **RETURN** true

Algorithm 1 defines the RSPC algorithm which executes a number of iterations d to randomly generate a point satisfying subscription s and checks whether it is a *point witness*. To generate a point within s costs $O(m)$, and verifying whether it lies inside any of $s_1, s_2, \ldots s_k$ can be done in $O(m \cdot k)$ steps. Overall, the algorithmic complexity of RSPC is $d(m + m \cdot k)$, or $O(d \cdot m \cdot k)$. However, our experiments in Section 6 show that this upper bound is a pessimistic estimate, since at any iteration, RSPC can output a definite NO if the guessed point is indeed a point witness. In addition, the complexity can be greatly reduced using the optimizations presented in Sections 4.2 and 4.3.

Proposition 1. RSPC returns NO when s is definitely not covered by S. It returns YES with a probability error δ upper bounded by

$$\delta = (1 - \rho_w)^d, \tag{1}$$

where ρ_w is the probability that a randomly generated point P inside s is a point witness.

Proof. If RSPC returns NO then a point witness was found, and thus s is definitely not subsumed by S. Therefore, the answer is correct. If s is not subsumed then RSPC returns YES only if none of the guessed points is a point witness. For each trial this happens with probability less than $1 - \rho_w$, therefore for d trials the probability RSPC returns YES is less than $(1 - \rho_w)^d$, since d trials are randomly generated and are thus assumed to be independent.   □

In problems with specific probability of error δ, we can compute the necessary number of trials, d, to answer the subsumption question with the required δ, using Equation 1 beforehand in polynomial time. The number of trials increases with a decrease of the error probability. The value of ρ_w depends on the number of existing point witnesses for the particular subscription s related to the set of subscriptions S, and the 'size' (number of integral solutions) of subscription s. Since the probabilistic algorithm may produce a wrong answer only if s is not subsumed by S, the worst situation is to assume that s is indeed not subsumed by the set. To compute the upper bound on d, we need to determine the lower bound on ρ_w, set by the smallest possible polyhedron witness.

Algorithm sketch for computing d. In order to compute d, the algorithm needs the value of ρ_w, which must be approximated, because knowing an exact value is equivalent to solving the subsumption problem. We approximate the lower bound on ρ_w as the product of the minimum distances for each attribute between the new subscription bounds and the bounds of each subscription in the set (possible minimum non-covered ranges). Then, the upper bound on d is extracted from Eq. 1, using the computed value for ρ_w and the given δ.

4.2 Minimized Cover Set of Subscriptions

To further reduce the number of subscriptions against which s needs to be checked, we introduce another algorithm, the minimized cover set algorithm (MCS). From the set of subscriptions S, MCS constructs a non-reducible set of subscriptions, by ignoring those that are redundant for the covering detection problem and filters out duplicate subscriptions (those covering the same parts of s), and subscriptions that do not intersect with s. The remaining subscriptions form the non-reducible set S' (which may not be the minimal covering set) against which s is subsequently checked by RSPC.

Definition 5. Two defined entries in the table, $T_{i_1}^{j_{i_1}}$ and $T_{i_2}^{j_{i_2}}$ are said to be conflicting if $i_1 \neq i_2$, and $s \wedge T_{i_1}^{j_{i_1}} \wedge T_{i_2}^{j_{i_2}}$ is not satisfiable. A defined entry $T_{i_1}^{j_{i_1}}$ is said to be *conflict-free* if it does not conflict with any other defined element $T_{i_2}^{j_{i_2}}$, where $i_1 \neq i_2$.

Conflict free entries are determined by comparing entries from the conflict table related to the same attribute, for different subscriptions. If a constraint conflicts with any other constraint defined by another subscription, the entry is conflicting. It is conflict free otherwise.

Figure 3 visualizes the set of 3 subscriptions, s_1, s_2 and s_3, as well as subscription s defined in Table 6, and Table 7 shows the corresponding conflict table. We can observe

Table 6. Conflict-free example: subscriptions

Subscription s
$[x_1 \leq 870 \wedge x_1 \geq 830 \wedge$
$x_2 \leq 1006 \wedge x_2 \geq 1003]$
Subscription s_1
$[x_1 \leq 850 \wedge x_1 \geq 820 \wedge$
$x_2 \leq 1007 \wedge x_2 \geq 1001]$
Subscription s_2
$[x_1 \leq 880 \wedge x_1 \geq 840 \wedge$
$x_2 \leq 1009 \wedge x_2 \geq 1002]$
Subscription s_3
$[x_1 \leq 890 \wedge x_1 \geq 810 \wedge$
$x_2 \leq 1005 \wedge x_2 \geq 1004]$

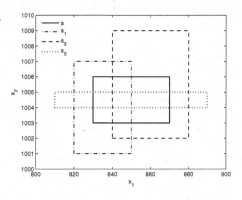

Fig. 3. An example with conflict free entries

Table 7. Conflict table for the example in Figure 3

s_i	$x_1 < low_i^1$	$x_1 > high_i^1$	$x_2 < low_i^2$	$x_2 > high_i^2$
s_1	undefined	$x_1 > 850$	undefined	undefined
s_2	$x_1 < 840$	undefined	undefined	undefined
s_3	undefined	undefined	$x_2 < 1004$	$x_2 > 1005$

that the defined entries for s_3 are conflict free: they are not conflicting with the entries from s_1 and s_2. On the other hand, s_1 and s_2 have conflicting entries because x_1 cannot simultaneously satisfy both conditions, $x_1 > 850$ and $x_1 < 840$.

Proposition 3. If the number of conflict-free elements in the i-th row of T, f_{c_i}, is greater than or equal to 1, or the number of defined elements in row i, $t_i \geq k$, then s_i is redundant. Proof is given in [15].

The MCS algorithm consists of two main steps, as defined in Algorithm 2. First, starting from the conflict table T, it counts the number of defined elements for each subscription s_i in the corresponding row, t_i and computes the number of conflict free elements, f_{c_i}. Then, it removes from the set all subscriptions for which t_i is equal to or greater than the current number of subscriptions in the set. It also removes subscriptions that have at least one conflict free element in the corresponding row of the conflict table. These two steps are repeated until there are no more subscriptions that fulfill any of the two conditions. The remaining subscriptions form the non-reducible cover set S' for answering the union covering problem.

Considering the conflict table from Table 7, in the first step none of the subscriptions has more defined entries than the total number of subscriptions ($t_1 = t_2 = 1$ and $t_3 = 2$ which is smaller than 3), while only s_3 has conflict free entries. Based on the elimination conditions (in this case, $f_{c_3} = 2 > 0$), MCS can remove subscription s_3 in the first iteration. In the second iteration, still no subscription has more defined entries

---

Algorithm 2. Minimized Cover Set

1: /* Find the minimized set of subscriptions S' relevant for subsumption detection */
2: /* Construct and use the conflict table T */
3: **repeat**
4:     $S' = S$
5:     **for** every row i in T **do**
6:         **compute** f_{c_i} /* number of conflict-free elements in row i in T */
7:         **compute** t_i /* number of defined entries in row i in T */
8:         **if** $f_{c_i} \geq 0$ **or** $t_i \geq k$ **then**
9:             **remove** row i from T
10:             **remove** subscription s_i from S'
11:             $k = k - 1$
12:         **end if**
13:     **end for**
14: **until** no s_i can be removed
15: **RETURN** S'

---

than the total number of subscriptions ($t_1 = t_2 = 1 < 2$) and there are no conflict free entries, thus the algorithm stops. The minimized cover set is $S' = \{s_1, s_2\}$.

Determining if a table entry is conflict free is $O(m \cdot k)$. Therefore computing each f_{c_i} costs $O(m^2 k)$, and in turn steps 1 and 2 in each iteration of the MCS algorithm cost $O(m^2 k^2)$. Steps 1 and 2 may be repeated k times since each time step 2 is performed at least one s_i is filtered out. As a result, the overall cost of the algorithm reduction is $O(m^2 k^3)$ in the worst case.

4.3   Fast Decisions Based on Sufficient Conditions

To summarize, in order to answer the subsumption problem, the algorithm first constructs the conflict table, runs the MCS algorithm to reduce the subscription set, and then applies the probabilistic RSPC algorithm which produces either a definite NO or a probabilistic YES. Nevertheless, for some specific cases, the algorithm can efficiently give a deterministic answer. Here we briefly present three specific cases.

1. Pairwise subsumption: As stated in Corollary 1, it is possible to detect if a subscription s is entirely covered by another subscription and produce a definite YES by analyzing the conflict table. If the row in the conflict table corresponding to subscription s_i contains only *undefined* values, then s_i covers the new subscription.
2. The outcome of the MCS algorithm can be an empty set, which means that there are no candidate subscriptions that could jointly cover s, and the algorithm will produce a definite NO.
3. Polyhedron witness: Detecting the existence of a polyhedron witness suffices to detect a non-cover relationship and output a definite NO as stated in Corollary 3. Based on the definitions of the polyhedron witness and conflict free entries, we can detect the presence of such a witness, depending on the number of defined entries in the conflict table without using either RSPC or MCS.

5 Subscription Propagation in a Distributed System

As in a distributed system subscription propagation affects the overall system performance, here we analyze the implications of incorrectly declaring a subscription as covered. Equation 1 gives the upper bound for the probability of error in incorrectly withholding the forwarding of a subscription, and therefore, it represents the likelihood of not finding a matching publication if it is available at the next broker. In a distributed publish/subscribe system, data is routed throughout the system, and we need to analyze the influence of our probabilistic algorithm on subscription propagation. We consider in Figure 4 a simple and illustrative case, where the new subscription s should be propagated along a chain of brokers $B_1, B_2, \ldots, B_n$.

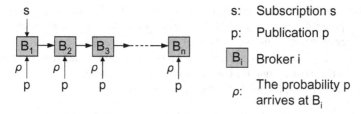

Fig. 4. New subscription propagation

We assume that the new subscription s is issued at broker B_1, while subscriptions $s_1, s_2, \ldots, s_k$ have already been propagated down the path to all brokers. Let ρ be the probability that a matching publication p (matches s but no s_i) is issued at any of the brokers B_i. The overall performance of the probabilistic algorithm is given by the probability of finding the matching publication, wherever it resides.

Proposition 4. The probability of finding the matching publication p under the condition that s is erroneously found to be covered by S, where $s_1, s_2, \ldots, s_k$ have been propagated to all brokers along the path, and all brokers have equal probability of ρ of receiving publication p is:

$$\sum_{i=1}^{n} \rho[(1 - \rho)(1 - (1 - \rho_w)^d)]^{i-1}, \qquad (2)$$

where ρ is determined by the network density and the communication distance of two neighboring brokers, and n is the total number of brokers in the path.

Equation 2 gives the lower bound for the overall algorithm performance. However, as we will show in the next chapter, the actual performance is much better in practice, even for loose error probabilities. On the other hand, the reduction in the global subscription traffic is more important for longer broker paths, reflecting the local reduction at each broker, exponentially amplified in the network diameter.

Note that we do not present in this paper the mechanism for dealing with subscriptions cancelation. This issue can be tackled by explicit forwarding of unsubscriptions between brokers or by associating an expiration time with each new subscription. According to our approach, the canceled subscription can either be covered, and then cancelation has only the effect of removing it from the passive set, either be present in the (active) subscription set, and then its covered subscription must be promoted to this set, to replace it.

6   Experimental Evaluation

In this section, we evaluate the performance of the proposed probabilistic approach in terms of *efficiency* and *effectiveness* using a number of subscription generation scenarios. Efficiency is measured as the number of actual algorithmic steps performed to answer the subsumption question, and effectiveness as the ratio of recognized redundant subscriptions to the total number of redundant subscriptions. Especially, we are interested in potential gains and costs when using the MCS algorithm in specific subscription generation scenarios. Next, we analyze the *number of false decisions* declaring a subsumption relationship when there was no subsumption. Finally, we compare our approach with the existing one for pair-wise coverage detection.

There are two main categories of subscription settings:

(1) Covering: s is covered by the set of subscriptions (with some of $s_i \in S$ being redundant).
(2) Non-cover: s is not covered by the set S (as such, all subscriptions are redundant).

In particular, we have considered the following subscription generation scenarios:

(1.a) Pairwise covering scenario; s is entirely covered by at least one subscription from the set of existing subscriptions.
(1.b) Redundant covering scenario; s is not covered by any single subscription, but is covered by the set, with a lot of subscriptions being redundant.
(2.a) No intersection scenario; s does not intersect with any existing subscription.
(2.b) Non-cover scenario; s is not covered by the set S, but overlaps with existing subscriptions over many attributes.
(2.c) Extreme non-cover scenario; similar to (2.b), but s has only a very small non covered gap.
(1-2) Comparison scenario; generate incoming subscriptions randomly.

Scenario (1.a) is straightforward as the covering relationship is determined efficiently by applying Corollary 1 after the construction of the conflict table, therefore the cost of detecting pairwise coverage is $O(m \cdot k)$. Scenario (2.a) is also straightforward because MCS determines non subsumption after the first iteration by removing all subscriptions from the set S' because all $s_i \in S$ have conflict-free elements in the conflict table. Scenarios (1.b), (2.b), and (2.c) are difficult settings for checking the covering relationship, as there are no pair-wise subsumptions which could help to reduce the set S'. We investigated these scenarios using the following subscription generation principle: Existing subscriptions overlap with a new subscription and each other for many attributes, but there are no pair-wise subsumptions. The last scenario (1-2) simulates a realistic setting

Table 8. Parameters used in simulations

	(1.b)	(2.b)	(2.c)	(1-2)
no. of subscriptions k	10-310 (30)	10-310 (30)	50	1 to 5000
no. of attributes m	10, 15, 20	10, 15, 20	5	10, 15, 20
error δ	10^{-10}	10^{-10}	$10^{-3}, 10^{-6}, 10^{-10}$	10^{-6}
no. of trial runs	1000	1000	3000	1
gap size	0	random	0.5-4.5% (0.5%)	NA

assuming that user interests are similar, and that the popularity of attributes appearing in subscriptions is Zipfian.

The parameters used in simulations are listed in Table 8. For the redundant covering and non-cover scenarios, the setting is similar, while the extreme non-cover scenario investigates different error probabilities. The comparison scenario is performed in a single run by generating a sequence of subscriptions. In the figures, each plotted point is the average of the values obtained over the number of trial runs.

6.1 Redundant Covering Scenario

This simulation scenario investigates algorithm performance when the subscription set S subsumes s. A high rate of redundant subscriptions is introduced to test the influence of the MCS algorithm on the overall performance: s is covered by 20% of the generated subscriptions and the remaining 80% are redundant and partly cover s.

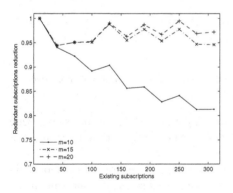

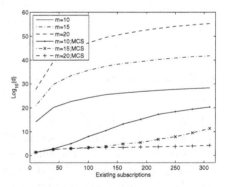

Fig. 5. Reduction for the redundant covering scenario

Fig. 6. Theoretical number of iterations for the redundant covering scenario

Figure 5 shows the effectiveness of the MCS algorithm: It successfully removed between 80% and 100% of redundant subscriptions. The performance increases for higher number of attributes because when increasing m, the probability of group coverage increases due to the specific subscription generation scenario.

Figure 6 shows the theoretically predicted number of iterations d needed to answer the subsumption question. The $log(d)$ plot is shown as a function of k, calculated using Equation 1. The plot is given for the initial set of subscriptions S, and the reduced set S' after running MCS. Due to the tight error probability, d is extremely high when using only the RSPC algorithm. However, MCS significantly reduces the number of needed iterations and becomes practically feasible: $d < 10^5$ for 100 subscriptions with 10 attributes, and decreases significantly for larger number of attributes. Further more, as the results obtained for non-cover show, we could reduce the number of trials further.

6.2 Non-cover Scenario

For the non-cover scenario, the experiment is constructed by forcing the non-covering of s by leaving a small range over x_1 uncovered. The values over the other attributes are generated randomly. The whole set of subscriptions S is actually redundant as s is not covered. In this scenario, the algorithm has always detected the non-coverage relationship due to optimizations and a low probability of error.

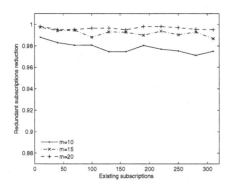 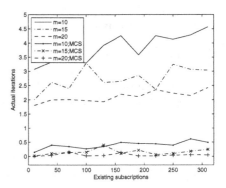

Fig. 7. Reduction for the non cover scenario   **Fig. 8.** Actual iterations for non cover

Figure 7 shows the effectiveness of the MCS algorithm which performs even better than for the redundant covering scenario because most of the subscriptions are removed quickly due to the non covering relationship.

Since non-cover can be detected prior to performing all d theoretical iterations, Figure 8 shows the actual number of iterations performed to discover a witness point. The average number of performed iterations is extremely low (< 0.5), due to the fact that in most of the cases, after running MCS, the reduced set is empty, thus $d = 0$. There are some evident fluctuations for this scenario caused by the probabilistic nature of the algorithm.

6.3 Extreme Non-cover Scenario

The extremeness of this scenario consists of covering the new subscription entirely, except for a narrow slice over one attribute, where we enforce a gap. We investigate the

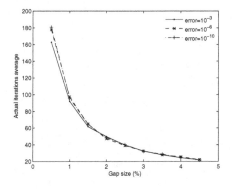

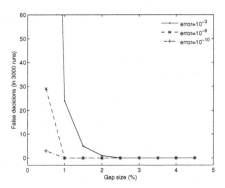

Fig. 9. Actual iterations performed

Fig. 10. Number of false negatives

total number of false decisions that result in non forwarding of a non covered subscription and the average number of performed trials.

Figure 9 shows that the average number of guesses is similar for all probabilities of error, even though the theoretical number of guesses increases for tighter error probabilities. This behavior is expected, as the chances of guessing a point witness depend on the ratio between the gap size and the total range size of the non covered attribute, but it does not depend on the error probability. This result suggests that we can also reduce the number of trials after which a subscription is declared covered.

In Figure 10 we can see the total number of false decisions increases with the error probability and decreases with larger gap sizes. In fact, for probabilities of error lower than 10^{-6} and gap sizes of more than 1%, the algorithm always takes the right decision. Even for a looser probability of error (10^{-3}), the number of false negatives remains quite low, if the gap is at least 2%. This shows that an error probability of 10^{-6} is sufficient for detecting non-coverage in most application scenarios because it has a low number of false decisions in case of a small non-covered subscription space while at the same time reducing the theoretical number of iterations d.

6.4 Comparison

Due to the lack of real-world subscription set, we have simulated a setting using power law distributions that are considered as good approximations of popularity both for the selection of attributes and attribute ranges. From the set of m attributes popular ones were chosen using a Zipf distribution (skew = 2.0). Attributes are generated in the following way: The center of a range is generated with a Pareto distribution (skew = 1.0) to simulate similar interests, while range sizes are generated with a normal distribution.

The experiment compares the growth of subscription set sizes in case of the pair-wise ([7,8]) and group subsumption (our approach) reductions.

Figure 11 shows the growth of the total number of active subscriptions when increasing the number of incoming subscriptions. It is interesting to observe the power of subscription set reduction using subscription coverage both for pair-wise and group

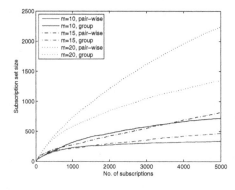

Fig. 11. Evolution of subscription set size

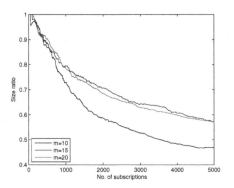

Fig. 12. Ratio of subscription set sizes

coverage in case of partly covered subscription space. The group coverage shows greater reduction compared to the pair-wise algorithm for all values of m. For $m = 10$ and $m = 15$ group coverage has reduced the original set of 5000 subscriptions to less than 10%, and pair-wise coverage to approx. 15% of the entire set, while for $m = 20$ the reduction is still significant (around 33% for group and less than 50% for pair-wise coverage). The set reduction is very important for subscriptions with a large number of attributes which increases complexity because of the absolute subscription set size, e.g. some brokers have limited resources and may not handle more than 1000 active subscriptions. When increasing m, the actual number of active subscriptions is also larger, and this is due to the fact that the probability of subsumption generally decreases in the applied subscription generation scenario when increasing subscription space dimensionality.

Figure 12 quantifies the actual gain of group coverage compared to the pair-wise coverage by showing the ratio between the subscription set sizes obtained with the 2 reduction mechanisms . The obtained results show the extreme reduction potential when increasing the number of incoming subscriptions. In case of 1000 received subscriptions, the ratio is between 70 and 80%, and keeps decreasing with new incoming subscriptions showing a stabilization tendency after 5000 subscriptions. The ratio is larger for large m, but still significant, and is almost similar for 15 and 20 attributes because the actual number of defined attributes does not significantly differ. Of course, the obtained results are highly dependent on subscription generation, but since our distributions follow a realistic popularity-based setting, it can be concluded that group coverage can greatly reduce the subscription set compared to the pair-wise approach.

To conclude, the reduction algorithm is both efficient and effective: It can significantly reduce the size of the subscription set with acceptable error probability and computational costs. RSPC should be used in combination with MCS because it dramatically reduced the number of performed trials. Finally, the comparison shows the supremacy of the group coverage algorithm over the classical pair-wise approach that will in general largely decrease the number of subscriptions in different distributed publish/subscribe systems.

7 Related Work

Most of the research efforts in publish/subscribe systems have so far focused on the problem of efficient matching and forwarding of publications [9,7]. Pairwise covering and merging of subscriptions are typically used to reduce the set of active subscriptions, and all algorithms rely on some version of the *counting algorithm*, originally defined in [16]. The importance of reducing the number of subscriptions in a distributed environment is stressed in [8]. The authors are dealing with a complementary problem— merging a set of subscriptions to reduce their number. In [7], modified binary decision diagrams are employed, to achieve pairwise covering and merging of subscriptions. The trade-off with merging is that the new subscription might contain parts of the subscription space not covered originally by the set, which leads to false positives, delivery of unrequested publications. A recently proposed solution relies on clustering of subscriptions based on a proximity metric in subscription space [17], and would greatly benefit from global subscription set reduction for both the total number of subscriptions and the generated traffic. None of these techniques supports group subsumption, and can filter out fewer subscriptions than the proposed probabilistic algorithm.

8 Conclusion

The paper presents a novel probabilistic algorithm for determining whether a subscription is covered by a set of subscriptions. Theoretically it solves the problem in $O(k \cdot m \cdot d)$. The probability of error is problem specific and very small, and an upper bound on the threshold d is determined in polynomial time prior to the execution of the algorithm. Our experiments have shown that the algorithm performs much better in practice when combing the probabilistic algorithm with the reduction algorithm that removes redundant subscriptions against which a new subscription needs to be checked. Even more, in case of the non covering relationship, it is possible to give a deterministic answer without applying the probabilistic tests. Therefore, we can conclude that the proposed algorithms can efficiently decide whether a subscription is covered by a group of subscriptions which is important for fast subscription forwarding and network congestion control in distributed publish/subscribe systems. The experimental results show that the algorithm performs much better than the pessimistic theoretical bounds even for settings where group coverage is difficult to detect. Finally, compared to the reduction based on the classical pair-wise coverage, the subscription set reduction achieved with our approach is significantly better, which, correlated with its good efficiency and the very tight achievable error probabilities, recommends it for distributed publish/subscribe systems.

References

1. Aguilera, M.K., Strom, R.E., Sturman, D.C., Astley, M., Chandra, T.D.: Matching events in a content-based subscription system. In: Proceedings of the 18th ACM Symposium on Principles of Distributed Computing, ACM Press (1999) 53–61
2. Altinel, M., Franklin, M.J.: Efficient filtering of XML documents for selective dissemination of information. In: The VLDB Journal. (2000) 53–64

3. Campailla, A., Chaki, S., Clarke, E., Jha, S., Veith, H.: Efficient filtering in publish-subscribe systems using binary decision diagrams. In: Proceedings of the 23rd International Conference on Software Engineering. (2001) 443–52
4. Fabret, F., Jacobsen, A., Llirbat, F., Pereira, J., Ross, K., Shasha, D.: Filtering algorithms and implementation for very fast publish/subscribe. In Sellis, T., Mehrotra, S., eds.: Proceedings of the 20th Intl. Conference on Management of Data (SIGMOD 2001), Santa Barbara, CA, USA (2001) 115–126
5. Carzaniga, A., Rosenblum, D.S., Wolf, A.L.: Design and evaluation of a wide-area event notification service. ACM Transactions on Computer Systems 19 (2001) 332–383
6. Mühl, G., L.Fiege, Gärtner, F.C., Buchmann, A.: Evaluating advanced routing algorithms for content-based publish/subscribe systems. In: Proceedings of the 10th IEEE International Symp. on Modeling, Analysis, and Simulation of Computer and Telecommunications Systems (MASCOTS'02), IEEE Computer Society (2002) 167–176
7. Li, G., Huo, S., Jacobsen, H.: A unified approach to routing, covering and merging in publish/subscribe systems based on modified binary decision diagrams. In: 25th International Conference on Distributed Computing Systems (ICDCS). (2005)
8. Crespo, A., Buyukkokten, O., Garcia-Molina, H.: Query merging: Improving query subscription processing in a multicast environment. IEEE Transactions on Knowledge and Data Engineering 15 (2003)
9. Carzaniga, A., Wolf, A.L.: Forwarding in a content-based network. In: Proceedings of ACM SIGCOMM 2003, Karlsruhe, Germany (2003) 163–174
10. Srivastava, D.: Subsumption and indexing in constraint query languages with linear arithmetic constraints. Annals of Mathematics and Artificial Intelligence 8 (1992) 315–343
11. Liu, H., Jacobsen, H.A.: Modeling uncertainties in publish/subscribe systems. In: ICDE '04: Proceedings of the 20th International Conference on Data Engineering, Washington, DC, USA, IEEE Computer Society (2004) 510
12. Chen, Y., Schwan, K.: Opportunistic overlays: Efficient content delivery in mobile ad hoc networks. In: Middleware 2005, ACM/IFIP/USENIX, 6th International Middleware Conference. (2005) 354–374
13. Dittrich, J.P., Fischer, P.M., Kossmann, D.: Agile: Adaptive indexing for context-aware information filters. In: Proceedings of the ACM SIGMOD International Conference on Management of Data, Baltimore, Maryland, USA, June 14-16, 2005. (2005) 215–226
14. Hauswirth, M., Schmidt, R.: An overlay network for resource discovery in Grids. In: 2nd International Workshop on Grid and Peer-to-Peer Computing Impacts on Large Scale Heterogeneous Distributed Database Systems (GLOBE'05). (2005)
15. Ouksel, A.M., Jurca, O., Podnar, I., Aberer, K.: Fast probabilistic subsumption checking for publish/subscribe systems. Technical Report LSIR-REPORT-2006-004, EPFL (2006)
16. Yan, T.W., García-Molina, H.: Index structures for selective dissemination of information under the Boolean model. ACM Transactions on Database Systems 19 (1994) 332–334
17. Voulgaris, S., Rivire, E., Kermarrec, A.M., van Steen, M.: Sub-2-sub: Self-organizing content-based publish and subscribe for dynamic and large scale collaborative networks. In: 5th Int'l Workshop on Peer-to-Peer Systems (IPTPS). (2005)

Dynamic Load Balancing in Distributed Content-Based Publish/Subscribe

Alex King Yeung Cheung and Hans-Arno Jacobsen

Middleware Systems Research Group
University of Toronto, Toronto, Ontario, Canada
{cheung,jacobsen}@eecg.utoronto.ca
http://www.msrg.utoronto.ca

Abstract. Distributed content-based publish/subscribe systems to date suffer from performance degradation and poor scalability caused by uneven load distributions typical in real-world applications. The reason for this shortcoming is due to the lack of a load balancing solution, which have rarely been studied in the context of publish/subscribe. This paper proposes a load balancing solution specific to distributed content-based publish/subscribe systems that is distributed, dynamic, adaptive, transparent, and accommodates heterogeneity. The solution consists of three key contributions: a load balancing framework, a novel load estimation algorithm, and three offload strategies. Experimental results show that the proposed load balancing solution is efficient with less than 1.5% overhead, effective with at least 91% load estimation accuracy, and capable of distributing all of the system's load originating from an edge point of the network.

Keywords: Publish/subscribe, load distribution, content-based routing, load balancing, load estimation, subscriber migration, offloading algorithm.

1 Introduction

Brokers in a distributed publish/subscribe system located at different geographical areas may suffer from uneven load distribution due to different population densities, interests, and usage patterns of end-users. A broker in a hotspot area where there is high message traffic resulting from a large number of publishers and subscribers may get overloaded in two ways. First, a broker can be overloaded if the incoming message rate into the broker exceeds the processing/matching rate supported by the matching engine. This effect is exacerbated if the number of subscribers is large because the matching rate is inversely proportional to the number of subscriptions in the matching engine [9]. Second, overload can also occur if the output transmission rate exceeds the total available output bandwidth. In both cases, queues accumulate with increasingly more messages waiting to be processed, resulting in increasingly higher processing and delivery delays. Worse yet, a broker may crash when it runs out of memory from queueing too many messages.

M. van Steen and M. Henning (Eds.): Middleware 2006, LNCS 4290, pp. 141–161, 2006.

Since the matching rate and both the incoming and outgoing message rates determine the load of a broker, and these factors depend on the number and nature of subscriptions that the broker services, load balancing is possible by offloading *specific* subscribers from higher loaded to lesser loaded brokers. Hence, we develop a load balancing algorithm that distributes load by offloading subscribers from heavily loaded brokers to less loaded brokers. Our contributions to support this idea include (1) a load balancing framework described in Section 3 that isolates subscribers to the edge brokers in the network and organizes load balancing activities into sessions between two brokers at a time; (2) a novel load estimation algorithm presented in Section 4 that profiles subscription load using bit vectors; (3) offload algorithms proposed in Section 5 to load balance on each performance metric of the broker by selecting the appropriate subscribers to offload based on their profiled load characteristics; and (4) experimental results shown in Section 6 that demonstrates the behavior and performance of our load balancing solution.

2   Background and Related Work

Content-based Publish/Subscribe is widely used in large-scale distributed applications because it allows processes to communicate asynchronously in a loosely-coupled manner. Publish/subscribe middleware can be readily found in online games [3], decentralized workflow execution [11], real-time monitoring systems [15], and the Enterprise Service Bus (ESB) of Service Oriented Architecture (SOA) infrastructures. In this communication paradigm, clients that send publication messages into the system are referred to as *publishers*, while those that only receive messages are called *subscribers*. Publishers issue publications in the form of attribute key-value pairs. Subscribers issue subscriptions to their nearest broker to specify the type of publications they want to receive. For the remainder of our discussion, we will assume that a subscription maps to a single subscriber. Subscriptions consist of predicates made up of attribute key-operator-value tuples to specify the filtering conditions on each attribute. A set of *brokers* connected together in an overlay network forms the publish/subscribe routing infrastructure (see Figure 3). In essence, brokers forward publication messages from the publishers to *matching* subscribers based on the routing paths established by subscriptions. Optimizations such as subscription aggregation [5], subscription merging [13], rendezvous nodes [14], and epidemic algorithms [7] may be employed to make the system more scalable or robust. However, hotspots can still arise because there is no load balancing mechanism.

The space of interest defined by a subscription's filtering conditions is called *subscription space*. A broker's *covering subscription set* (CSS) refers to the set of most general subscriptions whose subscription space is not covered by any other subscription. For example, a broker with the set of subscriptions shown in Figure 1a has a CSS identified by the subscriptions marked with an asterisk. For more efficient retrieval of a broker's CSS, the *partially-ordered set* (poset) [4] is used to maintain subscription relationships. The poset is a directed acyclic

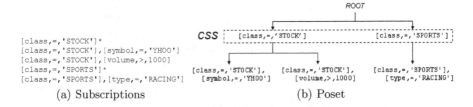

(a) Subscriptions   (b) Poset

Fig. 1. Example of the poset data structure

graph where each unique subscription is represented as a node in the graph as shown in Figure 1b. Nodes can have parent and children nodes where parent nodes have a subscription space that is a superset of its children nodes, while subscriptions with intersection or empty relationships will appear as siblings. As shown, the CSS is readily available as the immediate children nodes under the imaginary *ROOT* node.

Load Balancing has been a widely explored research topic for the past two decades since the introduction of parallel and distributed computing. Load balancing solutions can be found in the network layer [8], operating system layer [12], middleware layer [1], and application layer [2]. However, all of the above approaches cannot estimate the load of a subscription nor account for subscription spaces. These limitations prevent them from balancing load effectively in a heterogeneous content-based publish/subscribe system.

Load Balancing in Content-based Publish/Subscribe was never directly addressed in the past although distributed content-based publish/subscribe systems have been widely studied. Hence, the proposed solution in this paper is to the best of our knowledge the first dynamic load balancing algorithm for broker-based publish/subscribe systems to date.

Meghdoot [10] is a peer-to-peer content-based publish/subscribe system based on a distributed hash table that distributes load by replicating or splitting the locally heaviest loaded peer in half to share the responsibility of subscription management or event propagation. In general, their load sharing algorithm is only invoked upon new peers joining the system and peers are assumed to be homogeneous. Chen et al. [6] proposed a dynamic overlay reconstruction algorithm called *Opportunistic Overlay* that reduces end-to-end delivery delay and also performs load distribution on the CPU utilization as a secondary requirement. Load balancing is triggered only when a client finds another broker that is closer than its home broker. It is possible that subscriber migrations may overload a non-overloaded broker if the load requirements of the migrated subscription exceed the load-accepting broker's processing capacity. Our work differs from Meghdoot and Opportunistic Overlay by proposing a dynamic load balancing algorithm for non-DHT-based publish/subscribe systems that accounts for heterogeneous brokers and subscribers, and distributes load evenly onto all resources in the system without requiring new entities to join the federation. We also present a detailed subscriber migration protocol that enforces end-user transparency and best-effort delivery to minimize message loss.

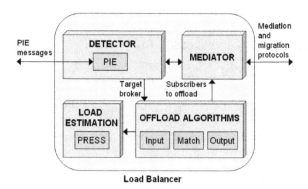

Fig. 2. Components of the load balancer

3   Load Balancing Framework

The components that make up the load balancing solution are shown in Figure 2. The solution consists of the detector, mediator, load estimation tools, and offload algorithms that determine which subscribers to offload. The detector detects and initiates a trigger when an overload or load imbalance occurs. The trigger from the detector tells the mediator to establish a load balancing session between the two entities, namely *offloading broker* (broker with the higher load doing the offloading) and the *load-accepting broker* (broker accepting load from the offloading broker). Depending on which performance metric is to be balanced, one of the offload algorithms is invoked on the offloading broker to determine the set of subscribers to delegate to the load-accepting broker based on estimating how much load is reduced and increased at each broker using the load estimation algorithms. Finally, the mediator is invoked to coordinate the migration of subscribers and ends the load balancing session between the two brokers. The following sections will describe the load balancing framework and the operations of each component in greater detail.

3.1   Underlying Publish/Subscribe Architecture

The Padres[1] Efficient Event Routing (PEER) architecture organizes brokers into a hierarchical structure as shown in Figure 3. Brokers with more than one neighboring broker are referred to as *cluster-head brokers*, while brokers with only one neighbor are referred to as *edge brokers*. A cluster-head broker with its connected set of edge brokers, if any, forms a *cluster*. Brokers within a cluster are assumed to be closer to each other in network proximity than brokers in other clusters. Publishers are serviced by cluster-head brokers, while subscribers are serviced by edge brokers.

PEER is designed with five goals in mind. First, PEER allows the load balancing scheme to move subscribers to control load in the edge brokers because they

---

[1] Our work is built onto the Padres [11] system.

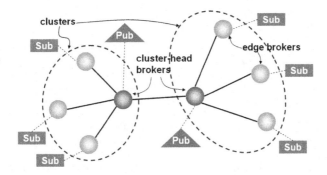

Fig. 3. PEER architecture

have no broker-to-broker through-traffic to route. Second, higher dissemination efficiency is achieved by having cluster-heads forward publication messages to all matching clusters almost simultaneously because cluster-heads have negligible processing delays since they do not service any subscribers. Third, cluster-head brokers may be load balanced by moving publishers and inter-broker subscriptions, as will be the focus of future work. Fourth, PEER's organization of brokers into clusters allows for two levels of load balancing: *local-level* (referred to as *local load balancing*) where edge brokers within the same cluster load balance with each other; and *global-level* (referred to as *global load balancing*) where edge brokers from two different clusters load balance with each other. Edge brokers only need to exchange load information with edge brokers in the same cluster, and neighboring clusters can exchange aggregated load information about their own edge brokers. Fifth, local load balancing preserves subscriber locality by keeping subscribers within their original cluster, assuming that subscribers connect to the closest broker in the first place. On the other hand, global load balancing trades off locality for a better balanced system by migrating subscribers between edge brokers in neighboring clusters.

3.2   Load Detection Framework

In order for brokers to know when and which brokers are available for load balancing, they have to exchange load information with each other. With this data, a detection algorithm can then trigger load balancing whenever it detects an overload or a wide load difference with another broker.

Protocol for Exchanging Load Information. *Padres Information Exchange* (PIE) is a distributed hierarchical protocol for exchanging load information between brokers using publish/subscribe primitives. Brokers publish PIE messages intermittently to let other brokers in the federation know of their existence and availability for load balancing. PIE, as well as other load balancing control messages described in later sections, has a higher routing priority than normal publish/subscribe traffic so that their delivery is not affected by the

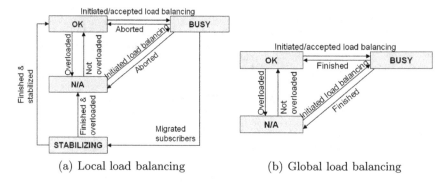

(a) Local load balancing   (b) Global load balancing

Fig. 4. State transition diagrams for an (a) edge broker and (b) cluster-head

brokers' load. A PIE message contains five attributes: (1) the broker's three performance metrics, specifically *input utilization ratio*, *output utilization ratio*, and average *matching delay* per message; (2) load balancing states, which can be one of *OK, BUSY, N/A*, or *STABILIZING*; (3) the set of edge brokers it is currently balanced with (more on this in Section 3.3); (4) the identifier of the cluster to which the broker belongs; and (5) the broker's unique identifier. Input utilization ratio (I_r) captures the broker's processing utilization as defined by the formula: $I_r = RateOfIncomingMessages/MaximumMatchRate$. Maximum match rate is obtained by taking the inverse of the average matching delay per message. Matching delay is defined as the time spent by the matching engine between taking a message as input and producing zero or more messages as output. Output utilization ratio (O_r) captures the broker's output bandwidth utilization as: $O_r = OutputBandwidthUsed/TotalOutputBandwidth$.

PEER's bi-level structuring allows for local and global-level PIE messages. Local PIE messages are published and subscribed by edge brokers within the same cluster to enable local load balancing. Global PIE messages are published and subscribed by cluster-head brokers to enable global load balancing. They only propagate one cluster-hop away and contain averaged load information from their cluster's local PIE messages. Cluster-head brokers without any edge brokers simply forward global PIE messages one extra hop to all of their neighbors.

Detection Algorithm. Detection allows a broker/cluster to monitor its current resource usage and also compare it with neighboring brokers/clusters so that a broker/cluster can invoke load balancing if necessary. Detection runs periodically at a broker/cluster only if it has a status of *OK, N/A*, and *STABILIZING*. An *OK* status means that the broker is available for load balancing, *N/A* means that it is overloaded, *STABILIZING* means that it is waiting for load to stabilize after load is exchanged, and *BUSY* means that it is currently in a load balancing session with another broker/cluster. A diagram showing the transition conditions between the local and global load balancing states are shown in Figures 4a and 4b, respectively.

The *local detection algorithm* running on an edge broker is composed of two steps. The first step identifies whether the broker itself is overloaded by examining four utilization ratios, namely input, output, CPU, and memory utilization ratio. The parameter *lower overload threshold* is introduced that prevents the broker from accepting further load by updating the broker's status to *N/A* when one of its utilization ratios exceeds 0.9. If a utilization ratio exceeds the *higher overload threshold* at 0.95, then load balancing is invoked immediately. In between the two thresholds is an inert period where the broker neither accepts nor invokes load balancing. All utilization ratios can be associated with different overload threshold values.

If the first step of the detection algorithm cannot find any overloaded resource, then the second step is to check if any one of the input utilization ratio, output utilization ratio, or matching delay differs from a neighbor by more than a threshold. Recall, load information about neighboring brokers is gathered through PIE. The threshold for utilization ratios is called the *local ratio triggering threshold*, and for matching delay is *local delay trigger threshold*. Both are set to 0.1 by default. The difference for utilization ratio is just the magnitude of the difference, while for matching delay, the following formula is used:

$$d_{\%Diff} = \left| \frac{d_1 - d_2}{N_f} \right| \tag{1}$$

d_1 and d_2 are the two delay values used in the comparison. N_f represents the normalization factor and is set to 0.1 by default so that delay differences much less than 0.1s do not yield high percentage differences and trigger unwanted load balancing. Then, a *broker-action* list of `<load-accepting broker, performance metric/offload action>` is generated that is sorted in descending order of highest performance metric difference. The list is passed to the local mediator to establish a load balancing session with an available load-accepting broker.

After a broker just finishes a load balancing session, its load information may mislead the broker into making an incorrect load balancing decision. For example, brokers accepting load may not experience an increase in utilization immediately. This may cause the broker to accept more load balancing sessions, which may cause its resource consumption to overshoot. To prevent this from occurring, both the offloading and load-accepting broker should inherit a status of *STABILIZING* for *stabilize duration* period (default is 30s) before setting its status back to *OK* (see Figure 4a). After this time, all performance metrics should not fluctuate more than the *stabilize percentage* (default is 0.05) between subsequent detection runs. When a broker has a *STABILIZING* status, it cannot accept load balancing requests nor invoke load balancing unless the broker is overloaded.

Alternatively, in place of their utilization ratio counterparts, it is also possible for the load balancer to use input queuing delay and output queuing delay as performance metrics. However, using queuing delay measurements do not accurately indicate the load of a broker at the instant the metric is measured because it is obtained after the message gets dequeued. Therefore, the measurement is lagging by the delay measured.

In the *global detection algorithm*, a cluster-head uses a subset of the status indicators in local load balancing (see Figure 4b) to indicate its cluster's load balancing status. The only difference here is that a cluster is N/A if one or more edge brokers are N/A. This allows the overloaded brokers to offload subscribers to brokers within the same cluster first to promote locality. The global detection algorithm is almost the same as the local detection algorithm, except that the global detector uses different threshold values (namely, *global ratio triggering threshold* and *global delay triggering threshold*, both default to 0.15) and it works with aggregated performance metric values.

3.3   Mediation Protocols

All load balancing activities are coordinated by exchanging messages using the underlying publish/subscribe infrastructure for simplicity and efficiency. Specifically, request-reply and one-way protocols are implemented in publish/subscribe to coordinate broker and subscriber activities.

Mediating Load Balancing Sessions. Once the local detection algorithm composes the broker-action list of candidate brokers for load balancing, the *local mediator* sends a load balancing request sequentially to brokers in the sorted list. When a load-accepting broker gets this request, its local mediator replies back with its current status. If the status is *OK*, the request is accepted and both brokers update their status to *BUSY*. In the *OK* case, the load-accepting broker also appends its load information in the reply so that the requesting broker can use this information for its load estimation and offload algorithms to compute which subscribers are suitable for offload. For all other states, the load-accepting broker rejects the load balancing request. In general, two or more load balancing sessions between a pair of brokers can occur concurrently, but a broker cannot participate in multiple load balancing sessions at the same time.

The *global mediator* running at the cluster-head broker uses the same protocol as the local mediator to set up global load balancing. The difference here is that after a successful handshake, both cluster-heads have to tell all edge brokers in their own clusters to subscribe to the other cluster's local PIE messages. This allows edge brokers from one cluster to load balance with edge brokers in the other cluster. Global load balancing ends when all edge brokers are balanced with each other as indicated by the *balanced set* field in local PIE messages. Local PIE subscriptions of the other cluster are undone by unsubscribing when global load balancing ends.

Mediating Subscriber Migration. Once the offloading algorithm is done with its computation, it returns back to the mediator a list of subscribers to offload. The mediator has to migrate the indicated subscribers to the new broker in the most efficient and timely manner with minimal delivery loss. First, the mediator sends a control publication message to each subscriber in the offload list telling them to issue their subscription to the new load-accepting broker. Subscribers issue a subscription to the load-accepting broker containing the ID of the load balancing session and the total number of migrating subscribers. These two pieces of information allow the load-accepting broker to know when it has received all migrating subscribers in the current load balancing session. For efficiency and best-effort guarantee of minimal delivery loss, the receiving broker waits for $N \times$ *migration timeout* seconds for all migrating subscribers to connect, where N is the total number of migrating subscribers. Meanwhile, subscribers need to detect and drop duplicate publications (by using a short message history) because they are subscribing to the same subscription at two brokers simultaneously. When all subscribers have connected to the load-accepting broker, or when the timeout occurs, the receiving broker sends a DONE control publication message back to the offloading broker to terminate the load balancing session. This message ensures that the publication paths for all migrated subscribers have been set up to flow to the load-accepting broker. When the offloading broker receives the DONE message, it tells the migrating subscribers to wait for all the messages currently in its input queue to be matched and delivered from the output queues before sending an unsubscribe message. This waiting period corresponds to the offloading broker's current input queuing delay, plus the matching delay, plus the output queuing delay. Once the migrating subscribers unsubscribe from the offloading broker, the migration process is complete. Note that all control and duplicate messages are handled transparently by a thin software layer on the client side that hides the intricate details of load balancing from the end-user application.

4   Load Estimation Algorithms

Load estimation is used by the offload algorithms to estimate a subscription's load contribution in the form of additional input and output publication rate on the load-accepting broker as well as the load reduced at the offloading broker.

4.1   Estimating Load Requirements of Subscriptions

Padres Real-time Event-to-Subscription Spectrum[2] (PRESS) is a space and time-efficient technique for estimating the bandwidth requirements and common publication set of two or more subscriptions based on current events. It uses bit vectors to record the matching pattern of subscriptions, hence the term *event-to-subscription*. It does not require the publish/subscribe system to use advertisements, nor does it assume that publications are in any sort of distribution. The operation of PRESS is best explained as part of the local load balancing algorithm after the mediation step where two brokers have agreed to load balance with each other.

First, the offloading broker *locally subscribes* to the CSS of the load-accepting broker (as supplied in the *OK* reply message from the replying broker). Locally subscribe means that subscriptions are sent to the matching engine, but never get forwarded to neighboring brokers. This is sufficient because the offloading broker

---

[2] *Real-time* refers to sampling using live incoming publications to the broker.

Table 1. Bit vector example $(\ldots \Rightarrow [class,=,\text{`}STOCK\text{'}])$

(a) Candidate subscriptions to offload

Candidate Subscriptions	Bit Vector
[class,=,'STOCK']	110111
...,[volume,>,15]	110100
...,[volume,>,150]	100000
[class,=,'SPORTS']	001000

(b) Load-accepting broker's CSS

Load-Accepting Broker's CSS	Bit Vector
...,[volume,>,50]	110000
...,[volume,<,5]	000001
[class,=,'MOVIES']	000000
CSS bit vector	110001

only wants to know which publications it currently sinks are also received by the load-accepting broker. Next, all client subscriptions in the matching engine are allocated a bit vector of length N initialized to 0, where N represents the number of samples. Sampling starts immediately after getting the load-accepting broker's *OK* reply message and ends after N publications have been received or a timeout T is met, whichever comes first. Both N and T are configurable parameters which default to 50 and 30s, respectively. The algorithm starts at the right-most position of the bit vector for all subscriptions. A '1' is set if the subscription matched the incoming publication, '0' otherwise, before moving onto the next bit on the left. During the sampling period, the total incoming publication rate is measured. Tables 1a and 1b show an example of the bit vectors measured at the offloading broker with $N = 6$ for subscriptions at the offloading broker and load-accepting broker, respectively, given the following publication arrival order:

1. [class,'STOCK'],[volume,0]
2. [class,'STOCK'],[volume,10]
3. [class,'STOCK'],[volume,20]
4. [class,'SPORTS'],[type,'racing']
5. [class,'STOCK'],[volume,100]
6. [class,'STOCK'],[volume,500]

Equation 2 shows the formula to calculate the publication rate matching a particular subscription represented by s_{PR}, where i_r represents the total input publication rate of the offloading broker, n_{BS} represents the number of bits set in the subscription's bit vector, and N represents the number of samples taken in PRESS.

$$s_{PR} = i_r \cdot \frac{n_{BS}}{N} \qquad (2)$$

For example, if the total input publication rate i_r at the offloading broker is assumed to be 3msg/s, then for the subscription [class,=,'STOCK'] having 5 out of the 6 bits set, its publication rate comes out to 2.5msg/s. Moreover, the additional incoming publication rate for each subscription can be calculated by using Equation 2 with the bit count obtained from the *ANDNOT* bit operation of the candidate subscription's bit vector with the aggregated load-accepting broker's CSS bit vector. Take the subscription [class,=,'STOCK'] as an example. After the *ANDNOT* bit operation, the bit vector for [class,=,'STOCK'] is:

$$110111 \; ANDNOT \; 110001 = 000110 \qquad (3)$$

With a bit count of 2 in 000110, and reusing 3msg/s for i_r, the additional incoming publication rate on the load-accepting broker for this subscription is 1msg/s.

In some cases, offloading a subscription may alter the CSS of the load-accepting broker. With PRESS, it is not necessary to resample all subscriptions again because the aggregated CSS bit vector can be updated by merging it with the offloaded subscription's bit vector using the *OR* bit operator. For example, if [class,=,'STOCK'] was chosen for offloading, then the load-accepting broker's CSS is updated to 110111.

Regarding the space and time efficiencies of PRESS: if there are 10,000 subscribers with N set to 100, PRESS only uses 1Mb of memory. Given that the load-accepting broker's CSS is usually small (it is just one in the case of [class,=,*]), an increase in the matching delay is negligible.

4.2   Estimation of Performance Metrics

Matching delay is estimated by the linear formula [9]:

$$d'_m = \left(\frac{n + \Delta n}{n} \right) \cdot d_m \qquad (4)$$

where d'_m is the new matching delay, d_m is the current matching delay, n is the number of subscriptions in the matching engine, and Δn is the change in the number of subscriptions. Estimating the input and output utilization ratios can be done simply by using their original equations but with new estimated values for incoming message rate and output bandwidth consumption using PRESS, respectively.

5   Offload Algorithms

After profiling all subscriptions using PRESS, the offloading broker will use the profiled data along with the load-accepting broker's load information to feed into the offload algorithm to compute the set of subscribers to offload. The offload algorithm to choose depends on what performance metric to balance, which is decided initially by the detector in the broker-action list as mentioned in Section 3.2. Table 2 summarizes the key properties of the three offload algorithms.

5.1   Input Offload Algorithm

This algorithm is invoked by the offloading broker when the input utilization ratio needs load balancing. The aim here is to reduce the offloading broker's input utilization ratio and increase the same metric on the load-accepting broker with minimal effect on the other performance metrics. There are two strategies to reduce the input utilization ratio: increase the rate at which messages are matched, or reduce the rate of incoming publication messages. Increasing the rate of matching is achieved by reducing the number of subscriptions in the matching engine. However, this action conflicts with the match offload algorithm that is trying to balance the matching delay and therefore is not applied here. Hence, the incoming publication rate can only be reduced by offloading subscriptions

Table 2. Properties of all offload algorithms

Offload Algorithm	Performance Metric Being Balanced	Methodology	Side Effects
Input	Input utilization ratio	Offload subscriptions in the CSS	Output utilization ratio is also decreased at offloading broker and increased at load-accepting broker
Match	Matching delay Overloaded CPU utilization ratio Overloaded memory utilization ratio	Offload subscriptions with least traffic	None
Output	Output utilization ratio	Offload subscriptions with highest traffic in Phase-I	None
		Offload subscriptions with highest traffic and minimal side-effects in Phase-II	Increases input utilization ratio of load-accepting broker

in the CSS because their subscription space is a superset of all subscriptions not in the CSS. With the poset [4], CSS lookup will take O(1) time. Once the subscriptions in the CSS are identified, a report card is calculated for each of them. A report card consists of the following fields:

1. **Number of subscribers** of this subscription to offload.
2. Resulting **load percentage difference** between the two brokers by offloading this subscription, where a negative value indicates that the offloading broker will become less loaded than the load-accepting broker. This value is calculated using the estimated input utilization ratios of the two brokers in the input offload algorithm, matching delays in the match offload algorithm, and output utilization ratios in the output offload algorithm.
3. Boolean value indicating if this **subscription is covered** by the load-accepting broker's CSS.
4. **Publication rate reduced** at the offloading broker estimated using PRESS.
5. **Output bandwidth required** per subscriber estimated using PRESS.

The number of subscribers to offload per unique subscription is restrained by two conditions. First, the offload should not overload any of the load-accepting broker's resources. Second, the performance metric of interest of the two brokers should be balanced within the *balanced threshold*, which is 0.005 by default; or bring the offloading broker's metric below the load-accepting broker's. The performance metric of interest for the input, match, and output offload algorithms are the input utilization ratio, matching delay, and output utilization ratio, respectively.

After calculating the report cards to determine the number of subscribers to offload for each subscription in the CSS, the subscription that results in the two brokers' input utilization ratio difference closest to zero is chosen for offloading. This selection scheme ensures that subscriptions with the highest input publication rate are chosen first, which helps to reduce the number of subscriptions offloaded, and in so doing, reduces the impact on the load-accepting broker's matching delay. If all subscriptions will result in a higher load difference than before, then the selection process terminates. This guarantees that all load balancing actions will always converge to a state where the brokers have smaller load differences.

Subscriptions chosen to be offloaded are removed from the poset to prevent future consideration for offloading. Load information about both brokers (the one obtained in the mediation process) is updated with estimated values according to the offloaded subscription's report card. Updated load information about both brokers are used on the next iteration of the subscription selection algorithm. The selection process ends when no more subscriptions are available for offloading, the offloading broker's input utilization ratio is below that of the load-accepting broker, or the absolute difference between the two brokers' input utilization ratios fall within the *balance threshold*.

5.2   Match Offload Algorithm

Although the input utilization ratio varies directly with the matching delay, balancing the input utilization ratio does not balance the matching delay. The objective of this offload algorithm is to balance the matching delays without affecting the input and output utilization ratios of the two brokers. Intuitively, subscriptions with the lowest publication traffic are most suited to this criterion. Furthermore, subscriptions that introduce less incoming traffic into the load-accepting broker are more favorable. In this algorithm, report cards are computed for all subscriptions in the offloading broker, then they are sorted by ascending output bandwidth. The number of subscribers to offload for each unique subscription is almost identical to the algorithm outlined in the input offload algorithm section. The only difference is that input utilization ratios are replaced by matching delays.

If the match offload algorithm is invoked because the broker is overloaded and wants to reduce its CPU utilization ratio, input utilization ratio, or memory utilization ratio, then subscriptions should continue to be offloaded until the CPU utilization ratio, input utilization ratio, and memory utilization ratio drops below the lower overload threshold. After a subscription is chosen to be offloaded, load information about both brokers are updated. The same criterion used in the input offload algorithm applies here for terminating the match offload process.

5.3   Output Offload Algorithm

This algorithm attempts to balance the output utilization ratios of two brokers by manipulating the amount of output bandwidth used at each broker. Prioritizing subscriptions for the offload process is divided into two phases. In *Phase-I*, subscriptions that are covered by or equal to the load-accepting broker's CSS are considered. These subscriptions are further classified into three types by using the fields computed for every subscription's report card. Offloading *Type-I* subscriptions will reduce the input publication rate of the offloading broker. These should be offloaded first because they reduce the overall input load of the system. *Type-II* subscriptions are similar to Type-I, except that they do not reduce the input publication rate because all subscribers for a subscription cannot be offloaded to produce a more balanced state. *Type-III* subscriptions are considered last in Phase-I because they do not reduce the input publication rate of the offloading broker even if all subscribers for that particular subscription are offloaded. The algorithm for calculating the number of subscribers to offload for each unique subscription is similar to the input offload algorithm shown previously, except that input utilization ratios are now replaced by output utilization ratios.

After a subscription is chosen to be offloaded, load information about both brokers is updated. If both brokers are balanced, then the algorithm stops and forwards the subscriber migration list to the mediator. Otherwise, *Phase-II* is invoked to further balance the output utilization ratio with some side-effects. All subscriptions considered in Phase-II are not contained in the CSS of the load-accepting broker. Therefore, these subscriptions may have the side-effect of significantly increasing the incoming publication rate of the load-accepting broker. What may happen is that there will be an oscillation between the input offload algorithm trying to balance the input utilization ratio disrupted by Phase-II of the output offload algorithm, and Phase-II of the output offload algorithm trying to balance the output utilization ratio disrupted by the input offload algorithm. To prevent this unstable situation from happening, Phase-II terminates when the input utilization ratios of both brokers are balanced, even if the output utilization ratios are not. An exception applies if the offloading broker is output overloaded, in which case the offloading broker will stop offloading once its output utilization ratio is below the *lower overload threshold*. With this exception, no oscillation occurs because the offloading broker cannot take back any subscriptions since it has a status of *N/A* at the *lower overload threshold*.

The sorting and selection scheme in Phase-II is exactly the same as in the input offload algorithm with the use of load differences. If the subscription offloaded in Phase-II covers other local subscriptions, then Phase-I is invoked to offload those covered subscriptions because they are now covered by the load-accepting broker's CSS. Otherwise, if the subscription offloaded in Phase-II does not cover any other subscriptions, then Phase-II continues to run.

6   Experiments

6.1   Experimental Setup

The proposed load balancing solution is implemented with 20,000 lines of Java code in Padres [11], a distributed content-based publish/subscribe system developed by the Middleware Systems Research Group (MSRG) from the University

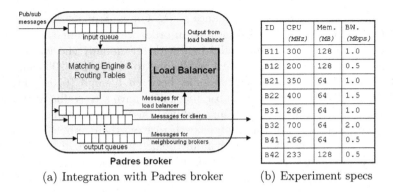

(a) Integration with Padres broker   (b) Experiment specs

Fig. 5. Evaluation scheme

of Toronto. The load balancer diagram previously shown in Figure 2 is integrated into the Padres broker as the *Load Balancer* component illustrated in Figure 5a. Our experiments are run with Padres brokers under a simulated environment that accounts for all processing delays such as matching, queuing, and bandwidth delays. Default values for the load balancing parameters are used unless otherwise specified. Publishers on creation are assigned to publish stock quote publications of a particular company at a defined rate. Publishers can be configured to change publication rates at any point in time in the experiment. Stock quote publications are real world values obtained from Yahoo! Finance containing a stock's daily closing prices. A typical publication looks like this:

```
[class,'STOCK'],[symbol,'YHOO'],[open,25.25],[high,43.00],[low,24.50],
     [close,33.00],[volume,17030000],[date,'12-Apr-96']
```

Subscribers are assigned to a fixed subscription based on one of the templates with the probabilities shown below. SUB_SYMBOL is randomly chosen out of the known stock symbols, with SUB_HIGH, SUB_LOW, and SUB_VOLUME replaced by a randomly chosen value of the same attribute from the stock's publication set.

```
20%   [class,=,'STOCK'],[symbol,=,'SUB_SYMBOL'],[high,>,SUB_HIGH]
20%   [class,=,'STOCK'],[symbol,=,'SUB_SYMBOL'],[low,<,SUB_LOW]
20%   [class,=,'STOCK'],[symbol,=,'SUB_SYMBOL'],[volume,>,SUB_VOLUME]
34%   [class,=,'STOCK'],[symbol,=,'SUB_SYMBOL']
5%    [class,=,'STOCK'],[volume,>,SUB_VOLUME]
1%    [class,=,'STOCK']
```

6.2   Local Load Balancing Experiments

The setup used for the local load balancing experiment involves four heterogeneous edge brokers connected to one cluster-head, labeled as *B0*, to form a star topology. *B0* has CPU speed of 2.0GHz with 256MB memory and 10Mbps bandwidth. *B1* has CPU speed of 100MHz with 64MB memory and 0.6Mbps. *B2* has twice the respective performance of *B1*, and *B3* has twice that of *B2*. *B4* has 10 times the respective performance of *B1*. On experiment startup, brokers *B0*, *B1*, *B2*, *B3*, and *B4* are instantiated in order within the first 0.5s. After 5s into the experiment, 40 unique publishers with a randomly chosen publication rate between 0 and 60msg/min start publishing to broker *B0*. 2000 subscribers join broker *B1* at a time chosen randomly between 10s and 1010s using a uniform random distribution. Of all subscribers, 25% have zero traffic, which means their subscriptions do not match any publications in the system. After 3000s, 50% of the publishers are randomly chosen to have their publication rates increased by 100%. This shows the dynamic behavior of the load balancer under changing load conditions. For the experiment on edge broker scalability shown in Figure 6g, all edge brokers have 500MHz CPU, 128MB memory, and 3Mbps bandwidth. All edge brokers are added to the same cluster.

Broker Load Distribution. Referring to Figures 6a, 6b, and 6c, broker *B1* becomes overloaded as all the subscribers attempt to connect to it as their first broker while *B1* attempts to offload them to other edge brokers simultaneously. At 1400s, *B1*'s utilization ratios drop to zero because it offloaded all subscriptions to counter the 100% CPU utilization ratio before that. Finally at 1800s, load balancing converges and all of the brokers' performance metrics are within the local triggering threshold, which was set to 0.1. The imbalance at 3000s is neutralized automatically by the load balancing algorithm and arrives at a balanced state at 3400s in the experiment. Although not shown here, by load balancing on the input and output utilization ratios, the input and output queuing delays are also balanced, respectively.

Client Perceived Delivery Delay. Figure 6d shows that an overloaded broker (*B1* in this case) can significantly increase the end-to-end delivery delay. In this experiment, the delivery delay is increased by 750 times. By having a load balancing algorithm in place, this overload period is dramatically reduced and high delay periods are minimized.

Subscriber Distribution Among Brokers. Figure 6e shows that the load balancing algorithm can account for heterogeneous brokers by assigning more subscribers to more powerful brokers. For instance, *B2* services twice as many subscribers as *B1* because *B2* is twice as powerful as *B1*. The same pattern is also observed for brokers *B3* and *B4* relative to *B1*.

Load Balancing Message Overhead. Figure 6f shows that the message overhead is 1.5% in the presence of load balancing from 1000s to 2000s, and 0.2% after load balancing has converged. Large spikes in this graph denote large batches of subscribers migrating at that instance in time. The decrease in overhead ratio in the first 2000s is because of the increase in publication traffic routed to new incoming subscribers.

Edge Broker Scalability. Figure 6g shows that by increasing the number of edge brokers in a cluster, the delivery delay is reduced because the load balancing algorithm evenly distributes load onto all available resources in the system.

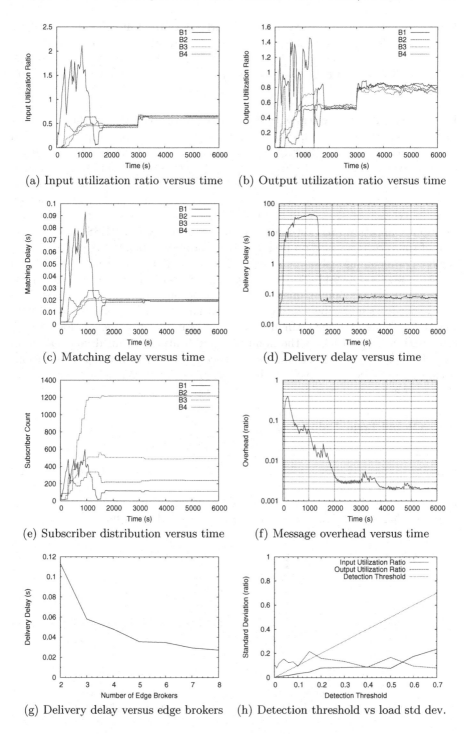

(a) Input utilization ratio versus time

(b) Output utilization ratio versus time

(c) Matching delay versus time

(d) Delivery delay versus time

(e) Subscriber distribution versus time

(f) Message overhead versus time

(g) Delivery delay versus edge brokers

(h) Detection threshold vs load std dev.

Fig. 6. Local load balancing results

Effect of Detection Threshold on Load Distribution. The input utilization ratio difference between all edge brokers is always kept well below the detection threshold as shown in Figure 6h. However, that is not the case for the output utilization ratio because of the stability constraint in the output load balancing algorithm.

Load Estimation Accuracy. Figure 7a shows the accuracy of the input utilization ratio estimation. Graphs for the matching delay and output utilization ratio estimation are not shown here because they have the same trends and exception cases as Figure 7a. Dots on the $y = x$ line denote 100% accuracy. Looking at the "offloading broker" and "load-accepting broker" data points, the input utilization ratio accuracy is the lowest of all three performance metrics with an average of 91%, including standard deviation. We expect the accuracy for input utilization ratio estimation to be lowest because PRESS' load estimation of the future is based on present data. Estimation points taken from $B1$ in the face of incoming subscribers are plotted using different point styles labeled as "B1 itelf" and "B1's load-accepting broker". These points are underestimated because load estimation does not account for the load imposed by newly incoming subscribers into the system that occurrs between 10s and 1010s. Figure 7b shows that the estimated input utilization ratio reaches closer to 0% error with less deviation as the number of publications sampled increases from 1 to 10. However, beyond 50 samples, the accuracy drops with higher deviations because publications sampled in the early stages no longer accurately portray the matching publication pattern of a subscription when sampling is done.

6.3   Global Load Balancing

The setup used for the global load balancing experiment involves 12 brokers organized into 4 clusters, with 2 edge brokers per cluster. Brokers $B11$ and $B12$ connect to their cluster-head $B10$, $B21$ and $B22$ connect to $B20$ as their cluster-head, and so forth for $B3x$ and $B4x$ clusters. Cluster-heads $Bx0$ connect to each other sequentially in a chain topology. All clusters have a cluster-head

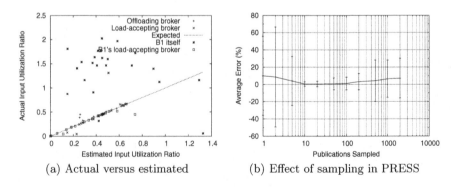

(a) Actual versus estimated   (b) Effect of sampling in PRESS

Fig. 7. Input utilization ratio estimation accuracy

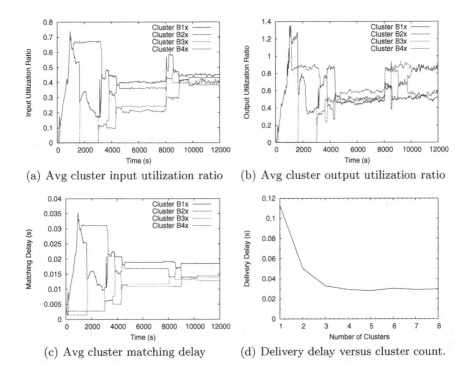

(a) Avg cluster input utilization ratio   (b) Avg cluster output utilization ratio

(c) Avg cluster matching delay   (d) Delivery delay versus cluster count.

Fig. 8. Global load balancing results

broker with 3000MHz CPU, 1GB RAM, and 10Mbps bandwidth. The CPU speed, memory size, and bandwidth of the edge brokers are given in Figure 5b. At the start of the experiment, all brokers join the federation. After 5s, 40 unique publishers with a randomly chosen publication rate between 0 and 60msg/min start publishing to broker *B10*. After 10s, 2000 subscribers join broker *B11*. Of the 2000 subscribers, 20% or 400 of them have zero traffic. At 8000s, 50% of the publishers are randomly chosen to have their publication rates increased by 100%. For the experiment on cluster scalability as shown in Figure 8d, each cluster has one cluster-head with 2GHz CPU, 512MB memory, and 10Mbps bandwidth; and two edge brokers with 500MHz CPU, 128MB memory, and 3Mbps bandwidth.

Cluster Load Distribution. The average load at each cluster is shown in Figures 8a, 8b, and 8c. Whenever a cluster performs global load balancing with another cluster, the two clusters' loads are merged on the graph because both clusters see the same set of edge brokers. Global load balancing takes longer to converge because the clusters are arranged in a chain topology which limits its parallelizing load balancing sessions. For example, cluster *B1x*'s load remains unchanged from 1000s to 3000s when *B2x* load balances with *B3x* as shown in Figure 8a. After 4500s, global load balancing converges, ending up with clusters further away from *B1x* having lesser load. The imbalance at 8000s results in a more balanced state for the input utilization ratios while the output utilization ratios diverges slightly to promote stability of the load balancing algorithm.

Cluster Scalability. When clusters are organized in a chain-like topology, there is a load diminishing effect on clusters further away from the source of load, namely cluster $B1x$. Figure 8d shows that with a global detection threshold of 0.15, clusters more than 3 cluster-hops away from cluster $B1x$ no longer reduce the overall delivery delay. This is consistent with the idea of preserving subscriber locality at the expense of a fully evenly loaded system.

7   Conclusions

In this paper, we presented a load balancing solution with three main contributions: a load balancing framework, load estimation methodologies, and three offload algorithms. The load balancing framework consists of the PEER architecture, a distributed load exchange protocol called PIE, and detection and mediation mechanisms at the local and global load balancing levels. The core of the load estimation is PRESS, which uses an efficient bit vector approach to estimate the input and output publication loads of a subscription. Each of the three offload algorithms are designed to load balance on a particular performance metric with minimal side-effects and proven stability. Both the load estimation and offload algorithms are independent of the load balancing framework. Our solution inherits all of the most desirable properties that make a load balancing algorithm flexible. PIE contributes to the *distributed* and *dynamic* nature of our load balancing solution by allowing each broker to invoke load balancing whenever necessary. *Adaptiveness* is provided by the three offload algorithms that load balance on a unique performance metric. The local mediator promotes *transparency* to the subscribers throughout the offload process. Finally, load estimation with PRESS allows the offload algorithms to account for broker and subscription *heterogeneity*. Experimental results show that our load balancing solution is well-controlled and effective at reducing high processing delays resulting from overload conditions while at the same time imposes minimal overhead.

In the near future, we plan on expanding our load balancing scheme onto cluster-head brokers, develop optimizations to our offload algorithms, and explore the possibilities of publisher migration in relation to load balancing.

Acknowledgements

Thanks to the Padres team members, in particular, Guoli Li, Shuang Hou, Vinod Muthusamy, Alex Wun, and Reza Sherafat Kazemzadeh for their assistance and comments. We are also very grateful to Serge Mankovski (CA), Cybermation/CA, Sun Microsystems, NSERC, and OCE/CITO for their support in this research.

References

1. T. Barth, G. Flender, B. Freisleben, and F. Thilo. Load distribution in a corba environment. In *Proceedings of DOA'99*, page 158, Washington, DC, USA, 1999.
2. F. Berman and R. Wolski. Scheduling from the perspective of the application. In *Proceedings of the HPDC'96*, page 100, Washington, DC, USA, 1996.
3. A. R. Bharambe, S. Rao, and S. Seshan. Mercury: a scalable publish-subscribe system for internet games. In *Proceedings of NetGames'02*, NY, USA, 2002.
4. A. Carzaniga, D. S. Rosenblum, and A. L. Wolf. Design and evaluation of a wide-area event notification service. *ACM TOCS*, 19(3):332–383, 2001.
5. R. Chand and P. A. Felber. A scalable protocol for content-based routing in overlay networks. In *Proceedings of NCA'03*, page 123, Washington, DC, USA, 2003.
6. Y. Chen and K. Schwan. Opportunistic Overlays: Efficient content delivery in mobile ad hoc networks. In *Proceedings of ACM Middleware'05*, 2005.
7. P. Costa, M. Migliavacca, G. P. Picco, and G. Cugola. Epidemic Algorithms for Reliable Content-Based Publish-Subscribe: An Evaluation. In *Proceedings of ICDCS'04*, pages 552–561, Tokyo, Japan, 2004.
8. D. M. Dias, W. Kish, R. Mukherjee, and R. Tewari. A scalable and highly available web server. In *Proceedings of COMPCON'96*, page 85, Washington, DC, 1996.
9. F. Fabret, H. A. Jacobsen, F. Llirbat, J. Pereira, K. A. Ross, and D. Shasha. Filtering algorithms and implementation for very fast publish/subscribe systems. *SIGMOD Rec.*, 30(2):115–126, 2001.
10. A. Gupta, O. D. Sahin, D. Agrawal, and A. E. Abbadi. Meghdoot: content-based publish/subscribe over P2P networks. In *Proceedings of ACM Middleware'04*, pages 254–273, NY, USA, 2004.
11. G. Li and H.-A. Jacobsen. Composite subscriptions in content-based publish/subscribe systems. In *Proceedings of ACM Middleware'05*, 2005.
12. M. J. Litzkow, M. Livny, and M. W. Mutka. Condor - a hunter of idle workstations. In *Proceedings of ICDCS'88)*, pages 104–111, 1988.
13. G. Mühl. Generic constraints for content-based publish/subscribe systems. In *Proceedings of CoopIS'01*, volume 2172, pages 211–225, 2001.
14. P. R. Pietzuch and J. M. Bacon. Hermes: A distributed event-based middleware architecture. In *Proceedings of the 1st International Workshop on DEBS*, 2002.
15. Vitria. http://www.vitria.com/.

Decentralized Message Ordering for Publish/Subscribe Systems

Cristian Lumezanu, Neil Spring, and Bobby Bhattacharjee

University of Maryland
College Park, MD 20742
{lume,nspring,bobby}@cs.umd.edu

Abstract. We describe a method to order messages across groups in a publish/subscribe system without centralized control or large vector timestamps. We show that our scheme is *practical*—little state is required; that it is *scalable*—the maximum message load is limited by receivers; and that it *performs well*—the paths messages traverse to be ordered are not made much longer than necessary. Our insight is that only messages to groups that overlap in membership can be observed to arrive out of order: sequencing messages to these groups is sufficient to provide a consistent order, and when publishers subscribe to the groups to which they send, this message order is a causal order.

1 Introduction

Publish/subscribe (commonly, "pub/sub") is a useful design approach for large-scale distributed information dissemination applications. Pub/sub systems support loosely-coupled asynchronous communication between information producers and consumers. Producers (publishers) inject messages into the system, which routes messages to consumers (subscribers) that register interest in certain messages using subscriptions. In this paper, we present a protocol for providing an *ordered view* of messages sent in a pub/sub system. The order we provide is maintained across groups and users.

System Model. Subscribers join *groups* that represent interests. The pub/sub system provides an API for nodes to **join** and **leave** groups, **send** messages to any group, and **receive** messages. Although it is reasonably easy to order messages to individual groups—simply elect a node to give each message a sequence number—ordering messages across groups is more challenging. Our ordering protocol enforces that the receive operation delivers messages in a consistent order across groups. More precisely, messages to groups that share subscribers are ordered so that the subscribers deliver messages to those shared groups in the same order.

1.1 Applications of Ordering

In the following applications, a centralized *coordinator* could order events. However, a single ordering authority limits feasible system size and introduces a single

M. van Steen and M. Henning (Eds.): Middleware 2006, LNCS 4290, pp. 162–179, 2006.

point of failure or compromise. We assert that a distributed protocol, such as the one we present, enables large deployment.

Network Games
Consider a multiplayer online game deployed using the publish/subscribe model [1], in which, for scalability, the virtual (game) world is divided into regions. Each player subscribes to the groups that represent nearby regions that it can affect or where events that can affect the player may occur [2,3]. If multiple players have overlapping areas of interest, they must see the common events in the same order to maintain consistency.

Ordered message delivery provides game consistency. Consider three players that are near enough to each other that every event *published* by one player will be received by the other two players. If one player shoots and hits another, all should see the events in order, else physical rules are violated. Causal ordering is essential for game correctness. However, unrelated events in distinct regions need not be ordered.

Stock Tickers
Consider an application in which messages correspond to stock market trades. Consumers at different brokerage firms may be interested in messages that satisfy different filters—by company size, geography, or industry, for example. The consumers will be members of groups based on their subscriptions, with every group receiving the same set of messages. An ordering protocol ensures that update operations that change state result in consistent states across the receivers that apply those updates in the same order.

Messaging
Internet messaging applications loosely follow the publish/subscribe model. For example, a user may choose to publish whether he is online or offline. Other users may subscribe to be notified of when a friend comes on-line by adding the user to their buddy list. A user may also join chat rooms (conferences) to converse with other users in the same rooms. Although ordering is not critical for "correctness" in messaging, enforcing that all messages appear in the same, likely causal, order should make such a system easier to use. For example, responses should always follow the messages to which they respond.

1.2   Overview of Our Ordering Protocol

We distribute the task of ordering messages across *sequencing atoms*. Sequencing atoms assign sequence numbers to messages addressed to groups that share subscribers. Our approach is scalable because sequencing atoms order no more messages than the most active receiver in the network—sequencing atoms exist to order the intersections of group memberships, so do not order more messages than receivers. We separate the task of sequencing across as many sequencing atoms as possible for flexibility in distributing load, then rely on placing related atoms on the same or nearby machines (*sequencing nodes*) to recover performance.

The insight that makes this possible is that the only destinations that can observe ambiguous order are those that subscribe to the same pairs of groups. Only messages to groups with at least two members in common must be ordered. By ordering those messages in the sequencing network and allowing unrelated messages to be ordered by end stations, we remove the requirement of centralized sequencing or long vector timestamps. The sequence numbers provided by sequencing atoms even allow events to be "committed" without ambiguity: receivers can tell when no prior messages are delayed.

For causal ordering, senders must subscribe to the groups to which they send. This requirement is simple and reasonable because receiving sent messages through the system also serves as an end-to-end reliability check. Our ordering is not total across all the users in the system: messages to unrelated groups may be delivered in any (perhaps globally inconsistent) order. Our distributed approach enables performance optimizations such as placing sequencers close to senders and receivers and trading message processing load against network load by combining sequencing atoms on the same node.

Our primary contribution is a method to order messages across groups of subscribers in a publish/subscribe system without centralized control. We present theoretical analysis to establish the correctness of our method and simulation results to verify its efficiency. Our broader goal is to develop primitives that improve the publish/subscribe model, that are scalable because they require no centralized servers or state, and that are practical by avoiding guarantees that applications do not need.

This paper is organized as follows. We survey related work in Section 2. We then describe the goals, assumptions, and procedures of our protocol in Section 3. We use simulations to measure performance in Section 4. We conclude in Section 5.

2   Related Work

The problem of ordered message delivery has been widely studied in distributed systems. Défago et al. [4] present an extensive survey, which we summarize here. Défago et al. organize algorithms by the assumptions they make on the underlying system (synchrony model, failure model, communication model, oracle model) and by the objectives they achieve. Here we focus on the ordering mechanisms.

Symmetric approaches are decentralized: each sender determines the order by appending information to all outgoing messages. The appended information reflects a causal order of messages, which may later be transformed into a total order using a predetermined function. Receivers use the attached information to decide whether to deliver or delay a message. Applications can append different types of information; most use timestamps or sequence numbers [5,6,7,8,9]. Including this information in each message typically requires nodes to keep a view of the messages they have received and sent.

In asymmetric protocols, order is built by a sender, destination, or sequencer. In sender-based protocols [10,11,12], the sender can multicast a message only when granted the privilege, *i.e.*, when it holds a token. In sequencer-based approaches, typically one node is elected as a sequencer and is responsible for ordering messages [13,14,15]. More than one sequencer can be present, but only one will be active or relevant at a time [16,17].

To preserve consistency among game states, networked multiplayer games enforce an unambiguous order of events. Typically, a centralized coordinator resolves all conflicts [18,19,20,21]. Although useful in a local area network, as the network grows, centralized approaches do not scale well and provide a central point of failure.

Although most work in decentralized ordering algorithms assumes only a single group, a few consider overlapping groups [14,22,23,24]. Our approach is closest to that of Garcia-Molina *et al.* [14]. In the taxonomy of this section, their approach is asymmetric and sequencer-based: they order messages as they deliver them through a tree of subscriber nodes. A total order of messages results when messages traverse this tree, assuming, among other typical assumptions for fault-tolerant behavior, that message delay is bounded. The graph is arranged so that messages are sequenced by the destination nodes that subscribe to the most groups, and the task of sequencing messages is overlapped with distribution. We separate these tasks to sequencing atoms, which may be placed on any nodes in the network, and to a distribution tree, which may be tailored to perform well despite distant nodes. Our sequencing atoms sequence only messages for double-overlaps, in which groups share multiple members in common, not all messages for a destination. Although we provide only causal ordering, we expect that our design makes it possible for sequencing atoms to marshal fewer messages and do less work for each message.

There has been little interest in applying these ordering protocols in distributed publish/subscribe systems [25,26,27,28]. As the network grows, centralized approaches do not scale because the sequencer becomes a bottleneck and central point of failure. Furthermore, token-based protocols introduce long delays when nodes must wait for the token or recover lost tokens. Distributed approaches based on vector timestamps are more scalable but they incur prohibitive network overhead due to the large timestamps. Our protocol is both scalable and incurs low overhead. By distributing the task of sequencing across a network of sequencers, we remove the requirement for a centralized coordinator or large vector timestamps. Unlike vector timestamp approaches, the additional information we append to each message does not depend on the size of the destination group and is proportional, in the worst case, to the number of groups.

3   Ordering Protocol

Our model of an ordered message delivery system consists of three phases: *ingress*, where messages move from senders to the sequencing network, *sequencing*, where messages traverse sequencing atoms while collecting sequence numbers, and *distribution* where packets leave the sequencing network and are sent to destination nodes. We focus on sequencing; existing multicast delivery schemes can support ingress and distribution.

Our goal is to ensure a consistent ordered delivery of messages to members of the same groups. A group is formed of all subscribers that share a common subscription. Our key observation is that when messages are sent to groups with overlapping membership, receivers may make inconsistent decisions about the order of those messages. We call groups that have two or more subscribers in common *double overlapped*, and our approach is to provide a sequence number space for each double-overlapped set of groups. These sequence numbers remove the possibility of inconsistent ordering decisions by receivers. By sending messages through sequencing atoms arranged into a sequencing network, the network determines the order of related messages in a decentralized way.

The sequencing graph is arranged so that sequencing atoms (also called sequencers) instantiated for double-overlapped groups form paths that group messages can follow. A group may have many sequencing atoms because it may have many double-overlaps with other groups. The paths of messages addressed to doubly-overlapped groups intersect at the sequencer associated with the overlap, ensuring that these messages are ordered.

Sequencing atoms are virtual. They need not be placed on different hosts; in fact, placing atoms on the same host may improve performance. A *sequencing node* is a machine that hosts sequencing atoms. We assume that the group membership matrix—which nodes belong to which groups—is globally known; it can be kept in a distributed data store such as a DHT or it can be provided by the underlying publish/subscribe system.

3.1   Operation

Each sequencing atom maintains the following state:

- A sequence number for its overlapped groups.
- A group-local sequence number for the groups it acts as ingress node for.
- A forwarding table to direct messages to the next sequencer for each destination group.
- A reverse-path table listing the previous sequencer in the network for each group.
- An output retransmission buffer for each subsequent sequencer.
- A buffer to store received messages from previous sequencers.

Upon receiving a new message from outside the sequencing network, a sequencer assigns it a group-local sequence number. The message can be forwarded immediately for distribution if its destination group has no double overlaps. Otherwise, if a group has a double overlap sequenced at this sequencer, the current sequence number for the overlap is added.

The message is then placed in the output buffer and transmitted to the next sequencer (if any) in the path for the group. The message can be removed from the buffer when this sequencer receives an acknowledgment from the next hop. We assume that there is a FIFO channel between any two sequencers. If the message is leaving the sequencer network, it will be sent to a delivery tree and on to group members.

This protocol provides two key properties. First, all members of the same group see messages in the same order, which is a causal order if the sender is also part of the group. Causal order expresses the "happens before" relationship among messages, as defined by Lamport [5]. Second, all destinations can make an immediate decision of whether to deliver or buffer arriving messages.

3.2   Sequencing Graph: Construction

The sequencing graph must meet two criteria:

C1: *A single path must connect sequencers associated with each group.*
C2: *The undirected sequencing graph must be loop-free.*

C1 ensures that each message is sequenced relative to all other groups with which the destination group shares a double overlap. When leaving the sequencing network, each message has sufficient information that it can be ordered relative to the messages to all overlapping groups. **C2** prevents messages from having circular dependencies, *e.g.*, message a before b, b before c, and c before a. A loop in the sequencing graph could allow an atom to make an ordering decision inconsistent with the ordering of messages not seen by that sequencing atom, as we illustrate with an example in the next subsection. The group- and sequencer-based sequence numbers and ordered inter-sequencer message channels ensure a consistent order of related messages at destinations.

Operations on a sequencing network include adding, removing, and modifying groups. They correspond to the operations of adding, removing and changing a subscription in the publish/subscribe system. When a subscriber node A adds a new subscription, if there is no other node with the same subscription, a new group is created with A as its only member. Otherwise, A joins the group that is associated with the subscription. Similarly, when A removes one of its subscriptions, it will leave the group associated with the subscription. If A was the only member of the group, the group is deleted.

We describe only addition and removal of groups; changing the graph when group membership changes can be accomplished by adding a group with the new membership and removing the old one. Figure 1 illustrates these operations.

Adding the first group G0 is trivial: an ingress-only sequencer is created—this sequencer orders all messages sent to the group. When the second group, G1 is added, if the memberships of G0 and G1 overlap with at least two nodes (are *doubly-overlapped*), a new sequencer, Q0, must represent G0 ∩ G1. All messages for both groups must transit this sequencer, and the G0-specific sequencer may be replaced or removed. This sequencer is *relevant* for all nodes in G0 ∩ G1; the rest need only use the group-local sequence number.

Adding each new group starts with the same basic procedure: a new sequencing atom is instantiated for any new double overlap. The new sequencing atoms must then be connected to the graph to form a path for the new group so that

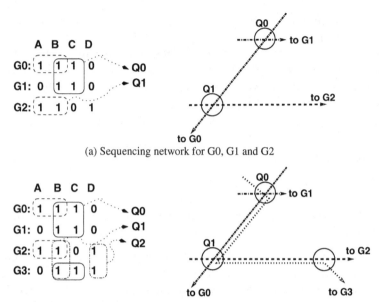

(a) Sequencing network for G0, G1 and G2

(b) G3 is added: Q0 and Q2 are associated to its overlaps; messsages to G3 are redirected through Q1 to avoid a loop in the sequencing graph

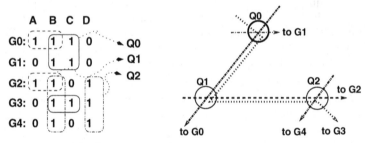

(c) G4 is added: messages to G4 traverse Q2 due to the overlap with G2 and G3

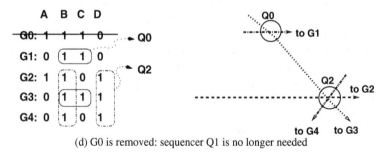

(d) G0 is removed: sequencer Q1 is no longer needed

Fig. 1. Adding and removing groups for a set of four nodes, A, B, C and D

C1 is satisfied. Unlike **C1**, **C2** is difficult to maintain using only local information. We use a global picture of the sequencing graph and subscription matrix state to find a new sequencer arrangement that satisfies **C1** and **C2**.

Removing a group may eliminate the overlaps that justify a sequencer's existence. Sequencers associated with a group can be removed lazily: adding ignored sequence numbers to a message does not hurt correctness, only efficiency. To remove a group, a termination message is sent to that group, signifying the end of the sequence space for that group, much like a TCP FIN. Each sequencer can inspect this termination message to determine if there is no longer overlap between the nodes this sequencer operates for. If the overlap is gone, the sequencer may retire by informing its parent to forward messages to its child for each sequenced group.

3.3   Sequencing Graph: Analysis

We present next an analysis of our protocol. We first describe how conditions **C1** and **C2** affect the sequencing graph and then we prove the unambiguity of the message delivery order across each group.

Let G be a group of subscribers that has double overlaps with other groups in the system. Each double overlap is associated with a sequencing atom and, according to **C1**, all the sequencers for the group form a single path in the sequencing graph. Since the graph is loop free and there are FIFO channels between each pair of sequencers, any order of arrival of two messages at a sequencing atom will be maintained by all the other sequencing atoms traversed by the messages afterward. We denote the sequence number assigned by sequencing atom Q to a message m addressed to group G by $Q(m)$ and the group-local sequence number with $G(m)$. The path of sequencing atoms traversed by a message m is $sp(m)$.

Definition 1. *Let G be a group with $|G| \geq 2$, let $A, B \in G$ and $M_{A,B}$ be the set of messages received by both A and B. We define a relation $\leq_{A,B}$ on the set $M_{A,B}$ such that $\forall m_1, m_2 \in M_{A,B}$, $m_1 \leq_{A,B} m_2$ if and only if $Q(m_1) \leq Q(m_2)$ when $sp(m_1)$ and $sp(m_2)$ have a common sequencer Q, or $G(m_1) \leq G(m_2)$ otherwise.*

Theorem 1. *$\forall G, \forall A, B \in G, A \neq B, \leq_{A,B}$ is a total order.*

Proof. $\leq_{A,B}$ is a total order if it is *reflexive, transitive, antisymmetric* and *total*. For simplicity we refer to $M_{A,B}$ and $\leq_{A,B}$ simply as M and $\leq_M$.

Reflexivity: $\forall m \in M$, $m \leq_M m$.
The property is obviously true.

Transitivity: $\forall m_1, m_2, m_3 \in M$ such that $m_1 \leq_M m_2$ and $m_2 \leq_M m_3$ then $m_1 \leq_M m_3$.
Case I: If all three messages are addressed to the same group, and traverse a sequencing atom Q then $m_1 \leq_M m_2 \Rightarrow Q(m_1) \leq Q(m_2)$ and $m_2 \leq_M m_3 \Rightarrow Q(m_2) \leq Q(m_3)$. Therefore $Q(m_1) \leq Q(m_3)$ and consequently $m_1 \leq_M m_3$. If the messages do not traverse a sequencing atom, transitivity is proved similarly using the group-local sequence numbers.
Case II: If two of the groups are identical and different from the third, there can be only one double overlap between them. All messages are sequenced by

the sequencer associated with the overlap and the proof is identical to the first subcase of *Case I.*

Case III: We now consider the case when messages are addressed to three different groups and travel on sequencing paths $sp(m_1)$, $sp(m_2)$ and $sp(m_3)$. Since a group may have different double overlaps with each of the other two groups, the sequencing paths pairwise intersect. Therefore the paths of m_1 and m_2 must have a common sequencing atom, Q_1, which establishes the order between the messages. The same applies for m_2 and m_3 (both sequenced by Q_2) and for m_1 and m_3 (sequenced by Q_3). If the paths have more than one common sequencing atom, we pick the one closest to the sender as the most significant one. Because the sequencing graph is loop-free, it is imperative that $Q_1 \subset sp(m_3)$, $Q_2 \subset sp(m_1)$ or $Q_3 \subset sp(m_2)$. We assume that $Q_1 \subset sp(m_3)$—for the other two cases the reasoning is similar. Then, message m_3 transits Q_1 (although it does not receive a sequence number from it). From the hypothesis, we have $m_1 \leq_{\mathcal{M}} m_2$ and $m_2 \leq_{\mathcal{M}} m_3$, therefore $Q_1(m_1) \leq Q_1(m_2)$ and $Q_2(m_2) \leq Q_2(m_3)$. Because m_2 arrives before m_3 at Q_2 and because the order of arrival of two messages at all sequencing atoms on a path must be consistent, m_2 arrives before m_3 at Q_1. m_1 arrives before m_2 at Q_1 and, using the transitivity of the "arrives before" relation, it results that m_1 arrives before m_3 at Q_1. The consistent arrival order on $sp(m_3)$ maintains this property at Q_3, which will assign a lower sequence number to m_1. Since $Q_3(m_1) \leq Q_3(m_3)$ then $m_1 \leq_{\mathcal{M}} m_3$.

Antisymmetry: $\forall m_1, m_2 \in \mathcal{M}$, if $m_1 \leq_{\mathcal{M}} m_2$ and $m_2 \leq_{\mathcal{M}} m_1$ then $m_1 = m_2$. If m_1 and m_2 travel through a sequencer Q then they will be assigned sequence numbers $Q(m_1)$ and $Q(m_2)$. If $m_1 \leq_{\mathcal{M}} m_2$ and $m_2 \leq_{\mathcal{M}} m_1$ then $Q(m_1) \leq Q(m_2)$ and $Q(m_2) \leq Q(m_1)$ and the total ordering of the natural numbers implies that $Q(m_1) = Q(m_2)$. A sequencing atom does not assign the same sequence number to two different messages therefore $m_1 = m_2$. If m_1 and m_2 do not traverse any sequencer they will be ordered based on the group local sequence number and the reasoning is the same.

Totality: $\forall m_1, m_2 \in \mathcal{M}$, either $m_1 \leq_{\mathcal{M}} m_2$ or $m_2 \leq_{\mathcal{M}} m_1$. Any two messages received by both A and B can either be addressed to a single group or to two different groups. If their destination is a single group, the group local sequence number will be used to establish a total order between them. On the other hand, if they go to two different groups, they have to traverse the sequencing atom instantiated by the overlap (A,B). The assigned sequence numbers are used to determine the order.   □

Any destination node can make an instant and deterministic decision of whether to deliver an arriving message to the application or to buffer it. The order of delivery is consistent over all members of the same group, but it does not reflect causal relationships between messages. This is because the sender and the receivers are completely decoupled and the ordering is enforced by the sequencing graph. We achieve causal ordering only when the sender is part of the group to which the message is sent. This happens because only then the sender can be aware of any *a priori* causal relationship between messages and can propagate it across the sequencing graph.

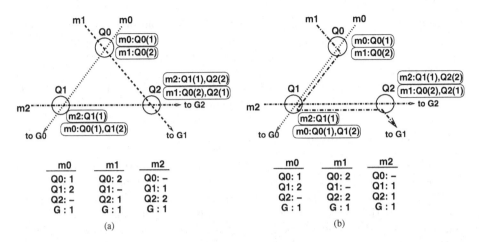

Fig. 2. Example of circular dependency among messages m_1, m_2 and m_3 and how it can be avoided; groups G0={A,B,D}, G1={A,B,C} and G2={B,C,D} are served by the sequencers Q0, Q1 and Q2. Each sequencer assigns a sequence number to each message that traverses it. (a) node B receives all three messages but cannot unambiguously decide on their order; (b) message m_1 is redirected through Q1 and the ambiguity is eliminated.

As mentioned in Section 3.2, a sequencing graph must meet two criteria to unambiguously order messages. The first condition, **C1**, is easy to justify: multiple paths create nondeterminism which may produce ambiguous sequence numbers for messages. We illustrate the need for the second condition through the following example.

Consider four nodes A, B, C, D and three groups with the following memberships: G0={A,B,D}, G1={A,B,C}, G2={B,C,D}. Figure 2(a) shows the resulting sequencing network—without **C2**—with the sequencers labeled Q0, Q1, Q2. Now, assume that messages m_0, m_1, m_2 are sent to groups G0, G1, G2. Without **C2**, these messages will gain inconsistent sequence numbers, shown in the table in Figure 2(a), by the following process. Messages m_0 and m_1 both traverse sequencer Q0 and receive a sequencer number. If m_0 reaches Q0 first, it is tagged with sequence number 1 and m_1 tagged 2. Next, they continue on the path towards the destination group, m_0 sent to Q1 and m_1 to Q2. Meanwhile message m_2 is sent to G2 and reaches sequencer Q1 before message m_0. Thus, at Q1, m_2 is tagged with 1 and m_0 with 2. So far, message m_0 passed through both Q0 and Q1, being assigned sequence numbers 1 and 2. Because these were the only two sequencers through which it had to pass, m_0 can now be delivered to the members of G0, nodes A, B and D. Message m_2, on the other hand is forwarded to Q2. If the connection between sequencers Q1 and Q2 is very slow compared to the one between Q0 and Q2, m_2 reaches Q2 after m_1 does. Then, at Q2, m_1 receives sequence number 1 and m_2 sequence number 2. We show in the table from Figure 2(a) the sequence numbers of each of the three messages after they exit the sequencing network. Because each is the first and only message sent to its group, all have group sequence number 1. As the table shows, the three messages have a circular dependency. B cannot deliver m_0 because it waits for m_1, which cannot be delivered because of m_2, while m_2 depends upon the successful delivery of m_0.

We eliminate the circular dependency in Figure 2(b) by redirecting message m_1 through sequencer Q1 to make the sequencing graph loop free, condition **C2**.

3.4   Placing the Sequencing Atoms

Randomly scattering sequencing atoms throughout the network would lead to poor performance: because messages must traverse the path of sequencing atoms for the group, many needless network hops would result. We have developed a two-step heuristic for co-locating sequencing atoms on the same machines. The heuristic is based on the relationship between the double overlaps associated to the sequencing atoms. In the first step, we place on the same machine any sequencing atoms whose corresponding overlaps have a subset relationship between them. For example, let there be two sequencing atoms, Q1 and Q2, such that Q1 is associated to an overlap containing nodes A, B and C and Q2 corresponds to an overlap formed by A and B. Since {A,B} ⊂ {A,B,C}, Q1 and Q2 are co-located on the same node. In the second step of the heuristic, we also co-locate overlaps that do not have subset relationships between them but share at least a common node as follows. For each overlap, we choose at random one of its nodes, find all other overlaps that contain the chosen node and place the corresponding sequencing atoms on the same machine. We impose the restriction that each sequencing atom be co-located only once. This arrangement of sequencing atoms on the same sequencing node preserves our scalability goal—that no sequencing machine sees more messages than the most loaded receiver—without needlessly distributing related sequencing atoms throughout the network.

The selection of the machine on which to place a related set of sequencing atoms is also important. Ideally, we want to minimize the extra delay that a message experiences when it traverses the sequencing path. We abstract a related set of sequencing atoms by a sequencing node and we seek to find an optimal mapping between sequencing nodes and physical machines. We propose a simple heuristic that is run on behalf of each group as follows:

- if no sequencing node associated to the group has been assigned to a physical node yet, assign one at random
- if there are sequencing nodes already assigned to machines, then pick the closest unassigned sequencing node on their sequencing paths and assign it to neighboring machines.

The heuristic tries to put neighboring sequencing nodes on a sequencing path on close machines in the publish/subscribe infrastructure. This placement makes messages traverse relatively few extra hops to be ordered and helps us show that acceptable performance is feasible.

4   Results

In this section, we present simulation results to validate the performance of our ordering scheme. We only focus on the properties of the protocol when group membership is static or does not change very often.

4.1   Experimental Setup

We developed a packet-level discrete event simulator to evaluate the sequencing protocol. We simulated using a 10,000 node topology generated by GT-ITM [29]. The simulator models the propagation delay between routers, but not packet losses or queuing delays.

We attach hosts to the topology by grouping them into similar size clusters, then distributing each cluster uniformly at random through the topology. Nodes in the same cluster are placed close to each other. We choose this mapping because it is consistent with online communities, in which users tend to cluster around the lowest-latency server. We do not place any constraints on the publish/subscribe system that uses the ordering scheme. Messages travel from publishers to subscribers on the shortest path and any router in the topology can serve as a forwarding node. This is acceptable because our experiments are concerned only with the characteristics of the ordering layer. We are interested in measuring the penalty in performance that our primitive introduces with respect to the underlying layer. The mapping between the sequencing graph and the underlying infrastructure is done using the heuristic described in Section 3.4. Better heuristics may give better results—our intent in this section is to show that acceptable performance is possible.

We vary the number of end-hosts between 32 to 128, and each host can subscribe to zero or more groups. We vary the number of groups from 8 to 32. We rank the groups based on their size and we generate the size of each group using a Zipf distribution with exponent 1. The sizes are proportional to the function $r^{-1}/H_{n,1}$, where r is the rank of the group, n is the number of hosts and $H_{n,1}$ is the generalized harmonic number of order n of 1. We choose the Zipf distribution because it is known to characterize the popularity of online communities [30,31]

4.2   Latency Stretch

We evaluate the extra delay messages encounter when traversing the sequencing network compared to taking the shortest unicast path. We measure the *latency stretch*: the ratio between the time taken for a message to traverse the network using the sequencers and the time taken using the direct unicast path. Similar metrics have been described by Chu *et al.* [32] (RDP) and Castro *et al.* [28] (RAD). RAD is defined per group and RDP per sender-destination pair; we believe latency stretch better represents the performance of our protocol because it captures the delay penalty of an individual node, when the node requires unambiguous delivery. To measure the latency stretch, each node sends a message to each of the groups it is part of, first using the sequencer network and then

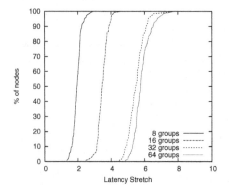 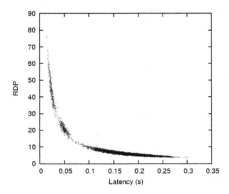

Fig. 3. Latency stretch for 128 subscriber nodes, when varying the number of groups

Fig. 4. Ratio between sequencing and unicast delay for each sender-destination pair versus the actual unicast delay, for 128 subscribers and 64 groups

directly. We average the results and index them by destination nodes. We leave group membership fixed during the experiment.

Figure 3 presents the cumulative distribution of the latency stretch computed for 128 nodes subscribing to 8, 16, 32, and 64 groups. When there are fewer groups, the sequencing network is smaller and traversing it takes less time. For example, when we used 8 groups, latency stretch did not exceed 2.5. As the number of groups increases, so do the number of overlaps and the number of sequencing nodes that must be traversed. The growth is sub-linear: for 64 groups, the maximum latency stretch observed is less than 8. We quantify next how the increase in delay incurred by ordering is distributed with respect to the actual latency between the publisher and its subscribers. For this we compute the Relative Delay Penalty (RDP [32])—the ratio between the sequencing and unicast delay for each sender-destination pair—and plot it against the corresponding unicast delay between the sender and the destination. Figure 4 shows the results for 128 subscribers arranged in 64 groups. The highest values for RDP correspond to the pairs in which the sender and the destination are very close to each other.

Increased delivery time in exchange for guaranteed order among messages is an inherent tradeoff of our approach. Delaying message delivery may be acceptable for Internet messaging or stock ticker applications, but generally it affects negatively the performance of network games. However, this section presents worst case results because we overestimate the performance of unicast: shortest unicast paths are rarely followed. To obtain faster delivery, the mapping of the sequencing graph should take into account the requirements of the applications that need ordering as well as the characteristics of the pub/sub infrastructure.

4.3   Sequencing Nodes

We next consider how adding groups affects the number of sequencing nodes and the stress on each node. We might worry that the number of sequencing

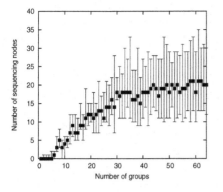 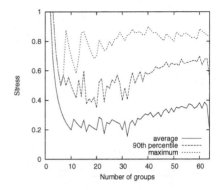

Fig. 5. Number of total sequencing nodes for 128 subscriber nodes, when varying the number of groups. Error bars indicate 10th and 90th percentiles.

Fig. 6. Ratio between number of groups associated to a sequencing node and total number of groups, when varying the number of groups

nodes and the number of groups associated with each of them would increase exponentially as we add more groups; such a protocol would be impractical. To simplify presentation, we consider only the sequencing nodes that host non-ingress-only sequencers: each group has at most one ingress-only sequencer, so the ingress-only sequencers may grow at most linearly with the number of groups.

Figure 5 shows the average number of sequencing nodes created as we vary the number of groups. We vary the number of groups formed by 128 subscriber nodes from 1 to 64, and run the experiment 100 times. The error bars range from 10th to 90th percentile. As the number of groups increases, there are more overlaps and thus more sequencing nodes. After 30 groups, the number of sequencing nodes grows more gradually because many of the new overlaps have common members with existing overlaps, and so can be mapped to existing sequencing nodes.

We define the stress of a sequencing node as the ratio between the number of groups for which it has to forward messages and the total number of groups. A sequencer with a stress value of 1 forwards messages to all groups. In Figure 6, we present the average, 90th percentile and maximum values of stress as the number of groups increases. We observe the same behavior as in Figure 5. Initially, as we add more groups, we also add more sequencing nodes and the stress decreases and stabilizes around the value 0.2. After 30 groups, when the number of sequencing nodes increases more slowly, the stress slightly increases because there are more groups to be sequenced by the same number of sequencing nodes. The heuristic we used to map sequencing atoms to sequencing nodes makes sure that all the groups associated to a sequencing node share at least a member. As such, the load of this member is an upper bound for the load on any sequencing node that lies on the path to it.

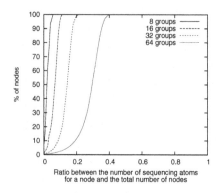
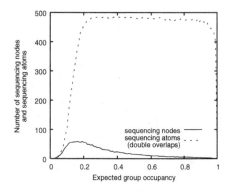

Fig. 7. Ratio between the number of sequencing atoms for each node and the total number of nodes, for 128 subscribers

Fig. 8. Number of sequencing nodes and double overlaps vs. expected occupancy of groups, for 128 subscriber nodes and 32 groups

4.4 Sequencing Atoms on a Path

Although the number of sequencing nodes remains small, the number of overlaps, and thus sequencing atoms, grows large. The size of the graph in atoms is less important, however, than the number of atoms each message must traverse, which represents how many sequence numbers a message must collect. Our approach is most attractive when the path length through the sequencing network is smaller than the number of nodes; that is, when the message overhead of sequence numbers provided by the sequencing network is less than that of system-wide vector timestamps. We compute the ratio between the number of sequencing atoms on a path and the total number of nodes, for different group sizes, and present it as a cumulative distribution in Figure 7. In the worst case, the number of sequencing atoms in the path of a message is less than half of the total number of nodes that participate. The path length through the sequencing network is bounded by the total number of groups, since a group can have an overlap with at most each of the other groups. As a result, our sequencer-based approach is attractive whenever the number of nodes exceeds the number of groups.

4.5 Varied Occupancy

Although we use a Zipf distribution to generate group sizes because we believe it models likely usage, we also wanted to explore worst-case usage scenarios. We define the expected occupancy as a measure of the density of the group membership. The value of the expected occupancy can be interpreted as the probability that a node is member of a group: an occupancy of 0 means that all groups are empty, while an occupancy of 1 means that every node subscribes to every group. Using 128 nodes and 32 groups, we vary the expected occupancy between 0 and 1 to see if the sequencing network approach is more efficient at some group densities.

Figure 8 illustrates how the expected occupancy of groups affects the average number of double overlaps and sequencing nodes. As the expected occupancy increases, the number of double overlaps and necessary sequencing nodes increase until approximately 0.2 occupancy. Beyond this, increasing group densities creates double overlaps that have common members with existing overlaps, and the number of sequencing nodes gradually decreases. When the group densities are very high (above 0.9), the overlaps include the entire population and the number of sequencing nodes drops to one.

5   Conclusion

Our primary contribution is a method for ordering messages in a pub/sub system without centralized control and without vector timestamps. We showed that it is practical and scalable, because little local and global state is maintained, because sequencing atoms can be placed to achieve good performance relative to a centralized sequencer, and because sequencing nodes order no more messages than destinations receive. Our insight is that only messages to groups with two or more common members must be ordered, and this provides a causal ordering when senders also subscribe.

This approach forms a new primitive for publish/subscribe systems. To investigate its applicability, we plan to apply the idea to the realistic workloads of these and other systems and measure when group membership is (or can be) geographically-correlated. We also intend to more completely understand the dynamic behavior of our algorithm. When changes in the group membership are infrequent or along existing patterns, we expect very little churn in the sequencing graph. However, we want to determine whether sequencing networks perform well even when incrementally updated as groups and nodes join and leave very often.

References

1. Bharambe, A.R., Rao, S., Seshan, S.: Mercury: A scalable publish-subscribe system for Internet games. In: NetGames. (2002)
2. Hu, S.Y., Liao, G.M.: Scalable peer-to-peer networked virtual environment. In chang Feng, W., ed.: NETGAMES, ACM (2004) 129–133
3. Morse, K.: Interest management in large-scale distributed simulations. Technical report, UC Irvine (1996)
4. Défago, X., Schiper, A., Urbán, P.: Total order broadcast and multicast algorithms: Taxonomy and survey. In: ACM Computing Surveys. (2004)
5. Lamport, L.: Time, clocks and the ordering of events in a distributed system. Communications of the ACM (1978)
6. Schiper, A., Eggli, J., Sandoz, A.: A new algorithm to implement causal ordering. In: 3rd International Workshop on Distributed Algorithms. (1989)

7. Peterson, L.L., Buchholz, N.C., Schlichting, R.D.: Preserving and using context information in interprocess communication. ACM TOCS **7**(3) (1989) 217–246

8. Dolev, D., Dwork, C., Stockmeyer, L.: Early delivery totally ordered multicast in asynchronous environments. In: 23rd Int'l Symposium on Fault-Tolerant Computing (FTCS-23). (1993)

9. Birman, K.P., Joseph, T.A.: Reliable communication in the presence of failures. ACM TOCS **5**(1) (1987) 47–76

10. Amir, Y., Moser, L.E., Melliar-Smith, P.M., Agarwal, D.A., Ciarfella, P.: The Totem single-ring ordering and membership protocol. ACM TOCS **13**(4) (1995) 311–342

11. Cristian, F.: Asynchronous atomic broadcast. In: IBM Technical Disclosure Bulletin. (1991)

12. Rajagopalan, B., McKinley, P.: A token-based protocol for reliable, ordered multicast communication. In: 8th Symposium on Reliable Distributed Systems (SRDS). (1989)

13. Kaashoek, M.F., Tanenbaum, A.S.: An evaluation of the Amoeba group communication system. In: ICDCS. (1996)

14. Garcia-Molina, H., Spauster, A.: Ordered and reliable multicast communication. ACM TOCS **9**(3) (1991) 242–271

15. Schiper, A., Birman, K., Stephenson, P.: Lightweight causal and atomic group multicast. ACM TOCS **9**(3) (1991) 272–314

16. Chang, J.M., Maxemchuk, N.F.: Reliable broadcast protocols. ACM TOCS **2**(3) (1984) 251–273

17. Whetten, B., Montgomery, T., Kaplan, S.M.: A high performance totally ordered multicast protocol. In: Selected Papers from the International Workshop on Theory and Practice in Distributed Systems. (1995)

18. Gautier, L., Diot, C.: Design and evaluation of mimaze, a multi-player game on the Internet. In: IEEE Int'l Conference on Multimedia Computing and Systems. (1998)

19. Ishibashi, Y., Tasaka, S., Tachibana, Y.: A media synchronization scheme with causality control in networked environments. In: IEEE LCN. (1999)

20. Ishibashi, Y., Tasaka, S., Tachibana, Y.: Adaptive causality and media synchronization control for networked multimedia applications. In: IEEE ICC. (2001)

21. Iimura, T., Hazeyama, H., Kadobayashi, Y.: Zoned federation of game servers: a peer-to-peer approach to scalable multi-player online games. In: NETGAMES. (2004)

22. Jia, X.: A total ordering multicast protocol using propagation trees. IEEE Trans. Parallel Distrib. Syst. **6**(6) (1995) 617–627

23. Ezhilchelvan, P.D., Macedo, R.A., Shrivastava, S.K.: Newtop: a fault-tolerant group communication protocol. In: ICDCS. (1995)

24. Aguilera, M.K., Strom, R.E.: Efficient atomic broadcast using deterministic merge. In: PODC. (2000)

25. Carzaniga, A., Rosenblum, D.S., Wolf, A.L.: Design and evaluation of a wide-area event notification service. ACM TOCS **19**(3) (2001) 332–383

26. Aguilera, M.K., Strom, R.E., Sturman, D.C., Astley, M., Chandra, T.D.: Matching events in a content-based subscription system. In: PODC. (1999) 53–61

27. Pietzuch, P., Bacon, J.: Hermes: A distributed event-based middleware architecture. In: 1st International Workshop on Distributed Event-Based Systems (DEBS'02). (2002)

28. Castro, M., Druschel, P., Kermarrec, A.M., Rowstron, A.I.: Scribe: A large-scale and decentralized application-level multicast infrastructure. IEEE Journal of Selected Areas in Communication (2002)
29. Zegura, E., Calvert, K., Bhattacharjee, S.: How to model an internetwork. In: IEEE Infocom. (1996)
30. Wolman, A., Voelker, G.M., Sharma, N., Cardwell, N., Karlin, A.R., Levy, H.M.: On the scale and performance of cooperative web proxy caching. In: SOSP. (1999)
31. Breslau, L., Cao, P., Fan, L., Phillips, G., Shenker, S.: Web caching and zipf-like distributions: Evidence and implications. In: INFOCOM. (1999)
32. Chu, Y.H., Rao, S.G., , Zhang, H.: A case for end system multicast. In: ACM Sigmetrics. (2000)

DBFarm: A Scalable Cluster for Multiple Databases

Christian Plattner[1], Gustavo Alonso[1], and M. Tamer Özsu[2]

[1] Department of Computer Science
ETH Zurich, Switzerland
{plattner,alonso}@inf.ethz.ch
[2] David R. Cheriton School of Computer Science
University of Waterloo, Canada
tozsu@uwaterloo.ca

Abstract. In many enterprise application integration scenarios, middleware has been instrumental in taking advantage of the flexibility and cost efficiency of clusters of computers. Web servers, application servers, platforms such as CORBA, J2EE or .NET, message brokers, and TP-Monitors, just to mention a few examples, are all forms of middleware that exploit and are built for distributed deployment. The one piece in the puzzle that largely remains a centralized solution is the database. There is, of course, much work done on scaling and parallelizing databases. In fact, several products support deployment on clusters. Clustered databases, however, place the emphasis on single applications and target very large databases. By contrast, the middleware platforms just mentioned use clustered deployment not only for scalability but also for efficiently supporting multiple concurrent applications. In this paper we tackle the problem of clustered deployment of a database engine for supporting multiple applications. In the database case, multiple applications imply multiple and different database instances being used concurrently. In the paper we show how to build such a system and demonstrate its ability to support up to 300 different databases without loss of performance.

Keywords: database clusters, scalability, replication, consistency.

1 Introduction

In many enterprise application integration scenarios, middleware has been instrumental in taking advantage of the flexibility and cost efficiency of clusters of computers. There exists a plethora of middleware solutions to create distributed deployments and to parallelize a wide range of application types. In addition, distributed deployment across a cluster of machines is most effective when the same platform can be used for concurrent applications. Thus, platforms such as J2EE or .NET are clearly designed to be used with multiple concurrent applications. In spite of this, the piece of the puzzle that still mostly remains a centralized solution is the database. Even though there is much work done in the area of cluster and parallel databases [20], the emphasis is always on improving access to a single database. This is not a trivial distinction. The problem with single instance optimizations is that they often conflict with the goal of supporting multiple database instances. For instance, crucial to be able to exploit clusters is the ability to

M. van Steen and M. Henning (Eds.): Middleware 2006, LNCS 4290, pp. 180–200, 2006.

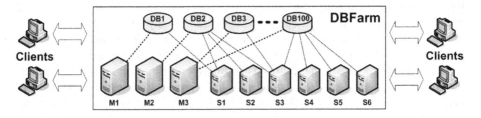

Fig. 1. Managing 100 Databases (DBx) on a DBFarm using 3 Master (Mx) and 6 Satellite (Sx) Servers. Each Database is installed on one Master and may be replicated on different Satellites.

freely move resources from machine to machine as needed and allocate more or less machines to different applications as load fluctuates. In the single database case, the clients simply connect to that database. In a cluster based solution, clients should see a single image of the system even when databases are dynamically moved around. Similarly, efficient use of the resources of the cluster imply that database instances might share computing nodes. Care must be taken that work on one instance does not negatively affect work on a different instance. Finally, clients should always see a consistent state but consistency needs to be accomplished without limiting the scalability of the cluster and without introducing unacceptable overhead.

These constraints point out to the need for some form of middleware based solution since database optimizations mostly apply to single instances and somebody has to coordinate the access to multiple, independent instances. The challenge in building such a middleware based solution is that it must be very light weight so as not to limit scalability. Handling, for instance, 100 databases each running 100 transactions per second does not allow to spend too much time on each transaction (and our goal is to scale well beyond that). Yet, that same middleware must guarantee consistency and a single system image.

In this paper we describe the architecture and implementation of *DBFarm*, a cluster based database server implemented as a thin middleware layer that can be used to support several hundred database instances. DBFarm is based on using two kinds of database servers: master database servers (see Figure 1) and satellites. Master servers can be made highly reliable by using specialized hardware, RAID systems, hot stand-by techniques, and sophisticated back-up strategies. This provides the necessary reliability and does it in a way that the resources are shared among all databases. Scalability is then provided by a cluster of unreliable satellite machines where copies of the individual databases are placed. A key aspect of DBFarm is that the users of the databases are not aware of the fact that they may be working with an unreliable copy rather than working on the master database. DBFarm ensures that they see a consistent state at all times. Another key feature of DBFarm is that the load distribution between the master databases and the satellite copies is done based on the read/write characteristics of the operations requested by the users. Writes are performed at the master databases, reads at the copies. This workload distribution allows to significantly reduce the load at the masters (and thus, be able to support a larger number of databases on the same machines) while providing a high level of parallelization for the satellites (and, thus, the basis for high scalability). The distribution also reflects the characteristics of most database loads where updates tend to be small operations with high locality while read-only transactions typically cause much more I/O (to retrieve data and indexes) and computation overhead (to perform operations such as joins, order, averages, or group by).

The feasibility and advantages of this approach are demonstrated through an extensive set of experiments. We show how DBFarm provides more stable and scalable performance (in both response time and throughput) for a set of up to 300 TPC-W databases than a stand alone database server installation. We also show the performance of DBFarm using the RUBBoS benchmark (much larger databases with a more complex load) and discuss how to assign priorities to individual databases so that they get a better performance than others.

In terms of applications, DBFarm can be used in a wide variety of settings. It can be used to turn a cluster of machines into a database service that is provided within a LAN setting (a company, a university), thereby localizing the maintenance and administration of the databases and the machines on which they run. It can also be used to implement database services as part of an Application Service Provider where small or medium companies place their databases at a provider's DBFarm. The sharing of resources implicit in DBFarm makes this an efficient solution and its simple scalability enables the support of a large number of users.

Our work exploits a novel form of replication and load distribution that is well suited to many modern applications such as web servers. Unlike many existing solutions, it provides consistency while remaining light weight. DBFarm does not involve complex software or hardware layers (e.g., specialized communication infrastructures, shared disks) or requiring the modification of the application (e.g., special clustering of the data or submission of complete transactions). Our approach also includes innovative algorithms for transaction routing across a database cluster that avoid many of the limitations of current database replication solutions. Finally, DBFarm provides a highly scalable clustering solution for databases.

2 Architecture

2.1 Load Separation

In order to provide scalability in databases, the load must be distributed across a number of machines. This is a well know problem in replicated, distributed and parallel databases. In DBFarm the added complication is that the load separation must happen on a per database instance basis while still maintaining consistency. There are many ways to implement load separation in single instance settings. [2, 5] use versioning and concurrency control at the middleware level to route transactions to the appropriate machines. [17] relies on clients to produce a well balanced load over a cluster, different cluster nodes are then synchronized using group communication primitives. [13, 18] assumes the database schema has been pre-partitioned into so called conflict classes, which are then used for load separation. [1] requires clients to specify the freshness level of the data and directs transactions to different nodes according to the freshness of the nodes (i.e., how up-to-date they are). This approach, however, already assumes that clients do not want to see the most up-to-date state and, thus, represents a relaxation of concurrency.

Unfortunately, none of these methods is feasible in the context of a multi instance cluster. Duplicating concurrency control at the middleware layer would result in a prohibitive overhead per transaction (aside of a complex maintenance issue since the middleware would have to be aware and maintain versioning and schema information for hundreds of instances). Group communication as a way to distribute load and maintain consistency is also out of the question because of the overhead of membership (each instance would have its own group membership) and the implicit synchronization of cluster nodes. Similarly, the use of conflict classes requires to parse the incoming transaction load to identify the conflict class being accessed which will immediately put a limit on the number of transactions the middleware can route per second.

The load separation approach used in DBFarm is a direct consequence of these restrictions. Rather than relying on schema or data partition information, we simply distinguish between read-only and update transactions. Update transactions are those that perform an update in the database (can nevertheless contain many read operations as well). Read-only transactions are those that do not result in a state change at the database. Such a load separation can be efficiently implemented at the middleware level without having to parse the statements of the transactions and without the need to maintain information on the schema of each database instance in the cluster. Such a separation also has important advantages. The update transactions determine the state of each instance and define what is consistent data. We only need this stream of transactions to determine correctness and consistency. Read-only transactions are used to provide scalability by re-routing them to different cluster nodes in the system. This is based on the nature of many database benchmarks (e.g., TPC-W or RUBBoS) that are used as representative loads and where the load is clearly dominated by read-only transactions (at least 50% of the transactions in most database benchmarks and typically far more complex than update transactions).

Load separation based on read/write transactions results in scalability that is limited only by the proportion of reads and writes in the load. Thus, DBFarm will not provide any scalability to a database with 100% updates (but such load also results in no scalability for any replicated solution -not just DBFarm- and would severely tax existing parallel database engines). However, in the common case that read-only transactions dominate the load, DBFarm provides significant scalability.

2.2 Master and Satellite Servers

As a direct result of the load separation technique used, DBFarm adopts a per instance primary copy, lazy propagation strategy. The primary copy of an instance is called the master database. Master databases are always located on master servers (*masters*). A master server processes all the update transactions of the hosted master databases. As such, it is always up-to-date. Each master database is responsible for maintaining its internal consistency using its own concurrency control and recovery mechanisms. Copies of the master databases (so called *satellite copies*) are placed in *satellite* servers. Satellites are used exclusively for executing read-only transactions. Hence, what is a consistent state is always dictated by the master servers. As a direct result, recovery of failed satellites and spawning of new database copies is not a complex issue in DBFarm (unlike other approaches where the transfer of state for creating or removing a copy involves complex synchronization operations [12, 17]). In addition, the master database of an instance is the fall back solution. If all copies fail, the master server allows clients to continue working on a consistent version of the managed data (albeit with a reduction in performance).

Generally, we assume the masters to be large computers with enough resources (main memory and disk capacity) to accommodate a large number of databases (see the experimental section for details). We also assume the masters to be highly available based on either software or hardware techniques. The capacity of a master will determine how many different databases can be supported by that master and how high the overall transaction load can be. DBFarm reaches saturation once all masters reach the limit of update transaction streams they can process. At that point, and unless they submit exclusively read-only transactions, clients cannot increase the rate at which they submit transactions since the speed at which the update part of the load is processed is determined by the masters which, at saturation, have no more available capacity. Scalability can, however, be easily increased by adding more masters and redistributing the databases across these machines.

Satellites in turn do not need to be as powerful as the masters, nor need they to be very reliable. There can be an arbitrary number of database copies in each satellite. Scalability for a single master database is provided by having copies in multiple satellites. The limit in scalability, aside of the limit imposed by the proportion of updates in the load, is reached when each concurrent read-only transaction executes in its own satellite server. Beyond that, additional copies will remain idle. Such an extreme degree of distribution can nevertheless be employed in a cluster without loss of efficiency by placing copies of different instances on the same satellite. Since satellites might be shared by different database copies, no resources are wasted because each copy is executing a single read-only transaction. On the other extreme, in DBFarm it is possible for an instance to be centralized and without any copy. In such a case, the master processes both the update and the read-only transaction streams for that database.

An advantage of the approach taken in DBFarm is that it provides a solution for realistic database applications. The master servers host normal databases. User defined functions, triggers, stored procedures, etc. can all be placed at the masters and do not need to be duplicated at the satellites. Most existing database replication solutions assume such features are either not used (e.g., when concurrency control or versioning happens at the middleware level) or require that they are replicated across all copies and behave deterministically at all cluster nodes - something not entirely feasible in the case of triggers in most existing database engines (e.g., when update propagation is done with group communication).

2.3   Transaction Scheduling in DBFarm

While the load separation approach of DBFarm enables scalability and makes sure that the master databases are always up-to-date, it does not by itself guarantee consistent views when copies are being accessed. Therefore, as long as no other measures are taken, the consistency from the client point of view will depend on how the transactional load generated by a client is split into read-only and update streams and how these streams are forwarded to the different database machines in the cluster.

From a client's perspective, what matters is what has been called _strong session serializability_ [8]. Briefly explained, strong session serializability requires that a client always sees its own updates. In other words, a read-only transaction from a given client must see not only a consistent state but one that contains all committed updates of that client. This prevents the client from experiencing _travel-in-time_ effects where suddenly a query returns correct but stale data. Although in principle strong session serializability would be enough, the approach we take in DBFarm goes a step beyond and makes sure that a read-only transaction executed at a copy will see all updates executed at the master database up to the point in time the read-only transaction has arrived at the system. In doing so, DBFarm effectively becomes transparent to the clients[1] since they will always read exactly the same they would have read using a single database server.

For simplicity in the explanations, and without loss of generality, we describe the details of the DBFarm transaction scheduling with a single master database server. As clients communicate only with masters, they are not aware of any satellites. Therefore, incoming read-only transactions need to be forwarded by the master to the satellites in a way that consistency is guaranteed. Update transactions for a given database instance are executed locally on the master database. The result is, conceptually, a series of consistent states of the database each of which contains the updates of all the transactions committed up to that point. The master takes advantage of this conceptual ordering by capturing the writesets of update transactions in commit order. A writeset is a precise representation of what has been changed (i.e., the tuple id and the new value). The master then uses this commit order to forward the writesets to all needed satellites using FIFO queues. Satellites then apply these writesets in the same order they are received. It is easy to see and formally prove that, if the execution of transactions at the master database was correct, then the application of changes to a copy in the commit order established by the master guarantees that the copy will go through the same sequence of consistent states as the master database and will eventually reach the same correct state as the master database.

Conceptually, the way this is done in a DBFarm is as follows. For every successful committed update transaction, the master sends back to the client a commit acknowledgment message. The latest sent commit acknowledgment therefore reflects the oldest state that any client should see when sending the next transaction. Hence, if DBFarm sends a commit acknowledgment to a client that executed transaction T_k, then all later incoming read-only transactions from any client must observe a state of the database that includes the effects of writeset WS_k (the writeset that includes the changes done by transaction T_k). Therefore, once a request for a read-only transaction arrives at the master, the master can deduce (by keeping track of the sent commit acknowledgment messages) the minimum state of the database that the read-only transaction must observe. Of course, the management of tracking commit acknowledgment messages and assuring consistency for read-only transactions must be done by DBFarm for each database separately. A possible approach to ensure that a read-only transaction sees no stale data

---

[1] Of course, by giving up transparency and using less strict forms of consistency, the system could offer even more scale-out for read-only transactions.

Algorithm 1: Master Transaction Handling

```
 1: INPUT DB: Database Name
 2: INPUT T: Incoming Transaction
 3: INPUT M: Mode of T, M ∈ {Read-Only, Update}

 4: if M == 'Update' then
 5:     /* T must be executed on the master */
 6:     Start a local update transaction in database DB
 7:     for all Incoming statements S in T do
 8:         if S == 'ROLLBACK' then
 9:             Abort the local transaction
10:             Send abort response back to client
11:             RETURN
12:         end if
13:         if S == 'COMMIT' then
14:             ENTER CRITICAL SECTION
15:             Commit the local update transaction
16:             if Commit operation failed then
17:                 LEAVE CRITICAL SECTION
18:                 Abort the local update transaction
19:                 Send error response back to client
20:                 RETURN
21:             end if
22:             Determine T's commit number CN
23:             Set CN(DB) := CN
24:             LEAVE CRITICAL SECTION
25:             Send successful commit reply to client
26:             Retrieve T's encoded writeset WS from DB
27:             Forward (DB, WS, CN) to all satellites that
                host a copy of database DB
28:             RETURN
29:         end if
30:         Execute S locally
31:         if Execution of S fails then
32:             Abort the local transaction
33:             Send error response back to client
34:             RETURN
35:         end if
36:         Send result of S back to client
37:     end for
38: end if
39: /* T is Read-Only, try to execute on a satellite */
40: if ∃ satellite N with a copy of DB then
41:     Use load balancing to select a satellite N
42:     MIN_CN := CN(DB)
43:     Forward (DB, T, MIN_CN) to N
44:     Relay all incoming statements S in T to N
45:     RETURN
46: end if
47: /* Need to execute T locally */
48: Start a local read-only transaction in database DB
49: for all Incoming statements S in T do
50:     if S ∈ {COMMIT, ROLLBACK} then
51:         Commit the local read-only transaction
52:         Send response back to client
53:         RETURN
54:     end if
55:     Execute S locally
56:     if Execution of S fails then
57:         Abort the local read-only transaction
58:         Send error response back to client
59:         RETURN
60:     end if
61:     Send result of S back to client
62: end for
```

Algorithm 2: Satellite Transaction Handling

```
 1: INPUT DB: Database Name
 2: INPUT T: Incoming Transaction
 3: INPUT CN_MIN: Min. committed State needed to exe-
    cute T

 4: Wait until CN(DB) ≥ CN_MIN
 5: /* Execute T locally in read-only mode */
 6: Start a local read-only transaction in database DB
 7: for all Incoming statements S in T do
 8:     if S ∈ {COMMIT, ROLLBACK} then
 9:         Commit the local read-only transaction
10:         Send response back to client
11:         RETURN
12:     end if
13:     Execute S locally
14:     if Execution of S fails then
15:         Abort the local read-only transaction
16:         Send error response back to client
17:         RETURN
18:     end if
19:     Send result of S back to client
20: end for
```

Algorithm 3: Satellite Writeset Application

```
 1: INPUT DB: Database Name
 2: INPUT WS: Writeset
 3: INPUT CN: Committed State produced by WS

 4: Turn WS into a set of SQL statements
 5: Wait until CN(DB) == (CN - 1)
 6: Start a local update transaction in database DB
 7: Apply the produced SQL statements
 8: Commit the local transaction
 9: if Application of WS failed then
10:     Report ERROR to the master
11:     Disable further processing for database DB
12:     RETURN
13: end if
14: Set CN(DB) := CN
```

is to block it on the master and then only forward its operations to the target satellite once it has reported the successful application of all needed writesets. However, this approach has several disadvantages: first, there is additional logic, communication and complexity; second, the master must implement transaction queuing; third, overhead is introduced due to the round-trip times of the involved messages and, as a result, read-only transactions may be unnecessarily blocked. In practice, the way the system works achieves the same result but without blocking transactions longer than needed and without imposing additional load on the master. The solution is based on a *tagging mechanism.* Every time an update transaction commits, the master not only extracts the writeset, but also atomically creates an increasing number which gets shipped together with the writeset. We call this number the *change number* for database DB (denoted by $CN(DB)$). Note that the change number is no longer client specific but applies to all update transactions executed on the database. When re-routing read-only transactions to satellite nodes, the master *tags* the begin operation of such transactions with the current change number of the respective database. This number is also maintained for the copies of database DB: if a satellite applies a writeset to a copy, then the copy is known to have achieved the writeset's assigned change number.

A satellite that receives a tagged read-only transaction will only start executing it after it has applied the needed writesets. This is how we make sure a read-only transaction sees all updates performed up to the point it starts executing, not only those from that particular client. The blocking of read-only transactions is therefore delegated to the satellites, where it can be efficiently handled.

It is important to note that other than checking that every read-only transaction observes the newest consistent state, no concurrency control is needed outside the databases and scheduling therefore has a low overhead in our approach. This is in contrast to existing replication strategies that require additional concurrency control and versioning mechanisms outside the databases [2, 6, 18].

The details of the algorithms used by DBFarm to handle transactions on the master and satellite servers, as well as writeset handling, are given in algorithms 1, 2 and 3.

Algorithm 1 describes the routing on a master. Lines 4-38 handle update transactions. These are executed locally on the master, statement by statement, until the client either decides to *rollback* (abort the transaction, in line 8) or to commit (line 13). In case of a rollback, the transaction can simply be aborted on the master. No further action is required. If the client wishes to commit, then the master commits the transaction on the master database DB, extracts the encoded (compressed) writeset and forwards it to all satellites that keep a copy of the database. Also, the master atomically updates the $CN(DB)$ value. The handling of read-only transactions is described in lines 39-62. Basically, such transactions are always tagged with $CN(DB)$ and re-routed if possible. If no copies are available, then the transaction has to be executed on the master.

Algorithms 1 and 2 describe the handling of read-only transactions and writesets on the satellites. Line 4 in algorithm 2 is where we make sure that read-only transactions never observe stale data. Transactions re-routed to satellites are always started in read-only mode. If a client inside a declared read-only transaction tries to update database elements, then the underlying database will automatically abort the transaction.

3 Implementation

The current implementation of DBFarm runs on top of PostgreSQL 8.1. The core part of DBFarm are the *adapters*, which are distributed middleware components used to integrate the concepts of the previous section (see Figure 2). As the adapters make up the main component of our implementation we are going to describe them first.

3.1 The Adapter Approach

Clients access the DBFarm by establishing a connection to an adapter at a master server. If the requested database instance is not locally hosted as a master database, then the connection is transparently forwarded to the correct master. Database copies hosted on satellites are not directly accessible by the clients. In Figure 2 the adapter on the master (the *master adapter*) intercepts all incoming client connections and re-routes read-only transactions to satellites. The actual routing is more fine grained, since clients never send transactions as a block. The master adapter therefore needs to inspect the data stream on each client connection and handle operations accordingly. To be able to identify read-only transactions the master adapter assumes that clients use the standard SQL mechanisms to either declare the whole session as read-only or decorate the begin operation of submitted read-only transactions with the *READ ONLY* attribute. In Java clients, for example, this can be forced by executing the *Connection.setReadOnly()* method. If a client does not give any information, then the adapter assumes that the client is starting an update transaction.

The master adapter also extracts the latest changes produced by each update operation (the *writesets*) from the master databases and sends them to the corresponding satellite adapters. In contrast to [6] we use writesets rather than the original SQL update statements since it has been shown that they are a more efficient way to propagate changes in replicated systems [14]. The writesets consist of a compact, encoded description of the tuples that need to be inserted, changed or deleted. At the target adapter, they are translated and executed as a minimal set of SQL statements. The extraction of the writeset for a given transaction occurs after the transaction commits and it is done for the entire transaction. Thus, when the master adapter propagates changes, it does so for all the changes of a given transaction.

Adapters on the satellites (*satellite adapters*) receive operations from read-only transactions and execute them on the locally installed copies making sure that consistency is preserved. To maintain consistency, satellite adapters constantly apply the received writesets and respect the tags at the beginning of re-routed read-only transactions.

Upon startup, each adapter configures and starts the local PostgreSQL installation (each PostgreSQL installation typically contains several master databases or satellite copies). All needed PostgreSQL configuration files are then dynamically generated so that the PostgreSQL database software only binds itself to the local *loopback* network interface. As a result, all PostgreSQL installations are not accessible by clients directly from the network. After the local PostgreSQL installation is up, the adapter connects to it and scans for installed databases. As a last step, the adapter starts its own listener on the external network interface. However, unless an adapter has been further configured by the administration console, it denies all client requests - until then it is simply not aware if it is running as a master or satellite. Information about the overall DBFarm configuration is at this stage centralized and provided by the administration console. Only after a master has been informed by the administration console about its mode and about other masters and the available satellite adapters (and the database copies that they host) it can establish all needed writeset and transaction re-routing connections and is then ready to process client transactions.

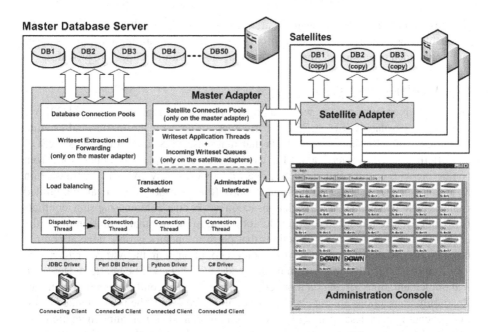

Fig. 2. Adapters in an example DBFarm with one Master Server and a set of Satellites

Currently, only the master adapters distribute read-only transactions across the satellites, for load-balancing purposes a round-robin assignment is used. At a later point of time, we plan to explore more sophisticated assignments to improve overall performance. The need for more sophisticated assignments arises from the fact that some read-only transactions may take a long time to execute (hours in some cases). If the scheduling would take load into consideration, it would do a better job distributing the incoming transactions. Nevertheless, for the purposes of demonstrating the characteristics of DBFarm, round robin scheduling suffices.

For efficiency reasons, connections from the master to other adapters are organized in pools: for each local database and for each known peer adapter there is a connection pool. The reason for using a pool for each local database (instead of one pool for the whole PostgreSQL installation) lies in a limitation of the PostgreSQL on-wire protocol: one cannot switch the selected schema and database user after a connection has been established and authenticated. Connections to other adapters are mainly used for two purposes: first, to send tagged read-only transactions and second, to stream writesets to the satellites. Connections are generated lazily; once a connection is no longer used, it will be put back into its pool. Pooled connections that are not used for a certain period of time will be closed and removed.

The adapters have been implemented as a thin layer of Java software. The software for the master and satellite adapters is the same, however, depending on its configuration an adapter either acts as the master or a satellite. The advantage of having identical adapters at both master and satellites is that it will eventually also allow us to move a master to one of the satellite machines. This makes DBFarm more dynamic but also changes the properties of the resulting architecture since the satellites are, in principle, unreliable. For reasons of space we do not further pursue such an approach in this paper but use the idea to emphasize the flexibility that the DBFarm architecture provides.

3.2 Assuring Consistency

Following up on our previous work on consistent database replication [23, 24, 22], we use snapshot isolation (SI) [3, 25] as correctness criteria for the master and satellite databases. Common database products that make use of SI are Oracle, PostgreSQL and Microsoft SQL Server 2005. SI is used to prevent complex read operations from conflicting with updates and viceversa. The way it works is by giving every transaction a snapshot of the database at the time it starts (the snapshot contains all committed changes up to that point). Since each transaction works on a different snapshot, conflicts between concurrent reads and writes do not occur. In the original definition of SI, the check for conflicts between transactions that perform updates is only done at commit time: if concurrent transactions try to modify a common item, the *first committer wins rule* is applied (the first one to commit succeeds, all others will be aborted). However, real implementations all rely on more efficient, incremental conflict detection methods. Read-only transactions are not checked for conflicts. SI avoids the four extended ANSI SQL phenomena as described in [3] (which is a prerequisite for an implementation of a SERIALIZABLE isolation level). However, one has to be aware that this is not the same as the classic definition of conflict serializability, e.g., as given in [4]. Fortunately, this does not impose problems in real applications, e.g., [11] has shown that transactions can be re-structured so that running them in SI based databases leads to serializable executions.

Using SI makes it relatively simple to implement consistency requirements by DBFarm to provide clients with a consistent view. Since a read-only transaction is executed in a copy using SI and the copy will provide consistent snapshots, a read-only transaction will always read a snapshot that has existed in the master database. This has important practical advantages since it allows a copy to constantly keep applying updates without having to abort or interfere with concurrently running read-only transactions from the clients.

3.3 PostgreSQL Frontend

In the current implementation of DBFarm a master adapter, as seen from the client side, looks like a normal PostgreSQL installation (the adapter listens on TCP port 5432). We have implemented server and client-side support for the low-level PostgreSQL protocol. The server side is used to implement the PostgreSQL frontend end, the client side is used to communicate with the locally installed PostgreSQL databases. When routing transactions between different adapters, the adapters use a slightly extended variant of the PostgreSQL client/server protocol (e.g., it is possible to switch the database schema/user for the current connection and transactions can be tagged with commit numbers; in addition, the mechanism for transportation of writesets was added).

Since master adapters implement the standard PostgreSQL server interface, DBFarm can be used by a plethora of application types and platforms: C, C++, Java, Perl, Phyton, .NET (with the PostgreSQL ADO provider), etc. - actually every application that is designed to be used with PostgreSQL. In fact, it can be used with already existing applications without requiring any changes as long as those applications use the standard PostgreSQL interface. This is in sharp contrast to other replication proposals, where clients need to be changed (or need special drivers) to be able to use the database system (e.g., [6, 17, 2]).

3.4 Writeset Extraction

We have implemented and tested different variants of writeset extraction. Currently, DBFarm supports two approaches. The basic, generic approach, is similar to what is being done in other systems (e.g., [6]): we simply collect all DML (data modification language) statements of transactions in the master adapter and use them as writeset. This method was only used for testing, since it has many open problems. For instance, one cannot handle updates that have been produced by triggers, since those are not visible to the adapter. Also, there are problems with statements that instruct the database to insert function based values into tuples (e.g., random numbers or the current time in milliseconds, which will, obviously, not lead to the same result when being executed on different cluster nodes).

The second approach is based on triggers: we have implemented a shared library which can be loaded into PostgreSQL at run-time. The library contains functions which will then be assigned by the master adapters as triggers to all tables that need replication. Whenever there is a change on a table, then our trigger function will capture the new values - no matter if the change was directly provoked by the user or by a stored procedure inside the database. The writeset is then simply collected in memory. At the end of a transaction a master adapter can then call another function in the shared library to extract the writeset. This is very fast, since writeset collection does not involve any disk accesses. Our implementation is also able to capture schema changes due to DDL (data definition language) commands (e.g., table and index creation) and to produce special writesets which lead to the corresponding changes of the database schema on the copies.

To keep different database copies synchronized, other replication systems often replay the server's complete redo-log on the replicas - e.g., [29] have implemented this for PostgreSQL. Unfortunately, such an approach only works for very simple setups, where each replicated PostgreSQL installation has the same content and page layout. This considerably reduces the flexibility. In DBFarm, the source and destination PostgreSQL installations may contain different sets of databases, and therefore we need to extract and apply writesets per database. Currently, we are working on an approach where it is possible to extract the redo-information for a subset of the databases in a PostgreSQL installation.

3.5 Administration Console

The administration console has been implemented as a platform independent graphical Java application. It is used to remotely start, stop and configure the adapters. Furthermore it helps to inspect the state of each cluster node. All communication between the administration console and the DBFarm cluster nodes is encrypted. What we require is that each node runs an OpenSSH [19] daemon. To be able to use the SSH-2 protocol from within Java, we use our own open source, pure Java SSH-2 client library [21].

4   Performance Evaluation

In general our approach makes no restrictions on how resources can be shared across different databases. However, in this paper we only evaluate the performance of static setups where a single powerful server hosts all master databases and a set of smaller, less reliable satellites are used to host the read-only copies. We present the results from our experiments involving a DBFarm deployment that uses 360 customer databases on a master database server and up to 30 additional satellite machines to offer improved performance for clients.

To produce realistic measurements, we used database setups based on two different standard benchmarks: TPC-W (as defined by the Transaction Processing Council [28]) and RUBBoS (defined by the Object Web Consortium [26]). The TPC-W benchmark models customers that access an online book store, while RUBBoS models a bulletin board similar to the Slashdot website [27]. For TPC-W we use the default *shopping mix* workload which consists of 80% read-only interactions. The workload defined by the RUBBoS benchmark consists of 85% read-only interactions.

We installed 300 TPC-W databases (using scaling factors 100/10,000, which results in 497 MB per database) on the master server, as well as 60 RUBBoS databases (using the *extended data set*, which results in 2,440 MB disk consumption per database). The denoted sizes include all the diskspace needed for a given single database (e.g., including index files). The overall disk space occupied by these databases on the master machine exceeds 417 GB. All databases were reasonably configured with indexes.

The master database server is a dual Intel(R) Xeon CPU 3.0 GHz machine with 4 GB RAM and an attached RAID-5 (ICP-Vortex GDT8586RZ PCI controller with 5 Hitachi HDS722525VLAT80 SATA 250 GB disks) which results in 931 GB of available space (we use a XFS partition which spawns the whole RAID-5), running Fedora Core 4 (2.6.13-1.1532smp). The thirty satellite machines have dual AMD Opteron(tm) 250 processors (2.4 GHz), 4 GB RAM and a Hitachi HDS722512VLAT80 disk (120 GB). These machines run Red Hat Enterprise Linux AS release 4 (2.6.9-11.ELsmp). All machines are connected with 100MBit links over a local area network (all machines are attached to the same ethernet switch). The adapter software was run with the Java-Blackdown 1.4.2-02 JVM. We used an unmodified version of PostgreSQL 8.1 for all experiments.

To measure the performance of our setups we use a Java based loadclient software that is able to reproduce the database loads that are generated by the TPC-W and RUB-BoS benchmarks. One has to emphasize that we are not running the entire benchmarks, but only the database part to stress DBFarm (e.g., a full TPC-W implementation would also have to measure the performance of the used web- and application servers).

The loadclient uses worker threads to simulate a number of clients. On startup, the loadclient generates a pool of connections to the target databases on the master. If the number of workers is less than the number of target databases, then for each database one connection is put into the pool. Otherwise, the loadclient generates connections

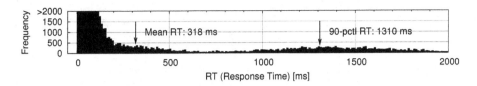

Fig. 3. A Section from an example Histogram

to the target databases in a round-robin fashion, until the amount of connections is as large as the set of worker threads. Also, for each connection per target database there is a state machine that dictates the next transaction type to be executed. Each worker thread, in an endless loop, randomly chooses a connection from the pool and executes a transaction according to the connection's state machine. After the transaction has been executed, the worker puts the connection back into the pool. It is important to note that between the executions of the different transactions the workers use no thinking time - each worker is intended to stress the tested setup as hard as possible.

When benchmarking the system, the loadclient uses varying numbers of workers. Whenever the number of workers changes, the loadclient uses a warm up time of several minutes until the system is stable. Then, a benchmarking phase of two minutes follows. During the benchmarking phase, the loadclient measures the response times for all executed transactions. At the end of a run it reports the mean response time as well as the 90-percentile response time. The data points in the following figures represent such runs.

To be able to calculate the 90-percentile response time, the loadclient keeps an internal histogram for each experiment. Please refer to Figure 3 for an example. The figure only shows a section of the overall collected historical data - internally the loadclient keeps track of all measured response times with a 1 ms resolution over the range from 0 to 20 seconds.

4.1 Part A: Handling Many Concurrent Databases

In the following experiments we show that DBFarm is able to handle situations where many databases are being accessed concurrently. We use a set of satellites to execute expensive read-only transactions, and therefore we can reduce the number of page fetches on the master. At the same time, more resources are available for update transactions on the master. In the experiments we use a simple satellite setup - for each database on the master we created only one satellite copy. These copies were then evenly spread over the available satellites.

Results for TPC-W. In these experiments we compared the achievable performance for a large amount of TPC-W databases that are accessed concurrently. First, we used the loadclient to stress the master alone. Then, we put the DBFarm system in place and measured the performance again.

In the first experimental round we used 100 concurrent TPC-W databases (Figure 4). One can observe that the master server already is at its limits with 300 concurrent

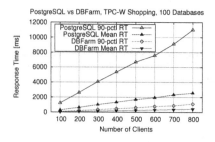
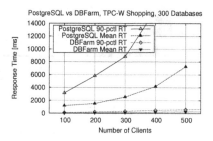

Fig. 4. TPC-W Results for 100 Databases   **Fig. 5.** TPC-W Results for 300 Databases

TPC-W shopping workers, since a mean response time of 1 second and a 90-percentile response time of almost 4 seconds is probably not acceptable for most interactive applications.

By applying the same load to DBFarm with 10 attached satellites (each containing 10 database copies), one can observe that the system is able to scale-up to a much higher number of concurrent clients while at the same time giving acceptable response times. These results are particularly telling since there is only one copy of each master database. Performance could be improved even more by adding more satellite machines and having 2 copies for each master database.

With the DBFarm setup, each satellite hosts 10 TPC-W database copies. This makes up a data set of about 5 GB that has to be handled by each satellite. Due to the fact that the TPC-W workloads mainly access hot-spot data (e.g., queries for the best seller books in the store), the 4 GB of main memory on each satellite is sufficient to keep the number of disk accesses low. Also the update transactions that appear in the TPC-W workload (mainly operating on the customer's shopping cart and placing new orders) need only on a small fraction of the data in each database. Therefore, the master server in the DBFarm setup (executing only update-transactions) can easily handle update-transactions for all accessed databases with the in-memory buffer cache. Most of its disk accesses are related to writing the latest changes to disk - this is also true for the satellites, which, after the warm-up phase, mainly access their disks to commit the latest received writesets.

Encouraged by the good results for 100 concurrent databases we also tried to handle 300 TPC-W databases. The results are given in Figure 5. Clearly, without the DBFarm approach the load of 300 concurrently accessed TPC-W databases is too much for our master server, the response times are not acceptable. Due to the fact that the machine is mainly doing disk I/O, the results are rather unstable - performance is dictated by the RAID-5 controller and seek times of the attached disks.

The same experiment over a DBFarm setup with the same 300 databases using thirty satellites (each holding 10 database copies) shows that DBFarm is able to handle the load and to offer acceptable response times for such a scenario.

Results for RUBBoS. The RUBBoS databases are not only larger (each database is over 2 GB) than the benchmarked TPC-W databases, but the used workload is also more complex, as the resulting transactions not only use hot-spot data but also touch a wide range of tuples inside the databases.

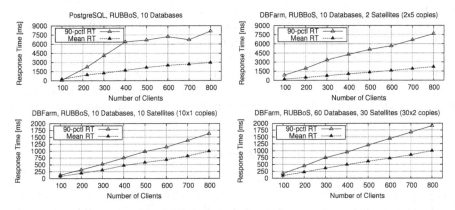

Fig. 6. RUBBoS Results

As before, we first measured the performance of the master server alone. The results are given in Figure 6. The results show that the master machine alone cannot handle many RUBBoS databases concurrently, already 10 databases lead to performance problems as shown by the large 90-percentile results.

By looking at the results for the DBFarm setup, one can observe that it is crucial that the number of copies on each satellite does not exceed a certain threshold. In the experiment where we used only two satellites (each containing 5 RUBBoS database copies) the performance improvement over a single master machine is insignificant. This is due to the fact that DBFarm has a similar problem as a single master server: the working set of 5 databases is too big for the available memory, and therefore the throughput on the satellites is limited by the available disk I/O-bandwidth. One can interpret the result as having moved the bottleneck from the master database server to the satellites. This may look like a waste of resources, but one should keep in mind that the overall setup has improved: by taking away load from the master, there is more available capacity for other concurrently accessed databases. We will point out this feature in the next section. To verify that the satellites are really the bottleneck, we then tested the same workload on a DBFarm setup with 10 satellites, therefore having only 1 RUBBoS copy per satellite. One can observe how the performance significantly improves over a setup with only 2 satellites.

In a last experiment set we tried to handle 60 concurrent RUBBoS databases with DBFarm. We used a setup with 30 satellites, each holding two database copies. It was impossible to perform the same experiment with a single master server, as the machine was stuck with disk-I/O and no stable results could be achieved (the throughput never got higher than a few transactions per second). The results in Figure 6 show that, again, DBFarm can handle such a scenario. Interestingly, the achieved performance is slightly lower than for the experiment based on 10 copies on 10 satellites. There are two reasons: first, by having two RUBBoS copies on each satellite, the buffer cache of the satellites is not big enough two hold both databases in memory. However, this is only a minor problem, as could be verified by observing the number of disk reads on the satellites during the experiment. Second, with 60 concurrent RUBBoS databases, the master server is becoming a bottleneck, since the data needed for each update transaction is not always in memory (the machine was performing more read operations than in the 10 databases experiment). One can learn the following from this experiment: when using a system like DBFarm, it is very important to optimize the structure of update-transactions: one has to try to keep the number of read operations (e.g., select operations or index scans for update statements) small, otherwise the master databases become the bottleneck of the system. This can, e.g., be achieved by introducing appropriate indexes specific to master databases.

4.2   Part B: Scaleout for Selected Databases

In the preceding experiments we used database copies on satellites to extend the capacity of a master database server. In all setups, we used no more than one copy per database on the master server. We could show that with such a system setup we can handle bursts over a set of databases.

In the last experiment we show how a single RUBBoS database can benefit from the DBFarm approach. For instance, one could think of having a high priority customer database that needs a certain guaranteed response time since there may be a service level contract with the customer. The approach to solve the problem is to assign a set of satellites, each holding exactly and exclusively one copy of the customer's database on the master server. In this way, the customer's read-only transactions can be load-balanced over different satellites which are at the same time guaranteed not to be affected by other customers. Again, there are two measurements: first we measured the performance of a pure PostgreSQL installation on the master server, then we measured the performance of the DBFarm setup. However, this time the load for the DBFarm was made much harder: to make things more interesting, in parallel to the RUBBoS load 200 TPC-W databases were also loaded by 100 worker threads with the shopping-mix. Copies of the 200 TPC-W databases were located on 20 separate satellites (each holding 10 copies). In case of the RUBBoS database, we used 3 satellites each holding exactly one copy. The results for the two experiments are given in Figure 7. Clearly one can observe that the high priority RUBBoS customer database is performing much better than with the single server setup - even though DBFarm has to concurrently deal with 200 TPC-W databases. The detailed results show that the throughput (given in *TPM*, transactions per minute) for the RUBBoS database has more than doubled.

5   Related Work

DBFarm builds upon the ideas developed in several previous projects in our group [23, 22, 15, 16] as well as on a wealth of related work on middleware based database replication. In [23, 22] we presented a system for replicating single database instances using snapshot isolation. The current version of DBFarm uses that implementation for providing snapshot isolation consistency to the clients.

On the theoretical side, [8] has extensively studied the problem of session consistency as a more meaningful correctness criterion for replicated databases than standard 1-copy-serializability. Their algorithms are targeted at offering serializability for a single, fully replicated database and they have so far only simulated the algorithms they

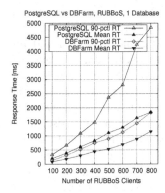

RUBBoS	DBFarm			PostgreSQL		
	RT			RT		
Clients	Mean	90-pctl	TPM	Mean	90-pctl	TPM
100	82	127	72,526	197	333	30,854
200	183	311	65,279	387	663	30,895
300	306	523	58,726	614	1,090	29,176
400	448	751	54,981	825	1,478	27,426
500	531	897	56,456	1,106	2,365	25,673
600	695	1,128	51,961	1,296	2,807	23,921
700	884	1,445	47,480	1,637	4,239	22,736
800	1,152	1,832	41,770	1,839	4,845	20,485

Fig. 7. Detailed Scale-Out Results for the RUBBoS Database. Note that DBFarm had to handle simultaneously 100 clients that randomly accessed 200 TPC-W databases (not included in TPM).

describe. DBFarm offers a stronger notion of consistency (not only one's own updates but all updates until a certain timestamp) using mechanisms that should not result in a loss of performance when compared to those presented in [8]. [9] proposes *generalized snapshot isolation*, a technique for replicated databases where readers may use older snapshots. Again, our system offers scale-out without giving up consistent views for all clients. In our current implementation, we also use snapshot isolation as a concurrency control mechanism. [11] investigated research in the serializability aspects of snapshot isolation. The consistency guarantees of systems that allow the use of other concurrency control mechanisms in parallel to snapshot isolation have been investigated in [10], these results directly apply to our system, as we are able to mix different concurrency control mechanisms on the different database nodes.

In terms of implemented systems, [1] applies the techniques presented in [22] to provide a travel-in-time feature where clients can requests older snapshots. Although this technique can easily be implemented in DBFarm, the goal of DBFarm is to support full consistency and On Line Transaction Processing (OLTP) loads ([1] uses TPC-R as benchmark, a data mining load). Note that once consistency is relaxed, scalability can be significantly increased (and, in fact, the concept of scalability changes since clients are accessing historical rather than actual data). The work described in [2] centers around a technique called distributed versioning. The key idea is to use a centralized middleware based scheduler which does bookkeeping of *versions* of tables in all the replicas. Every transaction that updates a table increases the corresponding version number. At the beginning of every transaction, clients have to inform the scheduler about the tables they are going to access. The scheduler then uses this information to assign versions of tables to the transactions. Our time tagging of transactions resembles the per table versioning of [2] but ours introduces clearly less overhead as it does not require any parsing of statements nor schema information at the middleware layer. C-JDBC [6], an open source database cluster middleware, has been primarily designed for fault tolerance. To be able to access a C-JDBC cluster, clients need to use a special Java JDBC driver. The system implements variants of the *Read-One Write-All* approach with consistency guaranteed through table level locking at the middleware level. The backend databases are accessed over JDBC, so the system can be used with different database implementations, they only need to provide a JDBC interface. The downside of this approach is the need for duplicating logic from the backend databases into the middleware, since JDBC does not supply mechanisms to achieve a fine grained control over an attached database. One example for this is *locking*, which, again, has to be done at the middleware level by parsing the incoming statements and then doing table-level locking. Another example is the writesets, which are not supported by the JDBC standard, so the middleware has to broadcast SQL update statements to all replicas to keep them in-sync. Also, when encountering peaks of updates, this leads to a situation where every backend database has to evaluate the same update statements. To circumvent these scalability problems, C-JDBC offers also the partition of the data on the backend replicas in various ways (called *RAIDb-levels*, in analogy to the RAID concept). However, static partitions of data restrict the queries that can be executed at every node. Like the solution in [2], C-JDBC cannot be used in the context of DBFarm because of the overhead it introduces at the middleware level it does not scale to hundreds of database instances. [7] presents a replication architecture based on partial replication and refresh transactions. To offer consistent views for readers, the system relies on the ordering properties of global FIFO multicast of the underlying network and as well as on maximum message delivery times.

There are also a number of systems that use group communication to implement single instance database replication [15,16,17]. These systems do not consider the problem of load balancing (they assume clients distribute themselves evenly across all copies) and impose severe restrictions on the transactional load. For instance, they require that transactions are submitted as a single block since the system can only reason about complete transactions. This is in contrast to DBFarm where clients can submit transactions statement by statement as it is done in most database applications. From the point of view of clustered databases with multiple instances, the biggest drawback of group communication based replication is the high overhead of group communication itself. With hundreds of database instances and several copies of each, the number of messages to be handled by the group communication system can be very high. Also, maintaining a membership group for each instance is very expensive and limits the flexibility in allocating copies to satellites. Since these system also adopt an update everywhere approach, each database copy must also duplicate application logic in addition to data (triggers, user defined functions, etc.). In the context of DBFarm this is simply not practical. Finally, group communication primitives rely on all nodes involved making suitable progress at roughly the same pace. In DBFarm, where a node may contain a potentially large amount of database instances, such forced synchronization will make it impossible for the system to scale. The approach proposed in [13] and [18] where load is partitioned using conflict classes is also not feasible in the context of multiple instances.

Oracle RAC (Real Application Clusters) is a commercial clustering solution that also uses snapshot isolation. It relies on the use of special hardware (all nodes in the database cluster need access to a set of shared disks) or the use of special network file systems. Therefore, unlike our approach, the system cannot easily be installed on a set of commodity servers.

6 Conclusions

This paper presents the architecture and implementation of DBFarm, a multi-instance database cluster solution that can handle hundreds of client databases concurrently. Additionally, it supports controlled scale-out for selected customer databases. DBFarm offers consistency at all times, to the clients it looks like an ordinary database server. There is no need to change any client code to be able to use the system. Our light weight adapter approach offers many advantages over classic middleware based replication solutions. Our experiments show that the approach is feasible and that the system can efficiently schedule transactions for relatively large amounts of customer databases while offering good performance for large sets of concurrent clients.

Our future work will concentrate on the dynamic aspects of the system. By allocating satellites and establishing database copies as demand requires, we plan to build an autonomic database service provider.

References

1. F. Akal, C. Türker, H.-J. Schek, Y. Breitbart, T. Grabs, and L. Veen. Fine-Grained Replication and Scheduling with Freshness and Correctness Guarantees. In *Proceedings of the 31st International Conference on Very Large Data Bases, Trondheim, Norway, August 30 - September 2, 2005*, pages 565–576.
2. C. Amza, A. L. Cox, and W. Zwaenepoel. A Comparative Evaluation of Transparent Scaling Techniques for Dynamic Content Servers. In *ICDE '05: Proceedings of the 21st International Conference on Data Engineering (ICDE'05)*, pages 230–241.
3. H. Berenson, P. Bernstein, J. Gray, J. Melton, E. O'Neil, and P. O'Neil. A Critique of ANSI SQL Isolation Levels. In *Proceedings of the SIGMOD International Conference on Management of Data*, pages 1–10, May 1995.
4. P. A. Bernstein, V. Hadzilacos, and N. Goodman. *Concurrency Control and Recovery in Database Systems*. Addison-Wesley, 1987.
5. E. Cecchet. C-JDBC: a Middleware Framework for Database Clustering. IEEE Data Engineering Bulletin, Vol. 27, No. 2, June 2004.
6. E. Cecchet, J. Marguerite, and W. Zwaenepoel. C-JDBC: Flexible Database Clustering Middleware. In *USENIX Annual Technical Conference, FREENIX Track*, pages 9–18, 2004.
7. C. Coulon, E. Pacitti, and P. Valduriez. Consistency Management for Partial Replication in a High Performance Database Cluster. In *Proceedings of the 11th International Conference on Parallel and Distributed Systems (ICPADS 2005), Fuduoka, Japan, July 20-22, 2005*.
8. K. Daudjee and K. Salem. Lazy database replication with ordering guarantees. In *Proceedings of the 20th International Conference on Data Engineering (ICDE 2004), 30 March - 2 April 2004, Boston, MA, USA*, pages 424–435.
9. S. Elnikety, F. Pedone, and W. Zwaenepoel. Database Replication Using Generalized Snapshot Isolation. In *SRDS '05: Proceedings of the 24th IEEE Symposium on Reliable Distributed Systems*.
10. A. Fekete. Allocating Isolation Levels to Transactions. In *PODS '05: Proceedings of the twenty-fourth ACM SIGMOD-SIGACT-SIGART symposium on Principles of database systems*, pages 206–215, June 2005.
11. A. Fekete, D. Liarokapis, E. O'Neil, P. O'Neil, and D. Shasha. Making Snapshot Isolation Serializable. *ACM Trans. Database Syst.*, 30(2):492–528, 2005.

12. R. Jiménez-Peris, M. Patiño-Martínez, and G. Alonso. An Algorithm for Non-Intrusive, Parallel Recovery of Replicated Data and its Correctness. In *21st IEEE Int. Conf. on Reliable Distributed Systems (SRDS 2002), Oct. 2002, Osaka, Japan*, pages 150–159.

13. R. Jiménez-Peris, M. Patiño-Martínez, B. Kemme, and G. Alonso. Improving the Scalability of Fault-Tolerant Database Clusters. In *IEEE 22nd Int. Conf. on Distributed Computing Systems, ICDCS'02, Vienna, Austria*, pages 477–484, July 2002.

14. B. Kemme. *Database Replication for Clusters of Workstations*. PhD thesis, Diss. ETH No. 13864, Dept. of Computer Science, Swiss Federal Institute of Technology Zurich, 2000.

15. B. Kemme and G. Alonso. Don't be lazy, be consistent: Postgres-R, a new way to implement Database Replication. In *Proceedings of the 26th International Conference on Very Large Databases, 2000*.

16. B. Kemme and G. Alonso. A New Approach to Developing and Implementing Eager Database Replication Protocols. *ACM Transactions on Database Systems*, 25(3):333–379, 2000.

17. Y. Lin, B. Kemme, M. Patiño-Martínez, and R. Jiménez-Peris. Middleware based Data Replication providing Snapshot Isolation. In *SIGMOD '05: Proceedings of the 2005 ACM SIGMOD international conference on Management of data*, pages 419–430.

18. J. M. Milan-Franco, R. Jiménez-Peris, M. Patiño-Martínez, and B. Kemme. Adaptive Distributed Middleware for Data Replication. In *Middleware 2004, ACM/IFIP/USENIX 5th International Middleware Conference, Toronto, Canada, October 18-22, Proceedings*, 2004.

19. OpenSSH. A free version of the SSH protocol suite. http://www.openssh.org/.

20. T. Ozsu and P. Valduriez. *Principles of Distributed Database Systems*. Prentice Hall, 1999.

21. C. Plattner. The Ganymed SSH-2 Library. http://www.ganymed.ethz.ch/ssh2.

22. C. Plattner and G. Alonso. Ganymed: Scalable Replication for Transactional Web Applications. In *Middleware 2004, 5th ACM/IFIP/USENIX International Middleware Conference, Toronto, Canada, October 18-22, Proceedings*, 2004.

23. C. Plattner, G. Alonso, and M. T. Özsu. Extending DBMSs with Satellite Databases. *Accepted for Publication in the VLDB Journal*, 2006. http://www.iks.inf.ethz.ch/publications/satellites.html.

24. C. Plattner, A. Wapf, and G. Alonso. Searching in Time. In *SIGMOD '06, 2006 ACM SIGMOD International Conference on Management of Data, June 27-29, 2006, Chicago, Illinois, USA*, 2006.

25. R. Schenkel and G. Weikum. Integrating Snapshot Isolation into Transactional Federation. In *Cooperative Information Systems, 7th International Conference, CoopIS 2000, Eilat, Israel, September 6-8, 2000, Proceedings*.

26. The ObjectWeb Consortium. RUBBoS: Bulletin Board Benchmark. http://jmob.objectweb.org/rubbos.html.

27. The Slashdot Homepage. http://slashdot.org/.

28. The Transaction Processing Performance Council. TPC-W, a Transactional Web E-Commerce Benchmark. TPC-C, an On-line Transaction Processing Benchmark. http://www.tpc.org.

29. S. Wu and B. Kemme. Postgres-R(SI): Combining Replica Control with Concurrency Control Based on Snapshot Isolation. In *ICDE '05: Proceedings of the 21st International Conference on Data Engineering (ICDE'05)*, pages 422–433.

Queryll: Java Database Queries Through Bytecode Rewriting

Ming-Yee Iu and Willy Zwaenepoel

School of Computer and Communication Sciences,
EPFL, Lausanne, Switzerland

Abstract. When interfacing Java with other systems such as databases, programmers must often program in special interface languages like SQL. Code written in these languages often needs to be embedded in strings where they cannot be error-checked at compile-time, or the Java compiler needs to be altered to directly recognize code written in these languages. We have taken a different approach to adding database query facilities to Java. Bytecode rewriting allows us to add query facilities to Java whose correctness can be checked at compile-time but which don't require any changes to the Java language, Java compilers, Java VMs, or IDEs. Like traditional object-relational mapping tools, we provide Java libraries for accessing individual database entries as objects and navigating among them. To express a query though, a programmer simply writes code that takes a Collection representing the entire contents of a database, iterates over each entry like they would with a normal Collection, and choose the entries of interest. The query is fully valid Java code that, if executed, will read through an entire database and copy entries into Java objects where they will be inspected. Executing queries in this way is obviously inefficient, but we have a special bytecode rewriting tool that can decompile Java class files, identify queries in the bytecode, and rewrite the code to use SQL instead. The rewritten bytecode can then be run using any standard Java VM. Since queries use standard Java set manipulation syntax, Java programmers do not need to learn any new syntax. Our system is able to handle complex queries that make use of all the basic relational operations and exhibits performance comparable to that of hand-written SQL.

1 Introduction

Queryll is a middleware system that uses bytecode rewriting to allow programmers to interface Java with other systems without needing to use an intermediary language. Currently, Queryll is focused on interfacing Java with SQL databases by providing database query facilities to Java. With Queryll, programmers can encode database queries using standard Java syntax for working with collections. No special compiler or IDE is needed. The queries are also semantically correct in that if they are executed as written, they will connect to a database, iterate through all the entries in the database, and find the desired entries (though executing queries in this way is obviously inefficient). When the compiled Java

M. van Steen and M. Henning (Eds.): Middleware 2006, LNCS 4290, pp. 201–218, 2006.

bytecode is fed into the Queryll bytecode rewriter, the queries in the bytecode stream are identified, and they are replaced with code that executes equivalent SQL queries instead. The bytecode rewriting acts, in fact, like a type of code optimization in which whole algorithms are replaced with more efficient substitutes.

Unlike Queryll, other middleware systems use special programming languages to interface Java to other systems. Databases, graphics cards, and symbolic computation engines all require the use custom languages to access their features. This approach can be very cumbersome. Not only does the Java programmer need to learn another programming language, but mismatches between the underlying models of these other languages and Java mean that programmers often have to write extra code for translating concepts between the two models. Since the Java compiler does not recognize the syntax of any of these other languages, their code has to be embedded in strings where they cannot be statically error-checked. Often parameters must be marshaled into special data structures before they can be passed to and from these other systems. Ultimately, these annoyances distract programmers from larger algorithmic and architectural issues.

One solution to these problems is to create hybrid programming languages that mix other languages with Java. For example, SQLJ [1] is a hybrid of Java and SQL. In SQLJ code, SQL queries can be intermixed with Java, and the queries can make reference to Java variables. Although hybrid languages do allow for static error-checking and do eliminate the need for data marshaling, they require special compilers and IDE changes. The approach also falls apart when multiple interface languages are merged with Java, resulting in a hybrid language with a complex tangle of additional language constructs.

Ideally, it should be possible to interact with databases and other systems using regular Java code. That way, programmers would not need to learn a new language but only a few new API calls to interface with a system. Programmers would not need special compilers, nor would they have to deal with issues such as data marshaling or embedding code inside strings. Unfortunately, it is impractical to use Java in this way. The primary language construct that these other interface languages have but Java lacks is a facility for inspecting and modifying one's own code. Queries written in a query language need to be understood and manipulated by a query optimizer to be executed on a database. A fragment shader program needs to be compiled into instructions that can be run on a graphics card. Java does support reflection, but it does not have APIs for understanding and manipulating code.

Unlike other database middleware layers for Java, Queryll provides a pure Java interface to databases that allows programmers to describe complex queries without resorting to another programming language. As such, programmers do not need to learn a new language, and the standard Java compiler can catch many potential errors at compile-time. There is also no unnatural split in the middleware API where a simplified API is available for performing basic queries and a more extensive API is needed for more complex queries. Queryll is able to achieve this behaviour because it is designed as a bytecode rewriting tool. As such, it does not make any changes to the Java language, meaning that a standard Java compiler and IDE can be used by programmers. The rewritten bytecode can also be run on a standard Java VM. Using bytecode rewriting for extending Java does not force programmers to change any of their existing tools, and it can be used to interface Java with multiple systems without adding new complexity to the Java language.

2   Related Work

There are many middleware languages and tools for interfacing Java with various databases. These different tools provide differing levels of abstraction and differing levels of integration with Java.

2.1   JDBC and SQLJ

The standard database middleware layer for Java is JDBC [2]. With JDBC, queries are described using SQL and are stored in strings. Programmers then pass these strings to the JDBC API, which executes the queries on a database. Although JDBC provides some helper methods to help with data marshaling, programmers must still manually pack parameters into queries and then manually read out and interpret individual fields from the query results.

As described earlier, SQLJ is a language that combines SQL with Java. Because of this integration, both the SQL and Java code can be checked for errors at compile time, programmers can reference Java variables from within SQL, and programmers can reference SQL results from within Java. Typically, a precompiler is used to compile SQLJ into Java code that uses JDBC.

2.2   ORM Tools

Both JDBC and SQLJ are tightly bound to the SQL table-oriented view of data, which is inconsistent with Java's object-oriented model. Object-Relational Mapping (ORM) tools such as Hibernate [3] or EJB [4] allow programmers to specify a mapping from SQL tables to an object representation. The ORM tool then generates code that allows programmers to manipulate these objects in Java and have these changes be persisted automatically to the corresponding SQL tables. Although these objects do hide data marshaling issues and allow programmers to execute simple queries with just a simple method call, they cannot be used for more complex queries. For complex queries, ORM tools typically supply a special object query language such as HQL or EJBQL (Fig. 1). Like JDBC, queries in these languages are encoded in strings, and programmers must manually encode parameters into their queries.

2.3   LINQ

In C# 3.0, Microsoft has added a feature called Language Integrated Query (LINQ) [5]. This feature allows programmers to inline queries with their C#

```
List l = em.createQuery("SELECT c FROM Customer c WHERE c.id = :id")
        .setParameter(":id", 2500)
        .getResultList();
```

Fig. 1. A sample EJBQL query

code. Unlike the approach used by Queryll, extensive changes to the C# compiler and language were made in order to support LINQ. Notably, C# now supports lambda expressions, and C# compiles lambda expressions into two forms: executable code and a data structure representation that can be inspected at runtime. The new language constructs in C# only provide support for queries. They cannot be used to interface C# with systems such as graphics cards, for example.

2.4   Bytecode Rewriting and Decompiling

All Java compilers compile Java programs into a machine independent intermediate representation known as bytecode. This bytecode is stored in files called classfiles. Java programs are distributed as classfiles which can be executed using a Java VM. Bytecode rewriting is a well-known Java technique for modifying the behaviour of compiled Java code. A typical example would be J-Orchestra [6] which can alter Java objects so that they can be invoked remotely without requiring changes to the original code. Many aspect-oriented programming tools also make use of bytecode rewriting to support dynamic aspect weaving [7]. And some ORM tools already make use of bytecode rewriting to transparently add persistence code to ordinary Java objects to enable those objects to be stored in databases. These uses of bytecode rewriting are limited to only modifying surface features of code such as intercepting method calls; however, some tools such as the automatic parallelization program javab [8] perform more detailed code analysis. One can consider classfile decompilation [9], where bytecode is converted to Java source files, to be an extreme form of bytecode rewriting. There are several Java decompilation tools, and Queryll borrows some of their techniques for its work.

3   Queries with Queryll

As mentioned earlier, Queryll is able to take database queries written in regular Java and rewrite the queries to use SQL. Clearly though, the Queryll bytecode rewriter is not able to convert arbitrary Java to SQL.

Queryll's query syntax is designed to conform with standard Java patterns for working with collections, resulting in a syntax that feels "natural" and consistent with existing Java code. It is also designed to have the properties of being executable and semantically correct. This means that if the query is compiled with a standard Java compiler and run on a standard Java VM, the code will not only execute but will return the correct query result as well. Although the

Queryll bytecode rewriter detects query code and rewrites them to use SQL, even if no rewriting occurs, the query code is perfectly functional. Admittedly, without rewriting, the query will be horribly inefficient since it will download the entire database and iterate through each row; nonetheless, the code will behave correctly. By forcing query code to be executable and semantically correct, we ensure that queries are expressed in sufficient detail that the standard Java compiler can verify much of the correctness of the query using its existing static type checking. These properties also preclude a syntax that introduces new domain-specific constructs to the Java language.

Queryll uses an object-relational mapping to allow database entities to be represented and manipulated as objects within Java. Queryll queries are expressed using iterations over collections of these objects. The current Queryll query syntax supports selection, projection, and join operations, thereby making Queryll functionally equivalent to basic relational algebra. Unfortunately, Queryll does not yet support aggregation operations or nested queries, meaning that it is not currently able to handle the extended query operations needed to express arbitrary SQL queries. Queryll does have support for SQL ordering and limit operations though.

3.1   Queryll ORM

Because SQL tables are a foreign concept to the object-oriented model of Java, they need to be translated into some sort of representation that can be manipulated by Java code. Queryll uses a custom light-weight ORM tool to map tables to classes. Like with other ORM tools, programmers must describe how table rows should map to objects, how table fields should be mapped into object fields, and the various relationships between tables. They are essentially defining an object representation of a database and defining how to convert between the SQL representation and the object representation.

So, consider a simple database describing bank clients, each of whom may have multiple bank accounts. This database might be composed of two tables (Fig. 2): Client and Account. Using the Queryll ORM tool, this database can be mapped to the class diagram in Fig. 3.

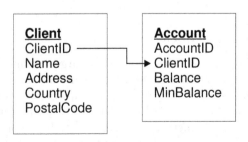

Fig. 2. A simple database

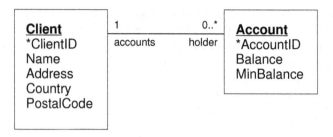

Fig. 3. Class diagram of database entities (* denotes primary keys)

From the mapping, Queryll generates the classes for each entity with accessor methods for fields and special methods for traversing relationships between objects (for example, retrieving a Collection of accounts belonging to a client). These objects act as a cache of database data and are all lazily instantiated. Queryll also creates a special class named EntityManager that is responsible for ensuring that the database data and their in-memory object representations remain consistent. Figure 4 shows how the generated classes may be used. Queryll's approach to object-relational mapping is fairly standard among existing ORM tools.

```
EntityManager em = db.beginTransaction();
Client c = em.findClient(1000);
System.out.println("Client 1000 lives at " + c.getAddress());
System.out.println("Client 1000 has " + c.getAccounts().size()
                    + " accounts");
db.endTransaction(em, true);
// Note: the findClient() method is used here for illustrative
// purposes. In actuality, no such method exists because Queryll
// supports using full queries instead.
```

Fig. 4. ORM tools can generate classes that allow programmers to access database data as objects instead of having to deal with SQL tables

3.2   Simple Queries and Selection

Since the main Java construct for working with large amounts of data is the for-each loop for iterating over arrays and Collections, we built our syntax around that construct. The for-each loop restricts our queries to using Collections to represent database contents. As such, we created a special type of Java Collection called a QuerySet. A QuerySet is a lazily initialized container of database entities. It holds a SQL query, and when any attempt is made to access any of the elements of a QuerySet, the QuerySet will execute the query on a database, and fill itself with the results of the query, and from then on behave like a normal Java Collection.

To write a simple Queryll query then, a programmer takes an existing Query-Set, iterates over each element of the QuerySet to find the elements that she is interested in, and adds these elements to a new QuerySet. All the elements of the original QuerySet must be iterated over (no premature loops exits), and the loop code can have no side-effects beyond adding elements to the new QuerySet. The query syntax is purposely based on adding elements to a new QuerySet as opposed to modifying an existing QuerySet. The elements added to the new QuerySet may be of a different type than the elements in the QuerySet being iterated over, so two different QuerySets are needed for everything to type-check correctly.

Finally, the programmer must also label the methods containing Queryll queries with the @Query annotation. Since bytecode rewriting is an expensive operation, the Queryll bytecode rewriter will only look at the bytecode of @Query methods when converting queries to their SQL equivalents.

Figure 5 shows a simple Queryll query that finds bank clients who come from Canada. Notice that the EntityManager object em has methods for returning a QuerySet of all the Client entities in the database. Since all queries must start with an existing QuerySet, the EntityManager provides the initial QuerySet objects on which queries can be constructed. As mentioned previously, the standard Java type rules impose a certain amount of correctness on the query. The string "country" acts as a parameter in the query, and the Java compiler ensures that this parameter is of the correct type. The Java compiler also ensures that the entity fields being examined during the query actually exist (otherwise the accessor methods would not exist) and that the result of the query is of the expected type.

```
QuerySet<String> canadian = new QuerySet<String>();
String country = "Canada";
for (Client c: em.allClient())
   if (c.getCountry().equals(country))
      canadian.add(c.getName());
```

Fig. 5. A simple query for finding all clients from Canada

The Queryll query syntax is flexible enough to allow programmers to express a wide variety of query operations in a natural way. For example, by simply changing the conditions in which an element is added to a new QuerySet, a programmer is writing a selection operation.

3.3   Projection

To support projection operations, Queryll supplies a Pair object that can hold two arbitrary values. Similar to a LISP list which also holds only two values (car and cdr), the Pair object can be used to construct simple data structures during a query, which can then be added to a new QuerySet. This ability to create new data structures is equivalent to using projection operations to create new columns for database relations or to remove columns from database relations. Projection operations themselves are not directly expressible in Queryll, as doing so would mean that Queryll would have to support the creation of new classes at runtime. The Java syntax for the creation of new classes is quite verbose and cumbersome, and working with a large number of these classes creates headaches for programmers because they would not work well with Java's type system. In fact, to support projection in LINQ, Microsoft had to create a new C# syntax for creating new classes at runtime and change the C# type system. Queryll's use of Pair objects to provide power equivalent to projection is much more consistent with existing Java syntax. Figure 6 shows how a programmer might use Pair objects to hold data about the penalty that should be applied to bank accounts that are below their minimum balance and hence overdrawn.

```
QuerySet<Pair<Account, Double>> overdrawn
    = new QuerySet<Pair<Account, Double>>();
for (Account a: em.allAccount()) {
   if (a.getBalance() < a.getMinBalance()) {
      double penalty = (a.getMinBalance() - a.getBalance()) * 0.001;
      overdrawn.add(new Pair<Account, Double>(a, penalty));
   }
}
```

Fig. 6. Queryll provides Pair objects, which can be used to create data structures for holding calculated values, thus providing power equivalent to projection

3.4   Join

Expressing join operations is quite easy in Queryll. Since the relationship between entities is described during the ORM phase, Queryll generates methods for navigating among objects, and these methods can be used during queries. Some types of joins, such as those where a single table row is joined with multiple rows from another table, are potentially difficult to express in Java, so Queryll provides a few utility methods for handling these cases. Figure 7 shows two different ways that joins can be used to find all the bank accounts belonging to clients in Switzerland.

3.5   Ordering and Limit

Currently, Queryll only has preliminary support for the SQL ordering and limit operations. The syntax for ordering is not yet finalized, but the current syntax requires programmers to create a sorter class that describes which fields of the elements should be used for sorting. This is similar to the existing use of the Comparator object in Java for sorting. Figure 8 shows an example of ordering in Queryll.

```
QuerySet<Pair<Client, Account>>
    swiss1 = new QuerySet<Pair<Client, Account>>(),
    swiss2 = new QuerySet<Pair<Client, Account>>();

for (Account a: em.allAccount())
    if (a.getHolder().getCountry().equals("Switzerland"))
        swiss1.add(new Pair<Client, Account>(a.getHolder(), a));

for (Client c: em.allClient())
    if (c.getCountry().equals("Switzerland"))
        swiss2.addAll(Pair.PairCollection(c, c.getAccounts()));
```

Fig. 7. Two different join queries that give the same results

```
QuerySet<Account> top10Accounts = em.allAccount();
top10Accounts = top10Accounts.sortedByDoubleDescending(
        new DoubleSorter<Account>() {
            public double value(Account val) {
                return val.getBalance();
            }
        });
top10Accounts = top10Accounts.firstN(10);
```

Fig. 8. Queryll supports ordering and limit operations as well

4   Implementation

The Queryll system (Fig. 9) is composed of two programs: an ORM tool and a bytecode rewriter. The bytecode rewriter is by far the more complicated of the two.

Suppose the query defined in Fig. 10 is given to the Queryll bytecode rewriter. As mentioned earlier, all methods containing queries should be labelled with a @Query annotation to help Queryll focus its optimizations on the right pieces of code. Queryll finds all such methods and feeds the bytecode of these methods into Sable's Soot [10] framework for conversion into Jimple code, a representation that is easier to analyze. Jimple is a three-address code for Java where all variables are typed (Java objects on the execution stack are usually typeless). Three-address code is useful because it eliminates Java's execution stack, resulting in one less structure that the bytecode rewriter needs to analyze and making it easier to rearrange code without having to worry about whether the state of the stack remains consistent. Queryll does not actually make use of the typing feature of Jimple, meaning that a simpler three-address code framework than Soot could be used if one becomes available. Figure 11 shows the Jimplified version of the compiled bytecode of the previous query. Being a three-address code, most instructions consist of an operation on two variables, the result of which is then assigned into third variable.

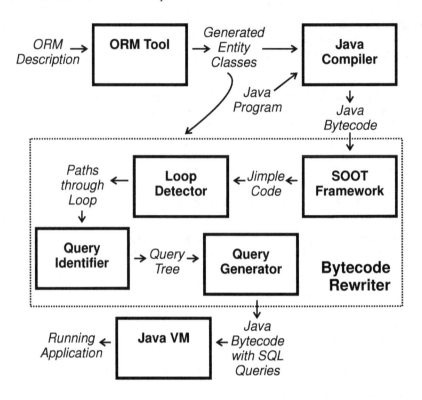

Fig. 9. Queryll system design

```
for (Office of: em.allOffice()) {
    if (of.getName().equals("Seattle"))
        westcoast.add(of);
    else if (of.getName().equals("LA"))
        westcoast.add(of);
}
```

Fig. 10. A simple query that can be analyzed by the Queryll bytecode rewriter

The next stage of the analysis then involves identifying loops within the code. Although loops are easy to identify in Java source code, compiled Java code uses only GOTO statements to describe its control flow. There are generally two approaches for extracting loops from program code that uses GOTOs for control flow. One approach is called GOTO-elimination [11] where code transformations are applied to individual GOTO statements to convert them into looping structures. Instead, Queryll uses the alternate approach where the control flow graph is analyzed as a whole and restructured to make use of loops [12]. This latter approach is used because it provides a deeper understanding of the loop structure than the former approach. Loops are defined as being strongly connected

```
          1:   $r12 = r1.<EntityManager: Set allOffice()>();
          2:   r6 = $r12.<Set: Iterator iterator()>();
          3:   goto label3;

label1:   4:   $r13 = r6.<Iterator: Object next()>();
          5:   r14 = (Office) $r13;
          6:   $r15 = r14.<Office: String getName()>();
          7:   $z3 = $r15.<String: boolean equals(Object)>("Seattle");
          8:   if $z3 == 0 goto label2;

          9:   r11.<Set: boolean add(Object)>(r14);
         10:   goto label3;

label2:  11:   $r16 = r14.<Office: String getName()>();
         12:   $z5 = $r16.<String: boolean equals(Object)>("LA");
         13:   if $z5 == 0 goto label3;

         14:   r11.<Set: boolean add(Object)>(r14);

label3:  15:   $z7 = r6.<Iterator: boolean hasNext()>();
         16:   if $z7 != 0 goto label1;
```

Fig. 11. When a query is rewritten to be in a Jimple representation, it is easier to analyze and manipulate

components in the control flow graph that have a single entry point. Queryll further restricts its definition of loops to require that all exits from the strongly connected component exit to the same instruction. Standard graph algorithms can be used to find pieces of code that satisfy these requirements and label that code as being a loop.

Since Queryll queries are all composed of a for-each loop over a QuerySet, the Queryll bytecode rewriter must be able to determine whether a loop is a for-each loop or not. A for-each loop that iterates over a Java Collection compiles down to code that creates an Iterator object from the Collection, and then continually advances the iterator until there are no more objects left to iterate over (see instructions 2, 4, 15, and 16 in Fig. 11). Queryll tries to identify this pattern in loops by looking for iterators being incremented within loops. Queryll also checks other properties of the loop such as whether each loop instruction has no side effects except for adding elements to a Collection or incrementing the iterator. If that is the case, the loop is labelled as a candidate for being a query, the Collection being iterated over is labelled as the source collection, and the Collection to which elements are added is labelled as the destination collection.

It then becomes necessary to interpret what sort of query is being performed by the loop. Since the loop might contain many variables and branching instructions, it can be difficult to understand what is going on. On the other hand, analyzing straight-line code is much easier because it is easy to calculate both the values of variables at any point in the code and dependencies between any instructions. To take advantage of that fact, Queryll breaks loops down into straight paths to do its analysis. It does this by examining every control flow path through a loop that results in a new element being added to the destination collection. The instructions that form a path are then treated as a straight-line piece of code. Table 1 shows the two paths that Queryll finds when examining the code in Fig. 11.

Table 1. There are two paths through the loop that lead to new elements being added to the destination collection

Path 1	Path 2
15: $z7 = r6.hasNext()	15: $z7 = r6.hasNext()
16: if $z7 != 0 goto label1	16: if $z7 != 0 goto label1
4: $r13 = r6.next()	4: $r13 = r6.next()
5: r14 = (Office) $r13	5: r14 = (Office) $r13
6: $r15 = r14.getName()	6: $r15 = r14.getName()
7: $z3 = $r15.equals("Seattle")	7: $z3 = $r15.equals("Seattle")
8: if $z3 == 0 goto label2	8: if $z3 == 0 goto label2
(branch not taken)	(branch taken)
9: r11.add(r14)	11: $r16 = r14.getName()
	12: $z5 = $r16.equals("LA")
	13: if $z5 == 0 goto label3
	(branch not taken)
	14: r11.add(r14)

For each path, Queryll determines what the values of local variables need to be for the path to be followed. So, essentially, for each branch instruction in the path, Queryll will make a note of what values a variable must take for the branch to be taken or not. These restrictions on the variables will be ANDed together to form an expression describing the conditions that need to hold for the path to be followed. These variables are likely only local variables holding intermediate calculations that do not directly refer to any concrete object fields though. To map these variables onto database entries, the bytecode rewriter starts at the last instruction in the path and goes over each instruction in the path backward. Since Jimple is a type of three-value code, most instructions are of the form where a binary operation on two variables is assigned to another variable. If the variable being assigned to is part of the expression representing the path, the right-hand side of the instruction (made up of the binary operation on two variables) is substituted for the left-hand variable in the path expression. When the first instruction of the path is reached, the resulting expression should be made up of operations acting on constants, outside variables, or entries from the source collection. For example, if Queryll was trying to construct an expression to describe the second path of Table 1, it would go through the steps shown in Table 2. Because Java bytecode instructions for conditional GOTOs can only work with conditions involving integers, when the above procedure is used on code that works with non-integers, the resulting expression contains redundant comparisons. So in Table 2, the expression for the path compares Office.Name with "Seattle", resulting in an integer, and then compares this integer with 0. These extra comparisons can confuse some SQL implementations, so Queryll always performs a simplification step on the final expression to remove them.

Table 2. For a given path, Queryll can construct an expression that describes when the path is executed

Instruction	Expression
Initial	$z3 = 0 AND $z5 != 0
14: r11.add(r14)	
13: if $z5 == 0 goto label3	
12: $z5 = $r16.equals("LA")	$z3 = 0 AND ($r16 = "LA") != 0
11: $r16 = r14.getName()	$z3 = 0 AND (r14.Name = "LA") != 0
8: if $z3 == 0 goto label2	
7: $z3 = $r15.equals("Seattle")	($r15 = "Seattle") = 0 AND (r14.Name = "LA") != 0
6: $r15 = r14.getName()	(r14.Name = "Seattle") = 0 AND (r14.Name = "LA") != 0
5: r14 = (Office) $r13	(((Office)$r14).Name = "Seattle") = 0 AND (((Office)$r13).Name = "LA") != 0
4: $r13 = r6.next()	(((Office)entry).Name = "Seattle") = 0 AND (((Office)entry).Name = "LA") != 0
16: if $z7 != 0 goto label1	
15: $z7 = r6.hasNext()	
Simplification	(((Office)entry).Name != "Seattle") AND (((Office)entry).Name = "LA")

Each path found by Queryll represents a different way in which a new entry can be added to the destination collection. So to construct a description of which elements of the source collection should appear in the destination collection, Queryll takes the expressions representing each path and ORs them together (Fig. 12). This giant expression can then be put into the WHERE clause of a SELECT..FROM..WHERE statement to create a SQL query. Similar techniques are used to create SQL queries that calculate new columns or which join together multiple tables.

```
SELECT ...
  FROM Office AS A
 WHERE (((A).Name   != "Seattle") AND ((A).Name = "LA"))
       OR ((A).Name  = "Seattle")
```

Fig. 12. Queryll ORs together the expressions for each path through the for-each loop to construct the WHERE clause of a SQL query

5   Benchmarks

The SQL query code generated by Queryll tends to be a little more verbose than hand-written SQL. Queryll also imposes some additional overhead at run-time because it uses various abstractions to allow it to construct SQL queries programmatically. These factors do negatively affect the performance of Queryll queries. Adopters of middleware must always deal with the trade-off between increased programmer productivity versus system performance, but ideally the overhead of Queryll should be tolerably low if not negligible.

We have built a microbenchmark based on TPC-W [13]. TPC-W is a benchmark suite that models the behaviour of database-driven websites. We have taken the Rice University implementation of TPC-W [14], which uses JDBC SQL queries, as a benchmark base. The full TPC-W benchmark makes use of application servers and web clients browsing through the website. Instead, we have taken a select number of queries from the benchmark and evaluated the throughput of these queries using JDBC and Queryll.

Of the queries in the Rice TPC-W implementation, all the queries involving updates were removed. Queryll uses an approach to persistence that is standard among other ORM tools whereby programmers load table rows into objects, programmers manipulate the fields of the objects, and the ORM tool will write the objects' data back to individual table rows before a transaction completes. Since this technique is already quite pervasive, evaluating update performance does not provide any new insight into the behaviour of Queryll. Queries making use of temporary tables, GROUP BY, aggregation functions, and LIKE were also removed as Queryll does not support these features yet. Of the remaining queries, many were similar (e.g. reading individual fields from a row in a table), so we have taken a representative sample of these for the microbenchmark. Table 3 lists the queries included in the microbenchmark. Each query is given a name, each query is described briefly, and the hand-written SQL used in the Rice TPC-W implementation of each query is shown.

We created a 600 MB database in PostgreSQL 8.1.3 [15] by populating the database using these parameters: the number of items was set to 10000 and the number of EBs was set to 100. During a run of the benchmark, each query was run 100 times using random valid parameters to warm the database cache, and then a measurement was taken of the time needed to execute the query 2000 times using random valid parameters. Each configuration was benchmarked at least 30 times, with only the last 20 runs included in the final measurement averages. This was needed to remove the effect of Java dynamic compilation from the measurements and to further warm the database cache. The database and the query code were both run on the same machine, a 2.5 GHz Pentium IV Celeron Windows machine, with 1 GB of RAM (though the benchmark harness was run using Java's default maximum heap size of 64 MB).

The results of the benchmark are shown in Table 4. Hand-written SQL queries are generally faster than the queries generated by Queryll except in the doSubjectSearch query. Most of the time differences can be explained by miscellaneous overhead in the generated Java query code or small differences in query execution

Table 3. Queries used in the benchmark

---

getName
Find a specific row in a table using its primary key
SELECT c_fname, c_lname
  FROM customer
WHERE c_id = ?

getCustomer
Find a specific row in a table and then join it to two other tables
SELECT ...
  FROM customer, address, country
WHERE customer.c_addr_id = address.addr_id AND address.addr_co_id = country.co_id AND customer.c_uname = ?

doSubjectSearch
Find all entries in a table with a field set to a certain value, join these entries to another table, sort them, and take the first 50
SELECT i.i_id, i.i_title, a.a_fname, a.a_lname
  FROM item i, author a
WHERE i.i_subject = ? AND i.i_a_id = a.a_id ORDER BY i.i_title (LIMIT 0,50)

getRelated
Find an entry in a table using its primary key, then follow its five references to other entries in the same table
SELECT J.i_id,J.i_thumbnail
  FROM item I, item J
WHERE (I.i_related1 = J.i_id or I.i_related2 = J.i_id or I.i_related3 = J.i_id or I.i_related4 = J.i_id or I.i_related5 = J.i_id) and I.i_id = ?

---

at the database. For example, the generated code for the getName query (Table 5) is essentially the same as the hand-written code, but the generated code sends a commit command to the database separately from its query, reads columns out from ResultSets by referring to columns by name instead of by index number, stores results in intermediate data structures, and has other additional overhead. When the hand-written JDBC code was modified to include some of the same inefficiencies, its running time shot up dramatically to almost match the time taken by the Queryll queries. This behaviour suggests that even though the time difference between hand-written queries and Queryll queries are large in percentage terms, in absolute terms the difference is quite small. Given sloppily hand-written JDBC code or highly optimized generated Queryll code, the time differences could be easily reversed.

In fact, the generated code for the doSubjectSearch query was consistently faster than the hand-written code for the query despite the extra overhead in the generated code. This fact suggests something unusual with the SQL queries, but the generated SQL query was essentially the same as the hand-written query, except that the ordering of the columns was different and each column was given

Table 4. Benchmark results

Query	Queryll		Hand-Written SQL		
	Time (ms)	Std Dev	Time (ms)	Std Dev	Difference (ms)
getName	3360	12.3	2053	19.3	1307
with extra processing			3030	18.9	330
getCustomer	7716	141.2	5163	69.1	2552
doSubjectSearch	21450	329.5	22384	25.3	-934
with modified query			20378	18.1	1072
doGetRelated	8124	16.8	3262	10.1	4862

Table 5. SQL queries generated by Queryll

---

getName
SELECT (A.C_FNAME) AS COL0, (A.C_LNAME) AS COL1
  FROM Customer AS A
WHERE ((((A.C_ID) = ?)))

getCustomer
SELECT ...
  FROM Customer AS A, Address AS B, Country AS C
WHERE ((((A.C_UNAME) = ?))) AND A.C_ADDR_ID = B.ADDR_ID AND
    B.ADDR_CO_ID = C.CO_ID

doSubjectSearch
SELECT (A.I_TITLE) AS COL1, (B.A_FNAME) AS COL2, (B.A_LNAME) AS
    COL3, (A.I_ID) AS COL0
  FROM Item AS A, Author AS B
WHERE ((((A.I_SUBJECT) = ?))) AND A.I_A_ID = B.A_ID ORDER BY
    (A.I_TITLE)

doGetRelated
SELECT ...
  FROM Item AS A, Item AS B, Item AS C, Item AS D, Item AS E, Item AS F
WHERE ((((A.I_ID) = ?))) AND A.I_RELATED1 = B.I_ID AND
    A.I_RELATED2 = C.I_ID AND A.I_RELATED3 = D.I_ID AND
    A.I_RELATED4 = E.I_ID AND A.I_RELATED5 = F.I_ID

---

a column alias. When we changed the hand-written query to match the generated one, its running time became better than that of the generated queries. We can only assume that the ordering of the columns somehow caused the database to execute the automatically generated queries in a slightly more optimal way than the hand-generated one.

The doGetRelated query is the only query that is significantly slower when using generated queries instead of hand-written ones. This likely results from the fact that the generated query is quite different from the original query. While the original query joins the Item table to itself once, the generated query joins the Item table to itself five times—one for each reference to another Item row.

This happens because Queryll does not currently support arbitrary cross joins between tables. Instead, the Queryll query is written exactly as it is described in Table 3. When Queryll analyzes the query, it sees one Item entity with five separate fields referring to five other Item entities, and it rewrites each reference to be a separate join operation.

Overall, the results show that in most cases, using generated queries instead of hand-written queries should not cause major performance problems. The use of generated queries does impose some overhead on the application (as opposed to the database) because it creates more intermediate data structures and uses more abstractions. Of course, even hand-written JDBC calls can suffer from similar overhead if programmers aren't careful. And much of this overhead can be reduced by improving the automatic code generation of Queryll.

6   Conclusion

Queryll is a middleware layer that allows Java programmers to access databases without having to resort to a separate interface language. The query syntax is consistent with existing Java syntax for searching Java collections. Unlike other database middleware, the Queryll API can handle both simple and complex queries. And database queries written using Queryll generally have comparable performance to hand-written queries even though Queryll provides a much higher level of abstraction.

7   Future Work

Although Queryll currently supports basic relational algebra, it would be useful to add aggregation and nested query support to Queryll to allow it to handle the extended algebra behind SQL. The existing code could also be made more robust through the addition of more error-checking. Additionally, it would be useful to formalize Queryll's query syntax and to rigorously define how it is converted to SQL. One difficult aspect of this is that since Queryll operates on Java bytecode, the query syntax needs to be defined in terms of bytecode. But this query syntax must then be backward translated to the regular Java that programmers would write.

Overall our success in using bytecode rewriting to add query support to Java makes us hopeful that the approach will also work well for integrating other interface facilities into Java. We would like to expand Queryll into a general bytecode rewriting framework that would allow programmers to plug-in various behaviours appropriate for different interfacing middleware.

References

1. Eisenberg, A., Melton, J.: SQLJ part 0, now known as SQL/OLB (object-language bindings). SIGMOD Rec. **27**(4) (1998) 94–100
2. Sun Microsystems: JDBC technology. (http://java.sun.com/products/jdbc/)
3. JBoss: Hibernate. (http://www.hibernate.org/)

4. Sun Microsystems: Enterprise JavaBeans technology. (http://java.sun.com/products/ejb/)
5. Microsoft: The LINQ project. (http://msdn.microsoft.com/netframework/future/linq/)
6. Tilevich, E., Smaragdakis, Y.: Portable and efficient distributed threads for Java. In: Middleware '04: Proceedings of the 5th ACM/IFIP/USENIX international conference on Middleware, New York, NY, USA, Springer-Verlag New York, Inc. (2004) 478–492
7. Pawlak, R., Seinturier, L., Duchien, L., Florin, G.: Jac: A flexible solution for aspect-oriented programming in Java. In: REFLECTION '01. Volume 2192 of LNCS., London, UK, Springer-Verlag (2001) 1–24
8. Bik, A.J., Gannon, D.B.: Javab—a prototype bytecode parallelization tool. Technical Report TR489, Indiana University (1997)
9. Miecznikowski, J., Hendren, L.: Decompiling Java bytecode: Problems, traps and pitfalls. In: CC 2002, Springer-Verlag (2002) 111–127
10. Vallée-Rai, R., Co, P., Gagnon, E., Hendren, L., Lam, P., Sundaresan, V.: Soot - a Java bytecode optimization framework. In: CASCON '99: Proceedings of the 1999 conference of the Centre for Advanced Studies on Collaborative research, IBM Press (1999) 13
11. Erosa, A.M., Hendren, L.J.: Taming control flow: A structured approach to eliminating GOTO statements. In: ICCL. (1994)
12. Peterson, W.W., Kasami, T., Tokura, N.: On the capabilities of while, repeat, and exit statements. Commun. ACM **16**(8) (1973) 503–512
13. Transaction Processing Performance Council (TPC): TPC Benchmark W (Web Commerce) Specification Version 1.8. Transaction Processing Performance Council (2002)
14. Amza, C., Cecchet, E., Chanda, A., Elnikety, S., Cox, A., Gil, R., Marguerite, J., Rajamani, K., Zwaenepoel, W.: Bottleneck characterization of dynamic web site benchmarks. Technical Report TR02-389, Rice University (2002)
15. PostgreSQL Global Development Group: PostgreSQL. (http://www.postgresql.org/)

Contory: A Middleware for the Provisioning of Context Information on Smart Phones

Oriana Riva

Helsinki Institute for Information Technology
P.O. Box 9800, FIN-02015 HUT, Finland
oriana.riva@hiit.fi

Abstract. Context-awareness can serve to make ubiquitous applications deployed for mobile devices adaptive, personalized, and accessible in dynamically changing environments. Unfortunately, existing approaches for the provisioning of context information in ubiquitous computing environments rarely take into consideration the resource constraints of mobile devices and the uncertain availability of sensors and service infrastructures. This paper presents the design, prototype implementation, and experimental evaluation of Contory, a middleware specifically designed to accomplish efficient context provisioning on mobile devices. To make context provisioning flexible and adaptive based on dynamic operating conditions, Contory integrates multiple context provisioning strategies, namely internal sensors-based, external infrastructure-based, and distributed provisioning in ad hoc networks. Applications can request context information provided by Contory using a declarative query language which features on-demand, periodic, and event-based context queries. Experimental results obtained in a testbed of smart phones demonstrate the feasibility of our approach and quantify the cost of supporting context provisioning in terms of energy consumption.

Keywords: Context-awareness, middleware, smart phones, energy consumption.

1 Introduction

Context-awareness is emerging as a promising enabler of various ubiquitous applications deployed for usage on mobile devices. In principle, mobile devices can acquire context data through a large variety of sensors embedded in the device and in the surrounding environment. In practice, making context information available for usage to applications running on such devices often turns out to be an ambitious demand [1]. Mobile devices are typically resource-constrained, while context provisioning is often a complex process consisting of several sequential and parallel sub-processes, which can lead to significant power consumption and memory utilization; for example, reasoning algorithms can require large storage space and complex computations. The integration of sensors in mobile devices should not compromise portability, usability (e.g., size, weight, design, and aesthetics), cost, and lifetime of everyday mobile devices. Some sensors may not be operative in every environment (e.g., GPS in indoor environments).

M. van Steen and M. Henning (Eds.): Middleware 2006, LNCS 4290, pp. 219–239, 2006.
© IFIP International Federation for Information Processing 2006

Typically, context-aware applications either directly sense and locally process context data (e.g., Context Toolkit [2]) or rely on external context infrastructures [3], which collect, process, and disseminate context data of multiple entities. Additionally, the increasing availability of ubiquitous connectivity, such as Bluetooth and WiFi, on mobile devices makes feasible a distributed provisioning approach, in which devices share context information of different types in mobile ad hoc networks. These three strategies for context provisioning are all valuable, but they build upon specific assumptions which might not be always and constantly verified. In ubiquitous environments, operating conditions of mobile clients can vary widely over time and space. For instance, in resource-rich environments, powerful context infrastructures can provide applications with required context data, thus reducing the computational load on single devices. Conversely, in resource-impoverished environments, devices can rely either on their own sensors and processing capabilities or on neighboring devices. In order to cope with the dynamism and heterogeneity of such environments, more flexibility is required in accomplishing context provisioning.

This paper proposes the CONTextfactORY (Contory) middleware for context provisioning on smart phones. Contory offers an SQL-like interface to generate context queries, in which applications can specify type and quality of the desired context items, context sources, push or pull mode of interaction, and other properties. Contory processes context queries and collects context data by employing multiple strategies for context provisioning, namely internal sensors-based, external infrastructure-based, and distributed provisioning in ad hoc networks. This approach presents two advantages. First, arranging different context strategies permits compensating for the temporary unavailability of one mechanism and coping with dynamic resource availability. Second, combining results collected through different context mechanisms allows applications to partly relieve the uncertainty of single context sources and to more accurately infer higher-level context information. Since smart phones are becoming increasingly interesting to academia and industry as platforms for realizing the ubiquitous computing vision, the smart phone was selected as development platform. To assess system performance and quantify the energy consumption on smart phones, we ran experiments in a testbed of Nokia Series 60 and Nokia Series 80 phones. Moreover, to evaluate the practical feasibility of the proposed approach, we built a prototype application for a sailing scenario.

Core concepts and design principles for the deployment of Contory have been previously presented in [4]. This paper makes the following contributions: *(i)* it presents full design and implementation of a middleware supporting multiple strategies for context provisioning; *(ii)* among these strategies, it offers an infrastructure-less approach to collect context data over mobile ad hoc networks; *(iii)* it describes a middleware and real-world applications implemented on a smart phone platform; *(iv)* it provides experimental results that give insights into the performance of smart phones in terms of energy consumption.

The rest of the paper is organized as follows. Section 2 discusses several existing context provisioning strategies. Section 3 presents requirements and design principles at the basis of Contory. Section 4 presents query model, software architecture, and programming interface of Contory, while implementation details are given in Section 5. Section 6 describes experimental results and a prototype application using Contory. Section 7 discusses related work. The paper concludes in Section 8.

2   Context Provisioning

Context can be defined as any information that can be used to characterize the situation of an entity [2]. Context provisioning is the process by which context information is acquired, processed, and made available for usage. Hereafter, we refer to *context providers* as the software components in charge of performing context provisioning. Sensors integrated in the handheld device and in the environment, tags and beacons, positioning systems, biosensors on user can be used to acquire raw context data about the user's physical and social environment. Context providers process raw data using mechanisms such as feature extraction, aggregation, classification, and clustering in order to infer the user's context. Finally, the extracted context is made accessible to the application and other external components.

A large number of approaches have been proposed to support context provisioning. As Fig. 1a shows, a first basic strategy, called **internal context provisioning**, consists of deploying specialized context providers to be installed on the device. The integration of these context providers into applications can lead to increased complexity, loss of generality and reuse, and expensive and time-consuming application development. Alternatively, context providers can be organized in libraries, toolkits (e.g., Context Toolkit [2]), frameworks (e.g., TEA framework [5]), middleware (e.g., RCSM [6]), thus providing application developers with uniform context abstractions. However, in many situations, it is unrealistic to assume that individual mobile devices will constantly carry any type of conceivable sensor or will be capable of interacting with any type of sensor embedded in the environment.

A second strategy consists of deploying autonomous context-service components, running on remote devices, accessible by multiple applications, and independent of the application logic. Existing examples are external service

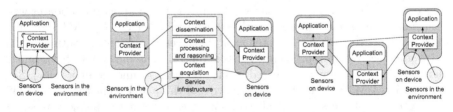

a) Internal context provisioning   b) External centralized context provisioning   c) External distributed context provisioning

Fig. 1. Context provisioning strategies

infrastructures [3] (e.g., Confab [7] and JCAF [8]), and shared servers (e.g., the Trivial Context System (TCoS) [9]). We call this approach, depicted in Fig. 1b, **external centralized context provisioning**. These shared context services are in charge of discovering suitable context sources and processing, storing, and disseminating gathered context data. Multiple context providers on different applications can pull or subscribe to these services to retrieve context information related to certain context entities. On the one hand, by sharing sensors and computing resources, this approach reduces the computational load on single devices and makes applications less tied to a specific sensor platform. On the other hand, relying on a centralized system presents scalability, extensibility, and fault-tolerance issues.

A third possibility, albeit rarely considered in this field, is a distributed model as the one depicted in Fig. 1c. We call this approach **external distributed context provisioning**. The key idea is to abstract context provisioning as the problem of supporting the access to a distributed database where data are provided by context providers located on the nodes of a Mobile Ad-hoc NETwork (MANET). Nodes equipped with the necessary sensors can acquire raw context data, process them, and make them accessible to neighboring nodes. Ubiquitous connectivity already available on commercial mobile devices enables proximity networks of this type.

3   Contory Requirements and Design

The deployment of a middleware for context provisioning stems from the necessity to move a number of core data and services for context sensing, management, and distribution from their multiple instances into a centralized provision of services. Requirements for the deployment of Contory were gathered from experiences with a context-based application developed in the DYNAMOS[1] Project. The DYNAMOS application, described in [10], aims to proactively provide mobile users with nearby services that are of interest based on the user's current context and needs. The application prototype runs on smart phones and was specifically designed to target the needs of a community of recreational sailboaters. In June and August 2005, we conducted two field trials with sailboats in which such an application was used by about 30 persons equipped with Nokia 6630 phones and GPS devices.

During the regatta, location-awareness was accomplished by means of GPS devices connected through Bluetooth (BT) to the phone. Location updates were encapsulated in events and constantly transmitted over GPRS/UMTS for storage in a remote repository. Collected location traces were fairly discontinuous due to several disconnection problems. First, several BT disconnections between the phone and the GPS device occurred (typically one disconnection per hour). Second, when a UMTS connection was active and the phone went through 2G/3G handover, the phone switched off (this did not occur if the phone was set to

---

[1] Dynamic Composition and Sharing of Context-Aware Mobile Services. URL: http://virtual.vtt.fi/virtual/proj2/dynamos/

operate only in 2G mode). Additionally, the traffic of events carrying context updates and going from the phone to the remote repository had to be optimized and largely reduced, in order to avoid the phone to switch off due to high memory consumption and network connectivity problems.

Besides these phone-specific issues, these experiences in the real field of action helped discover technical problems regarding context sensing and context management. We found that *(i)* context provisioning based exclusively on local sensors is often not reliable enough; *(ii)* sharing of context information owned by multiple users can provide useful services to the end-user, enlarge the spatial range of context monitoring, reduce global resource utilization, and permit coping with sensor unreliability; *(iii)* external infrastructures should be ready to cope with frequent user disconnections (e.g., by incorporating prediction or learning algorithms); and *(iv)* the client application should be ready to cope with frequent disconnections from remote repositories.

The design of Contory followed four main guiding principles:

- *Flexible and reliable context provisioning*: Ideally, context provisioning should take place without any interruption, e.g., due to hardware faults or temporary disconnections from context sources. In Contory, multiple context provisioning strategies are made available and can be dynamically and transparently interchanged based on sensor availability and resource consumption.
- *Common querying interface*: To formulate requests about heterogenous context items, Contory supports an SQL-like context query language. This common interface allows applications to specify type and qualifying properties of the required context data.
- *Push and pull access mode*: Context-aware applications can interact with Contory by using either a pull or a push mode; they can submit on-demand queries or long-running queries (periodic or event-based queries).
- *Modularity and extensibility*: Contory glues several context provider components together. Separation of semantic definition of the provided information and availability of modular context providers enhances adaptation to variable configurations. New sources of context information and processing algorithms, which will be developed in the forthcoming years, will need to be easily accommodated in the existing architecture.

4 Contory Middleware Architecture

Contory aims to provide specialized and transparent support for retrieving context items of different types and quality. This section describes core concepts for the design of Contory, its software architecture, and programming interface.

4.1 Context Items and Context Metadata

The context associated with a certain situation can be expressed as a set of *context items*, each describing a specific element of the situation. For instance, the situation *walking outside* could be represented by the triplet <*noise=medium, light=natural, activity=walking*>. Context items can describe spatial information (location, speed), temporal information (time, duration), user status (activity, mood), environmental information (temperature, light, noise), and resource availability (nearby devices, device power). In Contory, context data are exchanged by means of `cxtItem` objects. Each `cxtItem` consists of `type` (context category), `value` (current value(s) of the item), and `timestamp` (the time at which the context item had such a value). Optionally, it can have a `lifetime` (validity duration), a `source` identifier (e.g., sensor, infrastructure, and device addresses), and other `metadata` information. Types of metadata information include correctness (i.e, closeness to the true state), precision, accuracy, completeness (if any or no part of the described information remains unknown), and level of privacy and trust.

4.2   Context Query Language

From an application's point of view, Contory mostly acts as a data-retrieval system to which context-aware applications submit context queries. Although similar to a database system, the dynamism and fuzziness of context data lead to important differences. Context sources can provide large amounts of context data, hence some aggregation and filtering functions are required. Context monitoring is a continuous process, hence not only on-demand queries but also long-running queries have to be supported. Although different applications have usually different requirements, rather than deploying application-specific interfaces, we abstracted the functionality of several applications into one common SQL-like *context query language*. The query template has the following format.

```
SELECT <context name> [*]
FROM <source>
WHERE <predicate clause>
FRESHNESS <time>
DURATION <duration> [*]
EVERY <time> | EVENT <predicate clause>
```

The SELECT and DURATION clauses (marked with [*]) are mandatory. SELECT specifies the `type` of the requested context item. DURATION specifies the query lifetime as time (e.g, `1 hour`) or as the number of samples that must be collected in each round (e.g., `50 samples`).

Contory aims to offer different levels of transparency to the application developer. The maximum transparency is achieved when the FROM clause is unspecified and the middleware autonomously and dynamically selects the context provisioning mechanism to be employed. Alternatively, the FROM clause offers to the programmer several ways to control type and characteristics of the context sources to be employed. Context sources can be of three kinds according to the three context provisioning mechanisms supported: internal sensor-based (`intSensor`), external infrastructure-based (`extInfra`), and distributed context provisioning in ad hoc networks (`adHocNetwork`). In the case of `adHocNetwork` provisioning, the FROM clause also tells multiplicity (`numNodes`) and distance (`numHops`) of the context source nodes. For example, the search for suitable context items can involve all nodes that can be discovered (`numNodes=all`) or the first k nodes found within a distance lower than j hops (`numNodes=k, numHops=j`). Alternatively, the programmer can also specify the **destination** to which the query has to be sent. This destination can be the identifier of an entity (e.g., to know when a friend is nearby) or the coordinates of a region to be monitored (e.g., next exit on the highway).

WHERE contains filtering predicates expressed using the context item's `metadata`. FRESHNESS specifies how recent the context data must be. Finally, our query language provides support for long running queries by means of EVERY and EVENT clauses. These clauses are mutually exclusive. The EVERY clause allows the application to specify the rate at which context data should be collected (periodic query). The EVENT clause determines the set of conditions that must be met at the context provider's node before a new result is returned (event-based query).

In the following example, the query returns, for one hour, temperature values collected from the first 10 nodes found in an ad hoc network within a distance of at most 3 hops; data are not older than 30 seconds, have accuracy of 0.2 °C, and are sent every time the average temperature exceeds 25 °C.

```
SELECT temperature
FROM adHocNetwork(10,3)
WHERE accuracy=0.2
FRESHNESS 30 sec
DURATION 1 hour
EVENT AVG(temperature)>25
```

4.3 Contory Software Architecture

Fig. 2 depicts the conceptual architecture of Contory. *ContextFactory* is the core component of the overall architecture. One *ContextFactory* is instantiated on each device and made accessible to multiple applications. Based on the *Factory Method* design pattern [11], this design model aims to define an interface for creating objects, but let subclasses decide which class to instantiate. In our case, the *ContextFactory* offers an interface to submit context queries, but lets *Facade* components (subclasses) decide which *ContextProvider* components (classes) to instantiate. The *ContextFactory* provides support for *(i) context sensing and communication, (ii) context provisioning and sharing*, and *(iii) queries and providers management*. In the following, we describe each functionality along with their core architectural components.

Context Sensing and Communication. Context data can be sensed from a large variety of *CxtSources* such as external sensors (e.g., a GPS device), integrated monitors (e.g., a power management framework), external servers (e.g., a weather station). To provide discovery of *CxtSources* as well as to support communication with them, different types of *Reference* modules can be available on

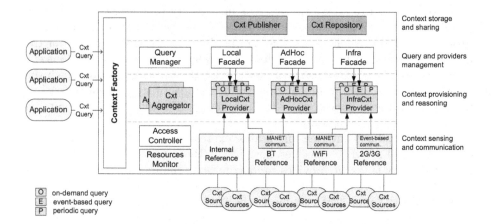

Fig. 2. Contory middleware architecture

the device. Typically, a *Reference* mediates the access to a certain communication module by offering useful programming abstractions. As shown in Fig. 2, Contory includes four types of *References*. The *InternalReference* is specialized to support communication with sensors integrated in the device. The *BTReference* provides support to discover BT devices and services, and to communicate with them. The *WiFiReference* manages communication in WiFi networks, but also provides abstractions for content-based routing, geographical routing, and multi-hop communication in ad hoc networks. The *2G/3GReference* manages communications with remote entities over the corresponding network standards and offers an event-based interface.

Mobile systems can undergo unexpected changes in the level of resource availability, for example, when a new application is started or when the host moves to a different network domain. Moreover, in wireless environments, disconnections and bandwidth fluctuations are common. These issues make necessary the adoption of dynamic resource allocation mechanisms. The *ResourcesMonitor* component is in charge of maintaining an updated view on the status of several hardware items (e.g., device drivers), on the device's overall power state, and on the available memory space. Each time, network, sensors, or device failures affect the functioning of a communication module, the corresponding *Reference* notifies the *ResourcesMonitor* module. This, in turn, will inform the *ContextFactory* which will enforce a reconfiguration strategy to take over. For example, if a BT-GPS device suddenly disconnects, the location provisioning task can be moved from a *LocalLocationProvider* (using the *BTReference*) to an *AdHocLocationProvider* (using the *WiFiReference*).

The *AccessController* module is responsible for controlling the interaction with external sources and requesters of context items. The *AccessController* keeps track of previously connected context sources (such as sensors or devices) and also of blocked context sources. This list is continuously refreshed so that only the most recent and the most often accessed sources are kept in memory. If the application requires high-security operating mode, every time a new context source is encountered, it is blocked or admitted based on explicit validation by the application. In low-security mode, every new entity is trusted.

Context Provisioning and Sharing. *CxtProviders* are responsible for accomplishing context provisioning. Optionally, they can also incorporate reasoning mechanisms for inferring higher-level context data. A *CxtAggregator* can be used to combine context items collected from single or multiple *CxtProviders*. Alternatively, advanced context processing mechanisms can be performed by external context infrastructures, distributed across remote components or implemented at the application level.

CxtProviders are of three types. *LocalCxtProviders* manage the access to local sensors which can be integrated in the device or be accessible via BT. These providers periodically pull sensor devices and report values that match WHERE and FRESHNESS requirements. *InfraCxtProviders* are responsible for retrieving context data from remote context infrastructures. *AdHocCxtProviders* are responsible for supporting distributed context provisioning in ad hoc networks; to gather context data from nodes in a MANET, these providers utilize the *BTReference* (only for one-hop routing) or the *WiFiReference* (also for multi-hop routing). Based on the EVENT and EVERY clauses specification, context providers offer three modes of interaction: *on-demand query*, *event-based query*, and *periodic query*.

The *CxtRepository* module is responsible for storing gathered context information, locally or remotely. Only a few recent context data are stored locally, while complete logs can be stored in remote repositories of context infrastructures. The *CxtPublisher* allows publishing context information in ad hoc networks by means of the *BTReference* or the *WiFiReference*. Each time a context item has to be published, two access modalities can be applied: public access allows any external entity to access the item, and authenticated access locks the item with a key that must be known by the requester.

Queries and Providers Management. The *QueryManager* is responsible for maintaining an updated list of all active queries and for assigning queries to suitable *Facade* components. For each of the three types of context provisioning mechanisms supported, a corresponding *Facade* module offers a unified interface for managing *CxtProviders* of that specific type. The purpose of utilizing the *Facade* design pattern [11] is to abstract the subsystem of *CxtProviders* to offer a more convenient (unidirectional) interface to the *ContextFactory*. The *Facade* knows which subsystem classes (i.e., *CxtProviders*) are responsible for a certain query and can direct actions or requests of the *ContextFactory* to the correct component.

The *QueryManager* invokes the factory method `processCxtQuery(CxtQuery q)` of the *ContextFactory* to assign the query to one or multiple *Facades*. The assignment is done base on the requirements specified in the query's FROM clause, based on sensor availability, and in the respect of the active control policies. For instance, a control policy can specify the maximum level of memory and power consumption that should be tolerated at runtime. Control policies are formulated as `contextRules` consisting of a condition and an action statements. Conditions are articulated as Boolean expressions, and the operators currently supported are `equal`, `notEqual`, `moreThan`, and `lessThan`. An example of condition is `<batteryLevel,equal,low>`. Through `and` and `or` operators, elementary conditions can be combined to form more complex ones. Whenever a condition is positively verified at runtime, the associated action becomes active and it is enforced by the *ContextFactory*. Actions currently supported are `reducePower`, `reduceMemory`, and `reduceLoad`. The enforcement of these actions can have different effects such as the switch from a certain provisioning mechanism to another one or the interruption of a query execution. For example, the activation of the `reducePower` action can cause the suspension or termination of high energy-consuming queries (e.g., those using the *2G/3GReference*) or the replacement of WiFi-based multi-hop provisioning with BT-based one-hop provisioning.

Once the query has been assigned to a *Facade*, in order to avoid redundancy and keep the number of active queries minimal, the *Facade* performs query aggregation. This process consists of two sub-processes: query merging and post-extraction. The *Facade* first checks whether the new submitted query `q1` can be merged with any other active query `q2`. If `q3 = merge(q1,q2)` can be found, `q3` is the new query to be processed. The post-extraction sub-process is applied to the received results for `q3` in order to extract the data matching the original queries `q1` and `q2`. The `merge` function implements a simplified version of the clustering algorithm defined in [12]. This algorithm builds on the definition of a "distance" metric between queries. The algorithm computes the distance between each pair of queries and if it is below a certain threshold, the two queries are put in the same cluster. In our design, for simplicity, we put in the same cluster queries with the same `SELECT` clause. Once clusters are formed, the merging is performed by applying clause-specific merging rules, as exemplified below:

```
q1:                      q2:                      q3:
SELECT temperature       SELECT temperature       SELECT temperature
FROM adHocNetwork(all,3) FROM adHocNetwork(all,1) FROM adHocNetwork(all,3)
FRESHNESS 10sec          FRESHNESS 20sec          FRESHNESS 20sec
DURATION 1hour           DURATION 2hour           DURATION 2hour
EVERY 15sec              EVERY 30sec              EVERY 15sec
```

Upon the aggregation process has completed, the *Facade* module either instantiates a new *CxtProvider* or updates the query parameters of an existing *CxtProvider* (e,g., in case the new query has been merged with an already active query). *CxtProviders* of different *Facades* can be assigned to the same query, but each *CxtProvider* is assigned only to one (single or merged) query at time.

4.4   Contory Programming Interface

The Contory API shields the programmer from the underlying communication platforms and context provisioning aspects. To interact with Contory, an application needs to implement a `Client` interface and implements the following methods:

- `receiveCxtItem(CxtItem cxtItem)` in order to handle the reception of collected context items;
- `informError(String msg)` to be called by several Contory modules in case of malfunctioning or failure;
- `makeDecision(String msg)` to be invoked by the *AccessController* to grant or block the interaction with external entities.

The application can access Contory services through the `ContextFactory` interface. As shown below, this interface offers methods for submitting and erasing context queries (line 2 and 3), for publishing or erasing context items (line 4), and for remotely storing context items (line 5). In order to be eligible to publish context items and made them accessible to other clients, the publisher must register and be authenticated (line 6). Likewise, the client can deregister (line 7).

```
1 public interface ContextFactory{
2    boolean processCxtQuery (CxtQuery query);
3    void cancelCxtQuery (String queryID);
4    boolean publishCxtItem (String cxtItem,boolean published);
5    void storeCxtItem (CxtItem cxtItem);
6    void registerCxtServer (CxtServer client);
7    void deregisterCxtServer (CxtServer client);
8 }
```

Different vocabularies are made available to the application developer: *(i)* the `CxtVocabulary` contains context types, context values, and metadata types for specifying context items and device resources; *(ii)* the `QueryVocabulary` contains parameters for specifying context queries; and *(iii)* the `CxtRulesVocabulary` contains operators and actions for specifying control policies.

5 Implementation

Contory has been implemented using Java 2 Platform Micro Edition (J2ME). Currently, two separate implementations exist: one for Connected Limited Device Configuration (CLDC) 1.0 and Mobile Information Device Profile (MIDP) 2.0 APIs, and one for Connected Device Configuration (CDC) 1.0. The J2ME platform was selected since it currently represents the most widespread computing platform for personal mobile devices. All software development was done using Nokia Series 60 and Nokia Series 80 phones. In the following, we provide specific insights into the implementation of *References* and distributed context provisioning. The *InternalReference* module has not been implemented yet because no sensors integrated in the phone platform used for the development were available at deployment time.

5.1 References Implementation

The *BTReference* utilizes the Java Specification Request 82 (JSR-82) available for CLDC. This specification defines a standard set of APIs for BT wireless technology and specifically targets devices that are limited in processing power and memory. The specification includes support for *(i)* discovery (device discovery, service discovery, and service registration), *(ii)* communication (establishing connections between BT devices and using those connections for BT communication), and *(iii)* device management (managing and controlling these BT connections).

Since no standardized support exists to program ad hoc networks, the *WiFiReference* provides device and service discovery, content-based routing, multi-hop communications in ad hoc networks by means of the Smart Messages (SM) [13] distributed computing platform. This was specifically designed for highly volatile networks such as MANETs. We utilize the portable version of SM [14] implemented for the J2ME CDC platform. An SM is a user-defined application, similar to a mobile agent, whose execution is sequentially distributed over a series of nodes using execution migration. The nodes on which SMs execute are named by properties, called *tags,* and discovered dynamically using application-controlled routing. Tags have a name, similar to a file name in a file system, which is used for content-based naming of nodes. To move between two nodes of interest, an SM explicitly calls for execution migration. An SM consists of *code bricks, data bricks* (mobile data explicitly identified in the program), and execution control state. To support SM execution, the SM runtime system runs inside a Java virtual machine and consists of: *(i) admission manager* that performs admission control and prevents excessive use of resources by incoming SMs, *(ii) code cache* that stores frequently executed code bricks, *(iii) scheduler* that dispatches ready SMs for execution on the Java virtual machine, and *(iv) tag space* that provides a shared memory addressable by names for inter SM communication and synchronization. The tag space offers a uniform view of the network resources in terms of naming and access to resources. We use SM tags to publish context items in the ad hoc network.

The *2G/3GReference* offers support for event-based communication by using the Fuego middleware [15]. This middleware is implemented in Java and provides a scalable distributed event framework and XML-based messaging service. This middleware also runs on mobile phones supporting Java MIDP 1.0.

5.2 Distributed Context Provisioning Using BT and SM

Distributed context provisioning has been implemented using the *BTReference* in one-hop ad hoc networks and using the *WiFiReference* in multi-hop ad hoc networks. Distributed context provisioning is accomplished in three phases: initialization, publishing, and execution.

In the BT-based implementation, the initialization phase places the BT device into inquiry mode and specifies an event listener that will respond to inquiry-related events. A context item can be published by advertising a context service on the BT server (service registration). The server creates a service record describing the offered context service and adds it to the server's Service Discovery Database (SDDB). This is visible and available to external BT entities. The *AdHocCxtProvider* first discovers accessible BT devices (in some cases a list of pre-known devices is used) and then looks for available services on the discovered devices.

In the WiFi-based implementation, the *WiFiReference* expresses its willingness to participate in the Contory ad hoc network by exposing the tag "contory". In such a way, every time an SM needs to be routed from a certain source to a certain destination, all nodes in the ad hoc network exposing the "contory" tag will collaborate with each other to forward the SM towards the destination. To publish a context item in the ad hoc network, the *AdHocCxtPublisher* exposes on the local node a tag whose name contains the type and whose value contains the value and metadata of the context item (e.g., ($temperatureTag :< name = temperature >, < value = 14^oC, 1^oC, trusted >$)). To discover context items of interest, the context query is encapsulated in an SM-FINDER that is routed towards nodes exposing the desired context tag (i.e., the tag whose name matches the SELECT clause of the carried query). To disambiguate between multiple messages, a unique identifier is associated with each query and with each result. If no valid result is received within a certain timeout, the query is cancelled. If nodes exposing context items of the type of interest are discovered, WHERE, FRESHNESS and EVENTS requirements specified in the query are evaluated. If positively verified, the value of the context item along with additional metadata properties are saved in the SM-FINDER which is routed back to the query issuer. In order to cope with nodes mobility, the SM-FINDER maintains a hopCnt that indicates how many hops the message has traversed until that moment. When the SM-FINDER is delivered to the *AdHocCxtProvider* issuer, if hopCnt>numHops the receiver discards the result because the *CxtPublisher* that provided such a result is out of the range of interest.

6   Evaluation

We evaluated Contory in two phases. We built an experimental testbed of smart phones and measured response times and energy consumption for different context operations. We then evaluated Contory by building a real-world application using it. This section presents experimental results and prototype application.

6.1   Experimental Results

The objective of this experimental analysis was to demonstrate the practical feasibility of the proposed approach, give an insight on the performance of our prototype implementation, and quantify its cost mostly in terms of energy consumption. Our experimental testbed consisted of a Nokia 6630 phone (Symbian OS 8.0a, 220 MHz processor, WCDMA/EDGE, 9 MB of RAM), a Nokia 7610 phone (Symbian OS 7.0s, 123 MHz processor, GPRS, 9 MB of RAM),

Table 1. Latency times of basic Contory operations

Entity acts as:	Operation	Elapsed time (msec) Avg [90% Conf interval]
ContextProvider	createCxtItem	0.078 [0.001]
	adHocNetwork, BT-based: publishCxtItem	140.359 [0.337]
	adHocNetwork, WiFi-based: publishCxtItem	0.130 [0.006]
	extInfra, UMTS-based: publishCxtItem	772.728 [158.924]
ContextRequester	createCxtQuery	0.219 [0.001]
	adHocNetwork, BT-based, one hop: getCxtItem	31.830 [0.151]
	adHocNetwork, WiFi-based, one hop: getCxtItem	761.280 [28.940]
	adHocNetwork, WiFi-based, two hops: getCxtItem	1422.500 [60.001]
	extInfra, UMTS-based: getCxtItem	1473.000 [275.000]

3 Nokia 9500 communicators (Symbian OS 7.0s, 150 MHz processor, WLAN 802.11b/EDGE, 64 MB of RAM), and a Bluetooth GPS Receiver InsSirf III.

Latency Experiments. Table 1 reports latency times for four main Contory operations: createCxtItem, publishCxtItem, createCxtQuery, and getCxtItem. The size of a context query object is 205 bytes, while the size of a context item varies from 53 bytes (e.g., a wind item) to 136 bytes (e.g., a location item). For these experiments, we used a lightItem whose size is 136 bytes. CxtItem and cxtQuery objects that are transmitted over UMTS using the event-based platform are encapsulated in event notifications whose size is 1696 bytes.

On the context publisher side, publishing a context item with the BT-based mechanism takes much longer than with the WiFi-based mechanism. The reason for this stems from the BT registering process. With BT, to make an item accessible, this needs to be encapsulated in a DataElement and registered into the BT ServiceRecord. With SM, this operation corresponds to simply creating a new SM tag and storing its name and value in the TagSpace hashtable. The variability of latency times for publishing a context item in the remote infrastructure is quite extreme and is due to the high delay variability in UMTS networks.

On the context provider side, adHocNetwork provisioning can be BT-based or WiFi-based. For the BT case, the latency time reported in the table represents the time needed to receive a context item, once device and service discovery has occurred (BT device discovery takes approximately 13 sec and BT service discovery takes approximately 1.12 sec). For the WiFi case, we ran experiments using a 2-hops topology with three communicators arranged in a line. The two latency times reported in the table represent the time needed to retrieve one context item located at a distance of one or two hops, once the route has been built. The additional time required to build the route is approximately twice the corresponding latency value in the table. The break-up analysis for SM experiments shows that connection establishment accounts for 4-5% of the total

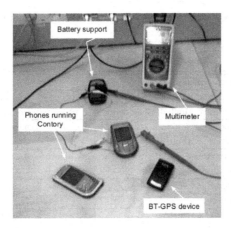

Fig. 3. Power measurements testbed setup

latency time, serialization for 26-33%, thread switching for 12-14%, and transfer time for 51-54%. The SM overhead is negligible. Finally, measured latency times for extInfra vary enormously, ranging from 703 msec up to 2766 msec.

Energy Consumption Experiments. Energy consumption remains one of the most critical issues that needs to be addressed in application development on mobile phones. While CPU speed and storage capacity have increased over the last 10 years, battery energy shows the slowest trend in mobile computing [16]. To measure energy consumption on phones, we inserted a multimeter in series between the phone and its battery. The testbed setup is shown in Fig. 3. We used a Fluke 189 multimeter, which was connected to a PC to record the readings. The meter read current inputs approximately every 500 ms. The precision of our measurements depends mostly on the precision of the multimeter and the stability of the voltage on the phone battery. The resistance of the wires was found to be negligible. The multimeter has an accuracy of 0.75% and precision of 0.15%. The stability of the voltage is important since this is used to compute the power consumption based on Ohm's law. We did some preliminary experiments to measure the voltage on the phone while performing different operations; we found out that under high load the battery deviated less than 2% from 4.0965 V for the first hour at least. To minimize the impact of the voltage variance, we ran short experiments and always with a full battery. Given that the shunt voltage of the meter is 1.8 mV/mA, we calculated that the maximum inaccuracy of our experiments was approximately 8%. We ran the experiments in an office environment with background noise due to other mobile phones, wireless LANs, BT, etc. Even though a noise-free environment would have been desirable, we ran all experiments in the same spot, thus emulating a daily life scenario with an almost constant level of background noise.

All experiments were performed from five to ten times. High energy consuming experiments were set to last no longer than 10 min. All numbers hereafter

Table 2. Energy consumption of different context provisioning mechanisms

Context provisioning method: operation	Energy consumption per cxtItem (Joule) Avg [90% Conf Interval]
adHocNetwork, BT-based: provideCxtItem	0.133 [0.002]
adHocNetwork, BT-based: getCxtItem (one-hop and on-demand query, including discovery)	5.270 [0.010]
adHocNetwork, BT-based: getCxtItem (one hop and periodic query, without discovery)	0.099 [0.007]
intSensor, BT-based: getCxtItem (periodic query, without discovery)	0.422 [0.084]
adHocNetwork, WiFi-based: getCxtItem (one hop and periodic query)	> 0.906 [a]
adHocNetwork, WiFi-based: getCxtItem (two hops and periodic query)	> 1.693 [a]
extInfra, UMTS-based: getCxtItem (on-demand query)	14.076 [0.496]

[a] Includes the cost of having back-light switched on.

reported were collected on a Nokia 6630 phone and a Nokia 9500 communicator (only when WiFi was used). Initially, we measured the cost of different operating modes when the GSM radio was turned off. When BT is turned off, back-light is switched on, and display is switched on, the average power consumption is about 76.20 mW. If the back-light is turned off, the consumption decreases to 14.35 mW. A consumption of 5.75 mW is achieved if also the display is turned off. Turning on BT in page and inquiry scan state increases the power consumption to 8.47 mW. Turning on Contory as well leads to a power consumption of 10.11 mW. We ran all experiments (except UMTS-based tests) with the GSM radio off, back-light off, and display off.

Table 2 reports energy consumption results for all three context provisioning mechanisms. On the provider side, the energy consumption for providing context items is relatively contained. On the requester side, we distinguish three cases.

For BT-based mechanisms, the cost of processing context queries is mostly due to the device discovery phase which lasts approximately 13 sec. Once the BT device is discovered, being periodically notified with context data is fast and the energy cost is definitely low. Results for intSensor were gathered by connecting the BT-GPS device to the phone. While the discovery cost is the same for BT-based intSensor and adHocNetwork, the cost for maintaining a periodic exchange of data is higher for intSensor. This is due to the larger size of the exchanged data (GPS-NMEA data are 340 bytes big) and the packet segmentation BT applies.

For WiFi-based provisioning, energy costs are much higher than in the BT cases. We encountered several problems in running these experiments. Each time a WiFi connection was established on the communicator inserted in the circuit, the communicator switched off after less than 30 sec. New smart phones are

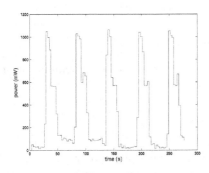

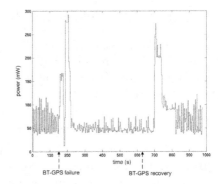

Fig. 4. Power consumption for extInfra provisioning

Fig. 5. Contory behaviour in the presence of BT-GPS failure

low-voltage devices operating from a single Lithium-Ion cell. During the startup phase, the high in-rush current causes the phone's voltage supply to drop due to the multimeter's internal resistance; hence, this drop triggers the internal power management protection circuit to turn off the phone. However, based on the logs we gathered, having WiFi connected at full signal (with back light on) drains a constant current of 300 mA, which leads to an average power consumption of 1190 mW. This also means that having WiFi connected is more than 100 times more energy-consuming than having BT in inquiry mode.

In the tests for extInfra provisioning, turning on the GSM radio produces an additional power consumption; this comes in peaks of 450-481 mW and every 50-60 sec. Fig. 4 shows the power consumption for a test in which 5 queries were sent to the infrastructure over UMTS, every 3 min. The maximum power consumption, which corresponds to when the connection is opened and the request for the item is sent, is 1000 mW. Such a high energy cost is mostly due to the cost of opening the UMTS connection. Sending and retrieving larger groups of items in the same time slot largely reduces the energy consumption per item.

To demonstrate how Contory is able to recover from sensor failures by dynamically switching from one context provisioning mechanism to another, we simulated a GPS failure. As Fig. 5 shows, initially the phone is retrieving location data from a GPS device connected through BT. After 155 sec, we caused a GPS failure by manually switching off the GPS device. As a reaction, Contory switches from sensor-based provisioning to ad hoc provisioning and starts collecting location data from a neighboring device. Later on, the GPS device becomes available again. Once the GPS device is discovered, Contory switches back to sensor-based provisioning. The cost in terms of power consumption of the switches is due mostly to the BT device discovery: this varies from 163 mW up to 292 mW.

Experiments Summary. These experimental results confirmed the practical feasibility of our approach. The combined use of different context provisioning strategies can bring several benefits. First, it allows to cope with failures of sensing devices by dynamically replacing one context strategy with another. Second, as each context provisioning strategy guarantees different performance at different costs, the possibility of flexibly switching from one mechanism to another permits optimizing the utilization of computing and communication resources at run time.

6.2 Sailing Application Prototype

Using the Contory API, we re-implemented the DYNAMOS sailing application [10] and add more context-based services. The use of Contory permitted to decouple the application implementation from underlying communication modules (e.g., the BT JSR-82, the Fuego Core event-based framework, the SM platform), from the repository system, and from sensor technology. The implementation of common services such as connecting BT sensors or communicating with the remote repository was accomplished by simply instantiating context query objects in few lines of code. Moreover, Contory offered support to: *(i)* extend the application's context monitoring range by collecting region-specific observations through ad hoc networks and making those data available to remote clients through the infrastructure support; *(ii)* share context information about multiple entities and across multiple devices; *(iii)* combine information from multiple context sources to enhance context estimation. In the following, we show two services that have been integrated into the previous DYNAMOS application and make use of these features.

WeatherWatcher: It allows users to retrieve weather information in a certain geographical region (e.g., the user wants to know the weather in the proximity of a guest harbor to visit). Weather information consists of temperature, wind, speed, humidity, atmospheric pressure, etc. In a sailing scenario, weather conditions represent an important element for selecting the sailing route, but as this type of information can change very quickly, the information owned by boats currently sailing in such a region is often more reliable than the one provided by official weather stations. Once the user has issued a weather request, if the target region is not dense enough or too far away to support multi-hop ad hoc network provisioning, the query is sent to the remote infrastructure. The infrastructure checks if any WeatherWatcher of users currently sailing in that region has recently provided weather information and returns this information to the requester. Fig. 6 shows the screen interface for this application.

RegattaClassifier: During a regatta competition, this service constantly provides an updated classification of the current winner of the regatta. Virtual checkpoints can be arranged along the route that the boats will take during the competition. Each time a boat reaches a checkpoint, the RegattaClassifier running on the phone's participant (see Fig. 7) communicates to the infrastructure location and speed of the boat (collected using GPS sensors). The infrastructure processes this information and provides each participant with an updated classification and additional statistics of the competition.

Fig. 6. WeatherWatcher screenshots   **Fig. 7.** RegattaClassifier screenshots

7   Related Work

As discussed in Section 2, most research projects investigating context support on mobile devices use sensor-based or infrastructure-based approaches. Approaches exploiting the communication support offered by ad hoc networks have rarely been employed for collecting dynamically changing context data. Our middleware differentiates from these approaches by making use of multiple provisioning mechanisms and by integrating a distributed approach deployed in ad hoc networks.

Our distributed context provisioning mechanism resembles work done to access data stored in sensor networks (e.g., Cougar [17], TinyDB [18]). However, these works consider only stationary sensors, whereas in our distributed model, there are both stationary and moving context providers. Furthermore, in sensor networks properties and data produced by nodes are known at the deployment time, while in MANETs properties and context data differ over time as nodes of different types move across the physical space. Declarative queries are also one of the preferred ways of accessing sensor data [19], [20]. We specialized our query language to offer support for expressing both type and quality of requested context items, and to support long running queries.

Few research projects have focused on implementing practical context support on mobile phones. The ContextPhone [21] is an open-source prototyping platform built on the Series 60 phone platform. It can be used to sense, process, store, and transfer context data. The blackboard-based framework of Korpipää [22] implements a ContextManager which provides a publish-subscribe mechanism and a database for context data on mobile devices. However, in both works the context sensing relies on information locally available on the device or through BT sensors, whereas in Contory, we provide flexible access to various types of internal and external sensors. According to the classification of Section 2, these works implement an internal sensor-based provisioning mechanism.

8   Conclusions

This paper presented Contory, a middleware specifically deployed to enable easy development of context-aware applications on mobile phones. Our approach provides high flexibility in supporting context provisioning by integrating several context strategies, namely internal sensors-based, infrastructure-based, and distributed provisioning in ad hoc networks. Additionally, Contory offers a unified SQL-like interface for specifying context queries. Using Contory allows context-aware applications to collect context information from different sources without the need to uniquely and continuously rely on their own sensors or on the presence of an external context infrastructure. We demonstrated the feasibility of our approach by deploying Contory in an experimental testbed of smart phones and quantifying its cost in terms of energy consumption. We also used Contory to implement a prototype application for a sailing scenario. Future directions in the development of Contory will focus on providing more efficient and reliable context provisioning in mobile ad hoc networks.

Acknowledgments

This work was partly supported by the DYNAMOS project. The author thanks Cristian Borcea for helpful comments on earlier drafts of this paper, Michael Przybilski for helping in setting up the experimental testbed, and Nishkam Ravi for providing Portable Smart Messages. She also would like to thank the anonymous reviewers who helped improve the paper.

References

1. Schmidt, A., Laerhoven, K.V.: How to Build Smart Appliances? IEEE Personal Communications, Special Issue on Pervasive Computing **8** (2001) 66–71
2. Dey, A.K., Salber, D., Abowd, G.: A Conceptual Framework and a Toolkit for Supporting the Rapid Prototyping of Context-Aware Applications. Human-Computer Interaction **16** (2001) 97–166
3. Hong, I., Landay, J.A.: An Infrastrucutre Approach to Context-aware Computing. Human-Computer Interaction **16** (2001) 287–303
4. Riva, O., di Flora, C.: Contory: A Smart Phone Middleware Supporting Multiple Context Provisioning Strategies. 2nd International Workshop on Services and Infrastructure for the Ubiquitous and Mobile Internet (SIUMI'06) (2006)
5. Schmidt, A., Adoo, K.A., Takaluoma, A., Tuomela, U., Laerhoven, K.V., de Velde, W.V.: Advanced Interaction in Context. In: Proceedings of the First Symposium on Handheld and Ubiquitous Computing (HUC'99), Karlsruhe, Germany (1999) 89–101
6. Yau, S., Karim, F.: A context-sensitive middleware for dynamic integration of mobile devices with network infrastructures. Journal Parallel Distributed Computing **64** (February 2004) 301–317
7. Hong, J., Landay, J.: An Architecture for Privacy-Sensitive Ubiquitous Computing. In: Proceedings of The Second International Conference on Mobile Systems, Applications, and Services (Mobisys'04), Boston, MA (2004) 177–189
8. Bardram, J.E.: The Java Context Awareness Framework (JCAF) - A Service Infrastructure and Programming Framework for Context-Aware Applications. In: Proceedings of the 3rd International Conference on Pervasive Computing (Pervasive'05). (2005)

9. Hohl, F., Mehrmann, L., Hamdan, A.: A Context System for a Mobile Service Platform. In: Proceedings of the International Conference on Architecture of Computing Systems(ARCS'02), London, UK, Springer-Verlag (2002) 21–33

10. Riva, O., Toivonen, S.: A Model of Hybrid Service Provisioning Implemented on Smart Phones. In: The 3rd IEEE International Conference on Pervasive Services (ICPS'06), IEEE Computer Society (2006) 47–56

11. Gamma, E., Helm, R., Johnson, R., Vlissides, J.: Design Patterns: Elements of Reusable Object-Oriented Software. Addison-Wesley (1995)

12. Crespo, A., Buyukkokten, O., Garcia-Molina, H.: Query Merging: Improving Query Subscription Processing in a Multicast Environment. IEEE Trans. Knowl. Data Eng. **15** (2003) 174–191

13. Borcea, C., Iyer, D., Kang, P., Saxena, A., Iftode, L.: Cooperative Computing for Distributed Embedded Systems. In: Proceedings of the 22nd International Conference on Distributed Computing Systems (ICDCS 2002), Vienna, Austria (2002) 227–236

14. Ravi, N., Borcea, C., Kang, P., Iftode, L.: Portable Smart Messages for Ubiquitous Java-Enabled Devices. In: The 1st Annual International Conference on Mobile and Ubiquitous Systems: Networking and Services (MobiQuitous '04). (2004) 412–421

15. Tarkoma, S., Kangasharju, J., Lindholm, T., Raatikainen, K.: Fuego: Experiences with Mobile Data Communication and Synchronization. In: 17th Annual IEEE International Symposium on Personal, Indoor and Mobile Radio Communications (PIMRC). (2006)

16. Paradiso, J.A., Starner, T.: Energy Scavenging for Mobile and Wireless Electronics. IEEE Pervasive Computing **4** (2005) 18–27

17. Yao, Y., Gehrke, J.: Query Processing in Sensor Networks. In: Proceedings of the First Biennial Conference on Innovative Data Systems Research (CIDR 2003), Asilomar, CA (2003) 233–244

18. Madden, S., Franklin, M.J., Hellerstein, J.M., Hong, W.: The design of an acquisitional query processor for sensor networks. In: Proceedings of The 2003 ACM SIGMOD International Conference on Management of Data (SIGMOD'03), San Diego, California, ACM Press (2003) 491–502

19. Bonnet, P., Gehrke, J., Seshadri, P.: Towards sensor database systems. In: Proceedings of the Second International Conference on Mobile Data Management (MDM '01), London, UK (2001) 3–14

20. Chen, A., Muntz, R.R., Yuen, S., Locher, I., Park, S.I., Srivastava, M.B.: A Support Infrastructure for the Smart Kindergarten. IEEE Pervasive Computing **1** (2002) 49–57

21. Raento, M., Oulasvirta, A., Petit, R., Toivonen, H.: ContextPhone: a prototyping platform for context-aware mobile applications. IEEE Pervasive Computing **4** (2005)

22. Korpipää, P.: Blackboard-based software framework and tool for mobile device context awareness. PhD Thesis. VTT Publications: 579, VTT Electronics, Espoo (2005) http://www.vtt.fi/inf/pdf/publications/2005/P579.pdf.

Efficient Semantic Service Discovery in Pervasive Computing Environments

Sonia Ben Mokhtar, Anupam Kaul, Nikolaos Georgantas, and Valérie Issarny

Inria Rocquencourt
78153 Le Chesnay, France
{Sonia.Ben_Mokhtar, Anupam.Kaul,
Nikolaos.Georgantas, Valerie.Issarny}@inria.fr

Abstract. Service-oriented architectures, and notably Web Services, are becoming an incontrovertible paradigm for the development of applications in pervasive computing environments, as they enable publishing and consuming heterogeneous networked software and hardware resources. Combined with Semantic Web technologies, in particular ontologies, Web services' descriptions can be unambiguously and automatically interpreted in open pervasive computing environments, where agreement on a single common syntactic standard for identifying service semantics cannot be assumed. Nevertheless, efficient matching of semantic Web services to effectively automate the discovery and further consumption of networked resources remains an open issue, which is mainly attributable to the costly underlying semantic reasoning. After analyzing the cost of ontology-based semantic reasoning, which is at the heart of the matching process, we propose a solution towards efficient matching of semantic Web services. We have further incorporated our solution into a service discovery protocol aimed at open pervasive computing environments that integrate heterogeneous wireless network technologies (i.e., ad hoc and infrastructure-based networking). Experimental results show that our solution enables better response times than of classical syntactic-based service discovery protocols.

1 Introduction

The pervasive computing vision is increasingly enabled by the large success of wireless networks and devices. In pervasive computing environments, heterogeneous software and hardware resources may be discovered and integrated transparently towards assisting the performance of daily tasks. Still, realizing this vision requires middleware support for dynamic and automated discovery and composition of software and hardware resources that populate the pervasive computing environment. Service-oriented architectures [11], and particularly Web Services[1], have proved to be an appropriate architectural paradigm offering middleware support for pervasive computing environments. Indeed, Service-Oriented Architecture (SOA) is an architectural style that aims at the development of highly autonomous, loosely coupled systems that are able to communicate, compose and evolve in open, dynamic and heterogeneous environments such as pervasive computing environments [5]. Web Services are then one of the realizations

---

[1] http://www.w3.org/2002/ws/

M. van Steen and M. Henning (Eds.): Middleware 2006, LNCS 4290, pp. 240–259, 2006.

of this architectural style. Using Web Services, each networked resource is abstracted as a service that is described in a declarative manner using the Web Services Description Language (WSDL) and is accessible by means of standard protocols such as the Simple Object Access Protocol (SOAP) on top of Internet protocols (HTTP, SMTP). Furthermore, Web Services have already been used in pervasive environments and have proved to be efficient when deployed on mobile, resource-constrained devices [7].

Abstracting software and hardware resources of the pervasive computing environment as Web services allows having a homogeneous vision of heterogeneous resources. Resources can then be discovered based merely on their WSDL interfaces. However, while using Web Services allows addressing substantially the heterogeneity issue in terms of technologies of service implementation, another issue remains, which is *syntactic heterogeneity*. Indeed, WSDL-based service discovery relies on the syntactic conformance of the required interfaces with the provided ones, for which common understanding is hardly achievable in open pervasive computing environments. A solution to this issue can be provided by introducing semantics into the service description. Combined with Semantic Web technologies[2], notably ontologies, for the semantic description of the services' functional and non-functional features, Web services can be automatically and unambiguously discovered and consumed in open pervasive computing environments. Specifically, ontology-based semantic reasoning enables discovering networked services whose published provided functionalities (or *capabilities*) match a required functionality, even if there is no syntactic conformance between them. A number of research efforts have been conducted in the area of semantic Web service specification, which have led to the development of various semantic service description languages, e.g., OWL-S[3], WSDL-S[4], WSMO[5], SWSO[6]. In this context, we have developed the Amigo-S service description language [2], which is specifically aimed at services in pervasive computing environments.

Building upon the features of Amigo-S that supports specifying services in rich, open pervasive computing environments, this paper focuses on associated middleware support for effectively enabling the discovery of networked Amigo-S services. Specifically, we introduce a dedicated Service Discovery Protocol (SDP) that enables advertising and discovering services in pervasive environments according to the semantics of networked services and of sought functionalities. This is to be contrasted with traditional SDPs that support the discovery of services according to syntactic interface descriptions, and thus assume worldwide knowledge and agreement about service interfaces. The key contribution of our work then comes not only from introducing an SDP for the discovery of semantic Web services in pervasive environments, but also from the fact that our SDP offers performance that makes it appropriate for use in highly dynamic networked environments populated by resource-constrained, wireless devices. The latter issue is a major challenge due to the performance and resource costs of ontology-based semantic reasoning. This has led us to introduce a solution to lightweight semantic matching

---

[2] http://www.w3.org/2001/sw/

[3] OWL-S: Semantic Markup for Web Services. http://www.daml.org/services/owl-s

[4] WSDL-S: http://lsdis.cs.uga.edu/projects/meteor-s/wsdl-s/

[5] WSMO: Web Services Modeling Ontology. http://www.wsmo.org/

[6] SWSO: Semantic Web Service Ontology. http://www.daml.org/services/swsf/1.0/overview/

of Web services towards the actual exploitation of semantic Web services in pervasive environments.

The next section provides an overview of semantic Web service technologies, and introduces Amigo-S and an associated matching relation for semantic Web services in pervasive environments. Based on Amigo-S, we present a solution to lightweight semantic matching of networked services (Section 3). Our solution optimizes ontology-based semantic reasoning, which is at the heart of the matching process. Furthermore, we propose a classification of service advertisements, towards efficient access and retrieval of services within cooperating service directories deployed on the network. We have further integrated our solution in the Ariadne service discovery protocol [12] extending it to S-Ariadne (i.e., Semantic-Ariadne), which is aimed at pervasive computing environments, for hybrid wireless networks combining ad hoc and infrastructure-based networking (Section 4). Experimental results show that S-Ariadne enables better response times than of classical service discovery protocols, and is further more scalable (Section 5). Finally, we summarize our contribution and sketch perspectives for our work (Section 6).

2   Semantic Web Services for Pervasive Computing

As pointed out in the previous section, semantic Web services can provide an adequate solution to effective service discovery in open pervasive computing environments. In this section, we briefly discuss base technologies supporting the provisioning of semantic Web services, and introduce basic elements of our approach for describing and matching semantic Web services in pervasive environments. We thus discuss semantic Web services (Section 2.1), the Amigo-S language for the description of pervasive services (Section 2.2), our definition of a base semantic matching relation (Section 2.3), and a study on the cost of semantic service matching (Section 2.4).

2.1   Semantic Web Services

Ontologies may conveniently be exploited to semantically model Web services. Indeed, while Web services interfaces all have a similar structure, thanks to the WSDL standard, the semantics underlying these interfaces cannot be inferred from their syntactic description. Similarly, it cannot be assumed that service providers and consumers will use worldwide the very same syntactic interface for describing the same service, as these descriptions are created by different organizations, communities and individuals all over the world. A natural evolution of Web services description has thus been the combination of the Semantic Web and Web Services paradigms towards the semantic representation of the services functional features, leading to *Semantic Web Services*. A number of research efforts have in particular been undertaken towards the concretization of this paradigm. In this area, various languages have been proposed to describe semantic Web services, e.g., WSDL-S, OWL-S, WSMO and SWSO.

Among them, OWL-S is the effort directly related to OWL[7] (the Ontology Web Language), which is a W3C recommendation. A service description in OWL-S is composed of three parts : the *service profile*, the *process model* and the *service grounding*.

---

[7] http://www.w3.org/TR/owl-ref/

The service profile gives a description of a service and its provider. It is generally used for service publication and discovery. The process model is a representation of the service conversation, i.e., the interaction protocol between a service and its client that is described as a process. The service grounding specifies the information that is necessary for the service invocation, such as the communication protocol, message formats and addressing information. The OWL-S service grounding is based on WSDL.

2.2 Amigo-S for Pervasive Services

OWL-S and the other languages mentioned above provide adequate solutions for the description of semantic Web services. However, these languages are primarily aimed at characterizing stationary services deployed on the core Internet and lack key features to thoroughly model services to be provisioned in the pervasive computing environment. Such features include characterizing the specifics of the underlying middleware platform that vary significantly among networked services. For example, services networked in the pervasive home environment illustrate such diversity, as they span the home automation, consumer electronics, mobile and personal computing application domains, and further require middleware-layer bridging to be interoperable [1,4]. Another key feature of pervasive services is the need for awareness of context and quality of service, as these two factors affect decisively the actual user's experience in pervasive environments that vary greatly in resource availability and contextual conditions [8,10]. Such specifics of pervasive services has led us to introduce the *Amigo-S* service description language that meets the requirements of pervasive services.

The key novel features of the Amigo-S language are that it supports heterogeneous service infrastructures and enables QoS- and context-awareness for service provisioning. Amigo-S is an ontology formally specified in OWL; it has been developed as part of the effort of the IST Amigo project[8]. The Amigo-S specification incorporates the OWL-S specification, and extends it by adding new classes and properties. In this way, we reuse established features of OWL-S and provide a new language that can easily be used by developers already familiar with OWL-S. In the following, we briefly introduce only the Amigo-S service profile; a more detailed description of Amigo-S may be found online [2]. In this paper, we mainly exploit the ability of the Amigo-s language for specifying service functional features, while other aspects of the language, such as the description of the services' underlying middleware, as well as the specification of QoS and context properties can be exploited like in [1,2].

As discussed above, the OWL-S service profile models a service as both a semantic concept by specifying the service category and a set of semantic IOPEs. In Amigo-S as well, a service is described with a service profile. However, we assume that a service may offer a number of *capabilities*, i.e., specific functionalities offered by the service, and we explicitly model such capabilities. OWL-S actually supports multiple profiles for a service; nevertheless, using a different profile for each capability of a service does not allow capabilities to share a set of common attributes, which may globally characterize the service. In Amigo-S, each such capability is defined as both a semantic concept and a set of semantic IOPEs. This enables describing richer services supporting several capabilities that may be functionally independent or even dependent. For instance a

---

[8] http://www.hitech-projects.com/euprojects/amigo/

complex capability may be composed of simpler capabilities, each one of which is also separately accessible. Further, we explicitly model *provided capabilities* as capabilities supported by a service, and *required capabilities* as capabilities needed by a service, which will be sought on other networked services. This enables support for any service composition scheme, such as a peer-to-peer scheme or a centrally coordinated scheme.

An example of service profiles as enabled by Amigo-S (restricted to service inputs, outputs and category) is depicted in the upper part of Figure 1. Along with service descriptions, the figure includes in its lower part two ontologies representing the concepts employed in the service descriptions. The service on the PDA *requires* a capability named GetVideoStream, which belongs to the service category VideoServer, takes as input a title of a VideoResource and provides as output an actual Stream. The service on the workstation *provides* two capabilities, SendDigitalStream and ProvideGame, which share common attributes such as the workstation resources available to them. For the former, service category is DigitalServer, input is DigitalResource and output is Stream, while for the latter, service category is GameServer, input is GameResource and output is Stream. These two capabilities are dependent, as SendDigitalStream *includes* ProvideGame, but are separately accessible. Thus, a peer service (in other words, a client) may access the former and have the option to access a video resource, a sound resource or a game; or access the latter, asking specifically for a game. The peer service on the PDA asking for a video resource should access SendDigitalStream, which also includes GetVideoStream. Making the right choice is supported by service matching, which is described in the following two sections.

2.3 Semantic Matching Relation

Based on the Amigo-S service specification, we define a matching relation, i.e., $Match$ (C_1, C_2), which allows identifying whether capability C_1 is equivalent or includes capability C_2, i.e., if C_1 can substitute C_2 in the provisioning of a service capability that is semantically characterized by C_2 (see the example of SendDigitalStream and GetVideoStream in Figure 1). The $Match$ relation then constitutes the basis of service discovery, as seeking a capability characterized by C amounts to discovering any networked service advertising a capability described by N such that $Match(N, C)$ holds. Additionally, the $Match$ relation may conveniently be exploited to group similar capabilities of networked services towards efficient service discovery, as further presented in the next section.

Specifically, the $Match$ relation is defined using the function $distance(concept_1, concept_2)$, hereafter denoted by $d(concept_1, concept_2)$, which gives the semantic distance between two concepts, $concept_1$ and $concept_2$, as given in the classified[9] ontology to which the concepts belong. Precisely, if $concept_1$ does not subsume $concept_2$ in the ontology to which they belong to, the distance between the two concepts does not have a numeric value, i.e., $d(concept_1, concept_2) = NULL$. Otherwise, i.e., if $concept_1$ subsumes $concept_2$, the distance takes as value the number of levels that separate $concept_1$ from $concept_2$ in the ontology hierarchy.

---

[9] Ontology classification is the result of semantic reasoning on ontology specifications. It allows inferring implicit relationships between concepts from the explicit definitions of these concepts.

Formally, let the provided capability C_1 be defined by the set of expected inputs $C_1.In$ and set of offered outputs $C_1.Out$, and the required capability C_2 be defined by the set of offered inputs $C2.In$ and the set of expected outputs $C_2.Out$. Furthermore, let the capability C_1 define a set of provided properties $C_1.P$, and the capability C_2 define a set of required properties $C_2.P$, where these properties describe all the information that can be required in the user request such as the service category and non-functional properties; currently, we only consider the former property. The relation $Match$ is then defined as:

$$
\begin{aligned}
Match(C_1, C_2) = &\forall in' \in C_1.In, \exists in \in C_2.In : d(in, in') \geq 0 \text{ and} \\
&\forall out' \in C_2.Out, \exists out \in C_1.Out : d(out, out') \geq 0 \text{ and} \\
&\forall p' \in C_2.P, \exists p \in C_1.P : d(p, p') \geq 0
\end{aligned}
$$

From the above, the relation $Match(C_1, C_2)$ holds if and only if all the expected inputs of C_1 are matched with inputs offered by C_2, all the expected outputs of C_2 are matched with outputs offered by C_1, and all the required properties of C_2 are matched with properties provided by C_1.

Furthermore, we define the function $SemanticDistance(C_1, C_2)$, which gives the semantic distance between the capability C_1 and the capability C_2:

$$
\begin{aligned}
SemanticDistance(C_1, C_2) = &\sum_{i=1}^{n_1} d(C_2.In_i, C_1.In_i) + \\
&\sum_{i=1}^{n_2} d(C_1.Out_i, C_2.Out_i) + \\
&\sum_{i=1}^{n_3} d(C_1.p_i, C_2.p_i)
\end{aligned}
$$

where n_1 is the number of inputs expected by C_1, n_2 is the number of outputs expected by C_2, and n_3 is the number of additional properties required by C_2. The semantic distance between capabilities corresponds to the sum of the distances between the pairs of related concepts in the advertisement and the request. This allows scoring service advertisements with respect to the requested capability with which they are being compared, and selecting the advertisement whose description best fits the user's requirements. An example of matching semantic service capabilities is shown in the middle part of Figure 1. In the figure, the requested capability GetVideoStream is matched with the provided capability SendDigitalStream, using the two underlying ontologies describing digital resources and servers. The relation $Match(SendDigitalStream, GetVideoStream)$ holds, and the semantic distance between these capabilities is equal to 3.

2.4 Cost of Semantic Matching

Practically, the semantic matching of service capabilities decomposes in three tasks:

1. Parsing the description of the requested and the provided capabilities;
2. Loading and classifying the ontologies used in both the requested and the provided capabilities using a semantic reasoner; and
3. Finding subsumption relationships between inputs, outputs and properties of the requested and provided capabilities in the classified ontologies.

Implementation and evaluation of semantic matching of service capabilities has been presented in the literature, e.g., see [9]. Results show that matching semantic service capabilities is a computation-intensive task with high response times compared to classical syntactic-based service discovery protocols. In particular, results show that the most

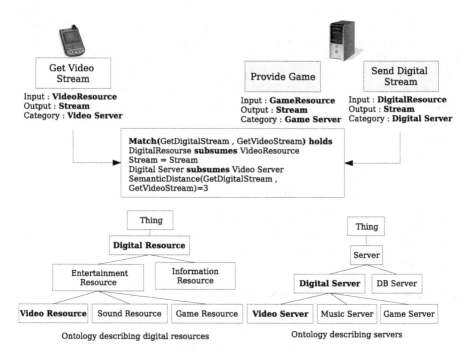

Fig. 1. Describing and matching capabilities of pervasive services

expensive phase in the process of matching semantic service capabilities is that of semantic reasoning (steps 2 and 3 above). As an illustration, Figure 2 shows an evaluation of the semantic matching of two capabilities using three different semantic reasoners: Racer[10], Fact++[11] and Pellet[12], which are the most popular semantic reasoning tools. The two capabilities have 7 inputs and 3 outputs each. The ontology used for the experiment contains 99 OWL classes, i.e., concepts, and 39 properties, i.e., relationships between the classes. We can notice that for any of the three reasoners, the average time to match two capabilities is around 4 to 5 seconds, which is much higher than classical syntactic-based matching of Web services (e.g., around 160 ms for a UDDI registry [13]). Furthermore, we notice that the time to load and classify ontologies takes from 76% to 78% of the total time for matching using any of the three reasoners.

The above results show that matching semantic Web service capabilities is an expensive task in terms of response time and resource consumption, which is not acceptable for a service discovery protocol aimed at pervasive computing environments, where service discovery needs to be efficient enough to ensure service availability despite the network's dynamics, and lightweight enough for use by thin, wireless devices. Thus, in order to enable actual deployment of semantic Web services in pervasive computing environments, a number of optimizations have to be introduced in the process of match-

---

[10] Racer: http://www.sts.tu-harburg.de/ r.f.moeller/racer/

[11] Fact++: http://owl.man.ac.uk/factplusplus/

[12] Pellet: http://www.mindswap.org/2003/pellet/

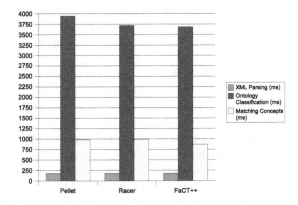

Fig. 2. Time taken to match a requested and a provided capability

ing semantic service capabilities, particularly, targeting acceptable response times. The next section introduces such solutions, building upon recent efforts in the area of efficient semantic service matching.

3 Achieving Lightweight Discovery of Semantic Web Services

Lightweight discovery of semantic Web services requires minimizing the overhead due to semantic reasoning, possibly performing it off-line so that semantic reasoners do not need to be used when advertising and seeking networked services. Specifically, optimization can be introduced at two levels. First, at the semantic reasoning level, by reducing the time spent to infer relationships between concepts in ontologies. Second, at the service discovery level, by classifying directories of services in a way that reduces the number of semantic matches performed to answer a user request. As discussed below (Section 3.1), related optimizations for both ontology-based semantic reasoning and classification of service advertisements have been proposed in the literature [3,13]. We then propose an effective solution to the discovery of semantic Web services in pervasive computing environments (Sections 3.2, 3.3).

3.1 Background

In [3], the authors emphasize the need of efficient indexes and search structures for directories. Towards this goal, they propose to numerically encode service descriptions given in OWL-S. This is done by numerically encoding ontology class and property hierarchies by intervals. More precisely, each class (resp. property) in a classified hierarchy is associated with an interval. Then, each service description maps to a graphical representation in the form of a set of rectangles defined by the sets of intervals representing properties combined with the set of intervals representing classes. Furthermore, for efficient service retrieval, the authors base their work on techniques for managing multidimensional data being developed in the database community. More precisely, they use the Generalized Search Tree (GiST) algorithm proposed by Hellerstein in [6] for creating and maintaining the directory of numeric services. Combining both encoding and indexing techniques allows performing efficient service search, in the order of milliseconds for trees of 10000 entries. However, insertion within trees of the previous size is still a heavy process that takes approximately 3 seconds.

In [13], the authors propose an approach to optimize service discovery in a UDDI registry augmented with OWL-S for the description of semantic Web services. This approach is based on the fact that the publishing phase is not a time critical task. Therefore, the authors propose to exploit this phase to pre-compute and store information about the incoming services. More precisely, a taxonomy that represents the subsumption relationships between all the concepts in the ontologies used by services is maintained. Then, each concept C in this taxonomy is annotated with two lists, one to store information about inputs of services while the other one is used to store information about outputs of services. More precisely, for each concept in the taxonomy, these lists specify to what degree any request pointing to that concept would match the advertisement. For example, for a particular concept C in the taxonomy, the list storing information about outputs is represented as $[< Adv_1, exact >, < Adv_2, subsumes >, ...]$, where Adv_i points to a service advertisement in the repository and $exact$ (resp. $subsumes$) specify the degree of match between C and the related concept in the corresponding advertisement. A performance evaluation of this approach shows that the publishing phase using this algorithm takes around seven times the time taken by UDDI to publish a service, under the assumption that no additional ontologies have to be loaded to the registry. On the other hand, the time to process a query is in the order of milliseconds. While the above increases the time spent for publishing service advertisements, it considerably reduces the time spent to answer a user request compared to approaches based on online reasoning (e.g., see Figure 2). Indeed, the querying phase is reduced to performing lookups in the hierarchical data structure that represents the classified ontology, and to performing intersections between the lists that store information about the service advertisements. Thus, no on-line reasoning is required to answer a user request. However, the publishing phase still requires semantic reasoning on service descriptions which is an expensive process in terms of consumed resources.

On the other hand, solutions to reduce the number of matches performed to answer a user request are generally based on service classification. OWL-S specification provides the mean of defining hierarchies of service descriptions called *profile hierarchies*. These hierarchies are similar to the object-oriented inheritance hierarchies. For instance, when a new service profile is defined it may be specified as a subclass of an existing profile class. This allows the new service to inherit all the properties of all the classes specified in its super-hierarchy of classes. While this approach allows the classification of service profiles according to the classes from which they inherit, it does not allow considering possible relationships between service profiles that do not have the same common set of properties but that still provide similar functional features. Service classification can also be based on the service category using existing taxonomies such as NAICS[13] or UNSPSC[14]. However, service categories alone does not give enough information about the service functionality.

---

[13] http://www.census.gov/epcd/www/naics.html
[14] http://www.unspsc.org/

Using the matching relation defined in the previous section, we propose an efficient semantic service discovery protocol for pervasive computing environments. Efficiency is addressed in terms of response time for both the discovery and advertisement of service capabilities. Towards this goal, we present below a number of optimizations of the semantic matching process. First, in order to reduce the time to load and classify ontologies, which is the most costly phase in the discovery process, we propose to encode classified ontologies (§ 3.2). Then, in order to reduce the number of semantic matches performed in the querying phase we propose to classify capabilities of networked services into hierarchies (§ 3.3).

3.2 Encoding Concept Hierarchies

In order to avoid semantic reasoning at runtime we propose to encode classified ontologies, represented by hierarchies of concepts, using intervals as described in [3]. These hierarchies represent the subsumption relationships between all the concepts in the ontologies used in the directory. The main idea of the encoding is that any concept in a classified ontology is associated with an interval. These intervals can be contained in other intervals but are never overlapping. The intervals are defined using a linear inverse exponential function $linKinvexpP(x) = \frac{1}{p^{int(\frac{x}{k})}} + (x \bmod k) * \frac{1}{k} * \frac{1}{p^{int(\frac{x}{k})}}$, where p and k are two parameters to be fixed. Regarding the scalability of this encoding solution, experiments show that for p=2 and k=5, and a system encoding real numbers as 64 bits doubles, the maximum number of entries that we can have on the first level of the hierarchy is 1071 and the maximum number of levels that we can have on the first entries of a level is 462 levels. Figure 3 taken from [3], shows an example of encoding a hierarchy of concepts with intervals.

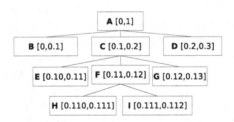

Fig. 3. Example of encoding a class hierarchy

Under the assumption that the classified ontologies are encoded and that service advertisements and service requests already contain the codes corresponding to the concepts that they involve, semantic service reasoning reduces to a numeric comparison of codes. Indeed, to infer whether a concept C1 represented by the interval I1 subsumes another concept C2 represented by the interval I2, it is sufficient to compare whether I1 is included in I2. In order to ensure consistency of codes along with the dynamics and evolution of ontologies, service advertisements and service requests specify the version of the codes being used. We assume that services periodically check the version of codes that they are using and update their codes in the case of ontology evolution.

3.3   Semantic Service Advertisement and Matching

Based on the encoding technique defined in the previous section, we present an algorithm for matching a requested capability with a set of capabilities of networked services. Service capabilities could be added or deleted at any time from the existing set of capabilities. When a request comes, the algorithm tries to find a capability that best matches the request minimizing the number of semantic matches performed with capabilities of networked services. At a pre-processing phase the algorithm classifies capabilities of networked services and constructs directed acyclic graphs (DAGs) of related capabilities. These graphs are indexed according to the ontologies being used in the capabilities that they contain. The relationship between capabilities that we consider to construct a graph is given by the relation $Match$ and the function $SemanticDistance$ defined in Section 2.3. Specifically, if both $Match(C_1, C_2)$ and $Match(C_2, C_1)$ hold and $SemanticDistance(C_1, C_2) = SemanticDistance(C_2, C_1) = 0$, then C_1 and C_2 will be represented by a single vertex in the graph. For all the other cases where $Match(C_1, C_2)$ holds, C_1 and C_2 will be represented in the graph by two distinct vertices with a directed edge from C_1 to C_2.

When a new service comes in the network the set of capabilities that it provides are classified among the existing hierarchies. The algorithm of classifying new capabilities in the existing hierarchies is described below.

When a request Req arrives, the algorithm first selects among the existing DAGs, graphs that contain services that are more likely to match the request. This is done using the indexes given to each graph, which correspond to the set of ontologies used by the capabilities of that graph. When a graph G is selected the algorithm performs a matching between the request and the most *generic* capabilities of this graph. These capabilities are said to be more generic than other capabilities contained in their subhierarchy because they provide a number of outputs that is greater or equal to the number of outputs of the other capabilities, and further because their provided outputs subsume the outputs of other capabilities (e.g., in Figure 1, the capability Send-DigitalStream is *more generic* than the capability ProvideGame). These capabilities correspond to the capabilities represented by vertices of this graph that do not have predecessors, i.e., the set $Roots(G)$. Similarly, we define $Leaves(G)$ as the set of vertices in the graph G that do not have successors. If $Match$ between Req and all the capabilities of $Roots(G)$ does not hold, the group G is filtered out, and another group is selected. Nevertheless, if the matching between the request and a capability C of $Roots(G)$ holds, i.e., $Match(C, Req)$ holds, we evaluate the semantic distance between C and Req. If the distance is equal to zero, C is selected, otherwise the algorithm tries to find a capability C' from the successors of C such that $SemanticDistance(C', Req) = Min(SemanticDistance(C_i, Req))$, where C_i is a successor of C. The algorithm for answering a user request is presented in more details later in this section.

Adding a New Service Advertisement. At a pre-processing phase, a set of DAG graphs are constructed and maintained. Each time a new service advertisement comes in the network, the graphs have to be updated with the set of capabilities provided by the new service. The algorithm of classifying the capabilities of a new service within a set of Graphs $G_1, G_2,..., G_n$ is given below. For each capability C_i provided by the new service, the algorithm tries to find a graph G_i in which this capability will be integrated (Steps (1), (2)). A subset of graphs is preselected according to the ontologies being used by C_i. The algorithm first checks whether C_i can be inserted in the sub-hierarchy of one of the root nodes of G. This is done by verifying if there exists a node $Root_i$ in $Roots(G_i)$ such that $Match(Root_i, C_i)$ holds (step (3)). If $Match(Root_i, C_i)$ holds (step 8), then C_i will have a predecessor in G_i. The next step is to find this node, N_i, among the successors of the node $Root_i$, such that the $Match(Succ(N_i), C_i)$ fails, and to draw an edge from C_i to N_i. Moreover, C_i could have a successor in G_i. Thus, the algorithm tries to find among the set $Leaves(G_i)$ if there is a node $Leaf_i$ such that $Match(C_i, Leaf_i)$(step (9)). If $Match(C_i, Leaf_i)$ holds, then C_i will have a successor in G_i. The next step is to find this node, N_i, among the predecessors of $Leaf_i$ such that $Match(C_i, Pred(N_i))$ fails, and to draw an edge from C_i to N_i (step (11)). On the other hand, if $Match(Root_i, C_i)$ does not hold (step(4)), C_i will not have a predecessor in G_i. Nevertheless, C_i could have a successor in G_i. Thus, the algorithms checks whether there is a node $Leaf_i$ in $Leaves(G_i)$ such that $Match(C_i, Leaf_i)$ holds (steps (5), (6) and (7)). These steps are similar to the aforementioned steps (9), (10) and (11).

input: $C_1, C_2, ..., C_n$ the set of capabilities of the new service,
        $G_1, G_2, ..., G_m$ the set of existing graphs.
output: $G'_1, G'_2, ..., G'_k$ the set of graphs after the insertion of the new capabilities.

InsertCapabilities(capabilities)

```
Forall the capabilities C_i in C_1, ..., C_n do{                           (1)
    For all the graphs G_i in G_1, ..., G_m that use the same ontologies as C_i
    until the insertion of C_i do{                                         (2)
        For (Root_i in Roots(G_i)) do{                                     (3)
            If (¬Match(Root_i, C_i)) then{                                 (4)
                For (Leaf_i in Leaves(G_i)) do{                            (5)
                    If (¬Match(C_i, Leaf_i)) then                          (6)
                        Fail;
                    Else{                                                  (7)
                        Test with Predecessors of Leaf_i
                        until ¬Match(C_i, Pred_j(Leaf_i))
                        Draw an edge from C_i to Pred_{j+1}(Leaf_i)
                }}
            }Else{                                                         (8)
                Test with Successors of Root_i
                until ¬Match(Succ_j(Root_i), C_i)
                Draw an edge from Succ_{j-1}(Root_i) to C_i
                For (Leaf_i in Leaves(G_i)) do{                            (9)
                    If (¬Match(C_i, Leaf_i)) then                          (10)
                        Fail;
                    Else{                                                  (11)
                        Test with Predecessors of Leaf_i
                        until ¬Match(C_i, Pred_j(Leaf_i))
                        Draw an edge from C_i to Pred_{j+1}(Leaf_i)
                }}}}}}
```

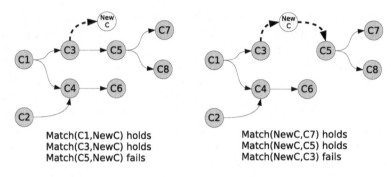

Match(C1,NewC) holds
Match(C3,NewC) holds
Match(C5,NewC) fails

Match(NewC,C7) holds
Match(NewC,C5) holds
Match(NewC,C3) fails

Fig. 4. Example of inserting a capability in a DAG

Figure 4 shows an example of inserting a capability, $newC$, in a DAG of capabilities, G. The first step (left part of the figure) is to match $newC$ with capabilities from $Roots(G)$ to find out whether $newC$ will have a predecessor in G. Indeed, $Match(C_1, newC)$ holds, which means that one of the successors of C_1 will be linked with $newC$, i.e., C_3. The next step (right part of the figure) is then to find out whether $newC$ will have a successor in G. This is done by matching the capabilities in $Leaves(G)$ with $newC$. Indeed, $Match(newC, C_7)$ holds, which means that $newC$ will be linked with one of the predecessors of C_7, i.e., C_5.

Answering User Requests. When a user request that contains a set of required capabilities comes, the algorithm below finds out a set of capabilities of networked services that best match the ones required by the user. More precisely, for each capability C_i in the user request the algorithm tries to find a graph that may contain capabilities that match C_i (steps (1) and (2)). A graph G_i is selected if it is indexed with the ontologies used in the request and if there exist a node $Root_i$ in the set $Roots(G_i)$ such that $Match(Root_i, C_i)$ holds (step 3). In this case, a node that has the minimal semantic distance with C_i is selected from the successors of $Root_i$ (step 5).

inputs: a set of capabilities required in the service description $C_1, C_2, ..., C_n$
         a set of graphs $G_1, G_2, ..., G_m$
outputs: a set of capabilities of networked services that match the capabilities given as input

MatchService(requested service)
For all the capabilities C_i required in the service description **do**{   (1)
     For all the graphs G_i in $G_1, ..., G_m$ that use the same ontologies as C_i
     until C_i is matched **do**{   (2)
         For all $Root_j$ in $Roots(G_i)$ **do** {   (3)
            If $(\neg Match(Root_i, C_i))$ **then**   (4)
                Try with the next node in $Root(G_i)$
            Else   (5)
                Return $Succ(Root_i)$ from the successors of $Root_i$ such that
                $SemanticDistance(Succ(Root_i), C_i)$ is minimal
    }}}

An example of matching a requested capability with capabilities of networked services is given in Figure 5. In this figure, the requested capability $NewC$ uses the ontology

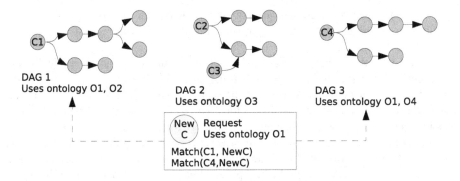

Fig. 5. Example of matching a user's requested capability

O_1 in its specification. This allows to filter out the DAG_2 as it is indexed with only the ontology O_3. The next step is to match $NewC$ with capabilities from $Roots(DAG_1)$ and $Roots(DAG_3)$, i.e., the capabilities C_1 and C_4. If the matching fails with one of these capabilities, we can infer that no capability will match $newC$ in the corresponding graph.

The benefits of using this solution to match user's required capabilities with capabilities of networked services is to reduce the number of semantic matches performed to answer a query. Indeed, it is sufficient to perform a semantic match with a subset of the capabilities of networked services rather than performing a semantic match with all the capabilities hosted by a directory of services. Furthermore, using the encoding of classified ontologies allows to reduce the semantic reasoning to a numeric comparison of codes.

4   S-ARIADNE Service Discovery Protocol

Towards the deployment of our solution in pervasive computing environments, we build upon the Ariadne middleware[15], which introduces a semi-distributed service discovery protocol for mobile ad hoc networks (MANETs) [12]. According to the design presented in [12], our discovery protocol, which we call S-Ariadne, relies on a backbone of directories constituting a *virtual network*. Directories are dynamically deployed, each directory performing service discovery in its vicinity. Then, service discovery in the global network is based on collaboration among deployed directories.

More precisely, S-Ariadne decomposes into a local and a global discovery process. The local discovery process is performed by each directory. Each directory is then responsible for:

(i) caching the Amigo-S descriptions of the services available in its vicinity, and classifying the capabilities provided by these services according to the grouping scheme discussed in Section 3.3, and

(ii) periodically advertising the presence of registered services to the vicinity.

---

[15] http://www-rocq.inria.fr/arles/download/ariadne/

When a directory receives a service request, specified as an Amigo-S service, it seeks capabilities of the cached services that semantically match the requested service as discussed in section 3.3.

To deal with the dynamics of pervasive networks, directories are dynamically and homogeneously deployed in the network using an on the fly election process. Specifically, if for a given period of time, a node does not receive any directory advertisement, the node initiates the election of a directory. The election process is done by broadcasting an election message in the network up to a given number of hops. Then, nodes can either accept or refuse to act as a directory, depending on a number of parameters such as network coverage, mobility and remaining/available resources. This mechanism allows electing directories with the best physical properties and distributing them efficiently since an election process is launched in the less covered areas. A node acting as a directory then periodically advertises its presence in its vicinity (i.e., up to a given number of hops).

The global service discovery process is based on collaboration among elected directories. However, the efficiency of the discovery process in terms of response time and generated traffic requires to query directories that are the most likely to cache service advertisements that do match the requested service. Towards this goal, we use directory categorization as introduced in [12], which gives a compact overview of the directory content. More precisely, we use Bloom filters for summarizing the content of a directory. The main idea is to compute a vector v of m bits, which corresponds to a Bloom filter. For any capability C, its semantic description relies on a set of ontologies $O(C) = \{O_1, O_2, ..., O_n\}$ to which belong the concepts describing its inputs, outputs and properties. Then, for each capability C provided by a networked service, and stored in a directory, the capability description in terms of used ontologies is hashed with k independent hash functions. Each ontology is considered in terms of its URI. The bits of the vector v whose positions are given by the results of the k hash functions are set to 1, i.e., the bits at position $h_1(O(C)), h_2(O(C)), ..., h_k(O(C))$ are set to 1. In order to determine whether a directory possibly caches a requested capability Req using the directory's Bloom filter, we check whether the bit positions $h_1(O(Req)), h_2(O(Req)), ..., h_k(O(Req))$ in the vector are all set to 1. If there is a bit that is not set to 1, the directory will not contain the required capability. Nevertheless, if all the bits are set to 1, the directory is likely to contain the required capability, and a concrete local service discovery is performed in that directory. The probability of a *false positive* depends on the parameters k that is the number of hash functions and m that is the size of the Bloom filter. These values can be chosen so that the probability of false positive is minimized.

The cooperation between directories is performed by exchanging the Bloom filters that give an overview of the directories content. The exchange of Bloom filters is done when new directories are elected and reactively, i.e., requested by another directory, when the percentage of false positives reaches a given threshold.

According to the deployment policy, each mobile node is associated to at least one directory. When the mobile node seeks a service characterized by a set of required capabilities, it sends a query message to the directory that is responsible of its network area (i.e., in its vicinity). The directory performs for each required capability a local service

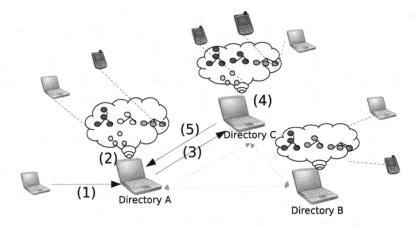

Fig. 6. S-Ariadne

discovery, as described in Section 3.3. If the required capabilities are not stored locally, the directory forwards the request to a subset of directories that are likely to cache capabilities that match the request. The directories to which the request is forwarded are selected according to their Bloom filters and additional parameters such as remaining battery lifetime and the distance between the respective directories.

Figure 6 provides an overview of the S-Ariadne architecture. In the figure, three nodes have been elected to act as directories. When a service request is issued, the directory node that is in the vicinity of the service requester, i.e., Directory A, receives the service request (Step(1)). The directory performs a local service discovery to find capabilities that semantically match the capabilities of the requested service (Step (2)). Service advertisements providing these capabilities are returned to the requester. If some capabilities have not been found locally, another request is sent to remote directories that are likely to store relevant capabilities according to their summarized description, i.e., Boom filters (Step (3)). These directories perform a local service discovery (Step (4)), and return the corresponding service advertisements (Step (5)), which are sent to the requester (Step(6)).

5   Prototype Implementation and Evaluation

We have implemented a prototype of our solution to efficient matching of semantic service capabilities as part of the Ariadne service discovery protocol extending it to S-Ariadne. We have evaluated the impact of introducing semantic service matching in Ariadne, which originally uses basic WSDL-based syntactic matching of Web services for the local service discovery. We have performed our evaluations on a Toshiba Satellite notebook with a 1.6 GHz Intel Centrino processor and 512 MB of RAM. In all the experiments that we performed, we increased the number of services from 1 to 100. The service descriptions are using 22 different ontologies, and each service description contains a single provided capability. Figure 7 shows the results of our first experiment, which evaluates the time to create graphs of services in an empty directory. A scenario for this experiment would be realized when a directory leaves the network and when another one is elected and has to host the set of service descriptions available in its vicinity. Figure 7 shows three measurements: (1) the time to parse the service descriptions; (2) the time to classify the service capabilities into graphs; and (3) the total time, i.e., time to parse and create the graphs. From this figure, we can notice that the time to create the graphs is negligible compared to the time to parse service descriptions, i.e., XML parsing time, which is mandatory due to the use of Web services and Semantic Web technologies.

The results given by the second experiment that we performed are depicted in Figure 8. This experiment shows the time to insert a new capability in a directory. This figure shows 3 measurements: (1) the time to parse the new service description; (2) the time to insert a capability in a directory; and (3) the total time, i.e., the time to parse and insert the new service description. Results show that the to time to classify a capability in a set of existing graphs is negligible compared to XML parsing time of the service description. We also notice that this time is nearly constant. This is due to the fact that the number of semantic matches performed in the directory in order to insert a capability depends neither on the total number of services on the directory nor on the number of graphs. The time to insert a capability depends on the number of capabilities contained in the graph in which the capability will be inserted. This is due to the fact that graphs are indexed using the ontologies that are being used in the capabilities' descriptions, which allows pre-selecting a subset of graphs that are likely to be appropriate for the insertion of the new capability. Thus, only a few number of semantic matches are performed in order to insert a capability in a directory. The results of the third experiment

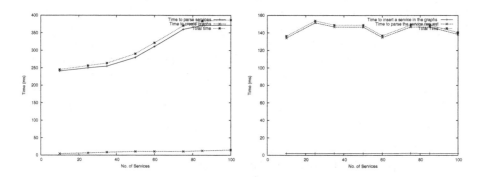

Fig. 7. Time to create graphs   **Fig. 8.** Time to publish a service advertisement

that we performed are depicted in Figure 9. In this experiment, we evaluate the time to match a service request with services hosted by a directory. Furthermore, we compare the time to match a request in a directory where capabilities are classified into a set of graphs, with the time to match a request in a directory without classification. Results are given without the XML parsing time of the request description. In this figure, we can notice that without classification the average overhead for matching is around 50% of the time to match when the capabilities are pre-classified. Moreover, we can notice that

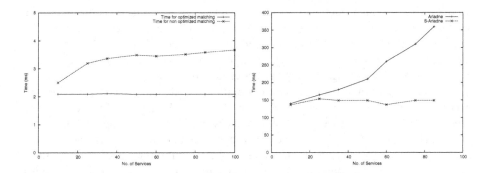

Fig. 9. Time to match a service request   **Fig. 10.** Ariadne vs S-Ariadne

the time to match a request in the classified directory is almost constant, which is due to the graphs indexing and the directory structuring. We can also notice that the response time to match a required capability, excluding XML parsing time, is in the order of few milliseconds.

The last experiment that we performed is a comparison of the response time given by the classical syntactic-based matching performed by Ariadne and the optimized semantic matching performed by S-Ariadne. The results are given in Figure 10. This figure shows that the response time given by Ariadne is increasing with the number of services available in the directory, while S-Ariadne has an almost stable response time, which is due to the following reasons: (1) using S-Ariadne, the services are parsed once at the publishing phase and their capabilities are classified, which avoids matching a request with all the services of the directory; (2) due to the numeric encoding of classified ontologies, the semantic matching performed by S-Ariadne reduces to a numeric comparison of codes, while using Ariadne the matching is performed by syntactically comparing the WSDL descriptions. We can conclude that, using S-Ariadne, semantic matching, which allows to leverage the openness of pervasive computing environments, can be performed more efficiently than classical syntactic matching. Furthermore, thanks to the indexing and classification of service capabilities, S-Ariadne is more scalable than Ariadne.

6 Conclusion

The pervasive computing vision implies that everywhere around us the environment is populated with networked software and hardware resources that can be discovered and integrated towards the realization of our daily tasks. Towards the realization of this vision, middleware support for the efficient dynamic discovery of software and hardware resources of the pervasive computing environment is a key requirement. Such middleware support has to deal with the heterogeneity of the networked resources. This can be partially addressed using service-oriented architectures, and particularly the Web services paradigm. Indeed, Web services enable having a homogeneous vision and access to the heterogeneous networked resources of the environments. Nevertheless, Web services discovery and interaction commonly relies on the syntactic conformance of service interfaces, for which common understanding is hardly achievable in open environments. The Semantic Web paradigm allows to overcome this limitation by introducing semantic specification of service functional and non-functional features, which enables semantic reasoning on Web services capabilities.

Building on semantic Web services, our approach to dynamic service discovery in pervasive computing environments relies on the Amigo-S language for the semantic specification of pervasive services, and introduces an efficient matching relation of service capabilities, which we have integrated in S-Ariadne extending Ariadne, a semi-distributed discovery protocol adapted to pervasive computing environments. Our solution optimizes the costly ontology-based semantic reasoning on one hand, and the number of semantic matches to be performed to answer a user request on the other hand. The optimization of the semantic reasoning is based on the encoding of classified concept hierarchies, which allows to reduce the semantic reasoning to a numeric comparison of codes, while the optimization of the matching process is based on the classification of service capabilities into hierarchies of related capabilities. Our results show that S-Ariadne provide better response time for the semantic matching of service capabilities than Ariadne, its syntactic ancestor, for the basic syntactic service matching. Furthermore, thanks to the indexing and the structuring of service directories, S-Ariadne is more scalable than a classical service directory.

Acknowledgments

This research is partially supported by the European IST AMIGO project[16] (EU-IST-004182).

References

1. Yerom-David Bromberg and Valerie Issarny. Indiss: Interoperable discovery system for networked services. In *Proceedings of ACM/IFIP/USENIX 6th International Middleware Conference (Middleware'05)*, 2005.
2. Amigo Consortium. Amigo middleware core: Prototype implementation and documentation. Project Deliverable D3.2, 2006.
3. Ion Constantinescu and Boi Faltings. Efficient matchmaking and directory services. In *Proceedings of the IEEE International Conference on Web Intelligence (WI'03)*, 2003.
4. N. Georgantas, S. Ben Mokhtar, Y.-D. Bromberg, V. Issarny, J. Kalaoja, A. Grodolle J. Kantarovitch, and R. Mevissen. The amigo service architecture for the open networked home environment. In *Proceedings of 5th Working IEEE/IFIP Conference on Software Architecture (WICSA'05)*, 2005.
5. Nikolaos Georgantas, Sonia Ben Mokhtar, Ferda Tartanoglu, and Valerie Issarny. *Architecting Dependable Systems III*, chapter Semantic-aware Services for the Mobile Computing Environment. Springer Verlag, 2005.
6. Joseph M. Hellerstein, Jeffrey F. Naughton, and Avi Pfeffer. Generalized search trees for database systems. In *Proceedings of the 21st International Conference of Very Large Data Bases, VLDB'95*, 1995.

---

[16] http://www.hitech-projects.com/euprojects/amigo/

7. Valerie Issarny, Daniele Sacchetti, Ferda Tartanoglu, Francoise Sailhan, Rafik Chibout, Nicole Levy, and Angel Talamona. Developing ambient intelligence systems: A solution based on web services. *Journal of Automated Software Engineering*, 2004.
8. Sonia Ben Mokhtar, Damien Fournier, Nikolaos Georgantas, and Valerie Issarny. Context-aware service composition in pervasive computing environments. In *Proceedings of the 2nd International Workshop on Rapid Integration of Software Engineering Techniques (RISE'05)*, 2005.
9. Sonia Ben Mokhtar, Anupam Kaul, Nikolaos Georgantas, and Valerie Issarny. Towards efficient matching of semantic web service capabilities. In *Proceedings of the workshop of Web Services Modeling and Testing (WS-MATE'06)*, 2006.
10. Sonia Ben Mokhtar, Jinshan Liu, Nikolaos Georgantas, and Valerie Issarny. Qos-aware dynamic service composition in ambient intelligence environments. In *Proceedings of the 20th IEEE/ACM International Conference on Automated Software Engineering (ASE'05)*, 2005.
11. Mike P. Papazoglou. Service -oriented computing: Concepts, characteristics and directions. In *Proceedings of the Fourth International Conference on Web Information Systems Engineering(WISE '03)*, 2003.
12. Francoise Sailhan and Valerie Issarny. Scalable service discovery for MANET. In *Proceedings of the 3rd IEEE International Conference on Pervasive Computing and Communications (PerCom'05)*, 2005.
13. Naveen Srinivasan, Massimo Paolucci, and Katia Sycara. Adding owl-s to uddi, implementation and throughput. In *Proceedings of the Workshop on Semantic Web Service and Web Process Composition*, 2004.

A Middleware System for Protecting Against Application Level Denial of Service Attacks

Mudhakar Srivatsa[1], Arun Iyengar[2], Jian Yin[2], and Ling Liu[1]

[1] College of Computing, Georgia Institute of Technology, Atlanta, GA 30332, USA
[2] IBM T. J. Watson Research Center, Yorktown Heights, NY 10598, USA
{mudhakar, lingliu}@cc.gatech.edu, {aruni, jianyin}@us.ibm.com

Abstract. Recently, we have seen increasing numbers of denial of service (DoS) attacks against online services and web applications either for extortion reasons, or for impairing and even disabling the competition. These DoS attacks have increasingly targeted the application level. Application level DoS attacks emulate the same request syntax and network level traffic characteristics as those of legitimate clients, thereby making the attacks much harder to be detected and countered. Moreover, such attacks usually target bottleneck resources such as disk bandwidth, database bandwidth, and CPU resources. In this paper we propose server-side middleware to counter application level DoS attacks. The key idea behind our technique is to adaptively vary a client's priority level, and the relative amount of resources devoted to this client, in response to the client's past requests in a way that incorporates application level semantics. Application specific knowledge is used to evaluate the cost and the utility of each request and the likelihood that a sequence of requests are sent by a malicious client. Based on the evaluations, a client's priority level is increased or decreased accordingly. A client's priority level is used by the server side firewall to throttle the client's request rate, thereby ensuring that more server side resources are allocated to the legitimate clients. We present a detailed implementation of our approach on the Linux kernel and evaluate it using two sample applications: Apache HTTPD micro-benchmarks and TPCW. Our experiments show that our approach incurs low performance overhead and is resilient to application level DoS attacks.

1 Introduction

Recently, we have seen increasing activities of denial of service (DoS) attacks against online services and web applications to extort, disable or impair the competition. An FBI affidavit [32] describes a case wherein an e-Commerce website, WeaKnees.com, was subject to an organized DoS attack staged by one of its competitors. These attacks were carried out using sizable 'botnets' (5,000 to 10,000 of zombie machines) at the disposal of the attacker. The attacks began on October 6th 2003, with SYN floods slamming into WeaKnees.com, crippling the site, which sells digital video recorders, for 12 hours straight. In response, WeaKnees.com moved to a more expensive hosting at RackSpace.com. However, the attackers adapted their attack strategy and replaced simple SYN flooding attacks with a HTTP flood, pulling large image files from WeaKnees.com. At its peak, it is believed that this onslaught kept the company offline for a full two weeks causing a loss of several million dollars in revenue.

M. van Steen and M. Henning (Eds.): Middleware 2006, LNCS 4290, pp. 260–280, 2006.

As we can see from the example above, sophisticated DoS attacks are increasingly focusing not only on low level network flooding, but also on application level attacks that flood victims with requests that mimic flash crowds [24]. Application level DoS attacks refer to those attacks that exploit application specific semantics and domain knowledge to launch a DoS attack such that it is very hard for any DoS filter to distinguish a sequence of attack requests from a sequence of legitimate requests. Two characteristics make application level DoS attacks particularly damaging. First, application level DoS attacks emulate the same request syntax and network level traffic characteristics as that of the legitimate clients, thereby making them much harder to detect. Second, an attacker can choose to send expensive requests targeting higher layer server resources like sockets, disk bandwidth, database bandwidth and worker processes [6][28][32].

As in the case of WeaKnees.com, an attacker does not have to flood the server with millions of HTTP requests. Instead, the attacker may emulate the network level request traffic characteristics of a legitimate client and yet attack the server by sending hundreds of resource intensive requests that pull out large image files from the server. An attacker may also target dynamic web pages that require expensive search operations on the backend database servers. A cleverly constructed request may force an exhaustive search on a large database, thereby significantly throttling the performance of the database server.

Problem Outline. There are two major problems in protecting an online e-Commerce website from application level DoS attacks. First, application level DoS attacks could be very subtle making it very hard for a DoS filter to distinguish between a stream of requests from a DoS attacker and a legitimate client. In section 2 we qualitatively argue that it would be very hard to distinguish DoS attack requests from the legitimate requests even if a DoS filter were to examine any statistics (mean, variance, etc) on the request rate, the contents of the request packet headers (IP, TCP, HTTP, etc) and even the entire content of the request packet itself. Second, the subtle nature of application level DoS attacks make it very hard to exhaustively enumerate all possible attacks that could be launched by an adversary. Hence, there is a need to defend against application level DoS attacks *without knowing* their precise nature of operation. Further, as in the case of WeaKnees.com, the attackers may continuously change their strategy to evade any traditional DoS protection mechanisms.

Our Approach. In this paper we propose middleware for protecting a website against application level DoS attacks. Our middleware solution carefully divides its operations between the server's firewall and application layer. The firewall component of our middleware is completely application transparent. The application layer component of our middleware exports an application programming interface (API) to the application programmers to improve the website's resilience to application level DoS attacks.

Our DoS protection middleware is functionally different from most traditional DoS filters. Our mechanism does not attempt to distinguish a DoS attack request from the legitimate ones. Instead, our mechanism examines the amount of resources expended by the server in handling a request, rather than the request itself. We use the utility of a request and the amount of server resources incurred in handling the request to compute a score for every request. We construct a feedback loop that takes a request's score as its input and updates the client's priority level. In its simplest sense, the priority level might encode the maximum number of requests per unit time that a client can issue. Hence, a high scoring request increases a client's priority level, thereby permitting the client to send a larger number of requests per unit time. On the other hand, a low scoring request decreases a client's priority level, thereby limiting the number of requests that the client may issue per unit time. Therefore, application level DoS attack requests that are resource intensive and have low utility to the e-commerce website would decrease the attacker's priority level. As the attacker's priority level decreases, the intensity of its DoS attack decreases.

Benefits. Our approach to guard an online service against application level DoS attacks has several benefits.

1. An obvious benefit that follows from the description of our DoS protection mechanism is that it is independent of the attack's precise nature of operation. As pointed out earlier it is in general hard to predict, detect, or enumerate all the possible attacks that may be used by an attacker.
2. A mechanism that is independent of the attack type can implicitly handle intelligent attackers that adapt and attack the system. Indeed any adaptation of an application level DoS attack would result in heavy resource consumption at the server without any noticeable changes to the request's syntax or traffic characteristics.
3. Our mechanism does not distinguish requests based on the request rate, the packet headers, or the contents of the request. As pointed out earlier (and discussed in Section 2) it is very hard to distinguish an attack request from the legitimate ones using either the request rate or the contents of the request.

Contributions. The key contributions of this paper include:

1. We propose a request throttling mechanism that allocates more server resources to the legitimate clients, while severely throttling the amount of server resources allocated to the DoS attackers. This is achieved by adaptively setting a client's priority level in response to the client's requests, in a way that can incorporate application level semantics. We provide a simple application programming interface (API) that permits an application programmer to use our DoS protection mechanism.
2. The proposed solution does not require the clients to be preauthorized. The absence of preauthorization implies that the server does not have to establish any out of band trust relationships with the client.
3. Our proposed solution is client transparent, that is, a user or an automated client side script can browse a DoS protected website in the same way as it browsed an unprotected website. Our DoS protection mechanisms do not require any changes to the client side software or require super user privileges at the client. The clients can seamlessly browse a DoS protected website using any standard web browser that supports HTTP cookies. All instrumentations required for implementing our proposal can be incorporated on the server side.
4. We present a detailed implementation of our proposed solution on the Linux kernel and a concrete evaluation using two sample applications: Apache HTTPD benchmark [2] and the TPCW benchmark [37] (running on Apache Tomcat [3] and IBM DB2 [20]). Our experiments show that the proposed solution incurs low performance overhead (about 1-2%) and is resilient to application level DoS attacks.

2   Application Level DoS Attacks

In this section, we present two examples of application level DoS attacks. Then, we discuss existing approaches for DoS protection, highlighting the deficiencies of those approaches in defending against application level DoS attacks.

2.1   Examples

Example 1. Consider an e-Commerce website like WeaKnees.com. The HTTP requests that pulled out large image files from WeaKnees.com constituted a simple application level DoS attack. In this case, the attackers (a collection of zombie machines) sent the HTTP requests at the same rate as a legitimate client. Hence, a DoS filter may not be able to detect whether a given request is a DoS attack request by examining the packet's headers, including the IP, the TCP and the HTTP headers. In fact, the rate of attack requests and the attack request's packet headers would be indistinguishable from the requests sent by well behaved clients.

Example 2. One could argue that a DoS filter that examines the HTTP request URL may be able to distinguish DoS attackers that request a large number of image files from that of the good clients. However, the attackers could attack a web application using more subtle techniques. For example, consider an online bookstore application like TPCW [37]. As with most online e-Commerce applications, TPCW uses a database server to guarantee persistent operations. Given an HTTP request, the application logic transforms the request into one or more database queries. The cost of a database query not only depends on the type of the query, but also depends on the query arguments. For instance, an HTTP request may require an exhaustive search over the entire database or may require a join operation to be performed between two large database tables. This makes it very hard for a DoS filter to detect whether a given request is a DoS attack request by examining the packet's headers and all its contents. In fact, the rate of attack requests and the attack request's packet headers and contents would be indistinguishable from those sent by any well behaved client unless the entire application logic is encoded in the DoS filter. However, this could make the cost of request filtering almost as expensive as the cost of processing the actual application request itself. Indeed a complex DoS filter like this could by itself turn out to be a target for the attackers.

2.2   Existing Approaches

Preauthorization. One way to defend from DoS attacks is to permit only preauthorized clients to access the web server. Preauthorization can be implemented using SSL [30] or IPSec [25] with an out of band mechanism to establish a shared key between a preauthorized client and the web server. Now, any packets from a non-preauthorized client can be filtered at the firewall. However, requiring preauthorization may deter clients from using the online service. Also, for an open e-Commerce web site like eBay or Amazon, it may not be feasible to make an exhaustive list of all clients that should be authorized to access the service. Further, it would be very hard to ensure all authorized clients will behave benignly. A DoS attack from a small subset of preauthorized clients may render the server unusable.

Challenge Mechanism. Challenge based mechanisms provide an alternative solution for DoS protection without requiring preauthorization. A challenge is an elegant way to throttle the intensity of a DoS attack. For example, an image based challenge [24] may be used to determine whether the client is a real human being or an automated script. A cryptographic challenge [40] may be used to ensure that the client pays for the service using its computing power. However, most challenge mechanisms make both the good and the bad clients pay for the service, thereby reducing the throughput and introducing inconvenience for the good clients as well. For instance, an image based challenge does not distinguish between a legitimate automated client script and a DoS attack script.

Network Level DoS Attacks. There are several network level DoS protection mechanisms including IP trace back [33], ingress filtering [13], SYN cookies [4] and stateless TCP server [18] to counter bandwidth exhaustion attacks and low level OS resource (number of open TCP connections) utilization attacks. Yang et al.[45] proposes a cryptographic capability based packet marking mechanism to filter out network flows from DoS attackers. However none of these techniques are capable of addressing application level DoS attacks. Nonetheless one should keep in mind that the application level DoS filters only augment the network level DoS filters but do not replace them.

Application Level DoS Attacks. The network layer DoS filters cannot handle application level DoS attacks primarily because they lack application level semantics. There have been some proposals that degrade the image/video quality [15][8][21] when the server experiences heavy overload. It is to be noted that such techniques are more effective in protecting the servers from overload than from DoS attacks.

2.3   Threat Model

We assume that the adversary can spoof the source IP address. We also assume that the adversary has a large but bounded number of IP addresses under its control. If an IP address is controlled by the adversary, then the adversary can both send and receive packets from that IP address. We assume that the adversary can neither observe nor modify the traffic to a client whose IP address is not controlled by the adversary. However, the adversary can always send packets with a spoofed source IP address that is not essentially controlled by the adversary. We also assume that the adversary has large, but bounded amounts of networking and computing resources at its disposal and thus cannot inject arbitrarily large numbers of packets into the IP network. We assume that the adversary can coordinate activities perfectly to take maximum advantage of its resources.

3   Trust Tokens

3.1   Overview

Figure 1 shows a high level architecture of our proposed solution. Our approach allocates more server resources to good clients, while severely limiting the amount of resources expended on DoS attackers. The maximum amount of resources allocated to a client is represented by the client's QoS level. We use *trust tokens* (denoted as TT in

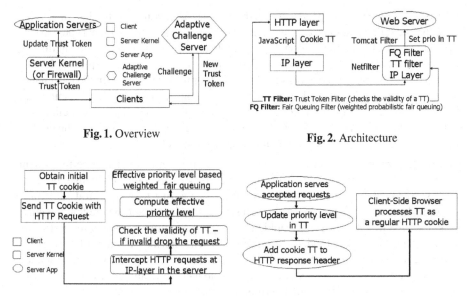

Fig. 1. Overview

Fig. 2. Architecture

Fig. 3. Control Flow

Figures 2 and 3) to encode the QoS level that a client is eligible to receive. Although our architecture is capable of supporting arbitrary QoS policies, for the sake of simplicity, we characterize a client's QoS level exclusively by its priority level (a totally ordered numeric value). A client's trust token is embedded in a standard HTTP cookie that is included in all responses from the server to the client. Using the standard cookie semantics, a legitimate client would include the trust token in all its future requests to the server. A client presenting a valid trust token to the server would be served at the priority level encoded in the token. Otherwise, the client's request would be dropped at the server's IP layer or firewall.

A client's priority level is used to rate limit its requests at the server's IP layer or the firewall. We use an IP level packet filter to filter HTTP requests from the clients. The packet filter uses weighted fair queuing [35] to throttle a client's request rate based on the client's priority level. Hence, requests from attackers attempting to issue a disproportionately large number of requests (relative to their priority level) are dropped at the IP layer itself. Filtering requests at the IP layer significantly reduces the amount of processor, memory, network, and disk resources expended on that request.

A client's priority level is adaptively varied by the application using application specific semantics and domain knowledge. For this purpose, we provide a simple and flexible API for application programmers. We describe the concrete API with three sample implementations in Section 3.3. Allowing the application to set a client's priority level permits us to incorporate application specific semantics (domain knowledge) and is thus highly flexible. IP level (firewall) request filtering ensures that illegitimate requests are dropped before they can consume much of the server's resources. In this paper we explore several algorithms which could be used to vary the client's priority level and study its effect on the performance of the web server.

Trust tokens are bootstrapped using an initial trust token issued by the challenge server when the client first attempts to access the web server. The trust token is encrypted in such a way that it would be computationally infeasible for a client to undetectably modify the token. We ensure the priority level of a client is kept up to date; since the priority level of a client is continuously varied it is very important for the server to retain the most recent value of a client's priority level, especially, if the client's priority level is dropping.

Our proposed solution is client transparent and requires no changes to the client side software. All our instrumentation is done at the server side thereby making the deployment very easy. The instrumentation at the server side includes:

Challenge Server. The challenge server poses a cryptographic challenge to a client, when the client first accesses the website. On correctly solving the challenge, the challenge server is responsible for initializing the client's trust token. A valid trust token allows a client to send requests to the web server. It is important to note that the client does not have to solve a cryptographic challenge every time it sends a request to the server. Further, we use an adaptive mechanism wherein the hardness of solving the challenge depends on the web server's load. Indeed, when the server is not overloaded, our system ensures that the client does not expend its computational resources on solving a challenge before it is granted permission to access the web server.

Server Kernel or Firewall. The IP layer at the server is modified to use the client's priority level to filter HTTP requests sent by a client. The priority level is enforced by fair queuing [35] requests at the IP level. Filtering requests at the IP layer saves a lot of computing and memory resources that are otherwise expended on the request as it traverses up the server's network stack.

Application Server. The application layer at the server is modified to use application specific rules to update a client's priority level. The client's new priority level is computed using a utility based model that considers the set of recent requests sent by the client and the amount of server resources consumed by these requests.

3.2 Design

In this section, we describe how a trust token is constructed. Then, we describe techniques to use the trust token to defend against application level DoS attacks.

Trust Token. A 24 Byte long trust token (tt) is constructed as follows: $tt = \langle prio, tv, H_{MK}(cip, sip, tv, prio)\rangle$, where cip (4 Bytes) denotes the client's IP address, sip (4 Bytes) denotes the server's IP address, tv (4 Bytes) denotes the time at which the trust token was issued (time is expressed as the number of seconds from 1st Jan 1970), $prio$ (4 Bytes) denotes the priority level assigned to the client by the server, MK denotes a secret cryptographic key used by the server and H denotes a keyed pseudo-random function (like HMAC-MD5 or HMAC-SHA1 [27]). A priority level of zero indicates that all requests from the client would be dropped by the server.

Client Side. Figure 2 below shows our architecture and Figure 3 shows the operational usage of the trust token. A legitimate client operates as follows. A client obtains its token tt when it solves a challenge. The token is stored as a HTTP cookie in the client's browser. The client includes the token tt in all its HTTP requests to the server.

Server Side Firewall. On the server side firewall, we perform two operations. First, we filter HTTP requests based on the validity of the trust token. Second, if the trust token is valid, the server extracts the client's priority level and throttles the client's request rate using fair queuing.

The server checks if the packet is a HTTP request and if so, it extracts the HTTP cookie tt. It validates the trust token tt as follows. A trust token tt is valid if the $tt.cip$ matches the client's IP address, $tt.sip$ matches the server's IP address, and $tt.tv$ is some time in the past ($tt.tv < cur\_time$). If so, the server extracts the priority level ($tt.prio$) from tt; otherwise the request is dropped by the firewall.

An adversary may behave benignly until it attains a high priority level and then begin to misbehave. Consequently, the server would issue a trust token with a lower priority level. However, the adversary may send an old trust token (with high priority level) to the server in its future requests. If all responses from the server to the client were tunneled via the firewall, then the firewall can record the client's updated priority level. However, for performance reasons, most application servers are configured in a way that requests are tunneled via the firewall but not the responses [19]. Under such a scenario, we prevent a DoS attack by computing the effective priority level as follows.

The server uses the request's priority level $prio$, the time of cookie issue ($tt.tv$) and the client's request rate r to compute the effective priority level $eprio$ as follows: $eprio = prio * e^{-\delta * max(cur\_time - tt.tv - \frac{1}{r}, 0)}$, where cur_time denotes the current time. The key intuition here is that if $cur\_time - tt.tv$ is significantly larger than the client's mean inter request arrival time ($\frac{1}{r}$) then the client is probably sending an old trust token. The larger the difference between ($cur\_time - tt.tv$) and $\frac{1}{r}$, the more likely it is that the client is attempting to send an old token. Hence, we drop the effective priority level $eprio$ exponentially with the difference between ($cur\_time - tt.tv$) and $\frac{1}{r}$. Note that the fair queuing filter estimates the client's request rate r for performing weighted probabilistic fair queuing.

Having validated the trust token and extracted its priority level, the server uses $eprio$ to perform weighted probabilistic fair queuing on all incoming HTTP requests from the client. Fair queuing limits the maximum request rate from a client to its *fair share*. Hence, requests from an attacker attempting to send requests at a rate larger than its fair share is dropped by the firewall. We set a client's fair share to be in proportion to its effective priority level ($eprio$). Hence, if a client has a low priority level, then only a very small number of requests from the client actually reach the web server. In the following portions of this section, we propose techniques to ensure that DoS attackers are assigned low priority levels, while the legitimate clients are assigned higher priority levels.

Server Side Application Layer. Once the request is accepted by the IP layer packet filter, the request is forwarded to the application. When the server sends a response to the client, it updates the client's priority level based on several application specific rules and parameters. For this purpose we use a benefit function $B(rq)$ that estimates the benefit of a client's request rq. The benefit of a request takes into account the utility of the request and the resources expended in handling that request. For instance, if the request rq is a credit card transaction, then the utility of request rq could be the monetary profit the server obtains from the transaction. We also define a priority update function G that updates the priority level of a client based on the benefit $B(rq)$.

In our first prototype, we propose to use a utility based benefit function $B(rq)$ = $F(rt, ut)$, where rq denotes the client's request, rt is the time taken by the server to generate a response for the request rq, and ut denotes the utility of rq. We use a simple benefit function $B(rq) = ut - \gamma * rt$, where γ is a tunable parameter. The response time rt is used as a crude approximation of the effort expended by the server to handle the request rq. Observe that in computing the benefit $B(rq)$, the response time rt (that denotes the effort expended by the server) is subtracted from the request's utility ut.

The new priority level $nprio$ could be computed as $nprio = G(eprio, B(rq))$, where $eprio$ is the current effective priority level of the client. In our first prototype, we use an additive increase and multiplicative decrease strategy to update the priority level as follows: If $B(rq) \geq 0$, then $nprio = eprio + \alpha * B(rq)$, and $nprio = \frac{eprio}{\beta*(1-B(rq))}$ otherwise. The additive increase strategy ensures that the priority level slowly increases as the client behaves benignly; while the multiplicative decrease strategy ensures that the priority level drops very quickly upon detecting a DoS attack from the client.

In summary, we perform request filtering at the server side IP layer or firewall. As we have pointed out earlier, filtering requests at the firewall minimizes the amount of server resources expended on them. However, the parameter that determines this filtering process (the client's priority level) is set by the application. This approach is highly flexible, since it is possible to exploit application specific semantics and domain knowledge in computing the client's priority level.

3.3   Implementation

Client Side. Our implementation neither requires changes to the client side software nor requires super user privileges at the client. We implement trust tokens using standard HTTP cookies. Hence, the client can use standard web browsers like Microsoft IE or FireFox to browse a DoS protected website in the same manner that it browses an unprotected website. An automated client side script with support for handling HTTP cookies is assumed; such scripts are commonly used on the web today.

Server Side IP Layer. On the server side, we use NetFilters [1] for filtering requests at the IP layer. NetFilters is a framework inside the Linux kernel that enables packet filtering, network address translation and other packet mangling. We use NetFilters to hook onto packet processing at the IP layer. Given an IP packet we check if it is a HTTP request and check if it has the tt cookie in the HTTP request header. If so we extract the trust token tt, check its validity and extract the priority level embedded in the token. We compute the effective priority level $eprio$ from its priority level $prio$ and the request rate r from the client. We have implemented a simple weighted probabilistic fair queuing filter to rate limit requests from a client using its effective priority level ($eprio$).

Server Side Application Layer. We use Apache Tomcat filters to hook on HTTP request processing before an incoming request is forwarded to the servlet engine. This filter is used to record the time at which request processing starts. Similarly, a filter on an outgoing response is used to record the time at which the request processing ended. This filter provides the application programmers the following API to use application specific rules and domain knowledge to update the client's priority level after processing a request rq: `priority updatePrio (priority oldPrio,`

URL `requestURLHistory`, `responseTime rt`), where `oldPrio` denotes the client's priority level before it issued the request rq, `requestURLHistory` denotes a finite history of requests sent from the client, and `rt` denotes the server response time for request rq. Additionally, this filter encrypts the trust token tt and embeds it as a cookie in the HTTP response.

Sample API Implementations. We now describe three sample implementations of our API to demonstrate its flexibility.

Resource Consumption. In Section 3.2 we presented a technique to update a client's priority level based on its request's response time and utility. Utility of the request can be computed typically from the requesting URL using application specific semantics and domain knowledge; note that client supplied parameters are available as part of the request URL. The response time for a request is automatically measured by our server side instrumentation.

Input Semantics. Many e-commerce applications require inputs from users to follow certain implicit semantics. For example, a field that requests a client's age would expect a value between 1 and 100. One can use the client supplied parameters (that are available as a part of the request URL) to estimate the likelihood that a given request URL is a DoS attack or not. Naive DoS attack scripts that lack complete domain knowledge to construct semantically correct requests (unlike a legitimate automated client side script), may err on input parameter values.

Link Structure. In many web applications and web servers the semantics of the service may require the user to follow a certain link structure. Given that a client has accessed a page P, one can identify a set of possible next pages $P_1, P_2, \cdots, P_k$ along with probabilities $tp_1, tp_2, \cdots, tp_k$, where tp_i denotes the probability that a legitimate client accesses page P_i immediately after the client has accessed page P. The server could lower a client's priority level if it observes that the client has significantly deviated from the expected behavior. Note that tracking a client's link structure based behavior requires a finite history of URLs requested by the client.

While heuristics like *Input Semantics* and *Link Structure* can guard the web server from several classes of application level DoS attacks, one should note that these heuristics may not be sufficient to mitigate all application level DoS attacks. For example, a DoS attacker may use requests whose cost is an arbitrarily complex function of the parameters embedded in the request. Nonetheless the *Resource Consumption* based technique provides a solution to this problem by actually measuring the cost of a request, rather than attempting to infer a DoS attack based on the request.

Challenge Server. We have implemented an adaptive challenge mechanism that is similar to the one described in [40]. Client side implementation of the challenge solver is implemented using Java applets, while the challenge generator and solution verifier at the server were implemented using C. Although using Java applets is transparent to most client side browsers (using the standard browser plug-in for Java VM), it may not be transparent to an automated client side script. However, a client side script can use its own mechanism to solve the challenge without having to rely on the Java applet framework.

Our experiments showed that the challenge server can generate about one million challenges per second and check about one million challenges per second. The challenge server can generate up to one million trust tokens per second. This rate is primarily limited by the cost of computing a message authentication code (MAC) on a 16 Byte input using HMAC-SHA1 ($0.91\mu s$). Given that the challenge server can handle very high request rates and it serves only two types of requests (challenge generation and solution verification) it would be very hard for an adversary to launch application level DoS attacks on the challenge server. Further, one can adaptively vary the cost of solving the challenge by changing the hardness parameter m. For example, setting the challenge hardness parameter $m = 20$ ensures that a client expends one million units ($=2^m$) of effort to solve the challenge and the server expends only one unit of effort to check a solution's correctness.

Our experiments showed that a client side challenge solver using a C program, a Java applet and JavaScript requires 1 second, 1.1 seconds and 1012 seconds (respectively) to solve a challenge with hardness $m=20$. A JavaScript based challenge solver is unfair to the legitimate clients since the attackers can use any mechanism (including a non-client transparent C program) to solve the challenge. Therefore, we chose to adopt the client transparent Java applet based challenge solver whose performance is comparable to that of a C program based challenge solver.

4   Evaluation

In this section, we present two sets of experiments. The first set of experiments quantifies the overhead of our trust token filter. The second set of experiments demonstrates the effectiveness of our approach against application level DoS attacks.

Table 1. Overhead

	No DoS Protection	Pre-auth	IPSec	Challenge	IP level tt Filter	App level tt Filter
Mix 1 (in WIPs)	4.68	4.67 (0.11%)	4.63 (1.11%)	1.87 (60%)	4.63 (1.11%)	4.59 (1.92%)
Mix 2 (in WIPs)	12.43	12.42 (0.06%)	4.67 (0.18%)	9.35 (24.8%)	12.37 (0.49%)	12.32 (0.89%)
Mix 3 (in WIPs)	10.04	10.04 (0.03%)	10.00 (0.37%)	6.19 (38.3%)	9.98 (0.61%)	9.91 (1.33%)
HTTPD (in WPPs)	100	100 (0.5%)	71.75 (3.2%)	0.3 (99.7%)	97.5 (2.4%)	96.25 (3.7%)

Table 2. TPCW Servlet Mean Execution Time (ms), Servlet Execution Frequency (percentage) and Servlet Utility

Servlet Name	Admin Req	Admin Resp	Best Seller	Buy Conf	Buy Req	Exec Search	Home	New Prod	Order Disp	Order Inq	Prod Detail	Search Req	Shop Cart
Latency (ms)	2.87	4666.63	2222.09	81.66	5.93	97.86	2.93	14.41	9.75	0.70	0.88	0.55	0.83
Frequency	0.11	0.09	5.00	1.21	2.63	17.20	16.30	5.10	0.69	0.73	18.00	21.00	11.60
Utility	0	0	3	10	4	0	0	0	2	1	1	0	2

Table 3. Attack Strategies

S1	always attack
S2	behave good and attack after reaching the highest Priority level

Table 4. Attack Types

T1	request flooding
T2	low utility requests
T3	old tt
T4	invalid tt

Table 5. Applications

A1	Apache HTTPD
A2	TPCW

All our experiments have been performed on a 1.7GHz Intel Pentium 4 processor running Debian Linux 3.0. We used two types of application services in our experiments. The first service is a bandwidth intensive Apache HTTPD service [2]. The HTTPD server was used to serve 10K randomly generated static web pages each of size 4 KB. The client side software was a regular web browser from Mozilla Fire-Fox [14] running on Linux. The web browser was instrumented to programmatically send requests to the server using JavaScripts [29]. We measured the average client side throughput in web pages per second (WPPs) as the performance metric. We have also conducted experiments using Microsoft IE running on Microsoft Windows XP. The results obtained were qualitatively similar to that obtained using FireFox on Linux, amply demonstrating the portability of our approach.

The second service is a database intensive web transaction processing benchmark TPCW 1.0 [37]. We used a Java based workload generator from PHARM [31]. We used Apache Tomcat 5.5 [3] as our web server and IBM DB2 8.1 [20] as the DBMS. We performed three experiments using TPCW. Each of these experiments included a 100 second ramp up time, 1,000 seconds of execution, and 100 seconds of ramp down time. There were 144,000 customers, 10,000 items in the database, 30 entity beans (EBs) and the think time was set to zero (to generate maximum load). The three experiments correspond to three workload mixes built into the client load generator: the browsing mix, the shopping mix and the ordering mix. The TPCW workload generator outputs the number of website interactions per second (WIPs) as the performance metric.

We simulated two types of clients: one good client and up to a hundred DoS attackers connected via a 100 Mbps LAN to the server. The firewall functionality described in Section 3.3 is implemented on the server. The good client was used to measure the throughput of the web server under a DoS attack. The intensity of the DoS attack is characterized by the rate at which attack requests are sent out by the DoS attackers. We measure the performance of the server under the same DoS attack intensity for various DoS filters. Our experiments were run till the *breakdown point*. The breakdown point for a DoS filter is defined as the attack intensity beyond which the throughput of the server (as measured by the good client) drops below 10% of its throughput under no attack. In the following experiments we show that under application level DoS attacks, the breakdown point for the trust token filter (tt) is much larger than that for other state of the art DoS filters.

4.1   Performance Overhead

Table 1 compares the overhead of our DoS filter ('tt') with other techniques. 'pre-auth' refers to a technique wherein only a certain set of client IP addresses are alone preauthorized to access the service. The 'pre-auth' filter filters packets based on the packet's source IP address. 'IPSec' refers to a more sophisticated preauthorization technique, wherein the preauthorized clients are given a secret key to access the service. All packets from a preauthorized client are tunneled via IPSec using the shared secret key. The 'pre-auth' and 'IPSec' filters assume that all preauthorized clients are benign. Recall that the trust token approach does not require clients to be preauthorized and is thus more general than 'pre-auth' and 'IPSec'. Nonetheless, Table 1 shows that the overhead of our trust token filter is comparable to the overhead of the less general 'pre-auth' and

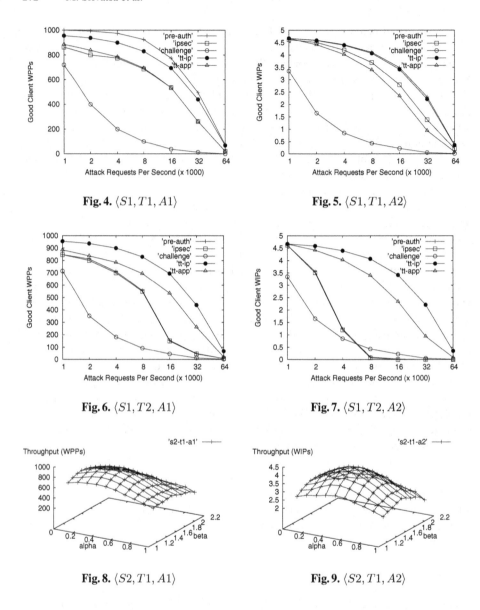

Fig. 4. $\langle S1, T1, A1 \rangle$

Fig. 5. $\langle S1, T1, A2 \rangle$

Fig. 6. $\langle S1, T2, A1 \rangle$

Fig. 7. $\langle S1, T2, A2 \rangle$

Fig. 8. $\langle S2, T1, A1 \rangle$

Fig. 9. $\langle S2, T1, A2 \rangle$

'IPSec' approaches. The cryptographic challenge mechanism has significantly higher overhead than the other approaches since it requires both the good and the bad clients to solve cryptographic puzzles each time they send a HTTP request to the server.

We also experimented with two implementations of the trust token filter: 'tt-ip' uses an IP layer implementation of the trust token filter, while 'tt-app' uses an application layer implementation of the same. 'tt-ip' offers performance benefits by filtering requests at the IP layer, while 'tt-app' offers the advantage of not modifying the server side kernel. Table 1 shows that the overhead of these two implementations are comparable; however, in section 4.2 we show that 'tt-ip' offers better resilience to DoS attacks.

4.2   Resilience to DoS Attacks

In this section, we study the resilience of our trust token filter against application level DoS attacks. We characterize an attack scenario along three dimensions: attack strategy S (Table 3), attack type T (Table 4) and application A (Table 5). The attack scenarios include all the elements in the cross product $S \times T \times A$. For example, a scenario $\langle S1, T2, A1 \rangle$ represents: `always attack` using `low utility requests` on `Apache HTTPD`. Note that these attacks cannot be implemented using standard well-behaved web browsers. Nonetheless, an adversary can use a non-standard malicious browser or browser emulators to launch these attacks.

For experimental purposes, we have assigned utilities to different TPCW servlets based on the application's domain knowledge (see Table 2). For HTTPD we assign utilities to the static web pages as follows. We assume that the popularity of the web pages hosted by the server follows a Zipf like distribution [44]. We assign the utility of a request to be in proportion to the popularity of the requested web page. A legitimate client accesses the web pages according to their popularity distribution. However, DoS attackers may attempt to attack the system by requesting unpopular web pages. In a realistic scenario, low popularity web pages are not cached in the server's main memory and thus require an expensive disk I/O operation to serve them. Further, the adversary may succeed in thrashing the server cache by requesting low popularity web pages.

Trust token filter is resilient to the `always attack` **strategy:** $\langle S1, T1, A1 \rangle$ and $\langle S1, T1, A2 \rangle$. Figures 4 and 5 show the performance of our trust token filter under the attack scenarios $\langle S1, T1, A1 \rangle$ and $\langle S1, T1, A2 \rangle$ respectively. For preauthorization based mechanisms this experiment assumes that only the good clients are preauthorized. In a realistic scenario, it may not be feasible to a priori identify the set of good clients, so the preauthorization based mechanism will not always be sufficient. If a bad client always attacks the system (strategy $S1$) then performance of the trust token filter is almost as good as the performance of preauthorization based mechanisms ('pre-auth' and 'IPSec'). This is because, when a client always misbehaves, its priority level would drop to level zero, at which stage all requests from that client are dropped by the server's firewall. Note that with 64K attack requests per second all the DoS filters fail. The average size of our HTTP requests was 184 Bytes; hence, at 64K requests per second it would consume 94.2 Mbps thereby exhausting all the network bandwidth available to the web server. Under such bandwidth exhaustion based DoS attacks, the server needs to use network level DoS protection mechanisms like IP trace back [33][45] and ingress filtering [13].

Trust token filter is resilient to application level DoS attacks: $\langle S1, T2, A1 \rangle$ and $\langle S1, T2, A2 \rangle$. Table 2 shows the mean execution time for all TPCW servlets. Some servlets like 'admin response' and 'best seller' are expensive (because they involve complex database operations), while other servlets like 'home' and 'product detail' are cheap. Figures 6 and 7 show an application level attack on HTTPD and TPCW respectively. In this experiment we assume that only 10% of the preauthorized clients are malicious. Figures 6 and 7 show the inability of network level filters to handle application level DoS attacks and demonstrate the superiority of our trust token filter. One can also observe from figures 6 and 7 that HTTPD can tolerate a much larger attack rate than TPCW. Indeed, the effectiveness of an application level DoS attack on a HTTPD server serving static web pages is likely to be much lower than a complex database intensive application like TPCW.

Several key conclusions that could be drawn from Figures 4, 5, 6 and 7 are as follows: (i) 'IPSec' and 'pre-auth' work well only when preauthorization for all clients is acceptable and if all preauthorized clients are well behaved. Even in this scenario, the performance of 'tt-ip' is comparable to that of 'IPSec' and 'pre-auth'. (ii) Even if preauthorization for all clients is acceptable and a small fraction (10% in this example) of the clients is malicious, then 'IPSec' and 'pre-auth' are clearly inferior to the trust token filter. (iii) If preauthorization for all clients is not a feasible option then 'IPSec' and 'pre-auth' do not even offer a valid solution, while the trust token filter does. (iv) The challenge based mechanisms incur overhead on both good and bad clients and thus significantly throttle the throughput for the good clients as well, unlike the trust token filter that selectively throttles the throughput for the bad clients.

4.3   Attacks on Trust Token Filter

In Section 4.2 we have studied the resilience of the trust token filter against DoS attacks. In this section, we study attacks that target the functioning of the trust token filter.

Additive increase and multiplicative decrease parameters α and β: $\langle S2, T1, A1 \rangle$ and $\langle S2, T1, A2 \rangle$. Figures 8 and 9 show the throughput for a good client for various values of α and β using applications HTTPD and TPCW respectively. Recall that α and β are the parameters used for the additive increase and multiplicative decrease policy for updating a client's priority level (see Section 3). The strategy $S2$ attempts to attack the trust token filter by oscillating between behaving well and attacking the application after the adversary attains the highest priority level. The figures show that one can obtain optimal values for the filter parameters α and β that maximize the average throughput for a good client. Note that the average throughput for a client is measured over the entire duration of the experiment, including the duration in which the adversary behaves well to obtain a high priority level and the duration in which the adversary uses the high priority level to launch a DoS attack on the web server. For HTTPD these optimal filter parameters ensure that the drop in throughput is within 4-12% of the throughput obtained under scenario $\langle S1, T2 \rangle$; while the drop in throughput for TPCW is 8-17%. These percentiles are much smaller than the drop in throughput using preauthorization or challenge based DoS protection mechanisms (see Figures 6 and 7).

Figure 10 shows the average client throughput when the adversary is launching a DoS attack on the web server. When the application is under a DoS attack, large values of α and β maximize the throughput for a good client. Note that a large α boosts the priority level for good clients while a large β penalizes the bad clients heavily. This suggests that one may dynamically vary the values of α and β depending on the server load.

Server resource utilization parameter γ: $\langle S2, T2, A1 \rangle$ and $\langle S2, T2, A2 \rangle$. Figures 11 and 12 show the average throughput for the good clients under the scenario $\langle S2, T2, A1 \rangle$ and $\langle S2, T2, A2 \rangle$ respectively. These experiments show the effect of varying the trust token filter parameter γ. Recall that we use the parameter γ to weigh a request's

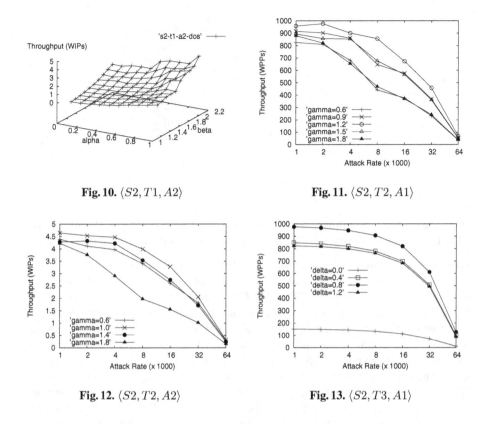

Fig. 10. $\langle S2, T1, A2 \rangle$ **Fig. 11.** $\langle S2, T2, A1 \rangle$

Fig. 12. $\langle S2, T2, A2 \rangle$ **Fig. 13.** $\langle S2, T3, A1 \rangle$

response time against the request's utility (see Section 3). If γ is very small, the filter ignores the response time which captures the amount of server resources consumed by a client's request. On the other hand, if γ is large, the utility of a request is ignored. This would particularly harm high utility requests that are resource intensive. For instance, a high utility request like 'buy confirm' has a response time that is significantly larger than the median servlet response times (see Table 2). The figures show that one can obtain optimal values for the filter parameter γ that maximizes the average throughput for a good client. The optimal value for parameter γ ensures that the drop in throughput for HTTPD and TPCW is within 7-11% of throughput measured under scenario $\langle S1, T2 \rangle$.

Attacking the trust token filter using old trust tokens: $\langle S2, T3, A1 \rangle$ and $\langle S2, T3, A2 \rangle$. Figures 13 and 14 shows the resilience of our trust token filter against attacks that use old trust tokens. An attacker uses strategy $S2$ to behave well and thus obtain a token with high priority level. Now, the attacker may attack the server using this high priority old token. These experiments capture the effect of varying the trust token filter parameter δ, which is used to penalize (possibly) old trust tokens. A small value of δ permits attackers to use older tokens while a large value of δ may result in rejecting requests even from well behaving clients. The figures show that one can obtain optimal values for the filter parameter δ that maximize the average throughput for a good client.

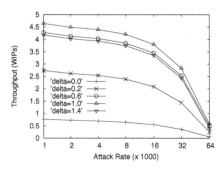

Fig. 14. $\langle S2, T3, A2 \rangle$

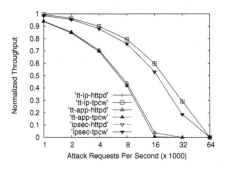

Fig. 15. $\langle S1, T4, A1 \rangle$ and $\langle S1, T4, A2 \rangle$

Using the optimal value for parameter δ we observed that the drop in throughput for HTTPD and TPCW is within 3-7% of throughputs measured under scenario $\langle S1, T2 \rangle$.

Attacking the filter using invalid (spoofed) trust tokens: $\langle S1, T4, A1 \rangle$ and $\langle S1, T4, A2 \rangle$. Figure 15 shows the effect of attacking the trust token filter by sending invalid cookies for both HTTPD and TPCW. Note that if the verification process for the trust token were to be expensive, then an attacker can launch a DoS attack directly on the verification process itself. We have already shown in Table 1 that the overhead of our trust token filter is comparable to that of the network layer DoS filters. This experiment shows that the drop in throughput on sending invalid tokens is comparable to sending packets with invalid authentication headers using IPSec. Observe from the figure that the drop in throughput for the IP layer implementation of the trust token filter and IPSec is the same for both the applications HTTPD and TPCW. Observe also that the throughput for the application layer implementation of the trust token filter ('tt-app') is significantly poorer than the IP layer implementation ('tt-ip'). Also, the application layer implementation for HTTPD and TPCW show slightly different impact on the throughput primarily because Apache HTTPD filters (written in 'C') are faster than Apache Tomcat filters (written in 'Java').

5   Discussion

5.1   Limitations and Open Issues

In this paper, we have so far assumed that one client IP address corresponds to one client. However, such an assumption may not hold when several clients are multiplexed behind a network address translation (NAT) router or a HTTP proxy. In the absence of a DoS attack there is no impact on the legitimate clients behind a NAT router or a HTTP proxy. However, a DoS attack from a few malicious clients may result in the blockage of all requests from the NAT router's or the HTTP proxy's IP address.

A closer look at the client-side RFC 1631 for the IP NAT [12] shows that client-side NAT routers use port address translation (PAT) to multiplex multiple clients on the same IP address. PAT works by replacing the client's private IP address and original source port number by the NAT router's public IP address and a uniquely identifying source port number. Hence, one can modify the trust token as: $tt = \langle prio, tv, H_{MK}(cip, cpn, sip, tv, prio)\rangle$, where cip denotes the IP address of the NAT router and cpn refers to the client's translated port number as assigned by the NAT router.

However, HTTP proxies do not operate using port address translation (PAT). One potential solution is to deploy a trust token filter at the HTTP proxy. The trust token filter at a HTTP proxy gets application specific priority updates for a client's request from the web server. While the web server may not know the set of requests that originated from one client, the HTTP proxy can aggregate priority updates of all requests on a per-client basis. It can use this per-client priority information to filter future HTTP requests from its clients. While such a solution retains client anonymity from the web server, it requires cooperation from the HTTP proxies. An efficient proxy transparent solution to handle application level DoS attacks is an open problem.

5.2 Related Work

Several past papers have addressed network level DoS attacks [4][33][13][18][45]. These techniques are useful in defending a server against network level bandwidth exhaustion attacks. However, the lack of application semantics and domain knowledge render network level DoS filters incapable of handling application level DoS attacks. Several tools have been proposed to perform preauthorization based DoS protection [25][30][26]. Our experiments show that even if preauthorization based techniques were feasible, an application level DoS attack by a small fraction of malicious preauthorized clients can jeopardize the system. Several authors have proposed challenge based mechanisms for DoS protection [24][40][22][36][41][39][11]. Our experiments show that the inability of a challenge based mechanism to selectively throttle the performance of the bad clients can significantly harm the performance for the good clients. Crosby and Wallach [10] present DoS attacks that target application level hash tables by introducing collisions. Section 2 provides a more detailed discussion on the above mentioned DoS protection mechanisms.

Recently, several web applications (including Google Maps [17] and Google Mail [16]) have adopted the Asynchronous JavaScript and XML (AJAX) model [42]. The AJAX model aims at shifting a great deal of computation to the Web surfer's computer, so as to improve the Web page's interactivity, speed, and usability. The AJAX model heavily relies on JavaScripts to perform client-side computations. Just as in the AJAX model, we use JavaScripts to perform client-side computations for handling HTTP cookies and solving cryptographic challenges. Recent surveys indicate that at least 97% of the client browsers support JavaScript and Java [43][38].

Jung et al. [23] characterizes the differences between flash crowds and DoS attacks. The paper proposes to use client IP address based clustering and file reference characteristics to distinguish legitimate requests from the DoS attack requests. An adversary can thwart IP address based clustering by employing a DDoS attack wherein the zombie machines are uniformly distributed over several IP domains. File reference characteristics may not be sufficient to mitigate application level DoS attacks since the cost of serving a request may be a complex function of the parameters embedded in the request. Siris et al. [34] suggests using request traffic anomaly detection to defend against DoS attacks. We have shown in Section 2 that an application level DoS attack may mimic flash crowds, thereby making it hard for the server to detect a DoS attacker exclusively using the request traffic characteristics.

Several papers have presented techniques for implementing different QoS guarantees for serving web data [7][9][5]. A summary of past work in this area is provided in [21]. These papers are not targeted at preventing DoS attacks and do not discuss application level DoS attacks.

6   Conclusion

In this paper we have proposed a middleware to protect a website against application level DoS attacks. We have developed a trust token filter that allocates more resources to the good clients, while severely restricting the amount of resources allocated to the DoS attackers. Our approach works by adaptively setting a client's priority level in response to the client's requests, in a way that incorporates application level semantics. Our DoS protection mechanism is proactive, client transparent, and capable of mitigating application level DoS attacks that may not be known a priori. We have described a concrete implementation of our proposal on the Linux kernel and presented a detailed evaluation using two workloads: a bandwidth intensive Apache HTTPD benchmark and TPCW (running on Apache Tomcat and IBM DB2). Our experiments demonstrate the advantages of the trust token filter over other network level DoS filters in defending against application level DoS attacks.

Acknowledgement. Most of this work was done while Mudhakar Srivatsa was a summer intern at IBM Research. At Georgia Tech, Mudhakar Srivatsa and Ling Liu were partially supported by NSF ITR, NSF CyberTrust and NSF CSR.

References

[1] Netfilter/IPTables project homepage. http://www.netfilter.org/.

[2] Apache. Apache HTTP server. http://httpd.apache.org.

[3] Apache. Apache tomcat servlet/JSP container. http://jakarta.apache.org/tomcat.

[4] D. J. Bernstein. SYN cookies. http://cr.yp.to/syncookies.html, 2005.

[5] V. Cardellini, E. Casalicchio, M. Colajanni, and M. Mambelli. Enhancing a web server cluster with quality of service mechanisms. In *Proceedings of 21st IEEE IPCCC*, 2002.

[6] CERT. Incident note IN-2004-01 W32/Novarg.A virus, 2004.

[7] S. Chandra, C. S. Ellis, and A. Vahdat. Application-level differentiated multimedia web services using quality aware transcoding. In *Proceedings of IEEE special issue on QoS in the Internet*, 2000.

[8] H. Chen and A. Iyengar. A tiered system for serving differentiated content. In *Proceedings of World Wide Web: Internet and Web Information Systems Vol. 6, No. 4*, December 2003.

[9] L. Cherkasova and P. Phaal. Session based admission control: a mechanism for web QoS. In *Proceedings of IEEE Transactions on Computers*, 2002.

[10] S. A. Crosby and D. S. Wallach. Denial of service via algorithmic complexity attacks. In *Proceedings of 12th USENIX Security Symposium, pp: 29-44*, 2003.

[11] C. Dwork and M. Naor. Pricing via processing or combatting junk mail. In *Proceedings of Crypto*, 1992.

[12] K. Egevang and P. Francis.   RFC 1631: The IP network address translator (NAT). http://www.faqs.org/rfcs/rfc1631.html, 1994.

[13] R. Ferguson and D. Senie. RFC 2267: Network ingress filtering: Defeating denial of service attacks which employ ip source address spoofing. http://www.faqs.org/rfcs/rfc2267.html, 1998.

[14] FireFox. Mozilla firefox web browser. http://www.mozilla.org/products/firefox, 2005.

[15] A. fox, S. D. Gribble, Y. Chawathe, E. A. Brewer, and P. gauthier. Cluster-based scalable network services. In *Proceedings of 16th ACM SOSP*, 1997.

[16] Google. Google mail. http://mail.google.com/.

[17] Google. Google maps. http://maps.google.com/.

[18] Halfbakery. Stateless TCP/IP server. http://www.halfbakery.com/idea/Stateless_20TCP_2fIP_20server.

[19] IBM. IBM network dispatcher features. http://www-3.ibm.com/software/network/about/features/keyfeatures.html.

[20] IBM. DB2 universal database. http://www-306.ibm.com/software/data/db2, 2005.

[21] A. Iyengar, L. Ramaswamy, and B. Schroeder. Techniques for efficiently serving and caching dynamic web content. In *Book Chapter in Web Content Delivery, X. Tang, J. Xu, S. Chanson ed., Springer*, 2005.

[22] A. Juels and J. Brainard. Client puzzle: A cryptographic defense against connection depletion attacks. In *Proceedings of NDSS*, 1999.

[23] J. Jung, B. Krishnamurthy, and M. rabinovich. Flash crowds and denial of service attacks: Characterization and implications for cdns and web sites. In *Proceedings of 10th WWW Conference*, 2002.

[24] S. Kandula, D. Katabi, M. Jacob, and A. Berger. Botz-4-sale: Surviving organized DDoS attacks that mimic flash crowds. In *Proceedings of 2nd USENIX NSDI*, 2005.

[25] S. Kent. RFC 2401: Secure architecture for the internet protocol. http://www.ietf.org/rfc/rfc2401.txt, 1998.

[26] A. Keromytis, V. Misra, and D. Rubenstein. SOS: Secure overlay services. In *Proceedings of the ACM SIGCOMM*, 2002.

[27] H. Krawczyk, M. Bellare, and R. Canetti. HMAC: Keyed-hashing for message authentication. http://www.faqs.org/rfcs/rfc2104.html, 1997.

[28] J. Leyden. East european gangs in online protection racket. www.theregister.co.uk/2003/11/12/east-european-gangs-in-online/.

[29] Netscape. Javascript language specification. http://wp.netscape.com/eng/javascript/.

[30] OpenSSL. Openssl. http://www.openssl.org/.

[31] PHARM. Java TPCW implementation distribution. http://www.ece.wisc.edu/~pharm/tpcw.shtml, 2000.

[32] K. Poulsen. FBI busts alleged DDoS mafia. www.securityfocus.com/news/9411, 2004.

[33] S. Savage, D. Wetherall, A. Karlin, and T. Anderson. Practical network support for IP traceback. In *Proceedings of ACM SIGCOMM*, 2000.

[34] V. A. Siris and F. Papagalou. Application of anomaly detection algorithms for detecting SYN flooding attacks. In *Proceedings of IEEE Globecom*, 2004.

[35] I. Stoica, S. Shenker, and H. Zhang. Core-stateless fair queuing: A scalable architecture to approximate fair bandwidth allocations in high speed networks. In *Proceedings of SIGCOMM*, 1998.

[36] A. Stubblefield and D. Dean. Using client puzzles to protect tls. In *Proceedings of 10th USENIX Security Symposium*, 2001.

[37] TPC. TPCW: Transactional e-commerce benchmark. http://www.tpc.org/tpcw, 2000.

[38] W3Schools. Browser statistics. http://www.w3schools.com/browsers/browsers_stats.asp.

[39] X. Wang and M. K. Reiter. Defending against denial-of-service attacks with puzzle auctions. In *Proceedings of IEEE Symposium on Security and Privacy*, 2003.

[40] X. Wang and M. K. Reiter. Mitigating bandwidth exhaustion attacks using congestion puzzles. In *Proceedings of 11th ACM CCS*, 2004.

[41] B. Waters, A. Juels, A. Halderman, and E. W. Felten. New client puzzle outsourcing techniques for dos resistance. In *Proceedings of 11th ACM CCS*, 2004.

[42] C. K. Wei. AJAX: Asynchronous Java + XML. http://www.developer.com/design/article. php/3526681, 2005.

[43] Wikipedia. Comparison of web browsers. http://en.wikipedia.org/wiki/Comparison_of_web_browsers.

[44] B. Yang and H. Garcia-Molina. Improving search in peer-to-peer networks. In *Proceedings of 22nd IEEE ICDCS*, 2002.

[45] X. Yang, D. Wetherall, and T. Anderson. A DoS-limiting network architecture. In *Proceedings of ACM SIGCOMM*, 2005.

Generalized Access Control of Synchronous Communication*

Constantin Serban and Naftaly Minsky

Computer Science Department
Rutgers University, Piscataway, NJ 08854 USA
{serban, minsky}@cs.rutgers.edu

Abstract. The security of modern networked applications, such as the information infrastructure of medical institutions or commercial enterprises, requires increasingly sophisticated access control (AC) that can support global, enterprise-wide policies that are sensitive to the history of interaction. The Law-Governed Interaction (LGI) mechanism supports such policies, but so far only for asynchronous message passing communication. This paper extends LGI to synchronous communication, thus providing advanced control over this important and popular mode of communication. Among the novel characteristics of this control are: the regulation of both the request and the reply, separately, but in a coordinated manner; regulated timeout capability provided to clients, in a manner that takes into account the concerns of their server; and enforcement on both the client and server sides.

Keywords: Access-control, Security, RMI, Synchronous communication, Law Governed Interaction.

1 Introduction

The economy and security of modern society relies on increasingly distributed infrastructures and institutions—such as the power grid, the banking system, transportation, medical institutions, government agencies, and commercial enterprises. This trend increases both the importance of *access control* (AC) technology and its complexity. The importance of access control is increased because such critical systems often communicate via the Internet and can no longer protect themselves by hiding within their local intranet behind their firewalls. Rather, they now depend on access control to protect them against malicious attacks by regulating the messages exchanged among their people and components and between them and the outside. Simultaneously, the complexity of access control is increasing due to the following needs: (a) the need to support increasingly sophisticated policies; (b) the need to regulate the interactions among the members of large and distributed communities of agents, via *communal* (overarching) policies; (c) the need to provide for *interoperability* between policies; and

---

* Work supported in part by NSF grant No. CCR-04-10485.

M. van Steen and M. Henning (Eds.): Middleware 2006, LNCS 4290, pp. 281–300, 2006.

(d) the need to organize policies into *hierarchies* in order to regulate complex systems such as those that serve enterprises—with their intrinsically hierarchical governance—and *federations* of enterprises, as in *grid computing*.

In previous papers [18,2,3] we have shown how these needs can be addressed by Law-Governed Interaction (LGI), which is a message-exchange mechanism that allows an open and heterogeneous group of distributed actors to engage in a mode of interaction governed by an explicitly specified and strictly enforced policy, called the law of this group. LGI is a significant generalization of the conventional concept of access-control. It also represents a radical departure from conventional AC mechanism in that it employs an inherently *decentralized* policy-enforcement technique.

However, LGI has been defined for asynchronous (message passing) communication, leaving unsupported the wide range of applications that employ *synchronous communication*—by which we mean here a *request-reply* type of interaction, when the client thread is blocked while waiting for the reply [1]. In this paper we argue that the control of synchronous communication requires different treatment than that of asynchronous one, particularly when dealing with communal and stateful policies. This is because there are some special needs that arise when regulating synchronous communication, which include: (a) the need to control both the request and the reply parts of a call, separately, but in a coordinated fashion; and (b) the need to provide clients with a *regulated timeout* capability, taking into account the concerns of both the server and the client. This paper addresses these needs, by extending LGI to support synchronous communication.

The rest of this paper is organized as follows. Section 2 motivates this paper by explaining some of the needs to generalize access control, particularly for synchronous communication—illustrating them via a case study, which will be used throughout the paper. Section 3 provides a brief overview of the concept of LGI. In Section 4 we describe the architecture of the proposed AC mechanism for synchronous communication, and we show how it supports the policy introduced in the case study. Section 5 describes the implementation of this mechanism for the RMI protocol, giving rise to what we call "Regulated RMI" (or RRMI). Section 6 discusses related work, and Section 7 concludes this paper.

2   On the Need for a Generalized Access Control Mechanism

We elaborate here on several needs of modern computing for a generalized AC mechanism. We start with a brief discussion of the need for more expressive

---

[1] The term "synchronous communication" as used here is not to be confused with the notion of "synchronous send", which requires the sender to wait for an acknowledgment of receivership before proceeding further in its computation; our definition assumes an exchange of payload information both at the request and at the reply time. Among the communication protocols supporting this type of synchronous communication are SunRPC, JAX-RPC, CORBA, DCOM, and Java RMI; the latter has been chosen as a starting point for the proof of concept implementation in this paper.

policies, for communal policies, and the need for decentralization; these properties apply to both asynchronous and synchronous communication equally, and they are already supported for message-passing communication in the previous version of LGI. We then discuss in greater detail the special needs of synchronous communication, namely the need to control both the request and the reply parts of a call, and the need to provide clients with a *regulated timeout* capability. We will motivate and start these discussions with a simple case study.

2.1   A Pay-Per-Service Interaction: A Case Study

In order to illustrate the types of policies we have in mind for the regulation of synchronous communication, consider a large, geographically distributed hospital, whose management decided that all internal services—such as drug acquisition (from internal pharmacies), printing, file-services, record databases, etc.—would operate as *cost centers*. This means that services need to be paid with internal currency, made available to various clients in their *e-wallets*. More specifically, the requests for such services and the budgeting of these requests are to be regulated by the following policy, to be called *PPS* for "pay-per-service".

1. *An agent that plays the role of a* budget officer *can provide any amount of currency to any agent in the enterprise, to be maintained in the* e-wallet *of that agent.*
2. *Each service request must carry a payment, which is to be deducted from the e-wallet of the client. When the service has been carried out successfully, this payment is to be deposited in the e-wallet of the server. (A service is considered successful if it does not terminate with an exception.)*
3. *A client can cancel a service while it is being handled by the server, incurring a penalty that amounts to a fraction f of the price of a normally completed service. This penalty is to be payed to the server, while the rest of the original payment is to be returned to the client.*

Note that policies of this kind can be used for budgetary control of systems, whether or not the budget has any monetary connotation.

2.2   The Need for More Expressive Policies

While the conventional access control mechanisms are still largely based on the *access control matrix* model, often upgraded into "role-based AC" (RBAC) [21], the limitations of this model have been long recognized in the context of commercial [7] and clinical [1] applications. These limitations are also becoming increasingly apparent in other application domains. We point out here two important, and closely related, features that are missing in the traditional AC model.

One such feature is *sensitivity to the history of interaction*, which gives rise to the so called *stateful*, or *dynamic* policies. Our example policy *PPS* is stateful in this sense, as one's ability to make service requests depends on the amount of currency in its e-wallet, which, in turn, depends on previous service requests it made. Throughout this paper, the state representing the history of interaction which is relevant to the policy at hand is called *control state*. The control state may include, among other things, the e-wallets of the agents subject to *PPS* policy.

The budgetary control in our example is critical in financial systems, but it is important in other kinds of systems as well. Other types of stateful policies include, in particular, *dynamic separation of duties* [10] and Chinese-Wall policies.

Another important feature, missing from traditional AC, is a degree of *initiative* that a policy can take. Conventional AC policies are limited to permitting or prohibiting messages. But one often needs to associate other actions with the sending or receipt of a message, such as sending a copy of the message to some audit trail server, or changing the state of the sender or receiver if the policy is stateful, as is required by our *PPS* policy above. Some of these capabilities have been introduced into several recent AC models. In particular, the AC model of Ryutov and Neuman [20] supports policies that can exhibit simple initiatives, but they do not support stateful policies; the same is true for XACML [12], a recent AC standard for web-services.

2.3   The Need for Communal Policies

Most conventional AC mechanisms are designed for *server-centric* policies. Such a policy is employed by an individual server to regulate the use of own its resources by its clients. Such a policy is usually expressed via Access Control Lists, or via a formalism like Keynote [6]. The enforcement mechanism for server-centric policies consists of a reference-monitor that mediates the interactions of the server with its clients. This reference monitor is usually run by the server itself, or is closely associated with it.

But the server-centric approach is inadequate for the growing class of applications where the interactions among the members of a distributed community of servers and their clients—or a community of peers—is subject to an overarching *communal* policy. Our example *PPS* policy is clearly communal, in particular, because the content of the e-wallet of an agent effects the ability of that agent to get services from any server in the AC domain, such as the enterprise.

2.4   The Need for Decentralization

The importance of communal, enterprise-wide policies has been recently recognized by some academic projects [9], as well as by commercial systems such as IBM-Tivoli [15], and by XACML [12]. They all employ a centralized reference monitor to mediate all interaction between agents in the enterprise, subject to a given communal policy. This reference monitor is often replicated, for the sake of scalability. But none of these mechanisms and models support fully stateful policies—and for a good reason. As argued in [2], it is hard to scale global stateful policies through the use of standard replication techniques because a state change sensed by one replica of the reference monitor may have to be propagated atomically to all other replicas.

We believe, therefore, that for an AC mechanisms to support communal and stateful policies in a scalable manner, it needs to be *decentralized*. As we shall see in Section 3, such decentralization can be accomplished efficiently and scalably by associating with every agent x a private reference monitor, called *controller*, that mediates all the interactions of x with other members of the community governed by the policy at hand. This controller also maintains the *local control state* of agent x, which reflect the history of its interaction with the rest of the community in question. It is this control state which would maintain the e-wallet of x under the PPS policy above.

2.5 The Need to Regulate Both the Request and the Reply Parts of a Call

Conventional access control mechanisms for synchronous communication regulate only the request step of a call, leaving the reply unregulated. Here we will argue that the reply to a call needs to be regulated as well, in coordination with the regulation of the request. Of course, regulation of the reply is a *post factum* decision, in so far as the execution of the server is concerned. But such regulation can have two types of effects: (a) it can update the control state, based on the nature of the reply, or on its timing; and (b) it can control the payload of the reply itself. The nature of these two types of effects, and the need for them, are discussed in the following subsections.

Updating the Control State: We have argued that an AC policy often needs to be sensitive to the history of interaction, as represented by the control state of the policy. But under synchronous communication such interaction consists of the reply as well as the request that triggered it. The reply may be important because it may matter to the policy whether or not the server replied, how long it took it to reply, and the nature of the reply itself.

An example of such sensitivity of a policy to the reply is provided by the PPS policy introduced in Section 2. Point 2 of this policy stipulates that payment for a service should be *moved* from the e-wallet of the client to that of the server. But this should happen only upon a successful completion of the service—that is, when the client receives a non-exception reply from the server. It is obvious that this policy can be implemented only if the reply is regulated; and if such reply control is coordinated with the control of the corresponding request.

Controlling the Payload of the Reply: Access control policies are often concerned with what information clients are allowed to access. Often, the sensitive information disclosed to the clients becomes explicit only at the time of reply, and not at the time of the request. The reply needs to be regulated in order to control the payload itself.

To show how this control may be useful, consider an elaboration of policy PPS of Section 2, via the following additional point:

Patient record servers may serve three kinds of clients: doctors, *who have access to an entire patient record;* researchers, *who have access to all the information within a record, except for the patient name and id; and* financial officers, *who are not allowed to see any medical information within a record.*

This part of our policy cannot be enforced at the request time, since the patient record information is not available at that time. Only after the server replies, the complete record of the patient is available, and the appropriate fields can be filtered based on the role of the caller.

2.6   The Need to Regulate Timeouts

Under synchronous communication the client thread is blocked until it gets the reply. This feature is intended to provide transparency of the network communication, by making remote calls appear to programmers as local calls [5]. But this transparency is often hard to maintain in practice because the duration of a service is unpredictable, due to communication uncertainties, particularly over WANs; and due to the lack of familiarity with the behavior of the server, particularly when it belongs to a different administrative domain.

The conventional technique for dealing with such unpredictability is for the client to terminate a given service call—if it takes too long to complete—simply by killing the requesting thread. But such an arbitrary, one-sided timeout may be harmful. The problem is that both the client and the server have stakes in the service, which might be undermined by its abrupt termination, unless the termination is done in an *orderly manner.* The meaning of "orderly" depends on the application at hand, as we shall see below. But whatever it may be, it ought to be defined explicitly in the policy regulating the communication, so that it can be enforced by the AC mechanism, and be visible to both the client and the server. There are many possible termination (timeout) policies, which may be suitable in different situations. We will consider two types of such policies below.

Predefined Timeouts: To provide a degree of predictability to the duration of a service, one can employ a policy under which every call would specify an upper limit $Tmax$ for the duration of requested service, which would be provided to the server as a parameter. This would mean that if the reply does not arrive at the client by the specified limit, the client would regain its control, and the server will be notified of the termination (assuming that the server implements proper interfaces that support such notification). This policy benefits the server as follows: if it knows that the requested service cannot be provided within the time $Tmax$, it might decide to decline the request immediately, and not waste its resources on attempting to provide it. The client would also benefit from this policy by not having to forcefully kill the thread that issued the call—measure that can leave the application in an inconsistent state.

Moreover, if the service in question is of a pay-per-service kind, then such a policy can mandate the return of the payment to the client, if the requested service has not been provided by the specified limit $Tmax$. This is appropriate because one can argue that the server does not deserve any payment for its effort, in this case, because it has been notified *a priori* of the time limit.

Note that the time in this policy can be strictly local, and the enforcement can be expressed in either client or server time. Distributed clocks, however, are often reasonably synchronized (using NTP, GPS, or other mechanisms), thus the two local times in practice are the same.

Unplanned Timeouts: Sometimes it is desirable to allow the client to interrupt a call while the call is still in progress. This may be the case if runtime conditions indicate to the client that the service it has requested is not necessary anymore, or if the thread that initiated the call needs to regain the control, for whatever reason. But even if unplanned, such a timeout needs to be done in an orderly fashion, according to a pre-specified policy.

A policy regarding unplanned timeouts is just what is provided for by Point 3 of the *PPS* policy in Section 2. This point stipulates that the server—whose work has been terminated for no fault of its own—be compensated by a specified fraction of the cost of a normal service; and that the rest of the payment be returned to the client. Thus, this policy ensures a degree of fairness to both the client and the server, whenever the client terminates its call. The implementation of this particular policy under the proposed AC mechanism is presented in Section 4.1.

3   An Overview of LGI

Broadly speaking, LGI is a message-exchange mechanism that allows an open and heterogeneous group of distributed *actors* to engage in a mode of interaction *governed* by an explicitly specified and strictly enforced policy, called the "law" of this group. By "actor" we mean an arbitrary process, whose structure and behavior is left unspecified. An actor engaged in an LGI-regulated interaction, under a law $\mathcal{L}$, is called an $\mathcal{L}$-*agent* (or simply an "agent," when the identity of the law does not matter); the messages exchanged under a given law $\mathcal{L}$ are called $\mathcal{L}$-*messages*; and the group of agents interacting via $\mathcal{L}$-messages is called an $\mathcal{L}$-*community*.

LGI thus turns a set of disparate actors, which may not know or trust each other, into a *community* of agents that can rely on each other to comply with the given law $\mathcal{L}$. This is done via a distributed collection of generic components called *private controllers*, one per $\mathcal{L}$-agent, which need to be *trusted* to mediate all interactions between these agents, subject to a specified law $\mathcal{L}$ (as illustrated in Figure 1).

The private controllers are actually hosted by what we call *controller pools*—each of which is a process of computation that can operate several (in the hundreds) private controllers, thus serving several different agents, possibly subject to different laws[2]. A prototype of LGI was released in October 2005 [17]; this

---

[2] We often use the term "controller" for either a controller-pool or for a private-controller—expecting the ambiguity to be resolved by the context.

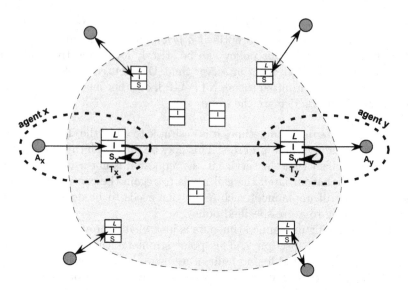

Fig. 1. Interaction via LGI: Actors are depicted by circles, interacting across the Internet (lightly shaded cloud) via their private controllers (boxes) operating under law L. Agents are depicted by dashed ovals that enclose (actor, controller) pairs. Thin arrows represent messages, and thick arrows represent modification of state.

section provides only a very brief overview of LGI. For more information, the reader is referred to the LGI tutorial and manual, available through the above mentioned website, and to a host of published papers.

Agents and their Private Controllers: An $\mathcal{L}$-agent x is a pair $x = \langle A_x, T_x^{\mathcal{L}} \rangle$, where A_x is an *actor*, and $T_x^{\mathcal{L}}$ is its *private controller*, which mediates the interactions of A_x with other LGI-agents, subject to law $\mathcal{L}$. The role of the controllers is illustrated in Figure 1, which shows the passage of a message from an actor A_x to A_y, as it is mediated by a pair of controllers, first by $T_x^{\mathcal{L}}$, and then by $T_y^{\mathcal{L}}$—both operating, in this case, under the same law.

The Structure and Operations of Private Controllers: Broadly speaking, a private controller, such as $T_x^{\mathcal{L}}$ above, can be described as a triple $\langle I, \mathcal{L}, S_x \rangle$ (depicted by boxes in Figure 1), where I is a generic interpreter and enforcer of LGI laws; $\mathcal{L}$ is the law under which this particular controller operates; and S_x is the *control state* (or, "cState") of agent x, whose content, semantics, and dynamic behavior are largely defined by law $\mathcal{L}$. The concept of law is defined in the following section.

To describe the behavior of a controller, we need to introduce its main features. First, a private controller $T_x^{\mathcal{L}}$ operates by responding to certain *regulated events* that occur at it, which includes, among others: (a) the arrival of various messages at the controller—messages sent by its own actor A_x to other agents, and messages sent by others to agent x; and (b) the coming due of an obligation.

Second, a private controller features a set of *primitive operations* that are carried out only if mandated by the law. They include operations on the cState S_x of the agent in question, and operations that cause messages to be forwarded to other agents.

A controller $T_x^{\mathcal{L}}$ operates *sequentially*, by reacting to the regulated events that occur at it, in the order of their occurrence (and in an arbitrary order for events that occur simultaneously). It reacts to each such event as follows: (a) it evaluates the *ruling* of law $\mathcal{L}$ for this event, where the ruling is a list of primitive operations; and (b) it carries out this ruling, by executing all the operations in it, in the order of their appearance in the ruling, and *atomically*—before the controller turns to the next event.

The Concept of Law, and the Semantics of LGI: Our concept of law differs structurally from the conventional concept of an AC policy (such as that of XACML) mostly in that it is **local**—in the sense that an LGI law can be complied with, by each member of the community subject to it, without having any direct information of the coincidental state of other members. This locality is important because it enables the decentralization of law enforcement, and thus provides for scalability even in the case of stateful policies.

It is important to note that, despite the fact that locality constitutes a strict constraint on the structure of LGI laws, it does not reduce their expressive power, as has been proved in [17]. In particular, despite its *structural locality*, an LGI law can have *global effect* over the entire $\mathcal{L}$-community—simply because all members of that community are subject to the same law—and can, thus, be used to establish *mandatory*, community-wide constraints.

The following is an **abstract definition** of LGI laws:

A law $\mathcal{L}$ is a function $L(e, s)$, which returns a list of primitive operations, called the ruling *of the law, for any possible regulated-event e and any possible control-state s.*

Note that the ruling of the law is not limited to accepting or rejecting a message, but can mandate any number of operations, providing laws with a strong degree of *initiative*, as discussed in the introduction. Also, the operations that can be included in the ruling may update the cState of the agent, thus providing for *stateful policies*. Finally, the ruling may impose an *obligation* on the agent, which provides a *proactive capability*.

This definition is abstract in that it is independent of the language used for specifying laws. We currently use two such languages—one is based on Prolog, and the other one on Java. But despite the pragmatic importance of a particular language being used for specifying laws, the semantics of LGI is basically independent of that language.

On the Basis for Trust Between Members of a Community: In order for an agent x to trust its peer y to operate under the same law $\mathcal{L}$, it is sufficient to have the assurance that the following three conditions are satisfied: (a) the exchange between x and y is mediated by *bona fide* private controllers T_x and T_y, respectively; (b) both controllers operate under law $\mathcal{L}$; and (c) the $\mathcal{L}$-messages exchanged between x and y are transmitted securely over the network.

The first of these conditions is the hardest to satisfy. LGI ensures this condition via certification. That is, a given law may require the controllers interpreting it to authenticate themselves by means of a certificate signed by a specified certification authority (CA). Such a CA that is willing to certify the controllers as correct is presumably associated with some reputed organization that manages and maintains an entire set of controllers.

To ensure condition (b), that is that the interacting controllers T_x and T_y operate under the same law, LGI adopts the following protocol: a controller T_x appends an *one way hash* [19] H of its law to every message it controls. The controller of the receiving peer, T_y, would accept this as a valid $\mathcal{L}$-message only if H is identical to the hash of its own law. Of course, such an exchange of hashes can be trusted only if condition (a) is satisfied.

Finally, to ensure the validity of condition (c) above, the messages sent across the internet—between actors and their controllers, and between pairs of controllers—should be digitally signed and encrypted. These conventional but rather expensive measures can be dispensed with if one is not concerned about monitoring and spoofing of messages.

4   Regulating Synchronous Communication

As we have already pointed out, synchronous communication differs from asynchronous one in that the former consists of two tightly coupled steps – the request and the reply – and because the client thread is blocked until it gets the reply. Conventional AC mechanisms for synchronous communication operate by regulating only its request part, usually intercepting the request at the server side, as shown in Figure 2. This is similar to the manner that conventional AC mechanisms for asynchronous communication operate.

In this paper we propose a generalized regulation mechanism that controls both the request and the reply separately, but in a coordinated manner, with respect to both the client and the server. This regulation takes place in four steps, as depicted in Figure 3. Any request placed by a client is intercepted first by the LGI-controller associated with the client, then by the controller of the server. When the server issues the reply, it is intercepted by the controller of the server, and then by the controller of the client. Each controller enforces the same communal law L, which can be written to coordinate the treatment of the reply with the request that triggered it, via the state it maintains.

The implementation of this AC mechanism is discussed in Section 5. In this section we will show how this mechanism can be used to implement the *PPS* policy of Section 2.1. For this purpose, we will express a law that implements this policy via a pseudocode; the actual formalization is in the Java-based law language of LGI, defined in [17]. This pseudocode consist of rules of the following type:

upon ⟨*event*⟩ *if* ⟨*condition*⟩ *do* ⟨*action*⟩

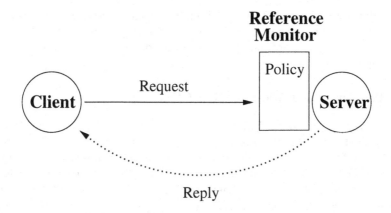

Fig. 2. Server Centric Access Control over RPC

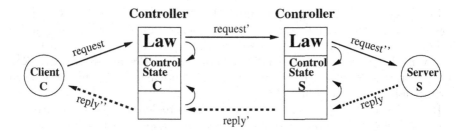

Fig. 3. Regulated Synchronous Communication

Each of these rules has three parts, briefly described below.

The **event** part of a rule specifies one of the events that may occur at a controller. Below are the four events which are directly involved in synchronous communication:

- *sentCall*: occurs at the controller of the client when a client performs a request.
- *arrivedCall*: occurs at the controller of the server when a request arrives at it.
- *sentResult*: occurs at the controller of the server after the server initiates the reply.
- *arrivedResult*: occurs at the controller of the client when the reply arrives at it.

The **condition** part of a rule is an arbitrary expression defined over the identity of the caller and the callee, the payload of the request or the reply, and the local control state.

The **action** part of a rule consists of a list of operations that mandate such activities as the forwarding of a message or the modification of the control state.

The modification of the control state is critical because it allows the recording of the relevant aspects of the history of interaction. In particular, the state can be used to facilitate the coordination between the control of request and the control of the reply.

4.1   The Implementation of the *PPS* Policy

Access to services under our Pay-Per-Service (*PPS*) policy introduced informally in Section 2.1 is regulated using a *currency* consumption scheme. The currency represents a form of credentials used for regulation purpose, thus the e-wallet of clients and servers are maintained securely, by their controllers as a form of state—the control state. The budget officer is recognized as such by having its controller maintain a `role(budgetOfficer)` credential in its control state. The acquisition of this credential and the initial setup of the corresponding state can be performed using either a digital certificate, an appointment, or a password scheme.

Figure 4 presents the law implementing the *PPS* policy. Rules $\mathcal{R}1$ - $\mathcal{R}4$ control how the currency is distributed among the clients and servers—corresponding to Point 1 in *PPS*, Rule $\mathcal{R}5$ - $\mathcal{R}8$ regulates the access to the server according to the available currency—corresponding to Point 2 in *PPS*, and Rules $\mathcal{R}9$ - $\mathcal{R}12$ regulate the cancellation of services using an unplanned timeout mechanism corresponding to Point 3 in *PPS*.

Rule $\mathcal{R}1$ specifies that everybody can request a replenishment of its currency, anytime during the interaction, via a `getBudget` request. $\mathcal{R}2$ prohibits such requests to be served by anybody but a proper budget officer. This is done as follows: each time an `arrivedCall(getBudget)` event arrives at a destination controller, the local control state is looked-up for `role(budgetOfficer)` credential. If the local state contains this credential, the target is allowed to handle the request. If not, a `NotBudgetOfficer` exception is returned to the caller. Rule $\mathcal{R}3$ allows the budget officer to reply with a certain currency amount, unhindered. Rule $\mathcal{R}4$ retrieves the assigned currency from the reply, and adds it to the e-wallet of the client. Since this currency constitutes a credential for the subsequent communication, it should be maintained by the client's controller in its state.

Rules $\mathcal{R}5$ to $\mathcal{R}8$ regulate the access of a client to a service, based on the cost of the service and the amount available in the client's e-wallet. We assume that the cost of a service is a fixed amount, denoted by the value `serviceCost`, while the name of the service (i.e., remote method, procedure) is represented by the variable S. The regulation is performed in a combined manner, on the request as well as on the reply path. In rule $\mathcal{R}5$, each time a client requests a service, the cost of the service is compared against the e-wallet of the client. If the cost exceeds the e-wallet amount, an `outOfCurrency` exception is returned to the caller. If the client has enough currency, the cost of the service is deducted from the e-wallet of the client. The state of the client is augmented with an item called *escrow*, which binds the cost with the request information (such as request_id, object_id, request signature). Finally the request is allowed to propagate. Rule

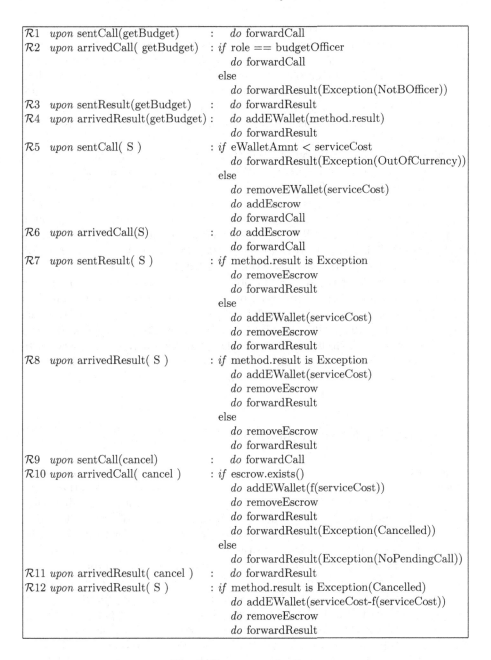

$\mathcal{R}1$	*upon* sentCall(getBudget)	:	*do* forwardCall
$\mathcal{R}2$	*upon* arrivedCall(getBudget)	: *if* role == budgetOfficer	
			do forwardCall
		else	
			do forwardResult(Exception(NotBOfficer))
$\mathcal{R}3$	*upon* sentResult(getBudget)	:	*do* forwardResult
$\mathcal{R}4$	*upon* arrivedResult(getBudget) :		*do* addEWallet(method.result)
			do forwardResult
$\mathcal{R}5$	*upon* sentCall(S)	: *if* eWalletAmnt < serviceCost	
			do forwardResult(Exception(OutOfCurrency))
		else	
			do removeEWallet(serviceCost)
			do addEscrow
			do forwardCall
$\mathcal{R}6$	*upon* arrivedCall(S)	:	*do* addEscrow
			do forwardCall
$\mathcal{R}7$	*upon* sentResult(S)	: *if* method.result is Exception	
			do removeEscrow
			do forwardResult
		else	
			do addEWallet(serviceCost)
			do removeEscrow
			do forwardResult
$\mathcal{R}8$	*upon* arrivedResult(S)	: *if* method.result is Exception	
			do addEWallet(serviceCost)
			do removeEscrow
			do forwardResult
		else	
			do removeEscrow
			do forwardResult
$\mathcal{R}9$	*upon* sentCall(cancel)	:	*do* forwardCall
$\mathcal{R}10$	*upon* arrivedCall(cancel)	: *if* escrow.exists()	
			do addEWallet(f(serviceCost))
			do removeEscrow
			do forwardResult
			do forwardResult(Exception(Cancelled))
		else	
			do forwardResult(Exception(NoPendingCall))
$\mathcal{R}11$	*upon* arrivedResult(cancel)	:	*do* forwardResult
$\mathcal{R}12$	*upon* arrivedResult(S)	: *if* method.result is Exception(Cancelled)	
			do addEWallet(serviceCost-f(serviceCost))
			do removeEscrow
			do forwardResult

Fig. 4. Pay-per-service Law

$\mathcal{R}6$ occurs when the server's controller detects a service request. In this case, a similar *escrow* state is saved in the local state, on behalf of the server. Rule $\mathcal{R}7$ occurs when the server replies to the client. Remember that PPS policy specifies that only a successful service is to be paid for; the non-success is determined by the return of an exception. If such an exception occurs, then the previously setup escrow is removed without crediting the e-wallet of the server. Otherwise, the e-wallet is credited with the service cost. Rule $\mathcal{R}8$ performs the corresponding activity on behalf of the client: if the result was an exception, then the client's e-wallet is credited back with the service cost and the escrow state is removed. Otherwise, the service is considered successful, and the escrow state is simply removed.

Rules $\mathcal{R}9$ to $\mathcal{R}12$ correspond to the *PPS* cancellation of service. $\mathcal{R}9$ allows anybody to cancel a service request. Whenever such a cancellation request is sensed by the controller of the server, $\mathcal{R}10$ is fired. This rule checks whether the server has already issued a reply, by checking the escrow state. If this is the case, the cancellation request cannot be satisfied and a `NoPendingCall` exception is returned. If the server is still handling the service, then the cancellation takes effect: the escrow is removed, the e-wallet of the server is credited with a fraction of the cost (denoted by the function `f(serviceCost)`), and two replies are issued automatically, without the server's involvement. First, a successful reply to the cancellation request is issued, followed by an exceptional reply to the cancelled service (`Canceled` exception). Rule $\mathcal{R}11$ allows the cancellation reply to reach the client, while $\mathcal{R}12$ handles the situation of the `Canceled` exception reply to a service. This rule is similar to Rule $\mathcal{R}8$ that handles any reply to a service. In this situation, however, the e-wallet of the client is replenished with the cost of the service minus the fraction penalty; similarly, the escrow is removed and the reply propagated to the client.

5   Regulated RMI Implementation

In this section we outline an implementation of the access control model for synchronous communication applied to Java Remote Method Invocation (Java RMI or simply RMI). RMI is a mechanism that allows remote procedure calls between objects located in different Java virtual machines. When a client performs a request, a method is transferred to the server along with its serialized arguments. When the server answers, the return data (or an exception) is serialized and transferred to the client. The data exchanged in this process consists of the method name and signature along with the argument or reply objects.

The implementation presented here, called Regulated RMI (or RRMI), is a modified version of Java RMI and is virtually source-level compatible with it.

This section has three parts. The first part describes the LGI laws that regulate RMI communication (also called RMI laws). The second part describes the changes we introduced in the RMI suite. Finally the performance of RRMI is discussed.

The Formulation of RMI Laws: In order to provide a fine-grained access to the information exchanged during an RMI method call, the RMI laws are written in Java. The use of Java for writing laws and their generic structure is described in detail in [17]. The access control rules are expressed in RMI laws by mapping the events introduced in Section 4 to specific methods, called *event methods*. The conditions are represented by Java code operating over the local state, the method name/signature and the arguments/reply values. The actions are represented by specific methods that mandate the handling of the request/reply and the modification of the local state. Each time an event occurs at the controller, the corresponding event method in the RMI law is invoked. The computation of such a method, in turn, produces a number of actions to be carried out by the controller. [3]

The RRMI suite: At application level, the RRMI suite is largely compatible with Java RMI. The only difference between the two suites appears in the initialization stage, when a security principal is associated with the stub of a caller and the skeleton of a remote object (or target). The important components of the RRMI suite are as follows: RRMI has an LGI-enabled transport protocol – different from JRMP or IIOP; there is a different stub compiler, called *LgiRMIC* instead of the standard *RMIC* compiler; a new *registry* application, *LgiRegistry* regulates the exchange of stubs between applications. Below we discuss these components.

The JRMP transport protocol is employed in the RMI stub-to-skeleton interaction. In order to enable control over RMI communication, we changed the transport protocol to our version of LGI-controllable transport layer. As opposed to JRMP, this new transport layer provides enough in-transit information permitting an adequate control decision based on the method name, its signature, and runtime arguments.

A control decision in LGI model can be based on the identity of the interacting principals: the client and the server. In order to perform a principal-based decision, the caller and the remote object are associated with their own principals. Since the communication endpoints are the stub and the skeleton, we modified the RMI compiler in order to allow the association of a principal to each stub and skeleton. The newly resulted compiler is called *LgiRMIC*.

We also developed a new registry entity. Our LgiRegistry is an LGI-enabled repository for stubs that offers LGI control over the propagation and publishing of remote object stubs.

Due to the nature of the above modifications, our implementation was based on NinjaRMI [24]. This is an open source RMI implementation developed as part of the Ninja project at UC Berkeley, and is source-level compatible with Java RMI.

Figure 5 presents a simple example of source code and the API provided by RRMI. In this example, *PMember* represents the principal member object, a principal subject to LGI regulation. LgiNaming represents the registry used to bind and lookup the published objects. The example shows the definition of a remote object, *RecordServerImpl*. The *principal* argument of the constructor establishes the identity of the principal exporting this object. The initialization

---

[3] An example of a formal RMI law implementing the *PPS* policy is available at:
http://www.moses.rutgers.edu/rrmi/examples/payperservice/ .

```
              /*remote object code*/
public class RecordServerImpl extends LgiRemoteObject implements RecordServer{
  public RecordServerImpl(PMember principal) throws RemoteException{
    super(principal);
  }
  public String getRecord() {
  ...// specific code
  }
}
              /*exporting server code*/
PMember callee = new PMember("http://lawurl","controller",port,"server").adopt();
LgiNaming Naming = new LgiNaming(callee);
RecordServer rs = new RecordServerImpl(callee);
Naming.rebind("registry_name/object_name", rs);

              /*client code*/
PMember caller= new PMember("http://lawurl","controller",port,"client").adopt();
LgiNaming Naming = new LgiNaming(caller);
RecordServer rs = (RecordServer) Naming.lookup("registry_name/object_name");
rs.getRecord(); //remote method invocation
```

Fig. 5. Sample RRMI client-server code

and the actual exporting of the object can be observed in the server code. The client code shows the initialization of the principal performing remote calls. The actual stub for the remote object is downloaded from the *Naming* registry using the *lookup* method. This method also attaches the identity of the principal of the caller to the downloaded stub. After these steps, any remote call will carry –in a seamless manner–the identity of both the caller and the recipient of the call. It can be observed that except for the principal initialization and stub downloading, the rest of the code is source compatible with Java RMI.

RRMI Performance Evaluation: We compared the performance of RRMI implementation with standard Java RMI/JRMP. The objective of our performance tests was to evaluate the overhead introduced by our mechanism compared to raw Java RMI (with *no* AC) . We measured the average completion time for RMI calls in the case of LAN and WAN networks using different scenarios. The LAN consisted of a 10Mbps Ethernet network connecting two SunUltra10 (440Mhz) workstations. For the WAN scenario, we used an additional Intel Pentium IV (1.5GHz) placed in a 100Mhz Ethernet LAN 25 hops away from the first LAN. For both scenarios we measured method calls with String and Vector arguments/return values of various sizes. In the case of Java RMI no access control was performed, and no security manager/class loader installed. In the

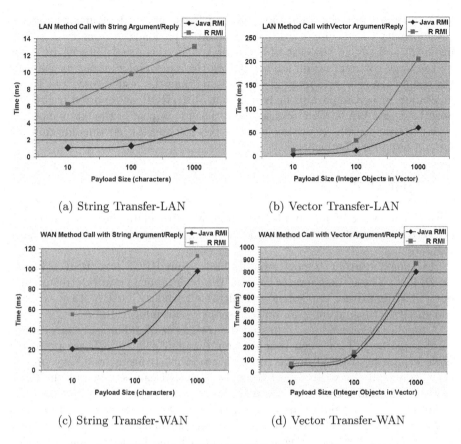

(a) String Transfer-LAN

(b) Vector Transfer-LAN

(c) String Transfer-WAN

(d) Vector Transfer-WAN

Fig. 6. RRMI vs. JavaRMI/JRMP Performance Comparison

case of RRMI we provided minimal control with a simple law that retrieved the method name and one argument and compared them to predefined values. In both cases, the actual implementation of the remote method was to simply return the argument.

The results in Figure 6 (a) and Figure 6 (c) show the comparison between the performance of RRMI and JavaRMI/JRMP when strings of 10, 100, and 1000 characters have been sent over and returned as part of a method call. The graphs in Figure 6 (b) and Figure 6 (d) show the same comparison when a Vector of Integers with 10,100, and 1000 items has been sent as an argument and returned as a result.

While the LAN measurements showed our implementation to be, on average, 2 to 4 times slower than that of Java RMI/JRMP, the overhead in the case of WAN was 8% for large sets of data. In a LAN, the serialization/deserialization and marshaling/unmarshalling are, by far, the dominant time-consuming component of an RMI call, and our solution requires the additional marshaling and serialization operations by two controllers. Additionally, Java RMI is optimized for communication of strings and small payloads, while RRMI incurs the constant penalty of carrying extra security-related payloads. As observed in Figure 6 (c) and (d), in the case of SANs or WANs, this disadvantages are offset by the large communication latency. Given the added value of our mechanism, the results are very encouraging. At the same time the results prove our implementation to be comparable or better than RMI/IIOP, as reported in [14], for both LAN and WAN. We also discovered that the impact of the law complexity over performance was relatively small in general (tens of μs) thus insignificant for end-to-end method calls.

6   Related Work

We are not aware of any published proposal to regulate the reply, and none of the conventional RPC-based middleware implementations provides for such regulation.

Predefined timeout is not available under Sun RPC, Java RMI [23], and DCOM [8]. These middlewares rely on the underlining network stream timeout (which is neither explicit nor predictable). Under CORBA [13,4], a client can specify a timeout interval, but the server is not informed of it.

A number of researchers addressed the treatment of unplanned timeout, and various protocols have been proposed for that [16] [22] [11]. These protocols, however, are hard-wired in the communication mechanisms, and they provide very little flexibility with respect to the actions that can be taken by the server or the client, and the effect of these actions.

Moreover, we are not aware of any prior attempt to incorporate timeouts in any access control mechanism or in any access control decision. In our approach, the timeout and its handling are made explicit in the access control policy, thus providing the flexibility required by both the application and by the access control policy.

7   Conclusions

This paper presented an extension of LGI which allows sophisticated and scalable regulation of synchronous communication. The following are the notable characteristics of the resulting regulation model: (a) it regulates both the request part and the reply part of a call; (b) the regulation is done both at the client and at the server side; and (c) it provides control over how the timeout is handled in a manner that can take into account the concerns of both the client and the server. The proposed model for access control has been implemented for Java RMI, giving rise to a mechanism called Regulated RMI (RRMI).

The full power of the proposed mechanism resides in its ability to handle stateful and communal policies. However, we believe that this mechanism is useful for access control even under less sophisticated requirements. RRMI can also be used for the customization of synchronous protocols even when the access control is not necessary.

References

1. J. R. Anderson. A security policy model for clinical information systems. In *Proceedings of the IEEE Symposium on Security and Privacy*, May 1996.
2. X. Ao, N. Minsky, and V. Ungureanu. Formal treatment of certificate revocation under communal access control. In *Proc. of the 2001 IEEE Symposium on Security and Privacy, May 2001, Oakland California*, May 2001. (available from http://www.cs.rutgers.edu/~minsky/pubs.html).
3. X. Ao and N. H. Minsky. Flexible regulation of distributed coalitions. In *LNCS 2808: the Proc. of the European Symposium on Research in Computer Security (ESORICS) 2003*, October 2003. (available from http://www.cs.rutgers.edu/~minsky/pubs.html).
4. K. Beznosov and Y. Deng. A Framework for Implementing Role-Based Access Control Using CORBA Security Service. In *ACM Workshop on Role-Based Access Control*, pages 19–30, 1999.
5. A. Birrell and J. B. Nelson. Implementing Remote Procedure Calls. *ACMTOCS*, 2(1):39–59, February 1984.
6. M. Blaze, J. Feigenbaum, J. Ioannidis, and A. Keromytis. The keynote trust-management systems, version 2. ietf rfc 2704. Sep 1999.
7. D.D. Clark and D.R. Wilson. A comparison of commercial and military computer security policies. In *Proceedings of the IEEE Symposium in Security and Privacy*, pages 184–194. IEEE Computer Society, 1987.
8. Microsoft Corporation. COM: Component Object Model Technologies. http://www.microsoft.com/com/default.mspx.
9. D. Ferraiolo, J. Barkley, and R. Kuhn. A role based access control model and reference implementation within a corporate intranets. *ACM Transactions on Information and System Security*, 2(1), February 1999.
10. S. Foley. The specification and implementation of 'commercial' security requirements including dynamic segregation of duties. In *Proceedings of the 4th ACM Conference on Computer and Communications Security*, April 1997.
11. I. Foster, C. Kesselman, and S. Tuecke. The Nexus task-parallel runtime system. In *Proc. 1st Intl Workshop on Parallel Processing*, pages 457–462. Tata McGraw Hill, 1994.
12. S. Godic and T. Moses. Oasis eXtensible Access Control Markup Language (XACML), vesion 2. March 2005. http://www.oasis-open.org/committees/xacml/index.shtml.
13. Object Management Group. OMG Security. http://www.omg.org/technology/documents/formal/omg_security.htm.
14. M.B. Juric, I. Rozman, M. Hericko, and T. Domajnko. CORBA, RMI and RMI-IIOP Performance Analysis and Optimization. In *SCI 2000, Orlando, Florida, USA*, July 2000.
15. G. Karjoth. The Authorization Service of Tivoli Policy Director. In *Proc. of the 17th Annual Computer Security Applications Conference (ACSAC 2001)*, December 2001.
16. M.C. Little and S.K. Shrivastava. An Examination of the Transition of the Arjuna Distributed Transaction Processing Software from Research to Products. In *Proceedings of the 2nd USENIX Workshop on Industrial Experiences with Systems Software (WIESS '02), Boston, MA, USA, 8 December 2002 (Co-located with OSDI '02) USENIX Association 2002*, 2002.

17. N. H. Minsky. Law Governed Interaction (LGI): A Distributed Coordination and Control Mechanism (An Introduction, and a Reference Manual). Technical report, Rutgers University, June 2005. (available at http://www.moses.rutgers.edu/documentation/manual.pdf).

18. N.H. Minsky and V. Ungureanu. Law-governed interaction: a coordination and control mechanism for heterogeneous distributed systems. *TOSEM, ACM Transactions on Software Engineering and Methodology*, 9(3):273–305, July 2000. (available from http://www.cs.rutgers.edu/~minsky/pubs.html).

19. R. Rivest. The MD5 message digest algorithm. Technical report, MIT, April 1992. RFC 1320.

20. T. Ryutov and C. Neuman. Representation and evaluation of security policies for distributed system services. In *In Proceedings of the DARPA Information Survivability Conference and Exposition, South Carolina*, pages 172–183, January 2000.

21. R. Sandhu, V. Bhamidipati, and M. Munawer. The ARBAC97 model for role-based administartion of roles. *ACM Transactions on Information and System Security*, 2(1):105–135, February 1999.

22. M. Sato, M. Hirano, Y. Tanaka, and S. Sekiguchi. OmniRPC: A Grid RPC facility for cluster and global computing in OpenMP. *Lecture Notes in Computer Science*, 2104:130–??, 2001.

23. Inc Sun Microsystems. RMI Wire Protocol. http://java.sun.com/j2se/1.4.2/docs/guide/rmi/spec/rmi-protocol.html.

24. Ninja Team. The Ninja Project Enabling Internet-scale Services from Arbitrarily Small Devices. http://ninja.cs.berkeley.edu/.

FMware: Middleware for Efficient Filtering and Matching of XML Messages with Local Data⋆

K. Selçuk Candan, Mehmet E. Dönderler, Yan Qi,
Jaikannan Ramamoorthy, and Jong W. Kim

Computer Science and Engineering Department
Arizona State University, Tempe, AZ 85287-8809
{candan, mdonder, yan.qi, jaikannan, jong}@asu.edu

Abstract. XML message filtering systems are used for sifting through real-time messages to support business data mining and reporting. An XML message filtering system needs to (a) process registered filter predicates on multiple distributed real-time streams and (b) match and validate the filter results with local data to identify the relevant data that can be used for higher-level processing. Although efficient real-time filtering schemes exists, the *matching* phase of the operation where filter results have to be matched against local data to select those matches that are relevant to the particular task remains to be expensive as it requires expensive join operations. In this paper, we present an efficient middleware (*FMware*) for filtering and matching XML messages against locally available data. The proposed operator relies on a novel cluster-domain matching scheme to reduce the cost of the process. We analytically study the cost of the proposed middleware and experimentally show that it adaptively reduces the number of local data accesses and provides large savings in matching time with respect to cluster-unaware matching.

Keywords: XML messaging, matching with local data, cluster-domain hashing.

1 Introduction

XML message brokers provide filtering, tracking, and routing services to enable processing and delivery of the message traffic within an enterprise. These tools (e.g. JMS [1] and IBM's MQSeries [2,3]) listen to (possibly multiple) XML data streams within an enterprise (or across enterprises) and identify message data fitting the registered user profiles or filter queries. These messages are then passed to appropriate business intelligence modules for further processing. Thus, efficient middleware support for filtering and publish/subscribe services is critical for effective use of system resources, reducing the messaging delays, and simplifying the design of enterprise business intelligence systems.

In this paper, we first note that such *basic XML document processing tasks can be off-loaded* to a middleware. In fact, there is an increasing number of XML

⋆ This research is funded by NSF grants ITR-0326544 and IIS-0308268.

M. van Steen and M. Henning (Eds.): Middleware 2006, LNCS 4290, pp. 301–321, 2006.
ⓒ IFIP International Federation for Information Processing 2006

message process off-loading technologies. Yet, most of these technologies provide either low-level XML parsing acceleration support [4], (usually proxy-based) publish/subscribe solutions (e.g. SemCast [5], CoDD [6], NiagaraCQ [7]), message validation through XML-gateways and XML-firewalls (e.g. DataPower [8] and Sarvega [9]), or purely network-level intelligent message routing solutions [10,11] which do not go beyond interpreting the request and reply message headers.

Existing work in publish/subscribe middleware focuses on the problem of routing of data and the filter queries in a way to ensure that right filter results reach the correct users in the shortest amount of time with minimal resources. For instance, CoDD [6] uses subscription queries to create a hierarchical tree structure which disseminates subsets of a data stream to consumers through loosely-coupled peer nodes. On the other hand, in an enterprise business intelligence context, it is not common that there are thousand of widely distributed subscribers for filter results. Therefore, routing and dissemination are less critical in this domain then efficiency in filtering and matching: since large volumes of data arrives continuously, it is essential that the filtering rate matches the data arrival rate to prevent the loss of valuable information. Therefore, the collection of query patterns need to be indexed in-memory to enable real-time filtering of the data. The state of the art in XML filtering schemes include YFilter [12], AFilter [13], TurboXPath [14], and XSQ [15]. Although, thanks to these in-memory based filtering techniques (relying on state machines, push down automata, or transducers), the filtering step itself can generally be performed in real-time (on the order of 100K filter statements), a major remaining challenge in business context is the *impedance mismatch* between the *in-memory filtering schemes* and the *locally relevant data in secondary storage*.

1.1 Challenge: Impedance Mismatch Between In-Memory Filtering Schemes and Locally Relevant Data in Secondary Storage

Consider an enterprise with multiple sales offices and multiple suppliers. Let us assume that the **product shipment office** of this enterprise needs to identify for each sale, (a) the productid of the sold item, (b) number of units sold, and the (c) appropriate warehouse for product shipment. Let us also assume that this enterprise is relying on XML messaging for communicating between the various offices and branches. Without getting into the details of the corresponding schema, let us further assume that the XML message filtering system can listen to the sales messages (with a registered filter statement of the form "$//productid//unit\_of\_sales$") to extract $\langle productid, unit\_of\_sales \rangle$ information for shipment. However, let us further consider the case where the sales messages arriving from the local sales offices **do not** contain the *warehouseid* information for the products. This is expected in this case, as *warehouseid* is relevant only to the **product shipment office** and "$//productid//warehouseid$" will only be available locally (possibly at a secondary storage).

Therefore, although in-memory message filtering (such as YFilter [12]) can be used for extracting "$productid//unit\_of\_sales$" from incoming sales messages, an efficient middleware is needed for matching these against locally stored data to identify $\langle productid, unit\_of\_sales, warehouseid \rangle$ matches (Figure 1).

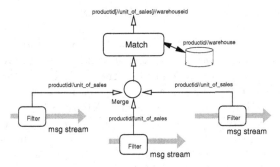

Fig. 1. Filtering and matching XML messages against locally available data

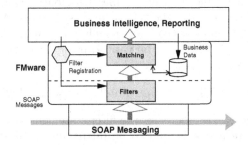

Fig. 2. FMware middleware for filtering and matching messages against local data

1.2   Contributions of This Paper

With the goal of supporting time critical filtering, tracking, and routing services for enterprises, in this paper we present a novel *FMware* middleware for efficient XML message stream filtering and matching against locally stored data (Figure 2 and Section 2). In particular, we focus on the post-processing phase required for validation of the message filter results against XML data in secondary storage and we develop an index-driven $\mathcal{C}$Match (clustered-matching) operator for efficient implementation of the *FMware* middleware.

To reduce the cost of message filtering, in-memory schemes (such as YFilter and AFilter) rely on structural similarities of the filter statements. When the matching phase requires access to data in the secondary storage, however, exploiting structural similarities is not straight-forward. Existing index-structures (such as [16]), that are used in XML DBMS context, rely on *prefix* clustering through an ancestor-descendant interval labeling (Section 3). $\mathcal{C}$Match operator, on the other hand, relies on a multi-interval scheme to exploit other structural clustering opportunities to adaptively reduce accesses to the secondary storage (Sections 3 and 3.7). In Section 4, we experimentally show that cluster domain processing not only reduces the matching cost, but knowledge about *clustering power* of the data can be exploited by FMware to choose the appropriate available index for matching.

2   Overview of the FMware Middleware

Traditional XML filtering systems are concerned with finding instances of a given set of patterns in a continuous stream of data trees (or XML messages). More specifically, if $\{x_1, x_2, ...\}$ denotes a stream of XML messages, where x_i is i^{th} XML message in the stream, and $\{q_1, ..., q_m\}$ is a set of filter predicates (described in an XML query language, such as XPath [17] or XQuery [18]) then an XML filtering system identifies (in real-time) $\langle x_i, q_j, PT_{ij} \rangle$ triplets, such that the message x_i satisfies the filter query q_j. The set PT_{ij} includes each instance of the query (referred to as path-tuples in [12]) in the message.

In order to enable (a) *filtering* of XML messages against registered queries and (b) *matching* filter results against locally stored data, *FMware* middleware needs to interface available filtering engines with data available in secondary storage. For example, consider the XPath filter statement $A[//B]//C$. Let us assume that the XML messages contain enough information to match the $A//B$ pattern, however the $A//C$ should be verified using local data. Thus, the filter statement can be split into two parts:

$$filterStmt = A[//B] \ and \ matchStmt = resMsg.A//C,$$

where $resMsg$ denotes the results for the filter statement $filterStmt$. Thus, the stream of filtering results will need to be further matched against the locally stored data for evaluating the $resMsg.A//C$ relationship.

Definition 1 (Filtering and Matching with Local Data). *Let*

- *the filter&match statement can be split into two sub-filter statements: filterStmt for filtering on XML message stream and matchStmt for local data,*
- *resMsg denotes the stream of message filtering results, where each result, $rmsg_i$, is a tuple (as in [12]) of nodes satisfying conditions specified in filterStmt,*

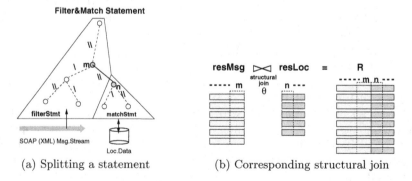

(a) Splitting a statement   (b) Corresponding structural join

Fig. 3. (a) A sample, tree-structured, filter statement which requires filter results from incoming messages matched against local data and (b) the corresponding structural join operation that needs to be performed efficiently

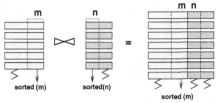

Fig. 4. Sort-merge-join based approaches assume that the inputs are structurally sorted in the joining nodes (m and n); naturally, the output can be sorted on only one of m or n (sorted on m in this example)

- $resLoc$ denotes the set of tuples, where each result, $rloc_j \in resLoc$, satisfies conditions specified in $matchStmt$, and
- Θ is a structural condition between node $node_m$ in $rmsg$ tuples and $node_n$ in $rloc$ tuples.

The filtered and matched result, R, consists of a stream of pairs, $\langle rmsg_i, rloc_j \rangle$, where $node_{i,m} \in rmsg_i$ and $node_{j,n} \in rloc_j$ satisfy the condition Θ (Figure 3).

Broadly speaking, there are two different ways to perform the *filtering and matching with local data* task:

- **Alternative I (Periodic matches):** (a) $filterStmt$ is evaluated on the XML message stream to identify a batch $resMsg\_Batch$ of matches. (b) $matchStmt$ is evaluated on the local data to identify local candidates $resLoc\_Batch$. (c) $resMsg\_Batch$ and $resLoc\_Batch$ is joined.
- **Alternative II (Streaming matches):** Each filter result $rmsg_i$ is matched against the local data using an *efficient* index structure to locate the local matches.

The disadvantages of the first alternative is that (a) it is blocking and (b) it requires explicit materialization of all candidate matches in advance. The second alternative requires neither blocking nor explicit materialization; however, it is essential that the matching is performed efficiently.

2.1 Alternatives for Streaming Matching Implementations

Structural relationships within XML data constitute significant information that has to be used in querying, indexing, and retrieval. Various structural join algorithms are devised for speeding up the processing of queries which involve ancestor/descendant type of structural relationships.

Structural join algorithms can be classified into two: holistic and binary. Holistic join operators take the entire query and match it against the data as a whole. Since in a streaming environment data itself is distributed and available in pieces, such holistic approaches, which are shown to work well for static XML data, are not applicable. Many existing (binary or holistic) structural join operators, including TwigStack, PathStack [19], iTwigJoin [20], Stack-Tree-Desc/Anc [21], $\mathcal{EE}/\mathcal{EA}$-Join [22], and TSGeneric [23], are specially designed variants of the standard **sort-merge join** algorithm: they require that the ancestor and descendant

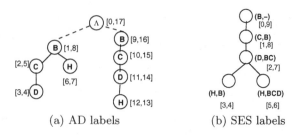

(a) AD labels   (b) SES labels

Fig. 5. (a) AD-labeling and (b) ViST-style SES-labeling of the same collection[26]

lists be available in a structurally sorted order before the join operation can be performed (Figure 4). Consequently, these sort-merge based schemes face the problems common in traditional sort-merge-joins: **(a)** they risk being blocking (for sorting the inputs) or **(b)** they constrain query plans to only those that can provide appropriately sorted inputs. Unfortunately, when the filter results for validation arrive from multiple message queues (with potentially different message structures and arrival orders) it is not possible to assume that the data for the corresponding join operation will be structurally sorted in a desirable manner. Thus, once again, they are not applicable in a filtering and matching environment.

A natural alternative to sort-merge join based schemes, more suitable for filtering with unpredictable arrival patterns, is to rely on structural index joins, where the data nodes (not necessarily structurally sorted) are checked against a pre-existing index structure which can return required ancestor or descendant nodes in the data. Index-joins can be performed on unsorted streaming input data as long as appropriate index structures are available on the local data. There are a variety of existing index structures, such as B+-trees, XR-trees [16], XB-trees [19], and R-trees [24,25] that can be used for indexing local data for efficient evaluation of structural conditions for identifying matching local data. The cost of this operation, per filtering result, $rMsg_i$ in the stream $resMsg$ is bound by the cost of the index access, which depends on the specific index structure used; but, generally, it is at least logarithmic in the local database size (depth of the index structure). When the arrival rate of the filtering results is high, on the other hand, the performance of existing index structures may not be sufficient (we experimentally evaluate this in Section 4). Therefore, for such operators to be useful in a real-time data filtering and matching middleware, they need to be implemented efficiently. In the next section, we propose a novel *clustered* matching approach addressing the needs of the *FMware* middleware.

3   Cluster Support for Efficient Indexed Matching

To implement structural matching (or join) operations efficiently, most index structures, such as B+-trees, XR-trees [16], XB-trees [19], and R-trees [24,25], assume an ancestor/descendant (AD) labeling scheme [22,27] which assigns intervals to nodes such that descendant nodes have intervals that are contained within the intervals of the ancestor nodes. The AD interval of an XML node n_i *clusters* all descendants of n_i based on their common prefixes up to n_i (Figure 5(a)). Therefore, the ancestor/descendant relationship can be checked using *containment* or *enclosure* ($=$ containment^{-1}) predicate on intervals. This renders interval-based AD labeling very common in implementation of structural joins.

3.1 Clustering Power and Precision

Since there is a one-to-one correspondence between the data nodes and the intervals, given an XML document, the number of interval labels assigned to it by an AD-based schemes is the same as the number of nodes in the data (Figure 5(a)). In contrast, in order to reduce the number of intervals that need to be considered, structure-encoded-sequence (SES) [28,29,26] based approaches try to further *cluster* structurally related nodes. They achieve this by using labeling schemes (such as Prufer sequences [29]) that can capture more than the ancestor/descendant relationships[1]. For example, Figure 5(b) shows ViST style [26] SES-labeling: each node $node_i$ is assigned a sequence seq_j and an SES interval $node_i.ses = (s_j, e_j)$. Once again, resulting intervals are either disjoint or contained within each other. However, as shown in Figure 5(b), some nodes with the same label are clustered under the same SES-label. For instance, the SES label [2, 7] in Figure 5(b) clusters two nodes in the original data (Figure 5(a)), both with tag D. Note that these two nodes tagged[2] D are also on similar paths on both trees. In other words, each structure-encoded interval *clusters* multiple data nodes. Based on this example, we can state that SES labels have higher cluster power than the AD labels.

Definition 2. Clustering Power of an SES-label ($cps(ses, l, d)$)**.** *The clustering power, $cps(ses, l, d)$, of an SES-label, ses, in a given data source, d, for the labeling scheme l is the number of nodes with this SES label.*   ◇

Since clustering applies to nodes with the same tags, given a data collection and a labeling scheme, we can also define the clustering power of a given tag:

Definition 3. Clustering Power of a Tag ($cpt(\tau, l, d)$)**.** *The clustering power, $cpt(\tau, l, d)$, of tag τ in a given data source, d, for the labeling scheme l is the average clustering power of the all SES labels corresponding to those nodes with tag τ.*   ◇

Clearly using SES-labels of the nodes, as opposed to their AD-labels during matching can reduce the number of index checks that have to be performed.

---

[1] There are a number of SES-labeling schemes. For instance, PRIX [29] uses Prüfer sequences, while [28] and other covering index based schemes consider path sequences. Details of SES-labeling processes have been omitted. Please refer to [28,29,26] for more details on SES-labeling schemes.

[2] A *tag* is the element name, attribute name, or the value associated with the XML node.

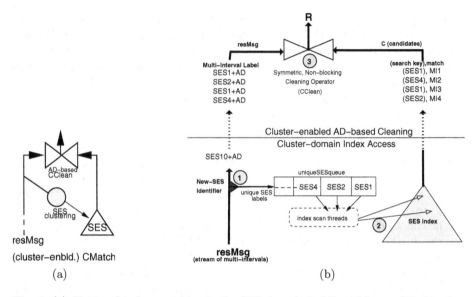

Fig. 6. (a) Clustered index matching in the SES domain is followed by an AD-domain cleaning phase: the faulty candidate nodes produced by the SES-based index scan are eliminated using AD-labels and (b) implementation of CMatch: nodes in $resMsg$ are first matched against indexed nodes using an SES-index, then candidates are cleaned using AD-labels; explained in Section 3

Furthermore, knowledge about the clustering powers of SES-labels and individual tags can enable the optimizer to decide whether a cluster-enabled scheme is likely to be effective (by reducing the number of inputs to consider) for a given matching condition. Thus we can benefit from the inherent clustering power of the SES-labels to reduce the number of times the existing index is accessed. However, this reduction in the number of index accesses do not come for free.

Unfortunately, SES-labels are not as precise as AD-labels in capturing structural relationships. In particular, unlike AD-labels, where $ancestor(node_i, node_j) \leftrightarrow contains(node_i.ad, node_j.ad)$, SES-labels satisfy only one direction of the implication: $ancestor(node_i, node_j) \rightarrow contains(node_i.ses, node_j.ses)$. Thus, a query of the form *"find all nodes with SES-labels contained within the SES label of a given node,"* might return more nodes than the descendants of the given node. Thus, although SES-labels can be used for clustering to reduce the number of disk accesses, to eliminate false retrievals that may result from the use of clustering, the filter-and-match operation would need a *cleaning phase*, based on the (unclustered) AD-labels (Figure 6(a)).

3.2   CMatch Operator for Multi-labeled Matching and Cleaning

To enable both *efficient* and *correct* operation, $FMware$ middleware relies on a **multi-labeling** scheme which uses SES-labels for clustering and AD-labels to prevent false retrievals. A *Multi-Interval* (MI) label combines the AD and SES interval labels. Formally, the MI-label of $node_i$ with AD-label $node_i.ad$ and SES-label $node_i.ses$ is $node_i.mi = \langle node_i.ad, node_i.ses \rangle$. FMware assigns MI-labels to each data node in the (global) XML data through exchange of structural information between distributed FMware entities.

Figure 6 provides an overview of the CMatch operator with which the $FMware$ middleware implements clustered index matching in the SES domain followed by an AD-domain cleaning phase: the faulty candidate nodes produced by the SES-based index scan are eliminated: *to reduce the number of accesses to the index, inputs are clustered based on their SES labels and the index is accessed only* **once** *for each SES label.* Since SES-based index access is not enough by itself to ensure correctness of the results, a symmetric, non-blocking CClean operator is used for cleaning the results from false hits.

Figure 6 shows the detailed implementation of the CMatch operator. The two complementary halves (cluster-domain index access and cluster-enabled cleaning) of the CMatch operator are described next.

3.3   Cluster-Domain Index Access (Steps 1,2)

As shown in **Step 1** of Figure 6(b), the CMatch operator first identifies unique SES-labels observed in the input stream of filtering results. These unique labels are then used for accessing an index structure to fetch the matching nodes. (**Step 2** of Figure 6(b)). The details of these steps are as follows:

(**Step 1. SES-clustering of Filter Results**). The stream of inputs, $resMsg$, is passed through a $newSES$ label identifier, which identifies unique SES labels in the input nodes and pushes each **unique** SES label encountered in the stream into a queue, $uniqueSESqueue$. In our implementation, this process of unique SES identification is piggy-backed on the SES-hashing process used for cleaning, discussed later in Section 3.4.

(**Step 2. SES-clustered Access to the Local Database**). Using an existing SES index, the unique SES labels in the $uniqueSESqueue$ are compared against the matching condition Θ (more specifically Θ_{ses}) to identify candidate matches. The individual Θ_{ses} matching operations are performed by the SES index-access threads that are available in a thread pool. For each ses_{new} in the $uniqueSESqueue$, the SES index is accessed only once (i.e., the search key, ses_{key}, is equal to ses_{new}). The index returns a stream, $C(ses_{key})$, of candidates, where

$$C(ses_{key}) = \{\langle ses_{key}, rloc_j \rangle | \ (\Theta_{ses}(ses_{key}, node_{j,n}.ses) = true) \ \wedge \ (node_{j,n} \in rloc_j)\}.$$

Given a search key, ses_{key}, each candidate in this stream is a multi-interval label of the matching nodes. Each candidate is also marked with the search key, ses_{key}; this is used in the second phase of the algorithm for the AD-based cleaning operation which will clean false hits.

Note that multiple SES-index scan threads pipe their results into a single stream, C. Therefore, this stream contains results for different SES labels (potentially interleaved due to simultaneously outputting index scan threads).

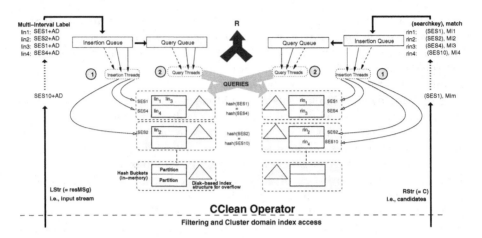

Fig. 7. Symmetric, non-blocking cleaning operator (𝒞Clean), explained in Section 3.4

3.4 AD-Based Cleaning (Step3)

The AD-based cleaning operator (**Step 3** of Figure 6(b)) matches the candidates (C) returned by SES index lookup with the original results in the message filter stream ($resMsg$) based on their SES labels used for index accesses and performs AD-based cleaning on Θ (more specifically Θ_{ad}) to remove faulty candidates. Thus, the result in the output stream, R, consists of pairs, $\langle rmsg_i, rloc_j \rangle$, where $node_{i,m} \in rmsg_i$ and $node_{j,n} \in rloc_j$ satisfy the condition Θ_{ad}:

$$R = \{\langle rmsg_i, rloc_j \rangle \mid (rmsg_i \in resMsg) \wedge (\langle ses_{key}, rloc_j \rangle \in C) \wedge$$
$$(n_{i,m}.ses = ses_{key}) \wedge \qquad \text{/*match for SES-clustering*/}$$
$$(\Theta_{ad}(node_{i,m}.ad, node_{j,n}.ad) = true)\} \quad \text{/*AD-based cleaning*/}$$

Therefore, simultaneously with the SES-based index access by the 𝒞Match operator, the original stream of filter results ($resMsg$) are passed to a symmetric, non-blocking operator for AD-based cleaning (**Step 3** of Figure 6(b)).

Before the AD-conditions can be checked for cleaning, however, $resMsg$ and C have to be **matched** based on the SES search key, ses_{key}, used for accessing SES clustered index. Unfortunately, neither of the streams is sorted or clustered on these SES values. In $resMsg$, results with the same SES values may be far apart from each other depending on how $resMsg$ has been computed prior to being passed to this operator. Similarly, since multiple SES-index access threads (each performing a separate index access with a different search key, ses_{key}) are writing onto the same stream C, the candidates are not likely to be clustered on the ses_{key} values to be used for cluster-based matching.

Overview of the 𝒞Clean Operator. The key for efficient cleaning, therefore, is symmetric non-blocking matching of tuples $n_{i,m} \in resMsg$ and $\langle ses_{key}, rloc_j \rangle \in C$, based on the condition, $(n_{i,m}.ses = ses_{key})$. Figure 7 shows the overview of the cluster-enabled cleaning operator, 𝒞Clean. The two left and right input streams ($LStr = resMsg$ and $RStr = C$) to the operator are streams of multi-interval labels. Each candidate element in $RStr$ is also annotated with the SES-based search key, ses_{key}, used for fetching this candidate from the index.

Since correct candidates must satisfy both $\Theta_{ad}(node_{i,m}.ad, node_{j,n}.ad) = true$) and $n_{i,m}.ses = ses_{key}$, inputs to the cleaning operator are clustered, using hash tables, based on their SES-labels: (a) for the nodes in $LStr$, the corresponding SES labels and (b) for the candidates in $RStr$, the search key (ses_{key}) used for fetching the candidate from the index are used for hashing. For those node pairs which satisfy the SES equality, the AD condition will be checked for cleaning. In a sense, SES labels are used for clustering the input nodes (and their AD labels), thereby reducing the number of nodes that need to be compared based on their AD-values.

Most importantly, to prevent the clustering phase itself from becoming a bottleneck, the CClean operator achieves both SES-based clustering and the AD-based joins *simultaneously*. To facilitate this, the operator keeps an **in-memory hash structure** for each of its input streams. Inputs are inserted into these hash structures based on their SES-labels:

- Each hash bucket contains inputs that have the same $hash(ses)$ value. Note that since multiple SES labels may have the same hash value, a bucket may contain input nodes with different SES labels.
- Partitions in buckets cluster nodes with the same SES.
- To achieve the non-blocking behavior, each stream queries the other one without waiting for all the data with the same SES label being available.

To prevent duplicate results, timestamps are associated with the inputs being inserted into hash tables.

Since the in-memory space allocated to each CMatch operator is limited, in addition to the in-memory hash tables, the operator also maintains **disk-based AD index structures** to manage overflow buckets. Note that these index structures are used for identifying descendants or ancestors, depending on which input stream they are indexing. Candidate index structures include XR-trees [16] and R-trees [24,25]. When a new SES label is hashed into a bucket with no empty partition, a victim partition is selected based on the *fullest least-recently-used* principle: the *fullest* partition that has not been used for the *largest* duration of time is selected to be the victim to be pushed onto the disk. In addition, if a partition becomes full and there is a new AD label to be inserted to that partition, it is pushed to disk (the *physical* partitions have a fixed size).

We are now ready to describe the functioning of the cluster-enabled hash-based cleaning operator, CClean, depicted in Figure 7 in detail.

CClean Algorithm. Figure 7 demonstrates the implementation and the operation of the symmetric, non-blocking CClean operator. The operator is non-blocking in that input streams are queued and processed as they are received. It is also symmetric in that the operator consumes and processes both its input streams, $LStr$ and $RStr$, simultaneously. The inputs to the operator are two streams, $LStr$ and $RStr$, of multi-interval labeled nodes ($LStr = resMsg$ and $RStr = C$).

(**Step 1.**) Data from both input streams are queued for insertion into the corresponding hash tables based on the corresponding SES labels as described above. A time-stamp that specifies the insertion time, called *insertion time-stamp*, is associated with each element in the hash table. These insertion time-stamps are used to prevent duplicate results. The insertion process is carried out by threads that are available in the corresponding insertion-thread pools.

(Case 1): If there is already a partition in the corresponding hash table with the SES label and the partition is not full, then the input is time-stamped and inserted into the partition. If the partition is already full, the partition is pushed to the disk, along with the new (time-stamped) input. The preempted partition is made available as a free partition.

(Case 2): If there is no partition in the corresponding hash bucket with the SES label of the input, then an empty partition is allocated. If there is also no empty partition, then a victim partition is pushed to the disk (into the disk-based index structures) and the partition is allocated for this SES. The input is time-stamped and inserted into the partition.

(**Step 2.**) Hashed or indexed inputs on both sides are pushed into the respective query queues to initiate AD-join queries on the other stream. These queries are executed by the query threads that are available in the query-thread pools. Each query thread initiates a query on the other stream:

1. If the corresponding SES partition is found on the in memory hash table of the other stream, the thread first performs an in-memory AD-join based on the AD condition, Θ_{ad}.
2. The thread, then, consults an SES bitmap which specifies whether the corresponding SES partition is in the disk or not:
   (a) if the SES partition is found on the disk, the appropriate AD range query is performed on the *index structure* corresponding to the given SES label.
   (b) if the partition is not on the disk either, the AD-join is not performed as there are no matches.

In order to prevent duplicate results, only those pairs of inputs, *lin* and *rin*, whose insertion time-stamps satisfy the following condition are included in the output stream:

1. if the input, for which the query is initiated, is from the *LStr* stream, then $ts_{lin} > ts_{rin}$, where *ts* denotes the insertion time-stamp.
2. if the input, for which the query is initiated, is from the *RStr* stream, then $ts_{rin} \geq ts_{lin}$.

For each pair of matching *lin* and *rin*, the concatenated multi-interval list $\langle lin, rin \rangle$ is inserted into the output.   ◇

Dynamic Hash Bucket Allocation. In $\mathcal{C}$Clean, nodes are hashed into the buckets based on SES-labels. All nodes having the same SES label are mapped into the same partition of the same bucket. If the variation in the clustering power of individual SES-labels in the data is extremely high (Section 3.1), it is possible that some buckets will be extremely full whereas others are relatively empty. Thus, instead of allocating fixed size buckets, $\mathcal{C}$Clean allocates memory to the hash buckets dynamically and goes to the disk **only** after all memory allocated for the cleaning task has been consumed. In our implementation, we are allocating memory dynamically to each bucket on per-need basis. Note that random hashing of the SES-labels ensures that the utilization of the in-memory pages is not low due to SES-labels with very low clustering powers.

Complexity of the $\mathcal{C}$Clean Operator. If during $\mathcal{C}$Clean, data is found in the in-memory hash tables, the cost of search is negligible. Otherwise, a search has to be done in the corresponding overflow structure. In the following discussion of the complexity of the $\mathcal{C}$Clean operator, for simplicity, we will consider the *worst case* where all insertions and searches go to disk.

Let $\mathcal{I} = |resMsg|$ be the number of input elements, $Suniq$ be the set of unique SES labels in $resMsg$, and $\mathcal{C} = |C|$ be the number of candidates returned by index accesses. Let also $r \in resMsg$ and $c \in C$ be two input nodes. Ignoring in-memory hash tables, nodes r and c will both require disk access and initiate searches in the opposite structure.

Insertion cost: The insertion cost of input $r \in resMsg$ is determined by the number of nodes in $resMsg$, with the SES label $s_r = r.ses$, that are already received and indexed. In particular, if we denote the number of nodes in $resMsg$ with SES label s_r, $\mathcal{I}(s_r)$, the worst case insertion cost of r is $O(log(\mathcal{I}(s_r)))$. Thus, the total insertion cost for elements in $resMsg$ can be computed as

$$\mathbf{O}\left(\sum_{\mathbf{s \in Suniq}} \mathcal{I}(\mathbf{s}) \times \mathbf{log}(\mathcal{I}(\mathbf{s}))\right).$$

The insertion cost of the candidate $c \in C$ with the corresponding SES search key k_c is, on the other hand, determined by the number of candidate nodes with the same SES key, k_c, already received in C. If the number of nodes in C with SES-based search key k_c is $\mathcal{C}(k_c)$, then the worst case insertion cost of c is $O(log(\mathcal{C}(k_c)))$. Since search keys are unique SES labels in $resMsg$, the total insertion cost for elements in C can be computed as $O\left(\sum_{s \in Suniq} \mathcal{C}(s) \times log(\mathcal{C}(s))\right)$. Thus, in the worst case, the insertion costs

$$\mathbf{O}\left(\sum_{\mathbf{s \in Suniq}} \mathcal{I}(\mathbf{s}) \times \mathbf{log}(\mathcal{I}(\mathbf{s})) + \mathcal{C}(\mathbf{s}) \times \mathbf{log}(\mathcal{C}(\mathbf{s}))\right).$$

Search cost: Ignoring the in-memory hash tables, the overall worst case search cost (in terms of disk accesses) is

$$\mathbf{O}\left(\sum_{\mathbf{s \in Suniq}} \mathcal{I}(\mathbf{s}) \times \mathbf{log}(\mathcal{C}(\mathbf{s})) + \mathcal{C}(\mathbf{s}) \times \mathbf{log}(\mathcal{I}(\mathbf{s}))\right).$$

Total cost: Based on these, we can compute the total $\mathcal{C}$Clean cost as

$$\mathbf{O}\left(2 \times \sum_{\mathbf{s \in Suniq}} (\mathcal{I}(\mathbf{s}) + \mathcal{C}(\mathbf{s})) \times \mathbf{max}\{\mathbf{log}(\mathcal{C}(\mathbf{s})), \mathbf{log}(\mathcal{I}(\mathbf{s}))\}\right).$$

If an SES label in $resMsg$ clusters a large number of nodes or returns a large number of candidates, this label is likely to impose high cleaning cost.

Nevertheless, index structures that maintain these intermediary nodes are likely to be smaller (and more efficient) than a large AD-index.

3.5   Complexity of the $\mathcal{C}$Match Operator

Since the clustering effect of the SES-labels reduces the number of requests that are sent to the SES index structure, higher clustering rates of SES-labels in the input stream would help the performance of the $\mathcal{C}$Match.

Cluster-domain index scan cost: Since the SES-domain index structure is accessed only once for each *unique* SES-label in the input, using the same notation as before, the access cost to the index structure could be written as

$$O\left(\sum_{s \in \mathbf{Suniq}} \mathbf{SES\_index\_access\_cost}\right).$$

AD-based cleaning cost: In Section 3.4, we computed the $\mathcal{C}$Clean operator used for AD-cleaning process as

$$O\left(2 \times \sum_{s \in \mathbf{Suniq}} (\mathcal{I}(s) + \mathcal{C}(s)) \max\{\log(\mathcal{C}(s)), \log(\mathcal{I}(s))\}\right).$$

Here, $\mathcal{I}(s) = \mathcal{I} \times rps(s, l, d)$, where rps denotes the relative clustering power of SES labels (in the data collection d and using labeling scheme l), as defined in Section 3.1. $\mathcal{C}(s) = match(\kappa, s)$ is the number of matches contained in the SES-interval s.

Total cost: We can compute the worst case overall cost (in terms of disk accesses) of the $\mathcal{C}$Match as the sum of the cluster-domain scan and AD-based cleaning costs given above. Since the two streams to $\mathcal{C}$Clean are processed in parallel, allocating independent resources to them would reduce the overall cleaning time. Similarly, since $\mathcal{C}$Clean is pipelined and non-blocking, cluster-domain index scan and AD-based cleaning phases can be performed *in parallel*. Thus, mostly, the observed execution time is only the maximum of the two phases, not their sum.

3.6 $\mathcal{C}$Match Versus AD-Only Matching

If the index scan was performed in the AD-domain rather than in the SES-domain, the total access cost to the existing AD index structure would be

$$O\left(\sum_{s \in \mathbf{Suniq}} \mathcal{I}(s) \times \mathbf{AD\_index\_access\_cost}\right).$$

Since, for AD-only match, there is no need for cleaning, this is also the total cost of the AD-only match operation. One major advantage of $\mathcal{C}$Match (versus AD-only match) is that for a given SES label, s, the index structure is accessed only once for $\mathcal{C}$Match, whereas the index is accessed $\mathcal{I}(s)$ times for AD-only matches (see equations above) Furthermore, since SES indexes are more compact than AD indexes, it is likely that searches on the existing SES index structures will be faster than searches on the AD index structures.

However, the $\mathcal{C}$Match operator has an AD-based cleaning overhead that has to be accounted for. Computation of the size of in-memory space needed to hold incoming inputs and candidates is trivial using the statistics described above. However, when the in-memory space is not large enough, $\mathcal{C}$Clean operator

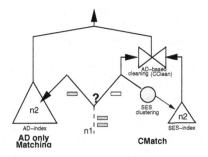

Fig. 8. Per-input choice between CMatch and AD-only index match in FMware

needs to use disk-based structures. Comparing the **worst case** CClean cost and the AD-only match cost, we see that cluster-domain scan followed by cleaning is worthwhile as long as the accesses to clustered intermediary structures are cheaper than scans on the large AD index structure.

3.7 Per-Query and Per-SES Adaptation in FMware

Given a matching statement with two query tags, based on the cost models and statistics presented above, we can estimate whether CMatch or AD-only match will cost less. One can also choose between different SES-labeling schemes based on the clustering rates they provide. We refer to this as *per-query adaptation*. Note that, it is also possible to consider each node in the input stream individually based on CMatch or AD-only match on a per-input basis (Figure 8). Furthermore, if the expected number of candidates is large, cluster-domain processing provides further opportunities. In the next section, we show that the *FMware* middleware benefits from both alternatives, based on available statistics.

4 Experimental Evaluation

In this section, we experimentally evaluate the effectiveness of cluster-domain matching, by comparing performances of CMatch and AD-only match. In particular, we show that the CMatch exploits available (per matching) task memory significantly better than an AD-only match, especially when the clustering powers of the nodes are high. We also show that the relative performances of CMatch and AD-only index join follow the cost patterns discussed earlier in the paper, thus it is possible to choose between CMatch and AD-only match, case-by-case, based on easy to collect statistics.

4.1 Setup

The operators presented here have been implemented in Java and ran on Redhat 7.2 Linux workstations, with 1.8 GHz Pentium IV processor. For the AD- and SES- index structures, we used B-tree implementation of BerkeleyDB [30]. The overflow data in CClean is indexed on disk.

Table 1. MQ1-MQ6 are the various matching queries used for comparing $\mathcal{C}$Match and AD-only match. $\mathcal{C}$Match can exploit available memory significantly better than AD-only index match, especially when the clustering powers are high.

AD:SES(Cl_Pow) InStream	AD:SES LocalDB	Matching Operator	Buffer(MB) Total	(BT+HT+OT)	#BScan	Cand	#Omiss	Exper.Tot.	Per Msg. Avg.
• No Clustering: AD-only matching is expected to perform better									
MQ1	1:1	ADMatch	1.11MB	(1.11+0+0)	1	n/a	n/a	498	498ms
	(1)	$\mathcal{C}$Match		(1+0.1+0.01)	1	5821	~22K	~87K	~87K ms = 87s
		ADMatch	2.1MB	(2.1+0+0)	1	n/a	n/a	455	**455ms**
		$\mathcal{C}$Match		(1+ 1+ 0.1)	1	5821	8	941	941ms
• Very Low Clustering Power: AD-only or $\mathcal{C}$Match									
MQ2	5821:5280	ADMatch	1.11MB	(1.11+0+0)	5821	n/a	n/a	558	0.096ms
	(1.1)	$\mathcal{C}$Match		(1+0.1+0.01)	5280	1	~22K	~86K	14.77ms
		ADMatch	2.1MB	(2.1+0+0)	5821	n/a	n/a	554	**0.095ms**
		$\mathcal{C}$Match		(1+ 1+ 0.1)	5280	1	8	490	**0.085ms**
• High Clustering Power: $\mathcal{C}$Match is expected to perform better									
MQ3	222:1	ADMatch	1.011MB	(1.011+0+0)	222	n/a	n/a	182	0.82ms
	(222)	$\mathcal{C}$Match		(1+0.01+0.001)	1	2	411	443	1.99ms
		ADMatch	1.11MB	(1.11+0+0)	222	n/a	n/a	220	0.99ms
		$\mathcal{C}$Match		(1+0.1+0.01)	1	2	8	65	**0.29ms**
MQ4	12897:1	ADMatch	2.1MB	(2.1+0+0)	12897	n/a	n/a	~ 6K	0.465ms
	(12897)	$\mathcal{C}$Match		(1+1+0.1)	1	4	~17K	~172K	13.33ms
		ADMatch	3.2MB	(3.2+0+0)	12897	n/a	n/a	~ 6K	0.465ms
		$\mathcal{C}$Match		(1+2+0.2)	1	4	8	722	**0.056ms**
• High Clustering Power: $\mathcal{C}$Match is expected to perform better									
MQ5	463:224	ADMatch	1.011MB	(1.011+0+0)	463	n/a	n/a	~30K	64.8ms
	(2.07)	$\mathcal{C}$Match		(1+0.01+0.001)	224	2	~1K	~1K	2.16ms
		ADMatch	1.11MB	(1.11+0+0)	463	n/a	n/a	~ 30K	64.8ms
		$\mathcal{C}$Match		(1+0.1+0.01)	224	2	8	115	**0.25ms**
MQ6	12897:1	ADMatch	1.11MB	(1.11+0+0)	12897	n/a	n/a	~900K	69.78ms
	(12897)	$\mathcal{C}$Match		(1+0.1+0.01)	1	5790	~82K	~506K	39.23ms
		ADMatch	2.1MB	(2.1+0+0)	12897	n/a	n/a	~900K	69.78ms
		$\mathcal{C}$Match		(1+ 1+ 0.1)	1	5790	~17K	~190K	**14.73ms**

We compared the AD-based index match and the $\mathcal{C}$Match operators under varying conditions. Both AD-only match and $\mathcal{C}$Match operator implementations are non-blocking and pipelined for fair comparison. Note that AD-only match does not need a cleaning phase. Table 1 provides a diverse set of matching conditions, selected for inclusion here as they illustrate the behavior of the $\mathcal{C}$Match under various matching characteristics. The table reports the following parameters:

- AD:SES, denotes the number of unique SES and AD labels in the inputs,
- Cl_Pow, denotes the clustering power of the SES labels in the input stream,
- Cand, is the number of candidates generated by cluster-domain index scan,
- Buffer, denotes the buffer allocated for each operator (more specifically, BT is buffers for B-tree, HT is hash table size, and OT is buffers for overflow-index trees),
- #BScan, denotes the number of accesses to existing (AD or SES) indexes,
- #Omiss is the number of misses from the overflow-index tree buffers
- Exper.Tot. is the execution time for the entire experiment
- Per Msg. Avg. is the average time (per message) required for matching. This is what we would like to have as small as possible.

In these experiments, we report results based on ViST-style SES-labels [26] and traditional Dietz style AD-labels [27]. As the local as well as streaming data, we used fragments of the DBLP XML data from [31].

Buffers are allocated (and varied) in such a way that AD-based matching and $\mathcal{C}$Match operators get to use the same amount of memory:

$$\underbrace{buf\_AD\_Btree}_{AD\ only\ index\ match} = \underbrace{\overbrace{buf\_SES\_Btree}^{1MB} + mem\_Hash\_Table + \overbrace{buf\_overflow\_index}^{0.1\times mem\_Hash\_Tables}}_{\mathcal{C}Match}$$

Since the index structures for SES-labels tend to be smaller than the index-structures for AD-labels, to evaluate the worst case behavior for the $\mathcal{C}$Match operator, we significantly constrain the available buffer (1-3MB per $\mathcal{C}$Match operator). This also reflects the situation observed in practice, where there are multiple filter-and-match operations to be processed in $FMware$ middleware and where the available buffer has to be shared among $\mathcal{C}$Match operations.

Finally, in the setup we used, the cost of each page miss was around $10ms$ and the access and processing cost for hits in the buffers was around $0.01ms$.

4.2   Experiment Results

Table 1 compares $\mathcal{C}$Match against AD-only matching for queries with different characteristics, including degrees of clustering of the involved tags and degree of expected candidates that need to be cleaned. Table 1 also presents results under constrained and non-constrained buffer availabilities for each query.

(**MQ1**). In this case, the input nodes in the filtered message stream have no clustering power. Since SES-based clustering **is not** applicable, as expected, AD-only match is relatively faster (though both alternatives are costly and realtime filtering and matching may not be applicable).

(**MQ2,MQ3,MQ4**). In these cases, the input stream of filtered nodes have some clustering power. On the other hand, for all three cases, the number of matching nodes in the local databases (and thus the candidates returned by the index accesses) are low.

In all three cases, the costs of the $\mathcal{C}$Match operator depends on whether the hash table is large enough for the required cleaning operation: If the hash table used during the cleaning phase is large enough to balance the expected number of hash misses with the savings from the access to the large B-tree index structures, then even a very low 1.1 clustering power can lead to savings. Note that in all three cases, the amount of hash-space allocated was less than the amount of buffer allocated for the AD-based index structures; in other words, when the clustering power is non-negligible $\mathcal{C}$Match uses the available memory more effectively than AD-only matching. Furthermore, the degree of saving increases predictably with the clustering power of the filtered nodes.

(**MQ5**). In this case, the clustering power of the nodes in the input stream is non-negligible ($\sim$2) and the number of relevant nodes in the local index structure is relatively high. However, the number of candidates returned by SES scan for cleaning is relatively low.

The clustering power ($\sim$2) of the input stream ensures that the number of index scans for CMatch is only half of those of AD-only match. *Thus leads to significant savings even with a relatively small hash table.*

(MQ6). In this case, the clustering power of the nodes in the input stream, the relevant number of nodes in the local database, as well as the number of matching candidates that are returned by the SES-scan are all high.

Due to its clustering power, CMatch provides significant savings, even when it has to rely on disk-resident trees in the cleaning phase. Note that since the index structures (used for efficient access to the overflow buckets) are significantly smaller than the B-trees used for AD-only matches, CMatch is able to provide better results even when the number of overflow-index access is significantly larger than the number of AD-index accesses.

Summary and Discussions: The experiment results show that

- cluster-domain processing helps the performance of *FMware by significantly reducing the total number of disk accesses to the local index structure*; and
- CMatch exploits available memory very effectively. In the experiments, increasing the buffer available for the AD index did not help reduce the cost of AD-only index match, yet when the same amount of increase is provided to the CMatch, we observed significant reductions in cost.

5   Related Work

In addition to the discussions in the Introduction, here we provide an overview of the work in adaptive query processing and index supported XML processing.

5.1   Adaptive Query Processing with Relational Data

In the relational domain, continuous query processing with unpredictable data arrival characteristics has been studied from various angles. Telegraph [32], for instance, is a dataflow engine which recognizes that cost of the operators, their selectivities, and the rates at which tuples arrive from the input vary during the processing of queries. Thus it routes data through operators adaptively, based on arrival characteristics. Aurora [33,34] focuses on QoS- and memory-aware operator scheduling and load shedding for coping with transient spikes in data.

Other works, which focus on adaptive query processing for continuous queries include [35,36,37]. Especially in the distributed relational query processing context, it has been long recognized that variations in the data arrival rates necessitate special join operator implementations. In particular, XJOIN [38] and HM-Join [39] are two non-blocking join operators suitable for deployment in systems where data with, high variable arrival rate, from remote sources have to be joined. The algorithms rely on symmetric non-blocking hash-joins.

5.2   Index- and Multi-index Support for XML Processing

Structural join schemes sometimes exploit on-the-fly-created index structures (such as B^+ trees or its augmented variations [19,40,16], R trees [24,25]) to skip unpromising ancestor (descendant) elements. DataGuides [28], IndexFabric [41], T-Index [42], BLAS [43], FB-Index [44], XJoinIndex [45], APEX [46], and other covering indices [47], on the other hand, use pre-computed indexes. A DataGuide [28] is a structural summary of the database, and provides an efficient mechanism to enumerate matching nodes when a tag path starting from the root is given as input. T-Index is also tailored to identify nodes matching a given path template, but paths are not limited to those starting from the root. IndexFabric indexes trees in a hierarchy of Patricia tries, reducing the number of disk accesses needed to find paths satisfying a path expression[41]. APEX[46] is similar to DataGuides and T-Indexes, but it only maintains frequent paths.

[20] notes that a combination of XML indexing methods can be useful for improving *stream*-based processing of structural queries, since different schemes are better for different classes of XML twig patterns. Similarly, in (XDG) [28], node labels are indexed by a term index *T-Index*, which gives the sequence of all nodes with the same label in the XDG. A second index, called *P-Index*, which is a path index, is used to determine the instances of a certain rooted tag path and also to identify the addresses of the physical data locations in an efficient way. ViST [26] also uses two index structures, namely *S-Index* (for SES-based labels) and *D-Index* (for ancestor-descendent labels). BLAS [43] uses a similar observation to develop a bi-labeling system for reducing the number of joins.

6   Conclusion

XML message filtering systems may need to match results with local data to identify those relevant for higher-level processing. We presented a *FMware* middleware for performing filtering in the presence of locally stored data which need to be matched against filter results. The *C*Match operator, underlying *FMware*, obtains its efficiency from the clustering effect of the structure-encoded labels, which significantly reduces the number of secondary storage accesses required for accessing the locally stored data. The operator also has a highly efficient, non-blocking cleaning phase to remove any spurious results that may have been created due to the imprecise clustering of structure-encoded labels. We experimentally showed that this approach provides significant savings in filter result validation time by reducing the total number of disk accesses to the local data.

References

1. JMS: Sun microsystem inc. http://java.sun.com/products/jms (2006)
2. Mohan, C., Dievendorff, D.: Recent work on distributed commit protocols, and recoverable messaging and queuing. IEEE Data Eng. Bull. **17**(1) (1994) 22–28
3. IBM-MQSeries. www.ibm.com (2005)
4. Letz, S., Zedler, M., Thierer, T., Schutz, M., Roth, J., Seiffert, R.: Xml offload and acceleration with cell broadband engine. In: XTech: Building Web 2.0. (2006)
5. Papaemmanouil, O., Çetintemel, U.: Semcast: Semantic multicast for content-based data dissemination. In: ICDE. (2005) 242–253

6. Anand, A., Chawathe, S.S.: Cooperative data dissemination in a serverless environment. In: CS-TR-4562, University of Maryland, College Park. (2004)
7. Chen, J., DeWitt, D.J., Tian, F., Wang, Y.: Niagaracq: a scalable continuous query system for internet databases. In: SIGMOD. (2000)
8. DataPower: Xs40 XML firewall. http://www.datapower.com/products/ (2006)
9. Sarvega: Xml security gateway.   http://www.sarvega.com/xml-guardian-gateway.html (2006)
10. DataPower: Xs40 XML router. http://www.datapower.com/products/ (2006)
11. Sarvega: Xml context router. http://www.sarvega.com/xml-context.html (2006)
12. Diao, Y., Franklin, M.: Query processing for high-volume xml message brokering. In: VLDB. (2003)
13. Candan, K., Hsiung, W.P., Chen, S., Tatemura, J., Agrawal, D.: Afilter: Adaptable xml filtering with prefix-caching and suffix-clustering. In: VLDB. (2006)
14. Josifovski, V., Fontoura, M., Barta, A.: Querying xml streams. The VLDB Journal **14**(2) (2005) 197–210
15. Peng, F., Chawathe, S.S.: Xsq: A streaming xpath engine. In: CS-TR-4493, University of Maryland, College Park. (2003)
16. Jiang, H., Lu, H., Wang, W., Ooi, B.C.: XR-Tree: Indexing XML data for efficient structural joins. In: ICDE. (2003)
17. Xpath. http://www.w3.org/TR/xpath (1999)
18. Xquery. http://www.w3.org/TR/xquery (2006)
19. Bruno, N., Srivastava, D., Koudas, N.: Holistic twig joins: Optimal XML pattern matching. In: SIGMOD. (2002)
20. Chen, T., Lu, J., Ling, T.: On boosting holism in xml twig pattern matching using structural indexing techniques. In: SIGMOD. (2005)
21. Al-Khalifa, S., Jagadish, H.V., Koudas, N., Patel, J.M.: Structural joins: A primitive for efficient XML query pattern matching. In: ICDE. (2002)
22. Li, Q., Moon, B.: Indexing and querying XML data for regular path expressions. In: VLDB. (2001)
23. Jiang, H., Wang, W., Lu, H.: Holistic twig joins on indexed XML documents. In: VLDB. (2003)
24. Chien, S.Y., Tsotras, V.J., Zaniolo, C., Zhang, D.: Efficient complex query support for multiversion XML documents. In: EDBT. (2002)
25. Grust, T.: Accelerating XPath location steps. In: SIGMOD. (2002)
26. Wang, H., Park, S., Fan, W., Yu, P.: ViST: A dynamic index method for querying XML data by tree structures. In: SIGMOD. (2003)
27. Zhang, C., Naughton, J.F., DeWitt, D.J., Luo, Q., Lohman, G.M.: On supporting containment queries in relational database management systems. In: SIGMOD. (2001)
28. Bremer, J., Gertz, M.: An efficient XML node identification and indexing scheme. In: VLDB. (2003)
29. Rao, P., Moon, B.: PRIX: Indexing and querying xml using Prüfer sequences. In: ICDE. (2004)
30. BerkeleyDB. http://www.sleepycat.com/ (2006)
31. UW XML Repos. http://www.cs.washington.edu/research/xmldatasets/ (2006)
32. M.A.Shah and S.Chandrasekaran: Fault-Tolerant, Load-Balancing Queries in Telegraph. SIGMOD Record **30**(2) (2001)
33. Carney, D., Cetintemel, U., Cherniack, M., Lee, C.C.S., Seidman, G., Stonebraker, M., Tatbul, N., Zdonik, S.B.: Monitoring Streams-A New Class of Data Managment Applications. In: VLDB. (2003)

34. Tatbul, N., Cetintemel, U., Zdonik, S.B., Cherniack, M., Stonebraker, M.: Load Shedding in a Data Stream Manager. In: VLDB. (2003)
35. S.Babu, *et al.*: Adaptive ordering of pipelined stream filters. In: SIGMOD. (2004)
36. Tian, F., DeWitt, D.: Tuple Routing Strategies for Distributed Eddies. In: VLDB. (2003)
37. Carey, M.J., Lu, H.: Load Balancing in a Locally Distributed DB System. SIGMOD Record **15**(2) (1986) 108–119
38. Urhan, T., Franklin, M.J.: XJoin: Getting fast answers from slow and bursty networks. Technical Report CS-TR-3994 (1999)
39. Mokbel, M., Lu, M., Aref, W.: Hash-merge join: A non-blocking join algorithm for producing fast and early join results. In: ICDE. (2004)
40. Chien, S.Y., Vagena, Z., Zhang, D., Tsotras, V., Zaniolo, C.: Efficient structural joins on indexed XML documents. In: VLDB. (2002)
41. Cooper, G.R.H.B., Franklin, M.J., Shadmon, M.: A fast index for semistructured data. In: VLDB. (2001)
42. Milo, T., Sicuo, D.: Index structures for path expressions. In: ICDT. (1999)
43. Yi Chen and Susan Davidson and Yifeng Zheng: BLAS: An Efficient XPath Processing System. In: SIGMOD. (2004)
44. Kaushik, R., Bohannon, P., Naughton, J., Korth, H.: Covering indexes for branching path queries. In: SIGMOD. (2002)
45. Bertino, E., Catania, B., Wang, W.Q.: XJoin Index: Indexing XML data for efficient handling of branching path expressions. In: ICDE. (2004)
46. Chung, J.M.C., Shim, K.: Apex: An adaptive path index for xml data. In: ACM SIGMOD. (2002)
47. Ramanan, P.: Covering indexes for xml queries: Bisimulation - simulation = negation. In: VLDB. (2003)

Synergy: Sharing-Aware Component Composition for Distributed Stream Processing Systems

Thomas Repantis[1], Xiaohui Gu[2], and Vana Kalogeraki[1,*]

[1] Dept. of Computer Science & Engineering, University of California, Riverside, CA 92521
{trep,vana}@cs.ucr.edu
[2] IBM T.J. Watson Research Center, Hawthorne, NY 10532
xiaohui@us.ibm.com

Abstract. Many emerging on-line data analysis applications require applying continuous query operations such as correlation, aggregation, and filtering to data streams in real-time. Distributed stream processing systems allow in-network stream processing to achieve better scalability and quality-of-service (QoS) provision. In this paper we present *Synergy*, a distributed stream processing middleware that provides sharing-aware component composition. Synergy enables efficient reuse of both data streams and processing components, while composing distributed stream processing applications with QoS demands. Synergy provides a set of fully distributed algorithms to discover and evaluate the reusability of available data streams and processing components when instantiating new stream applications. For QoS provision, Synergy performs QoS impact projection to examine whether the shared processing can cause QoS violations on currently running applications. We have implemented a prototype of the Synergy middleware and evaluated its performance on both PlanetLab and simulation testbeds. The experimental results show that Synergy can achieve much better resource utilization and QoS provision than previously proposed schemes, by judiciously sharing streams and processing components during application composition.

Keywords: Distributed Stream Processing, Component Composition, Shared Processing, Quality-of-Service, Resource Management.

1 Introduction

Stream processing applications have gained considerable acceptance over the past few years in a wide range of emerging domains such as monitoring of network traffic for intrusion detection, surveillance of financial trades for fraud detection, observation of customer clicks for e-commerce applications, customization of multimedia or news feeds, and analysis of sensor data in real-time [1,2]. In a typical stream processing application, stream processing *components* process continuous data streams in real-time [3] to generate outputs of interest or to identify meaningful events. Often, the data sources, as well as the components that implement the application logic are distributed across multiple sites, constituting distributed stream processing systems (DSPSs) (e.g., [4,5,6,7,8,9]). Stream sources often produce large volumes of data in high rates, while workload spikes

---

* The work of the third author is supported by NSF Award 0330481.

M. van Steen and M. Henning (Eds.): Middleware 2006, LNCS 4290, pp. 322–341, 2006.

cannot be predicted in advance. Providing low-latency, high-throughput execution for such distributed applications entails considerable strain on both communication and processing resources and thus presents significant challenges to the stream processing middleware design.

While a DSPS provides the components that are needed for an application execution, a major challenge still remains: Namely, how to select among different component instances to compose stream processing applications on-demand. While previous efforts have investigated several aspects of component composition [6,7] and placement [8] for stream applications, our research focuses on enabling *sharing-aware component composition* for efficient distributed stream processing. Sharing-aware composition allows different applications to utilize i) previously generated streams and ii) already deployed stream processing components. The distinct characteristics of distributed stream processing applications make sharing-aware component composition particularly challenging. First, stream processing applications often have minimum quality-of-service (QoS) requirements (e.g., end-to-end service delay). In a shared processing environment, the QoS of a stream processing application can be affected by multiple components that are invoked concurrently and asynchronously by many applications. Second, stream processing applications operate autonomously in a highly dynamic environment, with load spikes and unpredictable occurrences of events. Thus, the component composition must be performed quickly, during runtime, and be able to adapt to dynamic stream environments. Third, a DSPS needs to scale to a large number of streams and components, which makes centralized approaches inappropriate, since the global state of a large-scale DSPS is changing much faster than it can be communicated to a single host. Hence, a single host cannot make accurate global decisions.

Despite the aforementioned challenges, there are significant benefits to be gained from a flexible sharing-aware component composition: i) *enhanced QoS provision* (e.g., shorter service delay) since existing streams that meet the user's requirements can be furnished immediately, while the time-consuming process of new component deployment is triggered only when none of the existing components can accommodate a new request; and ii) *reduced resource load* for the system, by avoiding redundant computations and data transfers. As a result, the overall system's processing capacity is maximized to meet the scalability requirements of serving many concurrent application requests.

In this paper we present *Synergy*, a distributed stream processing middleware that provides sharing-aware component composition. Synergy is implemented on top of a wide-area overlay network and undertakes the composition of distributed stream processing applications. Synergy supports both data stream and processing component reuse while ensuring that the application QoS requirements[1] can be met. The decision of which components or streams to reuse is made dynamically at run-time taking into account the applications' QoS requirements and the current system resource availability. Specifically, this paper makes the following major contributions:

- We propose a decentralized light-weight composition algorithm that can discover streams and components at run-time and check whether any of the existing components or streams can satisfy the application's request. After the qualified candidate

---

[1] In this paper, we focus on the end-to-end execution time QoS metric, consisting of both processing delays at different components and network delays between components.

components have been identified, components and streams are selected and composed dynamically such that the application resource requirements are met and the workloads at different hosts are balanced.

- We integrate a QoS impact projection mechanism into the distributed component composition algorithm to evaluate the reusability of existing stream processing components according to the applications' QoS constraints. When a component is shared by multiple applications, the QoS of each application that uses the component may be affected due to the increased queueing delays on the processors and the communication links. Synergy's approach is to predict the impact of the additional workload on the QoS of the affected applications and ensure that a component reuse does not cause QoS violations in existing stream applications. Such a projection can facilitate the QoS provision for both current applications and the new application admitted in the system.

- We have implemented a prototype of Synergy and evaluated its performance on the PlanetLab [10] wide-area network testbed. We have also conducted extensive simulations to compare Synergy's composition algorithm to existing alternative schemes. The experimental results show that: i) Synergy consistently achieves much better QoS provision compared to other approaches, for a variety of application loads, ii) sharing-aware component composition increases the number of admitted applications, while scaling to large request loads and network sizes, iii) QoS impact projection greatly increases the percentage of admitted applications that meet their QoS requirements, iv) Synergy's decentralized composition protocol has low message overhead and offers minimal setup time, in the order of a few seconds.

The rest of the paper is organized as follows: Section 2 introduces the system model. Section 3 discusses Synergy's decentralized sharing-aware component composition approach and its QoS impact projection algorithm. Section 4 presents an extensive experimental evaluation of our system. Section 5 discusses related work. Finally, the paper concludes in Section 6.

2   System Model

In this section, we present the stream processing application model, describe the architecture of the Synergy middleware and provide an overview of its operation. Table 1 summarizes the notations we use while discussing our model.

2.1   Stream Processing Application Model

A data stream s_i consists of a sequence of continuous data tuples. A stream processing component c_i is defined as a self-contained processing element that implements an atomic stream processing operator o_i on a set of input streams $\sum is_i$ and produces a set of output streams $\sum os_i$. Stream processing components can have more than one inputs (*e.g.* a join operator) and outputs (*e.g.* a split operator). Each atomic operator can be provided by multiple component instances $c_1, \ldots, c_k$. We associate metadata with each deployed component or existing data stream in the system to facilitate the discovery

Table 1. Notations

Notation	Meaning	Notation	Meaning
c_i	Component	l_i	Virtual Link
o_i	Operator	s_i	Stream
ξ	Query Plan	λ	Application Component Graph
Q_ξ	End-to-End QoS Requirements	Q_λ	End-to-End QoS Achievements
p_{v_i}	Processor Load on Node v_i	b_{l_i}	Network Load on Virtual Link l_i
rp_{v_i}	Residual Processing Capacity on Node v_i	rb_{l_i}	Residual Network Bandwidth on Virtual Link l_i
τ_{c_i}	Processing Time for c_i	x_{c_i,v_i}	Mean Execution Time for c_i on v_i
σ_{s_i}	Transmission Time for s_i	y_{s_i,l_i}	Mean Communication Time for s_i on l_i
q_t	Requested End-to-End Execution Time	t	Projected End-to-End Execution Time
p_{o_i}	Processing Time Required for o_i	b_{s_i}	Bandwidth Required for s_i

process. Both components and streams are named based on a common ontology [11] (e.g., o_i.name = Aggregator.COUNT, s_i.name = Video.MPEGII.Birthday).

A stream processing request (query) is described by a *query plan*, denoted by ξ. The query plan is represented by a directed acyclic graph (DAG) specifying the required operators o_i and the streams s_j among them[2]. The CPU processing requirements of the operators $p_{o_i}, \forall o_i \in \xi$ and the bandwidth requirements of the streams $b_{s_j}, \forall s_j \in \xi$ are also included in ξ. The bandwidth requirements are calculated according to the user-requested stream rate, while the processing requirements are calculated according to the data rate and resource profiling results for the operators [12]. The stream processing request also specifies the end-to-end QoS requirements $Q_\xi = [q_1, ...q_m]$, such as end-to-end execution time and loss rate. Although our schemes are generic to additive QoS metrics, we focus on the end-to-end execution time metric denoted by q_t, which is computed as the sum of the processing and communication times for a data tuple to traverse the whole query plan.

The query plan can be dynamically instantiated into different *application component graphs*, denoted by λ, depending on the processing and networking availability. The vertices of an application component graph represent the components being invoked at a set of nodes to accomplish the application execution, while the edges represent virtual network links between the components, each one of which may span multiple physical network links. An edge connects two components c_i and c_j if the output of the component c_i is the input for the component c_j. The application component graph is generated by our component composition algorithm at run-time, after selecting among different component candidates that provide the required stream processing operators o_i and satisfy the end-to-end QoS requirements Q_ξ.

2.2 Synergy Architecture

Synergy is a wide-area middleware that consists of a set of distributed hosts v_i connected via virtual links l_i into an overlay mesh on top of the existing IP network. Synergy as a distributed stream processing middleware undertakes the component composition role to enable stream and component reusability while offering QoS management.

---

[2] In general, there may be multiple query plans that can satisfy a stream processing request. Query plan optimization however involves application semantics and is outside the scope of this paper. Thus, in this work we assume the query plan is given.

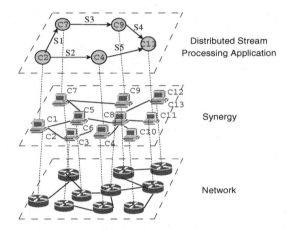

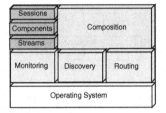

Fig. 1. Synergy system architecture   **Fig. 2.** Synergy node structure

Figure 1 shows an overview of our architecture. Synergy leverages the underlying overlay network for registering and discovering available components and streams in a decentralized manner. In our current Synergy prototype we implement a keyword-based discovery service [13] on top of the Pastry distributed hash table (DHT) [14]. However, our middleware can also be integrated with other DHTs, or unstructured overlays [15], since discovery is an independent module of our system. Synergy adopts a fully distributed architecture, where any node of the middleware can compose a distributed stream processing application. After a stream processing request is submitted and a query plan is produced, Synergy is responsible for selecting existing streams that satisfy the query and candidate components that can provide the required operators.

Each Synergy node, denoted by v_i, as illustrated in Figure 2, maintains a *metadata repository* of active stream processing sessions, streams, and components (including input and output buffers). Additionally, the architecture of a Synergy node includes the following main modules: i) a *composition module* that is responsible for running the component composition algorithm and uses: ii) a *discovery module* that is responsible for locating existing data streams and components; iii) a *routing module* that routes data streams between different Synergy nodes; and iv) a *monitoring module* that is responsible for maintaining resource utilization information for v_i and the virtual links connected to v_i. In the current implementation, the monitoring module can keep track of the CPU load and network bandwidth. The current processor load p_{v_i} and the residual processing capacity rp_{v_i} on node v_i are inferred from the CPU idle time as measured from the /proc interface. The residual available bandwidth rb_{l_j} on each virtual link l_j connected to v_i is measured using a bandwidth measuring tool (e.g., [16]). We finally use b_{l_j} to denote the amount of current bandwidth consumed on l_j.

2.3 Approach Overview

We now briefly describe the basic operations of the Synergy middleware. A stream processing application request is submitted directly to a Synergy node v_s, if the client is running the middleware, or redirected to a Synergy node v_s that is closest to the client based on a predefined proximity metric (e.g., geographical location). Alternative policies can select v_s to be the Synergy node closest to the source or the sink node(s) of the application. A query plan ξ is produced, that specifies the required operators and the order in which they need to be applied to execute the query. The processing requirements of the operators $p_{o_i}, \forall o_i \in \xi$ and the bandwidth requirements of the streams $b_{s_j}, \forall s_j \in \xi$ are also included in ξ. The request also specifies the end-to-end QoS requirements $Q_\xi = [q_1, ...q_m]$ for the composed stream processing application. These requirements (i.e., ξ, Q_ξ) are used by the Synergy middleware running on that node to initiate the distributed component composition protocol. This protocol produces the application component graph λ that identifies the particular components that shall be invoked to instantiate the new request.

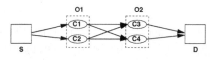

Fig. 3. Probing example

To avoid redundant computations, the system first tries to discover whether any of the requested streams have been generated by previously instantiated query plans, by querying the overlay infrastructure. To maximize the sharing benefit, the system reuses the result stream(s) generated during the latest possible stages in the query plan. Thus, the system only needs to instantiate the remaining query plan for processing the reusable existing stream(s), to generate the user requested stream(s). The system then probes those candidate nodes that can provide operators needed in the query plan, to determine: i) whether they have the available resources to accommodate the new application, ii) whether the end-to-end latency is within the required QoS, and iii) whether the impact of the new application would cause QoS violations to existing applications. Figure 3 gives a very simple example of how probes can be propagated hop-by-hop to test many different component combinations. Assuming components c_1 and c_2 offer operator o_1, while components c_3 and c_4 offer operator o_2, and assuming that the components can be located at any node in the system, probes will attempt to travel from the source S to the destination D through paths $S \to c_1 \to c_3 \to D, S \to c_1 \to c_4 \to D$, $S \to c_2 \to c_3 \to D$, and $S \to c_2 \to c_4 \to D$. A probe is dropped in the middle of the path if any of the above conditions are not satisfied in any hop. Thus, the paths that create resource overloads, result to end-to-end delays outside the requested QoS limits, or unacceptably increase the delays of the existing applications, are eliminated. From the successful candidate application component graphs, our composition algorithm selects the one that results in a more balanced load in the system and the new stream application is instantiated. The detailed operation of Synergy's sharing-aware component composition is described in the next section.

3   Design and Algorithm

In this section, we describe the design and algorithm details of our Synergy distributed stream processing middleware, that offers sharing-aware component composition. Synergy can i) reuse existing data streams to avoid redundant computations, and ii) reuse existing components if the new stream load does not lead to QoS violations of the

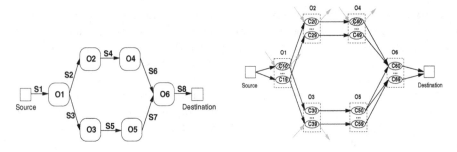

Fig. 4. Query plan example   **Fig. 5.** Synergy composition example

existing applications. We first describe the decentralized component composition pro-tocol, followed by the detailed algorithms for stream reuse and component sharing. Synergy's fully distributed and light-weight composition protocol is executed when in-stantiating a new application.

3.1 Synergy Composition Protocol

Given a stream processing request, the Synergy node first gets the locally generated query plan ξ and then instantiates the application component graph based on the user's QoS requirements Q_ξ. Figure 4 shows an example of a query plan, while Figure 5 shows a corresponding component composition example. To achieve decentralized, light-weight component selection, Synergy employs a set of probes to concurrently dis-cover and select the best composition. Synergy differs from previous work (e.g., [6,13]) in that it judiciously considers the impact of stream and component sharing on both the new and existing applications. The probes carry the original request information (i.e., ξ, Q_ξ), collect resource and QoS information from the distributed components, perform QoS impact projection, and select qualified compositions according to the user's QoS requirements. The best composition is then selected among all qualified ones, based on a load balancing metric. The composition protocol, a high level description of which is shown in Algorithm 1, consists of the following five main steps:

Step 1. Probe creation. Given a stream processing query plan ξ, the Synergy node v_s first discovers whether any existing streams can be used to satisfy the user's request. The goal is to reuse existing streams as much as possible to avoid redundant compu-tations. For example, in Figure 4, starting from the destination, v_s will first check if the result stream (stream s_8) is available. If not, it will look for the streams one hop away from the destination (streams s_6 and s_7), then two hops away from the destination (streams s_4 and s_5) and so on, until it can find any streams that can be reused. We denote this Breadth First Search on the query plan as identification of the *maximum sharable point(s)*. The nodes generating the reusable streams may not have enough available bandwidth for more streaming sessions or may have virtual links with unacceptable communication latencies. In that case all probes are dropped by those nodes and v_s checks whether there exist components that can provide the operators requested in the query plan, as if no streams had been discovered. The details about determining the maximum sharable points and about discovering sharable streams and components are

---

Algorithm 1. Synergy composition

Input: query $\langle \xi, Q_\xi, \rangle$, node v_s
Output: application component graph λ
v_s identifies *maximum sharable point(s)* in ξ
v_s spawns initial probes
for each v_i in path
    checks available resources **AND** checks QoS so far in Q_ξ **AND** checks *projected QoS impact*
    if probed composition qualifies
        performs transient resource allocation at v_i
        discovers next-hop candidate components from ξ
        spawns probes for selected components
    else
        drops the received probe
v_s selects the most load-balanced component composition λ
v_s establishes the stream processing session

---

described in Section 3.2. Next, the Synergy node v_s initiates a distributed probing process to collect resource and QoS states from those candidate components that provide the maximum sharable points. The goal of the probing process is to select qualified candidate components that can best satisfy ξ and Q_ξ and result in the most balanced load in the system. The initial probing message carries the request information (ξ and Q_ξ) and a probing ratio, that limits the probing overhead by specifying the maximum percentage of candidate components that can be probed for each required operator. The probing ratio can be statically defined, or dynamically decided by the system, based on the operator, the components' availability, the user's QoS requirements, current conditions, or historical measurement data [6]. The initial probing message is sent to the nodes hosting components offering the maximum sharable points. We do not probe the nodes that are generating streams before the maximum sharable points, since the overhead would be disproportional to the probability that they can offer a better component graph than the one starting after the maximum sharable points.

    Step 2. Probe processing. When a Synergy node v_i receives a probing message called probe P_i, it processes the probe based on its local state and on the information carried by P_i. A probe has to satisfy three conditions to qualify for further propagation: i) First, v_i calculates whether the requested processing and bandwidth requirements p_{o_i} and b_{s_j} can be satisfied by the available residual processing capacity and bandwidth rp_{v_i} and rb_{l_j}, of the node hosting the component and of the virtual link the probe came from respectively. Thus, both $rp_{v_i} \geq p_{o_i}$ and $rb_{l_j} \geq b_{s_j}$ have to hold[3]. ii) Second, v_i calculates whether the QoS values of the part of the component graph that has been probed so far already violate the required QoS values specified in Q_ξ. For the end-to-end execution time QoS metric q_t this is done as follows: The sum of the components' processing and transmission times so far has to be less than q_t. The time that was needed for the probe to travel so far gives an estimate of the transmission times, while the

---

[3] In the general case, where other node resources such as memory or disk space are to be taken into account in addition to the processing capacity, congruent equations have to hold for them as well.

processing times are estimated in advance from profiling [12]. iii) Third, v_i calculates the QoS impact on the existing stream processing sessions by admitting this new request. In particular, the expected execution delay increase due to the additional stream volume introduced by the new request is calculated. The details about the QoS impact projection are described in Section 3.3. Similarly, the impact of the existing stream processing sessions on the QoS of the new one is calculated. Both the new and the existing sessions have to remain within their QoS requirements.

If any of the above three conditions cannot be met, the probe is dropped immediately to reduce the probing overhead. Otherwise, the node performs *transient* resource allocation to avoid conflicting resource admissions (overallocations) caused by concurrent probes for different requests. The transient resource allocation is cancelled after a timeout period if the node does not receive a confirmation message to setup the stream processing application session.

Step 3. Hop-by-hop probe propagation. If the probe P_i has not been dropped, v_i propagates it further. v_i derives the next-hop operators from the query plan and acquires the locations of all available candidate components for each next-hop operator using the overlay infrastructure. Then v_i selects a number of candidate components to probe, based on the probing ratio. If more candidates than the number specified by the probing ratio are available, random ones are selected, or –if a latency monitoring service [17] is available– the ones with the smallest communication latency are selected. If no candidate components for the next operator are found, a new component has to be deployed. We choose to *collocate* this new component with the current one, deploying it in the same node, if processing resources are available, as this approach minimizes the communication delay between the two components. Other approaches for choosing an appropriate location with regards to future needs can also be employed [8,18]. Since the probe processing checks will take place for the new component as well, possible resource or QoS violations can be detected. While the resource allocation is transient, the component deployment is permanent. If the particular application session is not established through this path, the newly deployed component might serve other stream processing sessions.

After the candidate components have been selected, v_i *spawns* new probes from P_i for all selected next-hop candidates. Each new probe in addition to ξ (including p_{o_i} and b_{s_j}), Q_ξ, and the probing ratio, carries the up-to-date resource state of v_i, namely rp_{v_i} and rb_{l_j}, and of all the nodes the previous probes have visited so far. Finally, v_i sends all new probes to the nodes hosting the selected next-hop components.

Step 4. Composition selection. After reaching the destination specified in ξ, all successful probes belonging to a composition request return to the original Synergy node v_s that initiated the probing protocol. After selecting all qualified candidate components, v_s first generates complete candidate component graphs from the probed paths. Since the query plan is a DAG, v_s can derive complete component graphs by merging the probed paths. For example, in Figure 5, a probe can traverse $c_{10} \rightarrow c_{20} \rightarrow c_{40} \rightarrow c_{60}$ or $c_{10} \rightarrow c_{30} \rightarrow c_{50} \rightarrow c_{60}$. Thus, v_s merges these two paths into a complete component graph. Second, v_s calculates the requested and residual resources for the candidate component graphs based on the precise states collected by the probes. Third, v_s selects qualified compositions according to the user's operator, resource, and QoS requirements. Let V_λ be the set of nodes that is being used to instantiate λ. We use $c_i.o$ to represent the operator provided by the component c_i. The selection conditions are as follows:

$$operator\ \ constraints: c_i.o = o_i,\ \forall o_i \in \xi, \exists c_i \in \lambda \tag{1}$$

$$QoS\ \ constraints: q_r^\lambda \leq q_r^\xi, 1 \leq r \leq m \tag{2}$$

$$processing\ \ capacity\ \ constraints: rp_{v_i} \geq 0, \forall v_i \in V_\lambda \tag{3}$$

$$bandwidth\ \ constraints: rb_{l_j} \geq 0,\ \forall l_j \in \lambda \tag{4}$$

Among all the qualified compositions that satisfy the application QoS requirements, v_s selects the best one according to the following load balancing metric $\phi(\lambda)$. The qualified composition with the smallest $\phi(\lambda)$ value is the selected composition.

$$\phi(\lambda) = \sum_{v_i \in V_\lambda, o_i \in \xi} \frac{p_{o_i}}{rp_{v_i} + p_{o_i}} + \sum_{l_j \in \lambda, s_j \in \xi} \frac{b_{s_j}}{rb_{l_j} + b_{s_j}} \tag{5}$$

Step 5. Application session setup. Finally, the Synergy node v_s establishes the stream processing application session by sending confirmation messages along the selected application component graph. If no qualified composition can be found (*i.e.*, all probes were dropped, including the ones without stream reuse), the system node returns a failure message. If all probes were dropped, apparently the existing components are too overloaded to accommodate the requested application with the specified QoS requirements, or nodes in the probing path are too overloaded to host components that need to be deployed. New components can then be instantiated in strategically chosen places in the network [8,18].

The goal of the described protocol is to discover and select existing streams and components to share in order to accommodate a new application request, assuming components are already deployed on nodes. This is orthogonal to the policies that might be in place regarding new component deployment, which is outside the scope of this paper. Furthermore, Synergy is adaptable middleware, taking into account the current status of the dynamic system at the moment the application request arrives. Therefore, it does not compare to optimal solutions calculated offline that apply to static environments.

3.2 Maximum Stream Sharing

Synergy utilizes a peer-to-peer overlay of the nodes in the system for registering and discovering the available components and streams in a decentralized manner. As was mentioned in Section 2.2, the current Synergy implementation is built over Pastry [14]. We follow a simple approach to enable the storage and retrieval of the static metadata of components and streams in the DHT, which include the location (node) hosting the component or stream. As was described in Section 2.1, each component and stream is given a name, based on a common ontology [11]. This name is converted to a key, by applying a secure hash function (SHA-1) on it, whenever a component or stream needs to be registered or discovered. On the DHT this key is used to map the metadata to a specific node, with the metadata of duplicated components or streams being stored in the same node. Configuration changes caused by node arrivals and departures are handled gracefully by the DHT. Whenever components are instantiated or deleted, or streams are generated by new application sessions, or removed because they are not used by any sessions anymore, the nodes hosting them register or unregister their metadata with the DHT.

The stream processing query plan ξ specifies the operators o_i and streams s_j needed for the application execution. Using a *Maximum Sharing Discovery algorithm*, the Synergy node in which the query plan was submitted utilizes the peer-to-peer overlay for discovering existing streams and components. Since different users can submit queries that have the same or partially the same query plans, we want to reuse existing streams as much as possible to avoid redundant computations. The goal of the Maximum Sharing Discovery algorithm is to identify the *maximum sharable point(s)* in ξ. This is the operator(s) closest to the destination (in terms of hops in ξ), whose output streams currently exist in the system and can (at least partially) satisfy the user's requirements. An extreme case is that the final stream or streams already exist in the system, which can then be returned to the user directly without any further computation, as long as the residual bandwidth and communication latencies permit so. For example in Figure 4 if s_8 is already available in the system, it can be reused to satisfy the new query, incurring only extra communication but no extra processing overhead. In that case, the maximum sharable point in ξ is o_6 and Synergy will prefer to use no components if possible. If the final stream or streams are not available, the system node *backtracks* hop-by-hop the query plan to find whether preceding intermediate result streams exist. For example, in Figure 4, if result streams s_8 and s_7 are not found, but s_6 and s_5 are already available in the system, they may be reused to satisfy part of the query plan. By reusing those existing streams, the Synergy node will prefer to compose a partial component graph covering the operators after the reused streams, if the resource and QoS constraints permit so. In that case, the maximum sharable points in ξ are o_3 and o_4 and only components offering operators o_5 and o_6 will be needed. To discover existing streams and existing components that might be needed, the peer-to-peer overlay is utilized as was described.

3.3   QoS-Aware Component Sharing

To determine whether an existing candidate component can be reused to satisfy a new request, we estimate the impact of the component reuse to the latencies of the existing applications. An existing component can be reused if the additional workload brought by the new application will not violate the QoS requirements of the existing stream processing applications (and similarly the load of the already running applications will not violate the QoS requirements of the new application). To calculate the impact of admitting a new stream processing application to the QoS of the existing ones (and also the impact of the running applications to the potential execution of the one to be admitted), a Synergy node that processes a probe utilizes a *QoS Impact Projection algorithm*. This algorithm runs in all nodes with candidate components through which the probes are propagated. The QoS Impact Projection is performed for all the applications that use components on those nodes. If the projected QoS penalty will cause the new or the existing applications to violate their QoS constraints, these components are not further considered and are thus removed from the candidate set. For example, in

Figure 5, candidate components c_{10} and c_{40} are used by existing applications and with the new stream workload QoS violations are projected. Thus, c_{10} and c_{40} are not considered as candidate components for the operators o_1 and o_4 respectively. On the contrary, even though c_{20} and c_{39} are used by existing applications, they are still considered as candidate components for the operators o_2 and o_3 respectively, because no QoS violation is projected for them.

The QoS Impact Projection algorithm to estimate the effect of component reuse works as follows: For each component c_i, the node estimates its execution time. This includes the processing time τ_{c_i} of the component c_i to execute locally on the node and the queueing time in the scheduler's queue as it waits for other components to complete. The queueing time is defined as the difference between the arrival time of the component invocation and the time the component actually starts executing. We can then determine the mean execution time x_{c_i,v_i} for each component c_i on the node v_i. We assume a simple application behavior approximated by an M/M/1 queueing model for the execution time. Our experimental results show that this simplified model can provide good projection performance. If p_{v_i} represents the load on the node hosting component c_i, the mean execution time for component c_i on node v_i is given by:

$$x_{c_i,v_i} = \frac{\tau_{c_i}}{1 - p_{v_i}} \qquad (6)$$

The mean communication time y_{s_i,l_i} on the virtual link l_i for the stream s_i transmitted from component c_i to its downstream component c_j is estimated similarly: It includes the transmission time σ_{s_i} for the stream s_i, and also the queueing delay on the virtual link. If b_{l_i} represents the load (consumed bandwidth) on virtual link l_i connecting component c_i, the mean communication time y_{s_i,l_i} to transmit stream s_i through the virtual link l_i is then given by:

$$y_{s_i,l_i} = \frac{\sigma_{s_i}}{1 - b_{l_i}} \qquad (7)$$

Given the processing times τ_{c_i} and the transmission times σ_{s_i} required respectively for the execution of the components c_i and the data transfer of the streams s_i of an application, as well as the current respective loads p_{v_i} and b_{l_i}, a Synergy node can compute the projected end-to-end execution time for the entire application as:

$$\hat{t} = max_{path} \sum_{v_i \in V_\lambda, l_i \in \lambda} \left(\frac{\tau_{c_i}}{1 - p_{v_i}} + \frac{\sigma_{s_i}}{1 - b_{l_i}} \right) \qquad (8)$$

where the max_{path} is used in the cases where the application is represented by a graph with more than one paths, in which case the projected execution time of the entire application is the maximum path latency. The processing τ_{c_i} and transmission σ_{s_i} times are however easily extracted from the p_{o_i} and b_{s_i} values which are included for the corresponding operators o_i and streams s_i in the query plan ξ and have been calculated by combining the user requests with profiling [12]. The current loads p_{v_i} and b_{l_i} are known locally at the individual nodes. These values are used to estimate the local impact δ of the component reuse on the existing applications as follows:

Let $\frac{\tau_{c_i}}{1-p_{v_i}}$ denote the mean execution time required for invoking component c_i on the node v_i by the application. After sharing the component with the new application, the projected execution time would become: $\frac{\tau_{c_i}}{1-(p_{v_i}+\tau_{c_i})}$, where $(p_{v_i} + \tau_{c_i})$ represents the new processing load on the node after reusing the component. We can then compute the impact δ in the projected execution time for the entire application, as the difference of the projected end-to-end execution time after the reuse, $\hat{t}'$, from the one before the reuse, $\hat{t}$:

$$\delta = \hat{t}' - \hat{t} = \frac{\tau_{c_i}}{1-(p_{v_i}+\tau_{c_i})} - \frac{\tau_{c_i}}{1-p_{v_i}} \tag{9}$$

The projected impact δ is acceptable if $\delta + \hat{t} \le q_t$, in other words if the new projected execution time is acceptable. In the above inequality, q_t is the requested end-to-end execution time QoS metric that was specified by the user in Q_ξ. Similarly to ξ, it is cached for every application on each node that is part of the application. $\hat{t}$ is the current end-to-end execution time for the entire application. $\hat{t}$ is measured by the receiver of a stream processing session and communicated to all nodes participating in it using a feedback loop [15]. This enables the processing to adapt to significant changes in the resource utilization, such as finished applications or execution of new components. For an application that is still in the admission process, $\hat{t}$ is approximated by the sum of the processing and transmission times up to this node, as carried by the application's probe.

Equation 9 summarizes the QoS Impact Projection algorithm. A Synergy node has locally available all the required information to compute the impact δ for all applications it is currently participating in. This information is available by maintaining local load information, monitoring the local processor utilization, and caching ξ and Q_ξ for all applications it is running, along with their current end-to-end execution times. It uses the projected application execution time to estimate the effect of the component reuse on the existing applications, by considering the effects of increased processor load on the time required to invoke the components.

This projection is performed for all applications currently invoking a component to be reused, for all applications invoking other components located on the node, and also for the application that is to be admitted. If the projected impact is acceptable for all applications, the component can be reused. Otherwise, and if there are no other local components that can be reused, the probe is dropped.

4   Experimental Evaluation

We now present the experimental evaluation of Synergy, both through our prototype implementation over the PlanetLab [10] wide-area network testbed, and through simulations. The prototype provided a realistic evaluation. We used simulations in addition to the prototype, to be able to test larger network sizes.

4.1   Prototype over PlanetLab

Methodology. Our Synergy prototype was implemented as a multi-threaded system of about 18000 lines of Java code, running on each of 88 physical nodes of PlanetLab. The

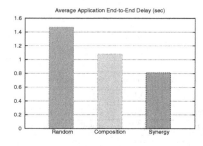

Fig. 6. Average application end-to-end delay

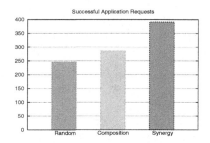

Fig. 7. Successful application requests

implementation was based on the SpiderNet service composition framework [13]. Uniformly across the nodes were instantiated 100 components, with a replication degree of 5. We used a probing ratio of 10%. Application requests asked for 2 to 4 components chosen randomly and for the corresponding streams between the components. We generated approximately 9 requests per second throughout the system. We generated queries using a Zipf distribution with $\alpha = 1.6$, expecting stream processing applications to follow trends similar to media streaming and web content provision applications [19]. We also experimented with different request distributions in the simulations.

We compared *Synergy* against two different composition algorithms: A *Random* algorithm that blindly selected one of the candidates for each application component. A *Composition* algorithm (such as [13]), that discarded those component candidates whose hosting nodes would not have the required processing power or communication bandwidth to support the request with the specified QoS and among the remaining candidates it chose the ones that resulted in the minimum end-to-end delay.

Results and Analysis. In this set of experiments we investigated Synergy's performance and overhead in a real setting.

Average Application End-to-End Delay. Figure 6 shows the average application end-to-end delay achieved by the three composition approaches for each transmitted data tuple. Synergy offers a 45% improvement over Random and a 25% improvement over Composition. The average end-to-end delay is in the acceptable range of less than a second. Reusing existing streams offers Synergy an advantage, since for some of the requests (fully or partially) only transmission and no processing time is required.

Successful Application Requests. An important metric of the efficiency of a component composition algorithm is the number of requests it manages to accommodate and meet their QoS demands, shown in Figure 7. Synergy successfully accommodates 27% more applications than Composition and 37% more than Random. Random does not take the QoS requirements into account, thus misassigns a lot of requests. While Composition takes operator, resource, and QoS requirements into account, it does not employ QoS impact projection to prevent QoS violations on currently running applications. This results to applications that fail to meet their QoS demands during their execution, due to dynamic arrivals of new requests in the system. Synergy's composition algorithm manages to increase the capacity of the system and also limit the QoS violations.

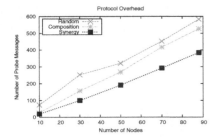

Fig. 8. Protocol overhead

Setup Time (ms)	Random	Composition	Synergy
Discovery	240	188	243
Probing	4509	4810	3141
Total	4749	4998	3384

Fig. 9. Breakdown of average setup time

Protocol Overhead. We show the overhead of the composition protocols which is attributed to the probe messages in Figure 8. To discover components and streams we use the DHT-based routing scheme of Pastry, which keeps the number of discovery messages low, while the number of messages needed to probe alternative component graphs quantifies our protocol's overhead. Synergy's sharing-aware component composition manages to reduce the number of probes: By being able to discover and reuse existing streams to satisfy parts or the entire query plan, it keeps the number of candidate components that need to be probed smaller. Also important is that the overhead grows linearly to the number of nodes in the system, which allows the protocol to scale to larger numbers of nodes. The probing ratio is another knob that can be used to tune the protocol overhead further [6]. While Random's overhead could also be tuned to allow less candidates to be visited, its per hop selections would still be QoS-blind.

Average Setup Time. Table 9 shows the breakdown of the average time needed for an application setup, for the three composition algorithms. The setup time is divided in time spent to discover components and streams and time spent to probe candidate components. As is shown, the discovery of streams and components is only a small part of the time needed to set up a stream processing session. The major part of the time is spent in transmitting probes to candidate components and running the composition algorithm in them. Sharing streams allows Synergy to save time from component probing, which effectively results to 32% faster setup time than Composition. The total setup time is only a few seconds. Having to discover less components balances out the cost of having to discover streams. Discovering a stream, especially if it is the final output of the query plan, can render multiple component discoveries unnecessary.

4.2 Simulations

Methodology. To further evaluate the performance of Synergy's sharing-aware composition algorithm we implemented a distributed stream processing simulator in about 7500 lines of C++ code. The network topology fed to the simulator was a transit-stub topology of 1500 routers, generated by the GT-ITM internetwork topology generator [20]. We simulated a large overlay network of 500 nodes chosen randomly from the underlying topology. Nodes and links were assigned processing and communication capacities from discrete classes, to simulate a heterogeneous system.

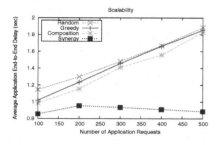

Fig. 10. Scalability

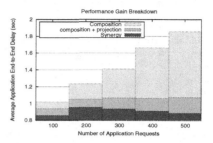

Fig. 11. Performance gain breakdown

A total of 1000 components were distributed uniformly across the nodes of the system, with a uniform replication degree of 5. In other words, 200 unique components and 800 component replicas were instantiated at the nodes. Application requests consisted of requests for 2 to 10 components chosen randomly and of streams of random rates transmitted between the components. For each application we set its QoS requirement 30% higher than its projected execution time. We made experiments to investigate both the performance of Synergy's composition algorithm and its sensitivity to the parameters mentioned above.

We compared *Synergy* not only against *Random* and *Composition*, but also against a *Greedy* algorithm that at each composition step selected the candidate component that resulted in the minimum delay between the two components. Note, that this does not necessarily result in the minimum end-to-end delay for the entire application. To implement this algorithm in a distributed prototype some latency monitoring service such as [17] would be needed. We included it in the simulations though, as a popular centralized approach that provides results with low overhead.

Other than the average application end-to-end delay, which includes processing, transmission, and queueing delays, our main metric for the algorithms' comparison was the success rate, defined as the percentage of application requests that get admitted and complete within their requested QoS limits. This effectively captures the success of a composition algorithm to provide the requested operators, resources, and QoS.

Results and Analysis. In this set of experiments we investigated the performance of Synergy's sharing-aware component composition algorithm for increasing loads.

Scalability. Figure 10 shows the average end-to-end delay of all the applications that are admitted in the system for increasing application load. Synergy consistently achieves the minimum average end-to-end delay. Furthermore, it manages to maintain the average end-to-end delay low, by not admitting more applications than those that can be supported by the system. This is not the case with Random, Greedy, or the Composition algorithm which do not employ QoS impact projection. As the number of deployed and requested applications increases, the probability that existing streams can be shared among applications increases as well. This gives Synergy an additional advantage, which explains the slight decline of the average end-to-end delay for large numbers of application requests.

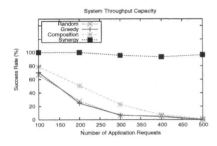
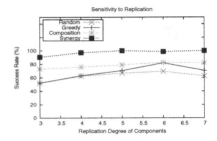

Fig. 12. System throughput capacity   **Fig. 13.** Sensitivity to replication

Performance Gain Breakdown. To investigate what part of the performance benefit of Synergy can be attributed to QoS Impact Projection and what part to Maximum Sharing Discovery, we incorporated QoS projection to the Composition algorithm. Figure 11 shows how Composition together with the QoS projection ("composition + projection") compares to Composition and Synergy, in terms of achieved end-to-end delay. QoS projection improves system performance particularly in high loads. While for 100 requests Composition enhanced with projection offers only 8% lower delay than plain Composition, that improvement rises to 42% for 500 requests.

System throughput capacity. Figure 12 shows the success rate for increasing request load. The benefit of sharing-aware component composition is evident, as Synergy is able to scale to much larger workloads, by reusing existing streams. QoS impact projection helps Synergy to achieve very high success rates by avoiding to disrupt currently running applications. Cases of applications that miss their deadlines even with Synergy can be explained by inaccurate estimations because of the current execution time update frequency, or because of inaccuracies in the approximation of the execution time of the admitted applications. As expected, random allocation results in poor QoS. Greedy allocation does not perform well either and the reason is that resources are assigned hop-by-hop ad hoc, blindly to the applications' end-to-end QoS requirements. Another interesting observation is that ensuring that there will be enough resources to run the admitted applications by eliminating resource violations, as the Composition algorithm does, does not suffice for these applications to meet their QoS requirements.

In the following set of experiments we kept the number of application requests at 100, which was a reasonable load for all algorithms as Figure 12 demonstrated. We then investigated the sensitivity of Synergy to various parameters.

Sensitivity to Replication. Figure 13 shows the success rate, as a function of the replication degree of the components in the system. The success of Synergy's composition, as well as its advantage over the other composition algorithms is clear, regardless of the replication degree of the components. Having more candidates to select from in the composition process does not seem to affect the QoS of the composed applications.

Sensitivity to QoS Requirements. Figure 14 shows the success rate as a function of the QoS demands of the applications. Even for very strict requirements, where applications can only tolerate a 10% of extra delay, Synergy's QoS impact projection is able to deliver in-time execution in more than 80% of the cases, whereas the other composition algorithms (Random, Greedy, Composition) fail in as many as 80% of the requests. As

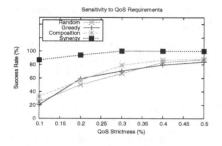

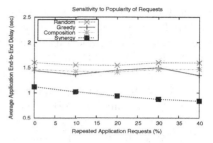

Fig. 14. Sensitivity to QoS requirements   **Fig. 15.** Sensitivity to popularity of requests

QoS requirements become more lax, the performance of those algorithms improves. Yet, even in the case of a 50% tolerance in the delay, the best of them, Composition, still delivers 12% less applications within their deadlines than Synergy.

Sensitivity to Popularity of Requests. To investigate how the distribution of user requests affects Synergy's performance in comparison to the rest of the composition algorithms, we assumed a non-Zipfian distribution of application requests with a varying percentage of repetitions. Figure 15 shows the average end-to-end delay of all the applications that are admitted in the system. Synergy utilizes stream sharing and thus can deliver results for the repeated application requests without extra processing. For a request repetition factor of 20% Synergy's Maximum Sharing Discovery algorithm offers 34% lower average end-to-end delay than Composition. For a repetition factor of 40% Synergy achieves an improvement of 25% in comparison to load without any repetitions. Since the rest of the composition algorithms do not offer stream reuse, their performance is not affected by the repetition in application requests. That is as long as the repetition factor is not extremely large, which would result in rejecting application requests due to resource contention.

5 Related Work

Distributed stream processing [4,9] has been the focus of several recent research efforts from many different perspectives. In [8] and [18] the problem of operator placement in a DSPS to make efficient use of the network resources and maximize query performance is discussed. Our work is complementary, in that our focus is on the effects of sharing existing operators, rather than deploying new ones. While [8] mentions operator reuse, they do not focus on the impact on already running applications. [7] describes an architecture for distributed stream management that makes use of in-network data aggregation to distribute the processing and reduce the communication overhead. A clustered architecture is assumed, as opposed to Synergy's totally decentralized protocols. Service partitioning to achieve load balancing taking into account the heterogeneity of the nodes is discussed in [21], while load balancing based on the correlation of the load distributions across nodes is proposed in [22]. While a balanced load is the final selection criterion among candidate component graphs in Synergy as well, our focus is on QoS provision. The distributed composition probing approach is first presented in [13,6]. Synergy extends this work by considering stream reuse and evaluating the impact of component sharing. Our techniques for distributed stream processing composition directly apply to multimedia streams [23,15] as well.

Application task assignment has also been the focus of many grid research efforts. GATES [5] is a grid-based middleware for distributed stream processing. It uses grid resource discovery standards and trades off accuracy with real-time response. While we also address real-time applications, our focus is on the composition of the application component graph. Similarly, work on grid resource management [24] focuses on optimally assigning individual tasks to different hosts, rather than instantiating *composite* network applications. Work on resource discovery such as SWORD [25] can assist in component composition, and is thus complementary to our work.

Component composition has also been studied in the context of web services from many aspects, such as coordinating among different services to develop production workflows [26], or providing reliability through replication [27]. Similar problems are also encountered when providing dynamic web content at large scales [28], or personalized web content [29], the changing and on-demand nature of which render them more challenging than static content delivery [30]. While we focus on component composition for stream processing, our techniques may be applicable to other applications with QoS requirements as well, such as composing QoS-sensitive web services.

6   Conclusion

In this paper we have presented Synergy, a distributed stream processing middleware that provides sharing-aware component composition. Synergy is built on top of a totally decentralized overlay architecture and utilizes a *Maximum Sharing Discovery algorithm* to reuse existing streams, and a *QoS Impact Projection algorithm* to reuse existing components and yet ensure that the QoS requirements of the currently running applications will not be violated. Both our prototype implementation of Synergy over PlanetLab and our simulations of its composition algorithm show that sharing-aware component composition can enhance QoS provision for distributed stream processing applications. Our future work includes the integration of iterative execution of Synergy's composition protocol with techniques for application migration. This can enable application adaptation to QoS-affecting changes in the environment, such as a node failure or overload.

References

1. Chandrasekaran, S., et al.: TelegraphCQ: Continuous dataflow processing for an uncertain world. In: Proceedings of CIDR, Asilomar, CA. (2003)
2. Arasu, A., Babcock, B., Babu, S., Cieslewicz, J., Datar, M., Ito, K., Motwani, R., Srivastava, U., Widom, J.: STREAM: The Stanford data stream management system. (to appear) (2005)
3. Golab, L., Ozsu, M.: Update-pattern-aware modeling and processing of continuous queries. In: Proceedings of 24th ACM SIGMOD Conference, Baltimore, MD, USA. (2005)
4. Abadi, D., et al.: The design of the borealis stream processing engine. In: Proceedings of CIDR, Asilomar, CA. (2005)
5. Chen, L., Reddy, K., Agrawal, G.: GATES: A grid-based middleware for distributed processing of data streams. In: Proceedings of IEEE HPDC-13, Honolulu, HI. (2004)
6. Gu, X., Yu, P., Nahrstedt, K.: Optimal component composition for scalable stream processing. In: 25th IEEE ICDCS, Columbus, OH. (2005)

7. Kumar, V., Cooper, B., Cai, Z., Eisenhauer, G., Schwan, K.: Resource-aware distributed stream management using dynamic overlays. In: 25th IEEE ICDCS, Columbus, OH. (2005)
8. Pietzuch, P., Ledlie, J., Shneidman, J., Roussopoulos, M., Welsh, M., Seltzer, M.: Network-aware operator placement for stream-processing systems. In: Proc. of 22nd ICDE. (2006)
9. Jain, N., Amini, L., Andrade, H., King, R., Park, Y., Selo, P., Venkatramani, C.: Design, implementation, and evaluation of the linear road benchmark on the stream processing core. In: Proceedings of 25th ACM SIGMOD Conference, Chicago, IL, USA. (2006)
10. PlanetLab Consortium: http://www.planet-lab.org/ (2004)
11. Arabshian, K., Schulzrinne, H.: An ontology-based hierarchical peer-to-peer global service discovery system. Journal of Ubiquitous Computing and Intelligence (JUCI) (2005)
12. Abdelzaher, T.: An automated profiling subsystem for QoS-aware services. In: Proc. 6th IEEE RTAS, Real-Time Technology and Applications Symposium, Washington, DC. (2000)
13. Gu, X., Nahrstedt, K., Yu, B.: SpiderNet: An integrated peer-to-peer service composition framework. In: Proceedings of IEEE HPDC-13, Honolulu, HI. (2004)
14. Rowstron, A., Druschel, P.: Pastry: Scalable, distributed object location and routing for large-scale peer-to-peer systems. In: Proceedings of IFIP/ACM International Conference on Distributed Systems Platforms, Heidelberg, Germany. (2001)
15. Chen, F., Repantis, T., Kalogeraki, V.: Coordinated media streaming and transcoding in peer-to-peer systems. In: Proceedings of 19th IPDPS, Denver, CO. (2005)
16. Hu, N., Steenkiste, P.: Exploiting internet route sharing for large scale available bandwidth estimation. In: Proc. of Internet Measurement Conference, IMC, New Orleans, LA. (2005)
17. Tang, C., McKinley, P.: A distributed approach to topology-aware overlay path monitoring. In: Proceedings of 24th IEEE ICDCS, Tokyo, Japan. (2004)
18. Seshadri, S., Kumar, V., Cooper, B.: Optimizing multiple queries in distributed data stream systems. In: 2nd Int. IEEE Workshop on Networking Meets Databases, NetDB. (2006)
19. Cherkasova, L., Gupta, M.: Analysis of enterprise media server workloads: Access patterns, locality, content evolution, and rates of change. IEEE/ACM Transactions on Networking, TON 12(5) (2004) 781–794
20. Zegura, E., Calvert, K., Bhattacharjee, S.: How to model an internetwork. In: Proceedings of IEEE INFOCOM, San Francisco, CA, USA. (1996)
21. Gedik, B., Liu, L.: PeerCQ: A decentralized and self-configuring peer-to-peer information monitoring system. In: Proceedings of 23rd IEEE ICDCS, Providence, RI, USA. (2003)
22. Xing, Y., Zdonik, S., Hwang, J.: Dynamic load distribution in the borealis stream processor. In: Proc. of 21st International Conference on Data Engineering, ICDE, Tokyo, Japan. (2005)
23. Kon, F., Campbell, R., Nahrstedt, K.: Using dynamic configuration to manage a scalable multimedia distributed system. Computer Communications Journal 24 (2001) 105–123
24. Cai, W., Coulson, G., Grace, P., Blair, G., L.Mathy, Yeung, W.: The gridkit distributed resource management framework. In: Proc. of European Grid Conference, EGC. (2005)
25. Oppenheimer, D., Albrecht, J., Patterson, D., Vahdat, A.: Design and implementation trade-offs for wide-area resource discovery. In: Proceedings of 14th IEEE HPDC-14. (2005)
26. Tai, S., Khalaf, R., Mikalsen, T.: Composition of coordinated web services. In: Proceedings of ACM/IFIP/USENIX 5th International Middleware Conference, Toronto, Canada. (2004)
27. Bartoli, A., Jimenez-Peris, R., Kemme, B., Pautasso, C., Patarin, S., Wheater, S., Woodman, S.: The adapt framework for adaptable and composable web services. IEEE Distributed Systems On Line, Web Systems Section (2005)
28. Amza, C., Cox, A., Zwaenepoel, W.: A comparative evaluation of transparent scaling techniques for dynamic content servers. In: Proceedings of 21st ICDE, Tokyo, Japan. (2005)
29. Colajanni, M., Grieco, R., Malandrino, D., Mazzoni, F., Scarano, V.: A scalable framework for the support of advanced edge services. In: Proc. of HPCC-05, Sorrento, Italy. (2005)
30. Karbhari, P., Rabinovich, M., Xiao, Z., Douglis, F.: ACDN: A content delivery network for applications. In: Proceedings of 21st ACM SIGMOD Conference, Madison, WI. (2002)

Enforcing Performance Isolation Across Virtual Machines in Xen

Diwaker Gupta[1], Ludmila Cherkasova[2], Rob Gardner[2], and Amin Vahdat[1]

[1] University of California, San Diego, CA 92122, USA
{dgupta, vahdat}@cs.ucsd.edu
[2] Hewlett-Packard Laboratories
{lucy.cherkasova,rob.gardner}@hp.com

Abstract. Virtual machines (VMs) have recently emerged as the basis for allocating resources in enterprise settings and hosting centers. One benefit of VMs in these environments is the ability to multiplex several operating systems on hardware based on dynamically changing system characteristics. However, such multiplexing must often be done while observing per-VM performance guarantees or service level agreements. Thus, one important requirement in this environment is effective performance isolation among VMs. In this paper, we address performance isolation across virtual machines in Xen [1]. For instance, while Xen can allocate fixed shares of CPU among competing VMs, it does not currently account for work done on behalf of individual VMs in device drivers. Thus, the behavior of one VM can negatively impact resources available to other VMs even if appropriate per-VM resource limits are in place.

In this paper, we present the design and evaluation of a set of primitives implemented in Xen to address this issue. First, *XenMon* accurately measures per-VM resource consumption, including work done on behalf of a particular VM in Xen's driver domains. Next, our *SEDF-DC* scheduler accounts for aggregate VM resource consumption in allocating CPU. Finally, *ShareGuard* limits the total amount of resources consumed in privileged and driver domains based on administrator-specified limits. Our performance evaluation indicates that our mechanisms effectively enforce performance isolation for a variety of workloads and configurations.

1 Introduction

Virtual Machine Monitors (VMMs)[1] are gaining popularity for building more agile and dynamic hardware/software infrastructures. In large enterprises for example, VMMs enable server and application consolidation in emerging on-demand utility computing models [2,3]. Virtualization holds the promise of achieving greater system utilization while lowering total cost of ownership and responding more effectively to changing business conditions.

Virtual machines enable *fault isolation*—"encapsulating" different applications in self-contained execution environments so that a failure in one virtual machine does not

---

[1] We use the terms *hypervisor* and *domain* interchangeably with VMM and VM respectively.

M. van Steen and M. Henning (Eds.): Middleware 2006, LNCS 4290, pp. 342–362, 2006.

affect other VMs hosted on the same physical hardware. *performance isolation* is another important goal. Individual VMs are often configured with performance guarantees and expectations, e.g., based on service level agreements. Thus, the resource consumption of one virtual machine should not impact the promised guarantees to other VMs on the same hardware.

In this paper, we focus on performance isolation mechanisms in Xen [1], a popular open source VMM. Xen supports per-VM CPU allocation mechanisms. However, it — like many other VMMs — does not accurately account for resource consumption in the hypervisor on behalf of individual VMs, e.g., for I/O processing. Xen's I/O model has evolved considerably over time. In the initial design [1] shown in Figure 1a, the Xen hypervisor itself contained device driver code and provided shared device access. To reduce the risk of device driver failure/misbehavior and to address problems of dependability, maintainability, and manageability of I/O devices, Xen moved to the architecture shown in Figure 1b [4]. Here, "isolated driver domains" (IDDs) host unmodified (legacy OS code) device drivers. Domain-0 is a privileged control domain used to manage other domains and resource allocation policies.

This new I/O model results in a more complex CPU usage model. For I/O intensive applications, CPU usage has two components: CPU consumed by the guest domain, where the application resides, and CPU consumed by the IDD that incorporates the device driver and performs I/O processing on behalf of the guest domain. However, the work done for I/O processing in an IDD is not charged to the initiating domain. Consider a guest domain limited to 30% CPU consumption. If the work done on its behalf within an IDD to perform packet processing consumes 20% of the CPU, then that domain may consume 50% of overall CPU resources. Such unaccounted CPU overhead is significant for I/O intensive applications, reaching 20%-45% for a web server [5].

The key contribution of this paper is the design of a set of cooperating mechanisms to effectively control total CPU consumption across virtual machines in Xen. There are a number of requirements for such a system. First, we must accurately measure the resources consumed within individual guest domains. Next, we must attribute the CPU consumption within IDDs to the appropriate guest domain. The VMM scheduler must be modified to incorporate the aggregate resource consumption in the guest domain and work done on its behalf in IDDs. Finally, we must limit the total amount of work done on behalf of a particular domain in IDDs based on past consumption history and target resource limits. For instance, if a particular domain is already consuming nearly its full

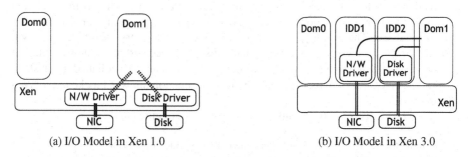

(a) I/O Model in Xen 1.0   (b) I/O Model in Xen 3.0

Fig. 1. Evolution of Xen's I/O Architecture

resource limits, then the amount of resources available to it in the IDDs must be scaled appropriately.

The analog of accounting resources consumed on behalf of a guest domain have come up in scheduling operating system resources across individual tasks [6,7,8,9,10,11,12], e.g., in accounting for resources consumed in the kernel on behalf of individual processes. Our work builds upon these earlier efforts, exploring the key challenges associated with constructing appropriate abstractions and mechanisms in the context of modern VM architectures. One of the interesting problems in this space is developing minimally intrusive mechanisms that can: i) account for significant asynchrony in the hypervisor and OS and ii) generalize to a variety of individual operating systems and device drivers (performance isolation will quickly become ineffective if even a relatively small number of devices or operations are unaccounted for). To this end, we have completed a full implementation and detailed performance evaluation of the necessary system components to enable effective VM performance isolation:

- XenMon: a performance monitoring and profiling tool that reports (among other things) CPU usage of different VMs at programmable time scales. XenMon includes mechanisms to measure CPU for network processing in net-IDDs (IDDs responsible for network devices) on behalf of guest domains.
- SEDF-DC: a new VM scheduler with feedback that effectively allocates CPU among competing domains while accounting for consumption both within the domain and in net-IDDs.
- ShareGuard: a control mechanism that enforces a specified limit on CPU time consumed by a net-IDD on behalf of a particular guest domain.

2   XenMon

To support resource allocation and management, we implemented an accurate monitoring and performance profiling infrastructure, called XenMon.[2] There are three main components in XenMon (Figure 2):

- xentrace: This is a lightweight event logging facility present in Xen. XenTrace can log events at arbitrary control points in the hypervisor. Each event can have some associated attributes (for instance, for a "domain scheduled" event, the associated attributes might be the ID of the scheduled domain and the event's time stamp). Events are logged into "trace buffers": shared memory pages that can be read by user-level Domain-0 tools. Note that xentrace was already implemented in Xen — our contribution here was to determine the right set of events to monitor.
- xenbaked: The events generated by XenTrace are not very useful on their own. xenbaked is a user-space process that polls [3] the trace buffers for new events and processes them into meaningful information. For instance, we collate domain sleep and wake events to determine the time for which a domain was blocked in a given interval.
- xenmon: This is the front-end for displaying and logging the data.

---

[2] Our implementation of XenMon has been integrated into the official Xen 3.0 code base.

[3] In the current implementation, events are posted via a virtual interrupt instead of periodic polling.

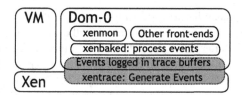

Fig. 2. XenMon Architecture

XenMon aggregates a variety of metrics across all VMs periodically (configurable with a default of 100 ms). For this paper, we only use the CPU utilization and network accounting facilities (Section 3) of XenMon. Details on all the metrics available from XenMon and some examples of using XenMon for analyzing CPU schedulers in Xen are available separately [13].

3 Network I/O Accounting

Recall that one of the challenges posed by the new I/O model in Xen is to classify IDD CPU consumption across guest domains. This work is focused on network I/O, so we summarize network I/O processing in Xen. As mentioned earlier, in the IDD model a designated driver domain is responsible for each hardware device and all guests wishing to use the device have to share it via the corresponding IDD. The IDD has a "back-end" driver that multiplexes I/O for multiple "front-end" drivers in guest VMs over the real device driver. Figure 3 shows this I/O architecture in more detail. Note that for the experiments reported in this paper, we use Domain-0 as the driver domain.

We briefly describe the sequence of events involved in receiving a packet — the numbers correspond to those marked in Figure 3. When the hardware receives the packet (1), it raises an interrupt trapped by Xen (2). Xen then determines the domain responsible for the device and posts a *virtual* interrupt to the corresponding driver domain via the *event channel* (3). When the driver domain is scheduled next, it sees a pending interrupt and invokes the appropriate interrupt handler. The interrupt handler in the driver domain only serves to remove the packet from the real device driver (4) and hand it over to the "back-end" driver (5), *netback* in Figure 3. Note that no TCP/IP protocol processing is involved in this step (except perhaps the inspection of the IP header).

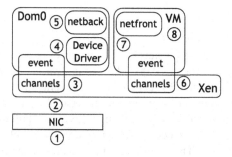

Fig. 3. I/O processing path in Xen

It is netback's responsibility to forward the packet to the correct "front-end" driver (*netfront* in Figure 3). The driver domain transfers the ownership of the memory page containing the packet to the target guest domain, and then notifies it with a "virtual interrupt" (6). Note that this involves no data movement/copying. When the target guest is next scheduled, it will field the pending interrupt (7). The netfront driver in the guest will then pass on the packet to higher layers of the networking stack for further processing (8). The transmit path of a packet is similar, except that no explicit memory page exchange is involved (see [1] for details).

Thus, I/O processing in a net-IDD primarily involves two components: the real device driver and the back-end (virtual) device driver. One natural approach for more accurate accounting is to instrument these components for detailed measurements of all the delays on the I/O path. However, this approach does not scale in Xen for two reasons: (1) since Xen uses legacy Linux drivers, this would require instrumenting *all* network device drivers, and (2) network drivers involve significant asynchronous processing, making it difficult to isolate the time consumed in the driver in the context of a given operation.

We therefore need some alternate heuristics to estimate the per-guest CPU consumption. Intuitively, each guest should be charged in proportion to the amount of I/O operations it generates. In [5], we used the number of memory page exchanges as an estimator. However, we found this method to be a rather coarse approximation that does not take into account what fraction of these page exchanges correspond to sent versus received packets, and that does not take into account the size of the packets.

Thus, we propose using the *number of packets* sent/received per guest domain for distributing the net-IDD CPU consumption among guests. Note that netback is an ideal observation point: all of the packets (both on the send and receive paths between driver domain and guest domain) *must* pass through it. We instrumented netback to provide detailed measurements on the number of packets processed by the corresponding net-IDD in both directions for each guest domain. In particular, we added XenTrace events for each packet transmission/reception, with the appropriate guest domain as an attribute. We then extended XenMon to report this information.

Of course, knowing the number of packets sent and received on a per-domain basis does not by itself enable accurate CPU isolation. We need a mechanism to map these values to per-domain CPU consumption in the IDD. In particular, we want to know the dependence of packet size on CPU processing overhead and the breakdown of send versus receive packet processing. To answer these questions, we perform the following two part study.

The Impact of Packet Size on CPU Overhead in Net-IDD: We performed controlled experiments involving sending packets of different sizes at a *fixed* rate to a guest VM. In particular, we fixed the rate at 10,000 pkts/sec and varied the packet size from 100 to 1200 bytes. Each run lasted 20 seconds and we averaged the results over 10 runs. We repeated the experiments to exercise the reverse I/O path as well – so the VM was *sending* packets instead of receiving them. To prevent "pollution" of results due to ACKS going in the opposite direction, we wrote a custom tool for these benchmarks using UDP instead of TCP. The other end point for these experiments was a separate

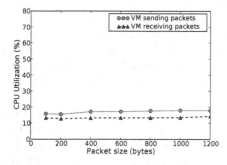 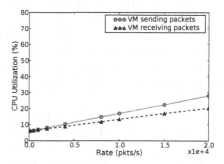

Fig. 4. CPU overhead in Domain-0 for processing packets at a fixed rate under different packet sizes

Fig. 5. CPU overhead in Domain-0 for processing packets of a fixed size under varying rates

machine on our LAN. Recall that in all of our experiments, we use Domain-0 to host the network device driver.

Our results show that CPU consumption in net-IDD does not depend on packet size as presented in Figure 4. The explanation is as follows: during driver packet processing there is no payload processing or copying; the driver largely deals with the packet header. For the rest of the I/O path within the net-IDD, there is no data copying (where CPU processing can depend on packet size) — only the ownership of memory pages changes to reflect data transfer.

CPU Overhead in Net-IDD for Send vs. Receive I/O Paths: In this experiment, we fixed the packet size at 256 bytes and varied the rate at which a VM sends or receives packets. We could thus selectively exercise the send and receive I/O paths within Xen and measure the resulting CPU overhead in net-IDD. We denote these as *Send Benchmark* and *Receive Benchmark*, respectively. As before, each run lasted 20 seconds and we averaged results over 10 runs.

Figure 5 presents our experimental results. An interesting outcome of this study is that the ratio of CPU consumption in net-IDD between send and receive paths is consistently the same for different packet rates. We denote this measured ratio as $weight$.

To validate the generality of presented results we repeated all of the experiments presented above for two different hardware configurations: a single CPU Intel Pentium-IV machine running at 2.66-GHz with a 1-Gbit Intel NIC (SYSTEM-1) and a dual processor Intel Xen 2.8-GHz with a 1-Gbit Broadcom NIC (SYSTEM-2). For both systems under test, the CPU consumption in net-IDD does not depend on packet size. Further, for both system under test, the ratio of CPU consumption in net-IDD between send and receive paths is consistent for different packet rates:

- SYSTEM-1: $weight = 1.1$ (standard deviation 0.07);
- SYSTEM-2: $weight = 1.16$ (standard deviation 0.15).

These results show that the number of packets in conjunction with the direction of traffic can be reasonably used to split CPU consumption among guests. Concretely, let $Send/Recv(Dom_i)$ denote packets sent/received by net-IDD to/from Dom_i and $Send/Recv(netIDD)$ denote the total packets sent/received by net-IDD. Then, we define the *weighted* packet count per domain as $weight \times Send(Dom_i) + Recv(Dom_i)$, where $weight$ is the ratio of CPU consumption in net-IDD for send versus receive paths. Similarly, we compute the weighted packet count for net-IDD: $wCount(netIDD)$. Then we can use the fraction $wCount(Dom_i)/wCount(netIDD)$ to charge CPU usage to Dom_i.

In the remainder of this paper, we use this weighted count to compute the CPU overhead in net-IDD for network processing on behalf of different guest domains. This approach is also attractive because it comes with a compact, portable benchmark that derives the weight coefficient between send/receive paths automatically for different systems and different network device drivers. It has the further advantage of being general to a variety of device drivers and operating systems (e.g., individual device drivers may be hosted on a variety of operating systems) without requiring error-prone instrumentation. Of course, it has the disadvantage of not explicitly measuring CPU consumption but rather deriving it based on benchmarks of a particular hardware configuration. We feel that this trade off is inherent and that instrumenting all possible device driver/OS configurations is untenable for resource isolation. A variety of middleware tools face similar challenges, i.e., the inability to modify or directly instrument lower layers, making our approach attractive for alternate settings as well.

With this estimation of CPU utilization per guest, we now turn our attention to SEDF-DC and ShareGuard.

4   SEDF-DC: CPU Scheduler with Feedback

Xen's reservation based CPU scheduler — SEDF (Simple Earliest Deadline First) — takes its roots in the Atropos scheduler [8]. In SEDF, an administrator can specify the CPU share to be allocated per VM. However, there is no way to restrict the aggregate CPU consumed by a domain and by driver domains acting on its behalf. We have extended SEDF to accomplish this goal.

4.1   Overview

Our modified scheduler, SEDF-DC for SEDF-*Debt Collector*, periodically receives feedback from XenMon about the CPU consumed by IDDs for I/O processing on behalf of guest domains. Using this information, SEDF-DC constrains the CPU allocation to guest domains to meet the specified combined CPU usage limit.

For each domain Dom_i, SEDF takes as input a tuple (s_i, p_i), where the *slice* s_i and the *period* p_i together represent the CPU share of Dom_i: Dom_i will receive at least s_i units of time in each period of length p_i. Such specifications are particularly convenient for dynamically adjusting CPU allocations: we can directly charge the CPU time consumed by IDDs for Dom_i by decreasing s_i appropriately. In CPU schedulers based on weights, one would need to continuously re-calculate weights of domains to achieve the same result.

We now describe SEDF-DC's operation, but limit our description only to places where SEDF-DC differs from SEDF. SEDF-DC maintains 3 queues:

- Q_r: the queue of runnable domains;
- Q_w: the queue of domains that have exhausted their slice and are awaiting the next period;
- Q_b: the queue of blocked domains.

A key concept in SEDF is *deadlines*. Intuitively, a deadline denotes the absolute time that a domain *should have* received its specified share of the CPU. Both Q_r and Q_w are sorted by deadlines, making the selection of the next domain to schedule a constant time operation.

Each domain D_i's deadline is initialized to $NOW + p_i$, where NOW denotes the current time. Let t denote the *feedback interval* (set to 500 ms in our current implementation). Let net-IDD be a driver domain with a networking device that is shared by $Dom_1, \ldots, Dom_n$. We will simplify the algorithm description (without loss of generality) by considering a single net-IDD. Using XenMon, we compute the CPU consumption $used_i^{IDD}$ of net-IDD for network I/O processing on behalf of Dom_i during the latest t-ms interval and provide this information (for all domains) to SEDF-DC.

For each domain Dom_i, the scheduler tracks three values $(d_i, r_i, debt_i^{IDD})$:

- d_i: domain's current *deadline* for CPU allocation, the time when the current period ends for domain Dom_i.
- r_i: domain's current *remaining time* for CPU allocation, the CPU time remaining to domain Dom_i within its current period.
- $debt_i^{IDD}$: CPU time consumed by Dom_i via the net-IDD's networking processing performed on behalf of Dom_i. We call this the *CPU debt* for Dom_i. At each feedback interval, this value is incremented by $used_i^{IDD}$ for the latest t-ms.

Note that the original SEDF scheduler only tracks (d_i, r_i). The introduction of $debt_i^{IDD}$ in the algorithm allows us to observe and enforce aggregate limits on Dom_i's CPU utilization.

Let a and b be integer numbers and let us introduce the following function $a \,\hat{-}\, b$ as follows:

$$a \,\hat{-}\, b = \begin{cases} 0 & \text{if } a \leq b \\ a - b & \text{otherwise} \end{cases}$$

We now describe the modified procedure for updating the queues (Q_r, Q_w, and Q_b) on each invocation of SEDF-DC.

1. The time $gotten_i$ for which the current Dom_i has been running is deducted from r_i: $r_i = r_i - gotten_i$.

   If $debt_i^{IDD} > 0$ then we attempt to charge Dom_i for its CPU debt by decreasing the remaining time of its CPU slice:
   - if $debt_i^{IDD} \leq r_i$ then $r_i = r_i - debt_i^{IDD}$ and $debt_i^{IDD} = 0$;
   - if $debt_i^{IDD} > r_i$ then $debt_i^{IDD} = debt_i^{IDD} - r_i$ and $r_i = 0$.
2. If $r_i = 0$, then Dom_i is moved from Q_r to Q_w, since Dom_i has received its required CPU time in the current period.
3. For each domain Dom_k in Q_w, if $NOW \geq d_k$ then we perform the following updates:

- r_k is reset to $s_k \stackrel{\wedge}{-} debt_k^{IDD}$;
- $debt_k^{IDD}$ is decreased by $min(s_k, debt_k)$;
- the new deadline is set to $d_k + p_k$;
- If $r_k > 0$ then Dom_k is moved from Q_w to Q_r.

4. The next timer interrupt is scheduled for $min(d_w^h + p_w^h, d_r^h)$, where (d_w^h, p_w^h) and (d_r^h, p_r^h) denote the deadline and period of the domains that are respective heads of the Q_r and Q_w queues.

5. On an interrupt, the scheduler runs the head of Q_r. If Q_r is empty, it selects the head of Q_w.

6. When domain Dom_k in Q_b is unblocked, we make the following updates:
   - if $NOW < d_k$ then
     - if $debt_k^{IDD} \leq r_k$ then $r_k = r_k - debt_k^{IDD}$, and $debt_k^{IDD} = 0$, and Dom_k is moved from Q_b to Q_r;
     - if $debt_k^{IDD} > r_k$ then $debt_k^{IDD} = debt_k^{IDD} - r_k$ and $r_k = 0$.
   - if $NOW \geq d_k$ then we compute for how many periods Dom_k was blocked. Since Dom_k was not runnable, this unused CPU time can be charged against its CPU debt:

$$bl\_periods = int \left\{ \frac{(NOW - d_k)}{p_k} \right\}$$

$$debt_k^{IDD} = debt_k^{IDD} - r_k - (bl\_periods \times s_k)$$

   - r_k is reset to $s_k \stackrel{\wedge}{-} debt_k^{IDD}$. If $r_k > 0$, then Dom_k is moved from Q_b to Q_r and can be scheduled to receive the remaining r_k;
   - $debt_k^{IDD}$ is adjusted by s_k: $debt_k^{IDD} = debt_k^{IDD} \stackrel{\wedge}{-} s_k$;
   - the new deadline is set to $d_k + p_k$

The SEDF-DC implementation described above might have bursty CPU allocation for domains hosting network-intensive applications, especially when a coarser granularity time interval t is used for the scheduler feedback, e.g., $t = 2s$. It might happen that domain Dom_i will get zero allocation of CPU shares for several consecutive periods until the CPU debt time $debt_i^{IDD}$ is "repaid". To avoid this, we implemented an optimization to SEDF-DC that attempts to spread the CPU debt across multiple execution periods.

We compute the number of times period p_i fits within a feedback interval — the intent is to spread the CPU debt of Dom_i across periods that happen during the feedback interval. We call this the *CPU period frequency* of domain Dom_i and denote it as $period\_freq_i$:

$$period\_freq_i = int \left(\frac{t}{p_i} \right)$$

If $period\_freq_i > 1$, then we can spread $debt_i^{IDD}$ across $period\_freq_i$ number of periods, where at each period the domain is charged for a fraction of its overall CPU debt:

$$spread\_debt_i = int \left(\frac{debt_i^{IDD}}{period\_freq_i} \right)$$

This optimized SEDF-DC algorithm supports more consistent and smoother CPU allocation to domains with network-intensive applications.

4.2   Evaluation

In this section we evaluate SEDF-DC beginning with a simple setup to demonstrate the correctness of the scheduler and continue with a more complex scenario to illustrate SEDF-DC's feasibility for realistic workloads. All tests were conducted on single processor Pentium-IV machines running at 2.8-GHz.

In the first experiment, we have a single VM (Domain-1) configured to receive a maximum of 60% of the CPU; Domain-0 is entitled to the remaining 40%. Domain-1 hosts a Web server, loaded using `httperf` [14] from another machine. We gradually increase the load and measure the resulting CPU utilization.

Figure 6a shows the results with the unmodified SEDF scheduler. We see that as the load increases, Domain-1 consumes almost all of its share of the CPU. Additionally, Domain-0 incurs an overhead of almost 35% at peak loads to serve Domain-1's traffic. Hence, while Domain-1 was entitled to receive 60% of the CPU, it had received a *combined* CPU share of 90% via additional I/O processing in Domain-0. We repeated the same experiment with SEDF-DC, with the results shown in Figure 6b. We can see that SEDF-DC is able to enforce the desired behavior, keeping the combined CPU usage of Domain-1 bounded to 60%.

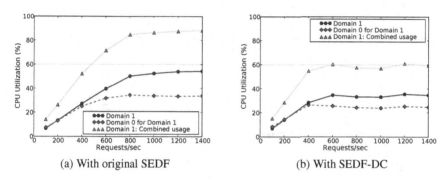

(a) With original SEDF   (b) With SEDF-DC

Fig. 6. Simple SEDF Benchmark

In practice, system configurations are likely to be more complicated: multiple VMs, each running a different service with different requirements; some VMs may be I/O intensive, others might be CPU intensive and so on. Our next experiment tries to evaluate SEDF and SEDF-DC under a more realistic setup.

For this experiment, we have two VMs (Domain-1 and Domain-2), each hosting a web-server. We configure both VMs and Domain-0 to receive a maximum of 22% of the CPU. Any slack time in the system is consumed by CPU intensive tasks running in a third VM. Domain-1's web-server is served with requests for files of size 10 KB at 400 requests/second, while Domain-2's web-server is served with requests for files of size 100 KB at 200 requests/second. We chose these rates because they completely saturate Domain-0 and demonstrate how CPU usage in Domain-0 may be divided between guest domains with different workload requirements. As before, we use `httperf` to generate client requests. Each run lasts 60 seconds.

We first conduct the experiment with unmodified SEDF to establish the baseline. Figure 7a shows the throughput of the two web-servers as a function of time. We also measure the CPU utilization's of all the VMs, shown in 7b. Note that Domain-1 consumes all of its 22% available CPU cycles, while Domain-2 consumes only about 15% of the CPU. Even more interesting is the split of Domain-0 CPU utilization across Domain-1 and Domain-2 as shown in Figure 7c. For clarify, we summarize the experiment in Table 1. The first column shows the average values for the metrics over the entire run. Domain-1 uses an additional 9.6% of CPU for I/O processing in Domain-0 (42% of overall Domain-0 usage) while Domain-2 uses an additional 13.6% of CPU via Domain-0 (58% of overall Domain-0 usage). Thus, the combined CPU utilization of Domains 1 and 2 (the sum of their individual CPU utilization and CPU overhead in Domain-0 on their behalf) is 29.2% and 27.7% respectively.

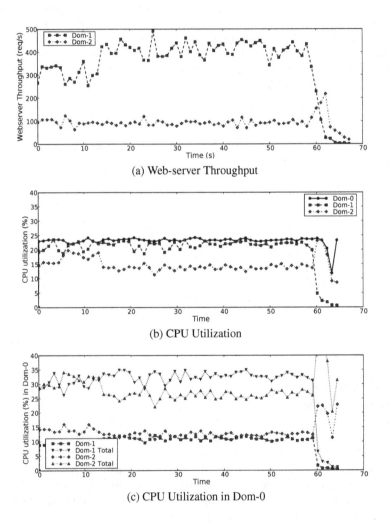

(a) Web-server Throughput

(b) CPU Utilization

(c) CPU Utilization in Dom-0

Fig. 7. With original SEDF

Table 1. SEDF-DC in action: metric values averaged over the duration of the run

Metric	SEDF	SEDF-DC
Dom-1 web-server Throughput	348.06 req/s	225.20 req/s
Dom-2 web-server Throughput	93.12 req/s	69.53 req/s
Dom-1 CPU	19.6%	13.7%
Dom-0 for Dom-1	9.6%	7.7%
Dom-1 Combined	29.2%	21.4%
Dom-2 CPU	14.5%	10.9%
Dom-0 for Dom-2	13.2%	10.6%
Dom-2 Combined	27.7%	21.5%

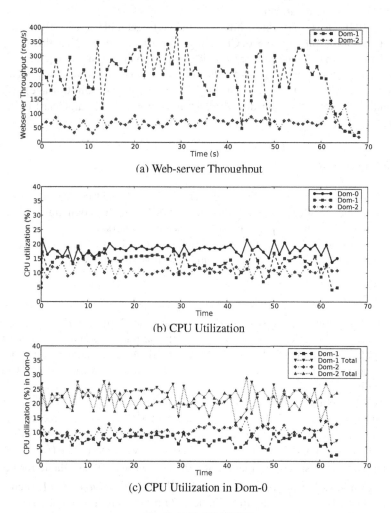

(a) Web-server Throughput

(b) CPU Utilization

(c) CPU Utilization in Dom-0

Fig. 8. With SEDF-DC

We then investigate whether we can limit the system-wide CPU usage of Domain-1 and Domain-2 to their 22% CPU share using SEDF-DC. Figure 8 shows the results of this experiment. Recall the operation of SEDF-DC: it computes the *debt* of a VM (work done by the IDD – in this case Domain-0 – on its behalf), and incrementally charges it back to the appropriate VM. This is clearly visible in Figure 8c: the *combined* utilization's of both Domain-1 and Domain-2 hover around 22% for the duration of the experiment. The oscillations result from discretization in the way we charge back debt.

Controlling combined CPU utilization for Domain-1 and 2 does impact the web servers' achievable throughput. Since the combined CPU usage of Domain-1 and 2 is limited to 22% under SEDF-DC—versus the uncontrolled values of 29.2% and 27.7% under the original SEDF scheduler—there is a drop in throughput as shown in Figure 8a. The second column of Table 1 gives the average throughput values over the run for a more concise comparison.

While SEDF-DC is capable of limiting the combined CPU usage across guest domains, it does not explicitly control CPU usage in a driver domain. Note that the split of the CPU utilization in Domain-0 for Domain-1 and Domain-2 is still unequal. Domain-1 is using 7.7% of CPU via Domain-0 (42% of overall Domain-0 usage) while Domain-2 is using 10.6% of CPU via Domain-0 (58% of overall Domain-0 usage). We turn our attention to controlling per-domain IDD utilization using ShareGuard in the next section.

5   ShareGuard

In the current Xen implementation, a driver domain does not control the amount of CPU it consumes for I/O processing on behalf of different guest domains. This lack of control may significantly impact the performance of network services. Such control is also required to enable SEDF-DC to enforce aggregate CPU usage limits. In this section we describe ShareGuard: a control mechanism to solve this problem.

5.1   Overview

ShareGuard is a control mechanism to enforce a specified limit on CPU time consumed by an IDD for I/O processing on behalf of a particular guest domain. ShareGuard periodically polls XenMon for CPU time consumed by IDDs, and if a guest domain's CPU usage is above the specified limit, then ShareGuard stops network traffic to/from the corresponding guest domain.

Let the CPU requirement of net-IDD be specified by a pair (s^{IDD}, p^{IDD}), meaning that net-IDD will receive a CPU allocation of at least s^{IDD} time units in each period of length p^{IDD} units (the time unit is typically milli-seconds). In other words, this specification is bounding CPU consumption of net-IDD over time to $CPUshare^{IDD} = \frac{s^{IDD}}{p^{IDD}}$. Let $limit_i^{IDD}$ specify a fraction of CPU time in net-IDD available for network processing on behalf of Dom_i such that $limit_i^{IDD} < CPUshare^{IDD}$. If such a limit is not set then Dom_i is entitled to unlimited I/O processing in net-IDD. Let t be the time period ShareGuard uses to evaluate current CPU usage in net-IDD and perform decision making. In the current implementation of ShareGuard, we use $t = 500\ ms$.

Using XenMon, ShareGuard collects information on CPU usage by net-IDD at every feedback interval, and computes the fraction of overall CPU time used by net-IDD for networking processing on behalf of Dom_i ($1 \leq i \leq n$) during the latest t interval. Let us denote this fraction as $used_i^{IDD}$. In each time interval t, ShareGuard determines the validity of the condition: $used_i^{IDD} \leq limit_i^{IDD}$. If this condition is violated, then Dom_i has exhausted its CPU share for network traffic processing in net-IDD. At this point, ShareGuard applies appropriate defensive actions for the next time interval t^{def}, where

$$t^{def} = t \times int \left(\frac{used_i^{IDD} + 1}{limit_i^{IDD}} \right)$$

ShareGuard performs the following defensive actions:

- **Stop accepting incoming traffic to a domain:** Since our net-IDDs run Linux, we use Linux's routing and traffic control mechanisms [15] to drop/reject traffic destined for a particular domain. In particular, we use `iptables` [16] — they are easily scriptable and configurable from user space. Similar techniques can be applied in other operating systems that may serve as wrappers for other legacy device drivers.
- **Stop processing outgoing traffic from a domain:** As in the previous case, we can use `iptables` to drop packets being transmitted *from* a domain. However, this will still incur substantial overhead in the IDD because `iptables` will only process the packet once it has traversed the network stack of the IDD. Ideally we want to drop the packet before it even enters the IDD to limit processing overhead.

    One approach would be to enforce `iptables` filtering *within* the guest domain. However, ShareGuard does not assume any cooperation from guests so we reject this option. However, we still have an attractive control point within the net-IDD where packets can be dropped before entering the net-IDDs network stack: the *net-back* driver (see Figure 3). ShareGuard sends a notification to netback identifying the target domain and the required action (drop or forward). This is akin to setting `iptables` rules, except that these rules will be applied within netback.

    Whenever netback receives an outbound packet from a domain, it will determine if there are any rules applicable to this domain. If so, it will take the specified action. This is both lightweight (in terms of overhead incurred by IDD) and flexible (in terms of control exercised by IDD).

After time interval t^{def}, ShareGuard restores normal functionality in net-IDD with respect to network traffic to/from domain Dom_i.

5.2 Evaluation

To evaluate the effectiveness of ShareGuard in isolating total domain CPU consumption, we ran the following experimental configuration. Three virtual machines run on the same physical hardware. Domain-1 and Domain-2 host web servers that support business critical services. These services have well-defined expectations for their throughput and response time. The CPU shares for these domains are set to meet these expectations. Domain-3 hosts a batch application that does some computation and performs occasional bulk data transfers. This VM supports a less important application that is not time sensitive, but needs to complete its job eventually.

In our first experiment, we observe overall performance of these three services to quantify the degree of performance isolation ShareGuard can deliver. We configure a dual-processor machine as follows: Domain-0 runs on a separate processor and set to consume at most 60% of the CPU. The second CPU hosts three VMs: Domain-1 and Domain-2 run web servers (serving 10 KB and 100 KB files respectively), and Domain-3 occasionally does a bulk file transfer. All these VMs have equal share of the second CPU, 33% each. In this initial experiment, we do not enable ShareGuard to demonstrate baseline performance characteristics. The experiments were conducted over a gigabit network, so our experiments are not network limited. In this experiment, we start a benchmark that loads web servers in Domain-1 and Domain-2 from two

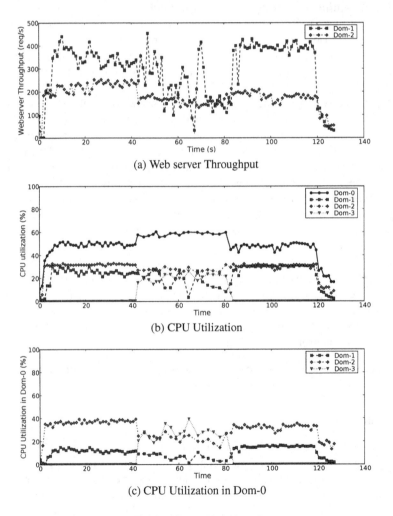

(a) Web server Throughput

(b) CPU Utilization

(c) CPU Utilization in Dom-0

Fig. 9. Without ShareGuard

separate machines using httperf for two minutes. Forty seconds into the benchmark, Domain-3 initiates a bulk-file transfer that lasts for 40 seconds.

Figure 9 shows the results as a function of time. We can clearly see the adverse impact of Domain-3's workload on both web servers' throughput (Figure 9a). Considering the split of CPU utilization in Domain-0 for the corresponding interval (Figure 9c), we find that Domain-3 uses between 20% to 30% of CPU for I/O processing in Domain-0 leaving insufficient CPU resources for I/O processing on behalf of Domain-1 and Domain-2.

The first column in Table 2 provides a summary of average metric values for the baseline case where Domain-1 and Domain-2 meet their performance expectations and deliver expected web server throughput. These metrics reflect Domain-1 and Domain-2 performance when there is no competing I/O traffic issued by Domain-3 in the experiment. Note that in this case the combined CPU utilization in Domain-0 for I/O processing by Domain-1 and Domain-2 is about 50%. Since Domain-0 is entitled to 60% of the CPU, this means that there is about 10% CPU available for additional I/O processing in Domain-0.

Table 2. ShareGuard at work: metric values are averaged over the middle 40 second segment of the runs

Metric	Baseline	Without ShareGuard	With ShareGuard
Dom-1 Web server	329.85	236.8	321.13
Dom-2 Web server	231.49	166.67	211.88
Dom-0 for Dom-1	11.55	7.26	11.9
Dom-0 for Dom-2	37.41	23.9	34.1
Dom-0 for Dom-3	N/A	23.92	4.42

The average metric values for this experiment (without ShareGuard) over the middle 40 second segment (where Domain-1, Domain-2, and Domain-3 all compete for CPU processing in Domain-0) are summarized in the second column of Table 2. Domain-3 gets 23.92% of CPU for I/O processing in Domain-0, squeezing in the CPU share available for Domain-1's and Domain-2's I/O processing. As a result, there is a significant decrease in achievable web server throughput: both web servers are delivering only 72% of their expected baseline capacity.

This example clearly indicates the impact of not controlling IDD CPU consumption by different guest domains. The question is whether ShareGuard can alleviate this problem. We repeat the experiment with ShareGuard enabled, and configure ShareGuard to limit the CPU consumption for Domain-3 in Domain-0 to 5%. Figure 10 shows the results.

Recall ShareGuard's operation: every 500 ms it evaluates CPU usage in the IDD; if a VM is violating its CPU share, it turns off all traffic processing for that VM for some time. We compute this duration such that over that interval, the average CPU utilization of the VM within the IDD will comply with the specification. This mode of operation is clearly visible in Figure 10c. We had directed ShareGuard to restrict Domain-3's consumption in Domain-0 to 5%. At $t = 40s$, ShareGuard detected that

Domain-3 had consumed almost 30% CPU in Domain-0. Accordingly, it disables traffic processing for Domain-3 for the next 2.5 seconds, such that the average utilization over this 3 second window drops to 5%. This pattern subsequently repeats ensuring that the isolation guarantee is maintained through the entire run.

Comparing Figure 9c and 10c, we see that with ShareGuard, Domain-1 and Domain-2 obtain more uniform service in Domain-0 even in the presence of Domain-3's workload. This is also visible in the CPU utilization (see Figure 10b). Finally, observe that the web-server throughput for Domain-1 and Domain-2 improve significantly under ShareGuard: both web servers deliver the expected throughput.

The third column in Table 2 provides a summary of average metric values over the middle 40 second segment with ShareGuard enabled. As we can see, CPU consumption by Domain-1 and Domain-2, as well as web server throughput are similar to the baseline

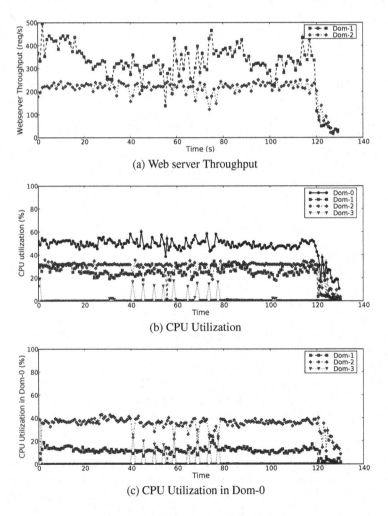

(a) Web server Throughput

(b) CPU Utilization

(c) CPU Utilization in Dom-0

Fig. 10. With ShareGuard

case. Web server performance does not degrade in presence of the bulk data transfer in Domain-3 because CPU processing in the IDD on behalf of Domain-3 is controlled by ShareGuard.

6 Discussion

All three of the components discussed in this play important, complementary tasks in enforcing performance isolation. Both SEDF-DC and ShareGuard depend on XenMon for detailed CPU utilization information. While ShareGuard is only relevant for workloads involving network I/O, SEDF-DC is agnostic to the choice of workloads — it only depends on accurate feedback on CPU utilization from XenMon.

However, SEDF-DC can only enforce guarantees on the aggregate CPU consumption of a guest and its IDD — it does not consider fair allocation of the driver domain's finite CPU resources. ShareGuard can be used to enforce such limits for networking workloads. Further, ShareGuard works irrespective of the choice of CPU scheduler. An artifact of Xen's current CPU schedulers in Xen is that SEDF-DC only works for single processor systems. ShareGuard, however, supports multi-processor systems as well. We expect that this limitation will be removed with future releases of Xen.

Finally, ShareGuard is more intrusive in the sense that it actively blocks a VM's traffic. In comparison, SEDF-DC is more passive and transparent. Also, as shown in Section 5, CPU allocation in ShareGuard is more bursty than in SEDF-DC (compare Figures 8c and 10c). All this underscores the fact that while on its own no single mechanism is perfect, working together they form a complete system.

7 Related Work

The problem of resource isolation is as old as time sharing systems. Most of the previous work in this area has focused on resource isolation between processes in an operating system or users on a single machine. In these systems, scheduling and resource management primitives do not extend to the execution of significant parts of kernel code. An application has no control over the consumption of many system resources that the kernel consumes on behalf of the application.

Consider network-intensive applications: most of the processing is typically done in the kernel and the kernel generally does not control or properly account for resources consumed during the processing of network traffic. The techniques used in ShareGuard have been inspired by earlier work addressing this problem with respect to receive live-locks in interrupt based networking subsystems. Mogul et al. [17] restrict the amount of I/O processing that the kernel does on behalf of user processes. In Lazy Receiver Processing [9] (LRP), the system uses better accounting information (such as hardware support for identifying which process an incoming packet is destined to) to improve resource isolation, e.g., such that packet processing on behalf of one process does not adversely affect the resource available to other processes.

Some of the ideas motivating LRP were extended to Resource Containers [12]. A resource container is an operating system abstraction to account for all system resources consumed by an *activity*, where an activity might span multiple processes. Resource

Containers separate the notion of resource principal from threads or processes and provide support for fine-grained resource management in operating systems. This distinction between a *protection domain* and a *resource principal* is also visible in Xen's new I/O model: a VM (the protection domain) may request service from several different IDDs, therefore the tracking of its resource usage needs to span across executions of all these domains.

One limitation of Resource Containers is that they only work for single processor systems. There does not seem to be any straightforward way of extending the notion of an *activity* to span multiple processors. This is further complicated by the fact that in most operating systems, each CPU is scheduled independently. SEDF-DC scheduler suffers from the same limitation. However, ShareGuard is both scheduler agnostic and it fully supports multi-processor systems.

The problem of performance isolation has been actively addressed by multimedia systems [8,18]. The Nemesis operating system [8] was designed to provide guaranteed quality of service (QoS) to applications. Nemesis aims to prevent *QoS crosstalk* that can occur when the operating system kernel (or a shared server) performs a significant amount of work on behalf of a number of applications. One key way in which Nemesis supports this isolation is by having applications execute as many of their own tasks as possible. Since a large proportion of the code executed on behalf of an application in a traditional operating system requires no additional privileges and does not, therefore, need to execute in a separate protection domain, the Nemesis operating system moves the majority of operating system services into the application itself, leading to a vertically structured operating system. QoS crosstalk can also occur when there is contention for physical resources, and applications do not have guaranteed access to the resources. Nemesis provides explicit low-level resource guarantees or reservations to applications. This is not limited simply to CPU: all resources including disks [19], network interfaces [20], and physical memory [21] – are treated in the same way.

The networking architecture of Nemesis still has some problems related to the charging of CPU time to applications. When the device driver transmits packets for an application, used CPU time is not charged to the application but to the device driver. Also, the handling of incoming packets before de-multiplexing it to the receiving application is charged to the device driver. We observe the same problem in the context of Xen VMM and the network driver domains, and suggest possible solution to this problem.

Exokernel [22] and Denali [23] provide resource management systems similar to vertically structured operating systems. The design goal for Exokernel was to separate protection from management. In this architecture, a minimal kernel — called Exokernel — securely multiplexes available hardware resources. It differs from the VMM approach in that it *exports* hardware resources rather than emulates them. VMMs have served as the foundation of several "security kernels" [24,25,26,27]. Denali differs from these efforts in that it aims to provide scalability as well as isolation for untrusted code, but it does not provide any specialized for performance isolation.

Most of the earlier work on VMMs focused on pursuing OS support for isolating untrusted code as a primary goal. While there is significant work on resource management in traditional operating systems, relatively less work has been performed in the context of virtual machines. Waldspurger [28] considers the problem of allocating memory across virtual machines; other systems such as Denali [23], HP SoftUDC [2] and Planetlab vServers [29] have also touched on some of these issues. Our work takes another step towards a general framework for strict resource isolation in virtual machines by considering the auxiliary work done on behalf of a guest in privileged or driver domains.

8   Conclusion and Future Work

Virtualization is fast becoming a commercially viable alternative for increasing system utilization. But from a customer perspective, virtualization cannot succeed without providing appropriate resource and performance isolation guarantees. In this work, we have proposed two mechanisms – SEDF-DC and ShareGuard – that improve CPU and network resource isolation in Xen. We demonstrated how these mechanisms enable new policies to ensure performance isolation under a variety of configurations and workloads.

For future work, we plan to extend these mechanisms to support other resources such as disk I/O and memory. Work is also underway on a hierarchical CPU scheduler for Xen: currently Xen ships with two CPU schedulers, but the choice of scheduler has to be fixed at boot time. We expect that in the future, many more CPU schedulers will become available (SEDF-DC being among the first), and that having a hierarchical scheduler that allows the use of different schedulers for different domains depending on the kinds of applications and workloads that need to be supported will enable more efficient resource utilization.

We believe that performance isolation requires appropriate resource allocation policies. Thus, another area for future investigation is policies for efficient capacity planning and workload management.

References

1. Barham, P., Dragovic, B., Fraser, K., Hand, S., Harris, T., Ho, A., Neugebauer, R., Pratt, I., Warfield, A.: Xen and the art of virtualization. In: Proc. of the 19th ACM SOSP, New York, NY (2003)
2. Kallahalla, M., Uysal, M., Swaminathan, R., Lowell, D.E., Wray, M., Christian, T., Edwards, N., Dalton, C.I., Gittler, F.: SoftUDC: A software based data center for utility computing. IEEE Computer (2004)
3. The Oceano Project.   http://www.research.ibm.com/oceanoproject/index.html: Last accessed 1/17/2006.
4. Fraser, K., Hand, S., Neugebauer, R., Pratt, I., Warfield, A., Williamson, M.: Reconstructing I/O. Technical Report UCAM-CL-TR-596, University of Cambridge (2005)
5. Cherkasova, L., Gardner, R.: Measuring CPU Overhead for I/O Processing in the Xen Virtual Machine Monitor. In: Proc. of USENIX Annual Technical Conference. (2005)
6. Chase, J.S., Levy, H.M., Feeley, M.J., Lazowska, E.D.: Sharing and protection in a single-address-space operating system. ACM Trans. Comput. Syst. 12(4) (1994) 271–307
7. Jones, M.B., Leach, P.J., Draves, R.P., J. S., .I.B.: Modular real-time resource management in the Rialto operating system. In: Proc. of the 5th HotOS, Washington, DC, USA, IEEE Computer Society (1995) 12

8. Leslie, I.M., McAuley, D., Black, R., Roscoe, T., Barham, P.T., Evers, D., Fairbairns, R., Hyden, E.: The design and implementation of an operating system to support distributed multimedia applications. IEEE Journal of Selected Areas in Communications **14**(7) (1996)

9. Druschel, P., Banga, G.: Lazy receiver processing (LRP): a network subsystem architecture for server systems. In: Proc. of the second USENIX OSDI. (1996) 261–275

10. Bruno, J., Gabber, E., Ozden, B., Silberschatz, A.: The Eclipse Operating System: Providing Quality of Service via Reservation Domains. USENIX Annual Technical Conference (1998)

11. Verghese, B., Gupta, A., Rosenblum, M.: Performance isolation: sharing and isolation in shared-memory multiprocessors. In: Proc. of the 8th International Conference on Architectural Support for Programming Languages and Operating Systems, New York, NY, USA, ACM Press (1998) 181–192

12. Banga, G., Druschel, P., Mogul, J.C.: Resource Containers: a New Facility for Resource Management in Server Systems. In: Proc. of the third USENIX OSDI, New Orleans, Louisiana (1999)

13. Gupta, D., Gardner, R., Cherkasova, L.: XenMon: QoS Monitoring and Performance Profiling Tool. Technical report, HPL-2005-187 (2005)

14. Httperf. http://www.hpl.hp.com/research/linux/httperf/

15. http://www.lartc.org/howto/: Last accessed 04/02/2006.

16. http://www.netfilter.org: Last accessed 04/02/2006.

17. Mogul, J.C., Ramakrishnan, K.K.: Eliminating receive livelock in an interrupt-driven kernel. ACM Trans. Comput. Syst. **15**(3) (1997)

18. Yuan, W., Nahrstedt, K.: Energy-efficient soft real-time cpu scheduling for mobile multimedia systems. In: Proc. of the 19th SOSP, New York, NY, USA, ACM Press (2003) 149–163

19. Barham, P.: A Fresh Approach to File System Quality of Service. In Proc. of NOSSDAV (1998)

20. Black, R., Barham, P., Donnelly, A., Stratford, N.: Protocol Implementation in a Vertically Structured Operating System. In: Proc. of IEEE Conference on Computer Networks. (1997)

21. Hand, S.M.: Self-paging in the Nemesis operating system. In: Proc. of the third USENIX OSDI, Berkeley, CA, USA, USENIX Association (1999) 73–86

22. Engler, D.R., Kaashoek, M.F., J. O'Toole, J.: Exokernel: an operating system architecture for application-level resource management. In: Proc. of the 15th ACM SOSP, New York, NY, USA, ACM Press (1995) 251–266

23. Whitaker, A., Shaw, M., Gribble, S.D.: Scale and performance in the Denali isolation kernel. In: Proc. of the 5th USENIX OSDI, Boston, MA (2002)

24. Karger, P.A.: A retrospective of the VAX VMM security kernel. IEEE Trans, on Software Engineering (1991)

25. Meushaw, R., Simard, D.: NetTop: Commercial Technology in high assurance applications. (2005)

26. Bugnion, E., Devine, S., Rosenblum, M.: Disco: running commodity operating systems on scalable multiprocessors. In: Proc. of the 16th ACM SOSP, New York, NY, USA, ACM Press (1997) 143–156

27. Creasy, R.J.: The origin of the VM/370 time-sharing system. IBM Journal of Research and Development (1982)

28. Waldspurger, C.A.: Memory resource management in VMware ESX server. In: Proc. of the 5th USENIX OSDI. (2002)

29. Chun, B., Culler, D., Roscoe, T., Bavier, A., Peterson, L., Wawrzoniak, M., Bowman, M.: PlanetLab: an overlay testbed for broad-coverage services. SIGCOMM Comput. Commun. Rev. **33**(3) (2003) 3–12

Low-Overhead Message Tracking for Distributed Messaging

Seung Jun[1] and Mark Astley[2]

[1] College of Computing, Georgia Institute of Technology, Atlanta, GA 30339, USA
[2] IBM T.J. Watson Research Center, 19 Skyline Drive, Hawthorne, NY 10532, USA

Abstract. As enterprise applications rely increasingly on commodity messaging middleware, message tracking has become instrumental in testing and run-time monitoring. However, building an effective message tracking system is challenging because of the large scale and high message rate of enterprise-wide applications. To address this challenge, we consider the case of message tracking for distributed messaging middleware. We desire to record the origin, path, and destination of every application message while imposing low overhead with respect to latency, memory and storage. To achieve our goal, we propose a tunable approximation approach based on Bloom filter "histories." Our approach is tunable in the sense that more accurate audit trails may be provided at the expense of storage space, or, conversely, storage overhead is reduced for applications requiring less accurate audit trails. We describe the design of the system and demonstrate its utility by analyzing the performance of a prototype implementation.

1 Introduction

The development of enterprise business applications has increasingly relied on commodity messaging middleware for component connectivity and interaction. Because the enterprise no longer implements the underlying communication framework, message traceback and audit trails will become an important administrative capability during development and for monitoring and problem determination at run-time. Past exploration in messaging middleware [5] suggests message rates on the order of thousands of messages per second, distributed to tens of thousands of clients. On this scale, a naive logging approach may impose unacceptable overhead and may rapidly exhaust persistent resources such as disk. Thus, we need an efficient message tracking system to accommodate high volume of traffic.

In this paper, we consider the specific case of message tracking for publish-subscribe messaging middleware based on the Java Messaging Service API [4]. We choose to focus on publish-subscribe, rather than more general messaging (*e.g.* queuing), because we believe that the large scale and high message rate of publish-subscribe middleware presents the greatest challenge for message tracking. Given a network of publish-subscribe message servers we wish to:

- Record the origin, path, and destination of every message routed by the system;
- Support traceback queries for previously sent messages; and
- Impose low runtime overhead with respect to latency, memory footprint, and disk storage.

M. van Steen and M. Henning (Eds.): Middleware 2006, LNCS 4290, pp. 363–381, 2006.
© IFIP International Federation for Information Processing 2006

To support tracking for publish-subscribe messaging, we have developed a tunable approximation approach based on Bloom filters [6], which trades accuracy for low overhead and efficient use of persistent resources. Our approach is tunable in the sense that more accurate audit trails may be provided at the expense of more frequent high-overhead operations (*e.g.* storing buffers to disk). Conversely, overhead can be reduced for applications which require less accurate audit trails.

While Bloom filters are often used as an efficient, approximate cache [8, 15], a novel feature of our approach is the organization of Bloom filters into "histories" which record an indefinite record of message paths for later query. We present theoretical results which specify clock synchronization and message jitter limits in order to maintain accurate histories. Similarly, we evaluate a prototype implementation in order to highlight trade-offs between performance, accuracy, and resource utilization.

The remainder of the paper is organized as follows. In Section 2, we define a tracking facility in the context of publish-subscribe messaging. In Section 3, we describe the design and implementation of our system, and analyze the accuracy of our design in Section 4. In Section 5, we evaluate performance. In Section 6, we describe related work. We summarize our results and discuss future work in Section 7.

2   Tracking for Distributed Messaging

Messaging middleware is a popular "glue" technology which provides the means for applications to interact with one another using a variety of interaction patterns. In addition to proprietary interfaces, most messaging middleware products support the Java Message Service (JMS) API, which defines messaging services within the Java 2 Enterprise Edition specification [3]. We focus on the publish-subscribe portion of JMS although our techniques are readily extended to other distribution patterns and/or other messaging APIs.

We define a tracking facility for publish-subscribe messaging as follows:

> *Given the unique ID of a message, the tracking facility will report the origin of the message, the messaging servers which routed the message, and the set of clients to which the message was delivered. The message may have been accepted for delivery at an arbitrary time in the past.*

We assume that the tracking facility is queried after a message has been completely routed. However, our techniques may be used to provide partial tracking information if earlier queries are necessary.

In the context of JMS, each message has a vendor specific unique ID which is assigned when the message has been accepted for delivery. A message has been accepted for delivery when the "publish" call returns at the publisher. Thus, the JMS message ID is a valid input to the tracking facility once the "publish" call completes. Although the message ID is first known to the publisher, we assume that any entity may issue a traceback query with an appropriate message ID.

The implementation of the tracking facility is divided into two distinct components. The *message tracking* component records the routes of messages as they are distributed through the messaging system. The *path reconstruction* component uses tracking records to reconstruct the complete path of a routed message. While we focus on efficient message tracking in this paper, we provide a brief description of how path reconstruction may be implemented in Section 3.3.

3 System Design

We develop our tracking facility as a component in the Gryphon system [1], which is a robust, highly-scalable messaging system that implements the publish-subscribe portion of JMS. Gryphon is representative of a large class of middleware routing infrastructures and consists of an overlay network of messaging *brokers*, each of which may host one or more network-connected *clients* (*i.e.* publishers and subscribers). A typical publish-subscribe message is routed as follows:

1. The message is created by the publisher and submitted to the associated broker for delivery.
2. The broker receives the message and determines (a) which locally attached subscribers (if any) should receive the message, and (b) which neighboring brokers (if any) should receive the message. It then routes the message to the appropriate local subscribers and neighboring brokers.
3. Neighboring brokers repeat this process until all appropriate brokers and subscribers have received the message.

In Gryphon, the network topology forms an arbitrarily connected graph. Routes are determined by spanning trees so that each broker receives a message from at most one neighbor. In addition, Gryphon provides ordered links between brokers and we assume that brokers do not arbitrarily reorder in-flight messages. Failures may require retransmission and hence introduce duplicate messages. For the moment, we assume there are no duplicate messages. We discuss modifications for handling duplicates in Section 4.3. Thus, the current discussion assumes ordered, tree-based routing without duplicate messages.

To facilitate tracking, the JMS ID of each message is augmented with a tuple $r = (p, b, t)$, where p is the unique ID of the publisher of the message, b is the unique ID of the broker to which the publisher is attached, and t is a monotonically increasing time stamp. The time stamp is generated locally by the publisher and may include a "skew adjustment" as described in Section 3.2. The values for p and b are stored at the publisher when it connects to a broker. The JMS ID is set by the publisher-side implementation of the JMS "publish" method.

3.1 Bloom Filter Histories

Each broker maintains one or more local Bloom filter "histories" which are a compressed record of message traffic. Histories consist of both in-memory and persisted (*i.e.* stored to disk) data, and are further partitioned according to message sender (as described in the next section).

A Bloom filter [6] is a data structure for representing a set of n elements called *keys*, comprised of an m-bit vector, v, (initialized to zeros) and associated with k hash functions whose range is $\{1, \ldots, m\}$. Let $v[i]$ $(1 \leq i \leq m)$ denote the ith element of the bit vector v. Given k hash functions $f_1, \ldots, f_k$, a Bloom filter supports two operations:

- ADD(r) adds the key r to the set of elements stored in the filter. That is, ADD(r) sets $v[f_j(r)] = 1$ for $j = 1, \ldots, k$.
- CONTAINS(r) returns *true* if the key r is stored in the filter or *false* otherwise. That is, CONTAINS(r) returns *true* if and only if $v[f_j(r)] = 1$ for each $j = 1, \ldots, k$.

Bloom filters are efficient in both speed and size because hash functions typically execute in constant time (assuming constant key size) and because the set of stored keys requires no more than m bits of storage. On the other hand, as hash functions may collide, Bloom filters are subject to *false positives*. That is, CONTAINS(r) may return *true* even if r is not actually stored in the filter. False positives affect the accuracy of the tracking facility and are discussed in Section 4.

Given a particular accuracy requirement, the capacity, n, of a Bloom filter is a function of m and k. Adding more keys beyond the capacity will degrade the accuracy of the filter. Therefore, when a filter reaches its capacity it is stored to disk, and a new filter is created to record subsequent keys. If a system failure occurs before a filter is stored, then the contents of the filter are lost. Therefore, to avoid excessive loss when message rates are low, filters are also periodically stored to disk according to the *persistence interval*, T_p, which specifies the maximum delay before which the current filter must be stored.

The in-memory filters and the set of filters stored to disk are paired with indexing information to form *filter histories*. That is, a filter history, H, is defined as a sequence $(B_1, R_1), \ldots, (B_j, R_j)$, where each B_i is a Bloom filter, and each R_i is a range of timestamps of the form $[t_{s,i}, t_{e,i}]$. The time range associated with each Bloom filter is used as a query index by the *path reconstruction* component. A history has at most one in-memory pair (B_j, R_j), called the *current filter*, with all other pairs being stored to disk.

Histories have a single operation: ADD(r, t). Given a history H with current filter (B_j, R_j), the ADD(r, t) operation invokes ADD(r) on B_j and updates R_j to include t as follows:

$$R_j = \begin{cases} [t, t] & \text{if previous } R_j \text{ is } \emptyset, \\ [t, t_b] & \text{if previous } R_j = [t_a, t_b] \text{ and } t < t_a, \\ [t_a, t] & \text{if previous } R_j = [t_a, t_b] \text{ and } t > t_b, \\ [t_a, t_b] & \text{otherwise.} \end{cases}$$

Given a filter history H and a time stamp t, we define the *matching set* as the set $M(H, t)$ of filters such that

$$M(H, t) = \{B_i \mid (B_i, R_i) \in H \text{ and } t \in R_i\}.$$

A matching set determines which filters should be queried when reconstructing the path of a message. We achieve the required accuracy and efficiency of our system by carefully managing the size of matching sets as explained in Section 4.

3.2 Message Tracking Component

Message tracking requires that we record JMS messages IDs at various points in the system. Messages are tracked in three phases. In the *publishing phase*, a publisher generates and sends a message to a local broker. This broker, called the publishing broker, is responsible for recording the originating publisher for each message. In the *routing phase*, the message is tracked at each intermediate broker to which it is forwarded. Finally, in the *delivery phase* the message is delivered by one or more brokers to interested local subscribers. The delivering brokers are required to record the set of subscribers which receive the message.

State Initialization. A publisher acquires its ID, p, and the broker ID, b, at connection time. Each publisher also maintains a skew adjustment, δ, which is used to adjust locally generated timestamps so that they remain within a certain bound relative to the broker's clock. The skew adjustment is necessary to bound matching set size, as explained in Section 4.2. At publisher connection time, δ is initialized to the value $t_b - t_p$, where t_b is the current local time at the broker, and t_p is the current time at the publishing client. To correct for clock drift, the value of δ is updated as described below.

Tracking information is only stored at brokers. Specifically, each broker is initialized with the following state:

- **Skew tolerance**, T_s, determines the maximum separation between the time stamp of a message submitted by a local publisher and the broker's local clock.
- **Persistence interval**, T_p, determines the persistence interval of each local filter history.
- **Publisher history**, H_P, is a filter history that is used to record the set of messages sent by local publishers.
- **Routing history**, H_b, is a filter history that is used to record the set of messages originated by each broker b. Thus, a broker maintains multiple routing histories as discussed later.
- **Subscriber history**, $H_{b,s}$, is a filter history that is used to record messages originated by broker b and delivered to local subscriber s. A broker maintains multiple subscriber histories depending on the number of brokers and subscribers.
- **Subscriber attachment map**, S_m, is a data structure which maintains the local subscriber membership and a sequence of local timestamps indicating when the membership last changed. This map is used to reconstruct the set of subscribers which may have received a message. Although subscribers may arrive or depart frequently, the set of changes at a particular point in time are assumed to be small. We assume membership changes (and the time stamp of the change) are stored reliably to disk.

The skew tolerance, T_s, and the persistence interval, T_p, are local values which may be different at each broker. However, some care is necessary when choosing these values as they affect the overall accuracy of the tracking system. We discuss how to determine the values for T_s and T_p to achieve the desired accuracy in Section 4. In each of the phases below, we assume that filters are automatically stored to disk when full or when the persistence interval expires as described in Section 3.1. We also assume that the Bloom filter parameters m, k, and n are global settings.

Publishing Phase. In the publishing phase, the publishing client creates a message, assigns an ID, and delivers the message to the broker. The ID is constructed as a tuple

$r = (p, b, t + \delta)$, where δ is the skew adjustment. The broker verifies $|t_b - (t + \delta)| \leq T_s$. If the message is out of tolerance, then δ is recomputed (e.g. $\delta = t_b - t$) and sent back to the publisher. The broker records the message in the local publisher history by invoking ADD$(r, t + \delta)$ on H_P.

Routing Phase. In the routing phase, the local broker extracts the message ID $r = (p, b, t')$ and creates the routing history H_b for the originating broker b if it does not already exist. Then, the broker records the message in H_b by invoking ADD(r, t') on H_b.

Delivery Phase. In the delivery phase, the local broker extracts the message ID $r = (p, b, t')$ and determines the unique IDs of the set of local subscribers $s_1, \ldots, s_j$ which should receive the message. For each subscriber s_i, the broker instantiates the subscriber history H_{b,s_i}, if necessary, and stores r in the subscriber history by invoking ADD(r, t') on H_{b,s_i}. Once each subscriber has been recorded, the message may be delivered.

3.3 Path Reconstruction Component

The path for a given message can be reconstructed by searching the broker network in a depth- or breadth-first manner. We first describe a basic algorithm for this process, and then consider optimizations and complexity.

Let $r = (p, b, t)$ be the ID of the message for which we wish to reconstruct a path. Note that b denotes the ID of the publishing broker where the message originated. We first initialize the following query state:

- K_r, initially $\emptyset$, is the set of brokers that routed the message.
- K_s, initially $\emptyset$, is the set of brokers which delivered the message to a subscriber.
- S_r is the set of subscriber IDs to which the message was delivered.
- K_a is the set of brokers to explore and is initialized to $\{b\}$.
- K_e is the set of brokers already explored and is initialized to $\emptyset$.

Starting from the originating broker b, the algorithm fills K_r, K_s, and S_r using K_a and K_e as follows:

- While $K_a \neq \emptyset$:
  1. Choose $i \in K_a$ and set $K_a \leftarrow K_a - \{i\}$. Set $K_e \leftarrow K_e \cup \{i\}$.
  2. If broker i contains the routing history H_b, it searches for the queried message in this history. Let $M(H_b, t)$ be the matching set for routing history H_b and time stamp t. If there exists $B_j \in M(H, t)$ such that CONTAINS(r) on B_j is true, then set $K_r \leftarrow K_r \cup \{i\}$.
  3. Let S_m be the set of subscribers retrieved from the subscriber attachment map which were attached to broker i at time t. For each subscriber s in S_m:
     (a) Let $H_{b,s}$ be the subscriber history with source broker b and subscriber s.
     (b) If there exists $B_j \in M(H_{b,s}, t)$ such that CONTAINS(r) on B_j is true, then set $S_r \leftarrow S_r \cup \{s\}$ and $K_s \leftarrow K_s \cup \{i\}$.
  4. For each neighbor j of broker i, such that $j \notin K_e$, set $K_a \leftarrow K_a \cup \{j\}$.

Upon termination, b, K_r and K_s can be used (along with the broker topology) to reconstruct the route of the message. Similarly, S_r gives the set of subscribers to which the message was delivered.

Reconstruction Complexity and Optimization. Assuming no false positives (we consider the effect of false positives in Section 4.3), the time required to reconstruct a path for a given message is proportional, namely $O(N)$, to the number of brokers, N, which routed the message. It is difficult to improve on this basic complexity result under the current design where filters act as membership tests and provide little information to simplify path reconstruction. However, the size of the constant term can be reduced as discussed below.

The constant search cost at each broker depends on the number of histories which must be queried, and the number of neighboring brokers which must be queried. At each broker (except the originating broker), an efficient search is accomplished by first sampling the local routing history, and then sampling the local subscriber histories if the routing history indicates that the local broker routed the message. Thus, in the worst case, if M is the matching set size, and the maximum number of subscribers a broker may host (at any time) is S, then at each step at most $S + 1$ histories will be queried or $(S + 1) \times M$ invocations of the CONTAINS operation. Since CONTAINS takes constant time (with constant key size) and S and M are constants, the history query cost is constant but tunable by adjusting S and M.

During the path reconstruction, a broker must query every neighboring broker about the traced message, which may incur unnecessary communication cost particularly when the message was delivered to only a small number of neighbors (*i.e.* when the message was sparsely routed). If communication cost is roughly constant, then let W be the cost of communicating with a neighboring broker, verifying that its local history did not track a message, and receiving the reply. If D is the maximum number of neighbors for any broker, then there is a constant communication cost no greater than $D \times W$ incurred during path reconstruction at each broker which routed a message.

There are at least two methods for reducing communication overhead. The first is to require brokers to store routing histories of the form $H_{b,d}$ where a message is recorded in $H_{b,d}$ if it originated from broker b and was forwarded to neighboring broker d. This eliminates unnecessary communication during path reconstruction (assuming no false positives) at the cost of complicating the configuration of T_s and T_p, which must be sensitive to the rate at which filters are filled (see Section 4.2). In particular, sparsely routed messages may yield drastically different fill rates for two given histories $H_{b,d}$ and $H_{b,d'}$.

A second approach is to store "routing set" information as part of the key recorded in routing histories. For example, if maximum out degree is D and neighboring brokers are numbered 0 through $D - 1$, then we can store a modified message ID $r' = (p, b, t', d)$ where d is a D-bit value with bit i set if neighbor i was forwarded the message. At path reconstruction time, we must now perform 2^D queries of the local routing history in order to determine where to continue the search. This approach is feasible when $O(\text{CONTAINS}) \times M \times 2^D$ is less than $W \times D$.

3.4 Discussion

As described in Section 4, applying skew adjustments to message timestamps is critical to ensuring tracking accuracy. However, skew adjustments could be eliminated if timestamps were assigned at the broker rather than the publisher. The decision to assign timestamps at the publisher is a deliberate choice to avoid a performance penalty. If timestamps were assigned at the broker, then each call to "publish" could not complete until a reply was received from the broker since message IDs include the time stamp and the ID must be valid before returning from "publish". This may not be significant when publishing reliably since the time stamp could be piggy-backed on the acknowledgment we expect for each message, but best-effort publishing does not require any acknowledgment. Therefore, we allow publishers to assign timestamps and use skew adjustments to manage disparate publisher clocks.

At a given broker, the current implementation uses separate router histories for each broker from which messages are originated. One may wonder if it is possible to simplify the design, for example by aggregating routing histories into a single history which records traces for all non-local brokers. In the current design, aggregation is undesirable for two reasons. First, aggregating incoming messages causes filters to be filled at a higher rate. Second, without careful clock synchronization, consecutive filters may have a larger than expected overlap in their range components. Both of these effects increase the size of the matching set which results in lower tracking accuracy as discussed in Section 4. The same reasoning applies to aggregation of subscriber histories.

Nonetheless, an aggregate history would be feasible under certain conditions. Namely, the filter capacity would need to be large enough to accommodate the higher aggregate input rate; and, T_p would need to be at least as large as the T_p of any broker for which messages are being aggregated. Such a history is essentially equivalent to the sum of the individual histories we use in the current design. In particular, the net effect on overall storage consumption (memory or disk) is identical since both approaches have the same capacity and the same total number of messages are recorded in either case.

4   Analysis

Bloom filters provide efficient space utilization at the expense of reduced accuracy. In this section, we describe how to compute the accuracy of our tracking facility in terms of Bloom filter accuracy and the size of history matching sets. We then describe how the tracking facility bounds matching set size in order to guarantee particular accuracy requirements.

4.1   Bloom Filter Accuracy

The *false positive probability* (*fpp*) of a Bloom filter is the probability that an invocation of CONTAINS will return *true* for a message that is not stored. Assuming that the output from the k hash functions is independent and uniformly distributed, *fpp* is determined by the expression [7]:

$$fpp = \left(1 - \left(1 - \frac{1}{m}\right)^{kn}\right)^k \tag{1}$$

where m is the size of the Bloom filter in bits, and n is the number of entries stored in the filter. Conversely, given a desired *fpp*, we can determine k, m, and n such that the required accuracy is met. We give an example of this process in Section 5.

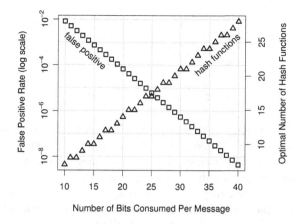

Fig. 1. False positive rate

Figure 1 helps determine the appropriate parameters. It shows that false positive rate decreases exponentially as the number of bits consumed per message (that is, m/n) grows with the optimal number of hash functions (that is, k) used for the given x-axis value.

We refer to the accuracy of the entire tracking system as the *expected false positive probability* (*efpp*). If all filters are identical (and hence have the same *fpp*), the *efpp* is determined by the size of the matching set:

$$efpp = 1 - (1 - fpp)^{|M|} \tag{2}$$

where $|M|$ is the maximum size of the matching set. If $|M|$ is known and bounded, it is possible to guarantee a particular *efpp*.

The choice of *efpp* affects both tracking and path reconstruction performance. During tracking, *efpp* constrains Bloom filter parameters and the required matching set size. These two values in turn affect the allowable skew among messages. If clocks can drift substantially, then more stringent *efpp* settings will require more frequent skew correction messages. During path reconstruction, the size of the matching set determines the number of filters which may need to be queried. Similarly, *efpp* reflects the likelihood of generating erroneous search results. Erroneous search results both increase path reconstruction overhead, by forcing searches down incorrect paths, and may corrupt results, by including incorrect brokers and subscribers on the path of a message. In the next section, we describe how matching set size is bounded by *efpp*. We discuss the effect of *efpp* on path reconstruction in Section 4.3.

4.2 Bounding Matching Sets

In this section, we derive a bound on matching set size in order to ensure a desired tracking accuracy (*i.e. efpp*). The size of matching sets is determined by the skew in timestamps of messages and the frequency of filter replacement (*i.e.* the rate at which filters in a history are stored).

Fig. 2. Persistence of Bloom filter

Recall that the time stamp of a message ID is adjusted according to a skew adjustment, δ, for each publisher. Given a skew tolerance, T_s, the skew adjustment in the publishing phase ensures that timestamps generated simultaneously by different publishers of the same broker never differ by more than $2\,T_s$.

A filter is stored to disk either when it has reached its capacity or when the persistence interval has expired. Let T_f represent the time required to exhaust filter capacity at the peak message rate. That is, if c denotes the filter capacity (number of messages), and r denotes the maximum aggregate publishing rate (messages per unit time) from all publishers attached to a broker, then $T_f = c/r$. Likewise, let T_p indicate the time after which a filter must be stored to disk to reduce the data loss from a failure.

As a filter is replaced for the two reasons described above, the minimum filter lifetime T_n is defined as the minimum of T_f and T_p. On the other hand, the maximum filter lifetime is T_p by definition.

Given a T_n defined as above, we first consider the bounds on the size of matching sets for the publisher history and then expand the result into the cases of the routing histories and the subscriber histories. Theorem 1 formalizes the intuition that more accurate clock synchronization results in smaller matching set.

Theorem 1. *If* $2\,T_s \leq w\,T_n$, *where* w *is a non-negative integer, the size of matching set does not exceed* $w + 1$.

Proof. Figure 2 illustrates the time line of Bloom filter persistence. Let B_i be the ith persisted Bloom filter for a publishing history. The filter B_i is used from time t_i, inclusive, to time t_{i+1}, exclusive, with respect to the broker's clock. The time interval T_i is defined as $t_{i+1} - t_i$. From the definition of T_n, it follows $T_n \leq T_i$ for all i. The function $\text{MAXTS}[B_i]$ returns the maximum of timestamps contained in B_i (*i.e.* the second element of the time stamp range R_i), and $\text{MINTS}[B_i]$ returns the minimum (*i.e.* the first element of R_i). It suffices to prove that the time stamp range of B_i never overlaps with that of B_{i+w+1}.

$$\text{MAXTS}[B_i] < t_{i+1} + T_s$$
$$\text{MINTS}[B_{i+w+1}] \geq t_{i+w+1} - T_s$$
$$= t_{i+1} + \left(\sum_{j=1}^{w} T_{i+j} \right) - T_s$$
$$\geq t_{i+1} + wT_n - T_s$$
$$\geq t_{i+1} + T_s$$

Since the maximum time stamp in B_i is less than the minimum time stamp in B_{i+w+1}, the two ranges never overlap.

We would like to derive a similar result in order to bound matching set size for routing and subscriber histories. However, before we can do so, there are three complications that must be considered. First, since JMS subscriptions support content-based filtering, many messaging systems, including Gryphon, avoid routing messages down paths where there are no matching subscribers. As a result, a downstream broker b_2 may not see all the messages originated at an upstream broker b_1. However, this reduced fill rate does not increase matching set size and therefore does not reduce accuracy.

Second, the relative T_p values may be different at the source and downstream brokers. This is only a concern if some downstream broker has a T_p less than T_n at the source. In that case, the downstream broker may store filters at a higher rate and potentially violate the matching set bounds. For the moment, we assume this is not the case, and describe modifications for $T_p < T_n$ in the discussion below.

Finally, during forwarding, messages are subject to jitter, the time between the shortest message latency and the longest. Message jitter can increase the size of the matching set unless we account for it when determining the skew constraints. The following corollary formalizes this intuition:

Corollary 2. *Suppose T_j is the maximum jitter of messages. If $2T_s + T_j \leq w\,T_n$, where w is a non-negative integer, the size of matching set does not exceed $w + 1$.*

The proof is similar to that of Theorem 1 and is omitted. If T_j includes the expected skew among brokers, then corollary 2 can be used to determine the required clock synchronization among brokers.

As a guide to configuration, the persistence interval, T_p, at a given broker should be slightly larger than T_f, the time required to fill a filter at the maximum aggregate publish rate. This ensures that filters are nearly full when stored. The value for *efpp* is determined according to administrative requirements. This value can be used to guide tradeoffs between desired Bloom filter parameters (and indirectly the maximum T_f that can be supported), and desired matching set size. Once matching set size is known, the skew tolerance, T_s, at a given broker should be set to maintain the bound provided by Theorem 1.

4.3 Discussion

Besides determining matching set size requirements, the choice of *efpp* also affects path reconstruction as described in Section 3.3. In particular, a false positive may cause an unnecessary search during path reconstruction, which occurs when a neighbor finds a false positive in a local routing history, causing all of the local subscriber histories to be erroneously searched, and causing further unnecessary queries to the next set of downstream brokers.

For typical *efpp* values, the expected number of unnecessary searches is quite small. If a given broker has at most D' neighbors which did **not** observe a message, then the expected number of unnecessary searches (of one hop) that this broker will conduct is just the expected value of a binomial expression with parameters D' and *efpp*:

$$\sum_{i=1}^{D'} i \binom{D'}{i} efpp^i (1 - efpp)^{D'-i} = D' \cdot efpp$$

Using the example *efpp* of 0.00001 from Section 5.1 and a D' of 5, this expected value is only 0.00005. At the highest *efpp* we tested, 0.05, the expected value is 0.25 (same D') or about one unnecessary one-hop search for every four brokers in the network. Note that if it is only critical to properly reconstruct the set of subscribers which received a message, then the probability of a false positive harmfully affecting the search results is reduced to $efpp^2 < efpp$ since both the local routing history and a subscriber history must report a false positive.

When applying Theorem 1 to the distributed case, we assumed that T_n at a source broker was less than the T_p at any downstream broker. In the event that there is some downstream broker b with T_p such that $T_p < T_n$, then b will store (partially full) filters more frequently than the source broker and will violate matching set size bounds. One way to avoid this problem is to retain the current filter even though it has been stored to disk, and overwrite the previous copy when filter capacity is finally reached. With this approach, only full filters are written and never at a rate higher than the source broker. The resulting filter is equivalent to the union [7] of the partially full filters that would normally have been stored separately to disk.

For space reasons, we have ignored the issue of retransmitted messages (*e.g.* retransmission due to failure), which are an unfortunate reality in large distributed systems. Retransmitted messages are only an issue when their time stamp is older than the oldest time permitted by the skew bounds in the current filter. We handle this case by adding a "singleton" set, S, to each filter history element, *e.g.* (B, R, S). The singleton set stores individual timestamps rather than a range. Retransmitted messages are stored in the current filter as usual except that their time stamp updates S rather than R. The notion of matching set is updated to include S, and filter capacity must now incorporate the maximum number of retransmissions which a filter may accommodate. This approach is tenable if the number of "old" messages per filter has a reasonable bound.

Finally, while the subscriber attachment map, S_m, is recorded using the clock of the broker hosting subscribers, the map is accessed during path reconstruction using the time stamp attached to the message, which may be skewed from the local broker. Thus, the time stamp should be adjusted by the clock skew between the two brokers. Since pairwise skews are difficult to maintain, the maximum possible skew among brokers is used for skew adjustment at the expense of potentially larger matching set. However, since this inaccuracy occurs only around join and departure, it should not affect the overall tracking accuracy in any significant way.

5   Implementation and Evaluation

We have implemented our tracking facility as an extension to the Gryphon messaging system. We refer to this implementation as the BF strategy. To evaluate our approach, we also implemented two other tracking strategies. The NULL strategy does not provide any tracking capability and serves as a baseline for performance comparisons. The ASYNC strategy is a "naive" logger which simply buffers each tracking event and periodically flushes the buffer to disk. This strategy is naive in the sense that in-memory records are not compressed and therefore the buffer must be flushed more frequently than a comparably sized BF buffer.

5.1 Implementation

In order to create message IDs with the proper tracking information, we have extended the Gryphon message ID implementation as illustrated in Table 1. The publisher is configured with a publisher ID and broker ID at connection time. The time stamp is recorded in milliseconds relative to the publisher's local time. A counter field is used to disambiguate messages which happen to be generated within the same millisecond. Our implementation synchronizes publisher clocks with local brokers so that $2\,T_s < T_n$ where T_n is either the time required to fill a filter at the peak messaging rate or T_p, whichever is smaller (see Section 4.2). This ensures that the size of the matching set is no greater than two.

Table 1. Message ID

Field	Length
Publisher ID	4 Bytes
Broker ID	4 Bytes
Time stamp	6 Bytes
Counter	2 Bytes

For a given *efpp* and the requirement that at most two filters overlap, we can generate corresponding Bloom filter parameters m, n and k. For example, an *efpp* of 0.00001 (five nines accuracy) corresponds to an *fpp* of less than $1 - \sqrt{0.99999} \approx 5 \times 10^{-6}$ for each filter. To satisfy this level of accuracy, we might choose $\frac{m}{n}$ to be 26 and k to be 16, so that the capacity of the each filter, n, is limited by the size of the filter m.

The number and range of the hash functions are determined by k and m, respectively. For our implementation, we derive hash functions using one or more applications of MD5 [13], with each application providing 128 hashed bits. To generate independent hashes, we prepend a random, unique prefix byte for each application. The output bits are then divided into k equal segments each addressing a range of m. For example, if $k = 16$ and $m = 65536$, we might use two applications of MD5 divided into 16 segments of 16 bits each.

5.2 Experimental Setup

We evaluated our approach by measuring experimental performance for each of the three strategies (BF, NULL and ASYNC). We consider two performance metrics for evaluation:

End-to-End Latency: The elapsed time from the publication of a message and its delivery to one matching client. This measure is an indirect indication of overhead which includes processor overhead (*i.e.* the per-message computation cost imposed by tracking) and I/O overhead (*i.e.* the per-message cost to store tracking records to disk).

Storage: The total disk storage used by each strategy. For the BF strategy, this is the size of the stored history of filters. For the ASYNC strategy, this is the size of the stored buffers.

For evaluation purposes we only considered measurements for a single broker. Since the various tracking strategies only impose processing and disk overhead (*i.e.* they do not alter routing protocols or introduce network traffic), the single broker case allows for more accurate measurements without loss of generality.

Each strategy was tested on a dedicated gigabit LAN consisting of 5 6-way 500 MHz PowerPC servers each with 4 GB of memory running AIX. The test setup consisted of one Gryphon broker hosting 200 publishers and 500 subscribers. A total of 500 topics were used, with each subscriber subscribing to a single topic, and each publisher publishing to ten topics. Subscribers were randomly distributed among the topics but a small portion of the topics had no subscribers. The aggregate input rate was 5000 messages per second (25 messages per second per publisher) divided evenly among all topics so that each subscriber received approximately ten messages per second (*i.e.* the aggregate output rate was 5000 messages per second). The broker ran on a dedicated machine, the publishers were spread evenly over two machines, and the subscribers were spread evenly over two machines. Each strategy was tested separately at a run length of 30 minutes.

Table 2. Test Configurations. If "stores full buffers" is "yes", then buffers were filled before T_p expired. For the BF strategy, we show the corresponding configurations for n (filter capacity), m (filter size in bits), and k (number of hash functions).

Strategy	Buffer Limit	Accuracy	T_p (seconds)	Stores Full Buffers?
NULL	N/A	N/A	N/A	N/A (baseline)
ASYNC	10K	100%	1	Yes
ASYNC	135K	100%	1	No
ASYNC	135K	100%	2	Yes
BF	10K	99.999% - n=2521, m=64K, k=16	1	Yes
BF	10K	99% - n=5461, m=64K, k=8	1	No
BF	10K	95% - n=7281, m=64K, k=8	1	No
BF	10K	99% - n=5461, m=64K, k=8	2	Yes
BF	10K	95% - n=7281, m=64K, k=8	2	Yes
BF	135K	99.999% - n=38836, m=1M, k=12	1	No
BF	135K	99% - n=87381, m=1M, k=6	1	No
BF	135K	95% - n=131072, m=1M, k=6	1	No
BF	135K	99.999% - n=38836, m=1M, k=12	2	No
BF	135K	99% - n=87381, m=1M, k=6	2	No
BF	135K	95% - n=131072, m=1M, k=6	2	No
BF	135K	99.999% - n=38836, m=1M, k=12	8	Yes
BF	135K	99% - n=87381, m=1M, k=6	8	No
BF	135K	95% - n=131072, m=1M, k=6	8	No
BF	135K	99% - n=87381, m=1M, k=6	18	Yes
BF	135K	95% - n=131072, m=1M, k=6	18	No
BF	135K	95% - n=131072, m=1M, k=6	27	Yes

We constructed two test scenarios which differed in the limits they placed on in-memory buffers. The first scenario limited buffers (*e.g.* publisher, routing or subscriber tracking records) to 10000 bytes. The second scenario limited buffers to 135000 bytes. For each scenario, we varied T_p so that we could observe the effects of storing full or partially full buffers. Finally, we used three different accuracy requirements when configuring the BF strategy. Table 2 summarizes the various test configurations.

5.3   Results

Latency was measured as the round trip time for a special latency message and includes both the tracking overhead for the message, as well as the overhead of competing with tracking for other in-flight messages. Figure 3 gives the average latency for our test configurations. The NULL strategy was also measured as a reference point.

In the first scenario, the BF strategy performs significantly better than the ASYNC strategy and imposes only slight overhead as compared to the NULL strategy. This behavior is easily understood by considering the frequency of disk operations. With a 10000 byte in-memory limit and message ID size of 16 bytes, the ASYNC strategy can record at most 625 messages between disk forces. With an aggregate message rate of 5000 messages per second, this corresponds to approximately eight disk forces per second. In contrast, the highest reliability BF strategy can accommodate 2521 messages in the given memory limit, or slightly less than two writes a second. With four times as many disk forces per second, the ASYNC strategy is at a severe disadvantage when in-memory constraints are tight. The second scenario shows that, not surprisingly, reducing the frequency of disk forces is the key to controlling latency. With the higher memory limit, ASYNC can accommodate about 8437 messages between disk forces and shows performance comparable with NULL. For the BF strategy, disk forces are never a critical factor and larger buffers do not impose any significant latency overhead.

Even with larger buffers, however, the lack of in-memory compression in the ASYNC strategy makes it highly sensitive to message rate and ID size. Thus, while ASYNC achieves acceptable performance for the message rate we tested, the BF strategy has more tolerance for significant increases in rate, and is not dependent on ID size. For example, quadrupling the message rate (*i.e.* 20000 messages per second) would cause slightly less than three disk forces per second for ASYNC whereas even the highest

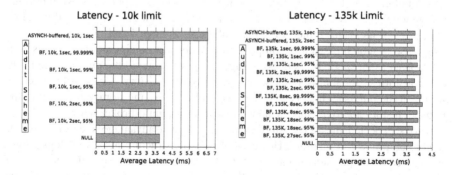

Fig. 3. Latency Comparison

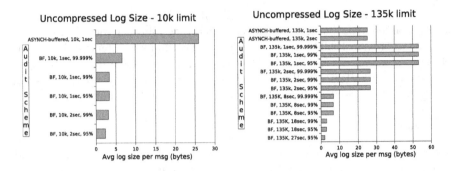

Fig. 4. Uncompressed storage use

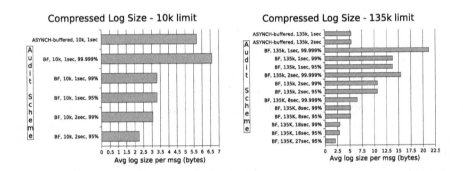

Fig. 5. Compressed storage use

accuracy BF configuration would still be storing nearly half-empty filters. Similarly, doubling the ID size halves the storage capacity of ASYNC without any effect on BF.

Neither ASYNC nor BF attempt further compression before forcing buffers to disk. It is reasonable to assume, however, that standard compression techniques might be applied to further reduce storage requirements. We simulate this effect by applying gzip to each buffer once it has been forced to disk. For evaluation purposes, we report the average number of bytes per message which is just the total disk log size divided by the number of messages routed for a particular test. Figures 4 and 5 give the average storage use (uncompressed and compressed) for our test configurations. Because our experiments use a single broker, the storage footprint is due to the publisher and subscriber histories. In a multi-broker setting, local routing history storage is bounded by the size of the publisher history at the source broker. Thus, the storage footprint of the publisher history approximates the added footprint in a multi-broker setting.

As to be expected, the ASYNC strategy is at a storage disadvantage since audit records are not compressed in memory. However, the simple structure of ASYNC logs allows for significant compression as can be seen in the figures. Conversely, the structure of filters used in the BF strategy does not allow significant compression. In fact, since the full Bloom filters must have random bit patterns with equal number of zeros and ones, compression is impossible in principle. Moreover, the BF strategy is at a significant disadvantage when only partially full filters are written to disk, particularly when high accuracy is required. In these cases, the underlying filters are sufficiently random to defy straightforward compression techniques. In cases where both ASYNC and BF are forced to persist partially full filters of roughly the same size at roughly the same rate (*e.g.* 135K buffers when $T_p = 1$), the ASYNC strategy will utilize disk space more efficiently. With larger buffers, the BF strategy does not offer an advantage unless disk forces can be delayed for several seconds.

Although the compressed ASYNC strategy consumes less storage than some of BF, the BF strategy still has advantage over ASYNC for two reasons. First, the ASYNC strategy requires more complex and larger indexing to avoid otherwise inefficient sequential search. By contrast, in the BF strategy, such indexing is constructed at the filter level, as opposed to at the message level, because each Bloom filter answers a membership query efficiently by applying k hash functions. Note that a filter has a capacity of at least thousands of messages. Second, since false positives are not correlated among brokers, many false positives can be deduced as such by comparing the results from neighboring brokers. For example, if only one broker, and none of its neighboring ones, claims to have seen a message, it is highly likely to be a false positive. Thus, low accuracy (that is, high *efpp*) at a single broker does not necessarily result in the overall low accuracy, which implies that it is rather safe to take low accuracy level.

6 Related Work

Our work is most similar to traceback facilities proposed at the IP layer. These systems are designed to help identify the source of distributed denial-of-service attacks (DDoS). There are two basic approaches: packet marking [14, 16], and route auditing as in SPIE [15]. Although developed independently, SPIE is very similar to our traceback facility in that both approaches use Bloom filters to track recent traffic. The main difference is that SPIE is intended to detect recent or in-progress DDoS attacks. As a result, only a single Bloom filter (per node) is required and stale data is periodically purged. In contrast, our traceback facility is designed to allow historical queries of message routes. Thus, Bloom filters are regularly persisted and we have developed new techniques to manage queries across a history of filters.

In the context of monitoring for middleware applications, various systems have been developed starting with CORBA monitors such as JEWEL [9], and more recently Enterprise Java Bean monitors [10]. These systems focus on component level interactions, rather than middleware messaging. In the context of messaging, recent work has focused on novel routing architectures [12] and various performance enhancements [11]. However, tracking facilities which specifically address messaging middleware do not appear in the literature. Nonetheless, commercial products such as WebSphere MQ [2] provide basic auditing facilities which log message information to disk. This solution works well for low message rates but is difficult to scale because of overhead. Our tracking facility attempts to provide scalability by reducing the cost of per-message operations while compressing persistent records.

Finally, Bloom filters [6] have enjoyed wide application in distributed systems, for example as a technique for caching web pages [8]. Broder and Mitzenmacher provide an interesting survey of Bloom filters as applied to networking in [7]. Typically, Bloom filters are used as a volatile cache for various types of data. In contrast, our message tracking facility persists and retains multiple Bloom filters. Thus, our main contribution is a scheme for indexing multiple Bloom filters for the purpose of managing false positive probability.

7 Conclusion

We believe that efficient mechanisms for monitoring and auditing middleware messaging will become increasingly important as enterprise business applications are more widely deployed. In this paper, we have defined a message tracking facility for distributed messaging middleware, and presented a low overhead system design which realizes such a facility. We expect future enterprise applications to require large scale deployments with tens of nodes and tens of thousands of clients. Thus, we believe that a key feature of our approach is the ability to tune accuracy (and hence overhead and resource requirements) to the needs of the application.

We have evaluated our design by measuring overhead as compared to a system with no tracking, and by illustrating trade-offs between absolute accuracy and high overhead. A key advantage of our approach is that it is tolerant of high message rates, and insensitive to the size of IDs being tracked. In particular, we have shown that low latency overhead is possible if accuracy can be relaxed to as little as 99.999% of a "perfect" system. Likewise, if only minimal memory is available for tracking, then low disk utilization is possible even with high-accuracy. If memory is not a constraining factor, then low disk utilization requires that disk writes be delayed until filters are full. We note that it is possible to remove this limitation by either merging partially full filters offline, or storing but retaining partially full filters in memory until they have reached capacity. We intend to implement these improvements as well as seek further optimizations as part of our future work.

Acknowledgments

The authors would like to thank the anonymous reviewers for their insightful comments.

References

1. Gryphon research project. http://www.research.ibm.com/gryphon/.
2. IBM WebSphere MQ. http://www.ibm.com/software/integration/wmq/.
3. Java 2 Platform Enterprise Edition. http://java.sun.com/j2ee/1.4/.
4. Java Message Service (JMS). http://java.sun.com/products/jms.
5. Sumeer Bhola, Robert E. Strom, Saurabh Bagchi, Yuanyuan Zhao, and Joshua S. Auerbach. Exactly-once delivery in a content-based publish-subscribe system. In *DSN*, pages 7–16. IEEE Computer Society, 2002.

6. Burton Bloom. Space/time trade-offs in hash coding with allowable errors. *Communications of the ACM*, 13(7):422–426, July 1970.
7. Andrei Broder and Michael Mitzenmacher. Network applications of Bloom filters: A survey. In *Proceedings of the 40th Annual Allerton Conference on Communication, Control and Computing*, pages 636–646, 2002.
8. Li Fan, Pei Cao, Jussara Almeida, and Andrei Z. Broder. Summary cache: A scalable wide-area web cache sharing protocol. In *Proceedings of ACM SIGCOMM*, 1998.
9. F. Lange, R. Kroeger, and M. Gergeleit. Jewel: Design and implementation of a distributed measurement system. *IEEE Transactions on Parallel and Distributed Systems*, 3(6):657–672, 1992.
10. Adrian Mos and John Murphy. A framework for performance monitoring, modelling and prediction of component oriented distributed systems. In *WOSP '02: Proceedings of the Third International Workshop on Software and Performance*, pages 235–236. ACM Press, 2002.
11. Lukasz Opyrchal, Mark Astley, Joshua Auerbach, Guruduth Banavar, Robert Strom, and Daniel Sturman. Exploiting IP multicast in content-based publish-subscribe systems. In *Middleware '00: IFIP/ACM International Conference on Distributed Systems Platforms*, pages 185–207. Springer-Verlag New York, Inc., 2000.
12. Peter R. Pietzuch and Jean Bacon. Peer-to-peer overlay broker networks in an event-based middleware. In *DEBS '03: Proceedings of the 2nd international workshop on Distributed event-based systems*, pages 1–8. ACM Press, 2003.
13. R. Rivest. RFC 1321. the MD5 message-digest algorithm, April 1992.
14. Stefan Savage, David Wetherall, Anna Karlin, and Tom Anderson. Practical network support for IP traceback. In *Proceedings of ACM SIGCOMM*, pages 295–306, 2000.
15. Alex C. Snoeren, Craig Patridge, Luis A. Sanchez, Christine E. Jones, Fabrice Tchakountio, Beverly Schwartz, Stephen T. Kent, and W. Timothy Strayer. Single-packet IP traceback. *IEEE/ACM Transactions on Networking (TON)*, 10(6):721–734, December 2002.
16. Dawn X. Song and Adrian Perrig. Advanced and authenticated marking schemes for IP traceback. In *Proceedings IEEE Infocomm 2001*, 2001.

Utility-Driven Proactive Management of Availability in Enterprise-Scale Information Flows

Zhongtang Cai[1], Vibhore Kumar[1], Brian F. Cooper[1], Greg Eisenhauer[1],
Karsten Schwan[1], and Robert E. Strom[2]

[1] College of Computing, Georgia Institute of Technology, Atlanta, GA 30332
{ztcai, vibhore, cooperb, eisen, schwan}@cc.gatech.edu
[2] IBM Watson Research Center, Hawthorne, NY 10532
robstrom@us.ibm.com

Abstract. Enterprises rely critically on the timely and sustained delivery of information. To support this need, we augment information flow middleware with new functionality that provides high levels of availability to distributed applications while at the same time maximizing the utility end users derive from such information. Specifically, the paper presents utility-driven 'proactive availability-management' techniques to offer (1) information flows that dynamically self-determine their availability requirement based on high-level utility specifications, (2) flows that can trade recovery time for performance based on the 'perceived' stability of and failure predictions (early alarm) for the underlying system, and (3) methods, based on real-world case studies, to deal with both transient and non-transient failures. Utility-driven 'proactive availability-management' is integrated into information flow middleware and used with representative applications. Experiments reported in the paper demonstrate middleware capability to self-determine availability guarantees, to offer improved performance versus a statically configured system, and to be resilient to a wide range of faults.

1 Introduction

Modern enterprises rely critically on timely and sustained delivery of information. An important class of applications in this context is a company's operational information system, which continuously acquires, manipulates, and disseminates information across the enterprise's distributed sites and machines. For applications like these, a key attribute is their availability - 24 hours a day, 7 days a week. In fact, system failures can have dire consequences, including loss of productivity, unhappy customers, or serious financial implications. For example, the average cost of downtime for financial companies, as reported in [1], is up to 6.5 million dollars per hour and hundreds of thousands of dollars per hour for retail companies. This has resulted in a strong demand for operational information systems that are available almost continuously.

Providing high availability in widely distributed operational information systems is complex for multiple reasons. First, because information flows are distributed, they are difficult to manage, and failures at any of a number of distributed components or sites can reduce availability. Second, multiple flows may use the same distributed resources, thereby increasing the complexity of the system and the difficulty of managing and preventing failures. Third, such systems often have high data rates and intensive processing

M. van Steen and M. Henning (Eds.): Middleware 2006, LNCS 4290, pp. 382–403, 2006.

requirements, and there are frequently insufficient system resources to replicate all this data and processing to achieve high reliability. Fourth, information flows must have negligible recovery times to limit losses to the enterprise. Finally, based on our experience working with industry partners like Delta Air Lines and Worldspan, systems must recover not only from transient failures but also from non-transient ones (e.g., failures that will recur unless some root cause is addressed) [2].

How can we provide high availability for information flows, given all of these requirements? Traditional techniques such as recovery from disk-based logs [3] may have recovery times that are unacceptable for the domain in question. Using active replicas [4] imposes high additional communication and processing overheads (since all data flow and processing is replicated) and therefore, may not be an economically viable option. Another option is to use an active-passive pair [4], where a passive replica of a component can be brought up to date by retransmitting messages that had gone to the failed, active one. This option reduces communication costs, since messages are only sent to the passive component at failure time. Unfortunately, this may result in long recovery times. A better solution would be a hybrid of the above approaches, accepting dynamically determined levels of additional processing and communication during normal operation in order to reduce recovery times when failures occur.

In this paper we extend the active-passive approach to dynamically tune the tradeoff between normal operation cost and recovery time. In particular, the passive replica will be periodically refreshed with 'soft-checkpoints': these checkpoints transfer the current state from the active node to the passive node (passive standby), but are not required for correctness (hence, they are 'soft'). If the passive replica has been recently brought up to date by a soft-checkpoint, then recovery will be relatively fast. The tradeoff between cost and recovery is tuned by changing the frequency at which soft-checkpoints are transmitted during normal operation. Such tuning is based on user-provided expressions of information utility, and it takes advantage of the following methods for failure prediction:

- *Availability-Aware Self-Configuration* – a user-supplied per information flow 'benefit-function' drives the level of additional resources used to guarantee availability. This ensures preferential treatment of flows that offer more benefit to the enterprise, with the aim of maximizing benefit across the system.
- *Proactive Availability-Management* – during its execution, a system may be at different levels of stability (e.g., a heavy memory load could mean an imminent failure). In many cases, the 'current stability' of the system can be quantified in order increase or decrease the resources expended to ensure desired levels of availability.
- *Handling Non-Transient Failures* – some failures will recur if the same sequence of messages that caused the failure is resent during recovery. In this case, we must use application-level knowledge to avoid fault recurrence. We present several techniques, based on real-world case studies, to deal with such faults.

Proactive availability-management techniques have been integrated into IFLOW, a high performance information flow middleware described in [5]. The outcome is a flexible, distributed middleware for running large-scale information flows and for managing their availability. In fact, experimentation shows that proactive availability-management not only imposes low additional communication and processing overheads on

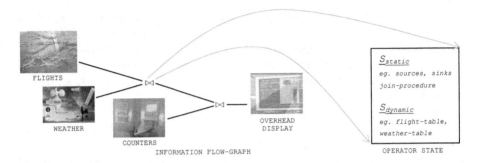

Fig. 1. Information Flow-Graph and Operator State

distributed information flows, but also, that proactive fault tolerance is an effective technique for recovering from failures, with a low recovery time of 2.5 seconds for an enterprise-scale information flow running on a representative distributed computing platform. Experiments further show that utility-based availability-management offers 1.5 times the net-utility of the basic active replica approach.

1.1 Example: Operational Information System

An operational information system (OIS) [2] is a large-scale, distributed system that provides continuous support for a company or organization's daily operations. One example of such a system we have been studying is the OIS run by Delta Air Lines, which provides the company with up-to-date information about all of their flight operations, including crews, passengers and baggage. Delta's OIS combines three different sets of functionality:

- *Continuous data capture* - for information like crew dispositions, passengers, airplanes and their current locations determined from FAA radar data.
- *Continuous status updates* - for low-end devices like airport flight displays, for the PCs used by gate agents, and even for large databases in which operational state changes are recorded for logging purposes.
- *Responses to client requests* - an OIS must also respond to explicit client requests, such as pulling up information regarding a particular passenger, and it may generate additional updates for events like changes in flights, crews or passengers.

In this paper, we model the information acquisition, manipulation, and dissemination done by such an OIS as an information flow graph (a sample flow-graph is shown in Figure 1). We then present techniques, based on this flow-graph formalization, to proactively manage OIS availability such that the net-utility achieved by the system is maximized. This is done by assigning per information flow availability guarantees which are aligned with the benefit that is derived from the information flow, and by proactively responding to perceived changes in system stability. We also present additional techniques, based on real-world case studies, that can help a system recover from non-transient failures.

2   System Overview

This section describes a model of the information flows under consideration, and it elaborates the fault model used for the proactive availability-management techniques explained later.

2.1   Information Flow Model

An information flow is represented as a directed acyclic graph $G(V_g, E_g, U_{net})$ with each vertex in V_g representing an information-source, an information-sink or a flow-operator that processes the information i.e. $V_g = V_{sources} \cup V_{sinks} \cup V_{operators}$. Edges E_g in the graph represent the flow of information, and may span multiple intermediate edges and nodes in the underlying network. The utility-function U_{net} is defined as:

$$U_{net} = Benefit - Cost \tag{1}$$

Both benefit and cost are expressed in terms of some unit of value delivered per unit time (e.g., dollars/second). Benefit is a user-supplied function that maps the delay, availability, etc. of the information flow to its corresponding value to the enterprise. Cost is also a user-supplied function; it maps resources such as CPU usage and bandwidth consumed to the expense incurred by the enterprise. We will expand the terms of this seemingly simple equation in upcoming sections.

2.2   Fault Model

We are concerned with failures that occur after the information flow has been deployed. In particular, we consider fail-stop failures of operators that process events. Such failures could result from problems in the operator code or in the underlying physical node. Other factors might also cause failures, but are not considered here, including problems with sources, problems with the sink, or link failures between nodes. While such issues can cause user-perceived failures, they must be addressed with other techniques. For example, link failures could be managed by retransmission or re-routing at the network level.

For the purpose of failure recovery, we assume that each flow-operator consists of a *static-state* S_{static} that contains the information about the edges connected to the operator and the enterprise logic embedded in the operator; in contrast, the *dynamic-state* $S_{dynamic}$ is the information that is a result of all the updates that have been processed by this operator (shown in Figure 1). Recovery therefore, is dependent upon the correct retrieval of the states S_{static} and $S_{dynamic}$, which jointly contain the information necessary for re-instantiation of flow-operator and information flow edges. However, as described next, simply recovering these states may not prevent the recurrence of a failure.

Transient Faults. A fault can be caused by a condition that is transient in nature (e.g., a memory overload due to a mis-behaving process). Such faults will not typically recur after system recovery. In our formulation, a transient fault would cause the failure of an operator, and correct retrieval of the two states associated with the operator would ensure permanent recovery from this fault. The techniques proposed in this paper are capable of effectively handling faults of this nature.

Non-transient Faults. Non-transient faults may be caused by some bugs in the code or some unhandled conditions. For information flows, this may mean recurrence of the fault even after recovery, particularly when recovery entails repeating the same sequence of messages that caused the fault. To deal with faults of this nature, we note that the output produced by a flow-operator in response to an input event E depends on the existing dynamic-state $S_{dynamic}$, the operator logic encoded as S_{static}, and the event E itself. Therefore, the failure of an operator on arrival of an event E is a result of the 3-tuple $< S_{dynamic}, S_{static}, E >$. Thus, any technique that aims to deal with non-transient failures must have application-level methods for retrieving and appropriately modifying this 3-tuple. Our prior work presents examples of such methods [2], and we generalize such techniques here.

3 Utility-Driven Proactive Availability-Management

Traditional techniques for availability-management typically rely on undo-redo logs, active-replicas, or active-passive pairs. A new set of problems is presented by information flows that form the backbone of an enterprise. For instance, using traditional on-disk undo-redo logs for information flows would lead to unacceptable recovery times for the enterprise domain in face of machine or disk failures. The other end of the availability-management spectrum, which uses active replicas, would impose large additional communication and processing overheads due to the high arrival rate of updates, typically making it economically infeasible for the enterprise to use this option. In response, we take the active-passive pair algorithm [4], and customize it for enterprise-scale information flows. To do this, we will incorporate our previous work on soft-checkpoints [6], and add the ability to dynamically choose checkpointing intervals to reduce communication and processing overheads. For completeness, we first describe the existing active-passive pair and soft-checkpoint techniques, and then describe our enhancements.

3.1 Basic Active-Passive Pair Algorithm

To ensure high-availability for the flow-operator, in its simplest form, the active-passive pair replication requires: a *passive node* containing the static-state S_{static} of the flow-operator hosted on the active node, an *event log* at the flow-graph vertices directly upstream to the flow-operator in question, a mechanism to *detect duplicates* at the vertices directly downstream to the flow-operator, and a *failure detection* mechanism for the active node hosting the primary flow-operator.

In case of a failure, recovery proceeds as follows: the failure detection mechanism detects the failure and reports it to the passive node. On receipt of the failure message, the passive node instantiates the flow-operator, making use of the static-state, S_{static}, already available at the node. The instantiated operator then contacts the upstream vertices for retransmission of the events in their event log. The newly instantiated operator node processes these re-transmitted events in a normal fashion, generating output events, and leaving it to the downstream nodes to detect the resulting duplicates. Once the retransmission of the event log has been completed, the resulting dynamic-state,

$S_{dynamic}$, will be recovered to the state of the failed operator, and normal operations can resume. Unfortunately, this simple algorithm can lead to long recovery times, large event logs at the upstream nodes, and large associated retransmission costs. The remedy to these problems is the 'soft-checkpoint' technique, described next.

The event logs at the upstream nodes and their retransmission to the recovered operator are required for reconstructing the dynamic-state $S_{dynamic}$, of the failed operator. However, in practice, it is advantageous to retain additional stable state at the passive node in order to avoid the need to re-transmit the entire event log. Such state saving is called soft-checkpointing, because it is not needed for correctness. Soft checkpoints can be updated on an intermittent basis in the background. Once taken, the component receiving the checkpoint no longer requires the events on which the state depends for reconstructing $S_{dynamic}$. This in turn permits upstream nodes to discard the event logs for which the soft-checkpoint has been taken. Soft-checkpointing, therefore, is an optimization that reduces worst-case recovery time and permits the reclamation of logs.

The introduction of soft-checkpoints requires small modifications to the recovery mechanism described earlier in this section. The flow-operator at the active node in the duration prior to failure would intermittently send messages to the passive node that contain information about the incremental change to its dynamic-state since the last message. The passive node, after the receipt of complete state update message from the active node, applies the incremental modifications to the state it holds and then sends a message to the flow-operator's upstream neighbors about the most recent event contained in the message from the active node. The upstream nodes can use such information to purge their event logs. In case of a failure, the algorithm proceeds exactly as described earlier, but only a small fraction of the events needs to be re-transmitted and processed.

3.2 Availability-Utility Formulation

In this section, we use a basic availability formulation to better describe the effects and trade-offs in soft-checkpoint-based active-passive replication. Availability $\mathcal{A_I}$ is described in terms of Mean-Time Between Failure, $MTBF$ and Mean-Time To Repair, $MTTR$.

$$\mathcal{A_I} = \frac{MTBF}{MTBF + MTTR} \tag{2}$$

As stated earlier, our approach contributes to a reduction in recovery time and also reduces the processing and communication overhead imposed as a result of ensuring a certain level of availability. The reduction in recovery time results in lower MTTR and a reduction in associated overheads diminishes cost. Jointly, both result in higher net-utility U_{net}, which is the actual utility provided by the system.

With our approach, MTTR depends on two factors: (1) the time to detect a failure, and (2) the time to reconstruct the dynamic-state of the operator. Failure detection mechanisms generally rely on time-outs to detect failures and therefore, depend on the coarseness of the timer used for this purpose. Some research in the domain of fault-tolerance has focused on multi-resolution timeouts [7], but to simplify analysis, henceforth, we assume that the time to detect a failure is a constant. The second factor contributing to MTTR depends on the soft-checkpoint algorithm. Specifically, a higher frequency f_{cp}, expressed in per unit time, of such checkpoints would lead to a smaller number of events required to reconstruct $S_{dynamic}$ in case of a failure. Therefore:

$$MTTR \propto \frac{1}{f_{cp}} \tag{3}$$

For simplicity, we next derive the availability-utility formulation for a single information flow (self-configuration across multiple information flows is addressed in Section 3.3), and we assume that the *Benefit* and *Cost* depend only on availability. In this case, in general, the benefit derived from a system is directly proportional to its availability. Thus:

$$Benefit \propto \frac{MTBF}{MTBF + k_1/f_{cp}} \tag{4}$$

The above formulation may lead one to believe that a higher f_{cp} is good for the system. Unfortunately, a higher f_{cp} also means more cost to propagate checkpoints from the active node to the passive node. Therefore:

$$Cost \propto f_{cp} \tag{5}$$

Note that a higher f_{cp} also results in fewer events retransmitted per soft-checkpoint; however, for large values of MTBF this effect is minor compared to the effects described above (increase in benefit due to better availability, and compared to the increase in cost due to a higher frequency of checkpoints). Experiments reported in Section 5.2 study the effects of soft-checkpoint frequency on the cost and availability of information flows.

Combining equations 1, 4, 5, and replacing proportionality using constants, we arrive at:

$$U_{net} = \frac{k_2 \times MTBF}{MTBF + k_1/f_{cp}} - k_3 \times f_{cp}, \tag{6}$$

which represents the business-utility calculation model and the constants are determined by business level objectives [8,5], or using more detailed formulation described later. This equation expresses the key insight that net-utility depends not only on MTBF, but also on the soft-checkpoint frequency used in a system, the latter both positively contributing to net-utility (by reducing the denominator) and directly reducing net-utility (by increasing the term being subtracted). Intuitively, this means that frequent checkpointing can improve utility by reducing MTBF, but that it can also reduce utility by using resources that would otherwise directly benefit the information flow.

3.3   Availability-Aware Self-configuration

Ideally, we would like to maximize the availability of an information flow, but given that there is an associated cost, our actual goal is to choose a value of availability that maximizes its net-utility. In our algorithm and its mathematical formulation, f_{cp} is the factor that governs availability. By setting the derivative of equation 6 equal to zero, we find that the value of f_{cp} that maximizes net-utility is:

$$f_{cp} = \sqrt{\frac{k_1 \times k_2}{k_3 \times MTBF}} - \frac{k_1}{MTBF} \tag{7}$$

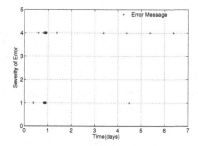

Fig. 2. Enterprise error-log showing predictable behavior of failures

In the presence of multiple information flows, each with a different benefit-function, the resource assignment for availability is driven by the need to maximize net-utility across all deployed information flows. Total net-utility of the entire system, then, is the sum of individual net-utilities of information flows. For a system with n information flows, we will need to calculate $\{f_{cp}^1, f_{cp}^2, ..., f_{cp}^n\}$, which will automatically determine resource assignments. The value of f_{cp} for each information flow can be calculated using partial differentials, and the involved calculations are omitted due to space constraints.

3.4   Proactive Availability-Management

We have established that net-utility depends on checkpoint frequency and MTBF. However, the MTBF in a real system is not a constant. Instead, the rate of failures fluctuates, with more failures occurring when the system is in an unstable state. For example, during periods of extreme overload, the system is likely to experience many component failures. If we can better approximate the current MTBF, and in particular predict when there will be many failures, we can make better decisions about checkpointing, increasing the checkpoint rate when the current MTBF is low (and failures are imminent.)

Failure Prediction. An effective way to estimate the current MTBF is to use failure prediction techniques to generate 'early alarms' when a failure seems to be imminent. By using failure prediction, our approach can be 'better prepared' for an imminent failure, by taking more frequent soft-checkpoints. Analysis logs provided to us by one of our industry partners strengthens our belief in the usefulness of dynamic failure prediction. These logs contain error messages and warnings that were recorded at a middleware broker over a period of 7 days, along with their time-stamps. Figure 2 shows the distribution and severity of errors recorded at the broker node. One interesting observation of these logs is that errors recur at almost the same time (around 9:00am as read from the log time-stamp) beginning from the 2nd day. Another interesting observation about the same set of logs is that 128 errors of severity level 1 occurred from 7:30pm in the first day before a series of level 4 errors occurred from 8pm. Based on such logs, it would be reasonable, therefore, to assume lower MTBF (i.e., predict imminent failures) for the 9am time period and the period when a large number of less severe errors occur, than for other time periods in which this application executes. We note that similar time- or load-dependent behaviors have been observed for other distributed applications[9].

We implemented the Sequential Probability Ratio Test(SPRT) used in MSET [10,11] failure prediction method, to predict failures injected by the FIMD [12] failure injection tool, including timing delay, omission, message corruption datatype, message corruption length, message corruption destination, message corruption tag, message corruption data, memory leak, and invalid memory access. The SPRT method is a run-time statistical hypothesis test that can detect statistical changes in noisy process signals at the earliest possible time, e.g., before the process crashes or when severe service degradation occurs. SPRT has been applied successfully to monitor nuclear power plants, and it has recently been used for software aging problems, e.g., for the database latch contention problem, memory leaks, unreleased file locks, data corruption, etc. For example, an early warning may be raised about 30 seconds (the 'early warning capability') before a memory leak fault causes the service to degrade dramatically or the process crashes. For database shared-memory-pool latch contention failures, early warning capabilities of 5 minutes to 2 hours have been observed. For additional information about SPRT and associated MSET method, please refer to [10] and to an extended version of this text in a technical report [13].

Modulating Checkpoint Frequency. The idea behind proactive availability-management is to use failure prediction to modulate f_{cp}. We first provide the important yet simple guideline regarding checkpoint frequency modulation, we then develop a detailed formulation for enterprise-scale information flows, and finally, present a formulation and method to meet some specific availability requirement while also maximizing net-utility.

General guideline. Intuitively, if a failure prediction turns out to be correct, the system 'benefits' because of reduced $MTTR$; if a prediction turns out to be a false-positive, the system still operates correctly, but it pays the extra 'cost' due to increased f_{cp}. Stated more formally, let:

$$\alpha = prediction\ false\text{--}positive\ rate$$
$$\beta = prediction\ false\text{--}negative\ rate$$
$$f'_{cp} = modulated\ checkpoint\ frequency\ after\ a\ failure\ is\ predicted$$
$$T_{proactive} = duration\ of\ increased\ checkpoint\ frequency$$
$$k = timeout\ after\ which\ an\ operator\ is\ concluded\ to\ have\ failed$$

Earlier, $Cost$ was shown to be proportional to soft-checkpoint frequency. The new cost, $Cost'$, due to modulated f'_{cp}, is:

$$Cost' = Cost \times f'_{cp}/f_{cp} \qquad (8)$$

This increased cost is incurred for a duration equal to $T_{proactive}$, and it is incurred each time a prediction is made. Therefore, the additional cost incurred per prediction is:

$$\delta Cost = (f'_{cp}/f_{cp} - 1) \times Cost \times T_{proactive} \qquad (9)$$

Table 1. Four types of cost

$Cost^{cp} = [1 - P(1 - \beta + \alpha)]f_{cp}C_1,$
$Cost^{fp} = \alpha P f'_{cp}t_o C_1,$
$Cost^{fn} = \beta P C_2/(2f_{cp}) + \beta P(k + 1/(2f_{cp}))C_3,$
$Cost^{ps} = (1 - \beta)P[C_2/(2f'_{cp}) + (k + 1/(2f'_{cp}))C_3 + f'_{cp}t_o C_1].$

The increase in f_{cp} also affects the availability of the system and therefore, the benefit, $Benefit'$, derived from the system. Using equation 4, we have:

$$Benefit' = \frac{MTBF + k_1/f'_{cp}}{MTBF + k_1/f_{cp}} \times Benefit \qquad (10)$$

Therefore, the increase in benefit due to a correct prediction that affects a period equal to $MTBF$ is:

$$\delta Benefit = (Benefit' - Benefit) \times MTBF \qquad (11)$$

Since λ is the fraction of false-positives and because there is no increase in benefit due to a false positive, the following condition expresses when proactive availability-management based on failure prediction is beneficial for an entire system:

$$\delta Cost < (1 - \alpha) \times \delta Benefit \qquad (12)$$

Proactive availability-management. Different systems could have different types and formulations of benefit and cost, and the above analysis provides the general guideline regarding proactive availability-management. For the enterprise information flow system targeted by this paper, the proactive availability-management problem can be formulated in more details as follows. Proactive availability-management regulates checkpoint frequency based on stability predictions to maximize net business utility. By considering 'total cost', including the cost of checkpointing and the utility loss because of a failure (i.e. the extra utility the system could offer if there had been no failure), the problem of maximizing net-utility can be converted to the problem of minimizing total cost. This total cost consists of the cost of normal checkpointing (at frequency f_{cp}), $Cost^{cp}$, the cost due to false-positive failure prediction (i.e., the failure predictor raises a false alarm), $Cost^{fp}$, the cost due to false-negative failure prediction (i.e., a failure is not predicted successfully), $Cost^{fn}$, and finally, the cost associated with failure recovery when a failure is successfully predicted, $Cost^{ps}$.

These four types of cost are summarized in Table 1. For the cost of normal checkpoints, $Cost^{cp}$, C_1 is the cost for each checkpoint update (e.g., the communication cost), and P is the possibility an operator could fail from any time t to t+1 (seconds). Here, $P(1 - \beta + \alpha)$ is the fraction of time when the checkpoint frequency is f'_{cp}, due to correct failure predictions and false alarms. For the cost of false-positive failure prediction, t_o is the average time a predictor raises an early alarm for a severe failure. In the equation for the cost due to false-negative prediction, $Cost^{fn}$, the first term is the total state recovery cost, i.e., the cost for the passive node to recover from the latest checkpointed state to the state when the failure occurred, including retransmission cost and re-computation cost. C_2 is the average recovery cost per unit time($/sec$). The second term is the total utility loss from the time when failure occurs to the time when the system recovers to normal operational status. In other words, this term represents the utility the system could provide if there had been no such failure. C_3 is the utility the system provides per second($/sec$)if there is no failure. The cost associated with failure recovery when a failure is successfully predicted, $Cost^{ps}$, is determined in a similar manner as $Cost^{fn}$.

To regulate checkpoint frequency, proactive fault tolerance finds the best checkpoint frequency, f_{cp}, when there is no failure predicted, and the best checkpoint frequency, f'_{cp}, after the time a failure is predicted. This is done by minimizing the total cost.

Meet specific availability requirement. Often, enterprises have specific requirements for system availability. For example, a 365 x 24 system with maximum allowed average downtime of 8.76 hours (i.e., 525 minutes) per year requires 99.9 percent availability, while a system with only 3 minutes of service outage must have at least a 99.999 percent availability. To achieve such availability is difficult due to the high cost of fault tolerance services and equipments. Proactive availability-management is able to strike a balance between these two factors by jointly considering availability and utility when regulating checkpoint frequency. Notice that MTTR can be expressed as:

$$MTTR = (1/2f_{cp} + k)\beta + (1/2f'_{cp} + k)(1 - \beta), \tag{13}$$

where k is the timeout after which we conclude that a module actually failed, the availability is given by:

$$A_I = \frac{MTBF}{MTBF + MTTR} = \frac{1 - P \cdot MTTR}{1}$$
$$= 1 - p[(1/2f_{cp} + k)\beta + (1/2f'_{cp} + k)(1 - \beta)] \tag{14}$$

Proactive fault tolerance meets the minimum availability requirement and also maximizes net utility by solving the following equation:

$$Minimize\{Cost = Cost^{cp} + Cost^{fp} + Cost^{fn} + Cost^{ps}\}, \text{ subject to:}$$

$$1 - p[(1/2f_{cp} + k)\beta + (1/2f'_{cp} + k)(1 - \beta)] \geq A_I^{required} \tag{15}$$

This optimization problem is of small size with two variables and one constraint, and is solved using standard Quasi-Newton method with inverse barriers.

3.5 Handling Non-transient Faults

Non-transient failures are a result of bugs or unhandled conditions in operator code. Traditional techniques for ensuring high-availability that use undo/redo logs [3,6] are useful for transient failures, but for non-transient failures, they may result in recurrence of faults during recovery. The same applies to replication-based approaches [14], for which all replicas would fail simultaneously for non-transient faults.

As described in Section 2.2, a non-transient failure of the information flow in our model is a result of the 3-tuple $< S_{static}, S_{dynamic}, E >$. The active-passive pair approach for ensuring high-availability has sufficient information during recovery to change this 3-tuple. The passive-node during recovery has access to S_{static}, a stale state $S'_{dynamic}$, and a set of updates T from the upstream nodes that when applied to $S'_{dynamic}$, would lead to $S_{dynamic}$. The rationale behind our approach to avoid non-transient failures is simple: avoid the 3-tuple that caused the failure. This can be done in a number of ways, and the retransmitted updates T along with application-level knowledge holds the key:

- *Dropping Updates*: the simplest solution to avoid recurrence of a fault is to avoid processing the update that caused the failure. Our earlier work on 'poison messages' used this technique [2].
- *Update Reordering*: changing the order in which updates are applied to $S'_{dynamic}$ during recovery can avoid $S_{dynamic}$. This makes use of application-level knowledge to ensure correctness.
- *Update Fusion*: combining updates to avoid an intermediate state could be an option. A simple example of this approach could be the use of this technique to avoid 'division by zero' error.
- *Update Decomposition*: decomposing an update into a number of equivalent updates can be an option with several applications, and this can potentially avoid the fault.

While seemingly simple, the techniques described above are often successful in realistic settings. For example, one of our collaborators, reported an occasional surge in the usage of resources connected to their Operational Information System (OIS) [15] that traced back to a particular uncommon message type. The resulting performance hit caused other subsystem's requests to build up, including those from the front ends used by clients, ultimately threatening operational failure (e.g., inappropriately long response times) or revenue loss (e.g., clients going to alternate sites). Such uncommon request/message, termed 'Poison Messages', were later found to be identifiable by certain characteristics. The solution then adopted was to either drop or re-route the poison message in order to maintain operational integrity.

4   Middleware Implementation

IFLOW [5] is an information flow middleware developed at Georgia Tech. IFLOW implements the information flow abstraction of Section 2.1 and provides methods to deploy and then optimize (by migrating operators) the information flow. For more details please refer to [16].

We now briefly describe the features that enable proactive availability-management in the IFLOW middleware. These features are implemented both at the *control plane* and the *data plane* of this middleware infrastructure.

4.1   Control Plane

The control plane in IFLOW is the basis for managing information flows. Self-management methods involve running a self-configuration and a self-optimization algorithm, carried out by exchanging control messages between physical nodes that are external to the data fast paths used to transport IFLOW data. Control actions involve operations like flow-control, operator re-instantiation, etc. The main new features of the IFLOW control plane that are used for proactive fault tolerance are described below:

- *Availability-aware self-configuration module*: the benefit-formulation in IFLOW allows for availability goals to be specified, and determines the best value of f_{cp} by using the formulation described in Section 3.2.
- *Failure detection & prediction*: IFLOW attempts to use the regular traffic from a node to determine its liveness, but it switches to specific detection messages if there is no regular traffic from the node to the monitoring node. We also have a provision for multi-resolution timeouts to reduce the load imposed by the failure detection algorithm. Finally, state can be maintained to use failure history for predicting failures, but we have not yet implemented any specific technique into IFLOW.
- *Control messages*: SOAP calls are used to notify active-node failure, to communicate log purge points to upstream vertices, etc.
- *Update re-direction in case of failure*: a simple control mechanism exists at the upstream vertices to re-direct updates to the passive node in case of failure. The connection between upstream vertices and the passive node is created at the time of flow deployment.

4.2   Data Plane

A *fast data-path* is one of the key design philosophies of the IFLOW middleware. We have taken care that the features required for proactive availability-management have minimal impact on the data-path. In order to ensure proactive availability-management, the state of an operator on the data plane needs to be soft-checkpointed and the changes need to be periodically communicated to the passive-node. The fact that a soft-checkpoint is not necessary for correctness of proactive availability-management ensures minimal impact on the data-path. Specifically, the active-node can transfer the soft-checkpoint to the passive node asynchronously, and this will not compromise the correctness of our algorithm. The specific features required for proactive availability-management are described below:

- *Logging at upstream vertices*: any update that is sent out from the source vertex is logged to enable retransmission in case of failure. Additional logs can be established at intermediate nodes (an operator vertex is a source for downstream vertices) to enable faster recovery. The log module also implements a mechanism to purge the log when a message is received from the downstream node after a soft-checkpoint is completed.
- *Soft-checkpoint module at operator vertices*: the soft-checkpoint module tracks the changes in $S_{dynamic}$ since the last soft-checkpoint. It is also responsible for sending soft-checkpoints to the passive node.
- *Duplicate detection at the downstream node*: the duplicate detection mechanism is based on the monotonic update system proposed in our earlier work [6]. When the updates cannot be ordered using the contained attributes, a monotonically increasing

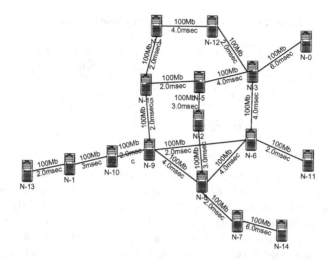

Fig. 3. Sample testbed. The testbed topology is generated using GT-ITM and is configured at emulab facility.

attribute (e.g., the real-time clock) is appended to the out-going update that uniquely identifies this update.

- *Additional edge between active-passive pair*: a supplementary data-flow between the active-passive pair delivers the soft-checkpoints to the passive vertex.
- *Maintaining checkpoints at passive-node*: the passive vertex contains the logic that applies an incoming soft-checkpoint to the recorded active node state.

5   Experiments

Experiments are designed to evaluate the performance our proactive availability-management techniques. First, simulations are used to better understand the behavior of the self-configuration module that determines the availability requirement based on the user-supplied benefit function. Next, an end-to-end setup is created on Emulab [17], representing an enterprise-scale information flow to compare our approach against the traditional approaches and to study the effect of different soft-checkpoint intervals and proactivity on aspects like MTTR, recovery cost, and net-utility. Results show that proactive availability-management is effective at providing low-cost failure resilience for information flow applications, while also maximizing the application's net-utility.

5.1   Simulation Study

A simulation study is used to compare utility-based availability management to simple approaches that are not availability-aware. The study uses a 128 node topology generated with the GT-ITM internetwork topology generator [18]. The formulation of net-utility U_{net} determines benefit as: $benefit = k_1 \times (k_2 - delay)^2 \times availability \times$

Table 2. Self-Determining Availability based on Benefit

Optimization Criterion	Utility	Cost	Delay
Net-Utility (dollars/sec)	431991	52670	2160
Cost (dollars/sec)	79875	14771	80315
Delay (msec)	222	444	191
f_{cp} (sec^{-1})	0.050	0.018	0.020
Availability (percent)	99.88	99.66	99.70

$availableBandwidth/requiredBandwidth$, and cost is calculated as: $cost = dataRate \times bandwidthCostPerByte$. Random costs are assigned to the network links, expressed in dollars per byte. We substitute ($k_1 = 1.0$, $k_2 = 150.0$) in the benefit formulation for this specific simulation [5]. The MTBF is assumed to be 86400sec. and the MTTR is assumed to be 864sec. for a f_{cp} value of 0.01Hz. (Many values are possible for these variables. However, we must choose some values when conducting our simulations, and the ones we chose are reasonable for the enterprise environment.) We first deploy the flow-graph using the net-utility specification from equation 1 as the optimization criteria, and the results are shown in Table 2 under the column labeled 'Utility'. The results show a high achieved net-utility with acceptable values for delay, f_{cp} and availability. The second deployment (under 'Cost') focuses instead on minimizing the cost, and it uses $1/cost$ as the optimization criteria. The effect of choosing a different criteria is evident in the reduced cost, achieved by allowing a higher delay and a lower availability (resulting from lower f_{cp}). The final experiment uses $1/delay$ to drive the deployment. This results in a reduction of delay achieved for the flow-graph, but at the expense of net-utility and availability.

5.2   Testbed Experiments Using IFLOW

This set of experiments is conducted on Emulab [17], and the network topology is again generated using the GT-ITM internetwork topology generator. In many cases, enterprises would hand tune their topology for availability and performance, instead of using an arbitrary topology. For example, an enterprise may explicitly designate a primary and secondary data center. An arbitrary topology is used in our experiments in order to understand how our techniques perform without the benefit of additional hand tuning. Figure 3 shows the testbed used for experimental evaluations. Background traffic is generated using cmu-scen-gen [19], injected into the testbed using rate-controlled udp connections. For the testbed depicted in Figure 3, background traffic is composed of 900 CBR connections. We use the utility formulation in Equation 15 to better study the net-utility and the costs associated with checkpointing and failures. Required availability is 99.9% if not stated otherwise.

Variation of Net-Utility for Different Approaches. The first experiment studies the variation of net-utility with different availability-management approaches in the presence of failures. For simplicity, only one failure is injected into the system. We conduct experiments with the active replication approach, the passive replication approach with varying soft-checkpoint intervals, and our proactive replication approach. Figure 4

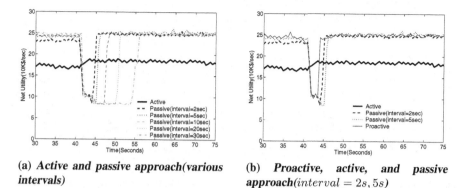

(a) *Active and passive approach(various intervals)*

(b) *Proactive, active, and passive approach(interval = 2s, 5s)*

Fig. 4. Net utility rate variations using active, passive or proactive fault tolerance approaches. A failure is injected into one operator node at the time $t = 40s$.

clearly demonstrates that the active replication approach provides lowest net-utility. This is because of the high amount of replicated communication traffic when using this approach. After a failure, net-utility of the active approach increases slightly; there is less replication traffic, because the failed node no longer sends replicated output updates. The experiment also corroborates the analysis in Section 3.2: a lower soft-checkpoint interval for the passive approach imposes higher communication cost on the system and therefore, results in lower net-utility. Note that if availability were a predominant factor in the net-utility formulation, then a lower soft-checkpoint interval could have resulted in higher net-utility. The cost of soft-checkpoints is almost negligible when the interval is greater than 5 seconds, but its effect is evident for an interval of 2 seconds.

Our proactive approach provides the highest net-utility overall, as it modulates the soft-checkpoint interval and takes into account the perceived system to offer preventive fault tolerance. For instance, it switches to a smaller soft-checkpoint interval just before the failure and is therefore able to recover as fast as the passive approach with a 2 seconds update interval, while performing as well as the passive approach with a 30 seconds update interval at other times. We note that evaluation of failure prediction techniques is not the focus of this paper (such kind of evaluations appear in [13]). To investigate how prediction accuracy affects the system, these experiments simulate a predictor for the proactive approach, with failure prediction statistically generated at various levels of accuracy. In particular, we notify the soft-checkpoint mechanism that a failure is imminent, no matter whether the prediction is correct or a false positive.

Variation of MTTR for Different Approaches. The variation of MTTR and its standard deviation with different approaches are shown in Figure 5. For each approach, nine experiments are used to obtain the mean and standard deviation. The active replication approach (not shown in the graph) has no explicit recovery time. This is because the node downstream of the replicated operator continues to receive processed updates even after the failure of one active replica. On the other hand, the passive replication approach which attempts to avoid the high cost of active replication incurs recovery

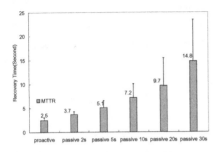
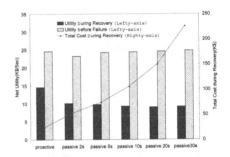

Fig. 5. MTTR and standard deviation of recovery time under three replication strategies. Standard deviation is represented by vertical error bars.

Fig. 6. Utility before failure and during recovery, and the total cost to recover from one failure

times that increase with the soft-checkpoint interval. The reason for this increase is the time taken for reconstructing the operator state: the higher the soft-checkpoint interval, the larger the number of updates required to rebuild the state. Recovery time for the passive replication approach depends on the soft-checkpoint interval. It ranges from 3.7 seconds (for a 2 second interval) to 14.8 seconds (for a 30 second interval). Our proactive approach, as expected, performs well as compared to other passive replication approaches, since it is able to change over to a very small soft-checkpoint interval just before the failure, and hence, has low MTTR. The experiment demonstrates the importance of choosing the right soft-checkpoint interval automatically to maximize availability at low cost and thereby maximize the net-utility of information flows.

Cost & Net-Utility During Recovery. Our proactive availability-management approach increases soft-checkpoint activity when a failure is predicted in the near future, but it maintains a low soft-checkpoint activity at other times. The analysis of net-utility value before failure, during failure recovery, and the total cost to recover from failure are summarized in Figure 6. Net-utility using proactive availability-management is higher than any other approach, because it contains a very recent soft-checkpoint for the operator state and therefore, incurs the least cost during recovery. Note that passive replication with an interval of 2 seconds also incurs a low cost during recovery, but this is achieved by losing non-negligible net-utility at normal operation time.

Effects of Checkpoint Frequency and Prediction Accuracy on Cost and Availability. The next experiment closely examines the effect of checkpoint frequency on the system, both in terms of system availability and the cost imposed to gain a unit amount of utility. As mentioned in Section 3.2, a higher f_{cp} leads to a higher number of soft-checkpoint messages from the active to the passive node, but it also leads to a smaller number of updates being required to reconstruct the operator state during recovery. The conflicting behavior of incurred cost due to f_{cp} is represented in Figure 7 by the two parabolic curves. Ideally, we would like to spend the minimum cost to achieve a unit amount of utility and would therefore, like to choose a value of f_{cp} that is located

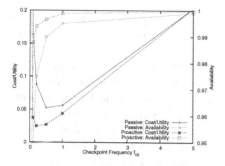

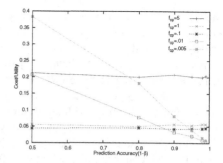

Fig. 7. Effect of checkpoint frequency on cost and availability. Checkpoint frequency affects the cost (left y-axis) in a non-linear way, and it is important to optimize it. Note that there is also a sweet spot in the graph, where cost is minimized and availability (right y-axis) is also high. Our proactive approach can achieve the same level of availability with significantly less cost compared to the passive approach.

Fig. 8. Effect of prediction accuracy on cost of ensuring availability. Better prediction accuracy helps reduce the cost incurred for ensuring high-availability, especially when the checkpoint frequency is low (the curve with the deepest slope). When checkpoint frequency is sufficiently large (the four curves with $f_{cp} \geq 1Hz$), higher accuracy has less effect on the cost due to the fact that less time is required to recover from an unpredicted failure.

at the dip of the parabolic curve. Note that the cost/utility ratio is consistently higher for the passive vs. the proactive approach. We also show the effect of f_{cp} on the availability of the system: the change is in line with the formulation described in Equation 4. However, the interesting insight from this experiment is the direct correspondence between the lowest achievable cost/utility and the flattening of the availability curve.

Our final experiment studies the effect of prediction accuracy λ, on the achieved cost/utility ratio. It is intuitive that better prediction accuracy would lead to lower cost/utility for proactive availability-management, and this is clearly depicted in Figure 8. It is interesting to note the behavior of proactive availability-management with a lower f_{cp} value. When prediction accuracy is low, a small f_{cp} leads to very high recovery times with low net-utility during that period. However, if f_{cp} is modulated properly to handle failures, recovery time decreases and a far lower cost/utility is achieved. Meanwhile, the effect of prediction accuracy is less prominent when a higher value of f_{cp} is used, as the recovery times don't improve much, even with a correct prediction.

6   Related Work

Traditional Fault-Tolerance. Redundancy is probably the earliest form of fault-tolerance; the approach popularly known as the active replication approach is well-studied, and a thorough description appears in [4]. Log-based recovery is well-know in the database domain. Here, a failure is handled with an undo-redo log [3]. Fault-tolerance has also been studied in the context of transactions [20] and distributed systems [21]. Dynamically trading consistency for availability is proposed in [22] using a continuous consistency model. A number of factors distinguish our approach from these traditional mechanism, the first and the foremost being its utility-awareness. Another distinction is our ability to use failure prediction to reduce the overhead of ensuring high-availability.

Failure Detection & Prediction. [7] focuses on the implementation of fault detection, and proposed a scalable fault detection/collection framework. More recently, researchers in the autonomic domain have used statistical monitoring techniques to detect failures in component-based Internet services [11,23]. MSET or multi-variate state estimation techniques [11] constitute an early warning system that enables failure prediction with low false alarm probability and has been successfully applied to the thermal control domain, and more recently, to software aging problems, including predicting memory leaks, data corruption, shared memory pool latching, etc. In [9], instrumentation data is correlated to system states using statistical induction techniques to identify system-level metrics that correlate with high-level performance states. In addition, these techniques are used to forecast service level objective violations, with prediction accuracy reported to be around 90%. Our system provides a framework in which several such failure detection and prediction techniques can be implemented to provide high-availability while imposing a low-overhead.

Fault-Tolerant Distributed Information Systems. Stars [21] presents a fault-tolerance manager for distributed application, using a distributed file manager which performs actions like message backups and checkpoints storage for user files. Its reliance on causal and atomic group multi-cast, however, demands additional solutions in the context of today's widely geographically distributed enterprise systems [24].

MTTR may be improved with solutions like Microreboot [25], which proposes a fast recovery technique for large systems. It is based on the observation that a significant fraction of software failures in large-scale Internet systems can be cured by rebooting. While rebooting can be expensive and cause nontrivial service disruption, microrebooting is a fine-grain technique for surgically recovering faulty application components, without disturbing the rest of the components of the application. Our work could benefit from such techniques.

GSpace [26] and replica management in Grids [27] studied dynamic data replication policy and modeling in distributed component-based systems when multiple replicas of data are desired, e.g., for global configuration data, or in a highly dynamic environment, to improve availability. For this kind of data replication management, efficient read-one write-all protocol [28] can be used when updates of the replicated data occur frequently.

IFLOW's techniques may be directly compared to the fault-tolerance offered in systems like Fault-Tolerant CORBA [29,30], Arjuna [31] and REL [32], which replicate selected application/service objects. Multiple replicas allow an object to continue to provide service even when one of its replicas fails. Passive replication is also provided. Here, the system records both the state of the currently executing member (primary member) and the entire sequence of method invocations. While CORBA focuses on the client-server model of communication, recent systems like Borealis [14] and SMILE [6] have focused on fault-tolerance for applications that process data streams. The former uses replication-based fault-recovery, and the authors propose to trade consistency for recovery time. The latter proposes the soft-checkpointing mechanism that can be used to implement a low-overhead passive replication scheme for fault tolerance. We differ from such earlier work because of our explicit consideration of system utility for managing system availability, and because our system also provides a framework for incorporating failure prediction techniques.

Utility-Functions. The specific notions of utility used in this paper mirror the work presented in [8], which uses utility functions for autonomic data-centers. Autonomic self-optimization according to business objectives is studied in [33], and self-management of information flow applications in accordance with utility functions is studied in [5]. A preliminary discussion about availability-aware self-configuration in autonomic systems appears in [34]. Our middleware carefully integrates the ideas from the above systems and other domains to build a comprehensive framework for fault-tolerant information flows.

7 Conclusion

We have proposed techniques for managing the tradeoff between availability and cost in information flow middleware. First, a net-utility-based formulation of the benefits an enterprise derives from its information flows combines both performance and reliability attributes of such flows. The goal is not simply to attain high utility, but to reliably provide high utility to large-scale information flow applications. Second, since reliability techniques incur costs, thereby reducing utility, proactive methods for availability-management regulates resources used to guarantee availability and take into account the fact that system and application behaviors change over time. A specific example is a higher likelihood of failure in high load vs. low load conditions. Reliability costs, therefore, are reduced by exploiting knowledge about the current 'perceived' system stability. Additional cost savings result from the use of failure prediction methods. Third, the implementation presented in this paper can deal with both transient and non-transient failures, the latter relying on application-specific techniques for fault avoidance. Finally, utility-driven proactive availability-management techniques has been integrated into our infrastructure for large-scale information flows, where it is shown to impose low additional communication and processing overheads on information flows. Experimental results with IFLOW attained on Emulab [17] demonstrate the effectiveness of proactive fault tolerance in recovering from failures.

Future work will experiment with richer failure prediction techniques, and investigate specific enterprise environments. For instance, we will model the redundant data-centers mandated by government rules, and will consider the attainment of high availability and net-utility in information flows that cross multiple organizational boundaries.

References

1. IBM: IBM global services: Improving systems availability. (http://www.cs.cmu.edu/~priya/hawht.pdf)
2. Gavrilovska, A., Schwan, K., Oleson, V.: A practical approach for zero' downtime in an operational information system. In: Proc. of ICDCS. (2002)

3. Gray, J., McJones, P.R., Blasgen, M.W., Lindsay, B.G., Lorie, R.A., Price, T.G., Putzolu, G.R., Traiger, I.L.: The recovery manager of the system R database manager. ACM Comput. Surv. **13**(2) (1981)

4. Randell, B., Lee, P., Treleaven, P.C.: Reliability issues in computing system design. ACM Comput. Surv. **10**(2) (1978)

5. Kumar, V., Cai, Z., Cooper, B.F., Eisenhauer, G., Schwan, K., Mansour, M., Seshasayee, B., Widener, P.: Implementing diverse messaging models with self-managing properties using iflow. In: Proc. of ICAC. (2006)

6. Strom, R.E.: Fault-tolerance in the smile stateful publish-subscribe system. In: Proc. of the Int'l Workshop on Distributed Event-Based Systems. (2004)

7. Stelling, P., Foster, I., Kesselman, C., Lee, C., Laszewski, G.V.: A fault detection service for wide area distributed computations. In: Proc. of HPDC. (1998)

8. Walsh, W.E., Tesauro, G., Kephart, J.O., Das, R.: Utility functions in autonomic systems. In: Proc. of ICAC. (2004)

9. Cohen, I., Goldszmidt, M., Kelly, T., Symons, J., Chase, J.: Correlating instrumentation data to system states: A building block for automated diagnosis and control. In: Proc. of OSDI. (2004)

10. Gross, K.C., Lu, W.: Early detection of signal and process anomalies in enterprise computing systems. In: Proc. of IEEE International Conference on Machine Learning and Applications. (2002)

11. Zavaljevski, N., Gross, K.C.: Uncertainty analysis for multivariate state estimation in mission-critical and safety-critical applications. In: Proc. MARCON. (2000)

12. Blough, D., Liu, P.: FIMD-MPI: A tool for injecting faults into mpi applications. In: Proc. of IPDPS. (2000)

13. Cai, Z., Kumar, V., Cooper, B.F., Eisenhauer, G., Schwan, K., Strom, R.: Utility-driven availability-management in enterprise-scale information flows. http://www.cercs.gatech.edu/tech-reports/ (2006) Technical report.

14. Balazinska, M., Balakrishnan, H., Madden, S., Stonebraker, M.: Fault-tolerance in the borealis distributed stream processing system. In: Proc. of the ACM SIGMOD international conference on Management of data. (2005)

15. Mansour, M., Schwan, K.: I-rmi: Performance isolation in information flow applications. In: Proc. of ACM/IFIP/IEEE Middleware. (2005)

16. Schwan, K., et al.: Autoflow: Autonomic information flows for critical information systems. In: Autonomic Computing: Concepts, Infrastructure, and Applications, ed. Manish Parashar and Salim Hariri, CRC Press. (2006)

17. Lepreau, J., et. al.: The Utah network testbed. (http://www.emulab.net/)

18. Zegura, E.W., Calvert, K., Bhattacharjee, S.: How to model an internetwork. In: Proc. of IEEE INFOCOM. (1996)

19. VINT Project: The network simulator - ns-2. (http://www.isi.edu/nsnam/ns/)

20. Wu, H., Kemme., B.: Fault-tolerance for stateful application servers in the presence of advanced transactions patterns. In: Proc. of SRDS. (2005)

21. Sens, P., Folliot, B.: STAR A fault-tolerant system for distributed applications. Software - Practice and Experience **28**(10) (1998)

22. Yu, H., Vahdat, A.: The costs and limits of availability for replicated services. In: Proc. of SOSP. (2001)

23. Fox, A., Kiciman, E., Patterson, D.: Combining statistical monitoring and predictable recovery for self-management. In: Proc. of SIGSOFT workshop on Self-managed systems. (2004)

24. Cheriton, D., Skeen, D.: Understanding the limitations of causally and totally ordered communication. In: Proc. of SOSP. (1993)

25. Candea, G., Kawamoto, S., Fujiki, Y., Friedman, G., Fox, A.: Microreboot - a technique for cheap recovery. In: Proc. of OSDI. (2004)
26. Russello, G., Chaudron, M., van Steen., M.: Dynamically adapting tuple replication for high availability in a shared data space. In: Proc. Int'l Conf. on Coordination Models and Languages. (2005)
27. Schintke, F., Reinefeld., A.: Modeling replica availability in large data grids. Journal of Grid Computing (2003)
28. Rabinovich, M., Lazowska, E.: An efficient and highly available read-one write-all protocol for replicated data management. In: Proc. of the Int'l Conf. on Parallel and Distributed Information Systems. (1993)
29. Group, O.M.: Final adopted specification for Fault Tolerant CORBA. In: OMG Technical Committee Document ptc/00-04-04. (2000)
30. Moorsel, A., Yajnik, S.: Design of a resource manager for fault-tolerant corba. In: Proc. of the Workshop on Reliable Middleware. (1999)
31. Parrington, G.D., Shrivastava, S.K., Wheater, S.M., Little, M.C.: The design and implementation of Arjuna. USENIX Computing Systems (1995)
32. Friese, T., Muller, J., Freisleben, B.: Self-healing execution of business processes based on a peer-to-peer service architecture. In: Proc. of ICAC. (2005)
33. Aiber, S., Gilat, D., Landau, A., Razinkov, N., Sela, A., Wasserkrug, S.: Autonomic self-optimization according to business objectives. In: Proc. of ICAC. (2004)
34. Chess, D.M., Kumar, V., Segal, A., Whalley, I.: Availability-aware self-configuration in autonomic systems. In: Distributed Systems Operations and Management. (2003)

Model Driven Provisioning: Bridging the Gap Between Declarative Object Models and Procedural Provisioning Tools

Kaoutar El Maghraoui[1], Alok Meghranjani[2], Tamar Eilam[3],
Michael Kalantar[3], and Alexander V. Konstantinou[3]

[1] Dept. of Computer Science, Rensselaer Polytechnic Institute, Troy, NY, USA
[2] École Polytechnique Fédérale de Lausanne, Lausanne, Switzerland
[3] IBM T.J. Watson Research Center, Hawthorne, NY, USA

Abstract. Today's enterprise data centers support thousands of mission-critical business applications composed of multiple distributed heterogeneous components. Application components exhibit complex dependencies on the configuration of multiple data center network, middleware, and related application resources. Applications are also associated with extended life-cycles, migrating from development to testing, staging and production environments, with frequent roll-backs. Maintaining end-to-end data center operational integrity and quality requires careful planning of (1) application deployment design, (2) resource selection, (3) provisioning operation selection, parameterization and ordering, and (4) provisioning operation execution. Current data center management products are focused on workflow-based automation of the deployment processes. Workflows are of limited value because they hard-code many aspects of the process, and are thus sensitive to topology changes. An emerging and promising class of model-based tools is providing new methods for designing detailed deployment topologies based on a set of requirements and constraints. In this paper we describe an approach to bridging the gap between generated "desired state" models and the elemental procedural provisioning operations supported by data center resources. In our approach, we represent the current and desired state of the data center using object models. We use AI planning to automatically generate workflows that bring the data center from its current state to the desired state. We discuss our optimizations to Partial Order Planning algorithms for the provisioning domain. We validated our approach by developing and integrating a prototype with a state of the art provisioning product. We also present initial results of a performance study.

1 Introduction

Today's enterprises are increasingly reliant on network-based services to implement mission-critical business processes. A typical enterprise supports thousands of business applications, composed of numerous heterogeneous distributed components, and deployed in multiple large data centers. The collection of business

M. van Steen and M. Henning (Eds.): Middleware 2006, LNCS 4290, pp. 404–423, 2006.

applications is in a constant state of flux. New applications are developed, tested on different test environments, staged and rolled into production. Existing applications are continuously updated, and often rolled-back. Data center operations personnel must provision and configure multiple networked environments and deploy applications into them. The capabilities of these environments have also evolved from basic services such as routing, naming, and hosting, to higher-level middleware services such as directory, messaging, and storage. Maintaining data center operational integrity and quality has thus become an extremely challenging task. In the absence of end-to-end operational methodologies and tools, enterprises and their customers are exposed to significant operational cost and risk.

While operators enjoy a large set of tools to perform local configuration tasks, they face major challenges in deploying complete applications. Current methodologies and tools provide fragmented and incomplete support for the end-to-end application deployment process. This process can be broken into four major logical steps, representing different domains of expertise. First, a deployment solution must be designed that satisfies functional application deployment requirements and non-functional deployment goals. Second, resources must be selected that can be used to implement the solution. Resource selection must take data center capabilities and constraints into account. Third, an ordering of bound provisioning operations must be established to bring the data center from its current to the desired state. Complex constraints exist between configuration parameters across the various tools and in provisioning operations that are far apart in the ordering sequence [1]. Implied or poorly documented ordering interdependencies are typically discovered in the process of deploying an application. Forth, the selected operations must be invoked across different management platforms and domains. Operation execution status must be monitored, and operational errors reported.

A new class of cross-platform management products, such as IBM Tivoli Provisioning Manager (TPM)[2], has emerged to address the bottom-up challenges of operating heterogeneous data centers. These provisioning technologies offer a large set of automation packages that expose a uniform data access and update layer to heterogeneous management platforms. In addition, they provide a platform for programming workflows for higher-level provisioning operations. Users can create workflows invoking primitive provisioning operations or other workflows to automate the deployment of a business application. Typically, such workflows statically encode significant aspects of the application design, resource selection, and operational ordering choices tied to a particular deployment environment. Development, testing and maintenance of such workflows in a changing environment is a significant challenge. Since these workflows are specific to a deployed application and a target environment, the potential level of reuse is minimal. Thus, the amortized complexity is not reduced.

More recently, a new class of model-based tools has emerged to address the top-down challenges of designing and binding applications to data center resources. In these tools, the current data center state and the desired deployment solution are both described declaratively using object-relationship models. These tools aid in the construction and validation of a model describing the desired solution, which may vary in its degree of concreteness. In particular, resource instances may or may not be identified by it. In [3,4] we described the design and implementation of such a tool, and the methods we used to guarantee that the deployment topology satisfies an input set of requirements and constraints. While these tools address the design and resource selection challenges, their output is a declarative model, and the generalized task of realizing this model using existing provisioning tools is an open problem.

We believe that representing configuration knowledge in object models will offer significant advantages and will be the basis for the next generation of configuration management tools [5]. Models provide easier visualization, conceptualization, extensibility, componentization, standardization, and reuse. Most technologies in this space are moving towards model-based solutions. However, there exists an inherent mismatch between a declarative model that is the basis for these modeling tools and the provisioning technologies that are in essence procedural. Moreover, the granularity does not match: models are typically fine grained, while provisioning operations are coarser grained. In particular, provisioning operations may have a complex effect on multiple resources. In modeling terms, multiple objects and relationships may change in a model describing the state of the data center before and after an execution of a provisioning operation.

In this paper we describe an approach which bridges the gap between the declarative model of a solution and the procedural provisioning operation tooling needed for its implementation. We use models to declaratively describe the required solution, as well as the operational capabilities of existing provisioning platforms. We then employ a planning algorithm to automatically infer the partial order of provisioning operations and their inputs to deploy a given application in a data center. The generated workflows maintain operational constraints while verifiably provisioning the desired data center state. Our approach supports the seamless integration of existing automation tools specializing in application solution design, resource selection, and cross-platform provisioning. We based and evaluated our models and algorithms on the capabilities of a state of the art provisioning product[2], in customer use.

The structure of the paper is as follows. In Section 2, we present an overview of our approach and architecture for model driven deployment planning. Next, in Section 3, we present a formal model for applying planning to the problem domain. In Section 4, we describe the planning algorithm and how we optimized it for our particular usage of deployment planning. In Section 5, we describe our prototypical implementation and integration with TPM [2], a state of the art provisioning product. In Section 6, we present empirical results of a multi-tier network provisioning experiment. Last, in Section 7, we review the related work, and in Section 8, we summarize the work and discuss future challenges.

2   Approach

2.1   Background: Data Center Operations Today

Data center operators use a large number of automation and configuration tools to deploy distributed applications and services on a set of managed resources. Every such tool provides a set of automated resource management functions, that we term *provisioning operations*. To accomplish a particular configuration task, the operator must identify a set of provisioning operations provided by the collection of available tools, instantiate them correctly, and execute them in an appropriate order. Hundreds of low-level provisioning operations may be required to deploy a single application. For example, servers must be selected from a free pool, network switches, firewalls and load balancers must be configured, operating systems, middleware, and application components must be installed and/or configured, and monitoring must be enabled. Some of these tasks, such as the selection of resources, are performed manually, others with tooling assistance. The ordering and parameterization of provisioning operation invocations is determined by operators in an ad hoc manner. Operators typically rely on past experience, product manuals, existing scripts and other unstructured and informal data sources.

Individual provisioning operations may incorporate complex logic. A provisioning operation often makes assumptions about the state of the affected resources and about other resources connected to them. Upon invocation, it may perform a large number of fine grained configuration actions effecting the state of a number of resources in the data center. For example, a provisioning operation to install an operating system may need to configure a DHCP server and a network image server, in addition to the target system of the installation. In secure environments, the OS install operation might have to configure a number of network devices to ensure connectivity between the install server and the target server. To determine a successful order of executions, operators must fully understand the preconditions and effects of each of the provisioning operations and their interdependencies. Due to the aforementioned complexities, operators often rely on step-by-step trial and error operation. Even a simple application migration from the developer's workstation to a testing environment can become a challenge, with studies indicating it accounts for 35% of the testing time[1].

2.2   A Case for Model Driven Deployment Using Planning

Increasingly, object models are used in order to formally describe resource configuration state. The objects in these models are typically typed and associated with attributes. For example, the Management Information Base (MIB) of an IP system will contain an object for each IP network interface, with attributes such as IP address and netmask. The IP interface node will also have a relationship to the network interface card (NIC) object on which it is defined. These configuration models can be navigated and queried at a fine level of granularity.

---

[1] Theresa Lanowitz, speaking at a Mercury Users Conference, 2004.

While configuration models offer uniform access and navigation, their update functions are typically not uniform or consistent. A single operation may have multiple parameters, pre-conditions and post-conditions. For example, the operation to configure an IP interface may take multiple parameters such as the IP address, netmask, NIC, and default gateway, where the IP address must be unique and must match the netmask, the NIC must be enabled and connected to a link-layer network associated with the netmask, and so on. The execution of the operation may result in changes at multiple attributes and nodes in the MIB.

The complexity of configuration operation parameterization and dependency ordering, necessitates the use of advanced algorithms for inferring and generating correct sequences of provisioning actions, termed *workflows*. The workflow generation problem can be naturally reduced to the AI planning problem. A planning system synthesizes a course of actions to change the world from its current state to a desired goal state. A planning domain defines a set of atomic *actions* that are capable of changing the state of the world. Each action can only be executed under some particular conditions of the world termed *preconditions*. Each action has certain *effects* on the state of the world. A *planner* generates a *plan*: a sequence of actions that will bring the world from its initial state to the goal state.

Use of planning for workflow generation allows users to focus on the declarative expression of data center resources, desired state and operation models. Models can be defined by different users, supporting separation of concerns across resource types and operational domains. For example, a CISCO router expert may model the pre-conditions and post-conditions of a CISCO IOS router configuration operation. A deployment expert may add a constraint that a route must exist between the boot server and a system being rebooted. These models can be created once, and reused many times to automatically generate multiple workflows to deploy multiple applications in different networked environments. Thus, the amortized complexity of managing the enterprise data center is significantly reduced using this approach.

Our approach to deployment planning and execution can be summarized as follows. (1) we formally capture both the current state of the data center, and the desired deployment solution using object-relationship models, (2) we formally capture the pre-conditions and effects of a key set of provisioning operations provided by the available tools using propositional logic, (3) we employ partial order planning algorithms to automatically generate sequences of provisioning operations to bring the data center from its current state to the desired state. We optimize partial order planning to the area of provisioning by utilizing domain knowledge and data center characteristics.

The detailed architecture of our approach is depicted in Fig. 1. The current state of data center resources is maintained in a configuration database in the form of an object-relationship model. Automation tools are integrated into the system by a specialized adapter. This adapter provides an abstraction layer and a common access layer to execute the functions that are provided by the tool.

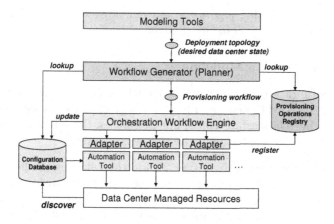

Fig. 1. Architecture

In addition, the pre-conditions and effects of key provisioning operations are formally modeled as predicates and transformers over the data center state and kept in a repository.

A workflow orchestration framework provides the means to author workflows, encoding sequences of invocations of provisioning operations, and to manage their execution. These worflows, in addition to invoking operations on the tools, update the configuration database, based on the expected or actual result of the execution. This is necessary since the tools are agnostic of the configuration database. Note that this will always be an approximation of the actual state of the data center. Discovery techniques can be employed to fix any inaccuracies in the state of the data center as it is recorded in the configuration database.

A workflow generator (planner) receives three inputs: the current state of the data center, the desired deployment topology, and the available provisioning operations. The desired topology is generated using a modeling tool, such as [4]. The workflow generator employs a planning algorithm to automatically generate orchestration workflows. The workflow generator component is the focus of this paper. The rest of paper focuses on the design, implementation, algorithms, and empirical studies of this architectural component.

3   Generating Workflows Using Planning

Given a model describing the desired deployment state of an application, the task of workflow generation involves identifying the provisioning operations to be performed, binding of operational parameters, and analyzing ordering dependencies between operations. The set of available provisioning operations is determined by the provisioning technology. In this section, we describe how we can use planning methods to generate the workflows by mapping the models representing current and desired state to first order logic that is the input to most planners, and modeling the provisioning operations as planner actions. Sect. 4

will focus on the planning algorithm and our adjustments and optimizations necessary for it to work well in this domain.

3.1   Problem Domain Modeling

State Modeling. Any resource object model (in fact any network model [6]) can be simply mapped to first-order logic. For a given object model, consisting of typed nodes and relationships containing attributes, the following construction will generate an equivalent planning initial or goal state:

- For each object instance N of type T, add the following predicates:
  - (exists N), to express that the object is in the *created* state.
  - (T N), to express the type of the object.
  - For object models with support for inheritance, add (T_1 N), (T_2 N), ... predicates for each supertype T_i of type T.
- For each relationship instance E of type T, between N_1 and N_2, add the following predicates:
  - (established E N_1 N_2), to express that the relationship is in the *established* state.
  - (T E), to express the type of the relationship.
  - For object models with support for relationship type inheritance, add (T_1 E), (T_2 E), ... predicates for each supertype T_i of relationship type T.
- For each object or relationship O, and an attribute A declared in type T with value V, add the following predicates:
  - (set O A), to express that the attribute is set.
  - ($T.A$ O V), to express the attribute's value.

The above rules are used to translate both the initial data center model and that of a desired topology (which represents the desired state of all the resources in the data center) into a first-order representation.

Figure 2 shows a sample object-relationship configuration model of a data center server and its logic representation. The server contains a network interface

Fig. 2. Example object model and logical representation

```
(:action moveSwitchPortToVlan
     : parameters        (?switch - Switch
                          ?sp      - SwitchPort
                          ?vlan1   - Vlan
                          ?vlan2   - Vlan
                          ?scs     - SwitchContainsSp
                          ?vdos    - VlanDefinedOnSwitch
                          ?vcs1    - VlanContainsSp
                          ?vcs2    - VlanContainsSp)
     : precondition (and (exists ?switch) (exists ?sp) (exists ?vlan2)
                          (established ?scs ?switch ?sp)
                          (established ?vdos ?vlan2 ?switch)
                          (established ?vcs1 ?vlan1 ?sp)
                          (set SwitchPort.spNumber ?sp) (set SwitchPort.spModule ?sp)
                          (set Vlan.vlanNumber ?vlan2))
     :effect        (and (established ?vcs2 ?vlan2 ?sp)
                          (not (established ?vcs1 ?vlan1 ?sp)))
```

Fig. 3. PDDL specification for the `moveSwitchPortToVlan` operation

card (NIC) which is connected to a switch port on switch `sw01`. The switch port is also configured to be a member of the virtual LAN (VLAN) `vlan1` defined on `sw01`. The `SwitchPort` type is inherited in our type system from the `Nic` type. `vlan1` has an attribute `vlanNumber` with value 201.

Action Modeling. Provisioning operations are modeled as planner actions. Typically, provisioning actions are implemented imperatively, thereby requiring additional declarative modeling of pre-conditions and post-conditions. The Planning Domain Definition Language (PDDL) [7] is a common language for expressing planning domains. Preconditions for each action may express restrictions on the life-cycle state of entities (e.g. exists), graph structure, and attribute values. The effects of the actions are similarly expressed.

An example of a configuration operation model expressed in PDDL is shown in Fig. 3. The operation `moveSwitchPortToVlan` configures a switch to assign a switch port into a particular VLAN. This allows the computer system connected to the port to communicate with other computer systems in that VLAN as if they were on the same local network. In order to move a switch port into a VLAN, the switch port, the switch and the VLAN must all exist and be interconnected. The preconditions clause in Fig. 3 express these requirements. The effects clause indicates that after the execution of this action, the switch port will be contained in the VLAN. For simplicity, we omitted the type predicates for both objects and relationships. They are implied from the definition of the parameters.

3.2 Planning

Planning algorithms are a class of search algorithms. They basically search and backtrack various possible plans until they find a solution. Classic planners adopt one of two approaches: searching the world state space or searching the plan space. In the first approach, the search space consists of a graph whose nodes represent the state of the world and whose edges represent the execution of actions (e.g. GraphPlan [8]). The planner can search world space starting from the initial state (progression planners) or starting from the goal state (regression planners). In the second approach, each node in the graph represents a partial plan, and each edge represents a plan refinement operation. Of these, some algorithms generate totally ordered plans (Total Order Planning), while others generate partially ordered plans (Partial Order Planning or Least Commitment Planning) [9,10].

For the task of provisioning workflow generation, we selected partial order planning (POP) for the following reasons:

1. A partially ordered plan can be efficiently executed in parallel. Provisioning a distributed application typically requires configuring multiple systems. These configurations can usually be done in parallel.
2. In any given data center state, there may be many possible actions that can be executed. The number of such actions is proportional to the size of the data center. Consequently, world state search approaches will have a high branching factor. A high branching factor is likely to increase planning cost.
3. Partially ordered planning algorithms are efficient when the number of possible actions to fulfill a given condition is small. This is the common case for distributed application provisioning: typically only a few provisioning operations will produce a particular configuration of a given resource.

3.3   Partial Order Planning

A partial order planner searches the plan space. Each node in the search space represents a *partial plan* while edges represent *plan refinement* operations. We briefly review partial order planning; for a more detailed description see, for example, [9].

A partial plan in POP is a set of action steps $S_0, S_1, \ldots, S_f$ and a set of ordering constraints $S_i < S_j$ which indicate the causal order of the action steps. In addition, the following meta information is maintained: (1) a set of causal links $S_i \rightarrow^c S_j$ that record that precondition c of step S_j is achieved by step S_i, (2) a set of *open conditions* which consist of action preconditions that still remained to be achieved, and (3) a set of *unsafe links* $S_i \rightarrow_c S_j$ indicating that precondition c is deleted by some step S_k in the partial plan.

Partial order planning begins with an initial unfinished plan comprising two dummy steps: Start Step S_0 and Finish step S_f. S_0 is a step with no preconditions and whose effects represent the world in the initial state. S_f is a step with no effects and whose preconditions represent the world in the goal state. This initial plan is iteratively refined by applying plan refinement operations also termed *flaw resolutions*. Flaw resolutions fall into two categories:

1. **Open Condition Achievement:** An open condition represents a unachieved precondition of an action already added to the partial plan. An open condition can be achieved by adding a new action to the partial plan or by reusing an action already in the plan.

2. **Unsafe Links Resolution:** An unsafe link indicates that an achieved condition may be invalidated by another action. In this case, ordering the actions avoids the conflict.

A partial plan is a complete plan when there are no flaws in it. A partial planner continues to refine the different partial plans generated until a complete plan is found or all the different possibilities have been tried and no solution is found. Observe that a POP planner generates a plan backwards by identifying actions that achieve the preconditions of actions already in the plan.

General-purpose planning algorithms suffer from poor scalability. The use of domain-specific knowledge is critical to developing practical planners [11]. We show in subsequent sections, how we have exploited the nature of the domain of network configurations in distributed application provisioning to achieve significant improvements in the efficiency of POP for this purpose.

4   Optimizing POP for Provisioning

4.1   Domain Characteristics

The domain of distributed application deployment poses efficiency challenges to the generic partial order planning algorithm:

Complex Provisioning Operations. Provisioning operations tend to be complex, ofter performing multiple configuration tasks. Consequently, even simple operations frequently have several parameters and effects. Their preconditions also tend to have many clauses. When adding an action to a partial plan, each parameter that must be instantiated acts as a multiplier to the number of possible variable instantiations, resulting in a high branching factor.

Data Center Size. A typical data center manages hundreds, if not thousands, of resources. This means that for a given action parameter, the planner needs to consider a large number of possible values. For example, when trying to instantiate a server variable in an action, there may be hundreds of possible instantiations. In partial order planning, if we naively attempt to fully instantiate each action that is added to a partial plan, the branching factor will be prohibitive.

Constrained Resource Modifications. Resources can be configured only in a limited number of ways, and data center policy typically introduces even more configuration constraints. For example, the set of NICs that a server contains is typically fixed. In addition, once a server is wired into a data center, its relationship (through its NIC) to a switch port on a particular switch is typically fixed. Consequently, a resource typically has a number of fixed relationships with other resources. Many provisioning operations tend to be local in nature: they operate on groups of closely related parameters. In subsequent sections we explore how a planner can take advantage of the fixed relationships between resources to efficiently instantiate parameters.

Runtime Parameter Determination. Not all parameters for provisioning operations are available at planning time. Some are only available at deployment time. For example, to enable communication, it is necessary to configure a server's network interface with an IP address. It is usually not possible to select any unused IP address; the selection is constrained by a runtime data center policy. As a consequence, at planning time, it is not possible to instantiate all variables. We discuss how we deal with this, using a concept that we term *deferred instantiation*, in Sect. 4.2 below.

4.2 Partial Order Planning for Provisioning

Prioritized Flaw Selection. Partial order planning proceeds by iteratively selecting flaws to resolve. This selection can be ordered to improve planning efficiency. In our workflow generator, we, as in [12] and [13], resolve unsafe links before open conditions. With regards to resolving open conditions, we use the following priority (in a descending order):

1. Open conditions of the form (exists ?<type>).
2. Fully instantiated open conditions.
3. Other partially instantiated open conditions.

Our highest priority is to instantiate unknown resources. We do so for two reasons: first, such open conditions have only one uninstantiated variable, helping to reduce branching. Second, once resources are bound, it is more likely that open conditions representing resource relationships and attribute values will be more constrained, again reducing branching.

Fully instantiated open conditions are given preference compared to partially instantiated open conditions because they constrain the problem more. They are least likely to introduce the uninstantiated open conditions.

When comparing two open conditions which are either fully instantiated or which are both partially instantiated, the flaw selection algorithm counts the number of partial plans that will be created to resolve each open condition. The open condition that generates the fewest new partial plans will be selected.

Condition Driven Variable Instantiation. Recall that one class of flaw resolutions are open condition achievement operations. These operations involve adding a new action to a partial plan or reusing an existing action in a partial plan to achieve the precondition of another action in the partial plan. When adding actions we can choose to instantiate all of its parameters with specific values or instantiate only some of them. If we choose to instantiate all of the parameters, we create a new partial plan for each combination of fully instantiated variables. Recall that provisioning operations typically have a large number of parameters and that data centers manage a large number of resources. Consequently, a large number of new partial plans will be generated. In search terms, the branching factor will be high. On the other hand, we may leave parameters uninstantiated until a consistency threat necessitates instantiation. If we leave parameters uninstantiated, the branching factor remains low, however, planning becomes more complex, as it is necessary to maintain variable binding constraints that specify whether two parameters are the same. Further, it is necessary to implement a unifier that takes into account the variable binding constraints to identify valid tuples of parameters. Unsafe link detection and action matching become more complex as well.

We adopted a hybrid approach that reduces the branching factor but which minimizes the complexity of the implementation and the performance overhead. In our approach, when adding a new action we instantiate only the parameters that are needed in order to satisfy the open condition. Note that adding an action may result in new open conditions corresponding to the unsatisfied preconditions of this new action with uninstantiated variables. Unlike the lazy approach described above, we do not allow these uninstantiated variables to be propagated to new actions at a subsequent step. Instead, when we select an open condition that is uninstantiated, we generate instantiations at that time. Our approach reduces the branching factor because the number of variables in an open condition is low for provisioning (typically one or two). Further, the need for variable binding constraints is minimized because uninstantiated variables are not propagated. This significantly reduces the complexity of the implementation and the performance overhead.

Model Guided Variable Instantiation. We take advantage of knowledge on resource and data center configurability constraints to minimize the number of tuples created when binding variables in an open condition. For example, the relationships between servers and their NICs, and also typically the relationships between the NICs and the switch ports to which they are connected, are all fixed. These fixed relationships limit the number of resources that need to be considered when instantiating an action.

As an example, consider the provisioning operation `addNetworkInterface` shown on the left side of Fig. 4, and its precondition (`established ?scn ...`), where scn is a relationship of type `SystemContainsNic`. Without our strategy, the planning algorithm would generate all pairs of systems and NICs in the data center, 8 combinations will be generated for the data center model piece shown in Fig. 4 (types and identities of relationships are omitted for simplicity). Most would lead to a search dead end since no action exists that can change the fixed relationships between servers and their NICs. Not only are a large number of possible instantiations generated, but they are not immediately eliminated from consideration. Using our strategy, on the other hand, only pairs connected by a relationship will be considered. Specifically, only the following pairs will be generated by the planning algorithm when instantiating this action: (`EJB-server, nic4`), (`EJB-server, nic5`), (`Data-server ,nic1`), and (`Data-server, nic2`). Clearly, if one of the variables in this example were already instantiated, the number of tuples is further reduced. As a further enhancement of this strategy, we not only look at the preconditions of the current action when instantiating variables, but also at other preconditions, associated with relationships that are know to be fixed, where the variables appear.

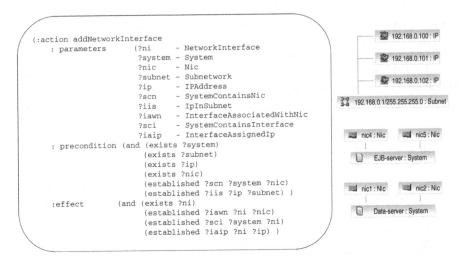

```
(:action addNetworkInterface
    : parameters      (?ni      - NetworkInterface
                       ?system  - System
                       ?nic     - Nic
                       ?subnet  - Subnetwork
                       ?ip      - IPAddress
                       ?scn     - SystemContainsNic
                       ?iis     - IpInSubnet
                       ?iawn    - InterfaceAssociatedWithNic
                       ?sci     - SystemContainsInterface
                       ?iaip    - InterfaceAssignedIp
    : precondition (and (exists ?system)
                        (exists ?subnet)
                        (exists ?ip)
                        (exists ?nic)
                        (established ?scn ?system ?nic)
                        (established ?iis ?ip ?subnet) )
    :effect        (and (exists ?ni)
                        (established ?iawn ?ni ?nic)
                        (established ?sci ?system ?ni)
                        (established ?iaip ?ni ?ip) )
```

Fig. 4. Specification of the `addNetweorkInterface` provisioning operation and part of initial state showing two servers, their NICs and several IP addresses

Deferred Variable Instantiation. A deployment topology describes how resources in a data center should be configured. While the deployment topology identifies all the resources needed, it may not have fully selected them. Recall that a data center may implement policies that prevent some types of resources from selection until deployment time. For example, to configure a network interface, it is necessary to have an IP address. While the planner knows, based on the data center model, what IP addresses are in use, it does not have control over the selection of IP addresses, as data center policies typically determine the selection at deployment time using a provisioning operation. This restriction prevents the planning system from instantiating the IP address in other network configuration actions, such as to configure network interfaces, routing, and access control. To address this challenge, we introduce the concept of *deferred variable instantiation*. For variables that can only be instantiated at deployment time, we create *placeholders* that represents the instantiated variables. Such a substitution can, however, take place only when the following conditions hold:

1. There is a provisioning operation (action) that can create a new unique instance of the required variable. For example, to resolve an IP address, the provisioning system may have an operation `getIPAddress` that generates a valid IP address.
2. The variable does not change in value once it is created.

The placeholder represents the output of a particular provisioning operation. It is treated as a read only instantiated variable that can be used as a parameter to other operations.

5 Prototype Implementation

We implemented a prototype of the workflow generator architecture and planning algorithm described in the previous sections. For the role of the workflow generator, we developed a custom Java-based partial order planner. The planner was implemented with configurable support for our domain specific variable instantiations, flaw selection, and deferred variable instantiation. For the role of the workflow engine, we used the IBM Tivoli Provisioning Manager (TPM) [2] v.3.1 product. TPM workflows are parameterized with strongly typed objects defined in a data center model (DCM). The DCM schema is DMTF CIM-based [14]. DCM instance data is populated manually, or automatically by discovery tools. TPM provides a device abstraction layer whereby logical device operations (LDOs) are declared against DCM types. This layer enables users to define workflows that can operate over different vendor implementations of a logical device. DCM objects are bound to device drivers that bundle device-specific implementations of logical device operations. We modeled a subset of the TPM LDOs relating to network configuration, as planner actions. We also implemented an importer from the DCM object model to logical representation. Finally, we implemented an Eclipse-based graphical user interface, with views for planner operations, initial and goal states, and generated operation partial orders.

Our prototype was also integrated with the SPiCE (Service Plan Composition Engine) model-driven data center design tool [3]. Using SPiCE, users could customize a logical application structure with deploy-time choices, and automatically generate the desired state of the data center. Our worflow generator would then be invoked, in the same Eclipse shell-sharing environment, to generate the the partial order of TPM LDOs required to provision the data center changes. A TPM workflow exporter was implemented to convert the planner's output to the TPM workflow language. Generated TPM workflows were submitted for execution to the TPM deployment engine.

6 Empirical Evaluation

We evaluated our prototype using the desired network structure of a three-tier clustered application consisting of a web, business logic, and data tier. An example of this structure is depicted in Fig. 5. An external browser system was defined to model remote access to the web tier. Browser traffic would be routed through a firewall, connected to a load-balancer, spreading requests across the servers in the web cluster. Web tier servers would invoke business logic functions by routing traffic over an internal firewall. Load balancing on the business tier would be performed at the application-level. Business tier servers were modeled as dual-homed, connecting to the data tier through another firewall. The figure is a screen shot of the SPiCE visualizer and depicts a filtered view over the desired state topology. Server, router and load-balancer network interface card (NIC), IP interface configuration, and routes were hidden. The switch and switch ports over which the VLANs were defined were also hidden.

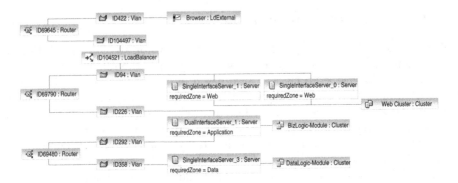

Fig. 5. Sample three-tier application network structure

The desired state models were varied in the number of servers per cluster. The models were generated by defining a SPiCE logical application structure and varying the cluster size. For our infrastructure modeling, we created a parameterized DCM generator that created data centers with the requisite number of switches, routers, load-balancers and servers. The number of NICs on each device was also parameterized. The generated data center resources were instrumented by a simulator device driver provided by TPM.

We modeled the network device logical device operations (LDOs) for creating a VLAN on a switch, assigning a port to a VLAN, creating IP network interfaces on systems (routers and servers), creating routes, access control lists, and virtual IP addresses, creating clusters and free-pools, and adding servers to clusters and free pools. We also modeled resource-selection operations for selecting IP addresses/subnets, assigning tiers, and determining cluster expansion sizes (for support of TPM dynamic orchestration features). Figure 6 lists a partial workflow generated for a minimal topology. The workflow represents a serial execution of the partial order generated by the planner (topological sort). It starts by creating the spare pool, customer and subnet logical resources defined in the desired state. Next it obtains a unique VLAN ID, and creates a new VLAN with the specified ID in the switch identified in the desired state. It configures the switch port to the newly created VLAN ID (must precede VLAN creation on switch). Note that this operation required the switch module containing the port as a parameter. This information was missing from the desired state. The planner used the module port lookup LDO to obtain the required parameter.

We focus on scalability studies that show our domain specific enhancements, described in Sect. 4.2, scale well and are better performing than the generic POP algorithm. We present two scalability experiments using the workflow generator. They investigated the scalability of the generator in terms of the infrastructure size and the size of the three-tier application desired state.

First, we varied the number of available resources in the data center keeping the number of resources in the desired state constant. Because the desired topology was unchanged, the number of provisioning operations was constant,

```
workflow SPiCEDeployOneTimeWorkflow LocaleInsensitive

  // variable declarations deleted ...

  CreateSparePool( "Pres-Module_pool", ID211)
  CreateCustomer( placeholder_2, ID213)
  CreateSubnet( ID92 )
  GetUniqueVLANNumber( placeholder_7)
  CreateVLAN( "1209", "ID68", placeholder_7, ID68)
  GetIPAddress( placeholder_10, "1219", ID92)
  AddNetworkInterface( "1218", "1219", ID92, placeholder_10, DT_ID75)
  CreateApplication( "MyAppStagEnv", ID213, ID214)
  GetPortModule( placeholder_24 )
  MovePortToVLAN( "1209", "1202", Vlan_DT_ID68, placeholder_24, "1")
  CreateRoute( "1218", ID152, ID94, ID75, ID193)
  GetClusterTier( placeholder_20 )
  GetClusterMinServers( placeholder_21 )
  GetClusterMaxServers( placeholder_22 )
  CreateCluster( "Pres-Module", placeholder_20, placeholder_22, placeholder_21, ID214, ID148 )
  AddServerToCluster( ID148, "1227" )
  AssociateClusterToPool( ID148, ID211 )
```

Fig. 6. A example of a generated workflow

modulo the selection of different servers. Therefore, the experiment measured the
performance of the planner's variable instantiation. Figure 7 shows the planning
time for infrastructures containing between 10 and 250 servers. We benchmarked
our POP planner performance with domain specific optimizations enabled and
disabled. The results show that the effect of our variable substitution optimizations result in a significant speedup for the base case, and are significantly less
sensitive to infrastructure size increases.

In our second scalability experiment, we varied the number of resources in the
desired state by increasing the number of servers in each tier cluster. We varied
the total number of servers from 4 to 128. In this case, we kept the number of
resources in the data center constant at 250 servers. Under these conditions, the

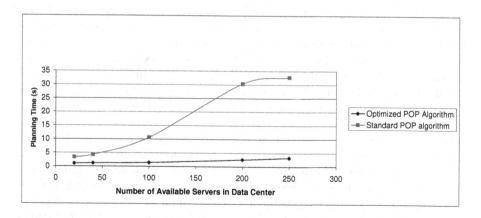

Fig. 7. Planning time vs. the number of servers in the infrastructure

number of provisioning operations will grow, resulting in a larger search space. Figure 8 shows the results of benchmarking our POP planner with optimizations enabled and one point with optimizations disabled. For problems with more than 4 servers we were unable to obtain solutions using the unoptimized planner.

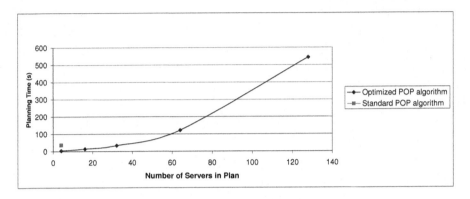

Fig. 8. the number of generated partial plans vs. the number of servers in the deployment topology

7   Related Work

Planning techniques are increasingly being adopted for distributed system management. Several projects have recently used planning techniques for the deployment of component-based applications [15,16,17], the composition of web services [18], and the management and execution of scientific workflows in the Grid [19,20]. There are several main differences in focus between these works and the work presented in this paper. All of these works focus on software (or service) level configurations. In contrast, our work is focused primarily on the low level network configuration aspect that is driven by the application requirements. The main usage of planning in these works is the optimization of resource placement, resource usage, and/or execution time, where a simplified model of the provisioning and configuration actions is assumed. In contrast, in our work we assume that an input desired state identifies the selected resources. Rather, we focus on the correct ordering and instantiation of complex real world provisioning and configuration actions with multiple preconditions and effects on the system state, and with a large number of input parameters.

Specifically, in [17], the authors addresses the issue of resource-aware deployment of component-based distributed applications in wide-area systems though planning. They provide a model, called the component placement problem (CPP), that describes the placement of application components onto computational, data, and network resources across a wide-area environment subject to constraints. The planner generates a plan of application components placement on a set of networked nodes. The work does not address the provisioning operations necessary to implement the solution and their ordering.

The CHAMPS system [16] focuses on Change Management, a process by which IT systems are changed through software upgrades, hot fixes, or, hardware changes. Upon the reception of a request for change, CHAMPS assesses the impact of the change and generates a change plan (as a BPEL workflow). Planning is used to optimize resource selection and execution time, while it is assumed that needed provisioning operations and their temporal dependencies are known.

Several techniques have been suggested to limit the search space when using planning for the dynamic composition of web services. Similar techniques might be applicable to our domain such as using business rules to guide the search space [21] and adopting a mixed-initiative approach where users can interact with the planner to drive the workflow composition process [22].

It is widely agreed on that proper modeling of the planning domain is key for correct and efficient planning. Several efforts have manually encoded the necessary domain knowledge [23,24]. This is error prone and requires extensive efforts which hinder the practicality and adoption of the approach. In this work, we advocate the usage of object models for representing the current and goal state. In addition, we sucessfully integrated our planner with a modeling tool that generates an object model representating the desired state [3], and with a provisioning engine that provides the current state.

8   Summary and Future Work

Separation of deployment concerns is key to improving data center reliability, as well as reducing capital and operational costs. Emerging model driven technologies are showing great promise in the direction of weaving functional application aspects, with non-fuctional aspects such as security, performance and availability, and data center resource availability and policies. Bridging the model to provisioning system gap is a key challenge in releasing the value of these tools. In this paper we demonstrated that with proper optimizations, planning algorithms can provide this bridge. Our initial results focused on generating network provisioning workflows driven by application requirements. Future work will focus on extending the operational models to the software domain. Resource selection can be performed in various stages of the deployment design process, and future work will examine usability and performance implications of alternatives. Existing workflows can be mined for dependencies, and compared to generated workflows to detect unusual ordering patterns. Desired state models may introduce non-functional operational dependencies, which should be honored by the planner.

Acknowledgements

The authors would like to thank the following people for discussions and ideas over the past three years: Giovanni Pacifici, Lily Mummert, John Pershing, Hendrik Wagner, Aditya Agrawal, Guerney Hunt and Andrew Trossman.

References

1. Brown, A.B., Keller, A., Hellerstein, J.: A model of configuration complexity and its applications to a change management system. In: International Symposium on Integrated Network Management. (2005)
2. IBM: Tivoli provisioning manager (http://www-306.ibm.com/software/tivoli/products/prov-mgr/) (2006)
3. Eilam, T., Kalantar, M., Konstantinou, A., Pacifici, G.: Reducing the complexity of application deployment in large data centers. In: International Symposium on Integrated Network Management. (2005)
4. Eilam, T., Kalantar, M., Konstantinou, A., Pacifici, G., Pershing, J., Agrawal, A.: Managing the configuration complexity of distributed applications in internet data centers. IEEE Communication Magazine **44** (2006) 166–177
5. Felfernig, A., Friedrich, G.E., et al.: UML as a domain specific knowledge for the construction of knowledge based configuration systems. In: SEKE'99 11th Int. Conf. on Software Engineering and Knowledge Engineering. (1999)
6. Taylor, R., Frank, R.: Codasyl data-base management systems. ACM Comput. Surv. **8** (1976) 67–103
7. Ghallab, M., Howe, A., Knoblock, C., McDermott, D., Ram, A., Veloso, M., Weld, D., Wilkins, D.: PDDL—the planning domain definition language (1998)
8. Blum, A.L., Furst, M.L.: Fast planning through planning graph analysis. Artif. Intell. **90** (1997) 281–300
9. Weld, D.S.: An introduction to least commitment planning. AI Magazine **15** (1994) 27–61
10. Minton, S., Bresina, J.L., Drummond, M.: Total-order and partial-order planning: A comparative analysis. Journal of Artificial Intelligence Research **2** (1994) 227–262
11. Knoblock, C.A., Yang, Q.: Relating the performance of partial-order planning algorithms to domain features. SIGART Bulletin **6** (1995) 8–15
12. McAllester, D., Rosenblitt, D.: Systematic nonlinear planning. In: Proceedings of the Ninth National Conference on Artificial Intelligence (AAAI-91). Volume 2., Anaheim, California, USA, AAAI Press/MIT Press (1991) 634–639
13. Penberthy, J.S., Weld, D.S.: UCPOP: A sound, complete, partial order planner for ADL. In Nebel, B., Rich, C., Swartout, W., eds.: KR'92. Principles of Knowledge Representation and Reasoning: Proc.s of the 3rd Int. Conf. Morgan Kaufmann, San Mateo, California (1992) 103–114
14. Force, D.M.T.: Common Information Model (CIM) Standards (http://www.dmtf.org/standards/cim) (2006)
15. Arshad, N., Heimbigner, D., Wolf, A.L.: Deployment and dynamic reconfiguration planning for distributed software systems. In: 15th IEEE Int. Conf. on Tools with Artificial Intelligence, IEEE Press (2003) 39–46
16. Keller, A., Hellerstein, J., Wolf, J., Wu, K., Krishnan, V.: The champs system: Change management with planning and scheduling. In: IEEE/IFIP Network Operations and Management Symposium (NOMS 2004), IEEE Press (2004)
17. Kichkaylo, T., Karamcheti, V.: Optimal resource-aware deployment planning for component-based distributed applications. In: HPDC '04: 13th IEEE Int. Symp. on High Performance Distributed Computing (HPDC'04), Washington, DC, USA, IEEE Computer Society (2004) 150–159
18. Su, X., Rao, J.: A survey of automated web service composition methods. In: SWSWPC 2004: First International Workshop on Semantic Web Services and Web Process Composition. (2004)

19. Blythe, J., Deelman, E., Gil, Y., Kesselman, C., Agarwal, A., Mehta, G., Vahi, K.: The role of planning in grid computing. In: 13th International Conference on Automated Planning and Scheduling (ICAPS), Trento, Italy (2003)
20. Deelman, E., Blythe, J., Gil, Y., Kesselman, C., Mehta, G., Vahi, K., Blackburn, K., Lazzarini, A., Arbree, A., Cavanaugh, R., Koranda, S.: Mapping abstract complex workflows onto grid environments. J. Grid Comput. 1 (2003) 25–39
21. Yang, J., Papazoglou, M.P., Orriëns, B., van den Heuvel, W.J.: A rule based approach to the service composition life-cycle. In: WISE, IEEE Computer Society (2003) 295–298
22. Kim, J., Spraragen, M., Gil, Y.: An intelligent assistant for interactive workflow composition. In: IUI '04: 9th international conference on Intelligent user interface, New York, NY, USA, ACM Press (2004) 125–131
23. Wu, J., Sirin, E., Hendler, J., Nau, D., Parsia, B.: Automatic web services composition using shop2. In: 2nd Int. Semantic Web Conference (ISWC). (2003)
24. McIlraith, S., Son, T., Zeng, H.: Semantic web services (2001)

Author Index

Lecture Notes in Computer Science

For information about Vols. 1–4206

please contact your bookseller or Springer